Java 17 for Absolute Beginners

Learn the Fundamentals of Java Programming

Second Edition

Iuliana Cosmina

Apress®

Java 17 for Absolute Beginners: Learn the Fundamentals of Java Programming

Iuliana Cosmina
Edinburgh, UK

ISBN-13 (pbk): 978-1-4842-7079-0
https://doi.org/10.1007/978-1-4842-7080-6

ISBN-13 (electronic): 978-1-4842-7080-6

Managing Director, Apress Media LLC: Welmoed Spahr
Acquisitions Editor: Steve Anglin
Development Editor: Matthew Moodie
Coordinating Editor: Mark Powers
Copyeditor: Anne Sanow

Cover designed by eStudioCalamar

Cover image by Shutterstock

Distributed to the book trade worldwide by Apress Media, LLC, 1 New York Plaza, New York, NY 10004, U.S.A. Phone 1-800-SPRINGER, fax (201) 348-4505, e-mail orders-ny@springer-sbm.com, or visit www.springeronline.com. Apress Media, LLC is a California LLC and the sole member (owner) is Springer Science + Business Media Finance Inc (SSBM Finance Inc). SSBM Finance Inc is a **Delaware** corporation.

For information on translations, please e-mail booktranslations@springernature.com; for reprint, paperback, or audio rights, please e-mail bookpermissions@springernature.com.

Apress titles may be purchased in bulk for academic, corporate, or promotional use. eBook versions and licenses are also available for most titles. For more information, reference our Print and eBook Bulk Sales web page at http://www.apress.com/bulk-sales.

Any source code or other supplementary material referenced by the author in this book is available to readers on GitHub. For more detailed information, please visit http://www.apress.com/source-code.

Printed on acid-free paper

To my first teacher, Moţa Dumitra.
You've instilled in me the hunger to learn.
Thank you!

Table of Contents

About the Author

Iuliana Cosmina is currently a software engineer for Cloudsoft, Edinburgh. She has been writing Java code since 2002. She has contributed to various types of applications, such as experimental search engines, ERPs, track and trace, banking, and cloud orchestration. During her career she has been a teacher, team leader, software architect, DevOps professional, and software manager.

She is a Spring-certified professional, as defined by Pivotal, the makers of Spring Framework, Boot, and other tools. She considers Spring the best Java framework to work with. When she is not programming, she spends her time reading, blogging, learning to play piano, travelling, hiking, or biking.

- You can find some of her personal work on her GitHub account at `https://github.com/iuliana`.

- You can find her complete CV on her LinkedIn account at `https://linkedin.com/in/iulianacosmina`.

- You can contact her at `Iuliana.Cosmina@gmail.com`.

About the Technical Reviewer

 **Manuel Jordan Elera** is an autodidactic developer and researcher who enjoys learning new technologies for his own experiments and creating new integrations. Manuel won the Springy Award–Community Champion and Spring Champion 2013. In his free time he reads the Bible and composes music on his guitar. Manuel is known as dr_pompeii. He has tech-reviewed numerous books for Apress, including *Pro Spring MVC with Webflux* (2020), *Pro Spring Boot 2* (2019), *Rapid Java Persistence and Microservices* (2019), *Java Language Features* (2018), *Spring Boot 2 Recipes* (2018), and *Java APIs, Extensions and Librarie*s (2018). Read his 13 detailed tutorials about many Spring technologies, contact him through his blog at `http://www.manueljordanelera.blogspot.com`, and follow him on his Twitter account, `@dr_pompeii`.

Acknowledgments

Writing books for beginners is tricky, because as an experienced developer, it might be difficult to find the right examples and explain them in such a way that even a nontechnical person would easily understand them. That is why I am profoundly grateful to the great people at Apress who have been with me for the full journey of writing this book for all the support and advice they provided to keep this book at beginner level. A special thank you to the tech reviewer of this book, Manuel Jordan; his recommendations and corrections were crucial for the final form of the book.

Apress has published many of the books that I have read and used to improve myself professionally. It is a great honor to publish my seventh book with Apress, and it gives me enormous satisfaction to be able to contribute to the making of a new generation of Java developers.

A special thank you to my Cloudsoft team, for being so supportive with my passion for writing technical books. Thank you all for being supportive and making sure I still had some fun while writing this book. You have no idea how dear you are to me.

A very grateful thank you to Vesa Kauranen, Ivan Duka, Süleyman Onur Otlu, and all developers who have identified bugs in the text and the code and helped me make this edition of the book better than the previous one.

And a very special thank you in advance to all the passionate Java developers who will find mistakes in the book and be so kind to write me about them, so that I can provide an erratum and make this book even better.

Finally, I want to thank the Bogza-Vlad family: Monica, Tinel, Cristina, and Stefan. You are all close to my heart and I miss you often.

CHAPTER 1

An Introduction to Java and Its History

According to Google Search, at the end of 2020, 9492 companies reportedly use Java in their tech stacks, including Google and the company that I, the author of this book, worked for while this book was being written. Even after 25 years, Java continues to be one of the most influential programming languages. It all started in 1990, when an American company that was leading the revolution in computer industry decided to gather its best engineers to design and develop a product that would allow them to become an important player in the new emerging Internet world. Among those engineers was James Arthur Gosling, a Canadian computer scientist who is recognized as the father of the Java programming language. It would take five years of design, programming, and one renaming (from Oak to Java because of trademark issues), but finally, in January 1996,[1] Java 1.0 was released for Linux, Solaris, Mac and Windows.

The general tendency when reading a technical book is to skip the introductory chapter altogether. But in this case I think it would be a mistake. I was never much interested in the history of Java until I wrote this book. I knew that James Gosling was the creator and that Oracle bought Sun, and that was pretty much it. I never cared much about how the language evolved, where the inspiration came from, or how one version was different from another. I started learning Java at version 1.5, and I took a lot of things in the language for granted. So when I was assigned to a project running on Java 1.4 I was quite confused, because I did not know why parts of the code I wrote was not compiling. Although the IT industry is moving very fast, there will always be that one client that has a legacy application. Knowing the peculiarities of each Java version is an advantage, because you know the issues when performing a migration.

---

[1] Reference: `https://en.wikipedia.org/wiki/Java_(software_platform)`.

I. Cosmina, *Java 17 for Absolute Beginners*, https://doi.org/10.1007/978-1-4842-7080-6_1

When I started doing research for this book, I was mesmerized. The history of Java is interesting because it is a tale of incredible growth, success of a technology, and an example of how a clash of egos in management almost killed the company that created it. Currently Java is the most-used technology in software development, and it is simply paradoxical that the company that gave birth to it no longer exists.

This chapter describes each version of Java, tracking the evolution of the language and the Java Virtual Machine.

Who This Book Is For

Most Java books for beginners start with the typical *Hello World!* example depicted in Listing 1-1.

Listing 1-1. The Most Common Java Beginner Code Sample

```java
public class HelloWorld {
    public static void main(String[] args) {
        System.out.println("Hello World!");
    }
}
```

This code, when executed, prints *Hello World!* in the console. But if you have bought this book it is assumed that you want to develop real applications in Java, and have a real chance when applying for a position as a Java developer. If this is what you want and if this is who you are, a beginner with the wits and the desire to make full use of this language's power, then this book is for you. And this is why I will give you enough credit to start this book with a more complex example.

Java is a language with a syntax that is readable and based on the English language. So if you have logical thinking and a little knowledge of the English language, it should be obvious to you what the code in Listing 1-2 does without even executing it.

Listing 1-2. The Java Beginner Code Sample a Smart Beginner Deserves

```java
package com.apress.ch.one.hw;

import java.util.List;

public class Example01 {
    public static void main(String[] args) {
        List<String> items = List.of("1", "a", "2", "a", "3", "a");

        items.forEach(item -> {
            if (item.equals("a")) {
                System.out.println("A");
            } else {
                System.out.println("Not A");
            }
        });
    }
}
```

In this code example, a list of text values is declared; then the list is traversed, and when a text is equal to "a", the letter "A" is printed in the console; otherwise, "Not A" is printed.

If you are an absolute beginner to programming, this book is for you, especially because the sources attached to this book make use of algorithms and design patterns commonly used in programming. So if your plan is to get into programming and learn a high-level programming language, read the book, run the examples, write your own code, and you should have a good head start.

If you already know Java you can use this book too, because it covers syntax and under-the-bonnet details for Java versions up to 17 (the Early Access Program or EAP[2] release), and you will surely find something you did not know.

---

[2] Early Access Program

How This Book Is Structured

The chapter you are currently reading is an introductory one that covers a small part of Java history, showing you how the language has evolved and providing a glimpse into its future. Also, the mechanics of executing a Java application are covered, so that you are prepared for **Chapter 2**. The next chapter will show you how to set up your development environment and will introduce you to a first simple application.

Starting with **Chapter 3**, fundamental parts of the language will be covered: packages, modules, classes, interfaces, annotations objects, operators, data types, records, statements, streams, lambda expressions, and so on.

Starting with **Chapter 8**, interactions with external data sources are covered: reading and writing files, serializing/deserializing objects, and testing and creating an user interface.

Chapter 12 is dedicated fully to the publish-subscribe framework introduced in Java 9 and reactive programming.

Chapter 13 will cover the Garbage Collector.

All the sources used in the listings in this book, and some that did not make it because the book must be kept to a reasonable size, are part of a project named java-17-for-absolute-beginners. This project is organized in modules (thus it is a multimodule project) that are linked to each other and have to be managed by something called Maven. Maven is something we developers call a build tool, and it provides the capability to build projects containing a lot of source code. To build a project means transforming the code written into something that can be executed. I choose to use multimodule projects for the books I write because it is easier to build them and also because common elements can be grouped together, keeping the configuration of the project simple and nonrepetitive. Also, by having all the sources organized in one multimodule project, you get the feedback if the sources are working or not as soon as possible, and you can contact the author and ask them to update them. I know that having a build tool introduces a certain level of complexity, but it gives you the opportunity to get comfortable with a development environment very similar to what you will work in as an employee.

Conventions

This book uses a number of formatting conventions that should make it easier to read. To that end, the following conventions are used within the book:

- code or concept names in paragraphs appear as follows:

  `java.util.List`

- code listings appear as follows:

  ```
  public static void main(String[] args) {
      System.out.println("Hello World!");
  }
  ```

- logs in console outputs will appear as follows:

  ```
  01:24:07.809 [main] INFO c.a.Application - Starting Application
  01:24:07.814 [main] DEBUG c.a.p.c.Application - Running in
  debug mode
  ```

- {xx} is a placeholder; the xx value is a pseudo-value giving a hint about the real value that should be used in the command or statement.

- ❶ appears in front of paragraphs you should pay specific attention to. There are similar icons for tips and warnings.

- *Italic* font is used for humorous metaphors and expressions.

- **Bold** font is used for Chapter references and important terms.

As for my style of writing, I like to write my books in the same way I have technical conversations with colleagues and friends: sprinkling jokes throughout, giving production examples, and making analogies to nonprogramming situations. Because programming is nothing but just another way to model the real world.

When Java Was Owned By Sun Microsystems

The first stable version of Java was released in 1996. Up until that point, there was a small team named the **Green Team** that worked on a prototype language named Oak, which was introduced to the world with a working demo—an interactive handheld home entertainment controller called the Star7. The star of the animated touch-screen user interface was a cartoon character named **Duke**, created by one of the team's graphic artists, Joe Palrang. Over the years, Duke (Figure 1-1) has become the official Java technology mascot, and every JavaOne conference (organized by Oracle once a year) has its own Duke mascot personality.

Figure 1-1. *Duke, the Java official mascot (image source: `https://oracle.com`)*

The Green Team released Java to the world via the Internet, because that was the fastest way to create widespread adoptions. You can imagine that they jumped for joy every time somebody downloaded it, because it meant people were interested in it. There are a few other advantages making software open source, such as the fact that contributions and feedback are provided by a big number of people from all over the world. Thus, for Java, this was the best decision, as it shaped the language a lot of developers are using today. Even after 25 years, Java is still among the top-three most-used programming languages.

The Green Team was working for an American company named **Sun Microsystems** and was founded in 1982. It guided the computer revolution by selling computers, computer parts, and software. One of their greatest achievements is the Java programming language. In Figure 1-2, you can see the company logo[3] that was used since Java's birth year until it was acquired by Oracle in 2010.

---

[3] The story behind the logo can be read at "Title," `https://goodlogo.com/extended.info/sunmicrosystems-logo-2385`, accessed October 15, 2021. You can also read more about Sun Microsystems.

Figure 1-2. *The Sun Microsystems logo (image source:* `https://en.wikipedia.org/wiki/Sun_Microsystems`*)*

It is quite difficult to find information about the first version of Java, but dedicated developers that witnessed its birth, when the Web was way smaller and full of static pages, did create blogs and shared their experience with the world. It was quite easy for Java to shine with its applets that displayed dynamic content that interacted with the user. But because the development team thought bigger, Java became much more than a Web programming language. In trying to make applets run in any browser, the team found a solution to a common problem: **portability**.

Developers nowadays face a lot of headaches when developing software that should run on any operating system. And with the mobile revolution, things got really tricky. In Figure 1-3 you can see an abstract drawing of what is believed to be the first Java Logo.

Figure 1-3. *The first Java logo, 1996–2003 (image source:* `https://oracle.com/`*)*

Java 1.0 was released at the first edition of the JavaOne conference with over 6000 attendees. Java started out as a language named Oak.[4] This language was really similar to C++ and was designed for handheld devices and set-top boxes. It evolved into the first version of Java, which provided developers some advantages which C++ did not:

- **security**: In Java, there is no danger of reading bogus data when accidentally going over the size of an array.

- **automatic memory management**: A Java developer does not have to check if there is enough memory to allocate for an object and then deallocate it explicitly; the operations are automatically handled by the garbage collector. This also means that pointers are not necessary.

- **simplicity**: There are no pointers, unions, templates, structures. Mostly anything in Java can be declared as a class. Also, confusion when using multiple inheritance is avoided by modifying the inheritance model and not allowing multiple class inheritance.

- **support for multithreaded execution**: Java was designed from the start to support development of multithreaded software.

- **portability**: One of the most known Java mottos is **Write once, run anywhere** (WORA). This is made possible by the Java Virtual Machine.

All this made Java appealing for developers, and by 1997, when Java 1.1 was released, there were already approximately 400,000 Java developers in the world. The JavaOne conference had 10,000 attendees that year. The path to greatness was set. Before going further in our analysis of each Java version, let's clarify a few things.

How Is Java Portable?

I mentioned a few times that Java is portable and that Java programs can run on any operating system. It is time to explain how this is possible. Let's start with a simple drawing, like the one in Figure 1-4.

---

[4] The language was named by James Gosling, after the oak tree in front of his house.

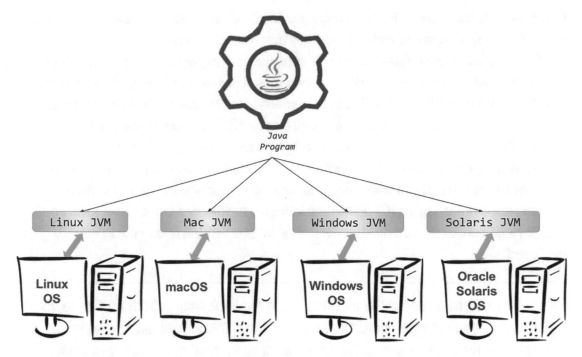

Figure 1-4. *Running a Java program on multiple platforms*

Java is what we call a **high-level programming language** that allows a developer to write programs that are independent of a particular type of computer. High-level languages are easier to read, write, and maintain. But their code must be translated by a compiler or interpreted into machine language (unreadable by humans because is it made up of numbers) to be executed, because that is the only language that computers understand.

In Figure 1-4, notice that on top of the operating systems, a **JVM** is needed to execute a Java program. JVM stands for **Java Virtual Machine**, which is an abstract computing machine that enables a computer to run a Java program. It is a platform-independent execution environment that converts Java code into machine language and executes it.

So what is the difference between Java and other high-level languages? Well, other high-level languages compile source code directly into machine code that is designed to run on a specific microprocessor architecture or operating system, such as Windows or UNIX. What JVM does is to mimic a Java processor, making it possible for a Java program to be interpreted as a sequence of actions or operating system calls on any processor regardless of the operating system. Sure, the compiling step makes Java slower than a pure compiled language like C++, but the advantage was and is still beautiful. Also, Java is not the only member of the JVM languages family. Groovy, Scala, Kotlin, and Clojure are all very popular programming languages that run on the JVM.

Because the Java compiler was mentioned, we have to get back to Java 1.1, which was widely used even as new versions were released. It came with an improved Abstract Window Toolkit (AWT) graphical API (collections of components used for building applets), inner classes, database connectivity classes (JDBC model), classes for remote calls (RMI), a special compiler for Microsoft platforms named JIT[5] Compiler (for **Just In Time**), support for internationalization, and Unicode. What also made it so widely embraced is that shortly after Java was released, Microsoft licensed it and started creating applications using it. The feedback helped further development of Java, and thus Java 1.1 was supported on all browsers of the time, which is why it was so widely deployed.

ⓘ   A lot of terms used in the introduction of the book might seem foreign to you now, but as you read the book, more information is introduced, and these words will start to make more sense. For now, just keep in mind that every new Java version has something more than the previous version, and at that time, every new component was a novelty.

So what exactly happens to the developer-written Java code until the actual execution? The process is depicted in Figure 1-5.

---

[5] Just In Time

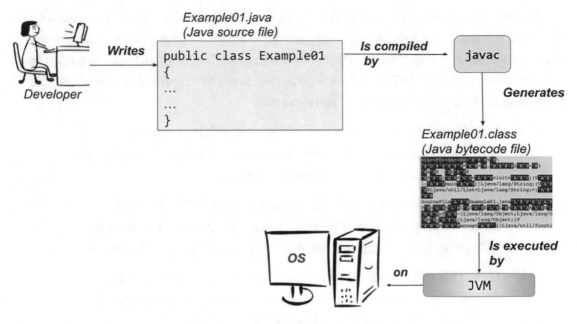

Figure 1-5. *From Java code to machine code*

Java code is compiled and transformed to bytecode that is then interpreted and executed by the JVM on the underlying operating system.

---

❶   Java is a compiled and interpreted general-purpose programming language with numerous features that make it well suited for the web.

Now that we've covered how Java code is executed, let's go back to some more history.

Sun Microsystem's Java Versions

The first stable Java version released by Sun Microsystems could be downloaded from the website as an archive named **JDK,** and its version at the time was 1.0.2. JDK is an acronym for **J**ava **D**evelopment **K**it. This is the software development environment used for developing Java applications and applets. It includes the **J**ava **R**untime **E**nvironment (**JRE**), an interpreter (loader), a compiler, an archiver, a documentation generator, and other tools needed for Java development. We will get into this more in the section about installing JDK on your computer.

Starting with version 1.2, released in 1998, Java versions were given codenames.[6] The Java version 1.2 codename was **Playground**. It was a massive release, and this was the moment when people started talking about **the Java 2 Platform**. Starting with this version, the releases up to J2SE 5.0 were renamed, and **J2SE** replaced JDK because the Java platform was now composed of three parts:

- **J2SE** (Java 2 Platform, Standard Edition), which later became JSE, a computing platform for the development and deployment of portable code for desktop and server environments.

- **J2EE** (Java 2 Platform, Enterprise Edition), which later became JEE, a set of specifications extending Java SE with specifications for enterprise features such as distributed computing and web services.

- **J2ME** (Java 2 Platform, Micro Edition), which later became JME, a computing platform for development and deployment of portable code for embedded and mobile devices.

With this release, the JIT compiler became part of Sun Microsystem's JVM (which basically means turning code into executable code became a faster operation and the generated executable code was optimized), the Swing graphical API was introduced as a fancy alternative to AWT (new components to create fancy desktop applications were introduced), and the Java Collections Framework (for working with sets of data) was introduced.

J2SE 1.3 was released in 2000 with the codename **Kestrel** (maybe as a reference to the newly introduced Java sound classes). This release also contained Java XML APIs.

J2SE 1.4 was released in 2002 with the codename **Merlin**. This is the first year that the Java Community Process members were involved in deciding which features the release should contain, and thus the release was quite consistent. This is the first release of the Java platform developed under the Java Community Process as JSR 59.[7] The following features are among those worth mentioning:

- **Support for IPv6**: Basically applications that run over a network can now be written to work using networking protocol IPv6.

---

[6] All codenames, for intermediary releases too, are listed at Oracle, "JDK Releases," `http://www.oracle.com/technetwork/java/javase/codenames-136090.html`, accessed October 15, 2021.

[7] If you want to see the contents and the list of Java Specification Requests, see Java Community Process, `http://www.jcp.org/en/jsr/detail?id=59`, accessed October 15, 2021.

- **Nonblocking IO:** IO is an acronym for input-output, which refers to reading and writing data—a very slow operation. Making IO nonblocking means to optimize these operations to increase speed of the running application.

- **Logging API**: Operations that get executed need to be reported to a file or a resource, which can be read in case of failure to determine the cause and find a solution. This process is called logging and apparently only in this version components to support this operation were introduced.

- **Image processing API**: Components developers can use this to manipulate images with Java code.

Java's coffee cup logo made its entrance in 2003 (between releases 1.4 and 5.0) at the JavaOne conference. You can see it in Figure 1-6.[8]

Figure 1-6. *Java official logo 2003-2006 (image source: `https://oracle.com`)*

J2SE 5.0 was released in 2004 with the codename **Tiger**. Initially it followed the typical versioning and was named 1.5, but because this was a major release with a significant number of new features that proved a serious improvement of maturity, stability, scalability, and security of the J2SE, the version was labeled 5.0 and presented like that to the public, even if internally 1.5 was still used. For this version and the next two, it was considered that 1.x = x.0. Let's list those features because most of them are covered in the book:

---

[8] The Java language was first named Oak. It was renamed to Java because of copyright issues. There are a few theories that you will find regarding the new name. There is one saying that the JAVA name is actually a collection of the initials of the names being part of the Green team: James Gosling, Arthur Van Hoff, and Andy Bechtolsheim, and that the logo is inspired by their love of coffee.

- **Generics** provide support for compile-time (static) type safety for collections and eliminates the need for most type conversions (which means the type used in a certain context is decided while the application is running, we have a full section about this in **Chapter 5**).

- **Annotations**, also known as **metadata**, are used to tag classes and methods to allow metadata-aware utilities to process them (which means a component is labeled as something another component recognizes and does specific operations with it).

- **Autoboxing/unboxing** refers to the automatic conversion between primitive types and matching object types (wrappers), also covered in **Chapter 5**.

- **Enumerations** define static final ordered sets of values using the enum keyword; covered in **Chapter 4**.

- **Varargs** provide a shorthand for methods that support an arbitrary number of parameters of one type. The last parameter of a method is declared using a type name followed by three dots (e.g., String...), which implies that any number of arguments of that type can be provided and are placed into an array; covered in **Chapter 3**.

- **Enhanced for each loop**: used to iterate over collections and arrays too, also covered in **Chapter 5**.

- Improved semantics for multithreaded Java Programs, covered in **Chapter 7**.

- Static imports also covered in **Chapter 4.**

- Improvements for RMI (not covered in the book), Swing (**Chapter 10**), concurrency utilities (**Chapter 7**), and introduction of Scanner class (**Chapter 11**).

Java 5 was the first available for Apple Mac OS X 10.4, and the default version installed on Apple Mac OS X 10.5. There were a lot of updates[9] released for this version up until 2015, to fix issues related to security and performance. It was a pretty buggy

---

[9] Let's call them what they actually are: hotfixes.

release, and it is pretty understandable, since quite a lot of features were developed in only two years.

In 2006, **Java SE 6** was released with a little delay, codename **Mustang**. Yes, this was yet another rename, and yes, yet again a serious number of features were implemented in quite a short period of time. A lot of updates were required afterward to fix the existing issues. This was the last major Java release released by Sun Microsystems, as Oracle acquired this company in January 2010. The most important features in this release are listed next.

- Dramatic performance improvements for the core platform (applications run faster, need less memory or CPU to execute).

- Improved web service support (optimized components that are required for development of web applications).

- JDBC 4.0 (optimized components that are required for development of applications using databases).

- Java Compiler API (from your code you can call components that are used to compile code).

- Many GUI improvements, such as integration of `SwingWorker` in the API, table sorting and filtering, and true Swing double-buffering (eliminating the gray-area effect); overall, improvement of components used to create interfaces for desktop applications.

Shortly after (*in Java terms*), in December 2008, **JavaFX** 1.0 SDK was released. JavaFX is suitable for creating graphical user interfaces for any platform. The initial version was a scripting language. Until 2008, in Java there were two ways to create a user interface:

- Using **AWT** (Abstract Window Toolkit) components, which are rendered and controlled by a native peer component specific to the underlying operating system; that is why AWT components are also called heavyweight components.

- Using **Swing** components, which are called lightweight because they do not require allocation of native resources in the operating system's windowing toolkit. The Swing API is a complimentary extension of AWT.

For the first versions, it was never really clear whether JavaFX would actually have a future and if it would grow up to replace Swing. The management turmoil inside Sun did not help in defining a clear path for this project either.

Oracle Takes Over

Although Sun Microsystems won a lawsuit against Microsoft in which they agreed to pay $20 million for not implementing the Java 1.1 standard completely, in 2008 the company was in such poor shape that negotiations for a merger with IBM and Hewlett-Packard began. In 2009, Oracle and Sun announced that they agreed on the price: Oracle would acquire Sun for $9.50 per share in cash, which amounted to a $5.6 billion offer. The impact was massive. A lot of engineers quit, including James Gosling, **the father of Java**, which made a lot of developers question the future of the Java platform.

Java 7

Java SE 7, codename **Dolphin**, was the first Java version released by Oracle in 2011. It was the result of an extensive collaboration between Oracle engineers and members of the worldwide Java communities, such as the OpenJDK Community and the Java Community Process (JCP). It contained a lot of changes, but a lot fewer than developers expected. Considering the long period between the releases, the expectations were pretty high. Project Lambda, which was supposed to allow usage of lambda expressions in Java (this leads to considerable syntax simplification in certain cases), and Jigsaw (making JVM and the Java application modular; there is a section in **Chapter 3** about them) were dropped. Both were released in future versions.

The following are the most notable features in Java 7:

- JVM support for dynamic languages with the new invoke dynamic bytecode (basically, Java code can use code implemented in non-Java languages such as Python, Ruby, Perl, Javascript, and Groovy).

- Compressed 64-bit pointers (internal optimization of the JVM, so less memory is consumed)

- Small language changes grouped under project **Coin:**
    - strings in switch statements (covered in **Chapter 7**)
    - automatic resource management in try-statement (covered in **Chapter 5**)
    - improved type inference for generics—the diamond <> operator (covered in **Chapter 5**)
    - binary integer literals: integer numbers can be represented directly as binary numbers, using the form 0b (or 0B) followed by one or more binary digits (0 or 1) (covered in **Chapter 5**).
    - multiple exceptions handling improvements (covered in **Chapter 5**)
- Concurrency improvements
- New I/O library (new classes added to read/write data to/from files, covered in **Chapter 8**)
- `Timsort` algorithm was introduced to sort collections and arrays of objects instead of merge sort because it has better performance. Better performance usually means reducing of consumed resources: memory and/or CPU, or reducing the time needed for execution.

Continuing development on a project with almost none of the original development team involved must have been a very tough job. That is obvious because of the 161 updates that followed; most of them were needed to fix security issues and vulnerabilities.

JavaFX 2.0 was released with Java 7. This confirmed that the JavaFX project had a future with Oracle. As a major change, JavaFX stopped being a scripting language and became a Java API. This meant that knowledge of the Java language syntax would be enough to start building user graphical interfaces with it. JavaFX started gaining ground over Swing because of its hardware-accelerated graphical engine called **Prism** that did a better job at rendering.

❶   Starting with Java 7, the OpenJDK was born, an open-source reference implementation of the Java SE Platform Edition. This was an effort from the Java developers' community to provide a version of the JDK that was not under an Oracle license, because it was assumed that Oracle will introduce stricter licensing for the JDK in order to make profit from it.

Java 8

Java SE 8, codename **Spider**, was released in 2014, and included features that were initially intended to be part of Java 7. Better late than never, right? Three years in the making, Java 8 contained the following key features:

- Language syntax changes

  - Language-level support for lambda expressions (functional programming features)

  - Support for default methods in interfaces (covered in **Chapter 4**)

  - New date and time API (covered in **Chapter 5**)

  - New way to do parallel processing by using streams (covered in **Chapter 8**)

- Improved integration with JavaScript (the Nashorn project). JavaScript is a web scripting language that is quite loved in the development community, so providing support for it in Java probably won Oracle a few new supporters.

- Improvements of the garbage collection process

Starting with Java 8, codenames were dropped to avoid any trademark-law hassles; instead, a semantic versioning that easily distinguishes major, minor, and security-update releases was adopted.[10] The version number matches the following pattern: `$MAJOR.$MINOR.$SECURITY`.

---

[10] Open JDK, "JEP 223: New Version-String Scheme," `http://openjdk.java.net/jeps/223`, accessed October 15, 2021.

When executing java -version in a terminal (if you have Java 8 installed), you see a log similar to the one in Listing 1-3.

Listing 1-3. Java 8 Log for Execution of java -version

```
$ java -version
java version "1.8.0_162"
JavaTM SE Runtime Environment build 1.8.0_162-b12
Java HotSpotTM 64-Bit Server VM build 25.162-b12, mixed mode
```

In this log, the version numbers have the following meaning:

- The 1 represents the major version number, incremented for a major release that contains significant new features as specified in a new edition of the Java SE Platform Specification.

- The 8 represents the minor version number, incremented for a minor update release that may contain compatible bug fixes, revisions to standard APIs, and other small features.

- The 0 represents the security level that is incremented for a security-update release that contains critical fixes, including those necessary to improve security. $SECURITY is not reset to zero when $MINOR is incremented, which lets the users know that this version is a more secure one.

- 162 is the build number.

- b12 represents additional build information.

This versioning style is quite common for Java applications, so this versioning style was adopted to align with the general industry practices.

Java 9

Java SE 9 was released in September 2017. The long-awaited **Jigsaw** project was finally here. The Java platform was finally modular.

❶ This is a big change for the Java world; it's not a change in syntax and it's not some new feature. It's a change in the design of the platform. Some experienced developers I know who have used Java since its first years have had difficulties adapting. It is supposed to fix some serious problems that Java has been living with for years (covered in **Chapter 3**). You are lucky because as a beginner, you start from scratch, so you do not need to change the way you develop your applications.

The following are the most important features, aside from the introduction of Java modules:

- The Java Shell tool, an interactive command-line interface for evaluation declarations, statements, and expressions written in Java (covered in **Chapter 3**)

- Quite a few security updates

- `private` methods are now supported in interfaces (covered in **Chapter 4**)

- Improved `try-with-resources`: final variables can now be used as resources (covered in **Chapter 5**)

- "_" is removed from the set of legal identifier names (covered in **Chapter 4**)

- Enhancements for the Garbage-First (G1) garbage collector; this becomes the default garbage collector (covered in **Chapter 13**)

- Internally, a new more compact String representation is used (covered in **Chapter 5**)

- Concurrency updates (related to parallel execution, mentioned in **Chapter 5**)

- Factory methods for collections (covered in **Chapter 5**)

- Updates of the image processing API optimization of components used to write code that processes images

Java 9 followed the same versioning scheme as Java 8, with a small change. The Java version number contained in the name of the JDK finally became the $MAJOR number in the version scheme. So if you have Java 9 installed, when executing `java -version` in a terminal, you see something similar to the log in Listing 1-4.

Listing 1-4. Java 9 Log for Execution of `java -version`

```
$ java -version
java version "9.0.4"
JavaTM SE Runtime Environment build 9.0.4+11
Java HotSpotTM 64-Bit Server VM build 9.0.4+11, mixed mode
```

Java 10

Java SE 10 (AKA Java 18.3) was released on March 20, 2018. Oracle changed the Java release style so that a new version is released every six months. Java 10 also uses the new versioning convention set up by Oracle: the version numbers follow a $YEAR.$MONTH format.[11] This release versioning style is supposed to make it easier for developers and end users to figure out the age of a release, so that they can judge whether to upgrade it to a newer release with the latest security fixes and additional features.

The following are a few features of Java 10.[12]

- A local-variable type inference to enhance the language to extend type inference to local variables (this is the most expected feature and is covered in **Chapter 5**)

- More optimizations for garbage collection (covered in **Chapter 13**)

- Application Class-Data Sharing to reduce the footprint by sharing common class metadata across processes (this is an advanced feature and it won't be covered in the book)

---

[11] Conventions described by Open JDK, "JEP 322: Time-Based Release Versioning," http:// openjdk.java.net/jeps/322, accessed October 15, 2021.

[12] The complete list can be found at Open JDK, "JDK 10," http://openjdk.java.net/projects/ jdk/10, accessed October 15, 2021, and the release notes containing the detailed list with API and internal changes can be found at Oracle, "JDK 10 Release Notes," https://www.oracle.com/ java/technologies/javase/10-relnote-issues.html, accessed October 15, 2021.

- More concurrency updates (related to parallel execution, mentioned in **Chapter 5**)

- Heap allocation on alternative memory devices (The memory needed by JVM to run a Java program—called heap memory—can be allocated on an alternative memory device, so the heap can also be split between volatile and nonvolatile RAM. More about memory used by Java applications can be read in **Chapter 5**.)

When JDK 10 is installed, running java -version in a terminal shows a log that is similar to the one in Listing 1-5.

Listing 1-5. Java 10 Log for Execution of `java -version`

```
$ java -version
java version "10" 2018-03-20
JavaTM SE Runtime Environment 18.3 build 10+46
Java HotSpotTM 64-Bit Server VM 18.3 build 10+46, mixed mode
```

Java 11

Java SE 11 (AKA Java 18.9),[13] released on September 25, 2018, contains the following features:

- Removal of JEE advanced components used to build enterprise Java applications and Corba (very old technology for remote invocation, allowing your application to communicate with applications installed on a different computer) modules.

- Local-variable syntax for lambda parameters allow the var keyword to be used when declaring the formal parameters of implicitly typed lambda expressions.

- Epsilon, a low-overhead garbage collector (a no-GC, so basically you can run an application without a GC), basically more optimizations to the garbage collection (covered in **Chapter 13**).

---

[13] The full list of features is at Open JDK, "JDK 11," http://openjdk.java.net/projects/jdk/11/, accessed October 15, 2021.

- More concurrency updates (related to parallel execution, mentioned in **Chapter 5**).

- The Nashorn JavaScript script engine and APIs are marked as deprecated with the intent to remove them in a future release. ECMAScript language constructs evolve pretty rapidly, so Nashorn was getting difficult to maintain.

Aside from these changes, it was also speculated that a new versioning change should be introduced because the $YEAR.$MONTH format did not go so well with developers. (Why so many versioning naming changes? Is this really so important? Apparently, it is.) The proposed versioning change is similar to the one introduced in Java 9.[14]

When JDK 11 is installed, running java -version in a terminal shows a log that is similar to the one in Listing 1-6.

Listing 1-6. Java 11 Log for Execution of `java -version`

```
$ java -version
java version "11.0.3" 2019-04-16 LTS
Java(TM) SE Runtime Environment 18.9 (build 11.0.3+12-LTS)
Java HotSpot(TM) 64-Bit Server VM 18.9 (build 11.0.3+12-LTS, mixed mode)
```

JDK 11 is a long-term support release with several years of support planned. This is what the **LTS** in the version name means.

Concomitant with the release of JDK 11, Oracle announced that they would start charging for Java SE 8 licenses, so small businesses that try to reduce their software costs started looking for alternatives. AdoptOpenJDK provides prebuilt OpenJDK binaries from a fully open-source set of build scripts and infrastructure, for multiple platforms.

OpenJDK has the same code as OracleJDK, depending on what provider you're using.

Another advantage is that while the Oracle, JDK cannot be modified to suit the needs of a business application; OpenJDK can be modified because is licensed under GNU General Public License, which is quite permissive.

Also, if money is not an issue Amazon's Coretto, Azul Zulu, and GraalVM are all alternate JDKs optimized in one way or another.

---

[14] If you are curious, you can read a detailed specification for it at Open JDK, "Time-Based Release Versioning."

Java 12

Java SE 12,[15] released on March 29, 2019, contains the following important features:

- A new experimental Garbage Collector (GC) algorithm named Shenandoah that reduces GC pause times.

- Modified syntax for the `switch` statement, allowing it to be used as an expression as well. It also removes the need for `break` statements (covered in **Chapter 7**).

- JVM Constants API, to model nominal descriptions of key class-file and run-time artifacts. This API can be helpful for tools that manipulate classes and methods.

- Minor improvements to the G1 garbage collector (covered in **Chapter 13**).

- CDS archives to improve the JDK build process.

- Approximately 100 microbenchmarks[16] are added to the JDK source.

When JDK 12 is installed, running java -version in a terminal shows a log that is similar to the one in Listing 1-7.

Listing 1-7. Java 12 Log for Execution of `java -version`

```
$ java -version
java version "12.0.2" 2019-07-16
Java(TM) SE Runtime Environment (build 12.0.2+10)
Java HotSpot(TM) 64-Bit Server VM (build 12.0.2+10, mixed mode, sharing)
```

JDK 12 is part of Oracle's six-month release cadence introduced with JDK 9 in September 2017. JDK 12 is a feature release with a short support lifespan. Two patches have been already released for this version.

---

[15] The full list of features is at Open JDK, "JDK 12," http://openjdk.java.net/projects/jdk/12/, accessed October 15, 2021.

[16] Based on Java Microbenchmark Harness, Open JDK, "Code Tools: jmh," https://openjdk.java.net/projects/code-tools/jmh/, accessed October 15, 2021.

Java 13

Java SE 13,[17] released on September 17, 2019, contains a few important features, hundreds of smaller enhancements, and thousands of bug fixes. The most important features of this version are:

- Dynamic CSD archives (an improvement of the CDS archive support added in JDK 12)

- Z Garbage Collector enhancements (covered in **Chapter 13**)

- A new implementation of the Legacy Socket API

- More improvements for the switch expressions (covered in **Chapter 7**)

- Support for text blocks (covered in **Chapter 5**)

When JDK 13 is installed, running java -version in a terminal shows a log that is similar to the one in Listing 1-8.

Listing 1-8. Java 13 Log for Execution of java -version

```
$ java -version
java version "13.0.2" 2020-01-14
Java(TM) SE Runtime Environment (build 13.0.2+8)
Java HotSpot(TM) 64-Bit Server VM (build 13.0.2+8, mixed mode, sharing)
```

JDK 13 is a feature release with a short support lifespan as well. Two patches have been already released for this version.

Java 14

Java SE 14,[18] released on March 17, 2020, contains a big list of important features, enhancements, and bug fixes. The most important features of this version are:

---

[17] The full list of features is at Open JDK, "JDK 13," http://openjdk.java.net/projects/jdk/13/, accessed October 15, 2021.

[18] The full list of features is at Open JDK, "JDK 14," http://openjdk.java.net/projects/jdk/14/, accessed October 15, 2021.

- Pattern matching for the `instanceof` operator (covered in **Chapter 7**)

- JFR Event Streaming API for collecting profiling and diagnostic data about a Java application and the JVM as they're running

- More enhancements of the G1 garbage collector (covered in **Chapter 13**)

- The CMS (Concurrent Mark Sweep) garbage collector was removed.

- Support for the Z Garbage Collector for macOS (covered in **Chapter 13**)

- `Records` were introduced to provide a compact syntax for declaring classes that are transparent holders for shallowly immutable data (covered in **Chapter 5**)

- Foreign Memory Access API provides support for Java programs to safely and efficiently access foreign memory outside of the Java heap

- Improvements of the `NullPointerException` class to provide more precise details to easily identify the variable being `null`

- The `jpackage` tool was introduced to provides support for native packaging formats to give end users a natural installation experience

When JDK 14 is installed, running java -version in a terminal shows a log that is similar to the one in Listing 1-9.

Listing 1-9. Java 14 Log for Execution of `java -version`

```
$ java -version
java version "14.0.2" 2020-07-14
Java(TM) SE Runtime Environment (build 14.0.2+12-46)
Java HotSpot(TM) 64-Bit Server VM (build 14.0.2+12-46, mixed mode, sharing)
```

Even if this release contains a lot of new features, most of them are available only in preview mode or are considered being in the `incubation` phase, making this release unstable and not a candidate for long-term support.

Java 15

Java SE 15,[19] released on September 15, 2020, contains considerable improvements to projects added in previous versions. The most notable features of this version are:

- Removal of the Nashorn JavaScript Engine

- Addition of sealed and hidden classes (covered in **Chapter 4**)

- The Edwards-Curve Digital Signature Algorithm (EdDSA) is now supported for cryptographic signatures

- More enhancements for the Legacy DatagramSocket API

- Biased Locking was disabled and deprecated, which leads to performance increase for multithreaded applications

When JDK 15 is installed, running java -version in a terminal shows a log that is similar to the one in Listing 1-10.

Listing 1-10. Java 15 Log for Execution of `java -version`

```
$ java -version
java version "15" 2020-09-15
Java(TM) SE Runtime Environment (build 15+36-1562)
Java HotSpot(TM) 64-Bit Server VM (build 15+36-1562, mixed mode, sharing)
```

JDK 15 is just a short-term release that was supported with Oracle Premier Support for six months until JDK 16 arrived in March 2021.

Java 16

Java SE 16,[20] released on March 16, 2021, is the reference implementation of the version of standard Java set to follow JDK 15. This means that everything unstable in JDK 15 is expected to be more stable in JDK 16. Aside from that, the most notable features of this version are:

---

[19] The full list of features is at Open JDK, "JDK 15," `http://openjdk.java.net/projects/jdk/15/`, accessed October 15, 2021.

[20] The full list of features is at Open JDK, "JDK 16," `http://openjdk.java.net/projects/jdk/16/`, accessed October 15, 2021.

- Introduction of a Vector API, to express vector computations that compile to optimal vector hardware instructions on supported CPU architectures, to achieve superior performance to equivalent scalar computations

- Strong encapsulation of JDK internals by default (covered in **Chapter 3**)

- Foreign linker API is introduced to provide statically typed, pure-Java access to native code

- Introduction of an Elastic Metaspace which promotes return of unused HotSpot class-metadata (i.e., metaspace) memory to the operating system more promptly

- Added support for C++ 14 language features

When JDK 16 is installed, running `java -version` in a terminal shows a log that is similar to the one in Listing 1-11.

Listing 1-11. Java 16 Log for Execution of `java -version`

```
$ java -version
openjdk version "16-ea" 2021-03-16
OpenJDK Runtime Environment (build 16-ea+30-2130)
OpenJDK 64-Bit Server VM (build 16-ea+30-2130, mixed mode, sharing)
```

JDK 16 is just a short-term release that was supported with Oracle Premier Support for six months until JDK 17 arrived in September 2021. At the time this chapter was being written, JDK 16 was available only via the early access program, which is why the "ea" string is present in the version name.

Java 17

JDK 17,[21] the next long-term support release, will be supported by Oracle for eight years. It was released on September 14, 2021, as per Oracle's six-month release cadence for Java SE versions.

---

[21] The full list of features is at JDK.java.net, "JDK 17 General-Availability Release," `https://jdk.java.net/17`, accessed October 15, 2021.

When this chapter was being written, JDK 17 was available only via the early access program, which is why the "ea" string is present in the version name; it means early access. It is quite difficult to use, as it is not supported by any editors or other build tools yet. The list of features is also incomplete and proposals for bug fixes and features are still welcome from the Java community.

By the time this book is released, Java 17 will be stable and ready to use. The book will fully cover all the important stable features of this release. Preview features are not included because they represent a risk for the stability of this project.

- Performance and implementation improvements for the Vector API introduced in JDK 16

- Refinements for sealed classes and interfaces

- Introducing Pattern Matching for switch expressions (feature preview)

- macOS specific improvements

- Enhancements for Pseudo-Random Number Generators: introduction of new interface and implementations for pseudorandom number generators (PRNGs), which including jumpable PRNGs and a new class of splittable PRNG algorithms (LXM)

- Enhancements on encapsulating JDK internals

- Deprecate the Applet API (prepare for removal in JDK 18)

- Deprecate the Security Manager (prepare for removal in JDK 18)

- Foreign Function & Memory API merges two previously incubating APIs the Foreign-Memory Access API and the Foreign Linker API, to allow developers to call up native libraries and process native data without the risks of JNI

The list of features for JDK 17 are focused on the JVM internals to improve performance and deprecate/discard old APIs.

When JDK 17 is installed, running java -version in a terminal shows a log that is similar to the one in Listing 1-12.

Listing 1-12. Java 17 Log for Execution of `java -version`

```
openjdk version "17" 2021-09-14
OpenJDK Runtime Environment (build 17+35-2724)
OpenJDK 64-Bit Server VM (build 17+35-2724, mixed mode, sharing)
```

This is where the details end. If you want more information on the first 25 years, you can easily find it on the Internet.[22]

Prerequisites

Before ending this chapter, it is only fair to tell you that to learn Java, you need a few things:

- Know your way around an operating system, such as Windows, Linux, or macOS.

- How to refine your search criteria, because information related to your operating systems is not covered in the book; if you have issues, you must fix them yourself.

- An Internet connection.

If you already know Java, and you bought this book out of curiosity or for the modules chapter, knowing about a build tool like Maven or Gradle is helpful, because the source code is organized in a multimodule project that can be fully built with one simple command. I've chosen to use a build tool because in this day and age, learning Java without one makes no sense; any company you apply to most definitely uses one.

Aside from the prerequisites that I listed, you also need install a JDK and a Java Editor. This is covered in **Chapter 2**. You do not need to know math, algorithms, or design patterns (though you might end up knowing a few after you read this book).

This being said, let's dig in.

---

[22] You can start your reading here, if you consider it necessary: Free Java Guide, "History of Java Programming Language," `https://www.freejavaguide.com/history.html`, accessed October 15, 2021.

Summary

Java has dominated the industry for more than 25 years. It wasn't always at the top of the most-used development technologies, but it has never left the top five either. Even with server-side JavaScript smart frameworks like Node.js, the heavy-lifting is still left to Java. Emerging programming languages like Scala and Kotlin run on the JVM, so maybe the Java programming language will suffer a serious metamorphosis in order to compete, but it will still be here.

The modularization capability introduced in version 9 opens the gates for Java applications to be installed on smaller devices, because to run a Java application, we no longer need the whole runtime—only its core plus the modules the application was built with.

Also, there are a lot of applications written in Java, especially in the financial domain, so Java will still be here because of legacy reasons and because migrating these titan applications to another technology is an impossible mission. Most of these applications are stuck on JDK 8, however, because they are complex and have a lot of dependencies that require upgrading too, which is not always possible.

Java will probably survive and be on top for the next 10 to 15 years. It does help that it is a very mature technology with a huge community built around it. Being very easy to learn and developer-friendly makes it remain the first choice for most companies. So you might conclude at this point that learning Java and buying this book is a good investment.

This chapter has a lot of references. They are an interesting read, but they are not mandatory to understand the contents of this book. The same goes for the rest of the chapters.

CHAPTER 2

Preparing Your Development Environment

To start learning Java, your computer needs to be set up as a Java development machine. Thus, here are the requirements:

- **Java** support on your computer is *kinda mandatory*.

- An integrated development environment, also known as an IDE, which is basically an application in which you write your code. An IDE assists you when writing code, compiling it and executing it.

  - The recommended IDE for this book is **IntelliJ IDEA.** You can go to their website to get the free community edition; for the purposes of the book, it will do.

  - Or you can choose the most popular free IDE for Java development: Eclipse.

  - Or you can try **NetBeans,**1 which is the default choice for most beginners because it was bundled with the JDK until version 8. It was taken out of the JDK in Java 9 and can now be downloaded from here: `https://netbeans.org/`.

- **Maven** is a build tool used to organize projects, easily handle dependencies, and make your work easier in big multimodule projects. (It is mandatory because the projects in this book are organized and built with a Maven setup.)

© Iuliana Cosmina 2022
I. Cosmina, *Java 17 for Absolute Beginners*, https://doi.org/10.1007/978-1-4842-7080-6_2

- **Git** is a versioning system that you can use to get the sources for the book, and you can experiment with it and create your own version. It is optional because GitHub, which is where the sources for this chapter are hosted, supports downloading them directly as an archive.[1]

To write and execute Java programs/applications, you only need the **J**ava **D**evelopment **K**it (JDK) installed. *Nothing stops you writing Java code in Notepad, if that is what you want.* All other tools that I've listed here are only needed to make your job easier and to familiarize you with a real development job.

---

❶   You probably need administrative rights if you install these applications for all users. For Windows 10, you might even need a special program to give your user administrative rights so that you can install the necessary tools. This book provides instructions on how to install everything—assuming your user has the necessary rights. If you need more information, the Internet is here to help.

If it seems like a lot, do not get discouraged; this chapter contains instructions on how to install and verify that each of tool is working accordingly. Let's start by making sure your computer supports Java.

Installing Java

Here you are with your computer, and you can't wait to start writing Java applications. But first you need to get yourself a JDK and install it. For this, you need an Internet connection. Open your browser and go to `https://developer.oracle.com/java`. The menu should have a **Downloads** section. Expand it and select Java SE, as shown in Figure 2-1.

---

[1] Any respectable software company uses a versioning system these days, so being comfortable with Git is a serious advantage when applying for a software developer position.

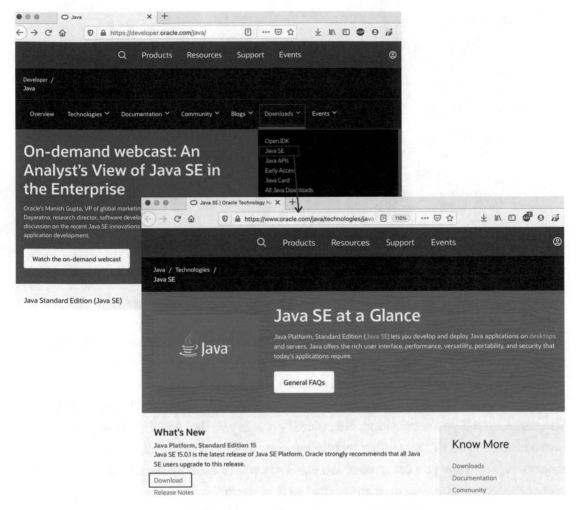

Figure 2-1. *Navigating the Oracle site to find the desired JDK*

On the Oracle site, you will find the latest stable Java version. Click on the Download link under the desired version. You should be redirected to a download page similar to the one in Figure 2-2.

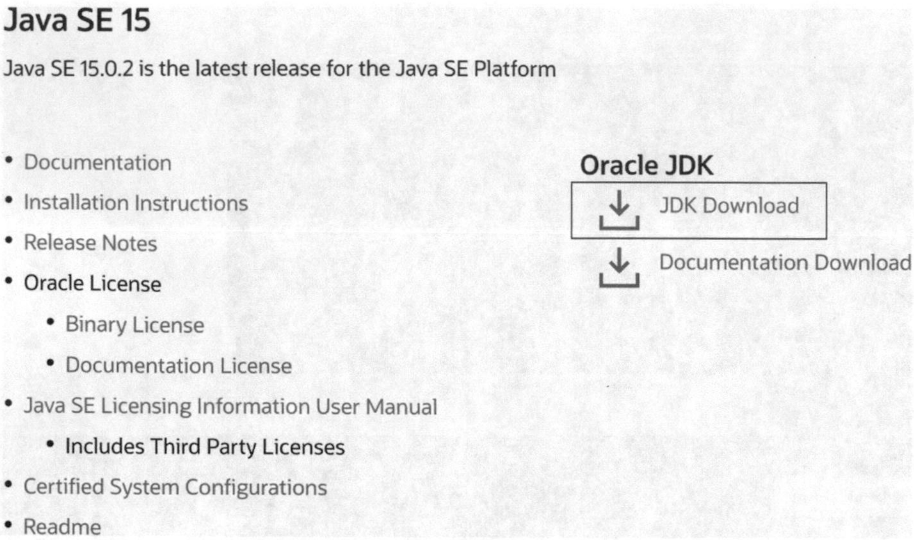

Java SE 15

Java SE 15.0.2 is the latest release for the Java SE Platform

- Documentation
- Installation Instructions
- Release Notes
- Oracle License
    - Binary License
    - Documentation License
- Java SE Licensing Information User Manual
    - Includes Third Party Licenses
- Certified System Configurations
- Readme

Oracle JDK

↓ JDK Download

↓ Documentation Download

Figure 2-2. *The Oracle page where you can download the desired JDK*

JDK is available for a few operating systems. You should download the one matching yours. For writing this book and writing the source code I am using a macOS computer, which means I will download the JDK with the ***.dmg** extension.

You need to accept the license agreement of you want to use Java for development. You can read it if you are curious, but basically it tells you that you are allowed to use Java as long as you do not modify its original components. It also tells you that you are responsible for how you use it, so if you use it to write or execute nefarious applications you are solely responsible in terms of the law and so on.

If you want to get your hands on an early version of JDK that was not officially released yet, this is the page where you have to go: `http://openjdk.java.net/ projects/jdk/`. At the time this chapter was being written, on that page, under **Releases**, versions 16 and 17 are listed as *in development*, and an early access (unstable) JDK 17 is available for download.

❗   This book will cover Java syntax and details for versions up to and including 17. That version is eight months away when this chapter is being written, thus some images and details might seem outdated (e.g. Oracle might change the theme of their site). There are common details that remain the same from a version to another. There is quite a small chance the JDK will no longer be called a JDK. Those won't be reviewed and changed, as the only thing that is different is the version number. As the book is planned to be released after Java 17 is released, it is recommended to download that version of the JDK to have full compatibility of the sources ensured.

After you have downloaded the JDK, the next step is to install it. Just double-click it and click Next until finish. This will work for Windows and macOS. The JDK is installed in a specific location.

In Windows, this is `C:\Program Files\Java\jdk-17`.

In macOS this is `/Library/Java/JavaVirtualMachines/jdk-17.jdk/Contents/Home`.

On Linux systems, depending on the distribution, the location where the JDK is installed varies. My preferred way is to get the *.tar.gz from the Oracle site that contains the full content of the JDK, unpack it, and copy it to a specific location. Also, my preferred location on Linux is `/home/iuliana.cosmina/tools/jdk-17.jdk`.

Using a PPA (repository; also known as a package manager) installer on Linux will put the JDK files where they are supposed to go on Linux automatically and update them automatically when a new version is released using the Linux (Global) updater utility. But if you are using Linux proficiently, you've probably figured out you can skip this section by now.

Another way to make things easy on a Linux or Unix system, is to use SDKMAN. Get it from here: `https://sdkman.io/`.

If you go to that location, you can inspect the contents of the JDK. In Figure 2-3, on the left are the contents of JDK 17, and on the right are the contents of the JDK 8.

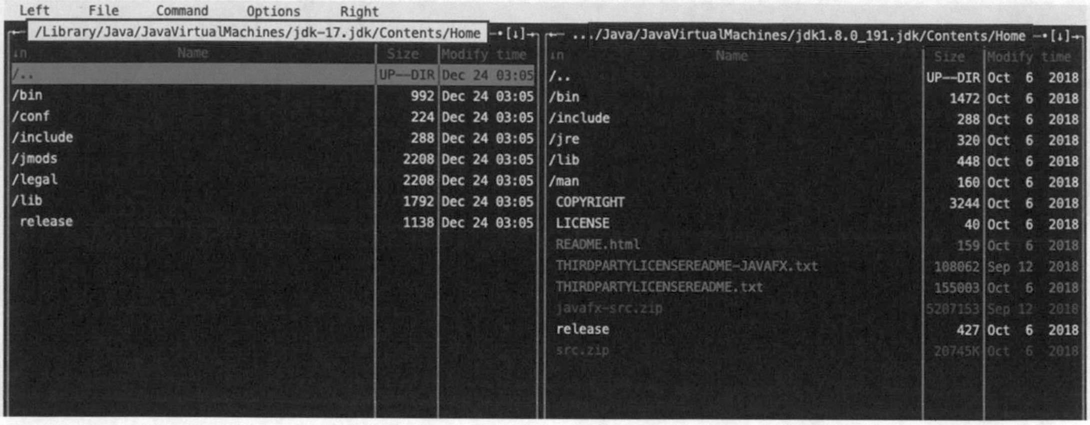

Figure 2-3. *JDK version 8 and 17 contents comparison*

I chose to make this comparison because starting with Java 9, the content of the JDK is organized differently. Until Java 8, the JDK contained a directory called jre that contained a Java Runtime Environment (JRE) used by the JDK. For people interested only in running Java applications, the JRE could be downloaded separately.

The lib directory contains Java libraries and support files needed by development tools.

Starting with Java 9, the JRE is no longer isolated in its own directory. Starting with version 11, Java has become fully modular. This means a customized JRE distribution can be created with specifically the modules needed to run an application. This means there are no JREs to download on the Oracle site starting with Java 11.

The most important thing you need to know about the JDK is that the bin directory contains executables and command-line launchers that are necessary to compile, execute, and audit Java code. The other directories are the jmods directory, which contains the compiled module definitions, and the include directory, which contains the C-language header files that support native code programming with the Java Native Interface (JNI) and the Java Virtual Machine (JVM) Debug Interface.

The JAVA_HOME Environment Variable

The most important directory in the JDK is the bin directory, because that directory has to be added to the path of your system. This allows you to call the Java executables from anywhere. This allows other applications to call them as well, without extra configurations steps needed. Most IDEs used for handling[2] Java code are written in Java, and they require knowing where the JDK is installed so that they can be run. This is done by declaring an environment variable named JAVA_HOME that points to the location of the JDK directory. To make the Java executables callable from any location within a system, you must add the bin directory to the system path. The next three sections explain how to do this on the three most common operating systems.

JAVA_HOME on Windows

To declare the JAVA_HOME environment variable on a Windows system, you need to open the dialog window for setting up system variables. On Windows systems, click the **Start** button. In the menu, there is a search box. In more recent versions, there is a search box on the horizontal toolbar; you can use this one too. Enter the word **environment** in there (the first three letters of the word should suffice). The option should become available for clicking. These steps, on Windows 10, are depicted in Figure 2-4.

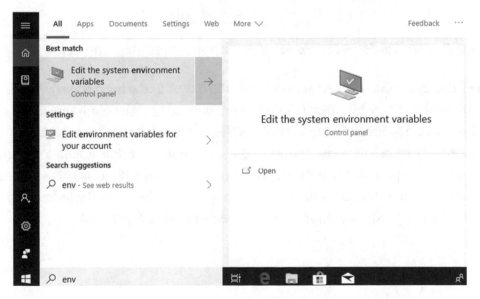

Figure 2-4. *Windows menu item to configure environment variables*

After clicking that menu item, a window like the one shown in Figure 2-5 should open.

---

[2] Includes operations like writing the code, analyzing the code, compiling it, and executing it.

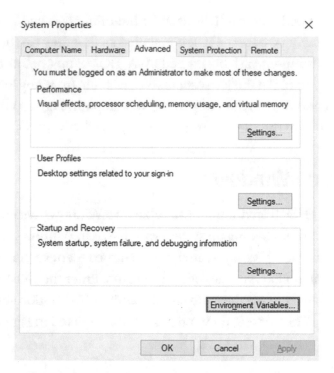

Figure 2-5. *First dialog window to set environment variables on Windows*

Click the **Environment Variables** button (the one with the hard edges). Another dialog window opens, which is split into two sections: user variables and system variables. You are interested in **System variables** because that is where we declare **JAVA_HOME**. Just click the **New** button, and a small dialog window appears with two text fields; one requires you to enter the variable name—JAVA_HOME, in this case, and one requires you to enter the path—the JDK path in this case. The second window and the variable information pop-up dialog window are depicted in Figure 2-6.

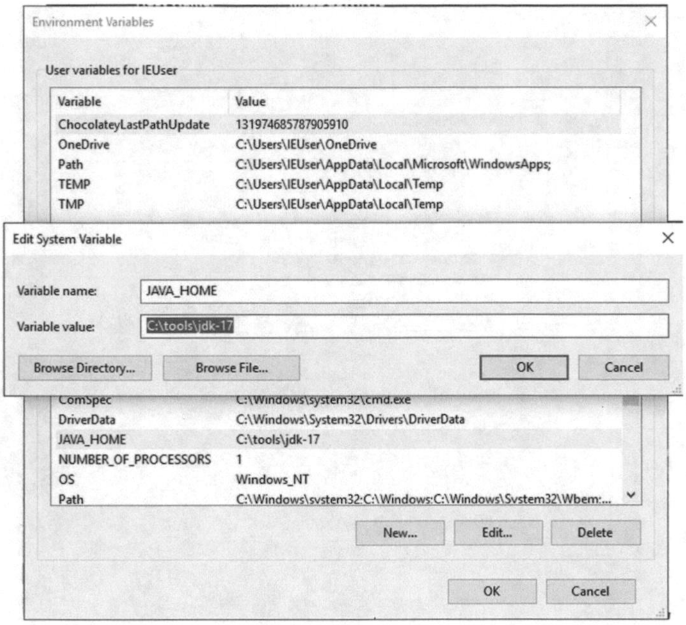

Figure 2-6. *Declaring JAVA_HOME as a system variable on Windows 10*

After defining the JAVA_HOME variable, you need to add the executables to the system path. This can be done by editing the Path variable. Just select it from the System Variables list and click the **Edit** button. Starting in Windows 10, each part of the Path variable is shown on a different line, so you can add a new line and add %JAVA_HOME%\ bin on it. This syntax is practical because it takes the location of the bin directory from whatever location the JAVA_HOME variable contains. The dialog window is depicted in Figure 2-7.

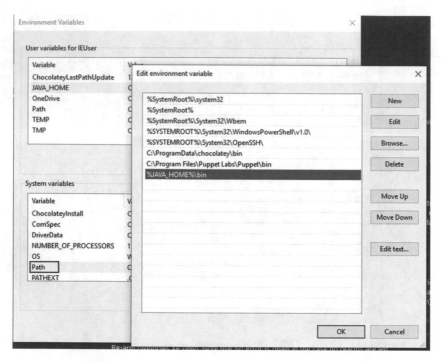

Figure 2-7. *Declaring the JDK executables directory as part of the system Path variable on Windows 10*

On older Windows systems, the contents of the Path are shown in a text field. This means that you must add the %JAVA_HOME%\bin expression in the **Variable** text field and separate it from the existing content by using a semicolon (;).

No matter which Windows system you have, you can check that you set everything correctly by opening **Command Prompt** and executing the set command. This lists all the system variables and their values. JAVA_HOME and Path should be there with the desired values. For the setup proposed in this section when executing the set the output is depicted in Figure 2-8.

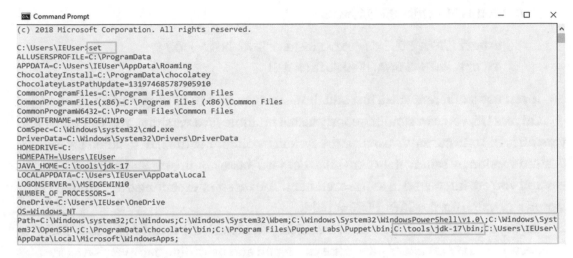

Figure 2-8. *Windows 10 system variables listed with the 'set' command*

If you execute the previous command and see the expected output, you can now test your Java installation by executing `java -version` in the **Command Prompt** window, which prints the expected result, similar to the contents of Listing 2-1.

Listing 2-1. Java 17 Log for Execution of `java -version`

```
$ java -version
openjdk version "17-ea" 2021-09-14
OpenJDK Runtime Environment (build 17-ea+3-125)
OpenJDK 64-Bit Server VM (build 17-ea+3-125, mixed mode, sharing)
```

JAVA_HOME on macOS

The location in which JDK is installed is /Library/Java/JavaVirtualMachines/jdk-17. jdk/Contents/Home. Your JAVA_HOME should point to this location. To do this for the current user, you can do the following:

- In the /Users/{your.user} directory,[3] create a file named .bash_ profile, if it doesn't exist already.

---

[3] Replace {your.user} with your actual system username.

- In this file, write the following:

```
export JAVA_HOME=$(/usr/libexec/java_home -v17)
export PATH=$JAVA_HOME/bin:$PATH
```

If you use a different shell, just add the same two lines in its own configuration file.

On macOS, you can simultaneously install multiple Java versions. You can set which version is the one currently used on the system by obtaining the JDK location for the desired version by calling the /usr/libexec/java_home command and giving the Java version you are interested in as the argument. The result of executing the command is stored as a value for the JAVA_HOME variable.

On my system, I have JDK 8 to 17 installed. I can check the location for each JDK by executing /usr/libexec/java_home command and providing each version as an argument. The commands and outputs for versions 8 and 17 are depicted in Listing 2-2.

Listing 2-2. Java 8 and 17 Locations Obtaind By Calling /usr/libexec/ java_home

```
$ /usr/libexec/java_home -v17
/Library/Java/JavaVirtualMachines/jdk-17.jdk/Contents/Home

$ /usr/libexec/java_home -v1.8
/Library/Java/JavaVirtualMachines/jdk1.8.0_162.jdk/Contents/Home
```

ℹ   Manually installing Java and declaring the JAVA_HOME environment variable can be avoided by using SDKMAN.

The line export PATH=$JAVA_HOME/bin:$PATH adds the contents of the bin directory from the JDK location to the system patch. This means that I could open a terminal and execute any of the Java executables under it. For example, I could verify that the Java version set as default for my user is the expected one by executing java -version.

Depending on the version given as argument, a different JDK location is returned. If you want to test the value of the JAVA_HOME, the echo command can help with that. Listing 2-3 depicts the outputs of the echo and java -version commands.

Listing 2-3. echo and java -version commands to check JAVA_HOME value and the Java version installed

```
$ echo $JAVA_HOME
/Library/Java/JavaVirtualMachines/jdk-17.jdk/Contents/Home

$ java -version
openjdk version "17-ea" 2021-09-14
OpenJDK Runtime Environment (build 17-ea+3-125)
OpenJDK 64-Bit Server VM (build 17-ea+3-125, mixed mode, sharing)
```

JAVA_HOME on Linux

> 🛈   If you are using Linux proficiently, you are either using a PPA or SDKMAN , so you can skip this section. However, if you like to control where the JDK is and define your own environment variables, keep reading.

Linux systems are Unix-like operating systems. This is similar to macOS, which is based on Unix. Depending on your Linux distribution, installing Java can be done via the specific package manager or by directly downloading the JDK as a *.tar.gz archive from the official Oracle site.

If Java is installed using a package manager, the necessary executables are usually automatically placed in the system path at installation time. That is why in this book we cover only the cases where you do everything manually, and choose to install Java only for the current user in a location such as /home/{your.user}/tools/jdk-17.jdk, because covering package managers is not the object of the book.[4]

After downloading the JDK archive from the Oracle site and unpacking it at /home/{your.user}/tools/jdk-17.jdk, you need to create a file named either .bashrc or .bash_profile in your user home directory. On some Linux distributions the files might already exist, and you just need to edit them. Add the following to lines:

```
export JAVA_HOME=/home/{your.user}/tools/jdk-17.jdk
export PATH=$JAVA_HOME/bin:$PATH
```

---

[4] Linux users do not really need this section anyway.

45

As you can see, the syntax is similar to macOS. To check the location of the JDK and the Java version, the same commands mentioned in the macOS section are used.

Installing Maven

ⓘ   The sources for the first edition of this book were organized in a Gradle multimodule project. As per readers' request, the sources for this book are organized in a Maven multimodule project.

The sources attached to this book are organized in small projects that can be compiled and executed using the Apache Maven. You can download it and read more about it on its official page: https://maven.apache.org. Apache Maven is a software project management and comprehension tool. It was chosen as a build tool for this book because of the easy setup (XML is pretty much omnipresent nowadays) and because of its long-term relationship with Java. It is practical to learn a build tool, because for medium-sized and large projects they are a must-have since they facilitate the declaration, download, and upgrade of dependencies.

Installing Maven is quite easy. Just download it, unpack it somewhere, and declare the M2_HOME environment variable. Instructions on how to do this are part of the official site, or you can use SDKMAN.

Once you have Maven installed you can check to see that it is installed successfully, and that it uses the JDK version you expect, by opening a terminal (or Command Prompt on Windows) and executing mvn -version. The output should look pretty similar to the one in Listing 2-4.

Listing 2-4. Output of Command mvn -version on macOS

```
$ mvn --version
Apache Maven 3.6.3 (cecedd343002696d0abb50b32b541b8a6ba2883f)
Maven home: /Users/iulianacosmina/.sdkman/candidates/maven/current
Java version: 17-ea, vendor: Oracle Corporation, runtime: /Library/Java/
JavaVirtualMachines/jdk-17.jdk/Contents/Home
Default locale: en_GB, platform encoding: UTF-8
OS name: "mac os x", version: "10.16", arch: "x86_64", family: "mac"
```

❶   If you are pursuing a career in Java development, knowing a build tool well is a valuable advantage. Most companies using Java have big projects, organized in interdependent modules that cannot be managed without a build tool. Apache Maven has been the de facto build tool for Java for a long time, so you might want to get familiar with it.

Installing Git

This is an optional section, but as a developer, being familiar with a versioning system is important, so here it is. To install Git on your system, just go to the official page at `https://git-scm.com/downloads` and download the installer. Open the installer and click **Next** until done. This works for Windows and macOS.[5] Yes, it is this easy; you do not need to do anything else. On Linux, it can be done using a PPA.

Just in case you need it, here is a page with instructions on how to install Git for all operating systems: `https://gist.github.com/derhuerst/1b15ff4652a867391f03`

To test that Git installed successfully on your system, open a terminal (**Command Prompt** in Windows, and any type of terminal you have installed on macOS and Linux) and run `git --version` to see the result that it is printed. It should be the version of Git that you just installed. The expected output should be similar to Listing 2-5.

Listing 2-5. Output of Command `git --version` to Verify Git Installation

```
$ git --version
git version 2.20.1
```

Now that you have Git installed, you can get the sources for this book by cloning the official Git repository in a terminal or directly from the IDE.

Installing a Java IDE

The editor that I recommend, based on my experience of more than 10 years, is IntelliJ IDEA. It is produced by a company called JetBrains. You can download this IDE from their official site at `https://www.jetbrains.com/idea/download/`. The Ultimate Edition

---

[5] For macOS, you can use homebrew (`https://brew.sh`) as well.

expires after 30 days; beyond that, a paid license is required. There is also a community edition available that can be used without a license. For simple projects that facilitate learning Java, this version suffices.

After you download the IntelliJ IDEA archive, double-click it to install it. After that, start it and configure your plug-ins first. Click the **Plug-ins** menu item and on the right side of the window, a list of plug-ins should appear. The list of plug-ins on the **Installed** tab is what you might want to check out (depicted in Figure 2-9).

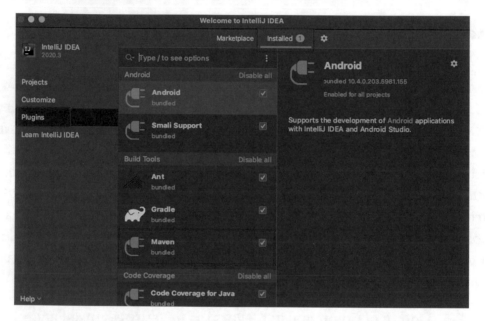

Figure 2-9. *IntelliJ IDEA Community Edition configure plug-ins window*

> ❶ The plug-ins necessary for diverse styles of Java projects are enabled by default in IntelliJ IDEA. You can modify that list and disable the ones you do not need. This will reduce the amount of memory IntelliJ IDEA needs to function.

The Maven plug-in is enabled by default; so is the Git plug-in. This means your IDE is suitable for use right away. This means that you need to get your hands on the sources for this book. There are three ways to get the sources for the book:

- Download the zipped package directly from GitHub.

- Clone the repository using a terminal (or Git Bash Shell in Windows) using the following command:

  ```
  $ git clone https://github.com/Apress/java-17-for-
  absolute-beginners.git
  ```

- Clone the project using IntelliJ IDEA.

Cloning from the command line or from IntelliJ IDEA, does not require a GitHub user when the HTTPS URL of the repository is used. Figure 2-10 shows the two steps necessary to clone the GitHub project for this book.

Figure 2-10. *IntelliJ IDEA Community Edition Clone from VCS windows*

When opening IntelliJ IDEA the first time, select the **Projects** menu item, then click the **Clone from VCS** button. A new dialog window appears and in it you can insert the repository URL and the location where the sources should be copied. After clicking the **Clone** button, the project will be copied, and IntelliJ IDEA will open it and figure out it uses Maven.

If you cloned the project using the command line, you can import it in IntelliJ IDEA using the **Open** Button and selecting the directory created by the cloning operation.

ⓘ IntelliJ IDEA has its own internal Maven bundle. If you want to tell IntelliJ IDEA to use your local installation, just open the **Preferences** menu item, go to **Build, Execution, Deployment ➤ Build Tools ➤ Maven** section and select the external Maven installation directory.

And this is it. Starting in the next chapter some code snippets are presented, so go ahead and build the project. This can be done by executing the maven install phase by double-clicking on it in the IntelliJ IDEA Maven view, as depicted in Figure 2-11.

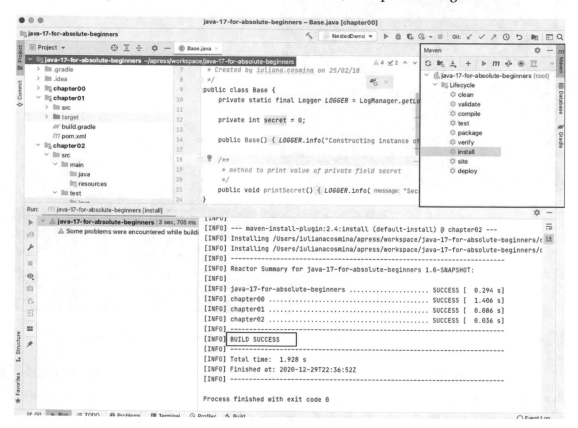

Figure 2-11. *IntelliJ IDEA Maven view*

It is expected that a window be opened at the bottom of the editor depicting the build progress, and if the sources are okay too, this process should end with the message BUILD SUCCESS being printed.

---

❶   If the build fails in IntelliJ IDEA, and you want to identify the problem, the first step is running outside the IDE. You can run the build in a terminal (or Command Prompt on Windows) by executing mvn clean install. If the build passes in the terminal, the sources and your setup is correct and there is a problem with the editor configuration for sure.

The Maven build follows a specific lifecycle to transform a Java project from sources to something that can be executed or deployed to an application server. Phases are executed in a specific order. Running a specific phase using the mvn {phase} command executes a number of steps named goals, each responsible for a specific task.

The mvn clean install command recommended previously executes a clean phase, that deletes previously generated bytecode files and then an install phase that compiles Java files into bytecode, executes tests, if there are any, packs them up in Java Archives (*.jar files) and copies them to the local Maven repository. If you want to read more about Maven just check out the official site: https://maven.apache.org, but for the scope as this book, everything has been made really easy for you as explained in **Chapter 3**.

Summary

If any of instructions are unclear to you (or I missed something), do not hesitate to use the World Wide Web to search for answers. All the software technologies introduced in this chapter are backed up by comprehensive official websites and by huge communities of developers eager to help. In the worst-case scenario, when you find nothing, you can always create an issue on the Apress GitHub official repository for this book or drop me an email. I'll do my best to support you if need be.

But I think you will be fine. Java is hardly rocket science.[6]

---

[6] It wasn't until Java 9, but this book should make it easier for beginner developers.

CHAPTER 3

Getting Your Feet Wet

This chapter covers the fundamental building blocks and terms of the Java language. Although it could be considered yet another introductory chapter, it is quite important. The previous chapter left you with a complete development environment configured for writing Java code. It is time to make use of it. The following topics are covered in this chapter:

- Core syntax parts
- Using JShell
- Java fundamental building blocks: packages, modules, and classes
- Creating a Java project with IntelliJ IDEA
- Compiling and executing of Java code
- Packing a Java application into an executable jar
- Using Maven

Core Syntax Parts

Writing Java code is easy, but before doing so, a few basic syntax rules are necessary. Let's analyze the code sample that started this book, now depicted in Listing 3-1.

Listing 3-1. The Java Beginner Code Sample a Smart Beginner Deserves

```
package com.apress.ch.one.hw;

import java.util.List;

public class Example01 {
    public static void main(String[] args) {
        List<String> items = List.of("1", "a", "2", "a", "3", "a");
```

© Iuliana Cosmina 2022

I. Cosmina, *Java 17 for Absolute Beginners*, https://doi.org/10.1007/978-1-4842-7080-6_3

```java
        items.forEach(item -> {
            if (item.equals("a")) {
                System.out.println("A");
            } else {
                System.out.println("Not A");
            }
        });
    }
}
```

The next list explains each line, or group of lines with the same purpose:

- ; (semicolon) is used to mark the end of a statement or declaration.

- `package com.apress.ch.one.hw;` is a package declaration. You can view this statement as an address the class declared in the file.

- `import java.util.List;` is an import statement. JDK provides a number of classes to use when writing code. Those classes are organized in packages too and when you want to use one of them, you have to specify the class to use and its package, because two classes might have the same name but are declared in different packages. And when the compiler compiles your code, it needs to know exactly which class is needed.

- `public class Example01` is a class declaration statement. It contains an accessor (`public`), the type (`class`) and the name of the class (`Example01`). A class has a body that is wrapped between curly braces.

- `{ ... }` (curly braces) are used to group statements together into code blocks. Blocks do not require to be ended with a ;. Blocks of code can represent a body of a class, a method, or just a few statements that have to be grouped together.

- `public static void main(String[] args)` is a method declaration statement. It contains an accessor (`public`), a reserved keyword (`static`) that will be explained later, the name of the method (`main`), and a section that declares parameters (`(String[] args)`).

- `List<String> items = List.of("1", "a", "2", "a", "3", "a");`
  is a statement declaring a variable named `items` of type
  `List<String>` and assigning the value returned by this statement to it:
  `List.of("1", "a", "2", "a", "3", "a")`.

- `items.forEach(...)` is a statement containing a function call on the
  `items` variable used to traverse all values in this list variable.

- `item -> { ... }` is a lambda expression. It declares a code block to
  be executed for each item in the list.

- `if (<condition>) { ... } else { ... }` is a decisional statement.
  The block of code being executed is decided by evaluating the
  condition.

- `System.out.println(<text>);` is a statement used to print an
  argument passed to it.

It's too early in the book to start explaining everything in the previous list in detail, but the most important rule when writing Java code is that except for package declarations and import statements, all code must be within a block. Also, if a statement is not spread on multiple lines, it must end with ";", otherwise the code will not compile.

Before starting to write more verbose Java classes, it is good to start writing simple Java statements and get used to the syntax. Starting with Java 9, this is possible using JShell, an interactive tool for learning the Java programming language and prototyping Java code. So instead of writing your code in a class, compiling it, and executing the bytecode, you can just use JShell to directly execute statements.

Using JShell

JShell is quite late to the party, as scripting languages like Python and Node introduced similar utilities years ago, and JVM languages like Scala, Clojure, and Groovy followed in their footsteps. But better late than never.

JShell is a Read-Eval-Print Loop (REPL), which evaluates declarations, statements, and expressions as they are entered and then immediately shows the results. It is practical to try new ideas and techniques quickly and without the need to have a complete development environment, nor an entire context for the code to be executed in.

JShell is a standard component of the JDK. The executable to start is in the `bin` directory located in the JDK installation directory. This means that all you have to do is open a terminal (Command Prompt in Windows) and type `jshell`. If the contents of the `bin` directory were added to the system path, you should see a welcome message containing the JDK version on your system. Also, the root of your terminal changes to `jshell>` to let you know you are now using `jshell`.

In Listing 3-2, jshell was started in verbose mode, by calling `jshell -v`, which enables detailed feedback to be provided for all statements executed until the end of the session.

Listing 3-2. Output of Command `jshell -v`

```
$ jshell -v
|  Welcome to JShell -- Version 17-ea
|  For an introduction type: /help intro

jshell>
```

If you are executing the commands as you are reading the book, go ahead and enter `/help` to view a list of all the available actions and commands. Assuming you are not, Listing 3-3 depicts the expected output.

Listing 3-3. Output of Command `/help` in `jshell`

```
jshell> /help
|  Type a Java language expression, statement, or declaration.
|  Or type one of the following commands:
|  /list [<name or id>|-all|-start]
|    list the source you have typed
|  /edit <name or id>
|    edit a source entry
|  /drop <name or id>
|    delete a source entry
|  /save [-all|-history|-start] <file>
|    Save snippet source to a file
...
|  /exit [<integer-expression-snippet>]
|    exit the jshell tool
...
```

In Java, values are assigned to groups of characters named **variables**. (More about how to choose them and use them in **Chapter 4**.) To begin using JShell, we'll declare a variable named `six` and assign the value 6 to it *(I know, smart right?)*. The statement and the `jshell` logs are depicted in Listing 3-4.

Listing 3-4. Declaring a Variable Using `jshell`

```
jshell> int six = 6;
six ==> 6
|  created variable six : int
```

As you can see, the log message is clear and tells us that our command was executed successfully, and a variable of type `int` named `six` was created. The six ==> 6 lets us know that value 6 was assigned to the variable that we just created.

You can create as many variables as you want and perform mathematical operations, string concatenations, and anything that you need to quickly execute. As long as the JShell session is not closed, the variables exist and can be used. Listing 3-5 depicts a few statements being executed with JShell and their results.

Listing 3-5. `jshell` Various Statements and Outputs

```
jshell> int six = 6
six ==> 6
|  modified variable six : int
|    update overwrote variable six : int
jshell> six = six + 1
six ==> 7
|  assigned to six : int
jshell> six +1
$14 ==> 8
|  created scratch variable $14 : int
jshell> System.out.println("Current val: " + six)
Current val: 7
```

The $14 ==> 8 depicted in the previous code listing shows the value 8 being assigned to a variable named $14. This variable was created by jshell. When the result of a statement is not assigned to a variable named by the developer, jshell generates a scratch variable and its name is made of the $(dollar) character and a number representing an internal index for that variable. It is not explicitly stated in the documentation, but from my observations while playing with jshell, the index value appears to be the number of the statement that lead to its creation.

---

❶   One of the most important building blocks of Java code is the **class**. Classes are pieces of code that model real-world objects and events. Classes contain two types of **members**: those modelling states, which are the class variables, also named **fields** or **properties**, and those modelling behaviors, named **methods**.

JDK provides a lot of classes that model the base components needed to create most applications. Classes are covered in more detail in the next chapter. Even if some concepts seem foreign now, just be patient and let them accumulate; they will make more sense later.

One of the most important JDK class is java.lang.String, which is used to represent text objects. This class provides a rich set of methods that manipulate the value of a String variable. Listing 3-6 depicts a few of these methods being called on a declared variable of type String.

Listing 3-6. jshell Method Calling Examples with String Variable

```
jshell> String lyric = "twice as much ain't twice as good"
lyric ==> "twice as much ain't twice as good"
|  created variable lyric : String

jshell> lyric.toUpperCase()
$18 ==> "TWICE AS MUCH AIN'T TWICE AS GOOD"
|  created scratch variable $18 : String
jshell> lyric.length()
$20 ==> 33
|  created scratch variable $20 : int
```

The task of writing Java code in jshell using variables of JDK types might look complicated, because you do not know what method to call, right? jshell is quite helpful because it tells you when the method does not exist. When trying to call a method, you can press the <Tab> key and a list of methods available is displayed. This is called **code completion** and smart Java editors offer it too.

In Listing 3-7, you can see the error message printed by jshell when you try to call a method that does not exist and how to display and filter methods available for a certain type.

Listing 3-7. More jshell Method Calling Examples with String Variable

```
jshell> lyric.toupper()
|  Error:
|  cannot find symbol
|    symbol:   method toupper()
|  lyric.toupper()
|  ^-----------^

jshell> lyric.to # <Tab>
toCharArray() toLowerCase( toString() toUpperCase(
jshell> lyric. # <Tab>
charAt( chars() codePointAt(
codePointBefore( codePointCount( codePoints()
...
```

JShell is quite obvious in telling us that the toupper() method is not known for String class.

When listing possible methods, methods ending in (require no arguments. The methods ending in a single open parentheses take none or more arguments and have more than one form. To view those forms, just write the method on your variable and press <Tab> again. Listing 3-8 depicts the multiple forms of the indexOf method.

Listing 3-8. jshell Listing All the Forms of the indexOf Method in the String Class

```
jshell> lyric.indexOf( # <Tab>
$1      $14     $18     $19     $2      $20     $5      $9      lyric   six

Signatures:
int String.indexOf(int ch)
int String.indexOf(int ch, int fromIndex)
int String.indexOf(String str)
int String.indexOf(String str, int fromIndex)

<press tab again to see documentation>
```

Right after the `lyric.indexOf(` line jshell lists the variables that were created during the session, to give you an easy choice of existing arguments.

Anything you would write in a Java project, you can write it in `jshell` as well. The advantage is that you can split your program in a sequence of statements, execute them instantly to check the result, and adjust as necessary. There are other things that `jshell` can do for you and the most important are part of this book.

All variables you declared in a JShell session are listed by executing the `/vars` command. Listing 3-9 depicts the variables declared in the session for this chapter.

Listing 3-9. `jshell>` `/vars` Output Sample for a Small Coding Session

```
jshell> /vars
|    int $1 = 5
|    int $2 = 42
|    int $5 = 8
|    int $9 = 8
|    int six = 7
|    int $14 = 8
|    String lyric = "twice as much ain't twice as good"
|    String $18 = "TWICE AS MUCH AIN'T TWICE AS GOOD"
|    int $19 = 9
|    int $20 = 33
```

If you want to save all your input from a JShell session, you can do so by executing the `/save {filename}.java`.[1]

Assuming all statements are valid Java statements, the statements in the resulting file can be executed into a new JShell session using the `/open {filename}.java` command.

There is a JShell complete user guide[2] available on the Oracle official site if you are interested in trying every command and every feature it has to offer.

---

[1] Replace {filename} with an actual name.

[2] The Oracle JShell user guide can be found at Oracle, "Java Shell User's Guide," `https://docs.oracle.com/javase/9/jshell/JSHEL.pdf`, accessed October 15, 2021.

Java Fundamental Building Blocks

⚠️   This is a consistent introduction into Java as a platform. To write code confidently, you need to have a grasp of what happens under the hood, what the building blocks are, and the order in which you have to configure/write them. If you want, you can skip the next section altogether, but in the same way some new drivers need a little knowledge of how the engine works before grabbing the driving wheel confidently, some people might feel more confident and in control when programming if they understand the mechanics a little. So I wanted to make sure that anyone reading this book gets a proper start.

To write Java applications, a developer must be familiar with the Java building blocks of a Java program. Think about it like this: if you are trying to build a car, you have to learn what wheels are and where they are placed, right? This is what I'm trying to achieve for Java in this book: to explain all the components and their purpose.

The core of this ecosystem is the **class**. There are other **object types**[3] in Java, but classes are the most important because they represent the templates for the objects making up an application. A class mainly contains **fields** and **methods**. When an object is created, the values of the fields define the state of the object, and the methods describe its behavior.

ℹ️   The Java object is a model of a real-world object. So if we choose to model a car in Java, we will choose to define fields that describe the car: manufacturer, modelName, productionYear, color, and speed. The methods of our car class describe what the car does. A car does mainly two things: accelerates and brakes, so any method should describe actions related to these two things.

Packages

When you are writing Java code, you are writing code to describe state and behavior of real-world items. The code must be organized in classes and other types that are used together to build an application. All types are described in files with the `.java` extension. Object types are organized in **packages**.

---

[3] Such as interfaces, enums, annotations, and records.

A package is a logical collection of types: some of them are visible outside the package, and some of them are not, depending on their scope.

💡 To understand the way packages work, imagine a box containing other boxes. Those boxes might be filled with other boxes, or they might be filled with some items that are not boxes. For the sake of this example, let's say those items are Lego pieces. This analogy works well, because Java types can be composed in the same way as Lego pieces are.

Package names must be unique, and their name should follow a certain template. This template is usually defined by the company working on the project. Good practices say that to ensure unicity and meaning, you typically begin the name with your organization's Internet domain name in reverse order, then add various grouping criteria.

In this project, package names follow the template depicted here: `com.apress. bgn.[<star>]+`. This template begins with the reversed domain name for Apress publisher (`www.apress.com`), then a term identifying the book is added (*bgn* is a shortcut for beginner) and at last, the `<star>` replaces the number of the package the source (usually) matches.

Considering the previously introduced boxes and Legos analogy, the `com` package is the big box containing the `apress` box. It could contain other Legos too, but for this example it does not.

The `apress` box represents the `com.apress` package and contains the `bgn` box.

The `bgn` represents the `com.apress.bgn` package box and contains boxes specific to each chapter, containing either other boxes and/or Legos. The Legos are the Java files, containing Java code. Figure 3-1 represents these boxes and Legos and the way they are nested.

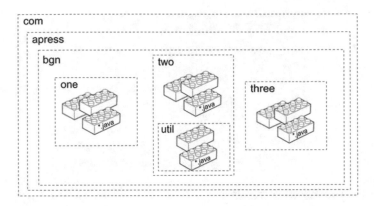

Figure 3-1. *Java packages with source code represented as nested boxes and Legos*

On your computer, a package is a hierarchy of directories. Each directory contains other directories and/or Java files. It all depends on your organizational skills. This organization is important, because any Java object type can be identified uniquely using the package name and its own name.

If we were to write a class named HelloWorld in a file named HelloWorld.java and put this file in package com.apress.bgn.one, in a Java project the com.apress.bgn.one. HelloWorld alliteration is the full class name that acts as an unique identifier for this class. You can view the package name as an address of that class.

Starting with Java 5, inside each package a file named package-info.java can be created that contains a package declaration, package annotations, package comments, and Javadoc annotations. The comments are exported to the development documentation for that project, also known as **Javadoc. Chapter 9** covers how to generate the project Javadoc using Maven. The package-info.java must reside under the last directory in the package. So if we define a com.apress.bgn.one package, the overall structure and contents of the Java project looks like Figure 3-2.[4]

---

[4] The chapter03.iml is an IntelliJ IDEA project file.

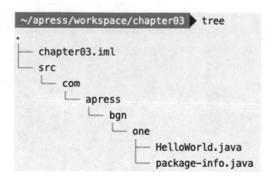

Figure 3-2. *Java package contents*

The package-info.java contents could be similar to the contents of Listing 3-10.

Listing 3-10. package-info.java Contents

```
/**
 * Contains classes used for reading information from various sources.
 * @author iuliana.cosmina
 * @version 1.0-SNAPSHOT
 */
package com.apress.bgn.one;
```

The files with .java extension containing type definitions are compiled into files with .class extension that are organized according to the same package structure and packaged into one or more **JAR**s (**J**ava **Ar**chives).[5] For the previous example, if we were to unpack the JAR resulted after the compilation and linkage, you would see what's shown in Figure 3-3.

---

[5] When JARs are hosted on a repository, such as The Maven Public Repository, they are also called artifacts. You can also read more about jars at Oracle, "JAR File Overview," https://docs.oracle.com/javase/8/docs/technotes/guides/jar/jarGuide.html, accessed October 15, 2021.

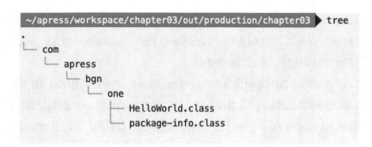

Figure 3-3. *Contents of a sample JAR*

The package-info.java file is compiled too, even if it only holds information about the package and no behavior or types.

---

❶   package-info.java files are not mandatory; packages can be defined without them. They are useful mostly for documentation purposes.

The contents of one package can span across multiple JARs, meaning that if you have more than one subproject in your project you can have the same package name in more than one, containing different classes. A symbolic representation of this is depicted in Figure 3-4.

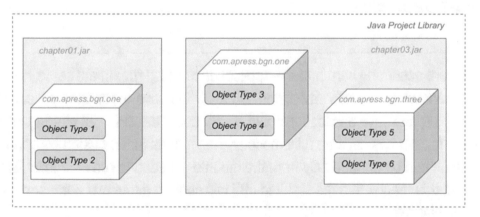

Figure 3-4. *Example of package contents that span across multiple JARs*

A library is a collection of JARs[6] containing classes used to implement a certain functionality. For example, JUnit is a very famous Java framework providing multiple classes that facilitate writing Java unit tests.

A moderately complex Java application references one or more libraries. To run the application, all its dependencies (all the JARs) must be on the classpath. What does this mean? It means that in order to run a Java application, a JDK, the dependencies (external JARs), and the application jars are needed. Figure 3-5 depicts this quite clearly.

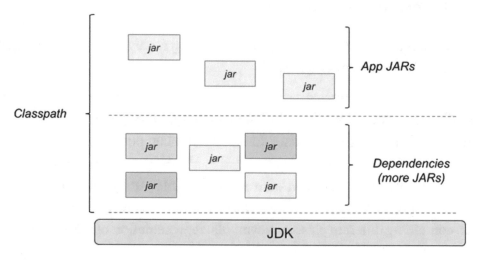

Figure 3-5. *Application classpath*

⚠   We are assuming here that the application is being run on the same environment where it was written, and so the JDK is used to run the application. Until JDK 11, any Java application could be run using the JRE. But starting with version 11, Java has become fully modular. This means that a customized "JRE" distribution can be created only from the modules needed to run an application. Indirectly, this means that the resulted JRE will contain a minimal number of JDK compiled classes.

---

[6] The most-used libraries are logging libraries like Log4J, "Apache Log4j 2," https://logging. apache.org/log4j/2.x and LogBACK, "Logback Project," https://logback.qos.ch, both accessed October 15, 2021.

The JARs that make up an application classpath are (obviously) not always independent of each other. For 21 years this organization style was enough, but in complex applications there were a lot of complications caused by:

- packages scattered in multiple jars. (remember Figure 3-4?) This might lead to code duplication and circular dependencies.

- transitive dependencies between jars which sometimes lead to different versions of the same class being on the classpath. This might lead to unpredictable application beahvior.

- missing transitive dependencies and accessibility problems. This might lead to an application crash.

All these problems are grouped under one name: **The Jar Hell.**[7] This problem was resolved in Java 9 by introducing another level to organize packages: **modules**. Or at least that was the intention. However, the industry has been reluctant to adopt Java modules. At the time this chapter was written, the majority of Java production applications are still not only stuck on Java 8, but developers avoid modules like they would avoid the plague.

However, before introducing modules, **access modifiers** should be mentioned. Java types and their members are declared with certain access rights within packages, and that is something quite important to understand before jumping to coding.

Access Modifiers

When declaring a type in Java—let's stick to the class for now—because it is the only one mentioned so far, you can configure its scope using access modifiers.

Access modifiers can be used to specify access to classes, and in this case we say that they are used at top-level.

They can be also be used to specify access to class members, and in this case they are used at member-level.[8]

At top-level only two access modifiers can be used: public and none.

---

[7] If you want to know more, a great article about the Jar Hell is Tech Read, "What Is Jar Hell?," https://tech-read.com/2009/01/13/what-is-jar-hell, accessed October 15, 2021 (though you might want to read it later, after you have written a little code of your own).
[8] We will not mention nested classes right now. We'll get there in **Chapter 4.**

A top-level class that is declared public must be defined in a Java file with the same name. Listing 3-11 depicts a class named Base that is defined in a file named Base.java located in package com.apress.bgn.zero.

Listing 3-11. Base Class

```java
package com.apress.bgn.zero;

// top-level access modifier
public class Base {
    // code omitted
}
```

The contents of the class are not depicted for the moment and replaced with ... to stop you from losing focus. A public class is visible to all classes anywhere in the application. A different class in a different package can create an object of this type, as depicted in Listing 3-12:

Listing 3-12. Creating an Object Using the Base Class

```java
package com.apress.bgn.three;

import com.apress.bgn.zero.Base;

public class Main {
    public static void main(String... args) {
        // creating an object of type Base
        Base base = new Base();
    }
}
```

The line Base base = new Base(); is where the object is created. The new keyword represents an operation called instantiation of a class, which means an object is created based on the specification described by the code that represents the Base class.

---

❶   A class is a template. Objects are created using this template and are called instances.

---

❶   For now, just let this affirmation sink in: a public class is visible to all classes everywhere.

When no explicit access modifier is mentioned, it is said that the class is declared as **default** or that it is **package-private**. I know it seems confusing that there are two ways to talk about the lack of access modifiers, but since you might read other books or blog posts that refer to this situation, it is better to have all the possibilities listed here.

This means if a class has no access modifier, the class can be used to create objects only by the classes defined in the same package. Its scope is limited to the package it is defined in. A class without an access modifier can be defined in any Java file: one that has the same name, or right next to the class that gives the file its name.

❶   When multiple classes are declared in the same file, the public class must have the same name as the file it is defined in, thus this is the class that names the file.

To test this, let's add a class named `HiddenBase` in the `Base.java` file introduced previously, as depicted in Listing 3-13.

Listing 3-13. Class with No Access Modifier

```
package com.apress.bgn.zero;

public class Base {
    // code omitted
}

class HiddenBase {
    // you cannot see me
}
```

Notice that the `Base` class is declared in the `com.apress.bgn.zero` package. If we try to create an object of type `HiddenBase`, in a class declared within package `com.apress.bgn.three`, the IDE will warn us by making the text read, and refusing to provide any code completion. Even more, a tab listing the problems of the current file will be opened with an error message that is more than obvious, as depicted in Figure 3-6.

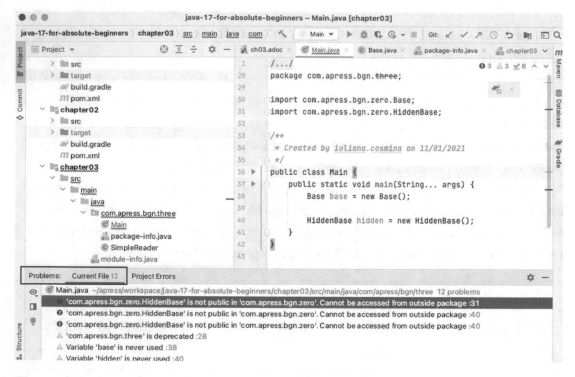

Figure 3-6. *Java class with no accessor modifier error*

---

❶ For now, take this affirmation and let it sink in as well: a class with no access modifier is visible to all classes (and other types) in the same package.

Inside a class the class members are defined: **fields** and **methods**.[9] At member-level two more modifiers can be applied, aside from the two previously mentioned: private and protected. At member-level the access modifiers have the following effect:

- public is the same as at top level; the member can be accessed from everywhere.

- private means that the member can only be accessed in the class where is declared.

---

[9] Aside from that, we can also define other Java types that will be referred to as being nested, but we'll cross that bridge when we come to it.

- protected means that the member can only be accessed in the package where the class containing it is declared or by any subclass of its class in another package.

- none means that the member can only be accessed from within its own package.

It seems complicated, but once you start writing code you get used to it. On the official Oracle documentation page, there is even a table with the visibility of members, shown in Table 3-1.[10]

Table 3-1. *Member-Level Accessors Scope*

Modifier	Class	Package	Subclass	World
public	Yes	Yes	Yes	Yes
protected	Yes	Yes	Yes	No
none (*default/package-private*)	Yes	Yes	No	No
private	Yes	No	No	No

To get an overall idea how that table applies into code, the class in Listing 3-14 is very helpful.

Listing 3-14. PropProvider a Java class with Members Decorated with Various Accessors

```
package com.apress.bgn.three.same;

public class PropProvider {
    public int publicProp;
    protected int protectedProp;
    /* default */ int defaultProp;
    private int privateProp;
```

---

[10] We depicted the table to avoid you the hassle of navigating to this URL at Oracle, "Controlling Access to Members of a Class," https://docs.oracle.com/javase/tutorial/java/javaOO/accesscontrol.html, accessed October 15, 2021.

```
    public PropProvider(){
        privateProp = 0;
    }
}
```

The class `PropProvider` declares four fields/properties, each with a different access modifier. The field `privateProp` can only be modified within the body of this class. This means that all other members of this class can read the value of this property and change it.

At this point in the book, only methods have been mentioned as being other types of members.

But classes can be declared inside the body of another class. Such a class is called a **nested class** and has access to all the members of the class that is wrapped around it, including the private ones. Figure 3-7 depicts the modified `PropProvider` class that has an extra method added, named `printPrivate`. This method reads the value of the private field and prints it. A nested class named `LocalPropRequester` is declared as well, and the private field is shown being modified in this class (line 56).

```
   © PropProvider.java ✕
28        package com.apress.bgn.three.same;
29
30  |≡  ⊟/**
31         * Table 3-1, column Class show in code
32       ⊟ */
33        public class PropProvider {
34            public int publicProp;
35            protected int protectedProp;
36            /* default */ int defaultProp;
37            private int privateProp;
38
39            // constructor
40       ⊟    public PropProvider(){
41                privateProp = 0;
42       ⊟    }
43
44            // method
45       ⊟    public void printPrivate(){
46                System.out.printf("Private member: %d ", privateProp);
47       ⊟    }
48
49            // nested class
50       ⊟    class LocalPropRequester {
51       ⊟        public LocalPropRequester() {
52                    PropProvider provider = new PropProvider();
53                    provider.publicProp = 1;
54                    provider.protectedProp = 2;
55                    provider.defaultProp =3;
56                    provider.privateProp = 4;
57       ⊟        }
58       ⊟    }
59        }
```

Figure 3-7. *Table 3-1, column class accessors in Java code*

Figure 3-7 is a screenshot of how the Java code is viewed in IntelliJ IDEA. If any field is not accessible, it is displayed in red.

The second column in Table 3-1, the `Package` column, covers the fields that are accessible to a class declared in the same package as class `PropProvider`. Figure 3-8 depicts a class named `PropRequester` class trying to modify all fields in class `PropProvider`. Notice the private field is shown in bright red. This means the field is not accessible, and IntelliJ IDEA is being quite obvious about it.

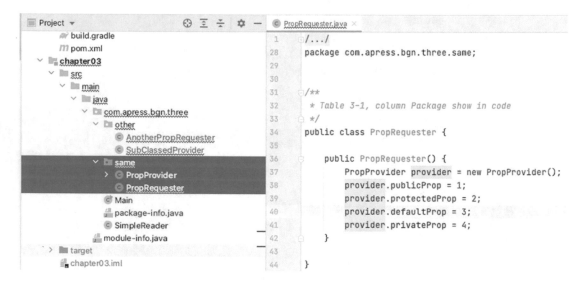

Figure 3-8. *Table 3-1, column package accessors in Java code*

The third column in Table 3-1, the `Subclass` column, covers the fields that are accessible to a subclass of class `PropProvider`. A `subclass` inherits states and behavior from a class it derives from that is called its `superclass`. The subclass is created using the `extends` keyword together with the superclass name. Figure 3-9 depicts a class named `SubClassedProvider` class trying to modify all fields inherited from `PropProvider`. Notice the private field and the field without an accessor shown in bright red. This means the fields are not accessible, and IntelliJ IDEA is being quite obvious about it.

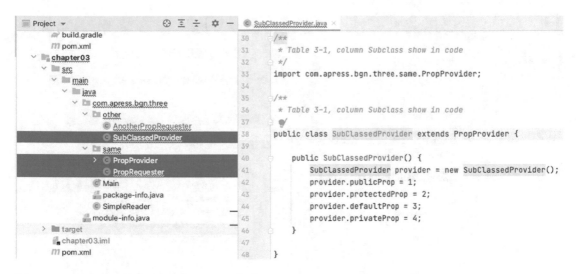

Figure 3-9. *Table 3-1, column subclass accessors in Java code*

---

❶   The field without an accessor is not accessible in the previous example, because the subclass in declared in a different package. If the subclass is moved in the same package, the rules from the `Package` column in Table 3-1 apply.

The third column in Table 3-1, the `World` column, applies to all classes outside the package where class `PropProvider` is declared, that are not subclasses of this class. Figure 3-10 depicts a class named `AnotherPropRequester` that tries to access all fields declared in `PropProvider`. As expected only the public field is accessible, and the rest are shown in red.

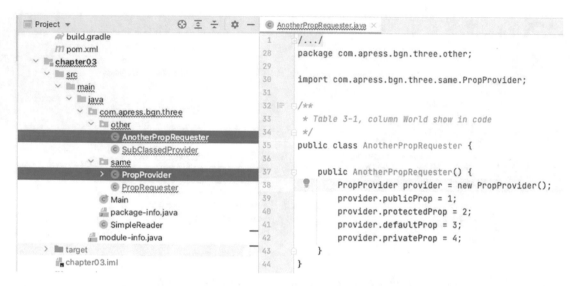

Figure 3-10. *Table 3-1, column world accessors in Java code*

---

❶   If you are trying to build a project outside a smart editor like IntelliJ IDEA, this won't work. The error messages will let you know that there is a compilation error, what is the cause, and where. For example, building the chapter03 subproject containing the AnotherPropRequester class using the Maven build tool fails. The following error messages are displayed in the terminal:

```
[ERROR] Failed to execute goal org.apache.maven.plugins:maven-compiler-
plugin:3.8.1:compile (default-compile) on project chapter03: Compilation
failure: Compilation failure:
[ERROR] /Users/iulianacosmina/apress/workspace/java-17-for-absolute-
beginners/chapter03/src/main/java/com/apress/bgn/three/other/
AnotherPropRequester.java:[42,17] protectedProp has protected access in
com.apress.bgn.three.same.PropProvider
[ERROR] /Users/iulianacosmina/apress/workspace/java-17-for-absolute-
beginners/chapter03/src/main/java/com/apress/bgn/three/other/
AnotherPropRequester.java:[44,17] defaultProp is not public in com.apress.
bgn.three.same.PropProvider; cannot be accessed from outside package
```

```
[ERROR] /Users/iulianacosmina/apress/workspace/java-17-for-absolute-
beginners/chapter03/src/main/java/com/apress/bgn/three/other/
AnotherPropRequester.java:[46,17] privateProp has private access in com.
apress.bgn.three.same.PropProvider
```

Build tools and editors are pretty good at letting you know when something is wrong in your Java code. Learn to use them well, trust them, and they will increase your productivity. Sure, there are hiccups, but not that many.

You will probably come back to Table 3-1 once or twice after you start writing Java code. Everything just mentioned is still valid even after the introduction of modules (if you configure module access properly, that is).

Modules

Starting with Java 9 a new concept was introduced: `modules`.[11] Java modules represent a more powerful mechanism to organize and aggregate packages. The implementation of this new concept took more than 10 years. The discussion about modules started in 2005, and the hope was for them to be implemented for Java 7. Under the name **Project Jigsaw,** an exploratory phase eventually started in 2008. Java developers hoped a modular JDK would be available with Java 8, but that did not happen.

Modules finally arrived in Java 9 after three years of work (and almost seven of analysis). Supporting them delayed the official release date of Java 9 to September 2017.[12]

A Java module is a way to group packages and configure more granulated access to package contents. A Java module is a uniquely named, reusable group of packages and resources (e.g., XML files and other types of non-Java files) described by a file named `module-info.java`, located at the root of the source directory. This file contains the following information:

- the module's name

- the module's dependencies (that is, other modules this module depends on)

---

[11] Build tools such as Maven or Gradle refer to subproject as modules as well, but their purpose is different from the one of the Java modules.

[12] The full history of the Jigsaw project can be found at Open JDK, "Project Jigsaw," `http://openjdk.java.net/projects/jigsaw`, accessed October 15, 2021.

- the packages it explicitly makes available to other modules (all other packages in the module are implicitly unavailable to other modules)

- the services it offers

- the services it consumes

- to what other modules it allows reflection

- native code

- resources

- configuration data

In theory, module naming resembles package naming and follows the reversed-domain-name convention. In practice, just make sure the module name does not contain any numbers and that it reveals clearly what its purpose is. The module-info.java file is compiled into a module descriptor, which is a file named module-info.class that is packed together with classes into a plain old JAR file. The file is located at the root of the Java source directory, outside of any package. For the chapter03 project introduced earlier, the module-info.java file is located in the src/main/java directory, at the same level with the com directory; the root of the com.apress.bgn.three package Figure 3-11.

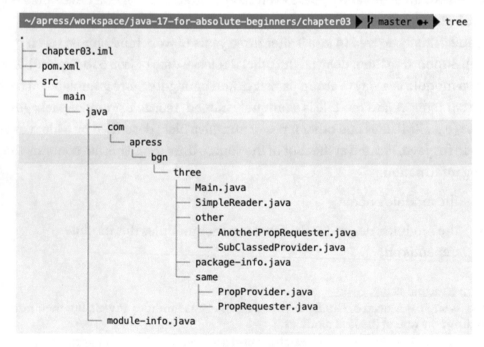

Figure 3-11. *Location of the module-info.java file*

As any file with *.java extension, the module-info.java is compiled into a *.class file. As the module declaration is not a part of Java type declaration, module is not a Java keyword, so it can still be used when writing code for Java types; as a variable name, for example. For package the situation is different, as every Java type declaration must start with a package declaration. Just take a look at the SimpleReader class declared in Listing 3-15.

Listing 3-15. SimpleReader Class

```
package com.apress.bgn.three;

public class SimpleReader {
    private String source;

    // code omitted
}
```

You can see the package declaration, but where is the module? Well, the module is an abstract concept, described by the module-info.java. So starting with Java 9, if you are configuring Java modules in your application, Figure 3-4 evolves into Figure 3-12.

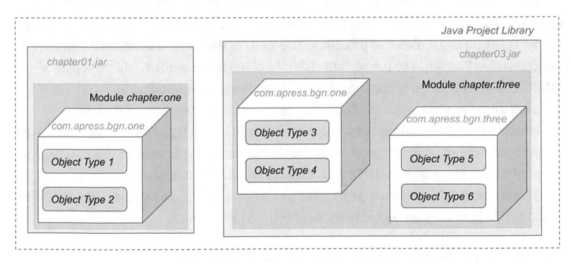

Figure 3-12. *Java modules represented visually*

A Java module is a way to logically group Java packages that belong together.

The introduction of modules allows for the JDK to be divided into modules too. The `java --list-modules` command lists all modules in your local JDK installation. Listing 3-16 depicts the output of this command executed on my personal computer where currently JDK 17-ea is installed.

Listing 3-16. JDK 17-ea Modules

```
$ java --list-modules
java.base@17-ea
java.compiler@17-ea
java.datatransfer@17-ea
java.desktop@17-ea

# output omitted
```

Each module name is followed by a version string @17-ea in the previous listing, which means that the module belongs to Java version 17-ea.

So if a Java application does not require all modules, a runtime can be created only with the modules that it needs, which reduces the runtime's size. The tool to build a smaller runtime customized to an application is called `jlink` and is part of the JDK executables. This allows for bigger levels of scalability and increased performance. How to use `jlink` is not an object of this book. The focus of the book is learning the Java programming language, so the technical details of the Java platform will be kept to a minimum—just enough to start writing and executing code confidently.

There are multiple benefits of introducing modules that more experienced developers have been waiting for years to take advantage of. But configuring modules for bigger and more complex projects is no walk in the park, and most software companies they either preffer to stick to JDK 8 or to avoid configuring modules altogether.

The contents of the `module-info.java` can be as simple as the name of the module and two brackets containing the body, as shown in Listing 3-17.

Listing 3-17. A Simple `module-info.java` Configuration

```
module chapter.three {
}
```

Advanced Module Configurations

A Java module declaration body contains one or more `directives` that are constructed using the keywords in Table 3-2. These directives represent access configurations and dependency requirements for the packages and classes contained in the modules.

Table 3-2. *Java Module Directives*

Directive	Purpose
requires	Specifies that the module depends on another module.
exports	One of the module's packages whose `public` types (and their `nested public` and `protected` types) should be accessible to code in all other modules.
exports ... to	This is the qualified version of the `exports` directive. It enables specifying in a comma-separated list precisely which module or module code can access the exported package.
open	Used at module level declaration (`open module mm {}`), and allows reflective access to all module packages. Java Reflection is the process of analyzing and modifying all the capabilities of a class at runtime and works on private types and members too. So before Java 9, nothing was really encapsulated.
opens	Is used inside the body of a module's declaration to selectively configure access through reflection only to certain packages.
opens ... to	This is the qualified version of the `opens` directive. It enables specifying in a comma-separated list precisely which module or module code can access its packages reflectively.
uses	Specifies a service used by this module—making the module a **service consumer**. A service in this case represents the full name of a interface/abstract class that another module provides an implementation for.
provides ... with	Specifies that a module provides a service with a specific implementation—making the module a **service provider**.
transitive	Used together with `requires` to specify a dependency on another module and to ensure that other modules reading your module also read that dependency—known as *implied readability*.

This book contains an appendix that provides examples for all directives. For the purpose of learning the Java language the only ones you really need are `requires` and `exports`. In this edition of the book I will explain each of these directives in depth as soon as the context will allow for them to be understood completely, and I will add analogies with real world events and scenarios to make sure the idea comes through. In this chapter only the two main directives will be explained first.

Modules can depend on one another. The project for this book is made of 13 modules, and most on them depend on module `chapter.zero`. This module contains the basic components used to build more complex components in the other modules. For example, classes inside module `chapter.three` need access to packages and classes in module `chapter.zero`. Declaring a module dependency is done by using the `requires` directive, as depicted in Listing 3-18.

Listing 3-18. A Simple `module-info.java` Configuration

```java
module chapter.three {
    requires chapter.zero;
}
```

The preceding dependency is an **explicit** one. But there are also **implicit** dependencies. For example, any module declared by a developer implicitly requires the JDK `java.base` module. This module contains the foundational APIs of the Java SE Platform, and no Java application could be written without it. This implicit directive ensures access to a minimal set of Java types, so basic Java code can be written. Listing 3-18 is equivalent to Listing 3-19.

Listing 3-19. A Simple `module-info.java` Configuration with an Explicit Directive of `requires java.base`

```java
module chapter.three {
    requires java.base;

    requires chapter.zero;
}
```

❶   Declaring a module as required, means that that module is required when the code is compiled—frequently referred to as *compile time* and when the code is executed—frequently referred to as *runtime*. If a module is required only at runtime, the **requires static** keywords are used to declare the dependency. Just keep that in mind for now, it will make sense when we talk about web applications.

Now chapter.three depends on module chapter.zero. But does this mean chapter.three can access all public types (and their nested public and protected types) in the all the packages in module chapter.zero ? If you are thinking that this is not enough, you are right. Just because a module depends on another, it does not mean it has access to the packages and classes it actually needs to. The required module must be configured to expose its *insides*. How can this be done? In our case, we need to make sure module chapter.zero gives access to the required packages. This is done by customizing the module-info.java for this module by adding the exports directive, followed by the necessary package names. Listing 3-20 depicts the module-info.java file for the chapter.zero module that exposes its single package.

Listing 3-20. The module-info.java Configuration File for the chapter.zero Module

```
module chapter.zero {
    exports com.apress.bgn.zero;
}
```

💡   Think about it like this: you are in your room cutting out Christmas decorations, and you need a template for your decorations. Your roommate has all the templates. But just because you need it doesn't mean that it will magically appear. You need to go and talk to your roommate. Needing your roommate's assistance can be viewed as the *requires room-mate* directive. After talking to your roommate, he will probably say: *Sure, come in, they are on the desk! Take as many as you need.* This can be considered the *exports all-templates-on-desk* directive. The desk is probably a good analogy for a package.

Using the configuration in Listing 3-20 we have just given access to the `com.apress.bgn.zero` package, to any module configured with a `requires module.zero;` directive. What if we do not want that? (Considering the previous tip, your roommate just left the door to his room open, so anybody can enter and get those templates!)

What if we want to limit the access to module contents only to the `chapter.three` module? (So your roommate has to give you his templates only to you.) This can be done by adding the `to` keyword followed by the module name to clarify, that only this module is allowed to access the components. This is the qualified version of the `exports` directive mentioned in **Table 3-2**.

If you were curious and read the recommended **Jar Hell** article, you noticed that one of the concerns of working with Java sources packed in Jars was security. This is because even without access to Java sources, by adding a jar as a dependency to an application, objects can be inspected, extended, and instantiated. So aside from providing a reliable configuration, better scaling, integrity for the platform, and improved performance, the goal for introduction of modules was in fact **better security**.

Listing 3-21 depicts the `module-info.java` file for the `chapter.zero` module that exposes its single package only to the `chapter.three` module.

Listing 3-21. Advanced `module-info.java` Configuration File for the `chapter.zero` Module

```
module chapter.zero {
    exports com.apress.bgn.zero to chapter.three;
}
```

More than one module can be specified to have access, by listing the desired modules separated by commas, as depicted in Listing 3-22.

Listing 3-22. Advanced `module-info.java` Configuration File for the `chapter.zero` Module with Multiple Modules

```
module chapter.zero {
    exports com.apress.bgn.zero to chapter.two, chapter.three;
}
```

The order of the modules is not important, and if there is a lot of them you can place them on multiple lines. Just make sure to end the declaration with a ; (semicolon).

This is all that can be presented about modules at this stage in the book, but fear not: all the other directives will be covered at the right time.

How to Determine the Structure of a Java Project

There are a few ways Java projects can be structured and this depends on the following:

- project scope
- build tool used

You might wonder why the project scope influences its structure, and you might expect there should be a standard for this, right? There is more than one standard, and that is dependent on the project scope. The reason for creating a Java project influences its size. If a project is small it might not require you to split the sources into subprojects, and it might not need a build tool either, since build tools come with their own standard way of organizing a project. Let's start with the smallest Java project ever, which should just print "Hello World!" to the console.

The "HelloWorld!" Project in IntelliJ IDEA

As a side note, you do not even need a project, because you have jshell. Just open a terminal (command Prompt for Windows), open jshell, and type the System.out.print("Hello World!") statement, as depicted in Listing 3-23.

Listing 3-23. jshell Hello World!

```
jshell>
|  Welcome to JShell -- Version 17-ea
|  For an introduction type: /help intro

jshell> System.out.print("Hello World!")
Hello World!
```

Since you have installed IntelliJ IDEA, let's create a Java project and check what project structure the editor chooses for us. Start with the first IntelliJ IDEA dialog window and click on the `Create New Project` option. A second dialog window will appear on top with the types of projects you can create being listed on the left. The two dialog windows mentioned here are depicted in Figure 3-13.

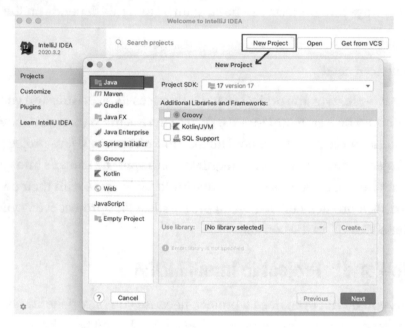

Figure 3-13. *Creating an IntelliJ IDEA project configuration starting dialog windows*

Select Java project type from the left and click `Next` without selecting any of the additional libraries and frameworks listed on the right.

The next dialog window allows you to select a template for your project. We're going to skip it by clicking `Next`.

The next dialog window allows you to select the project name and location. As we are using Java 17, you can notice at the bottom a section used to configure the Java module. This configuration window is depicted in Figure 3-14.

Figure 3-14. *IntelliJ IDEA project name and location configuration dialog window*

Use sandbox for both project name and module name and click on Finish. The next window is the editor window. This is where you write your code. If you expand the sandbox node on the left (that section is called the *Project view*), you can see that the project is built using the JDK you have installed (in this case 17). A src directory was created for you. Your project should look a lot like the one depicted in Figure 3-15.

Figure 3-15. *IntelliJ IDEA project view*

Before writing code, let's check out what other project settings are available. IntelliJ IDEA provides you access to view and edit project properties through the File > Project Structure menu item. If you click it a dialog window will open similar to the one depicted in Figure 3-16.

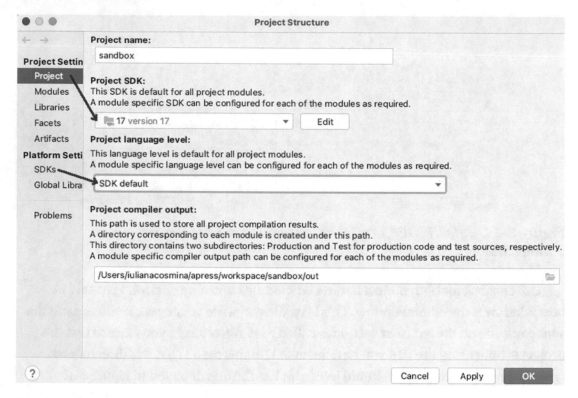

Figure 3-16. *IntelliJ IDEA project settings tab*

By default, the Project settings tab is opened. In the previous figure there are two arrows attracting your attention to the Project SDK: section which is actually depicting the JDK version for a Java project and the Project language level: section. At the time this chapter was written, JDK 17 EA is the most recent version. The most recent version of IntelliJ IDEA supports syntax and code completion for Java 17, and that is why is depicted here. This is the meaning of the project language level setting.

If you switch to the tab named Modules you will see the information depicted in Figure 3-17.

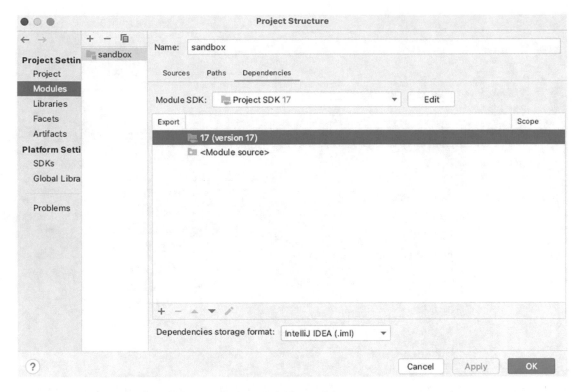

Figure 3-17. *IntelliJ IDEA project modules tab*

⚠   The previous image requires a clarification. Aside from Java modules, which wrap together packages, a module is also a way to wrap up together Java sources and resource files with a common purpose within a project. Before Oracle introduced the module concept as a way to modularize Java applications, the code making up these applications was already modularized by developers that needed to structure big projects in some practical way.

In the Modules tab, you can see how many parts (modules) a project has and the settings for each part. The sandbox project has one part, one module named also sandbox, and the source for this module is contained in the src directory. If we want to write a class that prints "Hello World!", the file called HelloWorld.java has to be placed under it. If you click-right on the src directory, the menu depicted in Figure 3-18 appears.

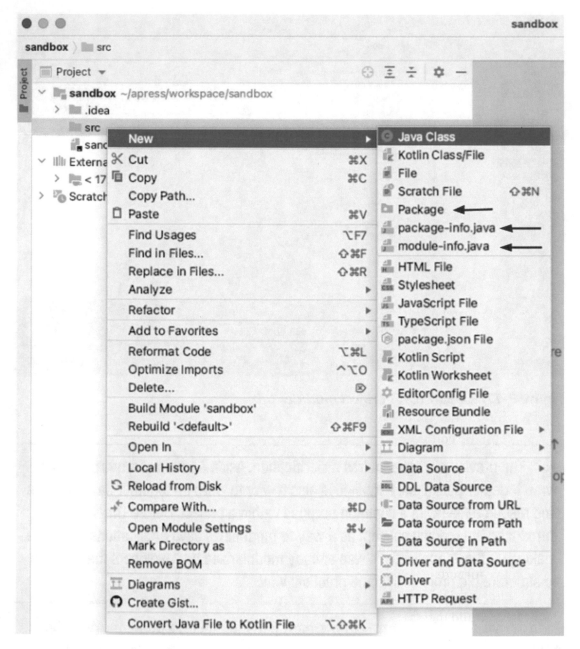

Figure 3-18. *IntelliJ IDEA menu listing which Java objects can be created in the src directory*

Aside from the Java Class option, there are a few red arrows showing you what other components can be in the src directory. Let's go ahead and create our class. Click on the Java Class menu option and after introducing the class name select Class from the list below the test field. In Figure 3-19 you can see all the Java types you can create.

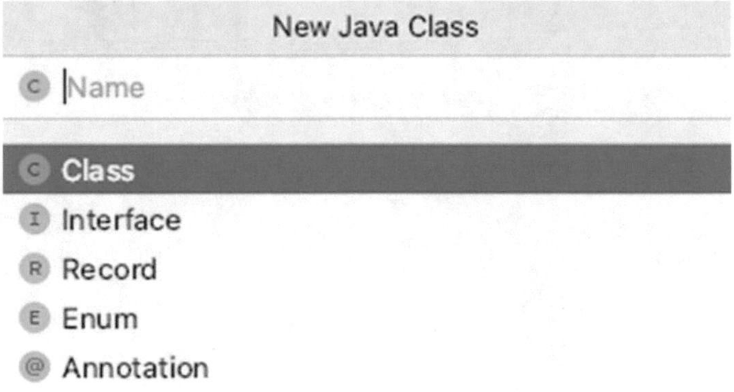

New Java Class
- © Name
- © **Class**
- ① Interface
- ® Record
- © Enum
- @ Annotation

Figure 3-19. *IntelliJ IDEA dialog window to create a Java type*

At the beginning of this chapter it was mentioned that the core building block of a Java application is the class, but that there are other types in Java except that. The list in the previous figure shows the five Java types are listed. Each of them is explained in detail later; for now, notice that a file named HelloWorld.java was created under the src directory and the contents of that file are as simple as shown in Listing 3-24.

Listing 3-24. The HelloWorld Class

```
public class HelloWorld {

}
```

You have just created your first Java class, in your first very simple Java project. It does nothing yet. The class is compiled by selecting the Build Project option from the IntelliJ IDEA Build menu, or by pressing a combination of keys that is different for each operating system. Compiling the class produces the HelloWorld.class file, containing the bytecode. By default, IntelliJ IDEA stores compilation results into a directory named out/production. The menu option for compiling your project and the result are depicted in Figure 3-20. The menu option is highlighted in green.

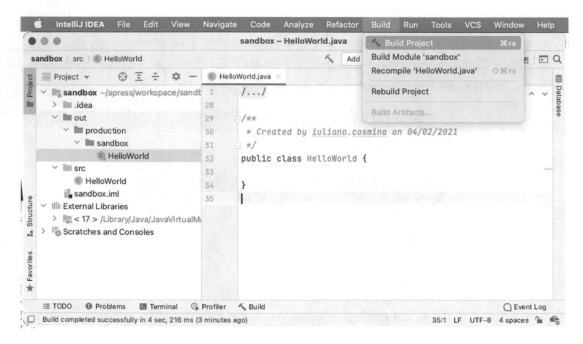

Figure 3-20. *IntelliJ IDEA: how to compile a Java project*

It is time we make the class print *Hello World!* For that we need to add a special method to the class. Any Java desktop application has a special method named `main` that has to be declared in a top-level class. This method is called by the JRE to run the Java program/application, and I call it the **entry point**. Without such a method, a Java project is just a collection of classes that is not runnable, cannot be executed, and cannot perform a certain function.

💡   Imagine it like this: it's like having a car, but you have no way of starting it, because the ignition lock cylinder is missing. By for all intents and purposes it is a car, but it cannot perform the main purpose of a car, which is to actually take you somewhere. You can imagine the `main` method as being the ignition lock cylinder, where the JRE will insert the key to get your application running. Let's add that method to the `HelloWorld` class.

> 💡   Because IntelliJ IDEA is an awesome editor, you can generate the `main` method by typing `psvm` and pressing the <Tab> key. The four letters represent the starting letter of all the components of the method declaration: **p**ublic, **s**tatic, **v**oid, and **m**ain.

The `HelloWorld` class with a `main` method that prints the text *Hello World!* is depicted in Listing 3-25.

Listing 3-25. The `HelloWorld` Class with the `main` Method

```
public class HelloWorld {
    public static void main(String... args) {
        System.out.println();
    }
}
```

Now that we have a `main` method, the code can be executed (or run). For this, in IntelliJ IDEA you have also two options:

- from the Run menu choose, option Run `[ClassName]`

- or just click-right on the class body and select Run `[ClassName]`. `main()` from the menu that appears.[13]

Figure 3-21 depicts both menu items that you can use to execute the class, as well as the result of the execution.

---

[13] Next to the *Run* menu item, a combination of keys is depicted that can be used to run the class.

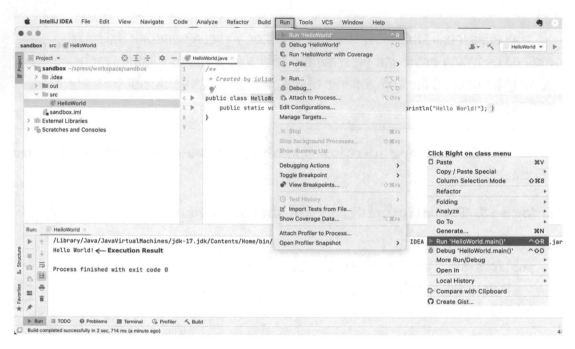

Figure 3-21. *IntelliJ IDEA: how to execute a Java class*

This is the most basic structure for a Java Project. This project is so simple that it can also be compiled manually from the command line. So let's do that!

The "HelloWorld!" Project Compiled and Executed from the Command Line

You've probably noticed the Terminal button in your IntelliJ IDEA. If you click that button, inside the editor a terminal will open. For Windows it will be a Command Prompt instance, for Linux and macOs will be the default shell. IntelliJ will open your terminal right into your project root. Here is what you have to do next:

- enter the src directory by executing the following command: cd src

- cd is a command that works under Windows and Unix systems as well and is short for change directory

- compile the HelloWorld.java file by executing: javac HelloWorld.java

- javac is a JDK executable used to compile Java files, that IntelliJ IDEA calls in the background as well

- run the resulting bytecode from the `HelloWorld.class` file by executing: `java HelloWorld`

Figure 3-22 depicts the execution of those commands, in a terminal in IntelliJ IDEA.

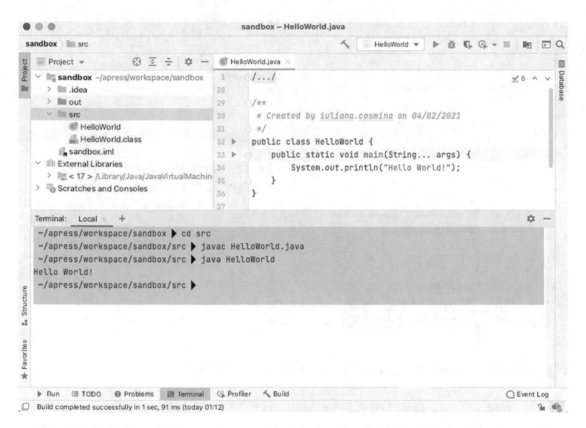

Figure 3-22. *Manually compiling and running the HelloWorld class in a terminal inside IntelliJ IDEA*

Looks simple, right? And it actually is that simple, because no packages or Java modules were defined. But wait, is that possible? Well, yes. If you did not define a package, the class is still part of an unnamed default package that is provided by default by the JSE platform for development of small, temporary, educational applications, like the one you are building here.

So let's make our project a little bit more complicated and add a named package for our class to be in.

Putting the "HelloWorld" Class in a Package

In Figure 3-18, in the menu listed contains a Package option. Click-right on the src directory and select it. A small dialog window will appear where you have to enter the package name. Enter com.sandbox. In Figure 3-23 the dialog window is depicted. If the package you are trying to create already exists, an error message is displayed in red.

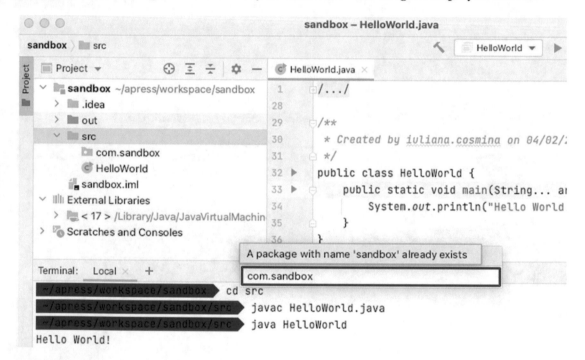

Figure 3-23. *Creating duplicate package in IntelliJ IDEA*

Now we have a package, but the class is not in it. To get the class there, just click on it and drag it. Another dialog window will appear to confirm that this is what you really want to do, as depicted in Figure 3-24.

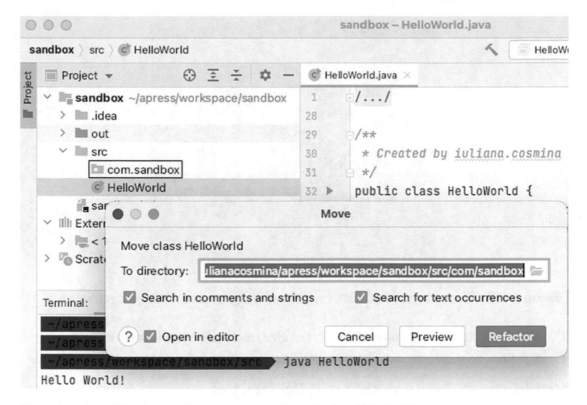

Figure 3-24. *Moving a class into a package in IntelliJ IDEA*

Click on the Refactor button and look at what happens to the class. The class should now start with a package com.sandbox; declaration. If you rebuild your project and then look at the production directory, you will see something similar to what is depicted in Figure 3-25.

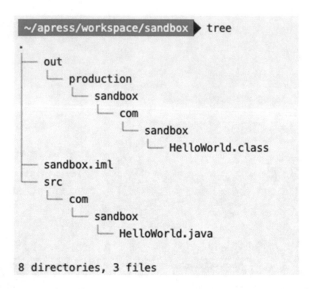

Figure 3-25. *New directory structure after adding the* com.sandbox *package*

Obviously if you compile and execute the class manually, you have to consider the package now, so your commands will change to:

```
~/sandbox/src/> javac com/sandbox/HelloWorld.java
~/sandbox/src/> java com/sandbox/HelloWorld
```

So what happens when modules are configured too? There is a default unnamed module, and all JARs, modular or not, and classes on the classpath will be contained in it. This default and unnamed module exports all packages and reads all other modules. Because it does not have a name it cannot be required and read by named application modules. Thus, even if your small project seems to work with JDKs with versions 9 or above, it cannot be accessed by other modules, but it works because it can access others. (This ensures backward compatibility with older versions of the JDK.) This being said, let's add a module in our project as well.

Configuring the "com.sandbox" Module

Configuring a module is as easy as adding a module-info.java file under the src directory. In Figure 3-18, the menu contains a module-info.java option and if you select that, the IDE will generate the file for you. All is well and fine, and if you do not like the module name that was generated for you, you can change it. I changed it to com.sandbox to respect the module naming convention established by Oracle developers. The file is initially empty, as depicted in Listing 3-26.

Listing 3-26. The `com.sandbox` Module Configuration File

```
module com.sandbox {
}
```

What happens now that we have a module? Not much from the IDEs point of view. But if you want to compile a module manually you have to know a few things. I compiled our module using the command in Listing 3-27.

Listing 3-27. Manually Compiling a Package Enclosed within a Module

```
~/sandbox/src/> javac -d ../out/com.sandbox \
    module-info.java \
    com/sandbox/HelloWorld.java
```

---

❶   "\" is a macOS/Linux separator. On Windows, either write the whole command on a single line or replace "\" with "^".

The previous command is built according to the template in Listing 3-28.

Listing 3-28. Template for Command to Manually Compile a Package Enclosed Within a Module

```
javac -d [destination location]/[module name] \
    [source location]/module-info.java \
    [java files...]
```

The `-d [destination]` determines where the results of the execution should be saved. The reason the command line in Listing 3-27 specifies the output folder as `/out/com.sandbox` is to make it clear that `com.sandbox` is the enclosing module. Under this directory, we'll have the normal structure of the `com.sandbox` package. The contents of the out directory are depicted in Figure 3-26.

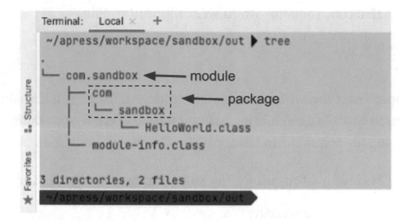

Figure 3-26. *Java module* `com.sandbox` *compiled manually*

As you have noticed in this example, the module does not really exist until we compile the sources, because a Java module is more of a logical mode of encapsulating packages described by the `module-info.class` descriptor. The only reason the `com.sandbox` directory was created is that we specified it as argument in the `javac -d` command.

Now that we've managed to compile a module, Listing 3-29 shows you how to run the `HelloWorld` class when it is enclosed in a module.

Listing 3-29. Manually Executing a Class Enclosed Within a Module

```
~/sandbox/> java --module-path out \
  --module com.sandbox/com.sandbox.HelloWorld
  Hello World!  # result
```

The previous command is built according to the template in Listing 3-30.

Listing 3-30. Template for Command to Manually Execute a Class Enclosed Within a Module

```
java --module-path [destination] \
    --module [module name] /[package name].HelloWorld
```

Oracle Magazine edition from September 2017 mentioned examples for the first time and although Oracle developers have decided that module names should follow the same rules as packages, to me this seems a little redundant, especially in complex projects where package names tend to become very long. Should you have module names just as long?

The truth is that people make the standards, and most times the practical becomes the standard. Since 2007, projects that have managed to embrace modules have chosen simpler, more practical module names. For example, the team that created the Spring Framework decided to name their modules `spring.core` instead of `org.springframework.core`, `spring.beans` instead of `org.springframework.beans,` and so on. So name your modules as you wish, as long as you avoid special characters and numbers.

Java Projects Using Build Tools, Mostly Maven

Apache Maven is a build automation tool used primarily for Java projects. Although Gradle is gaining ground, Maven is still one of the most-used build tools. Tools like Maven and Gradle are used to organize the source code of an application in interdependent project modules and configure a way to compile, validate, generate sources, test, and generate artifacts automatically. An artifact is a file, usually a JAR, that gets deployed to a Maven repository. A Maven repository is a location on a HDD where JARs get saved in a special directory structure.

Any discussion about build tools must start with Maven, because this build tool standardized a lot of the terms we use in development today. A project split into multiple subprojects can be downloaded from GitHub and build in the command line or imported into IntelliJ IDEA. This approach will make sure that you get quality sources that can be compiled in one go. It is also practical, because I imagine you do not want to load a new project in IntelliJ IDEA every time you start reading a new chapter. Also, it makes it easier for me to maintain the sources and adapt them to a new JDK, and with Oracle releasing so often, I need to be able to do this quickly.

The project you will use to test the code written in this book (and write your own code if you want to) is called `java-17-for-absolute-beginners`. It is a multimodule Maven project. The first level of the project is the `java-17-for-absolute-beginners project`, which has a configuration file named `pom.xml`. In this file, all dependencies and their versions are listed. The child projects, the ones on the second level, are the modules of this project. We call them *child* projects because they inherit those dependencies and modules from the parent project. In their configuration files, we can specify what dependencies are needed from the list defined in the parent.

These modules are actually a method of wrapping up together sources for each chapter, which is why these modules are named chapter00, chapter01, and so on. If a project is big and needs a lot of code to be written, the code is split again in another level of modules. Module chapter05 is such a case, and is configured as a parent for the projects underneath it. In Figure 3-27 you can see what this project looks like loaded in IntelliJ IDEA, and module chapter05 is expanded, so you can see the third level of modules. Each level is marked with the corresponding number.

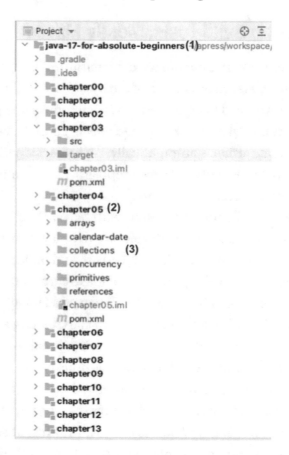

Figure 3-27. *Maven multilevel project structure*

If you have loaded it into IntelliJ IDEA like you were taught in **Chapter 2**, you can make sure everything is working correctly by building it. Here's how you do it:

- You can do it by using the IntelliJ IDEA editor, where in the upper right side you should have a tab called **Maven**. If the projects are loaded like they are depicted in Figure 3-28, the project was loaded

correctly. If the Maven tab is not visible just look for a label like
the one marked with (1) and click on it. Expand the java-17-for-
absolute-beginners (root) node until you find the build task,
marked with (2). If you double-click it and in the view at the bottom
of the editor you do not see any errors, all your projects were built
successfully. So yes, you should definitely see the BUILD SUCCESS
(3) message.

Figure 3-28. *Maven project view*

The second way to make sure the Maven project is working as expected is to build it from the command line. Open an IntelliJ IDEA terminal, and if you installed Maven on the system path as explained in **Chapter 2** just type mvn and hit <Enter>.

ℹ️   The main `pom.xml` file, located in the root of the project, has a default goal configured through the following line:

`<defaultGoal>clean install</defaultGoal>`

It declares the two Maven execution phases required to build this project. Without this element in the configuration, to build the project the two phases would be specified in the command, for example: `mvn clean install`.

In the command line you might see some warnings if the JDK 17 is still unstable when this book reaches you, but as long as the execution ends with BUILD SUCCESSFUL everything is all right.

Aside from the `sandbox` project, which is simple enough for you to create yourself, all the classes, modules, and packages mentioned in this section are part of this project. The `chapter00` and `chapter01` do not really contain classes specific to those chapters; I just needed them to be able to construct the Java module examples. IntelliJ IDEA sorts modules in alphabetical order, so the naming for the chapter modules was chosen this way so that they are listed in the normal order you should work with them.

Until now, this chapter has been focused on the building blocks of Java applications and we created a class that prints *Hello World!* by following the instructions, but not all of the details were explained. Let's do that now and even enrich the class with new details.

Explaining and Enriching the "Hello World!" Class

Previously, we wrote a class named `HelloWorld` in our `sandbox` project. This class is copied to the `chapter03` project, in package `com.apress.bgn.three.helloworld`. This chapter starts with a list of the main components of a class. The `HelloWorld` class contains a few of those elements that are explained in more detail. In Figure 3-29, the `HelloWorld` class is depicted in the IntelliJ IDEA editor.

Figure 3-29. *The HelloWorld class in the java-17-for-absolute-beginners project*

The lines contain different statements that are explained in the following list and the number of the line matches the number in the list.

1. **the package declaration:** when classes are part of a package their code must start with this line that declares the package enclosing them. package is a reserved keyword in Java and cannot be used for anything else but declaring a package.

   <empty for convenience>: left empty, so the picture looks nicer

8. **the class declaration:** this is the line where we declare our type:

   – it is public, so it can be seen from everywhere

   – it is a class

   – it is named HelloWord

   – it has a body enclosed in curly brackets and the opening bracket is on this line. But it can be on the next one too, since empty spaces are ignored.

9. **the main() method declaration:** in Java the method name and the number, type, and order of its parameters is referred to as **the method signature**. A method also has a **return type**, as in the type of result it returns. But there is also a special type that can be used to declare that a method does not return anything. In the order of the appearance, here is what every term of the main() method represents:

- **public method accessor:** the `main` method must be `public` otherwise JRE can't access it and call it.

- **static:** remember at the beginning of this chapter it was mentioned that a class has members (fields and methods)? When an object of that class type is created, it has the fields and methods as declared by the class. The class is a template for creating objects. Because of the `static` keyword, though, the `main` method is not associated with an object of a class type, but with the class itself. More details about this in the next chapter.

- **void:** this keyword is used here to tell us that the `main` method does not return anything, so it's like a replacement for *no type*, because if nothing is returned there is no need for a type.

- **string... args** or **String[] args:** methods are sometimes declared as receiving some input data; `String[] args` represents an array of text values. The three dots is another way to specify that a method can have more than one argument of the same type. The three dots notation can only be used in a method argument, and are called **varargs**. (The varargs argument also has to be the only parameter for the method, or the last one, otherwise resolving the arguments becomes an impossible job.) It means you can pass in an array of parameters without explicitly creating the array. Arrays are sets of data of fixed length, in mathematics they are known as *one-dimension matrix* or *vector*. `String` is the class representing text objects in Java. The [ ] means array and `args` is its name. But wait, we've run this method before and we did not need to provide anything! It is not mandatory, but you'll see how you can give it arguments (values provided to the method, that will be used by the code in its body) after this list.

10. **System.out.println("HelloWorld!");** is the statement used for writing *Hello World!* in the console.

11. } is the closing bracket of the `main` method body.

12. } is the closing bracket for the class body.

If we execute this class, we will see Hello World! being printed in the console. You were shown earlier in Figure 3-21 how to execute a class with a main() method in it. After executing a class that way, IntelliJ IDEA automatically saves the configuration for that execution in a **Run Configuration** and displays it in a drop-down list, next to a triangular green button, that can be used to execute that class by clicking on it, which are both placed on the header of the IDE and ostentatiously pointed to you in Figure 3-29.

Those two elements are really important, because a run configuration can be edited and arguments can be added for the JVM and the main method. Let's first modify the main method to do something with the arguments first.

Listing 3-31. Main Method with varargs

```
public class HelloWorld {
    public static void main(String... args) {
        System.out.println("Hello " + args[0] + "!");
    }
}
```

---

❶   Arrays are accessed using indexes of their elements, and the counting starts in Java from 0. Consequently, the first member of an array can be found at 0, the second at 1, and so on. But arrays can be empty, so in the previous code snippet if no argument is specified, the execution of the program will crash, and in the console, an explicit message will be printed in red.

```
Exception in thread "main" java.lang.ArrayIndexOutOfBoundsException: 0
at chapter.three/com.apress.bgn.three.helloworld.HelloWorld.main(HelloWorld.java:5)
```

When a Java program ends because an error during execution time, we say that **an exception was thrown**.

When we try to access an empty array, or an element of an array that does not exist, the JVM throws an object of type ArrayIndexOutOfBoundsException containing the line where the failure happened and the index of the element we were trying to access. Exception objects are used by the JVM to notify developers of exceptional situations when a Java execution does not work as expected, and these objects contain details regarding where in the code it happened and what caused the problem.

The modification we did in the previous code snippet will print the text value provided as argument when executing the class. Let's modify the run configuration for this class and add an argument. If you click on the small grey arrow next to the **Run Configuration** name, a menu will appear. Click on the **Edit Configurations** and inspect the dialog window depicted to you. Figure 3-30 depicts the menu and the dialog window.

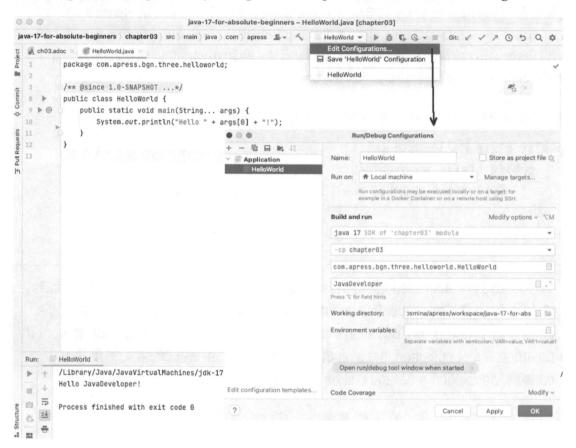

Figure 3-30. *Customizing a run configuration*

In the image, the key elements are highlighted in light blue. IntelliJ IDEA saves a few of your previous executions, including Maven build tasks, so you can run them again just with one click. In the left of the **Run/Debug Configurations** dialog window, IntelliJ IDEA groups run configurations by their type. By default, the last run configuration is opened on the right side of the window, in this case the run configuration for the HelloWorld class. As you can see there are a lot of options you can configure for an execution and most of them have been automatically decided by the IDE. The program arguments or the arguments for the main() method are introduced in the text field marked in red. In the figure we introduced *JavaDeveloper*, so if you click the Apply and then the Ok button and then execute the class, in the console instead of *Hello World!* you should see now *Hello JavaDeveloper!*

What else can we do with our class? Remember the code the book started with? Let's put it the main() method in this class. The code is depicted again in Listing 3-32.

Listing 3-32. A More Complex main Method

```java
package com.apress.bgn.three.helloworld;

import java.util.List;

public class HelloWorld {
    public static void main(String... args) {
        //System.out.println("Hello " + args[0] + "!");
        List<String> items = List.of("1", "a", "2", "a", "3", "a");

        items.forEach(item -> {
            if (item.equals("a")) {
                System.out.println("A");
            } else {
                System.out.println("Not A");
            }
        });
    }
}
```

The import java.util.List; statement is the only type of statement that can exist between a package and a class declaration. This statement is telling the Java compiler that an object type java.util.List will be used in the program. The import keyword is followed by the fully qualified name of the type. A fully qualified name of a type is made of the package name(java.util), a dot(.) and the simple name of the type(List). Without it, the HelloWorld class will not compile. Try it: just put "//" in front of the statement, which will turn the line into a comment that is ignored by the compiler. You will see the editor complain by making any piece of code related to that list bright red.

The statement List<String> items = List.of("1", "a", "2", "a", "3", "a"); creates a list of text values. Creating lists this way was introduced in Java 9. Specifying what type of elements are in a list by using <T> was introduced in Java 5, and it's called **generics**. The elements in the list are then traversed one by one by the forEach method, and each of them are tested to see if they are equal to the "*a*" character. The whole expression used to do this is called a **lambda expression** and this type of syntax was introduced in Java 8, together with the forEach method.

If you run the class now, in the console you should see a sequence of *A* and *Not A* printed, each on its own line.

```
Not A
A
Not A
A
Not A
A
```

The code we have written until now uses quite a few types of objects to print some simple messages in the console. The List object is used to hold a few String objects. The messages are printed using the println method that is called on the out object, which is a static field in the System class. And these are just the objects that are visible to you in the code. Under the hood, the List<T> elements are processed by a Consumer<T> object created on the spot that the lambda expression hides for simplicity reasons, so the preceding code can be expanded as in Listing 3-33.

Listing 3-33. A More Complex main Method

```java
package com.apress.bgn.three.helloworld;

import java.util.List;
import java.util.function.Consumer;

public class HelloWorld {
    public static void main(String... args) {
        List<String> items = List.of("1", "a", "2", "a", "3", "a");

        items.forEach(new Consumer<String>() {
            @Override
            public void accept(String item) {
                if (item.equals("a")) {
                    System.out.println("A");
```

```
        } else {
            System.out.println("Not A");
        }
    }
});
    }
}
```

Before ending this chapter, I would like to show you another neat thing. The contents of the forEach block can be written as a single line:

```
items.forEach(item → System.out.println(item.equals("a") ? "A" : "Not A"));
```

The previous line can be made even simpler my using something called a **method reference**. But more about that a little bit later in the book.

It might look scary now, but I promise that this book introduces each concept in a clear context and compared with real-world objects and events so you can understand it easily. And if that does not work there are always more books, more blogs, and of course the official Oracle page for each JDK, which has quite good tutorials. Where there's a will, there's a way.

---

❶   Also, take advantage of your IDE! By clicking on any object type in the code while pressing the Control/Command key, the code of the object class is opened and you can see how that class was written and you can read the documentation for it directly in the editor. As an exercise, do this for the forEach method and the System class.

❶   Most really smart editors have keymaps: groups of keys that when pressed together perform certain actions like navigation, code generation, execution, and so on. Print the IntelliJ IDEA keymap reference and get comfortable with it. Your brain is very fast, and when coding, the aim is to type as fast as you think, if possible. :)

Summary

In this chapter you were introduced to the fundamental blocks of a Java application. You were also taught how to use JShell to execute Java statements out of the context of an application. You found out how you can manually compile and Java code that declared packages and modules.

Many of the things you did while following this chapter you will probably do daily after getting a job as a Java developer (except for the days that you will spend hunting and fixing bugs in existing code). You will probably spend a lot of time reading documentation too, because the JDK has a lot of classes, with fields and methods you can use to write an application. With each released version things change, and you have to keep yourself up to date.

The brains has limited capacity; no employer will ever expect you to know every JDK class and method, but work smart and keep this URL `https://docs.oracle.com/en/java/javase/17/docs/api/index.html` (or the one matching the JDK version used) always opened in your browser. When you have doubts about a JDK class or method, just read about it on the spot.

CHAPTER 4

Java Syntax

Languages are means of communication, verbal or written, between people. Whether they are natural or artificial, they are made of terms and rules on how to use them to perform the task of communication. Programming languages are means of communication with a computer. The communication with a computer is a written communication; basically the developer defines some instructions to be executed, communicates them through an intermediary to the computer, and if the computer understands them, performs the set of actions and depending on the application type some sort of reply will be returned to the developer.

In the Java language, the communication is done through an intermediary—the Java Virtual Machine. The set of programming rules that define how terms should be connected to produce an understandable unit of communication is called **syntax**. Java borrowed most of its syntax from another programming language called C++. C++ has a syntax based on the C language syntax. C syntax borrows elements and rules form other languages that preceded it, but in essence all these languages are based on the natural English language. Maybe Java got a little cryptic in version 8 because of the introduction of lambda expressions, but still, when writing a Java program, if you are naming your terms properly in the English language, the result should be a code that is easily readable, like a story.

A few details have been covered in **Chapter 3**. Packages and modules were covered enough to give you a solid understanding of their purpose to avoid confusion regarding the organization of the project and avoid aimless fumbling through the code when trying to execute code mentioned in the book. But on other topics the surface has been barely scratched. Thus, let's begin our deep dive into Java.

© Iuliana Cosmina 2022
I. Cosmina, *Java 17 for Absolute Beginners*, https://doi.org/10.1007/978-1-4842-7080-6_4

Base Rules of Writing Java Code

Before writing Java code, let's list a few rules that you should follow to make sure your code not only works, but is easy to understand and thus maintain or extend. Let's depict the class we ended **Chapter 3** with, by adding a few details:

Listing 4-1. The HelloWorld Class with Comments

```
01. package com.apress.bgn.four.basic;
02.
03. import java.util.List;
04.
05./**
06.  * this is a JavaDoc comment
07. */
08. public class HelloWorld {
09.     public static void main(String... args) {
10.         //this is a one-line comment
11.         List<String> items = List.of("1", "a", "2", "a", "3", "a");
12.
13.         items.forEach(item -> {
14.             /* this is a
15.                 multi-line
16.             comment */
17.             if (item.equals("a")) {
18.                 System.out.println("A");
19.             } else {
20.                 System.out.println("Not A");
21.             }
22.         });
23.     }
24. }
```

Each section of the code gets its own section in this chapter. Let's start with the first line.

Package Declaration

A Java file starts with the **package declaration** if the type declared in the file is declared within a package. The package name can contain letters and numbers, separated by dots. Each part matches a directory in the path to the type contained in it, as shown in **Chapter 3**. The package declaration should reveal the name of the application and the purpose of the classes in the package. Let's take the package naming used for the sources of this book: `com.apress.bgn.four.basic`. If we split the package name in pieces, this is the meaning of each piece:

- `com.apress` represents the domain of the application, or who owns the application in this case.

- `bgn` represents the scope of the code, in this case the book who it is written for: **beginners**.

- `four` represents the purpose of the classes, to be used with **Chapter 4**.

- `basic` represents a more refined level of the purpose for the classes; these classes are simple, used to depict basic Java notions.

A package name like the one introduced here that is made of more parts is called a **qualified package name**. It has a hierarchical structure and package `com` is the root package. Assuming a type `MyType` is declared in this package, this type is referenced in classes in other packages using this import statement: `import com.MyType;`.

Package `apress` is a member of package `com` and is identified by a name composed of its own name prefixed by the enclosing package and a dot. Assuming a type `MyType` is declared in this package, this type is referenced in classes in other packages using this import statement: `import com.apress.MyType;`.

The same applies to package `bgn` which is a member of package `apress` and its type members, and so on down the package tree.

💡 You can imagine packages being the programming equivalent of Russian nesting Matryoshka dolls.

Thus, a type is referenced in other types via its **fully qualified name**. The fully qualified name of a type is formed by prefixing the type name with the qualified name of the package and a dot. Figure 4-1 should make things pretty clear.

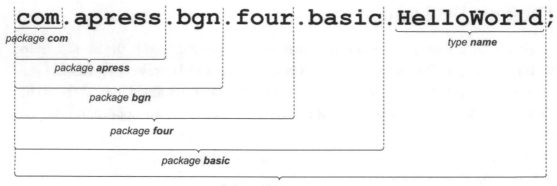

Figure 4-1. *Dissection of the fully qualified name of a Java type*

Import Section

After the package declaration, the **import section** follows. This section contains the fully qualified names of all classes, interfaces, and enums used within the file. Look at the code sample in Listing 4-2.

Listing 4-2. Small Code Snippet from the `java.lang.String` Class

```
package java.lang;

import java.io.ObjectStreamField;
import java.io.UnsupportedEncodingException;
import java.lang.annotation.Native;
import java.lang.invoke.MethodHandles;
import java.lang.constant.Constable;
import java.lang.constant.ConstantDesc;
import java.nio.charset.Charset;
import java.util.ArrayList;
// the rest of import statements omitted

public final class String
    implements java.io.Serializable, Comparable<String>, CharSequence,
               Constable, ConstantDesc {
```

```
private static final ObjectStreamField[] serialPersistentFields =
new ObjectStreamField[0];

// the rest of the code omitted
}
```

It is a snippet from the official Java String class. Every import statement represents a reference to the package, and the name of a class used within the String class body.

Special import statements can be used to import static variables and static methods as well. In the JDK there is a class used for mathematical processes. It contains static variables and methods that can be used by developers to implement code that solves mathematical problems. You can use its variables and methods without the need to create objects of this type, because static members do not belong to an object of a type, but to the type itself. Check out the code in Listing 4-3.

Listing 4-3. Using Static Imports for Members of Class Math

```
package com.apress.bgn.four;

import static java.lang.Math.PI;
import static java.lang.Math.sqrt;

public class MathSample {
    public static void main(String... args) {
        System.out.println("PI value =" + PI);
        double result = sqrt(5.0);
        System.out.println("SQRT value =" + result);
    }
}
```

By putting together import and static we can declare a fully qualified name of a class and the method or the variable we are interested in using in the code. This allows us to use the variable or method directly, without the name of the class it is being declared in. Without the static imports the code will have to be rewritten as in Listing 4-4:

Listing 4-4. Using Import of Class Math

```java
package com.apress.bgn.four;

import java.lang.Math;

public class MathSample {
    public static void main(String... args) {
        System.out.println("PI value =" + Math.PI);
        double result = Math.sqrt(5.0);
        System.out.println("SQRT value =" + result);
    }
}
```

---

❶   Fully qualified names are a powerful thing. Package names are unique within a module, but package names are not always unique within an application. Type names are not always unique within an application either, but fully qualified type names, formed by combining the two, are unique within an application.

💡   You can also think about packages as home addresses and types as persons. Two persons can have the same address, but they can't have the same name. Two persons can have the same name and live at different addresses. This is how banks and other institutions identify individuals uniquely in the UK or US, for example.

Fully qualified names are not limited to import statements. When two types have the same name and both are used to declare a third type, the only way to be able to tell the compiler within a type body which you intend to use is to use the fully qualified name. An example of this is shown in Listing 4-5, where a class Math from package com.apress. bgn.four.math is used within the body of a class where members of java.lang.Math class are used too.

Listing 4-5. Using a Member of Class `com.apress.bgn.four.math.Math`

```
package com.apress.bgn.four.math;

import java.lang.Math;

public class Sample {
    public static void main(String... args) {
        System.out.println("PI value =" + Math.PI);

        System.out.println("My PI value= " + com.apress.bgn.four.math.
        Math.PI);
    }
}
```

When more than one type is used from the same package, the type names can be replaced by a * (asterisk) that means any visible type from the package can be used in the code of the type being written. These are called **compact import statements**. Compacting imports is recommended when using multiple classes from the same package to write code, or multiple static variables and methods from the same class. When doing so, the import section of a file becomes verbose and difficult to read. This is where compacting comes to help. Compacting imports means replacing all classes from the same package or variables and methods from the same class with a wildcard, so only one import statement is needed. It works for static imports too. So the previous MathSample class becomes the one in Listing 4-6.

Listing 4-6. Using Compacted Imports

```
package com.apress.bgn.four;

import static java.lang.Math.*;

public class MathSample {
    public static void main(String... args) {
        System.out.println("PI value =" + PI);
        double result = sqrt(5.0);
        System.out.println("SQRT value =" + result);
    }
}
```

Java Grammar

The Java language is **case sensitive,** and this means that we can write a piece of code like the one depicted in Listing 4-7 and the code compiles and executes successfully.

Listing 4-7. Java Code Proving Its Case Sensitivity

```java
package com.apress.bgn.four;

public class Sample {
    public static void main(String... args) {
        int mynumber = 0;
        int myNumber = 1;
        int Mynumber = 2;
        int MYNUMBER = 3;
        System.out.println(mynumber);
        System.out.println(myNumber);
        System.out.println(Mynumber);
        System.out.println(MYNUMBER);
    }
}
```

All four variables are different, and the last four lines print the numbers: 0 1 2 3. Obviously, you cannot declare two variables sharing the same name in the same context (e.g., in the body of a method), because you would be basically redeclaring the same variable. The Java compiler does not allow this. If you try to do this your code will not compile, and even IntelliJ IDEA will try to make you see the error of your ways by underlining the code with red and showing you a relevant message, as in Figure 4-2, where variable mynumber was declared twice.

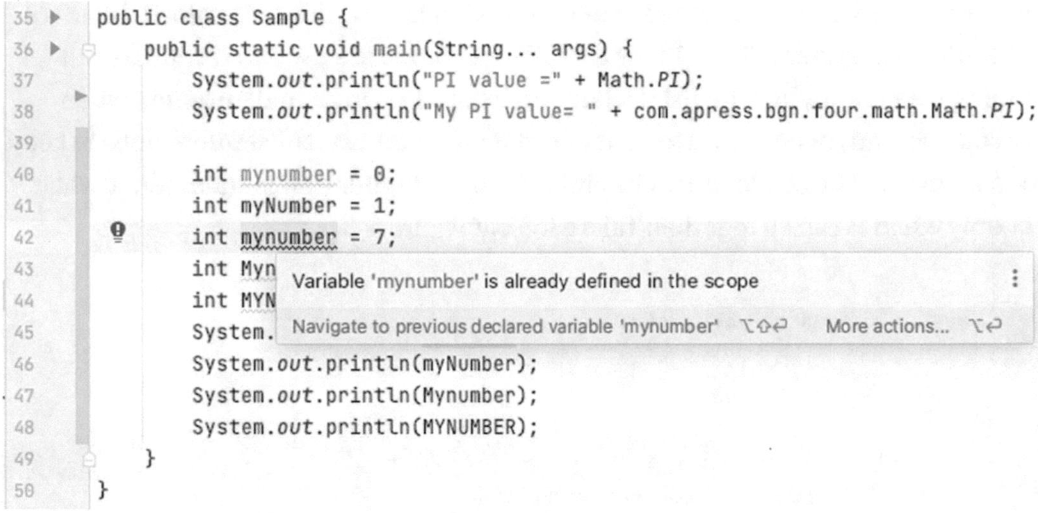

```
35 ▶   public class Sample {
36 ▶ ⊖     public static void main(String... args) {
37           System.out.println("PI value =" + Math.PI);
38 ▶         System.out.println("My PI value= " + com.apress.bgn.four.math.Math.PI);
39
40           int mynumber = 0;
41           int myNumber = 1;
42 ❾         int mynumber = 7;
43           int Myn ┌─────────────────────────────────────────────────────┐
44           int MYN │  Variable 'mynumber' is already defined in the scope  ⋮│
45           System. │                                                       │
46           System.out.println(myNumber);  Navigate to previous declared variable 'mynumber' ⌥↺↵   More actions... ⌥↵ │
47           System.out.println(Mynumber);
48           System.out.println(MYNUMBER);
49 ⊖     }
50   }
```

Figure 4-2. *Same variable name used twice*

There is a set of **Java keywords** that can be used only for fixed and predefined purposes in the Java code. A few of them have already been introduced: import, package, public, and class, but the rest of them will be covered at the end of this chapter with a short explanation for each of them, in Tables 4-2 and 4-3.

---

❶   Java keywords cannot be used as identifiers in code written by developers, so they cannot be used as names for variables, classes, interfaces, objects, and so on.

One or more types can be declared in a Java source file. Whether a class, interface (or @interface), enum, or class, the declaration of a type must be encased in curly brackets ({}). These are called **block delimiters**. import and package statements are not part of the type body. If you take a look at the code in Listing 4-1, you will notice the brackets are used there to wrap up the following:

- contents of a class, also called the body of the class (brackets in lines 08 and 23)

- contents of a method, also called the body of a method (brackets in lines 09 and 22)

- a set of instructions to be executed together (brackets in lines 13 and 21)

Line terminators: code lines are usually ended in Java by the semicolon (;) symbol or by the ASCII characters CR, or LF, or CR LF. Semicolons are used to terminate full functioning statements, like the list declaration in line 11. On a small monitor, when writing code you might be forced to split that statement on two subsequent lines to keep the code readable. The semicolon at its end tells the compiler that is statement that is correct only when taken all together. Take a look at Figure 4-3:

```
28      package com.apress.bgn.four;
29
30      import java.util.List;
31
32      /** Created by iuliana.cosmina on 15/02/2021 */
35  ▶   public class MultipleStatementsSample {
36  ▶       public static void main(String... args) {
37              List<String> items1 = List.of("1", "a", "2", "a", "3", "a");
38
39              List<String> item2 =
40                      List.of("1", "a", "2", "a", "3", "a");
41
42              List<String> items3 =
43                      List.of("1", "a", "2",
44                              "a", "3", "a");
45
46              List<String> badlist =;
47                      List.of("1", "a", "2", "a", "3", "a");
48          }
49      }
```

Figure 4-3. *Different statements samples*

The first three List declarations are equivalent. When declaring a List this way, you can even split its elements on multiple lines. The declaration on line 46, however, is written intentionally wrong. A semicolon is added in line 46, which ends the statement there. That statement is not valid, and the compiler will complain about it when you try to compile that class by printing an exception saying:

"Error:(13, 46) java: illegal start of expression".

If the message of the error seems not to fit the example think about it like this: the problem for the compiler is not the wrongful termination of the statement, but the fact that after the "=" symbol, the compiler expects to find some sort of expression that will produce the value for the badList variable, but instead it finds nothing.

Java Identifiers and Variables

An **identifier** is the name you give to an item in your Java code: class, variable, method, and so on. Identifiers must respect a few rules to allow the code to compile and also common-sense programming rules, called **Java coding conventions**. A few of them are listed here:

- An identifier cannot be one of the Java reserved words, or the code will not compile.

- An identifier cannot be a boolean literal (true, false) or the null literal, or the code will not compile.

- An identifier can be made of letters, numbers and any of _ (underscore), $(dollar sign).

- an identifier cannot start with a number

- Starting with Java 9, a single _(underscore) can no longer be used as an identifier, as it became a keyword. This is probably because in Java 7 numeric literals were introduced and numbers with multiple digits can be written in a more readable way (e.g., int i = 10_000;).

- Developers should declare their identifiers following **camel case** writing style, making sure each word or abbreviation in the middle of the identifier name begins with a capital letter (e.g., StringBuilder, isAdult).

A **variable** is a set of characters that can be associated with a value. It has a type, and based on it, the set of values that can be assigned to it are restricted to a certain interval, group of values, or just must follow a certain format defined by that type. For example: the item declared in line 11 in Listing 4-1 is a variable of type List, and the value associated with it is a list of values.

In Java there are three types of variables:

- **fields** (also known as **properties**) are variables defined in class bodies outside of method bodies, and that do not have the keyword `static` in front of them.

- **local variables** are variables declared inside method bodies, and they are relevant only in that context.

- **static variables** are variables declared inside class bodies with the keyword `static` in front of them. If they are declared as `public` they are accessible within the application wherever the enclosing type is. (Unless the module does not export the package where they are declared, that is.)

Java Comments

Java comments refer to pieces of explanatory text that are not part of the code being executed and are ignored by the compiler. There are three ways to add comments within the code in Java and depending on the characters used to declare them. All three types of comments were used in Listing 4-1, and the following list explains the purpose of each:

- `//` is used for single line comments (line 10). Developers use this type of comment for adding TODO statements or explain why a certain piece of code is needed. These comments are mostly intended for the team members working on the project.

- `/** ... */` JavaDoc comments, special comments that are exported using special tools into the documentation of a project called JavaDoc API (lines 05 to 07). Developers use this type of comments to document their code. There are plug-ins for build tools that can extract the JavaDoc from a project as a website, that can be then hosted publicly to help other developers using your project.

- `/* ... */` used for multiline comments (lines 14 to 16). Developers use this type of comment for adding TODO statements or explain why a certain piece of code is needed, when that explanation is quite long. These comments are mostly intended for the team members working on the project.

Java Types

In **Chapter 3** when introducing the Java building blocks only the class was mentioned, to keep things simple. It was mentioned that there are other types in Java, and this section introduces all of them. Classes are the most important, so they will be covered first.

Classes

It was mentioned before that classes are just templates for creating objects. Creating an object based on a **class** is called **instantiation**. The resulted object is referred to as **an instance of that class**. Instances are named **objects** because by default any class written by a developer implicitly extends class java.lang.Object, if no other superclass is declared. What this means is that in Java there is a basic template for all classes and that is represented by the java.lang.Object class. Any class is by default an extension of this class, so the class declaration in Listing 4-8 is equivalent to the one in Listing 4-9.

Listing 4-8. Simple Sample Class Implicitly Extending the java.lang. Object Class

```
package com.apress.bgn.four.basic;

public class Sample {
}
```

Listing 4-9. Simple Sample Class Explictly Extending the java.lang. Object Class

```
package com.apress.bgn.four.basic;

public class Sample extends Object {
}
```

Also, notice how importing the java.lang package is not necessary because the Object class, being the root class of the Java hierarchy, all classes (including arrays) must have access to extend it. Thus the java.lang package is implicitly imported as well.

❶   It was mentioned in **Chapter 3** that the `java.base` module is added as required implicitly in any Java project that declares a `module-info.java`. This module exports the `java.lang` package that contains the core components to writing Java code.

💡   Every human being is defined by a DNA molecule containing 23 pairs of chromosomes. They declare the organs and limbs a human should have to look and function as a ... human. You can view the `Object` class as the DNA molecule that declares all the components that a class should have to look and function as a class within a Java application.

There are other template types that can be used for creating objects in Java. In the following sections we will introduce them and explain what they are used for. But let's do so in a context. We will create a family of templates for defining humans. Most Java tutorials use templates for vehicles or geometrical shapes. I want to model something that anybody can easily understand and relate to. The purpose of the following sections is to develop Java templates that can be used to model different types of people. The first Java template that was mentioned so far is the **class**, so let's continue with that.

Fields

The operation through which instances are created is called **instantiation**. To design a class that models a generic human we should think about two things: human characteristics and human actions. What do all humans have in common? A lot, but for the purpose of this section, let's choose three generic attributes: they have a name, age, and height. These attributes map in a Java class to variables named **fields** or **properties**. The first version of the Human class is depicted in Listing 4-10.

Listing 4-10. Simple Human Class

```
package com.apress.bgn.four.base;

public class Human {
    String name;
    int age;
    float height;
}
```

In the previous code sample the fields have different types, depending on what values should be associated with them. For example, name can be associated with a text value, like "Alex," and texts are represented in Java by the String type. The age can be associated with numeric integer values, so is of type int. For the purpose of this section, we've considered that the height of a person is a rational number like 1.9, so we used the special Java type for this kind of values: float.

So now we have a class modelling some basic attributes of a human. How do we use it? We need a main(..) method and we need to create an object of this type: we need to instantiate this class. In Listing 4-11 a human named "Alex" is created.

Listing 4-11. Simple Human Object Being Created

```
package com.apress.bgn.four.base;

public class BasicHumanDemo {
    public static void main(String... args) {
        Human human = new Human();
        human.name = "Alex";
        human.age = 40;
        human.height = 1.91f;
    }
}
```

To create a Human instance, we use the new keyword. After the new keyword we call a special method called a constructor. We've mentioned methods before, but this one is special. Some developers do not even consider it a method. The most obvious reason for this is that it wasn't defined anywhere in the body of the Human class. So where is it coming from? It's a default constructor without parameters that is automatically generated by the compiler unless an explicit one is declared (with or without parameters). A class cannot exist without a constructor, otherwise it cannot be instantiated, which is why the compiler generates one if none was explicitly declared. The default constructor calls super(), which invokes the Object no argument constructor that initializes all fields with default values. This is tested by the code sample in Listing 4-12:

Listing 4-12. Simple Human Object Being Created Without Setting Values or Its Fields

```
package com.apress.bgn.four.base;

public class BasicHumanDemo {
    public static void main(String... args) {
        Human human = new Human();
        System.out.println("name: " + human.name);
        System.out.println("age: " + human.age);
        System.out.println("height: " + human.height);
    }
}
```

What do you think will happen? If you think that some default values (neutral) will be printed, you are absolutely right. Listing 4-13 depicts the output printed in a console when the code in Listing 4-12 is executed.

Listing 4-13. Default Values for the Fields of a Simple Human Object

```
name: null
age: 0
height: 0.0
```

Notice that the numeric variables were initialized with 0, and the String value was initialized with null. The reason for that is that the numeric types are primitive data types and String is an object data type. The String class is part of the java.lang package and is one of the predefined Java classes that is used to create objects of type String. It is a special data type that is used to represent text objects. We'll get deeper into data types in the following chapter.

Class Variables

Aside from attributes that are specific to each human in particular, all humans have something in common: a lifespan, which for the later period is assumed to be 100 years long. It would be redundant to declare a field called lifespan, because it would have to be associated with the same value for all human instances. So we will declare a field using the static keyword in the Human class, which will have the same value for all Human instances and that will be initialized only once. And we can go one step further and make sure that value never changes during the execution of the program by adding the `final` modifier in front of its declaration as well. This way we created a special type of variable called a **constant**. The new Human class is depicted in Listing 4-14:

Listing 4-14. Simple Human Class with a Constant Member

```
package com.apress.bgn.four.base;

public class Human {
    static final int LIFESPAN = 100;
    String name;
    int age;
    float height;
}
```

The LIFESPAN variable is also called a class variable, because it is not associated with instances, but with the class. *(And it was set to 100, which is a pretty optimistic value.)* This is made obvious by the code in Listing 4-15:

Listing 4-15. Code Sample Testing a Constant

```
package com.apress.bgn.four.base;

public class BasicHumanDemo {
    public static void main(String... args) {
        Human alex = new Human();
        alex.name = "Alex";
        alex.age = 40;
        alex.height = 1.91f;

        Human human = new Human();
        System.out.println("Alex's lifespan = " + alex.LIFESPAN);
        // prints 100
        System.out.println("human's lifespan = " + human.LIFESPAN);
        // prints 100
        System.out.println("Human lifespan = " + Human.LIFESPAN);
        // prints 100
    }
}
```

Encapsulating Data

The class we defined makes no use of access modifiers on the fields, and this is not acceptable. Java is known as an object-oriented programming language, and thus code written in Java must respect the **principles of object-oriented programming (OOP)**. Respecting these coding principles ensures that the written code is of good quality and totally aligns with the fundamental Java style. One of the OOP principles is **encapsulation**. The encapsulation principle refers to hiding of data implementation by restricting access to it using special methods called accessors (getters) and mutators (setters).

Basically, any field of a class should have private access, and access to it should be controlled by methods that can be intercepted, tested, and tracked to see where they were called. Getters and setters are a normal practice to have when working with objects; most IDEs have a default options to generate them, including IntelliJ IDEA. Just click right inside the class body and select the **Generate** option to see all possibilities and select **Getters and Setters** to generate the methods for you. The menu is depicted in Figure 4-4.

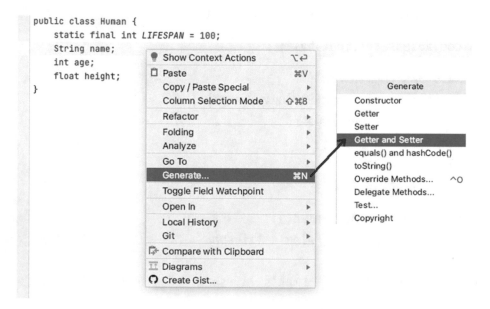

Figure 4-4. *IntelliJ IDEA code generation menu: Generate ➤ Getter and Setter submenu*

After making the fields private and generating the getters and setter, the Human class now looks like the one depicted in Listing 4-16.

Listing 4-16. Simple Human Class with Getters and Setters

```java
package com.apress.bgn.four.base;

public class Human {
    public static final int LIFESPAN = 100;
    private String name;
    private int age;
    private float height;

    public String getName() {
        return name;
    }

    public void setName(String name) {
        this.name = name;
    }

    public int getAge() {
        return age;
    }

    public void setAge(int age) {
        this.age = age;
    }

    public float getHeight() {
        return height;
    }

    public void setHeight(float height) {
        this.height = height;
    }
}
```

After looking at the previous code listing, you may be wondering what the purpose of the `this` keyword is. As the keyword hints, it is a reference to the current object. So `this.name` is actually the value of the field name of the current object, also referred to as an instance variable. Inside the class body, this is used to access fields for the current objects when there are parameters in methods that have the same name. And as you can see, the **setters** and **getters** that IntelliJ IDEA generates have parameters named exactly as the fields.

Getters are the simplest methods that are declared without any parameter, and return the value of the field they are associated with and the coding convention for their names to be made of the get prefix and the name of the field they access, with its first letter uppercased.

Setters are methods that return nothing and declare as a parameter a variable with the same type that needs to be associated to the field. Their names are made of the set prefix and the name of the field they access, with its first letter uppercased. When setters are generated by an editor, the parameter name matches the instance variable name, and the `this` keyword is needed to discern between the two in the context of the setter's body.

Figure 4-5 depicts the setter and getter for the name field.

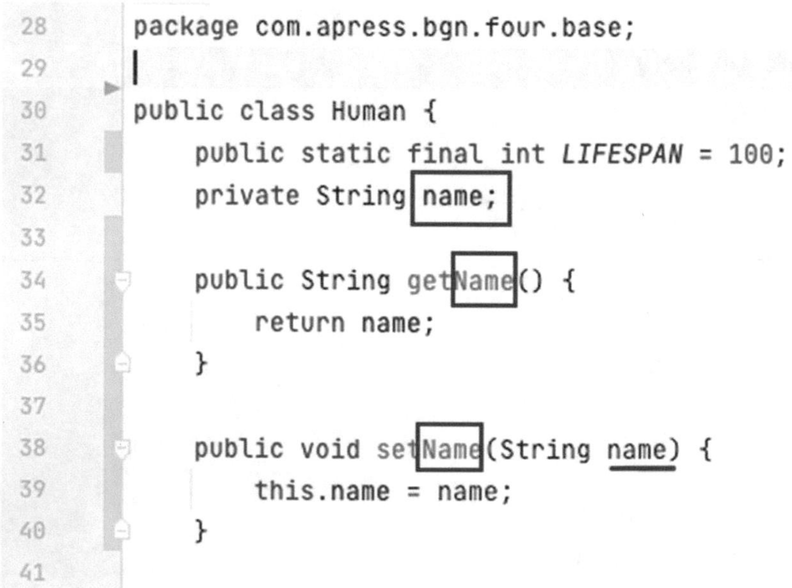

```
28    package com.apress.bgn.four.base;
29    |
30    public class Human {
31        public static final int LIFESPAN = 100;
32        private String name;
33
34        public String getName() {
35            return name;
36        }
37
38        public void setName(String name) {
39            this.name = name;
40        }
41
```

Figure 4-5. *Setter and getter methods used for the name field*

This means that when creating a Human instance, we have to use the setters to set the field values and the getters when accessing them. Therefore our class BasicHumanDemo changes to the one depicted in Listing 4-17.

Listing 4-17. BasicHumanDemo Class Using Human Instance with Getters and Setters

```
package com.apress.bgn.four.base;

public class BasicHumanDemo {
    public static void main(String... args) {
        Human alex = new Human();
        alex.setName("Alex");
        alex.setAge(40);
        alex.setHeight(1.91f);

        System.out.println("name: " + alex.getName());
        System.out.println("age: " + alex.getAge());
        System.out.println("height: " + alex.getHeight());
    }
}
```

Most Java frameworks look for getters and setters within classes to initialize or read the values of an object's fields. Setters and getters are considered by most developers as **boilerplate code** (or just boilerplate); sections of code that are repeated in multiple places with little to no variation. That is why the Lombok[1] library was born—to generate them at runtime, so developers don't have to pollute their code with them. The Kotlin language removed them altogether.

Java did something similar in version 14, when **records** were introduced. Records will be covered a little later in this chapter.

---

[1] Although practical, Lombok causes for setters and getters to be skipped when generating JavaDoc and other problems, but if you are interested you can read more about it at Project Lombok, Title Page, https://projectlombok.org, accessed October 15, 2021.

Methods

Since getters and setters are **methods,** it is time to start the discussion about methods too. A method is a block of code usually characterized by returned type, name, and parameters (when needed) that describes an action done by or on the object that makes use of the values of its fields and/or arguments provided. An abstract template of a Java method is depicted in Listing 4-18.

Listing 4-18. Method Declaration Template

```
[accessor] [returned type] [name] (type1 param1, type2 param2, ...) {
// code
[ [maybe] return val]
}
```

Following it, let's create a method for the class Human that computes and prints how much time a human still has to live, by making use of his age and the LIFESPAN constant. Because the method does not return anything, the return type used will be void. void is a special type that tells the compiler that the method does not return anything, thus no return statement is present in the method body. The code of this method is depicted in Listing 4-19.

Listing 4-19. Human#computeAndPrintTtl Method with No Return Value

```
package com.apress.bgn.four.base;

public class Human {
    static final int LIFESPAN = 100;
    private String name;
    private int age;
    private float height;

    /**
     * compute and prints time to live
     */
    public void computeAndPrintTtl(){
```

```
        int ttl = LIFESPAN - this.age;
        System.out.println("Time to live: " + ttl);
    }

    // some code omitted
}
```

---

❶   There is a coding convention regarding the naming of constants in Java that recommends using only uppercase letters, underscore (replaces space characters in a composed name), and numbers to make up their name.

The preceding method definition does not declare any parameters, so it can be called on a Human instance, as depicted in Listing 4-20.

Listing 4-20. The computeAndPrintTtl() Method Call

```
package com.apress.bgn.four.base;

public class BasicHumanDemo {
    public static void main(String... args) {
        Human alex = new Human();
        alex.setName("Alex");
        alex.setAge(40);
        alex.setHeight(1.91f);
        alex.computeAndPrintTtl();
    }
    // some code omitted
}
```

When the code in Listing 4-20 is executed, *"Time to live: 60"* is printed in the console.

The previous method can be modified to return the time to live value instead of printing it. The method must be modified to declare the type of the value being returned, and in this case the type is int, the same type of the value being computed inside the body of the method. The implementation is depicted in Listing 4-21.

Listing 4-21. The getTimeToLive() Method with Return Value

```
package com.apress.bgn.four.base;

public class Human {
    static final int LIFESPAN = 100;
    private String name;
    private int age;
    private float height;

    /**
     * @return time to live
     */
    public int getTimeToLive(){
        int ttl = LIFESPAN - this.age;
        return ttl;
    }

    // some code omitted
}
```

Calling the method will do nothing in this case, so we have to modify the code to save the returned value and print it, as depicted in Listing 4-22.

Listing 4-22. Using the getTimeToLive() Method

```
package com.apress.bgn.four.base;

public class BasicHumanDemo {
    public static void main(String... args) {
        Human alex = new Human();
        alex.setName("Alex");
        alex.setAge(40);
        alex.setHeight(1.91f);
        int timeToLive = alex.getTimeToLive();
        System.out.println("Time to live: " + timeToLive);
    }
    // some code omitted
}
```

Both methods introduced here declare no parameters, so they are called without providing any arguments. We won't cover methods with parameters, as the setters are more than obvious. Let's skip ahead.

Constructors

Now we've done it, we can no longer use alex.name in other classes without the compiler complaining about about not being able to access that property. Also, in calling all those setters it is quite annoying just to set those properties, so something should be done about that. Remember the implicit constructor? Constructors can be declared explicitly by developers too, and a class can have more than one. Constructors can be declared with parameters for each of the fields of interest. Listing 4-23 depicts a constructor for the Human class that initializes the class fields with the values of its parameters.

Listing 4-23. Human class with Explicit Constructor

```
package com.apress.bgn.four.base;

public class Human {
    static final int LIFESPAN = 100;
    private String name;
    private int age;
    private float height;

    /**
     * Constructs a Human instance initialized with the given parameters.
     * @param name - the name for the Human instance
     * @param age - the age for the Human instance
     * @param height - the height for the Human instance
     */
    public Human(String name, int age, float height) {
        this.name = name;
        this.age = age;
        this.height = height;
    }

    // some code omitted
}
```

A constructor does not require a `return` statement, even if the result of calling a constructor is the creation of an object. Constructors are different from methods in that way. By declaring an explicit constructor, the default constructor is no longer generated. So creating a Human instance by calling the default constructor, as depicted in earlier code listings, does not work anymore. The code no longer compiles, because the default constructor is no longer generated. To create a Human instance, we now have to call the new constructor and provide proper arguments in place of the parameters, having the correct types and respecting their declaration order.

```
Human human = new Human("John", 40, 1.91f);  // this works
Human human = new Human();  // this no longer works
```

But what if we do not want to be forced to set all fields using this constructor? It's simple: we define another with only the parameters we are interested in. Let's define a constructor that only sets the name and the age for a Human instance, as depicted in Listing 4-24.

Listing 4-24. Human Class with Explicit Constructors

```
package com.apress.bgn.four.base;

public class Human {
    static final int LIFESPAN = 100;
    private String name;
    private int age;
    private float height;

    public Human(String name, int age) {
        this.name = name;
        this.age = age;
    }

    public Human(String name, int age, float height) {
        this.name = name;
        this.age = age;
        this.height = height;
    }

    // some code omitted
}
```

Here is where we stumble upon another OOP principle called **polymorphism**. The term is Greek and translates to *one name, many forms*. Polymorphism applies to code design having multiple methods all with the same name, but slightly different signatures and functionality. It applies to constructors too. There are two basic types of polymorphism: **overriding**, also called run-time polymorphism, which will be covered a little bit later when the **inheritance** principle will be covered; and **overloading**, which is referred to as compile-time polymorphism.

The second type of polymorphism applies to the previous constructors, because we have two of them: one with a different set of parameters, that looks like it is an extension of the simpler one.

The second thing this should be noticeable in the most recent listing is that the two constructors contain two identical code lines. There is a common sense programming principle named DRY,[2] which is short for *Don't Repeat Yourself!* Obviously, the code in the most recent listing does not abide by it, so let's fix that by using the `this` keyword introduced previously in a new interesting way, as in Listing 4-25.

Listing 4-25. Human Class with Better Explicit Constructors

```java
package com.apress.bgn.four.base;

public class Human {
    static final int LIFESPAN = 100;
    private String name;
    private int age;
    private float height;

    public Human(String name, int age) {
        this.name = name;
        this.age = age;
    }
```

---

[2] Also one of the clean coding principles; you can read more about it at Aspire Systems Poland Blog, "Top 9 Qualities of Clean Code," https://blog.aspiresys.pl/technology/top-9-principles-clean-code, accessed October 15, 2021.

```java
    public Human(String name, int age, float height) {
        this(name,age);
        this.height = height;
    }

    // some code omitted
}
```

The constructors can call each other by using this(...). This is pretty useful to avoid writing the same code twice, thus promoting code reusability.

So now both constructors provide the means to create Human instances. If we use the one that does not set the height, the height field will be implicitly initialized with the default value for type float (0.0).

Now our class is quite basic, and we could even say that it models a Human in a quite abstract way. If we were to try to model humans with certain skill sets or abilities, we have to create new classes. Let's say we want to model musicians and actors. This means we need to create two new classes. The Musician class is depicted in Listing 4-26; getters and setter for the fields are skipped.

Listing 4-26. Musician Class

```java
package com.apress.bgn.four.classes;

public class Musician {
    static final int LIFESPAN = 100;
    private String name;
    private int age;
    private float height;
    private String musicSchool;
    private String genre;
    private List<String> songs;

// other code omitted
}
```

The Actor class is depicted in Listing 4-27; getters and setter for the fields are skipped.

Listing 4-27. Actor Class

```java
package com.apress.bgn.four.classes;

public class Actor {
    static final int LIFESPAN = 100;
    private String name;
    private int age;
    private float height;
    private String actingSchool;
    private List<String> films;

    // other code omitted
}
```

As you can see, there are more than a few common elements between the two classes. We've mentioned before that one of the clean coding principles requires developers to avoid code duplication. This can be done by designing the classes by following two more OOP principles: **inheritance** (which was mentioned briefly) and **abstraction**.

Abstraction and Inheritance

Abstraction is an OOP principle that manages complexity. Abstraction is used to decompose complex implementations and define core parts that can be reused. In our case, common fields of classes **Musician** and **Actor** can be grouped in the **Human** class that we defined earlier in the chapter. The **Human** class can be viewed as an abstraction, because any human in this world is more than their name, age, and height. There is no need to ever create Human instances, because any human will be represented by something else, such as passion, purpose, or skill. A class that does not need to be instantiated, but just groups together fields and methods for other classes to inherit or provide a concrete implementation for, is modelled in Java by an **abstract** class. Thus, the **Human** class is modified to make it abstract. Since we are abstracting this class, we'll make the LIFESPAN constant public to make it accessible from anywhere and make the getTimeToLive() method abstract to delegate its implementation to extending classes. The class contents are shown in Listing 4-28.

Listing 4-28. Human Abstract Class

```java
package com.apress.bgn.four.classes;

public abstract class Human {
    public static final int LIFESPAN = 100;
    protected String name;
    protected int age;
    protected float height;

    public Human(String name, int age) {
        this.name = name;
        this.age = age;
    }
    public Human(String name, int age, float height) {
        this(name, age);
        this.height = height;
    }

    /**
     * @return time to live
     */
    public abstract int getTimeToLive();

    // getters and setters omitted
}
```

An abstract method is a method missing the body, like the getTimeToLive() method declared in the previous code listing. This means that within the Human class there is no concrete implementation for this method, only a skeleton, a template. A concrete implementation for this method must be provided by the extending classes.

Oh, but wait, we kept the constructors! Why did we do that, if we are not allowed to use them anymore? And we aren't, because here is what IntelliJ IDEA does with the BasicHumanDemo class now in Figure 4-6:

Figure 4-6. *Java compiler error when trying to instantiate an abstract class*

Yes, that is a compile error. Constructors can be kept, as they can help further in abstracting behavior. Classes `Musician` and `Actor` must be rewritten to extend the `Human` class. This is done by using the `extends` keyword when declaring the class and specifying the class to be extended, also called **parent class** or **superclass**. The resulting class is called a **subclass**.

---

❶   When extending a class, the subclass inherits all the fields and concrete methods declared in the superclass. (Access to them is defined by access modifiers covered in **Chapter 3**.) The exception are abstract methods, for which the subclass is forced to provide a concrete implementation.

❶   The subclass must declare its own constructors that make use the ones declared in the superclass. The constructors from the superclass are called using the keyword `super`. The same goes for methods and fields, unless they have an access modifier that prohibits access.

Can you guess which one it is? It is `private`. A subclass cannot access private members of the superclass. If you did not know the answer, you might want to review **Chapter 3**.

Listing 4-29 depicts a version of the Musician class that is written by making use of abstraction and inheritance.

Listing 4-29. Musician Class That Extends Human

```
package com.apress.bgn.four.classes;

public class Musician extends Human {
    private String musicSchool;
    private String genre;
    private List<String> songs;

    public Musician(String name, int age, float height,
                    String musicSchool, String genre) {
        super(name, age, height);
        this.musicSchool = musicSchool;
        this.genre = genre;
    }

    public int getTimeToLive() {
        return (LIFESPAN - getAge()) / 2;
    }

    // getters and setters omitted
}
```

The songs field was not used as a parameter in the constructor for simplicity reasons here.

As you can see, the Musician constructor calls the constructor in the superclass to set the properties defined there. Also, notice the full implementation provided for the getTimeToLive() method. The Actor class is rewritten in a similar manner. There is a proposal implementation in the sources for the book, but try to write your own before looking in the classes package. In Figure 4-7 the Human class hierarchy is depicted, as generated by IntelliJ IDEA. Methods are omitted to keep the image simple.

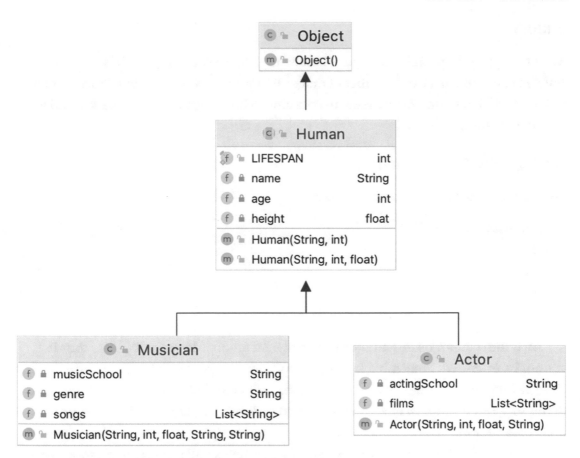

Figure 4-7. *UML diagram generated by IntelliJ IDEA*

The UML diagram clearly shows the members of each class, and the arrows point to the superclass. UML diagrams are useful tools in designing component hierarchies and defining logic of applications. If you want to read more about them, and the many types of UML diagrams that there are, you can do so here: `https://www.uml-diagrams.org`.

After covering so much about classes and how to create objects, we need to cover other Java important components that can be used to create even more detailed objects. Our Human class is missing quite a few attributes, such as gender, for example. A field that models the gender of a person can only have values from a fixed set of values. It used to be two, but because we are living in a brave new world that is quite fond of political correctness, we cannot limit the set of values for genders to two, so we will introduce a third, called UNSPECIFIED, which is to be used as a replacement for whatever a person identifies as. This means that we have to introduce a new class to represent gender that is only limited to be instantiated thrice. This would be quite tricky to do with a typical class, and this is the reason why enums were introduced in Java version 1.5.

Enums

The enum type is a special class type. It is used to define a special type of class that can only be instantiated a fixed number of times. An enum declaration groups together all instances of that enum. All of them are constants. The Gender enum can be defined as shown in Listing 4-30.

Listing 4-30. Gender Enum

```
package com.apress.bgn.four.classes;

public enum Gender {
    FEMALE,
    MALE,
    UNSPECIFIED
}
```

An enum cannot be instantiated externally. An enum is by default final, thus it cannot be extended. Remember how by default every class in Java implicitly extends class Object? Every enum in Java implicitly extends class java.lang.Enum<E> and in doing so, every enum instance inherits special methods that are useful when writing code using enums.

Being a special type of class, an enum can have fields and a constructor, **that can only be private**, as enum instances cannot be created externally. The private modifier is not needed explicitly, as the compiler knows what to do. Listing 4-31 shows the Gender enum implemented by adding an integer field that will be the numerical representation of each gender and a String field that will be the text representation. To access the enum properties, getters are needed.

Listing 4-31. A More Complex Gender Enum

```
package com.apress.bgn.four.classes;

public enum Gender {
    FEMALE(1, "f"),
    MALE(2, "m") ,
    UNSPECIFIED(3, "u");
```

```java
    private int repr;
    private String descr;

    Gender(int repr, String descr) {
        this.repr = repr;
        this.descr = descr;
    }

    public int getRepr() {
        return repr;
    }

    public String getDescr() {
        return descr;
    }
}
```

⚠ But wait, what would stop us from declaring setters as well and modifying the field values? Well, nothing. If that is what you need to do you can do it. **But this is not a good practice.**

Enum instances should be constant. So a correct enum design should not declare setters, and make sure the values of the fields will never be changed by declaring them final. When we do so, the only way the fields are initialized is by calling the constructor, and since the constructor cannot be called externally, the integrity of our data is ensured. An example of a good enum design is depicted in Listing 4-32.

Listing 4-32. Proper Gender Enum

```java
package com.apress.bgn.four.classes;

public enum Gender {
    FEMALE(1, "f"),
    MALE(2, "m") ,
    UNSPECIFIED(3, "u");

    private final int repr;
    private final String descr;
```

```
    Gender(int repr, String descr) {
        this.repr = repr;
        this.descr = descr;
    }

    public int getRepr() {
        return repr;
    }
    public String getDescr() {
        return descr;
    }
}
```

Methods can be added to enums, and each instance can override them. So if we add a method called comment() to the Gender enum, every instance will inherit it. But the instance can override it, as depicted in Listing 4-33.

Listing 4-33. Proper Gender Enum with Extra Method

```
package com.apress.bgn.four.classes;

public enum Gender {
    FEMALE(1, "f"),
    MALE(2, "m") ,
    UNSPECIFIED(3, "u"){
        @Override
        public String comment() {
            return "to be decided later: " + getRepr() + ", " + getDescr();
        }
    };

    private final int repr;
    private final String descr;

    Gender(int repr, String descr) {
        this.repr = repr;
        this.descr = descr;
    }
```

```java
    public int getRepr() {
        return repr;
    }
    public String getDescr() {
        return descr;
    }

    public String comment() {
        return repr + ": " + descr;
    }
}
```

---

❶   So how is this possible? How can an instance override a method of its class type? **Well, it doesn't**. The UNSPECIFIED enum actually extends the Gender class and overrides the comment() method.

This can be easily proven by iterating over the enum values and printing the result returned by the getClass() method, inherited from the Object class that returns the runtime type of the object. To get all the instances of an enum, the class java.lang. Enum<E>, which every enum extends implicitly, provides a method named values().

Listing 4-34 shows the code that does that and its output too.

Listing 4-34. Code Sample Listing Enum Items Classes

```java
package com.apress.bgn.four.classes;

public class BasicHumanDemo {
    public static void main(String... args) {
        for (Gender value : Gender.values()) {
            System.out.println(value.getClass());
        }
    }
}
// Output expected in the console
// class com.apress.bgn.four.classes.Gender
// class com.apress.bgn.four.classes.Gender
// class com.apress.bgn.four.classes.Gender$1
```

Notice the value printed for the UNSPECIFIED element. The Gender$1 notation means that the compiler, created an inner class by extending the original enum class and overriding the comment() method with the one provided in the declaration of the UNSPECIFIED element.

We're going to be playing with enums in future examples as well. Just remember that whenever you need to limit the implementation of a class to a fixed number of instances, or group related constants together, enums are the tools for you. Because we have introduced enums, our Human class can now have a field of type Gender, as depicted in Listing 4-35.

Listing 4-35. Human Class with a Gender Field

```java
package com.apress.bgn.four.classes;

public abstract class Human {
    public static final int LIFESPAN = 100;
    protected String name;
    protected int age;
    protected float height;

    private Gender gender;

    public Human(String name, int age, Gender gender) {
        this.name = name;
        this.age = age;
        this.gender = gender;
    }

    public Human(String name, int age, float height, Gender gender) {
        this(name, age, gender);
        this.height = height;
    }

    // other code omitted

    public Gender getGender() {
        return gender;
    }
```

```
    public void setGender(Gender gender) {
        this.gender = gender;
    }
}
```

In the previous sections **interfaces** were mentioned as one of the Java components used to create objects. It is high time we expand the subject.

Interfaces

⚲ One of the most common Java interview questions is: What is the difference between an interface and an abstract class? This section will provide you the most detailed answer to that question.

An **interface** is not a class, but it does help create classes. An interface is fully abstract; it has no fields, only abstract method definitions. I also like to call them *skeletons*. When a class is declared to implement an interface, unless the class is abstract, it must provide concrete implementations for all skeleton methods.

❶ The name skeleton method is quite important in Java 8+ versions, because from this version on, interfaces were enriched so that `static`, `default`, and `private` methods can be part of them.

Skeleton methods inside an interface are implicitly `public` and `abstract`, because skeleton methods must be abstract to force classes to provide implementations and must be public, so classes actually have access to do so. The only methods with concrete implementation in an interface until Java 8 were `static` methods.

In Java 8, **default** methods in interfaces were introduced, and in Java 9 **private** methods in interfaces were introduced.

The interfaces cannot be instantiated; they do not have constructors.

Interfaces that declare no method definitions are called **marker** interfaces and have the purpose to mark classes for specific purposes. The most renown Java marker interface is `java.io.Serializable`, which marks objects that can be serialized so that their state can be saved to a binary file or another data source and sent over a network to be deserialized and used. An interface can be declared in its own file as a top-level

151

component, or nested inside another component. There are two types of interfaces: *normal* interfaces and **annotations**.

The difference between abstract classes and interfaces, and when one or the other should be used, becomes relevant in the context of **inheritance**.

---

❶   Java supports only single inheritance. This means a class can only have one superclass.

Single inheritance might seem a limitation, however, consider the following example. Let's modify the previous hierarchy and imagine a class named `Performer` that should extend classes Musician and Actor. If you need a real human that can be modelled by this class, think of David Duchovny (he is an actor and musician).

In Figure 4-8 the class hierarchy mentioned previously is depicted.

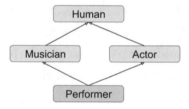

Figure 4-8. *Diamond class hierarchy*

The hierarchy in the previous image introduces something called the diamond problem, and the name is obviously inspired by the shape formed by the relationships between classes. What is actually wrong with the design? It should be obvious that if both `Musician` and `Actor` extend Human and inherit all members from it, what will `Performer` inherit and from where? It obviously cannot inherit members of Human twice, which would make this class useless and invalid. And how could we discern between methods with the same signature? So what is the solution in Java? As you probably imagine, considering the focus of this section: interfaces. *(Sort of, most times a combination of interfaces, and a programming concept named composition is required.)*

What has to be done is to turn methods in classes `Musician` and `Actor` into method skeletons and transform those **classes** into **interfaces**. The behavior from the `Musician` will be moved to a class called, let's say `Guitarist`, that will extend the `Human` class and implement the `Musician` interface. For the `Actor` class, something similar can be done, but we'll leave that as an exercise for you. Some help is provided though, by the hierarchy in Figure 4-9.

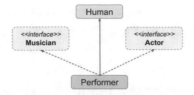

Figure 4-9. *Java hierarchy with interfaces for performer class*

So the Musician interface contains only method skeletons mapping what a musician does. It does not go into detail to model how. The same goes for the Actor interface. In Listing 4-36, you can see the bodies of the two interfaces.

Listing 4-36. Musician and Actor interfaces

```java
//Musician.java
package com.apress.bgn.four.interfaces;
import java.util.List;

public interface Musician {
    String getMusicSchool();
    void setMusicSchool(String musicSchool);
    List<String> getSongs();
    void setSongs(List<String> songs);
    String getGenre();
    void setGenre(String genre);
}

//Actor.java
package com.apress.bgn.four.interfaces;
import java.util.List;

public interface Actor {
    String getActingSchool();
    void setActingSchool(String actingSchool);
    List<String> getFilms();
    void setFilms(List<String> films);
    void addFilm(String filmName);
}
```

As you can see, the fields have been removed because they cannot be part of the interfaces, and all that is left is the method skeletons. The Performer class is depicted in Listing 4-37.

Listing 4-37. Performer Class Implementing Two Interfaces

```java
package com.apress.bgn.four.interfaces;

import com.apress.bgn.four.classes.Gender;
import com.apress.bgn.four.classes.Human;

import java.util.List;

public class Performer extends Human implements Musician, Actor {

    // fields specific to musician
    private String musicSchool;
    private String genre;
    private List<String> songs;

    // fields specific to actor
    private String actingSchool;
    private List<String> films;

    public Performer(String name, int age, float height, Gender gender) {
        super(name, age, height, gender);
    }

    // from Human
    @Override
    public int getTimeToLive() {
        return (LIFESPAN - getAge()) / 2;
    }

    // from Musician
    public String getMusicSchool() {
        return musicSchool;
    }
```

```java
    public void setMusicSchool(String musicSchool) {
        this.musicSchool = musicSchool;
    }

    // from Actor
    public String getActingSchool() {
        return actingSchool;
    }

    public void setActingSchool(String actingSchool) {
        this.actingSchool = actingSchool;
    }

    // other methods omitted
}
```

❶ What you should take from this example is that using interfaces and multiple inheritance is possible in Java to some extent, and that **classes extend only one class and can implement one or more interfaces**.

Inheritance applies to interfaces too. For example, both Musician and Actor interfaces can extend an interface named Artist that contains template for behavior common to both. For example, we can combine the music school and acting school into a generic school and define the setters and getters for it as method skeletons. The Artist interface is depicted in Listing 4-38 together with Musician.

Listing 4-38. Artist and Musician Interfaces

```java
package com.apress.bgn.four.interfaces;

// Artist.java
public interface Artist {
    String getSchool();
    void setSchool(String school);
}
```

```java
// Musician.java
import java.util.List;

public interface Musician extends Artist {
    List<String> getSongs();
    void setSongs(List<String> songs);
    String getGenre();
    void setGenre(String genre);
}
```

Hopefully, you understood the idea of multiple inheritance and when it is appropriate to use classes and when to use interfaces in designing your applications, because it is high time to fulfil the promise made in the beginning of this section and list the differences between abstract classes and interfaces. You can find them in Table 4-1.

Table 4-1. *Differences Between Abstract Classes and Interfaces in Java*

Abstract Class	Interface
Can have nonabstract methods.	Can only have static, abstract, default and private methods.
Single inheritance: a class can only extend one class.	Multiple inheritance: a class can implement more than one interface. Also, an interface can extend one or more interfaces.
Can have final, nonfinal, static and nonstatic variables.	Can only have static and final fields.
Declared with **abstract class**.	Declared with **interface**.
Can extend another class using keyword **extends** and implement interfaces with keyword **implements**.	Can only extend other interfaces (one or more) using keyword **extends**.
Can have nonabstract, package-private (default), protected or private members.	All members are by default abstract and public. (Except default and private methods starting with Java 9.)
If a class has an abstract method, it must be declared itself abstract.	(No correspondence).

Default Methods in Interfaces

One problem with interfaces is that if you modify their bodies to add new methods, the code will stop compiling. To make it compile, you have to add a concrete implementation for the newly added interface method(s) in every class that implements that interface. This has been a pain for developers for many years. An interface is a contract, it guarantees how a class will behave. When using third-party libraries in your project, you do so by designing your code to respect those contracts. When switching to a new version of a library, if that contract changes, your code will no longer compile.

💡 This situation is very similar to Apple changing the charging ports for their computers and phones from a version to another. If you buy a new Mac and try to use your old charger, it won't fit.

Sure, a solution would be to declare the new methods in a new interface and then creating new classes that implement both new and old interfaces (this is called composition, because the two interfaces are composed to represent a single contract). The methods exposed by an interface make up an API (Application Programming Interface), and when developing applications, the aim is to design them to have stable API. This rule is described by a programming principle called Open-Closed Principle. This is one of the 5 SOLID Programming Principles.[3] This principle states that you should be able to extend a class without modifying it. Thus, modifying the interface a class implements requires modifying the class too. Modifying interfaces tends to lead to breaking this principle.

Aside from interfaces composition mentioned previously, in Java 8 a solution for this was introduced: **default methods**. Starting with Java 8, methods with a full implementation can be declared in interfaces as long as they are declared using the `default` keyword. Default methods are implicitly public. Their main purpose is to modify the API to allow new implementations to override them, but without breaking existing implementations.

---

[3] A good article about them is available at Hackernoon, "SOLID Principles Made Easy," `https://hackernoon.com/solid-principles-made-easy-67b1246bcdf`, accessed October 15, 2021.

Let's consider the `Artist` interface. Any artist should be able to create something, right? So they should have a creative nature. Given the word we are living in, I won't give names, but some of our artists are actually products of the industry and are not creative themselves. The realization that we should have a method that tells us if an artist has a creative nature or not came after we decided our hierarchy depicted in Figure 4-10.

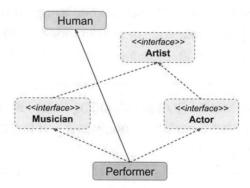

Figure 4-10. *Java hierarchy with more interfaces for performer class*

If we add a new abstract method to the `Artist` interface, the `Performer` class fails to compile. IntelliJ IDEA will make it really obvious that our application does not work anymore by showing a lot of things in red, as depicted in Figure 4-11.

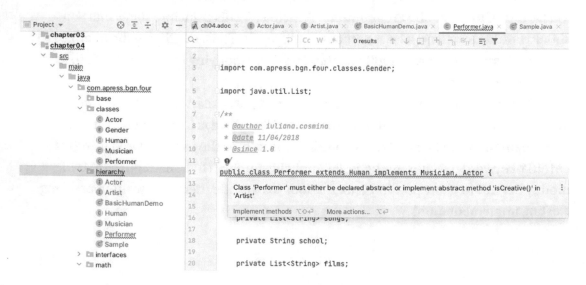

Figure 4-11. *Java broken hierarchy because of new method in interface*

The compiler errors that we see are caused by our decision to add a new abstract method named isCreative to the Artist interface, and if you hover with your mouse over the class declaration you can see why. Listing 4-39 depicts the abstract method breaking the code.

Listing 4-39. New Abstract Method Added to the Artist Interface

```java
package com.apress.bgn.four.hierarchy;

public interface Artist {
    String getSchool();

    void setSchool(String school);

    boolean isCreative();
}
```

To get rid of the compiling errors we'll transform the isCreative abstract method into a default method that returns true, because every artist should be creative. Default methods are by default public, so they can be called on every object of a type implementing the interface where the method is declared. Listing 4-40 depicts the body of the default method.

Listing 4-40. New default Method Added to the Artist Interface

```java
package com.apress.bgn.four.hierarchy;

public interface Artist {
    String getSchool();

    void setSchool(String school);

    default boolean isCreative(){
        return true;
    }
}
```

Now the code should compile again. Default methods are pretty practical, as they allow the modification of the contract represented by an interface without enforcing modification of existing classes implementing that interfaces. This will ensure binary compatibility with code written for older versions of that interface.

Classes that implement an interface containing a default method can use the existing default implementation or provide a new implementation for default methods (can override them). To show this, a class named `MiliVanili` is shown in Listing 4-41 that provides a new implementation for the default method in the `Artist` interface.

Listing 4-41. Default Method Being Overriden in Class Implementing the `Artist` Interface

```java
package com.apress.bgn.four.hierarchy;

import java.util.List;

public class MiliVanili implements Artist {

    @Override
    public boolean isCreative() {
        return false; // dooh!
    }

    // other code omitted
}
```

Interfaces extending other interfaces can be written to do any of the following (for a little more clarity the extended interface will be referred to as the super-interface):

- declare their own abstract methods and default methods

- redeclare the default method from the super-interface as an abstract method which forces classes extending this interface to provide an implementation

- redefine the default method from the super-interface

- declare a default method that provides an implementation for an abstract method from the super-interface

> 💡 Providing code samples for all these scenarios is a little bit too much for an absolute Java beginner book. If you are interested in what the code looks like and in testing the validity of these affirmations, check out the contents of the `com.ampress.bgn.four.interfaces.extensions` package.

Static Methods and Constants in Interfaces

In Java version 1 interfaces could only contain abstract methods and static constants. Interfaces have changed a lot since version 1, with the most important changes being the support for `default` and `private` methods.

Constants, or variables that once initialized never change, do not need an implementation, so it makes sense for developers to be allowed to declare them in an interface's body, right? You can do the same using enums, but sometimes you might want to keep related components together. In a previous example a `LIFESPAN` constant was declared in the `Human` class. Since any class implementing `Artist` will probably need the `LIFESPAN` for some calculation or another, we can move this constant in the `Artist` interface and use it in any class, as depicted in Listing 4-42.

Listing 4-42. The Constant `LIFESPAN` in the `Artist` Interface

```java
// Artist.java
package com.apress.bgn.four.hierarchy;

public interface Artist {
    public static final int LIFESPAN = 100;

    // other code omitted
}

// Performer.java
package com.apress.bgn.four.hierarchy;

public class Performer extends Human implements Musician, Actor {

    @Override
    public int getTimeToLive() {
        return (LIFESPAN - getAge()) / 2;
    }
```

```
    // other code omitted
}
```

When declaring constants in interfaces, the three accessors public static final are redundant because they are implied. The explanation for each is quite simple:

- Interfaces cannot have mutable fields, so by default they have to be final.

- Since interfaces cannot be instantiated; they cannot have fields that will become properties on instances, so they have to be static.

- Since anything in an interface body must be accessible to implementing classes, they have to be public.

As for static methods in interfaces, they are usually utility methods that are specific to certain operations within the hierarchy the interface is part of. Let's add a static method that checks to see if the name provided as an argument is capitalized, and capitalizes it if it isn't. The code is depicted in Listing 4-43, and the method capitalize is declared in the Artist interface and used in the Performer class.

Listing 4-43. Public Static Method in Interface

```
// Artist.java
package com.apress.bgn.four.hierarchy;

public interface Artist {

    public static String capitalize(String name){
        Character c = name.charAt(0);
        if(Character.isLowerCase(c)) {
            Character upperC = Character.toUpperCase(c);
            name.replace(c, upperC);
        }
        return name;
    }

    // other code omitted
}
```

```
// Performer.java
package com.apress.bgn.four.hierarchy;

public class Performer extends Human implements Musician, Actor {

    public String getCapitalizedName() {
        return Artist.capitalize(this.name);
    }

    // other code omitted
}
```

In Java 8 any method with a body that was not declared as default had to be declared public and static, because of reasons mentioned previously. If default or static methods share a lot of code, then a default or static method can group that code and have the others call it, right? The only problem appears when there is a need for that code to be private. That was not possible in Java 8, because everything in the body of an interface was public by default, but it became possible in Java 9.

Private Methods in Interfaces

Starting with Java 9, support for private and private static methods in interfaces was introduced. This means that the action performed by the default isCreative() method can be modified to also log an explanation for the returned value, by calling a private method, as shown in Listing 4-44.

Listing 4-44. New private Method Added to the Artist Interface

```
package com.apress.bgn.four.hierarchy;

public interface Artist {
    String getSchool();

    void setSchool(String school);

    default boolean isCreative(){
        explain();
        return true;
    }
```

```
private void explain(){
    System.out.println("A true artist has a creative nature.");
}
}
```

The same can be done for static methods as well, if there is a piece of code that is worth making private, just declare it in a `private static` method.

When doing development on a concrete project, you will find yourself using classes, interfaces, enums, and others. It is up to you how you design and organize your code. Just make sure to avoid repetition, and keep it clean, uncoupled, and testable.

Records

The Java `record` is a special type of class with a clear syntax for defining immutable data-only classes. The Java compiler takes the code of your record and generates constructors, getters, and other specialized methods such as `toString()`, `hashCode()`, and `equals()`.

ℹ The `hashCode()` and `equals()` specialized methods are defined in the `Object` class and thus they are implicitly defined in every Java class. They are very important in establishing the identity of an instance and will be covered in **Chapter 5**, the collections section.

Java records were introduced in JDK 14 as a preview feature, long after similar type of constructs were introduced in other programming languages as C#, Scala, or Kotlin. Java developers avoided the hassle of writing a lot of boilerplate code by using libraries such as Lombok. Lombok was already mentioned in the **Encapsulating Data** section of this chapter, where some disadvantages of using it were listed too.

Lombok requires annotating classes with special annotations that tell its annotation processor to generate the desired bytecode at compile time. It works for generation of all the components now supported using Java records.

Listing 4-45 shows how the Human class would be written using Lombok.

Listing 4-45. Human Class: the Lombok Version

```
package com.apress.bgn.four.lombok;

import com.apress.bgn.four.classes.Gender;
import lombok.*;

@NoArgsConstructor
@AllArgsConstructor
@RequiredArgsConstructor
@ToString
@EqualsAndHashCode
public class Human {
    @Getter @Setter
    @NonNull
    private String name;

    @Getter @Setter
    @NonNull
    private int age;

    @Getter @Setter
    private float height;

    @Getter @Setter
    private Gender gender;
}
```

Another issue with Lombok is that it becomes unpredictable in a Java project using modules. Manipulating code at compile time to inject extra functionalities is a sensitive operation that requires access to JDK internals that might not be exported for security reasons. For example, at the time this section was written, compiling the project using Lombok doesn't work because Lombok requires access to class com.sun.tools.javac. processing.JavacProcessingEnvironment from module jdk.compiler that doesn't export the com.sun.tools.javac.processing package.

Without Lombok, the class in Listing 4-45, would have a lot more lines, because all the annotations in code snippet essentially replace methods that the developer should write otherwise:

- @NoArgsConstructor tells Lombok to generate the bytecode for a default no-arguments constructor for the Human class.

- @AllArgsConstructor tells Lombok to generate the bytecode for a constructor requiring an argument for each field of the Human class.

- @RequiredArgsConstructor tells Lombok to generate the bytecode for a constructor requiring an argument for all required fields (the ones annotated with @NotNull).

- @ToString tells Lombok to generate the bytecode for the toString() method. The implementation of this method is decided by Lombok based on all the fields in the class.

- @EqualsAndHashCode tells Lombok to generate the bytecode for the equals() and hashCode() methods. The implementation of these methods is decided by Lombok based on all the fields in the class.

With the introduction of records, Lombok is no longer needed as long as the project is being compiled and run using on JDK 15. And you don't need your instances to be immutable. The resulted classes are immutable data-only classes, so there are no setters, but in the brave new world of reactivity, having immutable records is a must anyway. The record implementation of the Human class is shown in Listing 4-46 together with the code necessary to instantiate a Human.

Listing 4-46. Simple Human Record and Class Where Used

```java
// Human.java
package com.apress.bgn.four.records;

import com.apress.bgn.four.classes.Gender;

public record Human(String name, int age, float height, Gender gender) { }

// RecordDemo.java
package com.apress.bgn.four.records;
```

```
import com.apress.bgn.four.classes.Gender;

public class RecordDemo {

    public static void main(String... args) {
        Human john = new Human("John Mayer", 44, 1.9f, Gender.MALE);

        System.out.println("John as string: " + john);
        System.out.println("John's hashCode: " + john.hashCode());
        System.out.println("John's name: " + john.name());
    }
}
```

As you can see, records can be instantiated in the same way classes are by calling a constructor using the new keyword. After all, they are just another type of classes. Also, since there is no need for setters, because the objects are immutable, getters don't make much sense either. So to access the property values, methods with the same name as the field are generated that return the field value.

This can be proven by viewing the bytecode in the generated Human.class file using IntelliJ IDEA. Just look for this file in chapter04/target/classes directory and then select it, and from the menu select **View ➤ Show Bytecode**. A window should pop-up with contents pretty similar to the ones shown in Figure 4-12.

```
 R  records/Human.java  ×
  1      package com.apress.bgn.four.records;
  2      /*...*/
 29
 30      import com.apress.bgn.four.classes.Gender;
 31
 32      public record Human(String name, int age, float height, Gender gender) { }
 33
                                  Human Bytecode
// class version 61.0 (61)
// RECORD
// access flags 0x10031
public final class com/apress/bgn/four/records/Human extends java/lang/Record {

  // compiled from: Human.java
  // access flags 0x19
  public final static INNERCLASS java/lang/invoke/MethodHandles$Lookup java/lang/invoke/MethodHandles Lookup
  RECORDCOMPONENT    Ljava/lang/String; name
  RECORDCOMPONENT    I age
  RECORDCOMPONENT    F height
  RECORDCOMPONENT    Lcom/apress/bgn/four/classes/Gender; gender
```

Figure 4-12. *Bytecode of the Human record*

From the bytecode we can figure out yet another important thing about records: the class being shown in the bytecode is `final`, thus records cannot be extended. Also, all record classes implicitly extend class `java.lang.Record`.

Creation of subrecords is not possible.

Running the `main(..)` method in the `RecordDemo` class yields the following results:

```
John as string: Human[name=John Mayer, age=44, height=1.9, gender=MALE]
John's hashCode: -1637990649
John's name: John Mayer
```

The `toString()` implementation of a record is decent enough. The values of the properties of the `john` instance can be read and understood easily.

Records can be customized. Nothing stops you from providing a custom implementation for the `toString()`, `equals()`,`hashCode()` methods and providing various constructors in the record body, in the same way you would do it for a class. The only catch is the constructor must call the default constructor of the record using the `this` keyword. In Listing 4-47 you can see a constructor being added, which only requires name and age.

Listing 4-47. Simple Human Record with an Additional Constructor

```java
package com.apress.bgn.four.records;

public record Human(String name, int age, Float height, Gender gender) {
    public Human(String name, int age) {
        this(name, age, null, null);
    }
}
```

Since the default constructor and other methods generated for a record rely on the arguments of the record, no extra fields can be declared in a record's body. However, static variables and methods are supported. Figure 4-13 depicts a record with an extra constant and a field declared in its body, and the editor doesn't like the latter.

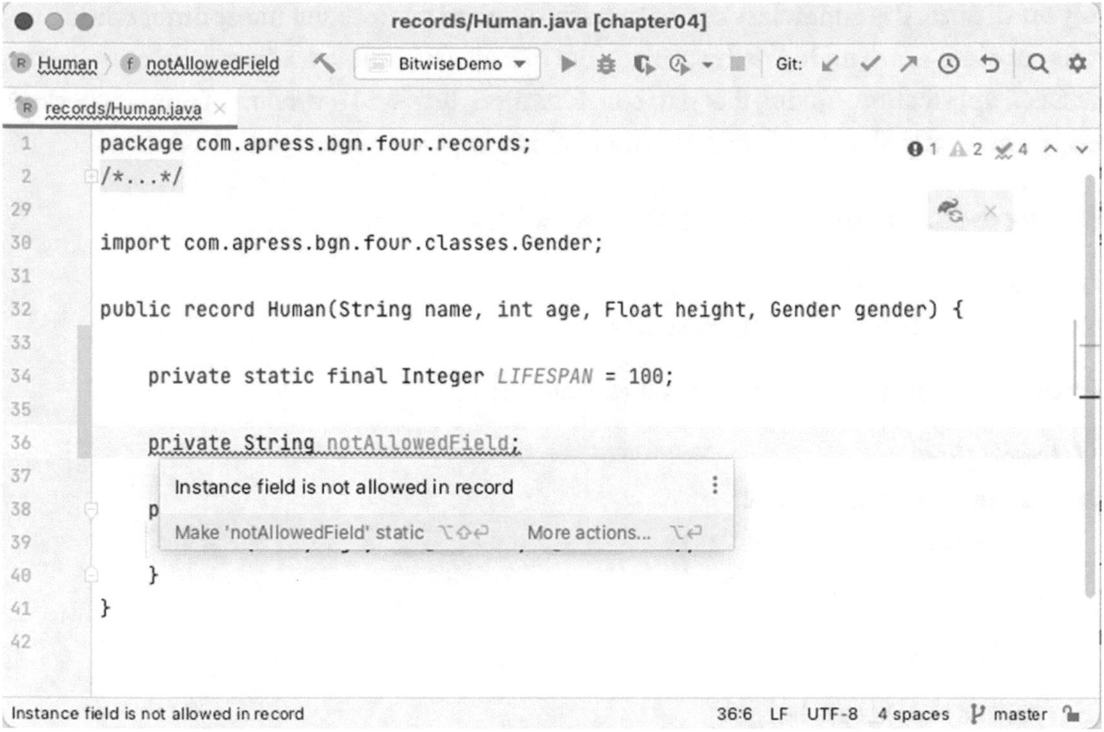

Figure 4-13. *Record with a constant and field*

Records are pretty practical when data immutability is a requirement, which is ... most of the time (e.g., DTOs or data transfer objects used to transfer data between software application subsystems). It can be done without records, but it requires a lot of effort from the developer. This is effort that old-school developers like me were doing whenever necessary, but *you youngsters have no idea how easy you have it nowadays!*

Sealed Classes

Sealed classes were a preview feature in JDK 15 and kept being a preview in JDK 16 as well. At the time this chapter was written, the list of Java 17 features is still pretty small and sealed classes are not mentioned. But the hope is that they will become an official feature in Java 17, so they merit a mention in this book.

A common problem developers have is choosing a scope modifier for their classes and interfaces. Security is always a concern and for some projects when classes need to be extended, making them public or protected is a risk. This is where the `sealed` modifier and its entire family should come in handy. It allows to `seal` a class to prevent it from being extended, except for a few subclasses declared using the `permits` keyword. Sure, the superclass seems to be doomed to be updated many times when new subclasses are added to the project, but it is an acceptable trade-off to have a better secured application. Taking this into consideration, let's seal a version of our Human class and permit only class Performer to extend it. Listing 4-48 depicts the two classes.

Listing 4-48. Sealed Class and Allowed Subclass

```java
// Human.java
package com.apress.bgn.four.sealed;

import com.apress.bgn.four.classes.Gender;

// Human.java
public sealed class Human
        permits Performer {
    protected String name;

    protected int age;

    protected float height;

    // other code omitted
}

// Performer.java
package com.apress.bgn.four.sealed;

import com.apress.bgn.four.classes.Gender;

public final class Performer extends Human {
    // other code omitted
}
```

If the extending classes are declared in the same source file, there is no need to list them after the permits keyword. And if there are no extending classes outside the file, the permits keyword can be omitted altogether.

Classes allowed to extend sealed classes should be sealed or final themselves. If we need one of those classes to allow being extended by unknown classes, the non-sealed modifier allows that. Listing 4-49 shows the class Engineer that is declared non-sealed; this class must be added to the list in the permits directive from the Human class.

Listing 4-49. Sealed Class and Allowed Subclass

```java
package com.apress.bgn.four.sealed;

import com.apress.bgn.four.classes.Gender;

public non-sealed class  Engineer extends Human {
    public Engineer(String name, int age, Gender gender) {
        super(name, age, gender);
    }

    public Engineer(String name, int age, float height, Gender gender) {
        super(name, age, height, gender);
    }
}
```

The sealed modifier can be applied to interfaces as well. The permits keyword specifies the classes that are permitted to implement the sealed interface.

✦ You would expect the permits keyword to also support interfaces that extend the sealed interface, but in the current version of JDK it doesn't. *(You can try it if you want.)*

The same rule applies for sealed interfaces as well: classes implementing a sealed interface are expected to be sealed, non-sealed, or final.

Listing 4-50 shows the sealed Mammal interface, which is implemented by the sealed Human class.

Listing 4-50. sealed Mammal Interface and the Sealed Human Class

```java
package com.apress.bgn.four.sealed;

public sealed interface Mammal permits Human {

}
```

```
public sealed class Human
        implements Mammal
        permits Performer, Engineer {
    // rest of the code ommitted
}
```

A limitation of sealed classes and interfaces is that any subclasses and implementing classes need to be in the same module.

Also, in case it wasn't obvious, any classes present after the `permits` keyword must extend the sealed class/implement the sealed interface. If a class is specified after the `permits` keyword and does not extend the sealed class/implement, the sealed interface the compiler won't like it.

Sealed classes are a good for `records`, since records are by default final.

Hidden Classes

Hidden classes are an interesting feature for developers working on developing frameworks such as Hibernate or Spring. It allows them to create classes that cannot be used directly by the bytecode of other classes, since they are destined to only be used internally by the framework. Internal classes should be declared with the `hidden` modifier, and they should not be discoverable. They could be generated dynamically by the framework, have a short lifespan, and be discarded when no longer needed, which will lead to improve performance of applications running on a JVM.

---

❶ At the time this chapter was written, hidden classes are more a concept than a reality.

Annotation Types

An `annotation` is defined similarly to an interface; the difference is that the interface keyword is preceded by the at sign (@). Annotation types are a form of interfaces, and most times are used as markers (look at the previous Lombok example). For example, you've probably noticed the @Override annotation. This annotation is placed on methods generated automatically by intelligent IDEs when classes extend classes or implement interfaces. Its declaration in the JDK is depicted in the code snippet in Listing 4-51:

Listing 4-51. The JDK @Override Declaration

```java
package java.lang;

import java.lang.annotation.*;

/**
 * documentation omitted
 */
@Target(ElementType.METHOD)
@Retention(RetentionPolicy.SOURCE)
public @interface Override { }
```

Annotations that do not declare any property are called marker or informative annotations. They are needed only to inform other classes in the application, or developers of the purpose of the components they are placed on. They are not mandatory, and the code will compile without them.

In Java 8, an annotation named @FunctionalInterface was introduced. This annotation was placed on to all Java interfaces containing exactly one abstract method, and that can be used in **lambda expressions**. Aside from the single abstract method, an interface can contain constants and other static members.

Lambda Expressions

Lambda expressions were also introduced in Java 8, and they represent a compact and practical way of writing code that was borrowed from languages like Groovy and Ruby. Listing 4-52 depicts the @FunctionalInterface declaration.

Listing 4-52. The JDK @FunctionalInterface Declaration

```java
package java.lang;

import java.lang.annotation.*;

/**
 * documentation omitted
 */
```

```
@Documented
@Retention(RetentionPolicy.RUNTIME)
@Target(ElementType.TYPE)
public @interface FunctionalInterface {}
```

Functional Interfaces are interfaces that declare a single abstract method. Because of this, the implementation of that method can be provided on the spot without the need to create a class to define a concrete implementation. Let's imagine the following scenario: we create an interface named Operation that contains a single method. We can provide an implementation for this interface by creating a class named Addition, or we can do it on the spot using a lambda expression. Listing 4-53 depicts the Operation interface, the Addition class, and a class named OperationDemo, showing the on-the-spot implementation being declared and used in the main(..) method.

Listing 4-53. Explicit Interface Implementation Compared to Lambda Expression

```
package com.apress.bgn.four.lambda;

@FunctionalInterface
interface Operation {
    int execute(int a, int b);
}

class Addition  implements Operation {
    @Override
    public int execute(int a, int b) {
        return a + b;
    }
}

public class OperationDemo {
    public static void main(String... args) {
        // using the Addition class
        Addition addition = new Addition();
        int result = addition.execute(2,5);
        System.out.println("Result is " + result);
```

```
        // implementation on the spot using a Lambda Expression
        Operation addition2 = (a, b) -> a + b;
        int result2 = addition2.execute(2, 5);
        System.out.println("Lambda Result is " + result2);
    }
}
```

By using a lambda expression the class `Addition` is no longer needed, which leads to less and more readable code. Lambda expressions can be used for a lot of things, and we'll cover them more later throughout the book whenever code can be written in a more practical way using them.

Exceptions

Exceptions are special Java classes that are used to intercept special unexpected situations during the execution of a program, so that the developer can implement the proper course of action. These classes are organized in a hierarchy that in depicted in Figure 4-14. `Throwable` is the root class of the hierarchy of classes used to represent unexpected situations in a Java application.

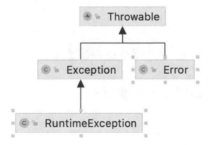

Figure 4-14. *Java exception hierarchy*

Exceptional situations in a Java Application can happen for a myriad of reasons:

- human error when writing the code

- hardware reasons (trying to read a file from a corrupted data disk)

- missing resources (trying to read a file that does not exist)

- and many more.

⚠ Sloppy developers, when in doubt, tend to write code that always catches a Throwable. You should obviously try to avoid that, as class Error is used to notify the developer that a situation the system cannot recover from has happened, and is a subclass of Throwable.

Let's start with a simple example. In Listing 4-54 we define a method that calls itself (its technical name is recursive), but we'll design it badly, to call itself forever and cause the JVM to run out of memory.

Listing 4-54. Bad Recursive Method

```java
package com.apress.bgn.four.exceptions;

/**
 * Created by iuliana.cosmina on 29/03/2021
 */
public class ExceptionsDemo {
    // bad method
    static int rec(int i){
        return rec(i*i);
    }
    public static void main(String... args) {
        rec(1000);
        System.out.println("ALL DONE.");
    }
}
```

If we run the ExceptionsDemo class, the *ALL DONE* is not printed. Instead, the program will end abnormally by throwing a StackOverflowError and mentioning the line where the problem is (in our case the line where the recursive method calls itself).

```
Exception in thread "main" java.lang.StackOverflowError
at chapter.four/com.apress.bgn.four.ex.ExceptionsDemo.
recExceptionsDemo.java:7
at chapter.four/com.apress.bgn.four.ex.ExceptionsDemo.
recExceptionsDemo.java:7
...
```

The StackOverflowError is indirectly a subclass of Error, and is obviously caused by the defective recursive method that was called. We could modify the code, and treat this exceptional situation and execute whatever has to be executed next, as shown in Listing 4-55.

Listing 4-55. Another Bad Recursive Method

```
package com.apress.bgn.four.exceptions;
public class ExceptionsDemo {
    // other code omitted
    public static void main(String... args) {
        try {
            rec(1000);
        } catch (Throwable r) { }
        System.out.println("ALL DONE.");
    }
}
```

In the console only the *ALL DONE* message is printed, with no trace of the error. That is expected since we caught it and decided not to print any information about it.

 This is also a bad practice called **exception swallowing**, never do this!

Also, the system should not recover from this, as the result of any operation after an Error being thrown is unreliable.

 This is why, it is a very bad practice to catch a Throwable!

The Exception class is the superclass of all exceptions that can be caught and treated, and the system can recover from them. Any subclasses of the Exception class that are not subclasses of RuntimeException are **checked exceptions**. These types of exceptions are known at compile time, because they are part of the methods declarations. Any method that is declared to throw a checked exception, when used in the code, enforces either the propagation of the exception further or it requires the developer to write code to treat the exception.

The `RuntimeException` class is the superclass of exceptions that are thrown during the execution of the program, so the possibility of them being thrown is not known when the code is written. Consider the code sample in Listing 4-56.

Listing 4-56. Code Sample That Might Throw an Exception

```java
package com.apress.bgn.four.exceptions;

import com.apress.bgn.four.hierarchy.Performer;

public class AnotherExceptionsDemo {
    public static void main(String... args){
        Performer p = PerformerGenerator.get("John");

        System.out.println("TTL: " + p.getTimeToLive());
    }
}
```

Let's suppose we do not have access to the code of the `PerformerGenerator` class, so we cannot see its code. We just know that calling the `get(..)` method with a name is supposed to return a `Performer` instance. So we write the preceding code and try to print the performer's time to live. What will happen if the p variable is not actually initialized with a proper object, because the `get("John")` call returns null?

The outcome is depicted in the next code snippet:

```
Exception in thread "main" java.lang.NullPointerException:
 Cannot invoke "com.apress.bgn.four.hierarchy.Performer.getTimeToLive()"
 because "p" is null at com.apress.bgn.four.exceptions.
AnotherExceptionsDemo.main(AnotherExceptionsDemo.java:39)
```

As you can see, the exception message telling you what is wrong is pretty explicit. It is actually more explicit than the one in the previous edition of this book. More precise NullPointerExceptions are a feature of Java 17.

But being smart developers (or a little paranoid), we prepare for this case. Depending on the requirements of the application we can do any of the following three things.

1. Catch the exception and print an appropriate message and exit the application. Catching an exception is done using a **try/catch** block. The syntax is pretty simple, and the behavior can be explained as follows: the JVM tries to execute the statements in the **try** block; if an exception is thrown that matches the type in the **catch** block declaration, the code in this block is executed.

This is recommended when the rest of the code cannot be executed without a `Performer` instance, as depicted in Listing 4-57.

Listing 4-57. Code Sample That Might Throw an Exception

```
package com.apress.bgn.four.exceptions;

import com.apress.bgn.four.hierarchy.Performer;

public class AnotherExceptionsDemo {
    public static void main(String... args){
        Performer p = PerformerGenerator.get("John2");

        try {
            System.out.println("TTL: " + p.getTimeToLive());
        } catch (Exception e) {
            System.out.println("The performer was not initialised properly
            because of: " + e.getMessage() );
        }
    }
}
```

The exception that was thrown here is of type `NullPointerException`, a class that extends `RuntimeException`, so a **try/catch** block is not mandatory. This type of exception is called an **unchecked exception**, because the developer is not obligated to check for them.

🖋 The `NullPointerException` is the exception type Java beginner developers struggle with a lot, because they do not have the "paranoia sense" developed well enough to always test objects with unknown origin before using them.

---

2. Throw an appropriate exception type. This is suitable when there is a different class calling the problematic code and that class will handle the exception appropriately, as depicted in Listing 4-58.

Listing 4-58. Code Sample That Wraps the Exception Into a Custom
Exception Type

```java
// ExtraCallerExceptionsDemo.java
package com.apress.bgn.four.exceptions;

import com.apress.bgn.four.hierarchy.Performer;

class Caller {

    public void printTTL(String name) throws EmptyPerformerException    {
    //    thrown exception declaration
        try {
            Performer p = PerformerGenerator.get(name);
            System.out.println("TTL: " + p.getTimeToLive());
        } catch (Exception e) {
            throw new EmptyPerformerException("There is no performer named
            " + name, e); // wrapping happens here
        }
    }
}

public class ExtraCallerExceptionsDemo {

    public static void main(String... args){
        Caller caller = new Caller();
        try {
            caller.printTTL("John2");
        } catch (EmptyPerformerException  e) {
            System.out.println(e.getMessage());
        }
    }
}

// EmptyPerformerException.java
package com.apress.bgn.four.exceptions;
```

```java
public class EmptyPerformerException extends Exception {

    public EmptyPerformerException(String message, Throwable cause) {
        super(message, cause);
    }
}
```

Notice the EmptyPerformerException class. This is a simple custom class that extends the java.lang.Exception class, making it a checked exception. They are declared as explicitly being thrown by a method, as you can see in the first bold line in the code. In this case, when invoking that method, the compiler will force the developer to treat that exception or throw it forward. If the printTTL(..) method would be declared without the throws EmptyPerformerException snippet, a compile time error will be thrown and the code will not be executed. IntelliJ IDEA being a very smart editor and using the JVM compiler to verify your code will notify you that something is not okay in your code by underlining it with a red line. This situation is depicted in Figure 4-15, where the throws EmptyPerformerException was commented to show the compiler being totally not okay with the situation.

```java
30      import com.apress.bgn.four.hierarchy.Performer;
31
32      /** Created by iuliana.cosmina on 29/03/2021 */
35
36      class Caller {
37
38          public void printTTL(String name) /*throws EmptyPerformerException*/ {
39              try {
40                  Performer p = PerformerGenerator.get(name);
41                  System.out.println("TTL: " + p.getTimeToLive());
42              } catch (Exception e) {
43                  throw new EmptyPerformerException("There is no performer named " + name, e);
44              }
45          }
46      }
47
48      public class ExtraCallerExceptionsDemo
49
50          public static void main(String... a
51              Caller caller = new Caller();
52              try {
53                  caller.printTTL( name: "John2");
54              } catch (EmptyPerformerException e) {
55                  System.out.println(e.getMessage());
56              }
57          }
58      }
59
```

Unhandled exception: com.apress.bgn.four.exceptions.EmptyPerformerException

Add exception to method signature ⌥⇧⏎   More actions... ⌥⏎

com.apress.bgn.four.exceptions.EmptyPerformerException
public EmptyPerformerException(String message,
                               Throwable cause)

· chapter04

Figure 4-15. *Compile errors caused by checked exception not being declared as being thrown by the printTTL(..) method*

Also, in the main(..) method, a try/catch block is required to catch and treat this type of exception, as shown in Listing 4-56. The main(..) method must be declared with throws EmptyPerformerException too, to be allowed to pass the exception further, in this case to the JVM.

💡 You can think of exceptions are like the CO2 bubbles in a frizzy drink: they tend to float up to the surface if not stopped by a filter. In Java the surface is represented by the JVM running the application. When JVM encounters an exception, it stops running the application.

Notice how in the line creating the EmptyPerformerException object, the original exception is provided as an argument, as per the constructor declaration. This is done so its message is not lost and can be used to debug the unexpected situation, since it will point directly to the problematic line.

3. Perform a dummy initialization. This is suitable when the code following the problematic call does different things depending on the performer instance returned, as depicted in Listing 4-59.

Listing 4-59. Code Sample That Performs a Dummy Initialization

```
package com.apress.bgn.four.exceptions;

import com.apress.bgn.four.classes.Gender;
import com.apress.bgn.four.hierarchy.Performer;

class DummyInitializer {

    public Performer getPerformer(String name) {
        Performer p = PerformerGenerator.get(name);
        try {
            System.out.println("Test if valid: " + p.getName());
        } catch (Exception e) {
            p = new Performer("Dummy", 0, 0.0f, Gender.UNSPECIFIED); //
            exception swallowing happens here
        }
        return p;
    }
}
```

```java
public class DummyInitExceptionDemo {
    public static void main(String... args) {
        DummyInitializer initializer = new DummyInitializer();
        Performer p = initializer.getPerformer("John2");

        if("Dummy".equals(p.getName())) { // different behaviour based on
        performer name
            System.out.println("Nothing to do.");
        } else {
            System.out.println("TTL: " + p.getTimeToLive());
        }
    }
}
```

Notice how here the original exception is not used anywhere; it is being **swallowed,** and thus in case of trouble, the root cause of the problem is hidden. In applications where the original exception is not critical, a curated warning log message is printed to notify the developer that there was some behavior there that should be taken a note of.

⚠ Keep in mind all the changes listed in this section apply to the code calling the PerformerGenerator.get("John") method, because it is assumed that we cannot modify the contents of this class. If the class is accessible, the method can be modified to return an Optional<Performer>. More about this type of object can be read in future chapters.

And since we are talking about exceptions, the **try/catch** block can be completed with a **finally** block. The contents of the finally block are executed if the exception does not match any of the types declared in the **catch** block (more than one type can be declared in a catch block, and it will be discussed later in the book), and is thrown further, or if the method returns normally. The only situation in which the finally block is not executed is when the program ends in an error. Listing 4-60 is an enriched version of the code shown in Listing 4-58 that includes a finally block for the Caller example.

Listing 4-60. Code Sample That Shows a `finally` Block

```
package com.apress.bgn.four.exceptions;

public class FinallyBlockDemo {
    public static void main(String... args) {
        try {
            Caller caller = new Caller();
            caller.printTTL("John");
        } catch (EmptyPerformerException e) {
            System.out.println("Cannot use an empty performer!");
        } finally {
            System.out.println("All went as expected!");
        }
    }
}
```

Later in this book, code that will end in exceptional situations will sometimes be used as example to provide the opportunity expand the exceptions topic even further when your knowledge will be a little more advanced.

Generics

Up to this point in the chapter we have covered only object types and Java templates used for creating objects. But what if we needed to design a class with functionality that applies to multiple types of objects? Since every class in Java extends the `Object` class, we can create a class with a method that receives a parameter of type `Object`, and in the method we can test the object type. It would be cumbersome, but it can be done, and it will be covered later.

In Java 5 the possibility to use a type as parameter when creating an object was introduced. The classes that are developed to process other classes are called **generics**. There are a lot of examples for generics, but I will start with the one that I needed first when learning Java.

When writing Java applications, you will most likely need at some point to pair up values of different types. The simplest version of a `Pair` class that can hold pair of instances of any types is shown in Listing 4-61.

Listing 4-61. Generic Class Pair<X,Y>

```java
package com.apress.bgn.four.generics;

public class Pair<X, Y> {

    protected X x;
    protected Y y;

    private Pair(X x, Y y) {
        this.x = x;
        this.y = y;
    }

    public X x() {
        return x;
    }

    public Y y() {
        return y;
    }

    public void x(X x) {
        this.x = x;
    }

    public void y(Y y) {
        this.y = y;
    }

    public static <X, Y> Pair<X, Y> of(X x, Y y) {
        return new Pair<>(x, y);
    }

    @Override public String toString() {
        return "Pair{" + x.toString() +", " + y.toString() + '}';
    }
}
```

We now have a generic Pair class declaration. X and Y represent any Java type in an application. The toString() method is inherited from the Object class and overridden in the Pair class to print the values of the fields. The next step is to use it. To prove that the Pair class can be used to couple instances of any type, in Listing 4-62, the following pairs of objects are created:

- a pair of Performers that we can only assume they sing together since the variable is named duet.

- a pair of a Performer instance, and a Double instance representing this performer's net worth; the variable is named netWorth.

- a pair of a String instance representing the genre of a performer and a Performer instance; the variable is named johnsGenre.

Listing 4-62. Using the Pair<X,Y> Generic Class

```java
package com.apress.bgn.four.generics;

import com.apress.bgn.four.classes.Gender;
import com.apress.bgn.four.hierarchy.Performer;

public class GenericsDemo {

    public static void main(String... args) {
        Performer  john = new Performer("John", 40, 1.91f, Gender.MALE);
        Performer jane = new Performer("Jane", 34, 1.591f, Gender.FEMALE);

        Pair<Performer, Performer> duet = Pair.of(john, jane);
        System.out.println(duet);

        Pair<Performer, Double> netWorth = Pair.of(john, 34_000_000.03);
        System.out.println(netWorth);

        Pair<String, Performer> johnsGenre = Pair.of("country-pop", john);
        System.out.println(johnsGenre);

    }
}
```

When the previous class is executed, the following messages are printed in the console.

```
Pair{com.apress.bgn.four.hierarchy.Performer@279f2327, com.apress.bgn.four.
hierarchy.Performer@2ff4acd0}
Pair{com.apress.bgn.four.hierarchy.Performer@279f2327, 3.400000003E7}
Pair{country-pop, com.apress.bgn.four.hierarchy.Performer@279f2327}
```

The `println(...)` method expects its argument to be a `String` instance, and if it isn't the `toString()` method will be called on the object given as argument. If the `toString()` method was not overridden in a class extending `Object`, the one from the `Object` class will be called that returns the full qualified name of the class and something called a **hashcode**, which is a numerical representation of the object.

There are a lot of generic classes in the JDK that you can use to write code, and some of them will be introduced later. This section is here just to introduce you to the typical generics syntax. This will help you recognize them easily and know how they are used.

var and the Diamond Operator

In Java 10, something developers have been asking for years happened: the possibility to declare variables without their type, leaving the compiler to infer it became possible by the introduction of the var keyword. Languages like Python, Groovy, and JavaScript provided this for years, and Java developers wanted it too.

It is not a big effort to write:

```
String message = "random message";
```

instead of

```
var message = "random message";  // compiler infers type String
```

But var becomes a lot more helpful when multilayered generic types are involved. For example, this statement:

```
HashMap<Long, Map<String, ? extends Performer>> performers = new
HashMap<Long, Map<String, ? extends Performer>>() ;
```

can be written as

```
var performers = new HashMap<Long, Map<String, ? extends Performer>>() ;
```

That same statement can be simplified by using **the diamond operator**, introduced in Java 7. The diamond operator allows omitting the names of the generic types used when instantiating a variable if they can be inferred by the compiler from the declaration. So the previous can also be written as:

```
HashMap<Long, Map<String, ? extends Performer>> performers3 =
    new HashMap<>();
```

---

❶   A statement like `var performers = new HashMap<>();` is valid, but the compiler has no way of deciding the type of the instances that can be added to the performers map. So a statement like `performers.put(null, null);` is correct since `null` does not have a type, but anything else like `performers.put("john", "mayer");` will cause a compile error.

The `var` keyword can simplify the code being written in Java, but it has a long way to go. For now, it is being allowed only in the body of methods, indexes for enhanced loops, lambda expressions, constructors, and loop and initialization blocks. It cannot be used in class field declarations or constants. Thus, the compiler can infer the type only for local variables.

`var` cannot be used to declare variables that are not initialized, because this doesn't give the compiler any information about the type of the variable. So the `var list;` statement causes a compiler error. But `var list = new ArrayList<String>();` works just fine.

---

❶   Although `var` cannot be used as an identifier this doesn't make it a keyword. That is why a class field named `var` can be declared, for example. Since it replaces the type name of a variable, `var` is actually a **reserved type name**.

Summary

The most often used elements of the Java language were introduced in this chapter. Hopefully after this chapter not much you will find in future code samples code will surprise you, so you can focus on learning the language properly. Do not worry if some things seem unclear at this point; they will become clearer later as your understanding of the language grows. Here are the things that you should be left with after reading this chapter:

- Syntax mistakes prevent Java code from being transformed into executable code. This means **the code is not compiling**.

- Static variables can be used directly when **static import statements** are used. The same applies to static methods.

- Java identifiers must respect naming rules. A single underscore _ is not an accepted Java identifier.

- Comments are ignored by the compiler and there are three types of comments in Java.

- Classes, interfaces, and enums are Java components used to create objects.

- Enums are special types of classes that can only be instantiated a fixed number of times.

- Records are special types of classes used to create data-immutable objects.

- Abstract classes cannot be instantiated, even if they can have constructors.

- Interfaces could only contain skeleton (abstract) and static methods until Java version 8, when default methods were introduced.

- Private methods and private static methods are allowed in interfaces starting with Java 9.

- In Java there is no multiple inheritance using classes.

- Interfaces can extend other interfaces.

- Java defines a fixed number of keywords named **reserved keywords** that can be used only for specific purposes, and cannot be used as identifiers. The list of Java keywords tends to stay quite constant between Java versions. This list will to be incomplete for versions bigger than Java 17. The reserved keywords are covered in the following section.

Java Keywords

At the beginning of this chapter it was mentioned that there is a list of Java keywords that can be used only for their fixed and predefined purpose in the language. This means they cannot be used as identifiers: you cannot use them as names for variables, classes, interfaces, enums, or methods. You can find them in Tables 4-2 and 4-3.

Table 4-2. *Java Keywords (Part 1)*

Keyword	Description
abstract	Used to declare a class or method as abstract—as in, any extending or implementing class, must provide a concrete implementation.
assert	Used to test an assumption about your code. Introduced in Java 1.4, it is ignored by the JVM, unless the program is run with "-ea" option.
boolean byte char short int long float double	Primitive type names.
break	Statement used inside loops, to terminate them immediately.
continue	Statement used inside loops, to jump to the next iteration immediately.
switch	Statement name, used to test equality against a set of values known as cases.
case	Statement used to define case values in a switch statement.
default	Used to declare a default case within a switch statement. And starting with Java 8 it can be used to declare default methods in interfaces.
try catch finally throw throws	Keywords used in exception handling.
class interface enum	Keywords used to declare classes, interfaces and enums .
extends implements	Keywords used in extending classes and implementing interfaces.

(continued)

Table 4-2. (*continued*)

Keyword	Description
const	Not actually used in Java, is a keyword borrowed from C where it is used to declare constants, variables that are assigned a value, that cannot be changed during the execution of the program.
final	The equivalent of the const keyword in Java. Anything defined with this modifier, cannot change after a final initialization. A final class cannot be extended. A final method cannot be overridden. A final variable has the same value that was initialized with throughout the execution of the program. Any code written to modify final items, will lead to a compiler error.

❶   Surprisingly, record is not a keyword.

Table 4-3. *Java Keywords (Part 2)*

Keyword	Description

do
for
while
	Keywords used to create loops: do{..} while(condition),
	while(condition){..},
	for(initialisation;condition;incrementation){..}

goto	Another keyword borrowed from C , but that is currently not used in Java, because it can be replaced by labeled break and continue statements.
if else	Used to create conditional statements: if(condition) {..}, else {..}, else if (condition) {..}
import	Used to make classes and interfaces available in the current source code.
instanceof	Used to test instance types in conditional expressions.
native	This modifier is used to indicate that a method is implemented in native code using JNI (Java Native Interface).
new	Used to create Java instances.

(*continued*)

Table 4-3. (*continued*)

Keyword	Description
package	Used to declare the package the class/interface/enum/annotation/record is part of. It should be the first Java statement line.
public private protected	Access level modifiers for Java items (templates, fields, or methods).
return	Keyword used within a method to return to the code that invoked it. The method can also return a value to the calling code.
static	This modifier can be applied to variables, methods, blocks and nested class. It declares an item that is shared between all instances of the class where declared.
stricfp	Used to restrict floating-point calculations to ensure portability. Added in Java 1.2.
super	Keyword used inside a class to access members of the super class.
this	Keyword used to access members of the current object.
synchronized	Used to ensure that only one thread executes a block of code at any given time. This is used to avoid a problem cause race-condition.[4]
transient	Used to mark data that should not be serialized.
volatile	Used to ensure that changes done to a variable value are accessible to all threads accessing it.
void	Used when declaring methods as a return type to indicate that the method does not return a value.
_(underscore)	Cannot be used as an identifier starting with Java 9.

[4] A detailed article describing this problem and ways to avoid it can be found at Devopedia, "Race Condition (Software)," https://devopedia.org/race-condition-software, accessed October 15, 2021.

Important mentions:

- `true` and `false` are boolean literals, but they are not reserved keywords. For example, `true` and `false` are valid package names.

- `var` is a reserved type name. For example, `var` can be used as a field name or a package name.

- `null` is not a reserved keyword either. It is a literal used to represent missing object, but it is a valid name for a package, for example.

- `yield` and `record` are not reserved keywords, but restricted identifiers.

- after modules were added the word `module` and the names of all directives became **restricted keywords**. They are special words to be used only for their sole purpose to declare and configure modules.

CHAPTER 5

Data Types

In the previous chapter a lot of Java code was written, but when designing the class only the simplest data types were used: a few numeric ones and texts. In the JDK a lot of data types are declared for a multitude of purposes: for modelling calendar dates; for representing multiple types of numerics; and for manipulating texts, collections, files, database connections, and so on. Aside from JDK, there are libraries created by other parties that provide even more functionality. The data types provided by the JDK are fundamental types, the bricks every Java application is built from. Depending on the type of application you are building, you might not need all of them. For example, I've never had the occasion to use the `java.util.logging.Logger` class. Most applications I have worked on were already set up by a different team when I came along, and they were using external libraries like `Log4j`, `Logback`, or logging abstractions like `Slf4j`.

This section will cover the basic Java Data Types that you will need to write about 80% of any Java application.

Stack and Heap Memory

Java types can be split in two main categories: primitive and reference types. Java code files are stored on the HDD, Java bytecode files as well. Java programs run on the JVM which is launched as a process by executing the `java` executable. During execution, all data is stored in two different types of memory named: **stack** and **heap** that are allocated for a program's execution by the operating system.

The **stack** memory is used during execution (also referred to as at *runtime*) to store method primitive local variables and references to objects stored in the heap. A stack is also a data-structure represented by a list of values that can only be accessed at one end, also called a LIFO order, which is an acronym for Last In First Out. The name fits, because every time a method gets called, a new block is created in the stack memory

195

© Iuliana Cosmina 2022
I. Cosmina, *Java 17 for Absolute Beginners*, https://doi.org/10.1007/978-1-4842-7080-6_5

to hold local variables of the method: primitives and references to other objects in the method. When the call ends, the block is removed (popped out) and new blocks are created for methods being called after that.

---

❶   A stack data structure is very similar to a stack of plates: you can only add or remove extra plates on the top. The first element in a stack is called *head*. Operations performed on a stack have specific names: adding an element to the stack is called a *push* operation, inspecting the first element in the stack is called a *peek* or *top*, and extracting the first element in the stack, its head, is called *pop*. A stack gets emptied by calling *pop* repeatedly until its size is zero.

Each JVM execution thread has its own stack memory, and its size can be specified using JVM parameter -Xss (or equivalent and more explicit -XX:ThreadStackSize). If too many variables are allocated—or the method being called is recursive and badly designed—the condition to return is never fulfilled and thus keeps calling itself forever, and you will run into a java.lang.StackOverflowError, which means there is no stack memory left because every method call will cause a new block to be created on the stack. The size of the stack memory depends on the platform running the JVM, and it is 1024KB for Unix based systems (Linux and macOS) and for Windows, it depends on the virtual memory. There is a way to check its size on your computer. Just open a terminal or command prompt and run this command: java -XX:+PrintFlagsFinal -version. The command returns a list of JVM configurations referred to as flags. Some of them are used to configure the memory JVM is allowed to manage.

Listing 5-1 shows the command being executed on my computer which is a macOS. The grep command filters the output for the criteria provided as argument, thus resulting in a cleaner and scoped output.

Listing 5-1. Showing the Stack Size Default Values on macOS

```
> java -XX:+PrintFlagsFinal -version | grep ThreadStack
  # Data Type  # Flag Name  # = # Flag Value
    intx ThreadStackSize    = 1024
```

The **heap** memory is used at runtime to allocate memory for objects and JRE classes. Objects are instances of JDK classes or developer defined classes. Any object created with new will be stored inside the heap memory. Objects created inside the heap memory can be accessed by all threads of the application. Access and management of the heap memory are a little more complex and will be covered more in **Chapter 13**. The -Xms and -Xmx JVM parameters are used to set initial and maximum size of the heap memory for a Java program during execution. The heap size may vary depending on the number of objects created by the program, and if all heap memory allocated to a Java program is full, then a java.lang.OutOfMemoryError is thrown. The default size for the heap memory depends on the physical available memory of the computer running the JVM, and its minimum and maximum values and other additional data can be extracted from the output of the java -XX:+PrintFlagsFinal -version too.

Listing 5-2 shows the command being executed on my computer which is a macOS with a total physical memory of 16GB. The grep command filters the output for the criteria provided as argument, thus resulting in a cleaner and scoped output.

Listing 5-2. Showing the Heap Size Default Values on macOS

```
> java -XX:+PrintFlagsFinal -version | grep HeapSize
#  Data Type  # Flag Name   #  = # Flag Value
    size_t MaxHeapSize         = 4294967296
    size_t MinHeapSize         = 8388608
```

> 💡 If you want to learn more about JVM flags, the Useful JVM Flags article series on this technical blog is quite a good source: https://blog.codecentric.de/en/?s=JVM+Flags&x=0&y=0.

> ❗ Although it is probably too early to see the importance of this information, there are a lot of Java command line options that you might find useful when working on real-world applications. So add this link to your must-have collection as well: https://docs.oracle.com/en/java/javase/17/docs/api/index.html.

The java.lang.String class is the most-used class in the Java programming language. Because text values within an application might have the same value, for efficiency reasons this type of objects are managed a little different within the heap. In the heap there is a special memory region named the **String Pool** where all the String instances are stored by the JVM. This has to be mentioned here because the following piece of code that will be analyzed to explain how memory is managed in Java contains a definition of a `String` instance, but the String Pool and other details about the `String` data type will be covered in detail in its own section later in the chapter.

Let's consider the executable class in Listing 5-3 and imagine how the memory is organized during its execution.

Listing 5-3. Code Sample Used to Discuss Memory Usage

```
01. package com.apress.bgn.five;
02.
03. import java.util.Date;
04.
05. public class PrimitivesDemo {
06.     public static void main(String... args) {
07.         int i = 5;
08.         int j = 7;
09.         Date d = new Date();
10.         int result = add(i, j);
11.         System.out.print(result);
12.         d = null;
13.     }
14.
15.     static int add(int a, int b) {
16.         String mess = new String("performing add ...");
17.         return a + b;
18.     }
19. }
```

Just by looking at this code, can you figure out which variables are saved on the stack and which on the heap? Let's go over the program line by line and see what is happening:

- As soon as the program starts, Runtime classes that JVM needs are loaded in the heap memory.

- The `main(..)` method is discovered in line 06, so a stack memory is created to be used during the execution of this method.

- Primitive local variable in line 07, i=5, is created and stored in the stack memory of main(..) method.

- Primitive local variable in line 08, j=7, is created and stored in the stack memory of main(..) method. At this point the program memory looks like the one depicted in Figure 5-1.

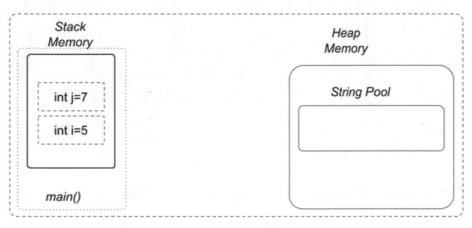

Java Runtime Memory

Figure 5-1. *Java stack and heap memory, after declaring two primitive variables*

- In line 09 an object of type java.util.Date is declared, so this object is created and stored in the heap memory and a reference named d is saved on the stack. At this point the program memory looks like the one depicted in Figure 5-2.

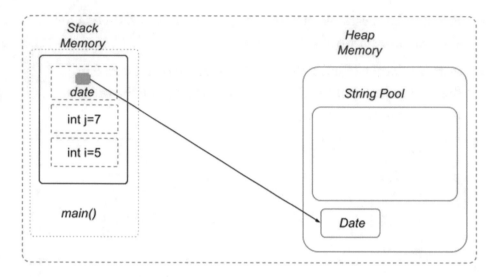

Java Runtime Memory

Figure 5-2. *Java stack and heap memory, after declaring two primitive variables and an object*

- In line 10 method add(..) is called with arguments i and j. This means their values will be copied into the local variables for this method named a and b and these two will be stored in the memory block for this method.

- Inside the add(..) method body in line 16, a String instance is declared. So the String object is created in the heap memory, in the String Pool memory block, and the reference named mess is stored in the stack, in the memory block for this method. At this point the program memory looks like the one depicted in Figure 5-3.

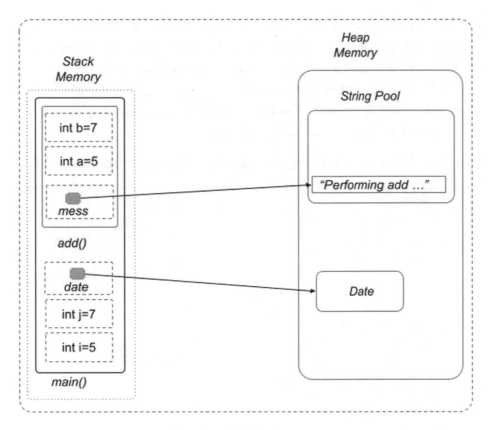

Java Runtime Memory

Figure 5-3. *Java stack and heap memory, after calling the add(..) method*

- Also in line 10, the result of the execution of method add(..) is stored into the local variable named result. At this point the add(..) method has finished its execution, so its stack block is discarded. Thus, we can conclude that variables that are stored on the stack exist for as long as the function that created them is running. In the stack memory of the main(..) method the result variable is saved.

- In line 11, the print method is called, but we'll skip the explanation for this line for simplicity reasons.

- In line 12, the d reference is being assigned a null value, which means the object of type Date is now only in the heap and not linked to the execution of the main(..) method in any way. In that line the JVM is instructed that that object is no longer needed and thus it can be safely discarded. Which means the space containing it can be collected and used to store other objects.

At this point the program memory looks like the one depicted in Figure 5-4.

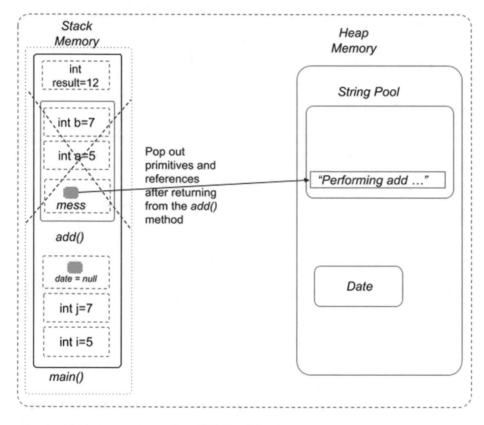

Java Runtime Memory

Figure 5-4. *Java stack and heap memory, before the ending of the main(..) method execution*

Obviously, after the program execution ends all memory contents are discarded.

From version to version small changes have been introduced to the way Java does memory management—the algorithms deciding how and when space should be allocated and freed in the heap have been optimized—but the overall memory organization hasn't change much over the years.

❶ When applying for a Java developer position, you will most likely be asked what the difference between stack and heap memory is. So if the previous section did not clarify these two notions for you, please feel free to consult additional resources, such as this very good article: `https://www.journaldev.com/4098/java-heap-space-vs-stack-memory`.

Introduction to Java Data Types

As you have noticed in the previous example, the data types can be split in Java in two big groups based on where and how they are stored during execution: **primitive** types and **reference** types. Let's introduce them briefly and later explain their most important members.

Primitive Data Types

Primitive types are defined by the Java programming language as special types that do not have a supporting class and are named by their reserved keyword. Variables of these types are saved on the stack memory and when values are assigned to them using the =(equals) operator, the value is actually copied. So if we declare two primitive variables of type int as in Listing 5-4:

Listing 5-4. Code Sample Used to Discuss Primitives

```java
package com.apress.bgn.five;

public class AnotherPrimitivesDemo {

    public static void main(String... args) {
        int k = 42;
        int q = k;
        System.out.println("k = " + k);
        System.out.println("q = " + q);
    }
}
```

We end up with two variables, k and q, both having the same value: 42. When passed as arguments to other methods, the values of primitive values are copied and used without the initial variables being modified.

---

❶ This means that in Java methods, primitive arguments are passed by value.

This can be proved by creating a method to swap the values of two int variables. The code for the method and how to use it are depicted in Listing 5-5.

Listing 5-5. Code Sample Used to Show Primitives Are Passed By Value

```java
package com.apress.bgn.five;

public class SwappingPrimitivesDemo {
    public static void main(String... args) {
        int k = 42;
        int q = 44;
        swap(k, q);
        System.out.println("k = " + k);
        System.out.println("q = " + q);
    }

    static void swap(int a, int b) {
        int temp = a;
        a = b;
        b = temp;
    }
}
```

So what do you think will get printed as values for k and q? If you thought the output is the same as the one listed here, you are correct.

```
k = 42
q = 44
```

This happens because in Java passing arguments to a method is done through their value, which means for primitives, changing the formal parameter's (the method arguments) value doesn't affect the actual parameter's value. If you read the previous section, you can already imagine what happens on the stack. When the swap(..) method is called a new stack memory block is created to save the values used by this method. During the execution of the method the values might change, but if they are not returned and assigned to variables in the calling method, the values are lost when the method execution ends. Figure 5-5 depicts the changes that take place on the stack during the execution of the code previously listed.

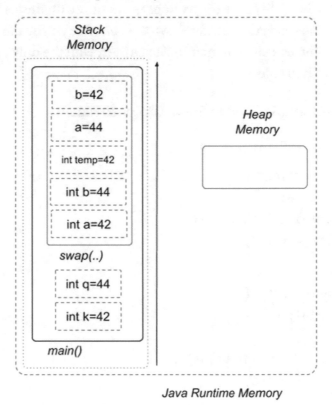

Figure 5-5. *Java passing primitive arguments by value*

Reference Data Types

There are 6 **reference types** in Java:

- class types

- interface types

- enums

- array types

- records

- annotations

Reference types are different from primitive types, because these types are instantiable (except interfaces and annotations). Instances (objects) of these types are created by calling constructors. Variables of these types are actually just references to objects stored in the heap. Because the references are stored on the stack as well, even if we modify the previous code to use references, the behavior will be the same.

Listing 5-6 introduces a class named IntContainer, with the only purpose to wrap int primitive values into objects.

Listing 5-6. Code Sample Used to Show IntContainer

```
package com.apress.bgn.five;

public class IntContainer {
    private int value;
    public IntContainer(int value) {
        this.value = value;
    }

    public int getValue() {
        return value;
    }
    public void setValue(int value) {
        this.value = value;
    }
}
```

Listing 5-7 shows the creation of two objects of this type and two references for them, and new version of the swap method.

Listing 5-7. Code Sample Used to Show Swap of Two int Values Using References

```
package com.apress.bgn.five;

public class ReferencesDemo {

    public static void main(String... args) {
        IntContainer k = new IntContainer(42);
        IntContainer q = new IntContainer(44);
        swap(k,q);
        System.out.println("k = " + k.getValue());
        System.out.println("q = " + q.getValue());
    }

    static void swap(IntContainer a, IntContainer b) {
        IntContainer temp = a;
        a = b;
        b = temp;
    }
}
```

If we run the main(..) method, you will notice that we still get:

```
k = 42
q = 44
```

How can this be explained? Java still uses the same style of arguments passing, **by value**, only this time the value of the reference is the one passed. Figure 5-6 depicts what is going on in the memory managed by the JVM for the execution of the previous code.

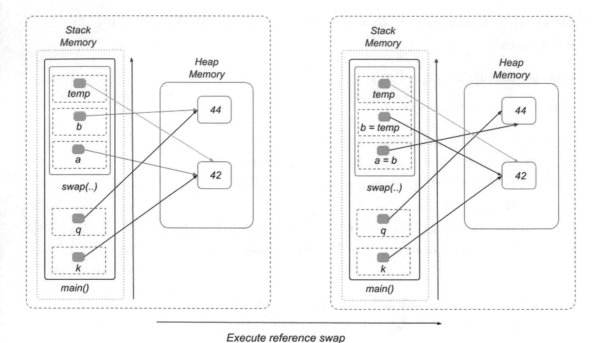

Figure 5-6. Java passing reference arguments by value

The references to the objects are interchanged in the body of the swap(..) method, but they have no effect on the k and q references, nor on the objects they point to in the heap. To really exchange the values, we need to exchange the content of the objects by using a new object. Look at the new version of the swap(..) method depicted in Listing 5-8.

Listing 5-8. Code Sample Used to Show Swap of Two int Values Using References That Actually Swaps the Values

```
package com.apress.bgn.five;

public class ReferencesSwapDemo {

    public static void main(String... args) {
        IntContainer k = new IntContainer(42);
        IntContainer q = new IntContainer(44);
        swap(k,q);
        System.out.println("k = " + k.getValue());
        System.out.println("q = " + q.getValue());
    }
```

```
static void swap(IntContainer a, IntContainer b) {
    IntContainer temp = new IntContainer(a.getValue());
    a.setValue(b.getValue());
    b.setValue(temp.getValue());
}
}
```

By making use of setters and getters, we exchange the values of the objects, because the references are never modified inside the body of the method. Figure 5-7 depicts what happens within the memory during execution of the previous piece of code.

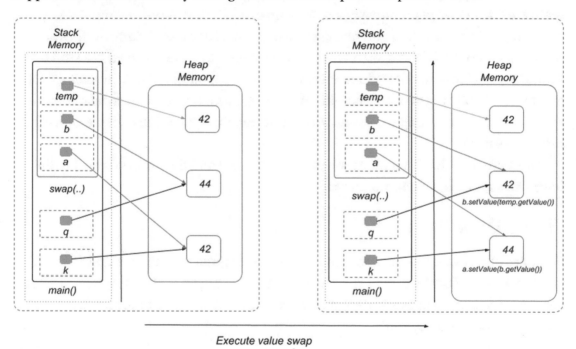

Figure 5-7. *Java passing reference arguments by value, swapping object contents*

Maybe this example was introduced too early, but it was important so you could witness as early as possible the major differences between primitive and reference types. We'll list all the differences in the summary; until then, let's introduce the most-used data types in Java.

If we run the `main(..)` method in Listing 5-8, you will notice that the values of k and q are swapped, as shown in the output depicted here.

```
k = 44
q = 42
```

Java Primitive Types

Primitive types are the basic types of data in Java. Variables of this type can be created by directly assigning values of that type, so that they are not instantiated. In Java there are eight types of primitive types: six of them are used to represent numbers, one to represent characters, and one to represent `boolean` values. Primitive types are predefined into the Java language, and they have names that are reserved keywords. Primitive variables can have values only in the interval or dataset that is predefined for that type. When being declared as fields of a class at instantiation time, a default value specific to the type is assigned to the field. Primitive values do not share state with other primitive values.

Most Java tutorials introduce the numeric types first and the last two later, but this book will start with the non-numerics.

The **boolean** Type

Variables of this type can have only one of the two accepted values: `true` and `false`. If you ever heard of boolean logic, this should be familiar to you. In Java this type of values are used to set/unset flags and design execution flows. The values `true` and `false` are themselves reserved keywords.

---

❶ Default value for a `boolean` variable is **false**.

Another observation: when a field is of type `boolean` the getter for it has a different syntax. It is not prefixed with `get` but with `is`. Java IDEs respect this and generate the getters as expected. This makes sense because of what boolean values are used for. They are useful for modelling properties with only two values. For example, let's say we are writing a class to model a conversion process. A boolean field can be used to mark the process state as done or still in process. If the name of the field is done, a getter named getDone() would be pretty unintuitive and quite stupid, but one named isDone() would be quite the opposite.

Listing 5-9 depicts that class and also shows a main(...) method to test the default value of the done field.

Listing 5-9. Code Sample Used to Show Usage of boolean Fields

```java
package com.apress.bgn.five;

public class ConvertProcessDemo {
    /* other fields and methods */
    private boolean done;
    public boolean isDone() {
        return done;
    }
    public void setDone(boolean done) {
        this.done = done;
    }
    public static void main(String... args) {
        ConvertProcessDemo cp = new ConvertProcessDemo();
        System.out.println("Default value = " + cp.isDone());
    }
}
```

And as expected, the output printed is:

```
Default value = false
```

The boolean type is not compatible with any other primitive type; assigning a boolean value to an int variable by simple assignment (using =) is not possible. Explicit conversion is not possible either. So writing something like this:

```java
boolean f = false;
int fi = (int) f;
```

211

causes a compilation error like the one shown here.

```
> javac com/apress/bgn/five/PrimitivesDemo.java
com/apress/bgn/five/PrimitivesDemo.java:39: error: incompatible types:
boolean cannot be converted to int
        int fi = (int) f;
                       ^
1 error
```

We'll be adding more information about this type in **Chapter 6**.

The `char` Type

The char type is used to represent characters. The values are 16-bit unsigned integers representing UTF-16 code units. The interval of the possible values for char variables is from '\u0000' to '\uffff' inclusive; as numbers, this means from 0 to 65535. This means that we can actually try to print the full set of values. As the representation of the characters is numeric, this means we can convert int values from the previously mentioned interval to char values.

Listing 5-10 prints all the numeric values of the char interval and their matching characters.

Listing 5-10. Code Sample Used to Print All `char` Values

```
package com.apress.bgn.five;

public class CharListerDemo {
    public static void main(String... args) {
        for (int i = 0; i < 65536; ++i ) {
            char c = (char) i;
            System.out.println("c[" + i + "]=" + c);
        }
    }
}
```

❶   The last `char` value the `for` loop statement prints is 65535. The 65536 value is used just as an upper maximum value. So if `i=65336`, then nothing gets printed, and the execution of the statement ends. The `for` loop will be covered in detail in **Chapter 7**.

Depending on the operating systems, some of the characters might not be supported. This means they won't be displayed, or that they will be replaced with a bogus character. The same goes for white spaces characters.

If you think the interval dedicated to represent characters is too big, just scroll the console and you will understand why. The UTF-16 character set contains all numbers as characters, all separators, characters from Chinese and Arabic, and a lot more symbols.[1]

Numeric Primitive Types

In the code samples presented so far to introduce Java language basics, we mostly used variables of type `int`, but there is more than one numeric primitive type in Java. Java defines six primitive numeric types. Each of them has a specific internal representation on a certain number of bits, which obviously means they are bounded by a minimum and a maximum value. There are four numeric types to represent integer values and two numeric types to represent real numbers. In Figure 5-8 you can see the integer (nonreal) types and the interval of the values for each of them.

---

[1] A complete list of the symbols and their meaning can be found at FileFormat info, "Complete Character List for UTF-16," `https://www.fileformat.info/info/charset/UTF-16/list.htm`, accessed October 15, 2021.

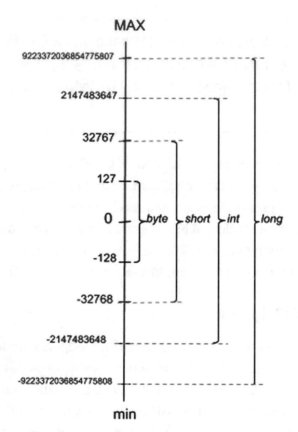

Figure 5-8. *Java numeric integer (nonreal) types*

Anything in a computer is represented using bits of information; each bit can only have a value of 1 or 0, which is why it is called **binary representation**. Binary representation is not the focus of this book, but a short mention will be made because it is important. You might be wondering now why the binary representation was chosen for our computers. This is primarily because data (in memory and on hard disks) is stored using a series of ones (on) and zeros (off) binary representations; also, binary operations are really easy to do, and this makes computers very fast.

Let's take math for example: we widely use the decimal system, which is made of 10 unique digits from 0 to 9. Internally computers use a binary system, which uses only two digits: 0 and 1. To represent numbers bigger than 1, we need more bits. So in a decimal system we have 0, 1, 2, 3, 4, 5, 6, 7, 8, 9, 10, 11, and so on. In a binary system to represent numbers we only have two digits, so we'll have 0, 1, 10, 11, 100, 101, 110, 111, 1000, and so on. If you imagine a bit like a box, in which you can only put ones and zeroes, to represent numbers like a computer does, you need more and more as the numbers get bigger. As a bit can only have two values, the number of values to represent is defined by a power of 2. Just look at Figure 5-9.

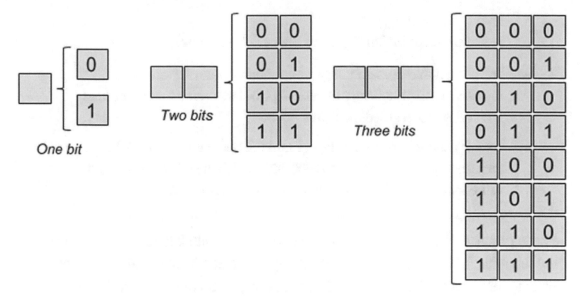

Figure 5-9. *Binary numeric representation*

On one bit we can represent two values, which is 2^1; on two bits we can represent four values, which is 2^2; and so on. This is how we will refer to Java primitive numeric types representation boundaries, sometimes including a bit for the sign as well.

Java Integer Primitive Types

The following list contains the integer primitive types and their boundaries.

- byte is used to represent numbers between -2^7 and 2^7-1 inclusive ([-128, 127]). Default value for a byte field is 0 and is represented on 8 bits.

- short is used to represent numbers between -2^{15} and $2^{15}-1$ inclusive ([-32768, 32767]). The interval for this type is a superset of the byte interval; thus a byte value can be safely assigned to a short variable without the need for an explicit conversion. This goes for all types that have the interval a superset of the one for the byte type. In the next code snippet, a byte value is assigned to a short variable and the code compiles and when executed prints 23. Default value for a short field is 0 and is represented on 16 bits.

```
byte bv = 23;
short sbv = bv;
System.out.println("byte to short: " +   sbv);
```

- int is used to represent integer numbers between -2^{31} and $2^{31}-1$ inclusive ([-2147483648, 2147483647]). Default value for an int field is 0 and is represented on 32 bits.

- long is used to represent integer numbers between -2^{63} and $2^{63}-1$ inclusive ([-9223372036854775808, 9223372036854775807]) Default value for a long field is 0 and is represented on 64 bits.

---

❶   In practice, there is sometimes the need to work with integer numbers outside the interval. For these situations there is a special class (a class, not a primitive type) in Java named BigInteger that allocates just as much memory is needed to store a number of any size. Operations with BigInteger might be slow, but this is the trade-off to work with huge numbers.

Java Real Primitive Types

When it comes to arithmetics, aside from integer numbers we also have real numbers, and they are quite useful because most prices and most arithmetic operations executed by programs do not result in an integer numbers. Real numbers contain a decimal point and decimals after it. To represent real numbers in Java two primitive types are defined, called **floating-point types**. The floating-point types are float and double. Each of them are covered in a little more detail here:

- float is used to represent single-precision 32-bit format IEEE 754 values as specified in IEEE Standard for Binary Floating-Point Arithmetic, ANSI/IEEE Standard 754-1985 (IEEE, New York). The default value is 0.0. A floating-point variable can represent a wider range of numbers than a fixed-point variable of the same bit width at the cost of precision. Values of type int or long can be assigned to variables of type float. What is actually happening, and why the loss of precision? A number is represented as a floating-point number and an exponent, which is actually a power of 10. So when the floating-point number is multiplied with 10 at this exponent power, the initial number should result. Let's take the maximum long value and assign it to a float variable and check what is printed.

```
float maxLongF = Long.MAX_VALUE;
System.out.println("max long= " + Long.MAX_VALUE);
System.out.println("float max long= " + maxLongF);
```

The Long.MAX_VALUE is a final static variable that has the maximum long value assigned to it: 9223372036854775807. What will the preceding code print? The following:

```
max long= 9223372036854775807
float max long= 9.223372E18
```

As you can see, the maxLongF number should be equal to 9223372036854775807, but because it is represented as a smaller number and a power of 10, precision is lost. If we were to reconstruct the integer number by multiplying 9.223372 with 10^{18}, it would give us 9223372000000000000. It's close, but not close enough. So what are the interval edges for float? Float is used to represent real numbers between $1.4E^{-45}$ and $2^{128} * 10^{38}$.

- double is used to represent single-precision 64-bit format IEEE 754 values as specified in IEEE Standard for Binary Floating-Point Arithmetic, ANSI/IEEE Standard 754-1985 (IEEE, New York) and is used to represent numbers between $4.9E^{-324}$ and $2^{127} * 10^{308}$. The default value is 0.0.

---

❶ Values 0 and 0.0(double) are different in Java. To a normal user they both mean zero, but in mathematics, the one with the decimal point is more precise. Still, in Java we are allowed to compare an int value to a float value, and if we compare 0 and 0.0, the result will be that they are equal. Also, positive zero and negative zero are considered equal; thus the result of the comparison 0.0==-0.0 is also true.

At the end of this section, it should also be emphasized that developers cannot define a primitive type, either by defining it from scratch or by extending an existing primitive type. Type names are **reserved Java keywords** that cannot be redefined by the developer. It is prohibited to declare fields, methods, or class names that are named as those types.

As you have noticed until now, a variable that we intend to use must be declared first and used later. When it is declared, a value can be associated as well. For primitive values, a number can be written in many ways. In Listing 5-11 you can see a few samples of how numeric values can be written when variables are initialized or assigned afterward.

Listing 5-11. Code Sample Used to Print Primitive Values in Multiple Ways

```java
package com.apress.bgn.five;

public class NumericDemo {
    private byte b;    // default value 0
    private short s;   // default value 0
    private int i;     // default value 0
    private long l;    // default value 0
    private float f;   // default value 0.0
    private double d;  // default value 0.0

    public static void main(String... args) {
        NumericDemo nd = new NumericDemo();

        nd.b = 0b1100;
        System.out.println("Byte binary value: " + nd.b);

        nd.i = 42 ;   // decimal case

        nd.i = 045 ; // octal case - base 8
        System.out.println("Int octal value: " + nd.i);

        nd.i = 0xcafe ; // hexadecimal case - base 16
        System.out.println("Int hexadecimal value: " + nd.i);

        nd.i = 0b101010101010101010101010101011;
        System.out.println("Int binary value: " + nd.i);

        //Starting with Java 7 '_' can be used in numeric values
        nd.i = 0b1010_1010_1010_1010_1010_1010_1010_1011;
        System.out.println("Int binary value: " + nd.i);

        nd.l = 1000_000l; // equivalent to 1000_000L
        System.out.println("Long value: " + nd.l);
```

```
            nd.f = 5;
            System.out.println("Integer value assigned to a float variable:
            " + nd.f);

            nd.f = 2.5f; // equivalent to nd.f = 2.5F;
            System.out.println("Decimal value assigned to a float variable:
            " + nd.f);

            nd.d = 2.5d; // equivalent to nd.d = 2.5D;
            System.out.println("Decimal value assigned to a double variable:
            " + nd.f);
    }
}
```

As you can figure out from the previous listing, integer numbers can be represented in Java in four ways:

- **decimal**: base 10, written using digits 0 to 9.

- **octal**: base 8, written using digits 0 to 7 and prefixed by 0(zero); this means number 8 is represented in octal as the 010 digits.

- **hexadecimal**: base 16, written using digits 0 to 9 and letters A to F, lowercase or upper case, and prefixed by 0x or 0X; this means number 10 is represented in hexadecimal as 0x00A, 11 as 0x00B and so on until the letters in the set end, and 16 is represented as 0x010.

- **binary(base 2)**: base 2, written using digits 0 and 1 and prefixed by 0b or 0B. This was already covered when explaining bits.

You can read more about numeric representation in a computer programming book, but unless you end up working on some project requiring you to do mathematical operations, you will seldom get to play with representations other than decimal.

Starting with Java 7, the "_"(underscore) is permitted to be used when declaring numeric values to group together digits and increase clarity. There are some limitations, such us:

- "_" cannot be used at the start or end of a numeric value.

- "_" cannot be used for byte values.

- "_" cannot be used next to digits or symbols representing the base (0b/0B for binary, 0 for octal,0x/0X for hexadecimal).

- "_" cannot be used next to the decimal point.

The output of the code in Listing 5-11 being executed is depicted in Listing 5-12.

Listing 5-12. Output Resulted by Executing the Code in Listing 5-11

```
Byte binary value: 12

Int octal value: 37
Int hexadecimal value: 51966
Int binary value: -1431655765
Int binary value: -1431655765
Long value: 1000000
Integer value assigned to a float variable: 5.0
Decimal value assigned to a float variable: 2.5
Decimal value assigned to a double variable: 2.5
```

As no formatting is done when the variables are printed, the values depicted in the console are in the decimal system.

For now, this is all that can be said about the primitive types. Each of the primitive types has a matching reference type defined within the JDK that will be mentioned later in the chapter.

Java Reference Types

A short description of the Java Reference Types was given earlier to highlight the difference between primitive and reference types as early as possible. It is now time to expand that description and give some examples of the most-used JDK reference types when programming.

Objects or *instances* are created using the new keyword followed by the call of a constructor. The constructor is a special member of a class, used to create an object by initialising all fields of the class with their default values, or values received as arguments. A class instance is created by calling the class constructor (one of them, because there might be more than one defined within the class). Consider the example that we had in Chapter 4, the `Performer` class, to declare a reference to an object of type `Performer` the following expression is used:

```
Performer human = new Performer("John", 40, 1.91f, Gender.MALE);
```

The interface reference types cannot be instantiated, but objects of class types that implement that interface can be assigned to references of that interface type. The hierarchy used in Chapter 4 is depicted in Figure 5-10.

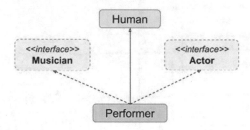

Figure 5-10. *Class and interface hierarchy*

Based on this hierarchy, the four statements in Listing 5-13 are valid; they compile, and the code can be executed successfully.

Listing 5-13. Code Sample Showing Different Reference Types

```
package com.apress.bgn.five;

import com.apress.bgn.four.classes.Gender;
import com.apress.bgn.four.hierarchy.*;

public class ReferencesDemo {

    public static void main(String... args) {
        Performer performer = new Performer("John", 40, 1.91f,
        Gender.MALE);
        Human human = new Performer("Jack", 40, 1.91f, Gender.MALE);
        Actor actor = new Performer("Jean", 40, 1.91f, Gender.MALE);
        Musician musician = new Performer("Jodie", 40, 1.71f, Gender.
        FEMALE);
    }
}
```

In the previous example we created four objects of type `Performer` and assigned them to different reference types, including two interface reference types. If we were to inspect the stack and heap contents for the preceding method, here is what we would find (Figure 5-11):

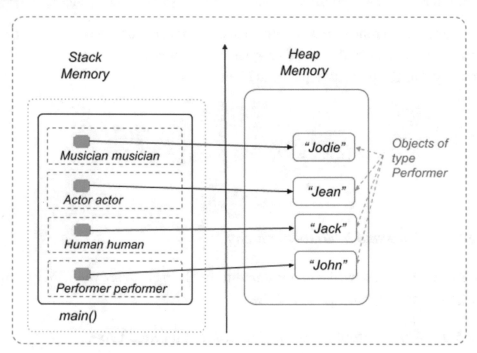

Figure 5-11. *Multiple reference types*

All the references in the previous example point to different objects in the heap. Having refferences of different types pointing to the same object is possible too, as shown in Listing 5-14.

Listing 5-14. Code Sample Showing Different Reference Types Pointing to the Same Object

```
package com.apress.bgn.five;

import com.apress.bgn.four.classes.Gender;
import com.apress.bgn.four.hierarchy.*;
```

```
public class ReferencesDemo {

    public static void main(String... args) {
        Performer performer = new Performer("John", 40, 1.91f,
        Gender.MALE);
        Human human = performer;
        Actor actor = performer;
        Musician musician = performer;
    }
}
```

In the previous code snippet, we've created only one object, but multiple references to it, of different types. If we were to inspect the stack and heap contents again, for the preceding method, here is what we would find (Figure 5-12):

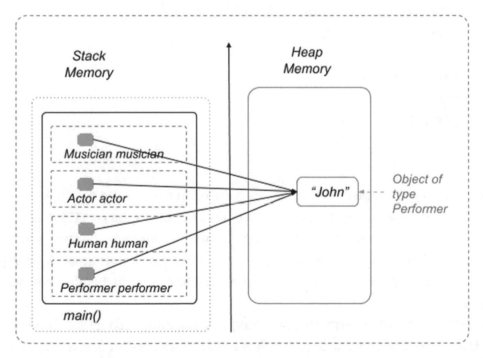

Figure 5-12. *Multiple reference types, second example*

References can only be of type or super-type of an assigned object, so the assignments in Listing 5-15 will not compile.

Listing 5-15. Code Sample Showing Assignments Failing at Compile Time

```java
package com.apress.bgn.five;

import com.apress.bgn.four.classes.Gender;
import com.apress.bgn.four.hierarchy.*;

public class BadReferencesDemo {

    public static void main(String... args) {
        Performer performer = new Performer("John", 40, 1.91f,
        Gender.MALE);
        Human human = performer;
        Actor actor = performer;
        Musician musician = performer;
        //these will not compile!!!
        performer = musician;
        //or
        performer = human;
        //or
        performer = actor;
    }
}
```

This is because the methods are called on the reference type, so the object the reference is pointing to must have those methods. That is why the Java Compiler complains, and that is why smart editors notify you by underlining the statement with a red line. The easiest way to fix the compiling erros in the previous example is an explicit cast (or conversion) to the Performer type. But this doesn't mean that the code will be runnable.

The easiest way to prove this is by creating a class named Fiddler that implements Musician and assign an instance of this class to a Performer reference. An explicit conversion of the Fiddler instance to Performer is necessary to trick the compiler into accepting this code as valid, as shown in the marked line in Listing 5-16.

Listing 5-16. Code Sample Showing Assignments Failing at Runtime

```java
package com.apress.bgn.five;

import com.apress.bgn.four.classes.Gender;
import com.apress.bgn.four.hierarchy.*;

public class BadReferencesDemo {

    public static void main(String... args) {
        Musician fiddler = new Fiddler(true);
        Performer performer = (Performer) fiddler;
        System.out.println("Learned the skill at: " + performer.
        getSchool());
        System.out.println("Appeared in movies: " + performer.getFilms());
    }
}

class Fiddler implements Musician {
    private boolean ownsFiddle = false;

    public Fiddler(boolean ownsFiddle) {
        this.ownsFiddle = ownsFiddle;
    }

    @Override
    public String getSchool() {
        return "Irish Conservatory";
    }

// other methods omitted
}
```

The Fiddler instance was explicitly converted to Performer and the compiler accepted this, because it assumes we know what we are doing. The converted instance is then assigned to a reference of type Performer and then methods getSchool() and .getFilms() are called on it.

When running the previous code, you would expect the performer.getSchool() method to be executed correctly and "Learned the skill at: Irish Conservatory" to be printed in the console, because after all, class Fiddler implements Musician and provides a concrete implementation for getSchool(). You would also expect an exception to be thrown when the next line is executed; calling performer.getFilms() is not possible since class Fiddler does not implement Actor and does not provide a concrete implementation for the getFilms() method.

But this is not how JVM does things. Actually, when running this code, an exception will be thrown exactly when executing the conversion line, because a Fiddler instance cannot be converted to a Performer instance. A message looking like this will be printed in red in the console.

```
Exception in thread "main" java.lang.ClassCastException:
    class com.apress.bgn.five.Fiddler cannot be cast to class com.
    apress.bgn.four.hierarchy.Performer (com.apress.bgn.five.Fiddler is
    in module chapter.five.primitives of loader 'app'; com.apress.bgn.
    four.hierarchy.Performer is in module chapter.four of loader 'app')
    at chapter.five.primitives/com.apress.bgn.five.BadReferencesDemo.
    main(BadReferencesDemo.java:56)
```

Arrays

The new keyword can also be used to create arrays, in a similar way it is used to create objects. An array is a data structure that holds a group of values together. Its size is defined when created and cannot be changed. Each variable can be accessed using an index, which starts from 0 and goes up to the length of the array -1. Arrays can hold primitive and reference values. Listing 5-17 contains a class with a declaration of an array field that groups together int values.

Listing 5-17. Class with int Array Field

```
package com.apress.bgn.five;

public class ArrayDemo {

    int array[];

    public static void main(String... args) {
        ArrayDemo ad = new ArrayDemo();
        System.out.println("array was initialized with " + ad.array);
    }
}
```

❶ There are two ways to declare an array, depending on where the brackets are positioned: after the array name or after the array element types:

```
int array[];
```

```
int[] array;
```

This is important to know because if you are ever interested of getting your Java knowledge certified,[2] the exam might contain questions regarding the correct ways to declare arrays.

What do you think will be printed in the console when the preceding code is executed? If you assumed that the `ad.array` field will be initialled with `null` and the message printed will be "array was initialized with null," you are quite right in your assumption.

Arrays are reference types, even when they contain elements of a primitive types and thus when left to the JVM to initialize fields of this type with a default value, `null` will be used, as this is the typical default value for reference types. The `null` keyword was mentioned before, but let's emphasize its importance. The `null` keyword is used to represent a nonexisting value. A reference that is assigned this value does not have a concrete object assigned to it; it does not point to an object in the heap. That is why when writing code, if an object is used (through its reference) before being initialized, a `NullPointerException` is thrown. That is why developers test equality to `null` before using the object (or array).

The previous code snippet could be written a little better to take the possibility of the array being `null` into account, and exiting from the `main(..)` method gracefully using the `return` keyword, as shown in Listing 5-18.

---

[2] OCA and OCP certification details can be found at Oracle, "Oracle Certification," `https://www.oracle.com/uk/corporate/features/oracle-certification.html`, accessed October 15, 2021.

Listing 5-18. Class with int Array Field That Can Be Null

```java
package com.apress.bgn.five;

public class ArrayDemo {

    int array[];

    public static void main(String... args) {
        ArrayDemo ad = new ArrayDemo();
        if (ad.array == null) {
            System.out.println("Array unusable. Nothing to do.");
            return;
        }
    }
}
```

---

❶ When a method is declared to return nothing using the void keyword, a correct return from the method can be enforced by the return; statement without a value. The return; statement is not really necessary in the previous code sample, is just provided as an example on how to write code to return from the method in an explicit point of the execution.

Why do we need the null keyword to mark something that does not exist yet? Because it is common practice in programming to declare a reference first and initialize it only when first time used. This is useful especially for objects that are big and require allocating a lot of memory. This programming technique is called **Lazy Loading** (also known as asynchronous loading).

Listing 5-19 depicts a more evolved version of the ArrayDemo class where the array field it is initialized, and a size is set for it.

Listing 5-19. Class with int Array Field That is Initialized Properly

```java
01. package com.apress.bgn.five;
02.
03. public class ArrayDemo {
```

```
04.
05.    int array[] = new int[2];
06.
07.    public static void main(String... args) {
08.        ArrayDemo ad = new ArrayDemo();
09.        if (ad.array == null) {
10.            System.out.println("Array unusable. Nothing to do.");
11.            return;
12.        }
13.
14.        for (int i = 0; i < ad.array.length; ++i) {
15.            System.out.println("array["+ i +"]= " + ad.array[i]);
16.        }
17.    }
18. }
```

The initialization of the array takes place in line 5. The size of the array is 2. The size of the array is given as a parameter to what it looks like a constructor call, only instead of parentheses, square brackets are used, prefixed by the type of elements the array groups together. By setting the dimension of the array to 2, we are telling the JVM that two adjacent memory locations will have to be put aside (allocated) for this object to store two int values in. Because no values were specified as the array contents, what do you think will they be filled with when the array is created? This is a simple one: the previous array is defined to be made of two int values, so when the array is initialized, the default value for the int type will be used.

Figure 5-13 depicts what happens in the stack and heap memory when the previous code is executed.

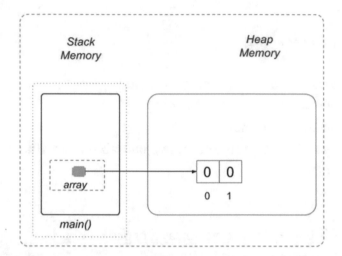

Figure 5-13. *Declaring an int array of size 2*

In lines 14 to 16 a for loop is used to print the values of the array. The `int i` variable is what we call an index variable, and is used to traverse all values of the array by incrementation with 1 in each step of the loop. The `array.length` is the property containing the size of the array—how many elements the array contains. As you probably expected, the output printed in the console is:

```
array[0]= 0
array[1]= 0
```

To put some values in an array we have the following choices:

- we access the element directly, and we set the values:

```
array[0] = 5;
array[1] = 7;
//or
for (int i = 0; i < array.length; ++i) {
    array[i] = i;
}
```

- we initialize the array explicitly with the values we intend to store:

```
int another[] = {1,4,3,2};
```

Arrays can group references as well. Listing 5-20 depicts how a Performer array can be declared and used.

Listing 5-20. Class Creating a Performer Array

```
package com.apress.bgn.five;

import com.apress.bgn.four.classes.Gender;
import com.apress.bgn.four.hierarchy.Performer;

public class PerformerArrayDemo {
    public static void main(String... args) {
        Performer[] array = new Performer[2];
        for (int i = 0; i < array.length; ++i) {
            System.out.println("performer[" + i + "]= " + array[i] );
        }
        array[0] = new Performer("Julianna", 35, 1.61f, Gender.FEMALE);
        array[1] = new Performer("John", 40, 1.91f, Gender.MALE);
        for (int i = 0; i < array.length; ++i) {
            System.out.println("performer[" + i + "]= " + array[i].
            getName() );
        }
    }
}
```

Before explicit initialization, elements of the array are initialized with the default value for the Performer type. Since Performer is a reference type, that value is null.

Because depicting the memory contents makes it more obvious what happens with our array and objects, I give to you Figure 5-14.

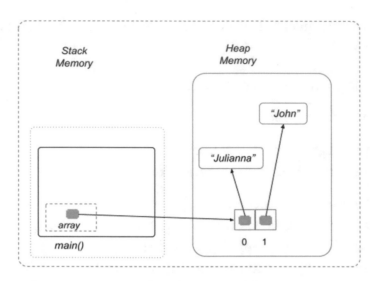

Figure 5-14. *Declaring an array of performers with size 2*

So yes, we actually have an array of references, and the object they point to can be changed during the program.

A last thing I need to cover here is that arrays can be multidimensional. If you studied advanced math you probably remember the *matrix* concept, which was a rectangular array arranged in rows and columns. In Java, you can model *matrices* by using arrays. If you want a simple matrix with rows and columns, you just define an array with two dimensions. A very simple example is depicted in Listing 5-21.

Listing 5-21. Class Modelling a Matrix Using a 2-Dimensional Array

```java
package com.apress.bgn.five;

public class MatrixDemo {

    public static void main(String... args) {
        // bi-dimensional array: 2 rows, 2 columns
        int[][] intMatrix = {{1, 0}, {0, 1}};
        int[][] intMatrix2 = new int[2][2];
        for (int i = 0; i < intMatrix2.length; ++i) {
            for (int j = 0; j < intMatrix2[i].length; ++j) {
                intMatrix2[i][j] = i + j;
                System.out.print(intMatrix[i][j] + " ");
            }
        }
```

```
        System.out.println();
    }
  }
}
```

You can even go multidimensional, and define as many coordinates you want. In Listing 5-22 we modelled a cube by using a three-dimensional array.

Listing 5-22. Class Modelling a Cube Using a 3-Dimensional Array

```java
package com.apress.bgn.five;

public class CubeDemo {

    public static void main(String... args) {
        // three-dimensional array with three coordinates
        int[][][] intMatrix3 = new int[2][2][2];
        for (int i = 0; i < intMatrix3.length; ++i) {
            for (int j = 0; j < intMatrix3[i].length; ++j) {
                for (int k = 0; k < intMatrix3[i][j].length; ++k) {
                    intMatrix3[i][j][k] = i + j + k;
                    System.out.print("["+i+", "+j+", " + k + "]");
                }
                System.out.println();
            }
            System.out.println();
        }
    }
}
```

When it comes to arrays, make them as big as you need them and your memory allows, but make sure to initialize them and make sure in your code that you do not try to access indexes outside the allowed range. If the size of an array is **N**, then its last index is **N-1** and its first is **0**. Try to access any index outside that range and an exception of type java.lang.ArrayIndexOutOfBoundsException will be thrown at runtime. So if you write code like this:

```java
int array = new int[2];
array[5] =7;
```

Although it compiles, the execution fails, because of an exception being thrown. The following will be printed in the console:

```
Exception in thread "main" java.lang.ArrayIndexOutOfBoundsException: Index
5 out of bounds for length 2 at chapter.five.arrays@1.0-SNAPSHOT/com.apress
    .bgn.five.ArrayDemo.main(ArrayDemo.java:49)
```

For easier handling of arrays in Java there is a special class: `java.util.Arrays`. This class provides utility methods to sort and compare arrays, to search elements, or to convert their contents to text or to a stream (**Chapter 8**), so that they can be printed without writing the tedious for loop used so far in the examples. Listing 5-23 depicts a few of these utility methods.

Listing 5-23. `java.util.Arrays` Useful Methods

```java
package com.apress.bgn.five;

import java.util.Arrays;

public class ArrayUtilitiesDemo {
    public static void main(String... args) {
        int[] array = {4, 2};
        System.out.println(Arrays.toString(array));
        // or
        Arrays.stream(array).forEach(ai -> System.out.println(ai));
        // or using a method reference
        Arrays.stream(array).forEach(System.out::println);

        Arrays.sort(array);

        array = new int[]{4, 2, 1, 5, 7};
        int foundAt = Arrays.binarySearch(array, 5);
        System.out.println("Key found at: " + foundAt);
    }
}
```

```
// output
[4, 2]
4
2
4
2
Key found at: -11
```

A short explanation each statement in the previous code listing can be found in the following list:

1. `int[] array = {4, 2}` is an array declaration and initialization. The `new int[]` is not required as the compiler can figure out the type of elements from the declaration of the array, and the size of the array from the size of the set of values provided for initialization.

2. `Arrays.toString(array)` returns String representation of the contents of the specified array. The elements string representations are separated by commas, and the resulting string is enclosed in square brackets(`[]`).

3. `Arrays.stream(array)` returns a sequential `IntStream` with the specified array as its source. Streams are covered in a dedicated chapter (**Chapter 8**), and these classes provide methods to process elements one by one, without the need of a `for` loop. In the previous code snippet the elements of the resulting stream are processed using the `System.out.println(..)` method, which means they are printed in the console one by one.

4. `Arrays.sort(array)` sorts the specified array into ascending numerical order. This method does not return a new sorted array, so the elements change positions within the original array. The algorithm used to perform the sorting is called **Dual-Pivot Quicksort** and is one of the most efficient sorting algorithms.[3]

---

[3] An interesting comparison of sorting algorithms, if you are interested, can be found at Toptal, "Sorting Algorithms Animations," `https://www.toptal.com/developers/sorting-algorithms`, accessed October 15, 2021.

5. `array = new int[]{4, 2, 1, 5, 7}` is a reinitialization of the array. This means a new array value is assigned to the `array` reference. So the declaration must specify the new keyword together with the type and the array size, unless a set of elements is used for the intialization; which is exactly the case of this statement, so the size is not mandatory.

6. `Arrays.binarySearch(array, 5)` searches the array for the value provided as argument (in this case, 5) and returns a value representing the position of the element in the array (ergo, its index). The algorithm used for the search is called **Binary Search** and works by splitting the array repeatedly in two parts until the element is found. This technique is called Divide-et-Impera (or **Divide-and-conquer**), and it involves splitting a big problem into smaller problems repeatedly (recursively) until they can be easily solved. Binary search on an array is the most efficient when the array is sorted.

💡 Feel free to search the web for the algorithms mentioned in this section, because they are useful to understand when you need to develop your own solutions. **Chapter 7** will show you how to write code following a few simple and well-known algorithms.

The **String** Type

The next special Java data type on our list is `String`. Together with the primitive `int`, this is one of the most-used type in Java. `String` instances are used to model texts and perform all kind of operations on them. The String type is a special type, because objects of this type are given special treatment by the JVM. If you remember the first image with memory contents, the `String` object was allocated in the heap in a special place called **String Pool**. In this section dedicated to it this type will be covered in detail, and a lot of questions you might have had so far will hopefully get an answer.

Until now `String` variables were declared in this book, as depicted in Listing 5-24:

Listing 5-24. A few `String` Statements Used in This Book

```
package com.apress.bgn.five;

public class SimpleStringDemo {
    public static void main(String... args) {
01.        String text1 = null;
02.
03.        String text21 = "two";
04.        String text22 = "two";
05.        String text23 = new String ("two");
06.
07.        String piece1 = "t";
08.        String piece2 = "wo";
09.        String text24 = piece1 + piece2;
10.
11.        char[] twoCh = {'t', 'w', 'o'};
12.        String text25 = new String(twoCh);
    }
}
```

As you can see, each one of the lines 3, 4, 5, 9, and 12 define a `String` object with the same content *'two'*. I intentionally did this for reasons that will become obvious soon enough. In real-world applications, especially in this big-data hype period, applications handle a lot of data, most of it in text form. So being able to compress the data and reuse it would reduce the memory consumption. Reducing memory access attempts increases speed by reducing processing which in turn will reduce costs.

`String` variables can be initialized with text values directly (lines 3 and 4). In this case the JVM looks first in the String Pool for a `String` object with the same value. If found, the new `String` variable is initialized with a reference to it. If not found, memory is allocated, the text value is written to it, and the new `String` variable is initialized with a reference to it.

In line 5, the constructor of the class `String` is used to create a `String` object. Notice the new keyword is being used. This means that allocation for memory to store the text provided as parameter is being explicitly requested.

Before continuing this section, we have to make a small but important side note and mention what **object equality** means in Java. Objects are handled in Java using references to their memory location. The ==(double equals) operator compares memory locations the references point to, so two objects are equal if and only if they are stored in the same memory address. That is why objects should be compared using the equals(..) method. This is a special method inherited from the Object class, but each class must provide its own implementation that is truly relevant to its own structure. As expected, the equals(..) implementation in the Object class defaults to the == behavior.

𝕎 Think about two red balls. They have the same diameter, the same color, and are made of the same material. They are identical, which translates to Java as being equal, but they are not the same ball; they were just created using the same specifications. If you take two random kids, like Jim and Jane, each can play with their own ball. But if Jim and Jane play with the same ball, just throwing it from one to the other, this is pretty similar to equality of references in Java. Figure 5-15 is an abstract representation of this situation.

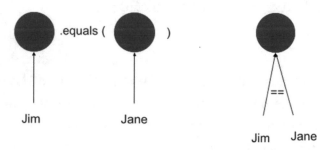

Figure 5-15. *Showing the difference between equals and == using red balls*

Listing 5-25 depicts a simple version the Ball class, and an executable code sample that creates two separate ball objects and compares them, but also creates a single ball to test equality of references. Since Jim and Jane could be considered references to a ball, the code was written as such.

Listing 5-25. Code Sample Showing Differences Between equals(..) and == on References

```
package com.apress.bgn.five;

import java.util.Objects;

public class EqualsDemo {

    public static void main(String... args) {

        Ball jim = new Ball(10, "red", "rubber");
        Ball jane = new Ball(10, "red", "rubber");

        System.out.println("-- Playing with different balls -- ");
        System.out.println("Jim and Jane have equal balls? A:" +
        jim.equals(jane));
        System.out.println("Jim and Jane have the same ball? A:" +
        (jim == jane));

        System.out.println("-- Playing with the same ball -- ");
        Ball  extra = new Ball(10, "red", "rubber");
        jim= extra;
        jane = extra;
        System.out.println("Jim and Jane have equal balls? A:" +
        jim.equals(jane));
        System.out.println("Jim and Jane have the same ball? A:" +
        (jim == jane));
    }
}

class Ball {
    int diameter;
    String color;
    String material;

    @Override
    public boolean equals(Object o) {
        Ball ball = (Ball) o;
        return diameter == ball.diameter
```

```
            && Objects.equals(color, ball.color)
            && Objects.equals(material, ball.material);
    }

    // other code omitted
}
```

Executing the code in the previous listing should produce the following output:

```
-- Playing with different balls --
Jim and Jane have equal balls? A:true
Jim and Jane have the same ball? A:false
-- Playing with the same ball --
Jim and Jane have equal balls? A:true
Jim and Jane have the same ball? A:true
```

This previous code sample points out pretty well the difference between the '=='
operator and the equals(..) method on references: the == operator tests references
equality, and the equals(..) method tests the equality of the objects those references
point to. The equals(..) method implementation introduced here is naive, because
the nullability and comparison with an object of a different type should be taken into
consideration. And then there is also the hashCode() method that must be implemented
when equals(..) is, otherwise your classes won't function correctly with some
collection classes that will be covered later in this chapter. But for now, I really hope the
difference between object equality and reference equality is clear, so that the next rest of
the String section makes sense.

Object equality parentheses now closed.

In Java String instances are **immutable**, which means they cannot be changed once
created. The String class is also declared final, so developers cannot extend it. There
are multiple reasons why String instances are immutable in Java, some of them being
related to security of applications, but those reasons are too stuffy to cover in this book.
In this section the focus is on the most obvious reason.

Since String instances cannot be changed once created, this means that the JVM
can reuse existing values that were already allocated to form new String values, without
consuming additional memory. This process is called **interning**. One copy of each text
value (literal) is saved into a special memory region called **the String Pool**. When a new
String variable is created and a value is assigned to it, the JVM first searches the pool

for a String of equal value. If found, a reference to this memory address will be returned without allocating additional memory. If not found, it'll be added to the pool and its reference will be returned. This being said, considering the sample code in Listing 5-24 (the one before the equality parentheses), we expect for `text21` and `text22` variables to point to the same `String` object in the pool, which means references are equal too. Listing 5-26 depicts code that tests the assumption.

Listing 5-26. Code Sample Showing Differences Between `equals(..)` and `==` on String References

```
package com.apress.bgn.five;

public class SimpleStringDemo {
    public static void main(String... args) {
        String text21 = "two";
        String text22 = "two";

        if (text21 == text22) {
            System.out.println("Equal References");
        } else {
            System.out.println("Different References");
        }
        if (text21.equals(text22)) {
            System.out.println("Equal Objects");
        } else {
            System.out.println("Different Objects");
        }
    }
}
```

When running the preceding code, the following will be printed in the console, proving the previous affirmations and the existence of the **String Pool**.

```
Equal References
Equal Objects
```

In Figure 5-16 you can see an abstract representation of the memory contents when the previous code is executed.

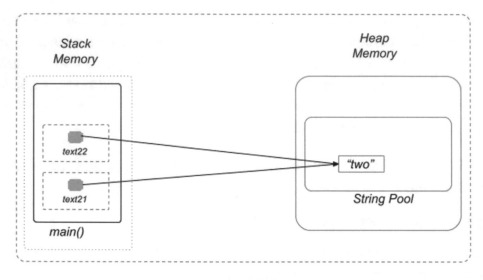

Java Runtime Memory

Figure 5-16. *Abstract representation of the string pool area created in the heap memory*

When a new String object is created using the new operator, the JVM will allocate new memory for the new object and store it in the heap, so the String pool won't be used. This results in every String object created like this having its own memory region with its own address.

⚠ I think it is obvious at this point that using String constructors (there are more than one) to create String objects is in fact equivalent to wasting memory.

This is why if we were to compare variable text22 and variable text23 from the initial code sample we would expect their references to be different, but the objects should be equal. Listing 5-27 depicts code that tests this assumption.

Listing 5-27. Code Sample Showing Differences Between equals(..) and == on String References

```
package com.apress.bgn.five;

public class SimpleStringDemo {
    public static void main(String... args) {
        String text22 = "two";
        String text23 = new String ("two");

        if (text22 == text23) {
            System.out.println("Equal References");
        } else {
            System.out.println("Different References");
        }
        if (text22.equals(text23)) {
            System.out.println("Equal Objects");
        } else {
            System.out.println("Different Objects");
        }
    }
}
```

When running the preceding code, the following will be printed in the console, proving everything the assumption was correct:

```
Different References
Equal Objects
```

I leave it up to you to imagine how the stack and heap memory looks like for the previous example.[4]

---

[4] If you want to check if you understood memory management and strings correctly, you are welcome to draw your own picture and send it to the author for a review and a technical discussion.

> ❶ The **String Pool** had a default size of 1,009 entries until Java 6. Starting with this version its size can be modified using the -XX:StringTableSize command line option. Since the size varies from one Java version to another and the memory available to the program, my recommendation is just to run java -XX: +PrintFlagsFinal -version and look for StringTableSize in the returned output to get the real size of the String Pool on your machine.

In Listing 5-24, lines 11 and 12 depict how a String instance can be created from a char[3] array. Until Java 8, internally that was the initial representation for String values—arrays of characters. A character is represented on 2 bytes, which means a lot of memory was consumed for Strings. In Java 9 a new representation was introduced called Compact String, which uses byte[] or char[] depending on the content. This means that the memory consumed by a String processing application will be significantly lower starting with Java 9.

The String class provides a huge set of methods to manipulate strings; an entire book could probably be written only about this Java type. These methods will be explained when used in the book, but if you are curious you can consult the online JavaDoc here (https://docs.oracle.com/en/java/javase/17/docs/api/java.base/ java/lang/String.html) or just look them up using your smart editor.

Escaping Characters

There are special characters that cannot be part of a String value. As you have probably noticed, String values are defined between double quotes ("sample"), and this makes the "(double quote) character unusable as a value. To be able to use it as a String value or part of one, it has to be escaped. Aside from this character there is also the \(backslash), the \a(alert), and a few others. In Figure 5-17 you can see how IntelliJ IDEA tries to tell you that you cannot use those characters in the content of a String value.

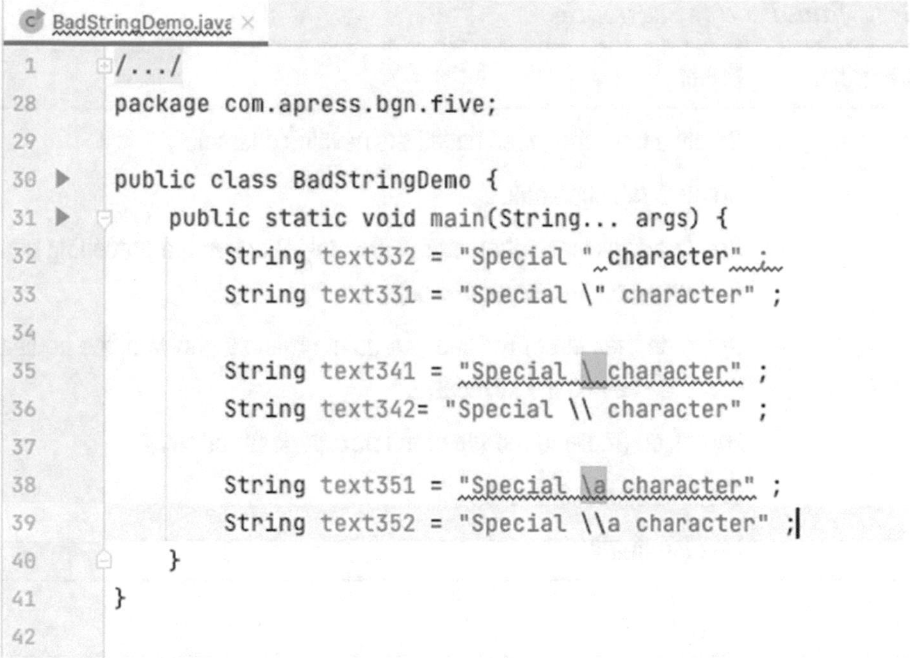

```
 C  BadStringDemo.java ×
 1      /.../
28      package com.apress.bgn.five;
29
30  ▶   public class BadStringDemo {
31  ▶       public static void main(String... args) {
32              String text332 = "Special " character" ;
33              String text331 = "Special \" character" ;
34
35              String text341 = "Special \ character" ;
36              String text342= "Special \\ character" ;
37
38              String text351 = "Special \a character" ;
39              String text352 = "Special \\a character" ;
40          }
41      }
42
```

Figure 5-17. *Code samples with special characters*

So a single \(backslash) is not allowed to be part of a String value, but two of them are, and it tells the compiler that the String value contains a \(backslash) character.

```
System.out.println(" Example using \\.")
//Prints
 Example using \.
```

As for the \a alliteration, it is not allowed in a String value because the \(backslash) is used to construct escape sequences, but \a is not an escape sequence.

The '(single quote) must be escaped as well when used as a character value.

```
char quote = '\";
```

There are a few Java escape sequences that can be used in String values to get a certain effect, and the most important are listed in Table 5-1.

Table 5-1. *Java Escape Sequences*

Escape Sequence	Effect
\n	Create a new line (often called the newline character).
\t	Create a tab character.
\b	Create a backspace character (which might delete the preceding character, depending on the output device).
\r	Return to the start of the line (but do not make a new line, the equivalent of the Home key on the keyboard).
\f	Form feed (move to the top of the next page for printers).
\s	Create a space character.
\	Line terminator.

> ℹ️ The full list of characters to be escaped in String values can be found in the Java Language Specification documentation here: `https://docs.oracle.com/javase/specs/jls/se16/html/jls-3.html#jls-3.10.7`.

> ⚠️ According to the JLS, it is a compile-time error if the character following a backslash in an escape sequence is not a \ or an ASCII b, s, t, n, f, r, ", ', \, 0, 1, 2, 3, 4, 5, 6, or 7.

The newline \n and the tab \t character are used quite often in programming to properly format console output. If we declare a `String` instance like this one:

```
String perf = "The singers performing tonight are: \n\t Paolo Nutini \n\t
Seth MacFarlane\n\t John Mayer";
```

When printed in the console the text will be formatted and will look like this:
The singers performing tonight are:

```
    Paolo Nutini
    Seth MacFarlane
    John Mayer
```

That last thing that should be mentioned about Java `String` is that in JDK 15, support for text blocks was introduced. This means that instead of splitting a big `String` value into multiple smaller values written on multiple lines and concatenating them to keep the code readable, you can now declare a single block of text and assign it to a String reference. Before Java 15, if you wanted to declare a multiline string value you had a few options, which included concatenations (using the '+' operator), explicit line terminators, and delimiters. A few of these options are depicted in Listing 5-28. Depending on the solution you are building, you can choose any of them, and a discussion about the efficiency and drawbacks is out of scope for this book.

Listing 5-28. Multiline Java `String` Value Before JDK 15

```
package com.apress.bgn.five;

import java.io.PrintWriter;
import java.io.StringWriter;

public class MultiLineDemo {

    public static void main(String... args) {
        // this statement extracts the newline character specific to the
        // operating system
        String newLineCh = System.getProperty("line.separator");

        // method 1: simple concatenation using the '+' operator
        String multilineStr = "line one of the text block" +
                newLineCh +
                "line two of the text block" +
                newLineCh +
                "last line of the text block" ;

        // or method 2 using `String#concat(..)` method
        multilineStr = "line one of the text block"
                .concat(newLineCh)
                .concat("line two of the text block")
                .concat(newLineCh)
                .concat("last line of the text block") ;
```

```java
// or method 3 using `String.join` utility method
multilineStr = String.join("line one of the text block" ,
        newLineCh ,
        "line two of the text block" ,
        newLineCh ,
        "last line of the text block");

// or method 4 using a StringBuffer instance
multilineStr = new StringBuffer("line one of the text block")
        .append(newLineCh)
        .append("line two of the text block")
        .append(newLineCh)
        .append("last line of the text block").toString();

// or method 5 using a StringBuilder instance
multilineStr = new StringBuilder("line one of the text block")
        .append(newLineCh)
        .append("line two of the text block")
        .append(newLineCh)
        .append("last line of the text block").toString();

// or method 5 using a StringWriter instance
StringWriter stringWriter = new StringWriter();
stringWriter.write("line one of the text block");
stringWriter.write(newLineCh);
stringWriter.write("line two of the text block");
stringWriter.write(newLineCh);
stringWriter.write("last line of the text block");
multilineStr = stringWriter.toString();

// or method 6 using a StringWriter and PrintWriter instance
stringWriter = new StringWriter();
PrintWriter printWriter = new PrintWriter(stringWriter);
printWriter .println("line one of the text block");
printWriter.println("line two of the text block");
```

```
        printWriter.println("last line of the text block");
        multilineStr = stringWriter.toString();

        System.out.println(multilineStr);
    }
}
```

---

❶ **StringBuffer** represents a thread-safe, mutable sequence of characters. This means any action on a **StringBuffer** is executed after single access is ensured. This is why using **StringBuffer** to concatenate string is slower than using **StringBuilder**, which is its non–thread-safe equivalent. So when designing your code, unless there is a risk for your string concatenation block to be executed by multiple threads in parallel, go with **StringBuilder**.

In JDK 15, support for declaring text blocks was added which enables to embed multiline texts in the code exactly as they are without modifying them to add line terminators, delimiters or concatenation operators. A text block is thus an alternative form of Java String representation that starts with three double-quote characters followed by a line terminator and ends with three double-quote characters. So the previous multiline text can be written the new syntax, as shown next:

```
String multilineStr = """
        line one of the text block
        line two of the text block
        last line of the text block
    """;
```

The new syntax is designed only for declaring multiline texts, so it cannot be used to declare single line texts. Doing so will result in a compile error. The same will happen if the starting three double-quote characters are followed by text instead of the expected line terminator. Figure 5-18 depicts two wrong ways to declare multiline text blocks, and the explanation provided by the IDE.

```
  BadStringDemo.java ×
1     /.../
28    package com.apress.bgn.five;
29
30 ▶  public class BadStringDemo {
31 ▶      public static void main(String... args) {
32        |
33            String text361 = """Wrong way to use this""";
34            String text362 = """Another wong way
35                    to use this""";            Illegal text block start: missing new line after opening quotes
36        }
37    }
```

Figure 5-18. *Invalid syntax for declaring multiline texts*

A few mentions:

- The "(double-quote) does not need to be escaped in a multiline text block unless there is three of them grouped together within the value. In this case the compiler might be a little confused as to where the text block ends, so in this case at least one of them must be escaped.

- When the lines that make the text block need to be indented, either spaces or tabs should be used; using them both might lead to unpredictable results (e.g., irregular indentation can break a YAML configuration)

- Text blocks support two extra escape sequences:

    - \<line-terminator> suppresses the inclusion of an implicit new line character. For example, a text block declared as shown previously is equivalent to:

```
String multilineStr = "line one of the text block" +
                "\n" +
                "line two of the text block" +
                "\n" +
                "last line of the text block" +
                "\n" ;
```

If the last new line is not needed there are two options. The text block can have the terminator specified inline with the last line of text.

```
String multilineStr = """
    line one of the text block
    line two of the text block
    last line of the text block""";
```

But this is not recommended, since it might affect indentation. The recommended way is to use the \<line-terminator> escape character since this better frames the text block and allows the closing delimiter to manage indentation.

```
String multilineStr = """
        line one of the text block
        line two of the text block
        last line of the text block\
    """;
```

-   \s escape sequence translates to space. This is useful when we want some spaces at end of the lines in the text block.

```
String multilineStr = """
        line one of the text block\s
        line two of the text block\s
        last line of the text block\
    """;
```

In the official Oracle documentation there is section dedicated to the new multiline blocks added in JDK 15. If you ever need more information, this is the best place to look: https://docs.oracle.com/en/java/javase/17/text-blocks/index.html - new-escape-sequences.

Wrapper Classes for Primitive Types

It was mentioned in the primitive section of this chapter that each primitive type has a corresponding reference type. Before covering each of them and why they are needed, please take a look at Table 5-2.

Table 5-2. *Java Primitive Types and Equivalent Reference Types*

Primitive Type	Reference Type
char	java.lang.Character
boolean	java.lang.Boolean
byte	java.lang.Byte
short	java.lang.Short
int	java.lang.Integer
long	java.lang.Long
float	java.lang.Float
double	java.lang.Double

The Java wrapper classes wrap a value of the primitive type with the same name. In addition, these classes provide methods for converting primitive values to String and vice-versa, as well as constants and methods useful when dealing with primitive types, that need to be treated as objects. The numeric wrapper classes are related, all of them extend the Number class, as depicted in Figure 5-19.

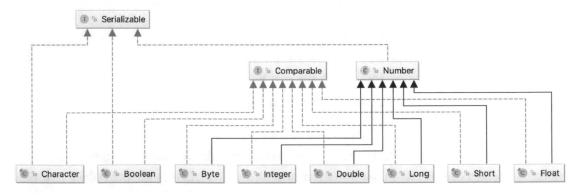

Figure 5-19. *Java primitive and equivalent reference types*

The following code samples will use mostly the Integer class, but the other numeric wrapper classes can be used in a similar way. Converting a primitive value to its equivalent reference is called **boxing**; the reverse process is called **unboxing**. JVM does these conversions automatically in most situations, the term **autoboxing** was introduced to refer to the process of boxing, while for some reason automatic unboxing is still called **unboxing**.

The code sample depicted in Listing 5-29, contains a few operations with `Integer` and int values.

Listing 5-29. Autoboxing and Unboxing in Action

```java
package com.apress.bgn.five;

public class WrapperDemo {
    public static void main(String... args) {
        // upper interval boundary for int
        Integer max = Integer.MAX_VALUE;
        System.out.println(max);

        //autoboxing Integer -> int
        int pmax = max;

        //autoboxing int -> Integer
        Integer io = 10;

        //creating primitive utility method
        //exception is thrown, if string is not a number
        int i1 = Integer.parseInt("11");

        //constructor deprecated in Java 9
        //exception is thrown, if string is not a number
        Integer i2 = new Integer("12");

        //exception is thrown, if string is not a number
        Integer i3 = Integer.valueOf("12");

        //convert int into to String
        String s0 = Integer.toString(13);

        //convert int to float
        float f0 = Integer.valueOf(14).floatValue();

        //creating string with binary representation of number 9 (1001)
        String s1 = Integer.toBinaryString(9);
```

```
        //introduced in Java 1.8
        Integer i4 = Integer.parseUnsignedInt("+15");

        //method to add to integers
        int sum = Integer.sum(2, 3);

        //method to get the bigger value
        int maximum = Integer.max(2, 7);
    }
}
```

The Character and Boolean types are a little different because these types are not numeric, so they cannot be converted to any numeric values. They cannot be converted one to another either. Oracle provides good documentation for its classes, so if you are curious about using these two types just check out the official JDK API documentation at https://docs.oracle.com/en/java/javase/17/docs/api/index.html.

Date Time API

A lot of applications make use of calendar date types to print the current date, deadlines, and birthdays. No matter what application you will decide to build, you will most likely need to use calendar dates. Until Java 8, the main class to model a calendar date was java.util.Date. There are a few problems with this class and others involved in handling calendar dates. But before we get into that, take a look at Listing 5-30 and check out how we can get the current date and create a custom date and print certain details.

Listing 5-30. java.util.Date Code Sample

```
package com.apress.bgn.five;

import java.text.SimpleDateFormat;
import java.util.Date;

public class DateDemo {
    public static void main(String... args){
        SimpleDateFormat sdf = new SimpleDateFormat("dd-MM-yyyy");
        Date currentDate = new Date();
        System.out.println("Today: " + sdf.format(currentDate));
```

```
    //deprecated since 1.1
    Date johnBirthday = new Date(77, 9, 16);
    System.out.println("John's Birthday: " + sdf.format(johnBirthday));

    int day = johnBirthday.getDay();
    System.out.println("Day: " + day);
    int month = johnBirthday.getMonth() + 1;
    System.out.println("Month: " + month);
    int year = johnBirthday.getYear();
    System.out.println("Year: " + year);
    }
}
```

The get the current date set on your system is simple; just call the default constructor of the Date class:

```
Date currentDate = new Date();
```

The contents of the currentDate can be displayed directly, but usually an instance of java.text.SimpleDateFormat is used, to format the date to a pattern that is country specific or just more readable. The formatter can also be used to convert a String with that specific format intro a Date instance. If the text does not match the pattern of the formatter, a specific exception will be thrown (type: java.text.ParseException)

```
try {
    Date johnBirthday = sdf.parse("16-10-1977");
} catch (ParseException e) {
    // do something with the exception
}
```

To create a Date instance from the numbers representing a date (year, month, and day), a constructor that takes those values as arguments can be used. That constructor, however, has been deprecated since Java 1.1, so some developers prefer using the sdf.parse(..) method instead. The constructor has a few particularities regarding its arguments:

- the year argument must be the year value –1900.

- the months are counted from 0, so the month provided as argument must be the month we want –1.

  The code to construct a Date from the numeric values for year, month, and day is depicted here:

```
//deprecated since 1.1
Date johnBirthday = new Date(77, 9, 16);
System.out.println("John's Birthday: " + sdf.format(johnBirthday));
//it prints: John's Birthday: 16-10-1977
```

If we want to extract the year, month and day of the month from the date, there are methods for that, only again a peculiarity: the method to extract the day of the month is named getDate(). Also keep in mind, since months are numbered from 0 to 11, to the real month value you have to add 1 to the result returned by getMonth(). Listing 5-31 shows the code to create a Date instance, extract, then day, month, and year and print them.

Listing 5-31. Printing Components of a Calendar Date

```
package com.apress.bgn.five;

import java.text.ParseException;
import java.text.SimpleDateFormat;
import java.util.Date;

public class PrintDateDemo {
    public static void main(String... args) {
        try {
            SimpleDateFormat sdf = new SimpleDateFormat("dd-MM-yyyy");
            Date johnBirthday = sdf.parse("16-10-1977");
            System.out.println("John's Birthday: " + sdf.format(johnBirthday));

            //day of the month
            int day = johnBirthday.getDate();
```

```java
        System.out.println("Day: " + day);

        int month = johnBirthday.getMonth() + 1;
        System.out.println("Month: " + month);

        int year = johnBirthday.getYear();
        System.out.println("Year: " + year);

    } catch (ParseException e) {
        e.printStackTrace();
    }
  }
}
```

⚠ The `java.util.Data` class has two methods that can be easily confused.

The `getDate()` method returns the day of the month of a Date object.

The `getDay()` method returns the day of the week of a Date object.

Both are deprecated as of JDK version 1.1, and better, less confusing ways to extract that information are presented later in this section.

If you inspect the demo classes of this section in the IntelliJ IDEA editor, you will notice that some constructors and methods are written with a strikethrough font. This means that they are deprecated and might be removed in future versions of Java and thus they should not be used. This is why there is another way to do all of this: by using the `java.util.Calendar` class. The code to do the same as in Listing 5-31, but using the Calendar class is depicted in Listing 5-32.

Listing 5-32. Code Sample for Handling Calendar Dates Using the Calendar Class

```java
package com.apress.bgn.five;

import java.text.SimpleDateFormat;
import java.util.Calendar;
import java.util.Date;
import java.util.GregorianCalendar;
```

```java
public class CalendarDateDemo {
    public static void main(String... args) {
        SimpleDateFormat sdf = new SimpleDateFormat("dd-MM-yyyy");
        Calendar calendar = new GregorianCalendar();
        Date currentDate = calendar.getTime();
        System.out.println("Today: " + sdf.format(currentDate));

        calendar.set(1977, 9, 16);
        Date johnBirthday = calendar.getTime();
        System.out.println("John's Birthday: " + sdf.format(johnBirthday));

        int day = calendar.get(Calendar.DAY_OF_MONTH);
        System.out.println("Day: " + day);
        int month = calendar.get(Calendar.MONTH);
        System.out.println("Month: " + month);
        int year = calendar.get(Calendar.YEAR);
        System.out.println("Year: " + year);
    }
}
```

Unfortunately some of the peculiarities mentioned earlier remain, as the central class for representing dates is still the java.util.Date, but at least we are not using deprecated methods anymore.

The java.util.Date class and the java.text.SimpleDateFormat class are not thread safe, so in complex applications with multiple execution threads, developers must synchronize access to those type of objects explicitly. Objects of those types are not immutable and working with timezones is a pain. This is the main reason why in Java 8 a new API to model calendar date operations was introduced that is better designed, and date instances are thread-safe and immutable.

The central classes for the API are java.time.LocalDate and java.time.Local DateTime, used to model calendar dates and calendar dates with time. Listing 5-33 shows how to get the current date and how to create a custom date looks like with the new API.

Listing 5-33. Code Sample for Handling Calendar Dates Using the New DateTime API Introduced in the JDK 8

```java
package com.apress.bgn.five;

import java.time.LocalDate;
import java.time.LocalDateTime;
import java.time.Month;

public class NewCalendarDateDemo {

    public static void main(String... args) {
        LocalDateTime currentTime = LocalDateTime.now();
        System.out.println("Current DateTime: " + currentTime);
        LocalDate today = currentTime.toLocalDate();
        System.out.println("Today: " + today);

        LocalDate johnBd = LocalDate.of(1977, Month.OCTOBER, 16);
        System.out.println("John's Birthday: " + johnBd);

        int day = johnBd.getDayOfMonth();
        System.out.println("Day: " + day + ", " + johnBd.getDayOfWeek());
        int month = johnBd.getMonthValue();

        System.out.println("Month: " + month + ", " + johnBd.getMonth());
        int year = johnBd.getYear();
        System.out.println("Year: " + year);
    }
}
```

To get the current date and time a static method named now() is called, which returns an instance of type LocalDateTime. This instance can be used to get the current date by calling toLocalDate(). This method returns the current date as an instance of type LocalDate. This class has a toString() method that prints the formatted date according to the default Locale set on the system. To create a custom date, the actual year and day of month can be used as arguments, and the month can be specified using one of the values of the java.time.Month enum. Extracting information regarding a date can be done easily by calling methods with intuitive names. Just look at the getDayOfMonth() and getDayOfWeek() methods in the previous snippet. Their name

259

reflects exactly what data they are returning. As you can see, classes LocalDate and LocalDateTime simplify the development where timezones are not required. Working with time zones is quite an advanced subject, so it won't be covered within this book.

Collections

One of the most important family of types in JDK that you will probably use a lot are the collections. Classes and interfaces in the collections family are used to model common data collections such as sets, lists, and maps. All the classes are stored under package java.util and can be split into two categories: tuples and collections of key-value pairs. The tuples are unidimensional sets of data: if the values are unique, any class implementing the java.util.Set interface should be used to model them; if not, any class implementing the java.util.List interface should be used. For collections of key-value pairs classes, implementing java.util.Maps should be used. Starting with Java version 1.5 collections have become generic, which allowed developers more precision and security when working with them. Before Java 1.5, collections could contain any type of objects. Developers can still write code like the one depicted in Listing 5-34:

Listing 5-34. Code Using Collections Up to Java 1.5

```
package com.apress.bgn.five;

import com.apress.bgn.four.classes.Gender;
import com.apress.bgn.four.hierarchy.Performer;

import java.util.ArrayList;
import java.util.List;

public class CollectionsBasicDemo {

    public static void main(String... args) {
        List objList = new ArrayList();
        objList.add("temp");
        objList.add(Integer.valueOf(5));
        objList.add(new Performer("John", 40, 1.91f, Gender.MALE));
    }
}
```

You probably do not see any problem with this; the compiler sure doesn't, but when you iterate this list it is quite difficult to determine which objects are you handling without complicated code analyzing the type of each object. This was mentioned before at the end of **Chapter 4** when generics were introduced. The code to iterate the list and process the elements differently based on their type is depicted in Listing 5-35, just to show you why this is a bad idea and bad practice in this day and age of Java.

Listing 5-35. More Code Using Collections Up to Java 1.5

```java
package com.apress.bgn.five;

import com.apress.bgn.four.classes.Gender;
import com.apress.bgn.four.hierarchy.Performer;

import java.util.ArrayList;
import java.util.List;

public class CollectionsBasicDemo {

    public static void main(String... args) {
        List objList = new ArrayList();
        objList.add("temp");
        objList.add(Integer.valueOf(5));
        objList.add(new Performer("John", 40, 1.91f, Gender.MALE));

        for (Object obj : objList) {
            if (obj instanceof String) {
                System.out.println("String object = " + obj.toString());
            } else if (obj instanceof Integer) {
                Integer i = (Integer)obj;
                System.out.println("Integer object = " + i.intValue());
            } else {
                Performer p = (Performer) obj;
                System.out.println("Performer object = " + p.getName());
            }
        }
    }
}
```

Maybe this is not clear to you now, but to be able to use the contents of the list you have to know exactly all the types of the objects that were put in the list. This might be doable when you are working alone on a project, but in a bigger project, when multiple developers are involved, this can get messy really fast.

This is where **generics** come to help. Generics help define at compile time what types of objects should be put into a collection, and thus if the wrong object type is added to the collection, the code no longer compiles. Both lists and sets implement the same interface: `java.util.Collection<T>`, which means their API is almost the same. The simplified hierarchy of the collections containing the classes and interfaces most used in programming is depicted in Figure 5-20.

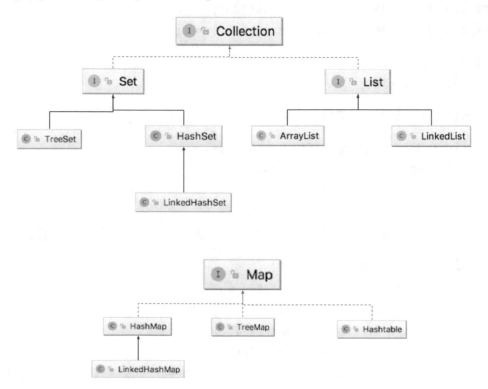

Figure 5-20. *Collection hierarchy*

Listing 5-36 depicts the creation of a List of String values, and the loop statement needed to traverse it and print its elements.

Listing 5-36. Code Using Collections Starting with Java 1.5

```java
package com.apress.bgn.five;

import java.util.ArrayList;
import java.util.List;

public class GenericListDemo {
    public static void main(String... args) {
        List<String> stringList = new ArrayList<String>();
        stringList.add("one");
        stringList.add("two");
        stringList.add("three");

        for (String s : stringList) {
            System.out.println(s);
        }
    }
}
```

A List contains an unsorted collection of nonunique data, null elements included. In the previous example we declared a reference of type List<T> and an object of type ArrayList<T>. We did this because as all implementations have the same API; we could easily switch ArrayList<T> with LinkedList<T> and the code will still work.

```java
List<String> stringList = new ArrayList<String>();
stringList = new LinkedList<String>();
```

---

❶ Declaring abstract references is a good programming practice, because it increases the flexibility of your code.

The syntax in the previous examples is pre–Java 1.7. In Java1.7 the <> (diamond operator) was introduced. This allowed more simplification of collections initializations, because it only required declaring the type of the elements in the list in the reference declaration. So the two lines in the previous code snippet become:

```java
List<String> stringList = new ArrayList<>();
stringList = new LinkedList<>();
```

Every new Java version has added changes to the collection framework starting with Java 1.5. In Java 1.8, support for lambda expression has been added by adding a default method named forEach in the java.lang.Iterable<T> interface (Figure 5-20), which is extended by the java.lang.Collection<T>. So the code to print all the values in the list, like we did previously using a for loop, can be replaced with:

```java
stringList.forEach(element -> System.out.println(element));
```

In Java 9, yet another improvement was introduced: factory methods for collections. Our collection was populated with elements by repeatedly calling add(..), which is a little redundant, especially since we have the full collection of elements we want to put in the list. That is why in Java 9 methods to create collection objects in one line of code were introduced. For example:

```java
List<String> stringList = List.of("one", "two", "three");
```

The resulting List<T> is an immutable collection: it can no longer be modified, and elements cannot be added or removed from it.

Moving even further close to the present, in Java 10 support for local variable type inference was added, which means that we no longer have to explicitly specify the reference type because it will be automatically be inferred based on the object type, so the following declaration:

```java
List<String> stringList = List.of("one", "two", "three");
```

This becomes:

```java
var stringList = List.of("one", "two", "three");
```

Similar code can be written with Set<T>, HashSet<T>, and TreeSet<T>, and similar methods exist for this family of classes as well.

---

❶ Collections is a common topic at Java entry-level position interviews, so don't be surprised if you are asked what the difference is between a List<T> and Set<T>.

When working with Set<T> implementations, you just have to make sure the objects added to the set have equals(..) and hashCode() implemented correctly. The reason for this is that Set<T> models the mathematical *set* abstraction that allows no duplicate elements.

The equals(..) indicates whether the object passed as an argument is "equal to" the current instance. The default implementation provided by the Object class considers two objects to be equal if they are stored in the same memory location.

The hashCode(..) returns an integer representation of the object memory address. The default implementation provided by the Object class returns a random integer that is unique for each instance. This value might change between several executions of the application. This method is useful when objects are used as keys in hash tables, because it optimizes retrieving elements from them. If you want to learn more about hash tables, the Internet is your oyster; as for Java, a hash table can be modelled by an instance of java.util.HashMap<K,V>.

As per the official documentation, if two objects are equal, then calling hashCode() on each of them must yield the same result. But it is not a must for two unequal objects to have different hashCodes.

This being said, the Ball class introduced earlier will be used to create some ball instances; add them into a Set. The code sample in Listing 5-37 shows a version of the Ball class containing proper implementations for the equals(..) and hashCode();

Listing 5-37. Basic equals(..) and hashCode() Implementations

```java
package com.apress.bgn.five;

import java.util.HashSet;
import java.util.Set;

public class SetDemo {

    public static void main(String... args) {
        Set<Ball> ballSet = new HashSet<>();
        ballSet.add(new Ball(2, "RED", "rubber"));
        ballSet.add(new Ball(4, "BLUE", "cotton"));

        System.out.println("Set size: " + ballSet.size());
        Ball duplicate = new Ball(2, "RED", "rubber");
        boolean wasAdded = ballSet.add(duplicate);
```

```java
        if(!wasAdded) {
            System.out.println("Duplicate ball not added to the set. ");
            System.out.println("Set size: " + ballSet.size());
        }
    }
}

class Ball {
    private int diameter;
    private String color;
    private String material;

    @Override
    public boolean equals(Object o) {
        if (this == o) return true;
        if (o == null || getClass() != o.getClass()) return false;
        Ball ball = (Ball) o;
        return diameter == ball.diameter &&
                color.equals(ball.color) &&
                material.equals(ball.material);
    }

    @Override
    public int hashCode() {
        int result = 17 * diameter;
        result = 31 * result + (color == null ? 0 : color.hashCode());
        result = 31 * result + (material == null ? 0 : material.hashCode());
        return result;
    }
    // other code omitted
}
```

Running the code in the previous listing produces the following output:

```
Set size: 2
Duplicate ball not added to the set.
Set size: 2
```

Before Java 1.7 developers had to write equals(..) and hashCode()
implementations similar to the ones in the previous listing for all classes that might have
been used in a Set<T> or as key in a Map<K,V>. The implementations have to be based on
the values of the most important fields in the class. The 17 and 31 are just two random
integers used to compute the hashCode value.

In Java 1.7 class java.util.Objects was introduced providing utility methods
to make implementing these methods easier. Listing 5-38 depicts equals(..) and
hashCode() implementations after Java 1.7.

Listing 5-38.   Basic equals(..) and hashCode() Implementations After Java 1.7

```java
package com.apress.bgn.five;

import java.util.Objects;

class Ball {
    private int diameter;
    private String color;
    private String material;

    @Override
    public boolean equals(Object o) {
        if (this == o) return true;
        if (o == null || getClass() != o.getClass()) return false;
        Ball ball = (Ball) o;
        return diameter == ball.diameter &&
                Objects.equals(color, ball.color) &&
                Objects.equals(material, ball.material);
    }

    @Override
    public int hashCode() {
        return Objects.hash(diameter, color, material);
    }

    // other code omitted
}
```

Starting with Java 14, things became even simpler because now a class like Ball can be written as a record, as depicted in Listing 5-39.

Listing 5-39. Class Ball Written as a Record to Avoid Implementing equals(..) and hashCode()

```
package com.apress.bgn.five;

import java.util.HashSet;
import java.util.Set;

record Ball(int diameter, String colour, String material) {}

public class RecordSetDemo {
    public static void main(String... args) {
        // same as Listing 5-37
    }
}
```

Executing the code in the previous listing yields the same result as before, thus proving that the equals(..) method generated by the Java compiler is valid.

Map<K,V> implementations come with a few differences, because they model collections of key-value pairs. The code in Listing 5-40 depicts the creation and initialization of a map that uses keys of type Ball and values of type Integer. You can imagine this map instance to represent the number of identical balls in a bucket.

Listing 5-40. Map<Ball, Integer> Code Sample

```
package com.apress.bgn.five;

import java.util.HashMap;
import java.util.Map;

public class MapDemo {
    public static void main(String... args) {
        Map<Ball, Integer> ballMap = new HashMap<Ball, Integer>();
        ballMap.put(new Ball(2, "RED", "rubber"), 5);
        ballMap.put(new Ball(4, "BLUE", "cotton"), 7);
```

```
    for (Map.Entry<Ball, Integer> entry : ballMap.entrySet()) {
        System.out.println(entry.getKey() + ": " + entry.getValue());
    }
  }
}
```

As you can notice from the for loop, you can infer that a map is actually a collection of Map.Entry<K, V> elements. If we were to move ahead to the Java 1.7 syntax, the declaration of the map becomes simpler by applying the <>(diamond) operator:

```
Map<Ball, Integer> ballMap = new HashMap<>();
```

Moving further to Java 1.8, traversal and printing values in map becomes more practical as well, because of the introduction of the forEach(..) method and lambda expressions:

```
ballMap.forEach((k,v) -> System.out.println(k + ": " + v));
```

And in Java 9, declaring and populating a map becomes easier too.

```
Map<Ball, Integer> ballMap = Map.of(new Ball(2, "RED", "rubber"), 5, new
Ball(4, "BLUE", "cotton"), 7);
```

Java 10 adds in var to simplify the declaration even more.

```
var ballMap = Map.of(new Ball(2, "RED", "rubber"), 5, new Ball(4, "BLUE",
"cotton"), 7);
```

Another thing that needs to be mentioned before ending this section is what happens when a key-pair value is added to the map and the key already exists. As you probably expect, the existing key-pair in the map is overwritten. Before Java 8, writing code to prevent this situation when a set of values is lost required checking if the key is present, and if not present then adding the new key-pair, as depicted in Listing 5-41.

Listing 5-41. Preventing Key-Pair Overwriting Before Java 8

```
package com.apress.bgn.five;

import java.util.HashMap;
import java.util.Map;
```

```
public class MapDemo {
    public static void main(String... args) {
        Map<Ball, Integer> ballMap = new HashMap<>();
        Ball redBall = new Ball(2, "RED", "rubber");

        ballMap.put( redBall, 5);
        ballMap.put(new Ball(4, "BLUE", "cotton"), 7);

         //ballMap.put( redBall, 3); // this overrides entry <redBall, 5>

        if(!ballMap.containsKey(redBall)) {
            ballMap.put(redBall, 3);
        }

        for (Map.Entry<Ball, Integer> entry : ballMap.entrySet()) {
            System.out.println(entry.getKey() + ": " + entry.getValue());
        }
    }
}
```

In Java 8 a practical set of utility methods were added to the Map<K,V> interface to simplify code written using maps, including the method putIfAbsent(..) depicted inListing 5-42, which replaces the statement marked in the previous code listing.

Listing 5-42. Preventing Key-Pair Overwriting Before Java 8

```
package com.apress.bgn.five;

import java.util.HashMap;
import java.util.Map;

public class MapDemo {
    public static void main(String... args) {
        Map<Ball, Integer> ballMap = new HashMap<>();
        Ball redBall = new Ball(2, "RED", "rubber");

        ballMap.put( redBall, 5);
        ballMap.put(new Ball(4, "BLUE", "cotton"), 7);

        ballMap.putIfAbsent(redBall, 3);
```

```
    for (Map.Entry<Ball, Integer> entry : ballMap.entrySet()) {
        System.out.println(entry.getKey() + ": " + entry.getValue());
    }
  }
}
```

The JDK classes for working with collections cover a wide range of functionality, such as sorting, searching, merging collections, intersections, conversions to/from arrays, and so on. As the book advances the context of the code samples will widen, and we will be able to use collections to solve real-world problems.

Concurrency Specific Types

Previously in the book it was mentioned from time to time that a Java program can have more than one execution thread. By default, when a Java program is executed, a thread is created for the code that is called from the main(..) method. A few other utility threads are created and executed in parallel for JVM related things. These threads can easily be accessed using static utility methods defined in the java.lang.Thread class. The code in Listing 5-43 does just that: it extracts the references to the Thread instances and prints their name to the console.

Listing 5-43. Code Used to Show All Threads Necessary to Run a Simple Java Application and Its Output

```
package com.apress.bgn.five;

public class ListJvmThreads {
    public static void main(String... args) {
        var threadSet = Thread.getAllStackTraces().keySet();
        var threadArray = threadSet.toArray(new Thread[threadSet.size()]);
        for (int i = 0; i < threadArray.length; ++i) {
            System.out.println("thread name: " + threadArray[i].getName());
        }
    }
}
```

```
/// Output
thread name: main
thread name: Finalizer
thread name: Common-Cleaner
thread name: Monitor Ctrl-Break
thread name: Signal Dispatcher
thread name: Reference Handler
thread name: Notification Thread
```

The output shown in Listing 5-43 was produced when running the code on JDK 17-ea on a macOS computer in IntelliJ IDEA. The threads listed have the following responsibilities:

- The thread named main is the thread that executes the developer written code. The developer can write code to start its own threads from the main thread.

- The thread named Reference Handler is the thread that takes unused objects and adds them to a queue to be evicted.

- The thread named Finalizer is a low priority JVM thread that executes the finalize() method of each object in a queue waiting to be evicted from memory. This method can be overwritten by developers to explicitly free resources linked to objects about to be evicted.

- The thread named Common-Cleaner is also a low priority JVM thread in charge of lightweight cleanup of object without using finalization.

- The thread named Monitor Ctrl-Break is a thread created by IntelliJ IDEA, since the code is executed using this editor.

- The thread named Signal Dispatcher handles native signals sent by operating system to the JVM.

- The thread named Notification Thread is a thread handling notification sent by operating system to the JVM.

Except main, Monitor Ctrl-Break (which is not a JVM application thread), Common-Cleaner, and all the other three are system threads that ensure the JVM collaborates with the operating system. Except for main, all other threads are called

daemon threads. They have low priority, and they provide services to **user threads**, which is what the main thread is. These are the only two types of threads in Java.

The developer can write code to start its own threads from the main thread. The most simple way to create a custom thread is to create a class that extends the Thread class.

The Thread class implements an interface named Runnable that declares a single method named run().

The Thread class declares a method named start(). When this method is called, the body of the run() method is executed in a separate execution thread than the one calling start().[5]

Thus, when extending the Thread class or implementing the Runnable interface directly, the run() method must be overridden.

The example in Listing 5-44 depicts a class named RandomDurationThread. The contents of the run() method pauses the execution at random times by calling the Thread.sleep(..) utility method. The body of the method is wrapped in two lines of code that print the name of the thread: a starting message and an ending message. The Thread.sleep(..) ensures that each thread execution has a different duration, so that we can clearly see they are executed in parallel.

Listing 5-44. Code Sample Declaring Threads with Random Execution Durations By Extending the Thread Class

```java
package com.apress.bgn.five;

public class RandomDurationThread extends Thread {

    @Override
    public void run() {
        System.out.println(this.getName() + " started...");
        for (int i = 0; i < 10; ++i) {
            try {
                Thread.sleep(i * 10);
```

---

[5] The internals of thread management is much more complicated, but this section will just scratch the surface.

273

```
        } catch (InterruptedException e) {
            e.printStackTrace();
        }
    }
    System.out.println(this.getName() + " ended.");
  }
}
```

The code using the RandomDurationThread to create multiple threads and starting them is shown in Listing 5-45.

Listing 5-45. Code Sample to Run Multiple Threads in Parallel

```
package com.apress.bgn.five;

public class MultipleUserThreadsDemo {
    public static void main(String... args) {
        for (int i = 0; i < 10; ++i) {
            new RandomDurationThread().start();
        }
    }
}
```

In the previous code listing, 10 instances of class RandomDurationThread were created and the start() method was called for each of them. When the previous code is executed a log similar to the one depicted in Listing 5-46 should be printed in the console.

Listing 5-46. Output Resulted By Running the Code in Listing 5-45

```
Thread-6 started...
Thread-4 started...
Thread-2 started...
Thread-1 started...
Thread-3 started...
Thread-7 started...
Thread-5 started...
Thread-0 started...
```

```
Thread-8 started...
Thread-9 started...
Thread-2 ended.
Thread-0 ended.
Thread-4 ended.
Thread-3 ended.
Thread-8 ended.
Thread-1 ended.
Thread-9 ended.
Thread-7 ended.
Thread-6 ended.
Thread-5 ended.
```

As it is obvious from this output, the threads start and end in a random order.

Another way to create threads is by creating a class that implements the Runnable interface. This is useful when we want to extend another class, or, considering that the Runnable declares a single method, lambda expressions can be used too. Listing 5-47 shows the equivalent Runnable implementation of the RandomDurationThread.

Listing 5-47. Code Sample Declaring Threads with Random Execution Durations By Implementing the Runnable Interface

```java
package com.apress.bgn.five;

public class RandomDurationRunnable implements Runnable {
    @Override
    public void run() {
        System.out.println(Thread.currentThread().getName() + "
        started...");
        for (int i = 0; i < 10; ++i) {
            try {
                Thread.sleep(i * 10);
            } catch (InterruptedException e) {
                e.printStackTrace();
            }
        }
```

```
        System.out.println(Thread.currentThread().getName() + " ended.");
    }
}
```

Because we no longer have access to the name of the thread, to print it we must use another utility method called `Thread.currentThread()` to retrieve a reference to the current thread in execution so we can get its name.

The `Thread` class provides a constructor with a parameter of type `Runnable`, which means it can be called with any argument of a type that implements `Runnable`. Thus to create threads using our `RandomDurationRunnable` declared previously, code similar to the one in Listing 5-48 can be written.

Listing 5-48. Code Sample to Run Multiple Threads in Parallel Using a Class Implementing `Runnable`

```
package com.apress.bgn.five;

public class RunnableDemo {
    public static void main(String... args) {
        for (int i = 0; i < 10; ++i) {
            new Thread(new RandomDurationRunnable()).start();
        }
    }
}
```

Running the code in the previous listing produces an output just as random as the one in Listing 5-46.

It was previously mentioned that this particular case is a good candidate for using lambda expressions, because `Runnable` can be implemented on the spot. This means that the code in Listing 5-48 and Listing 5-47 can be combined as depicted in Listing 5-49.

Listing 5-49. Code Sample to Run Multiple Threads in Parallel Using Lambda Expressions

```
package com.apress.bgn.five;

import static java.lang.Thread.currentThread;
import static java.lang.Thread.sleep;
```

```java
public class LambdaThreadsDemo {
    public static void main(String... args) {
        for (int i = 0; i < 10; ++i) {
            new Thread(
                    //Runnable implemented on the spot
                    () -> {
                        System.out.println(currentThread().getName() + "
                        started...");
                        for (int j = 0; j < 10; ++j) {
                            try {
                                sleep(j * 10);
                            } catch (InterruptedException e) {
                                e.printStackTrace();
                            }
                        }
                        System.out.println(currentThread().getName() + "
                        ended.");
                    }).start();
        }
    }
}
```

Java provides thread management classes that can create and manage threads, so the developer mustn't declare the threads explicitly. The concurrency framework is a subject too advanced for this book, but if this section has made you so curious and you want to know more, you can have a look at the Oracle Concurrency tutorial here: `https://docs.oracle.com/javase/tutorial/essential/concurrency/index.html`.

Summary

In this chapter we learned how memory for a Java program is administered by the JVM and the basics of the most-used Java data types. A few important details that should remain with you from this chapter are listed here:

- There are two types of memory managed by the JVM: stack and heap.

- The difference between primitive and reference types.

- Primitive values are stored in the stack memory, and objects values are stored in the heap.

- There are eight primitive data types in Java: `boolean`, `char`, `short`, `byte`, `int`, `long`, `float`, `double`.

- References can only be of the super-type of an assigned object.

- The size of an array is defined when it is created and it cannot be changed afterward.

- In Java `String` instances are **immutable**, which means they cannot be changed once created.

- If calendar dates need to be handled, use the new DateTime API.

- `null` is useful and powerfull.

- Collections can group objects types together in tuples or key-value pairs.

- Concurrency in Java is fun in small doses.

Some examples in this chapter might seem complicated, but do not be discouraged. It is difficult to explain certain concepts without providing working code that you can execute, test, and even modify yourself. Unfortunately, this requires the use of concepts that will be introduced in later chapters (such as `for` and `if` statements). Just make a note of every concept that it is not clear now and the page number, and return to this chapter after you read about the concept in detail later in the book.

CHAPTER 6

Operators

The previous chapters have covered basic concepts of Java programming. You were taught how to organize your code, how your files should be named, and which data types you can use, depending on the problem you are trying to solve. You were taught how to declare fields, variables, and methods and how they were stored in memory, to help you design your solutions so the resource consumption will be optimal.

After declaring variables, in this chapter you will learn to combine them using operators. Most Java operators are the ones you know from math, but because programming involves other types than numeric, extra operators with specific purposes were added. In Table 6-1, all Java operators are listed with their category and their scope.

Table 6-1. *Java Escape Sequences*

Category	Operator	Scope
casting	*(type)*	Explicit type conversion.
unary, postfix	expr++, expr−	Post increment/decrement.
unary, prefix	++expr, −expr	Pre increment/decrement.
unary, logical	!	Negation.
unary, bitwise	~	Bitwise complement Performs a bit-by-bit reversal of an integer value.
multiplicative, binary	*, /, %	For numeric types: multiply, divide, divide and return remainder.
additive, binary	+, -	For numeric types: addition, substraction; "+" is used for String concatenation as well.

(continued)

279

© Iuliana Cosmina 2022
I. Cosmina, *Java 17 for Absolute Beginners*, https://doi.org/10.1007/978-1-4842-7080-6_6

Table 6-1. (*continued*)

Category	Operator	Scope
bit shifting, binary	>>, >>, >>>	For numeric types: multiply and divide by a power of two, signed and unsigned.
conditional, relational	`instanceof`	Test whether the object is an instance of the specified type (class or subclass or interface).
conditional, relational	==, !=, <, >, <=, >=	Equals, differs from, lesser than, greater than, less than or equals, greater than or equals.
AND, binary	&	Bitwise logical AND.
exclusive OR, binary	^	Bitewise logical XOR.
inclusive OR, binary	|	Bitewise logical OR.
conditional, logical AND	&&	Logical AND.
conditional, logical OR	||	Logical OR.
conditional, ternary	? :	Also called *the Elvis operator.*
assignment	=, +=, -=, *=, /= %=, &=, ^=, <<=,>>=, >>>= ,|=	Simple assignments, combined assignments.

Let's start this chapter with the most common operator in programming: the assignment operator, "=".

The Assignment Operator

The "=" assignment operator is obviously the most used in programming, as nothing can be done without it. Any variable that you create, regardless of the type, primitive or reference, has to be given a value at some point in the program. Setting a value using the assignment operator is quite simple: on the left side of the "=" operator you have the variable name and on the right it will be a value. The only condition for an assignment to work is that the value matches the type of the variable.

To test this operator you can play a little using jshell: just make sure you start it in verbose mode, so you can see the effect of your assignments. The statements executed for this chapter are shown in Listing 6-1.

Listing 6-1. jshell Play

```
jshell -v
|  Welcome to JShell -- Version 17-ea
|  For an introduction type: /help intro

jshell> int i = 0;
i ==> 0
|  created variable i : int

jshell> i = -4;
i ==> -4
|  assigned to i : int

jshell> String sample = "text";
sample ==> "text"
|  created variable sample : String

jshell> List<String> list = new ArrayList<>();
list ==> []
|  created variable list : List<String>

jshell> list = new LinkedList<>();
list ==> []
|  assigned to list : List<String>
```

In the previous example, we declared primitive and reference values and assigned and reassigned values to them. Assignment of values with types that mismatch the initial type is not permitted. In the code sample in Listing 6-2, we are trying to assign a text value to a variable that was previously declared as having the int type.

Listing 6-2. More jshell Play

```
jshell> i = -5;
i ==> -5
|  assigned to i : int

jshell> i = "you are not allowed";
|  Error:
|  incompatible types: java.lang.String cannot be converted to int
|  i = "you are not allowed";
|      ^--------------------^
```

Introduction of type inference in JDK 10 does not affect this, and the type of the variable will be inferred depending on the type of the first value assigned. Obviously, this means you cannot declare a variable using the var keyword without specifying an initial value. This obviously excludes the null value, as it has no type.

This can be forced though by casting the null value to the type we are interested in, as shown in Listing 6-3.

Listing 6-3. jshell Failed Variable Declaration

```
jshell> var j;
|  Error:
|  cannot infer type for local variable j
|    (cannot use 'var' on variable without initializer)
|  var j;
|  ^----^

jshell> var j = 5;
j ==> 5
|  created variable j : int

jshell> var sample2 = "bubulina";
sample2 ==> "bubulina"
|  created variable sample2 : String
```

```
// this does not work, obviously
jshell> var funny = null;
|  Error:
|  cannot infer type for local variable funny
|    (variable initializer is 'null')
|  var funny = null;
|  ^--------------^

// yes, this actually works !
jshell> var funny = (Integer) null;
funny ==> null
|  created variable funny : Integer
```

Explicit Type Conversion **(type)** and **instanceof**

These two operators are covered together because it is easier to provide code samples pretty similar to what you might need to write for real scenarios.

It was mentioned in the book before that it is better to keep the reference type as generic as possible to allow for changing of the concrete implementation without breaking the code. This is called **type polymorphism**. Type polymorphism is the provision of a single interface to entities of different **types** or the use of a single symbol to represent multiple different types.

Sometimes we might need to group objects together, but execute different code depending on their types. Remember the Performer hierarchy mentioned in the previous chapter? We're going to make use of these types here to show you how to use these operators. If you do not want to go back to the previous chapter to remember the hierarchy, in Figure 6-1 here it is again, but with a twist: an extra class named Graphician that implements interface Artist and extends class Human[1] was added to the hierarchy.

---

[1] The implementation of the new class is not relevant for this chapter so it won't be detailed here, but you can find it in the project attached to this book.

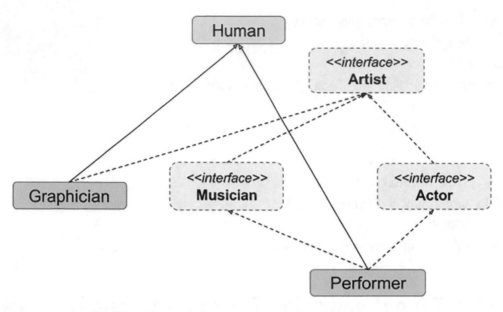

Figure 6-1. *The Human hierarchy*

In the following code sample, an object of type Musician and one of type Graphician are created and both are added into a list containing references of type Artist. We can do this because both types implement the interface Artist. The code in Listing 6-4 shows a few classes in this hierarchy being used to create objects added to the same list and then extracted from it, and having their type tested.

Listing 6-4. Code Sample Showing instanceof and (type) Operators

```
package com.apress.bgn.six;

import com.apress.bgn.four.classes.Gender;
import com.apress.bgn.four.hierarchy.*;

import java.util.ArrayList;
import java.util.List;

public class OperatorDemo {

    public static void main(String... args) {
        List<Artist> artists = new ArrayList<>();

        Musician john = new Performer("John", 40, 1.91f, Gender.MALE);
        List<String> songs = List.of("Gravity");
```

```
john.setSongs(songs);
artists.add(john);

Graphician diana = new Graphician("Diana", 23, 1.62f,
Gender.FEMALE, "MacOs");
artists.add(diana);

for (Artist artist : artists) {
    if (artist instanceof Musician) {          // (*)
        Musician musician = (Musician) artist; // (**)
        System.out.println("Songs: " + musician.getSongs());
    } else {
        System.out.println("Other Type: " + artist.getClass());
    }
}
}
```

The line marked with (*) shows how to use the instanceof operator. This operator is used to test whether the object is an instance of the specified type (class, superclass, or interface). It is used in writing conditions to decide which code block should be executed.

The line marked with (**) does an explicit conversion of a reference, also known as a **cast** operation. Since the instanceof operator helps figure out that the object the reference points to is of type Musician, we can now convert the reference to the proper type so methods of class Musician can be called.

Notice how the instanceof operator is used to test the type and then, to use the reference, an explicit conversion needs to be written. Starting with Java 14 the instanceof operator was enriched to include conversion which allows for a clearer and simpler syntax, as depicted in Listing 6-5.

Listing 6-5. Java 14 New instanceof Syntax

```
for (Artist artist : artists) {
    if (artist instanceof Musician musician) {
        System.out.println("Songs: " + musician.getSongs());
```

```
    } else {
        System.out.println("Other Type: " + artist.getClass());
    }
}
```

But what happens if an explicit conversion fails? For this we will try to convert the previously declared Graphician reference to Musician. The following line can be added to the previous code listing, and it won't stop the code from compiling.

```
Musician fake = (Musician) diana;
```

The Graphician class has no relation to the Musician type, so the code will not run. A special exception will be thrown in the console to tell you what was wrong. The error message printed in the console will be quite explicit and is depicted in the next log snippet.

```
Exception in thread "main" java.lang.ClassCastException: class com.apress
.bgn.six.Graphician cannot be cast to class com.apress.bgn.four.hierarchy
.Musician (com.apress.bgn.six.Graphician is in module chapter.six of
loader 'app'; com.apress.bgn.four.hierarchy.Musician is in module chapter
.four@1.0-SNAPSHOT of loader 'app')
    at chapter.six/com.apress.bgn.six.OperatorDemo.main
    (OperatorDemo.java:25)
```

The message clearly states that the two types are not compatible, and the package and module names are included.

Explicit conversion is not limited to reference types; it works for primitives too. In the previous chapter it was mentioned that any variable of a type with values in a smaller interval can be converted to a type with a bigger interval, without explicit conversion. The reverse is possible too, by using explicit conversion, but if the value is too big, bits will be lost and the value will be unexpected. Just look at the examples of conversions between byte and int depicted in Listing 6-6.

Listing 6-6. jshell Conversions Examples

```
jshell> byte b = 2;
b ==> 2
|   created variable b : byte
```

```
jshell> int i = 10;
i ==> 10
|   modified variable i : int
|      update overwrote variable i : int

jshell> i = b
i ==> 2
|   assigned to i : int

jshell> b = i
|   Error:  \\
|   incompatible types: possible lossy conversion from int to byte
|   b = i
|        ^

jshell> b = (byte) i
b ==> 2
|   assigned to b : byte

jshell> i = 300_000
i ==> 300000
|   assigned to i : int

jshell> b = (byte) i
b ==> -32  // oops! value outside of byte interval
|   assigned to b : byte
```

As a general rule, just use explicit conversion to widen the scope of a variable, not to narrow it, as narrowing it can lead to exceptions or loss of precision.

Numerical Operators

This section groups together all operators that are mostly used on numerical types. The numerical operators you know from math: +, -, /, * and comparators are found in programming too, but they can be combined to obtain different effects.

Unary Operators

Unary operators require only one operand, and they affect the variable they are applied to.

Incrementors and Decrementors

In Java (and some other programming languages) there are unary operator named incrementors(++) and decrementors(--). These operators are placed before or after a variable to increase or decrease its value by 1. They are usually used in loops as counters, to condition the termination of the loop. When they are placed before the variable, they are called **prefixed** and when are placed after it, they are called **postfixed**.

When they are prefixed, the operation is executed on the variable before the variable is used in the next statement. This means that in Listing 6-7, the value of the i variable will be incremented and then assigned to j.

Listing 6-7. Prefixed Incrementor Example

```
package com.apress.bgn.six;
public class UnaryOperatorsDemo {
    public static void main(String... args) {
        int i = 1;
        int j = ++i;
        System.out.println("j is " + j + ", i is " + i);
    }
}
```

The expected result of the preceding code is that j=2, because the value of the i variable is modified to 2, before it is assigned to j. Thus, the expected output is j is 2, i is 2.

When they are postfixed, the operation is executed on the variable, after the variable is used in the next statement. This means that in Listing 6-8, the value of i first assigned to j, and incremented after that.

Listing 6-8. Prefixed Incrementor Example

```
package com.apress.bgn.six;
public class UnaryOperatorsDemo {
    public static void main(String... args) {
        int i = 1;
        int j = i++;
        System.out.println("j is " + j + ", i is " + i);
    }
}
```

The expected result of the preceding code is that j=1, because the value of the i variable is modified to 2, after it is assigned to j. Thus, the expected output is j is 1, i is 2.

The decrementor operator can be used in the same way; the only effect is that the variable is decreased by 1.

Try to modify the UnaryOperatorsDemo to use the - - operator instead.

Sign Operators

Mathematical operator +(plus) can be used on a single operator to indicate that a number is positive (quite redundant and mostly never used). So basically:

```
int i = 3;
```

Is the same as:

```
int i = +3;
```

Mathematical operator can be used to declare negative numbers.

```
[jshell> int i = -3
i ==> -3
| created variable i : int
```

Or negate an expression:

```
[jshell> int i = -3
i ==> -3
| created variable i : int
```

```
[jshell> int j = - ( i + 4 )
j ==> -1
| created variable j : int
```

As you can see in the previous example, the result of the (i + 4) is 1, because i = -3, but because of the - in front of the parentheses, the final result that is assigned to the j variable is -1.

Negation Operator

There is one more unary operator, and its role is to negate variables. Operator "!" applies to boolean variables and is used to negate them. So true becomes false and false becomes true as shown in Listing 6-9.

Listing 6-9. Negating Boolean Values in jshell

```
[jshell> boolean t = true
t ==> true
| created variable t : boolean
[jshell> boolean f = !t
f ==> false
| created variable f : boolean
[jshell> boolean t2 = !f
t2 ==> true
| created variable t2 : boolean
```

Binary Operators

There are quite a few binary operators, and some of them can even be combined to perform new operations. This section starts with the ones you probably know from math.

The +(plus/addition/concatenation) Operator

"+" is used to add two numeric variables, as shown in the statements from Listing 6-10.

Listing 6-10. Adding Numeric Values in jshell

```
jshell> int i = 4
i ==> 4
|  created variable i : int
```

```
jshell> int j = 6
j ==> 6
|  created variable j : int

jshell> int k = i + j
k ==> 10
|  created variable k : int

jshell> int i = i + 2
i ==> 6
|  modified variable i : int
|    update overwrote variable i : int
```

The last statement int i = i + 2 has the effect of incrementing the value of i with 2 and as you can see, there is a little redundancy there. That statement can be written without mentioning i twice, because its effect is to increase the value of i with 2. This can be done by using the += operator, which is composed of the assignment and the addition operator. The optimal statement is i += 2.

The + operator can also be used to concatenate String instances, or String instances with other types. The JVM decides how to use the + operator depending on the context. For example, try to guess the output of the code in Listing 6-11 being executed.

Listing 6-11. Concatenating String and int Values

```
package com.apress.bgn.six;

public class ConcatenationDemo {
    public static void main(String... args) {
        int i1 = 0;
        int i2 = 1;
        int i3 = 2;
        System.out.println(i1 + i2 + i3);
        System.out.println("Result1 = " + (i1 + i2) + i3);
        System.out.println("Result2 = " + i1 + i2 + i3);
        System.out.println("Result3 = " + (i1 + i2 + i3));
    }
}
```

So how did the guessing go?

If the code executed, the following will be displayed in the console.

```
1. 3
2. Result1 = 12
3. Result2 = 012
4. Result3 = 3
```

The explanation for each line int this output is shown here:

- The result in line 1 can be explained as follows: all operands are of type `int`, so JVM adds the terms as `int` values, and the `System.out.println` method prints this result.

- The result in line 2 can be explained as follows: parentheses isolate the addition of two terms (`i1+i2`). Because of this, the JVM executes the addition between the parentheses as a normal addition between to `int` values. But after that, what we are left with is `"Result1 = "` + `1 + i3`, and this operation includes a `String` operand, which means the + operator must be used as a concatenation operator, since adding a number with a text value does not work otherwise.

- The result in line 3 explanation should be obvious at this time: we have three `int` operands, and a `String` operand, and thus the JVM decides that the context of the operation cannot be numeric, so concatenation is required.

- The result in line 4 can be explained in a similar way as the case in line 2. The parentheses ensure that the context of the operation is numeric, and thus the three operands are added.

This is a typical example to show how JVM decides the context for operations involving the + operator that you might find in other Java tutorials as well. But the int variables can be replaced with `float` or `double` and the behavior will be similar. Concatenation works with reference types too, since the any Java type is by default an extension of `Object` and thus can be converted to `String`, by calling its `toString()` method. Listing 6-12 shows the concatenation between a `String` and a `Performer` instance.

Listing 6-12. Concatenating String and Performer Values

```
package com.apress.bgn.six;

import com.apress.bgn.four.classes.Gender;
import com.apress.bgn.four.hierarchy.Musician;
import com.apress.bgn.four.hierarchy.Performer;

public class ReferenceConcatenationDemo {
    public static void main(String... args) {
        Musician john = new Performer("John", 43, 1.91f, Gender.MALE);

        System.out.println("Singer: " + john);
        // or convert explicitly
        System.out.println("Singer: " + john.toString());
    }
}
```

The -(minus) Operator

Mathematical operator -(minus) is used to subtract two variables or to subtract a value from a variable. In Listing 6-13 you can see how this operator and the -= operator, which is composed of the assignment, and the subtraction operator are used.

Listing 6-13. Subtracting Numeric Values in jshell

```
jshell> int i = 4
i ==> 4
|  created variable i : int

jshell> int j = 2
j ==> 2
|  created variable j : int

jshell> int k = i - j
k ==> 2
|  created variable k : int
```

```
jshell> int i = 4
i ==> 4
|  modified variable i : int
|    update overwrote variable i : int

jshell> i  = i - 3
i ==> 1
|  assigned to i : int

jshell> int i = 4
i ==> 4
|  modified variable i : int
|    update overwrote variable i : int

jshell> i -=3
$7 ==> 1
|  created scratch variable $7 : int
```

The *(multiply) Operator

The "*" (multiply) operator is used to multiply two variables or to multiply a value with a variable. It can be used in similar statements as "+" and -, and there is also composed operator "*=" that can be used to multiply the value of a variable and assign it on the spot. In Listing 6-14, you can see this operator in action.

Listing 6-14. Multiplying Numeric Values in jshell

```
jshell>  int i = 4
i ==> 4
|  created variable i : int

jshell> int j = 2
j ==> 2
|  created variable j : int

jshell> int k = i * j
k ==> 8
|  created variable k : int
```

```
jshell> int i = 4
i ==> 4
|  modified variable i : int
|    update overwrote variable i : int

jshell> i  = i * 3
i ==> 12
|  assigned to i : int

jshell> int i = 4
i ==> 4
|  modified variable i : int
|    update overwrote variable i : int

jshell>  i *= 3
$7 ==> 12
|  created scratch variable $7 : int
```

The /(divide) Operator

The "/"(divide) operator is used to divide two variables or to divide a value by a variable. It can be used in similar statements as "+" and "-", and there is a composed operator "/=" that can be used to divide the value of a variable and assign it on the spot.

The result of a division is named **quotient,** and it is assigned to the variable on the left side of the assignment operator ("="). When the operands are integers, the result is an integer too, and the remainder is discarded. In Listing 6-15, you can see this operator in action.

Listing 6-15. Divide Numeric Values in jshell

```
jshell> int i = 4
i ==> 4
|  created variable i : int

jshell> int j = 2
j ==> 2
|  created variable j : int
```

```
jshell> int k = i / j
k ==> 2
|   created variable k : int

jshell> int i = 4
i ==> 4
|   modified variable i : int
|     update overwrote variable i : int

jshell> int i = i / 3
i ==> 1
|   modified variable i : int
|     update overwrote variable i : int

jshell> int i = 4
i ==> 4
|   modified variable i : int
|     update overwrote variable i : int

jshell> i /= 3
$7 ==> 1
|   created scratch variable $7 : int
```

The %(modulus) Operator

"%" is also called the **modulus** operator and is used to divide two variables, but the result is the remainder of the division. The operation is called **modularization,** and there is also a composed operator "%=" that can be used to divide the value of a variable and assign the remainder on the spot. In Listing 6-16, you can see this operator in action.

Listing 6-16. Modulus Numeric Values in jshell

```
jshell> int i = 4
i ==> 4
|   created variable i : int

jshell> int j = 3
j ==> 3
|   created variable j : int
```

```
jshell> int k = i % j
k ==> 1
|  created variable k : int

jshell> int i = 4
i ==> 4
|  modified variable i : int
|     update overwrote variable i : int

jshell> i = i % 3
i ==> 1
|  assigned to i : int

jshell> int i = 4
i ==> 4
|  modified variable i : int
|     update overwrote variable i : int

jshell> i %= 3
$7 ==> 1
|  created scratch variable $7 : int
```

The modulus operator returns the remainder, but what happens when the operands are real numbers?

The short answer is that operations with floating point numbers are tricky. It depends on the digits after the decimal point, and the operand used for the division. Take a look at Listing 6-17.

Listing 6-17. Modulus Numeric Operations with Floating Point Numbers in jshell

```
jshell> double d = 5.28d
d ==> 5.28
|  created variable d : double

jshell> d / 2
$2 ==> 2.64
|  created scratch variable $2 : double
```

```
jshell> d % 2
$4 ==> 1.2800000000000002
|  created scratch variable $4 : double
```

The explanation for the previous result is loss of precision because of how floating-point numbers are represented internally.

Also, if the remainder is a real number with an infinite number of decimals after the decimal point, representing it is not possible, so some rounding is necessary. This is shown in Listing 6-18.

Listing 6-18. Loss of Precision in `jshell` for a Remainder with an Infinite Number of Decimals After the Decimal Point

```
jshell> float f = 1.9f
f ==> 1.9
|  created variable f : float

jshell> float g = 0.4f
g ==> 0.4
|  created variable g : float

jshell> float h = f % g
h ==> 0.29999995      // remainder
|  created variable h : float
```

The reminder returned in `jshell` is `0.29999995`, which can be rounded to `0.3` for some cases. But rounding can be dangerous when the data is used for sensitive operations, such as determining the volume of a tumour for a robot to operate on or the perfect trajectory for a rocket to be sent to Mars.

⚠ Rounding of floating-point numbers is problematic, because it causes a loss of precision.

The loss of precision when working with floating point numbers is not a Java problem, since operations with floating point numbers are supported according to the rules of the IEEE754[2] arithmetic.

If a project needs mathematical operations with a better precision, the `java.lang.Math` class provides methods for different types of rounding and other types of floating point number operations.

Relational Operations

In certain cases, when designing the solution for a problem, you need to introduce conditions to drive and control the execution flow. Conditions require the evaluation of a comparison between two terms using a **comparison** operator. In this section all comparison operators used in Java are described and code samples are be provided. Let's proceed.

The == Equals Operator

`"=="` tests equality of terms. Because in Java a single equals ("=") sign is used to assign values, the double equals was introduces to test equality and avoid confusion. This operator is very often used to control execution flows. Controlling execution flows is the topic of the following chapter, but to show how the `"=="` operator should be used, a few simple code samples involving control statements such as `if` and `for` are introduced in this chapter. In Listing 6-19, you can see an example of testing the `"=="` comparator in searching value 2 in an array. If the value is found, the index where it was found is printed in the console.

Listing 6-19. Example for Using the `"=="` Operator to Test a Value in an Array

```java
package com.apress.bgn.six;

public class ComparisonOperatorsDemo {
    public static void main(String... args) {
        int[] values = {1, 7, 9, 2, 6,};
        for (int i = 0; i < values.length; ++i) {
```

---

[2] A description of the IEEE Standard for Floating-Point Arithmetic can be found at Wikipedia, "IEEE 754," https://en.wikipedia.org/wiki/IEEE_754, accessed October 15, 2021.

```
    if (values[i] == 2) {
        System.out.println("Fount 2 at index: " + i);
    }
  }
 }
}
```

The condition in the marked line is evaluated, and the result is a boolean value. When the result is false, nothing is done, but if the result is true the index is printed. Because the result is of type boolean, if you make a mistake and use = instead of ==, the code will not compile.

⚠️ You just have to be extra careful when comparing boolean values. The code in Listing 5-20 compiles and runs, but it doesn't work as expected.

Listing 6-20. Example of an Unexpected Initialization of a Boolean Variable Instead of an Evaluation of Its Value

```java
package com.apress.bgn.six;

public class BadAssignementDemo {
    public static void main(String... args) {
        boolean testVal = false;

        if(testVal = true) {
            System.out.println("TestVal got initialized incorrectly!");
        } else {
            System.out.println("TestVal is false? " + (testVal == false));
        }
    }
}
```

The "==" sign works just fine for primitives. For reference types, you need to use the equals() method that was covered previously in the book at the beginning of **Chapter 5,** when explaining the difference between stack and heap memory.

The Other Comparison Operators

The other comparison operators work only on primitive types. Since there is not that much to say about each of them individually, this section covers them all.

- != tests inequality of terms. It is the opposite of the == operator. This operator also works on reference types, but it compares reference values instead the objects themselves, exactly as ==.

As an exercise, modify the example in Listing 6-19 to print a message when the array element value is different from 2.

- < and <= have the same purpose as the one you probably learned in math class. The first one (<) tests if the item on the left of the operator is less than the one on the right. The next one (<=) tests if the item on the left of the operator is less or equal to the one on the right. This operator cannot be used on reference types.

- > and >= have the same purpose as the one you probably learned in math class. The first one (>) tests if the item on the left of the operator is greater than the one on the right. The next one (>=) tests if the item on the left of the operator is greater or equal to the one on the right. This operator cannot be used on reference types.

Almost all numeric operators can be used on variables of different types, as they are automatically converted to the type that has a wider interval representation. The code in Listing 6-21 reflects a few situations, but in practice you might need to make even more extreme things that do not always abide to the common sense rules of programming, nor follow good practices. Just try to avoid doing that if you can, though!

Listing 6-21. Different Primitive Types Comparison Examples

```
package com.apress.bgn.six;

public class MixedOperationsDemo {
    public static void main(String... args) {
        byte b = 1;
        short s = 2;
        int i = 3;
        long l = 4;
```

```
        float f = 5;
        double d = 6;
        int ii = 6;

        double resd = l + d;
        long resl = s + 3;
        //etc

    if (b <= s) {
        System.out.println("byte val < short val");
    }
    if (i >= b) {
        System.out.println("int val >= byte val");
    }
    if (l > b) {
        System.out.println("long val > byte val");
    }
    if(d > i) {
        System.out.println("double val > byte val");
    }
    if(i == i) {
        System.out.println("double val == int val");
    }
    }
}
```

Just make sure if you are ever in a situation where you need to make shady things *(nonoptimal code constructs)* like these to test a lot and think your conversions well, especially when floating point types are involved. This is because (for example) the piece of code in Listing 6-22 can have quite unexpected results.

Listing 6-22. Unexpected Comparison Results with Floating Numbers

```
package com.apress.bgn.six;

public class BadDecimalPointDemo {
    public static void main(String... args) {
        float f1 = 2.2f;
```

```
        float f2 = 2.0f;
        float f3 = f1 * f2;
        if (f3 == 4.4) {
            System.out.println("expected float value of 4.4");
        } else {
            System.out.println("!! unexpected value of " + f3);
        }
    }
}
```

If you expect for the message *expected float value of 4.4* to be printed in the console, you will be quite surprised.

Any IEEE 754 floating point number representation will present issues, because some numbers that appear to have a fixed number of decimals in the decimal system actually have an infinite number of decimals in the binary system. So obviously we cannot compare floats and doubles using ==. One of the solutions that is easiest to implement is to use the compare method provided by the wrapper class, in this case Float.compare, as shown in Listing 6-23.

Listing 6-23. Correct Comparison Results with Float.compare

```
package com.apress.bgn.six;

public class GoodDecimalPointDemo {
    public static void main(String... args) {
        float f1 = 2.2f;
        float f2 = 2.0f;
        float f3 = f1 * f2;
        if (Float.compare(f3,4.4f) == 0) {
            System.out.println("expected float value of 4.4");
        } else {
            System.out.println("!!unexpected value of " + f3);
        }
    }
}
```

Using the previous example, the expected message is now printed in the console: *expected float value of 4.4.*

Bitwise Operators

In Java there are a few operators that are used at bit level to manipulate variables of numerical types. Bitwise operators are used to change individual bits in an operand. Bitwise operations are faster and usually use less CPU processing power because of the reduced use of resources. They are most useful in programming visual applications (e.g., games) where color, mouse clicks, and movements should be quickly determined to ensure a satisfactory experience.

Bitwise NOT

Operator ~ is sort of a binary **negator**. Is performs a bit-by-bit reversal of an integer value. This affects all bits used to represent the value. So if we declare

```
byte b1 = 10;
```

The binary representation is 00001010. The Integer class provides a method named toBinaryString(), which can be used to print the binary representation of the previously defined variable, but it won't print all the bits because the method doesn't know on how many bits we want the representation on. So we need to use a special String method to format the output. The method depicted in Listing 6-24 can be used to print the b1 value in binary on 8 bits, exactly as mentioned previously.

Listing 6-24. Method Used to Print Each Bit of a byte Value

```
public static void print8Bits(byte arg) {
    System.out.println("decimal:" + arg);
    String str =
        String.format("%8s", Integer.toBinaryString(arg)).replace(' ', '0');
    System.out.println("binary:" + str);
}
```

If we apply the ~ operator on the b1 value, the binary value resulted is 11110101. In case you did not notice, this value is out of the byte interval range, and is converted to int automatically. This is how negative numbers are represented internally in Java—according to the Java Language Specification, a representation called **2's complement**. (This will be covered toward the end of the chapter.)

So the result will be -11, as displayed by the code in Listing 6-25:

Listing 6-25. Testing the ~ Bitwise Negator Operator

```
package com.apress.bgn.six;
BitwiseDemo

public class BitwiseDemo {
    public static void main(String... args) {
        byte b1 = 10;
        print8Bits(b1);
        byte b2 = (byte) ~b1;
        print8Bits(b2);
    }

    // print8Bits method omitted
}
// execution result
decimal:10
binary:00001010
decimal:-11
binary:11111111111111111111111111110101
```

In the previous code listing, you probably noticed this statement byte b2 = (byte) ~b1 and you are expecting an explanation. The bitwise complement expression operator requires an operand that is convertible to a primitive integral type, or a compile time error occurs. Internally, Java uses one or more bytes to represent values. The ~ operator converts its operand to the int type, so it can use 32-bits when doing the complement operation; this is needed to avoid loss of precision. That is why an explicit cast to byte is needed in the previous example. And because everything is clearer with images, in Figure 6-2 you can see the effect of the ~ on the bits of the b1 variable, in parallel with its value.

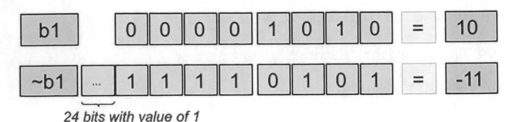

24 bits with value of 1

Figure 6-2. *The effect of the ~ negator operator on every bit of a byte value*

Bitwise AND

The bitwise AND operator is represented by & and it compares two numbers bit by bit. If the bits on identical positions have the value of 1, the bit in the result will be 1. The code sample in Listing 6-26 depicts the result of the & operator.

Listing 6-26. Testing the & Bitwise AND Operator

```
package com.apress.bgn.six;

public class BitwiseDemo {
    public static void main(String... args) {
        byte b1 = 117;  // 01110101
        print8Bits(b1);
        byte b2 = 95;   // 01011111
        print8Bits(b2);
        byte result  = (byte) (b1 & b2);  // 01010101
        print8Bits(result);
    }

    // print8Bits method omitted
}

// execution result
decimal:117
binary:01110101
decimal:95
binary:01011111
decimal:85
binary:01010101
```

The effect of the & operator can be seen better in Figure 6-3. The 01010101 value is the binary representation of decimal number 85.

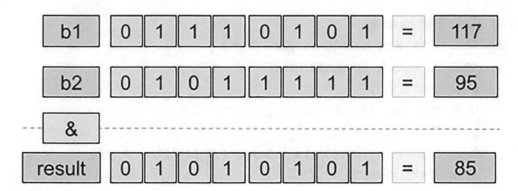

Figure 6-3. *The effect of the & operator on every bit*

Also, for practical reasons the composed operator &= is available in Java so that the bitwise AND operation can be done on the same variable to which the result is assigned, as shown in Listing 6-27. The advantage of this is that the result is automatically converted to byte, so no explicit conversion is required.

Listing 6-27. Testing the &= Bitwise AND Operator in jshell

```
jshell> byte b1 = 117
b1 ==> 117
|  created variable b1 : byte

jshell> b1 &= 95
$2 ==> 85
|  created scratch variable $2 : byte
```

Bitwise Inclusive OR

The bitwise OR operator (also known as inclusive OR) is represented by |(pipe) and it compares two numbers bit by bit, and if at least one of the bit is 1, the bit in the result is set to 1. The code in Listing 6-28 depicts the result of the | operator.

Listing 6-28. Testing the | Bitwise OR Operator

```
package com.apress.bgn.six;

public class BitwiseDemo {
    public static void main(String... args) {
        byte b1 = 117; // 01110101
        print8Bits(b1);
        byte b2 = 95; // 01011111
        print8Bits(b2);
        byte result  = (byte) (b1 | b2); // 01111111
        print8Bits(result);
    }

    // print8Bits method omitted
}

// execution result
decimal:117
binary:01110101
decimal:95
binary:01011111
decimal:127
binary:01111111
```

The effect of the | operator can be seen better in Figure 6-4. The 01111111 value is the binary representation of number 127.

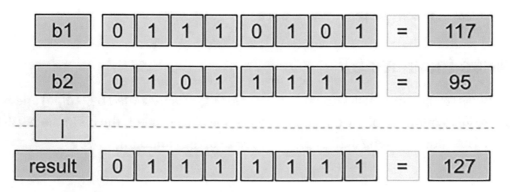

Figure 6-4. *The effect of the | operator on every bit*

Also, for practical reasons the composed operator |= is available in Java so that the bitwise inclusive OR operation can be done on the same variable to which the result is assigned to, as shown in Listing 6-29. The advantage of this is that the result is automatically converted to byte, so no explicit conversion is required.

Listing 6-29. Testing the |= Bitwise OR Operator in `jshell`

```
jshell>  byte b1 = 117
b1 ==> 117
|   created variable b1 : byte

jshell> b1 |= 95
$2 ==> 127
|   created scratch variable $2 : byte
```

Bitwise Exclusive OR

The bitwise exclusive OR or XOR operator is represented by ^ and it compares two numbers bit by bit, and if the values of the bits are different the bit in the result is set to 1. The code sample in Listing 6-30 depicts the result of the ^ operator.

Listing 6-30. Testing the ^ Bitwise XOR Operator

```
package com.apress.bgn.six;

public class BitwiseDemo {
    public static void main(String... args) {
        byte b1 = 117; // 01110101
        print8Bits(b1);
        byte b2 = 95; // 01011111
        print8Bits(b2);
        byte result  = (byte) (b1 ^ b2); // 00101010
        print8Bits(result);
    }

    // print8Bits method omitted
}
```

```
// execution result
decimal:117
binary:01110101
decimal:95
binary:01011111
decimal:42
binary:00101010
```

The effect of the ^ operator can be seen better in Figure 6-5. The 00101010 value is the binary representation of number 42.

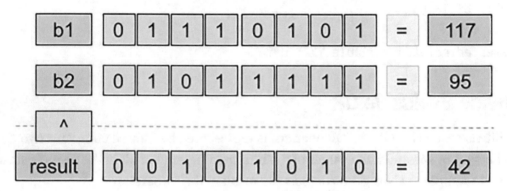

Figure 6-5. *The effect of the ^ operator on every bit*

Also, for practical reasons the composed operator ^= is available in Java so that the bitwise exclusive OR operation can be done on the same variable to which the result is assigned to, as shown in Listing 6-31. The advantage of this is that the result is automatically converted to byte, so no explicit conversion is required.

Listing 6-31. Testing the ^= Bitwise OR Operator in jshell

```
jshell> byte b1 = 117
b1 ==> 117
|  created variable b1 : byte

jshell> b1 ^= 95
$2 ==> 42
|  created scratch variable $2 : byte
```

Logical Operators

When designing conditions for controlling the flow of the execution of a program, sometimes there is need for complex conditions to be written: composed conditions constructed from multiple expression. There are four operators that can be used to construct complex conditions. Two of them are bitwise operations that can be reused &(AND) and |(OR), but they require evaluation of all the parts of the condition. The other operators &&(AND) and ||(OR) have the exact effect as the previously mentioned ones, but the difference is that they do not require evaluation of all the expression, which is why they are also called shortcut operators. To explain the behavior of these operators, there is a typical example that can be used.

In Listing 6-32 we declare a list of 10 terms (some of them null) and a method to generate a random index used to select an item from the list. Then we test the selected element from the list to see if it is not null and equal to an expected value. If both conditions are true, then a message is printed in the console. Let's check out the first example.

Listing 6-32. Testing the & Operator to Control the Execution Flow

```java
package com.apress.bgn.six;

import java.util.ArrayList;
import java.util.List;
import java.util.Random;

public class LogicalDemo {
    static List<String> terms = new ArrayList<>() {{
        add("Rose");
        add(null);
        add("River");
        add("Clara");
        add("Vastra");
        add("Psi");
        add("Cas");
        add(null);
        add("Nardhole");
        add("Strax");
    }};
```

```java
public static void main(String... args) {
    for (int i = 0; i < 20; ++i) {
        int index = getRandomIndex(terms.size());
        String term = terms.get(index);
        System.out.println("Generated index: " + index);
        if (term != null & term.equals("Rose")) {
            System.out.println("Rose was found");
        }
    }
}

private static int getRandomIndex(int listSize) {
    Random r = new Random();
    return r.nextInt(listSize);
}
}
```

To make sure we get the expected result, we repeat the operation of selecting a random element from the list 20 times. As you can probably notice in the marked line, the bitwise & is used to compose the two expressions. You would expect the text *"Rose was found"* to be printed in the console only if the value of the term variable is not null and is equal to Rose. But when the preceding code is run, this gets printed:

```
Exception in thread "main" java.lang.NullPointerException: Cannot invoke
"String.equals(Object)" because "term" is null
    at chapter.six/com.apress.bgn.six.LogicalDemo.main(LogicalDemo.java:56)
```

This is because both expressions are evaluated. But think about it! If the term variable is null, should we even evaluate its equality to Rose, especially since calling a method on a null object causes a runtime error? Obviously not, which is why the & is not suitable for this case. If the term is null it fails the first condition and there is no point in evaluating the second, so enter the && shortcut operator, which does exactly this. This works because when using the logical AND operator, if the first expression is evaluated to false, it does not really matter what the second expression is evaluated to; the result will always be false. So we can correct previous code sample to the one in Listing 6-33.

Listing 6-33. Testing the && Operator to Control the Execution Flow

```
package com.apress.bgn.six;

import java.util.ArrayList;
import java.util.List;
import java.util.Random;

public class LogicalDemo {
    static List<String> terms = new ArrayList<>() {{
        /* list elements omitted */}};

    public static void main(String... args) {
        for (int i = 0; i < 20; ++i) {
            int index = getRandomIndex(terms.size());
            String term = terms.get(index);
            System.out.println("Generated index: " + index);
            if (term != null && term.equals("Rose")) {
                System.out.println("Rose was found");
            }
        }
    }

    // getRandomIndex method omitted
}
```

When the code is executed, no exception will be thrown, because if the term is null the second expression is not evaluated. Thus, this code is technically more efficient because it evaluates less conditions, but it is also designed better because it avoids failures.

Now, let's modify the previous code sample and this time let's print a message if we find a null or if we find Rose. For this an OR operator is needed, so we'll try first to use the bitwise version (Listing 6-34):

Listing 6-34. Testing the && Operator to Control the Execution Flow

```
package com.apress.bgn.six;

import java.util.ArrayList;
import java.util.List;
import java.util.Random;
```

```java
public class LogicalDemo {
    static List<String> terms = new ArrayList<>() {{
        /* list elements omitted */}};

    public static void main(String... args) {
        for (int i = 0; i < 20; ++i) {
            int index = getRandomIndex(terms.size());
            String term = terms.get(index);
            System.out.println("Generated index: " + index);
            if (term == null | term.equals("Rose")) {
                System.out.println("null or Rose was found");
            }
        }
    }

    // getRandomIndex method omitted
}
```

If we run the previous code, a NullPointerException is thrown when the random index happens to match the index of a null element in the list. This is because the | operator requires both expression to be evaluated, so if term is null calling term. equals(..) will cause the exception to be thrown. So to make sure the code works as expected, the | must be replaced with ||, which shortcuts the condition and does not evaluate the second expression in it, except if the evaluation result of the first condition is false. This works because when using the logical OR operator, if the first expression evaluates to true, it does not really matter what the second expression gets evaluated to, the result will always be true. We'll leave that as an exercise for you.

Conditions can be made up from more than one expression and more then one operator, whether is && or ||. The code in Listing 6-35 depict a few complex conditions.

Listing 6-35. Complex Conditions Composed from Multiple Expressions

```java
package com.apress.bgn.six;

import java.util.ArrayList;
import java.util.List;
import java.util.Random;
```

```java
public class ComplexConditionsDemo {
    static List<String> terms = new ArrayList<>()  {{
        /* list elements omitted */}};

    public static void main(String... args) {
        for (int i = 0; i < 20; ++i) {
            int rnd = getRandomIndex(terms.size());
            if (rnd == 0 || rnd == 1 || rnd <= 3) {
                System.out.println(rnd + ": this works...");
            }
            if (rnd > 3 && rnd <=6 || rnd < 3 && rnd > 0) {
                System.out.println(rnd + ": this works too...");
            }
        }
    }

    private static int getRandomIndex(int listSize) {
        Random r = new Random();
        return r.nextInt(listSize);
    }
}
```

Beware of conditions that become too complex; make sure you cover that piece of code with a lot of tests. When writing complex conditions it is possible that some expressions become redundant, and IntelliJ IDEA and other smart editors display warnings of dead code on expressions that are redundant and unused to help the developer improve the design of the code.

Shift Operators

The **shift operators** are operators working at bit level. Because moving bits around is a sensitive operation, the requirement of these operands is for arguments to be integers. The operand to the left of the operator is the number that will be shifted, and the operand to the right of the operator is the number of bits that will be shifted.

There are three shift operators in Java, and each of them can be composed with the assignment operator to do the shifting and assign the result to the original variable on the spot. This section analyzes all shift operators with simple example and images to make things clear.

The << Shift Left Operator

As its name says, given a number represented in binary, this operator is used to shift bits to the left. The code in Listing 6-36 shows the << shift left operator in action.

Listing 6-36. Testing the << Operator

```
package com.apress.bgn.six;

public class ShiftDemo {
    public static void main(String... args) {
        byte b1 = 12; // 00001100
        print8Bits(b1);
        byte b2 = (byte) (b1 << 3); // 01100000
        print8Bits(b2);
    }

    // print8Bits method omitted
}

// execution result
decimal:12
binary:00001100
decimal:96
binary:01100000
```

When bits are shifted to the left, the remaining positions are filled with 0. Also, the number becomes bigger, and the new value is its old value multiplied with 2^N, where N is the second operand.

The code in Listing 6-36 can be written like as b1 <<= 3, using the composed operator, without the need to declare another variable. The result is 12 * 2^3. The bits are shifted as displayed in Figure 6-6.

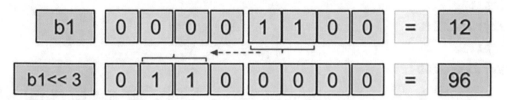

Figure 6-6. *The effect of the `<<` operator*

⚠️ Shifting operators promote byte values to int, to avoid loss of precision. In the previous code sample, the number of bits to shift was small enough to result in a value inside the byte type interval. That is why explicit conversion to byte works and the result is still valid. This is not always possible, as you will see further in this section.

The >> Signed Shift Right Operator

As its name says, given a number represented in binary, this operator is used to shift bits to the right. The code in Listing 6-37 shows the >> shift right operator in action.

Listing 6-37. Testing the >> Operator

```
package com.apress.bgn.six;

public class ShiftDemo {
    public static void main(String... args) {
        byte b1 = 96; // 01100000
        print8Bits(b1);
        byte b2 = (byte) (b1 >> 3); // 00001100
        print8Bits(b2);
    }
```

```
    // print8Bits method omitted
}

// execution result
decimal:96
binary:01100000
decimal:12
binary:00001100
```

When bits are shifted to the right, the remaining positions are filled with 0 if the number is positive. If the number is negative, the remaining positions are replaced with 1. This is done to preserve the sign of the number. Also, the number becomes smaller, and the new value is its old value divided by 2^N, where N is the second operand.

The code in Listing 6-37 can be written as b1 >>= 3, using the composed operator, without the need to declare another variable. The result is 12 * 2^3. The bits are shifted as displayed in Figure 6-7.

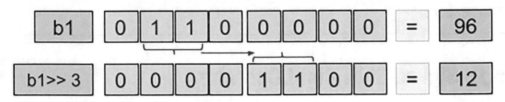

Figure 6-7. *The effect of the `>>` operator*

Figure 6-7 and Listing 6-37 both show the shift right operator applied to a positive number. When it comes to negative numbers things get complicated, because negative numbers are represented internally as 2's complement. What does this mean? It means that to get the representation of a negative number, we get the representation of the positive number, and we flip the bits and then add 1. Figure 6-8 depicts the process of obtaining the internal representation of -7, starting from the representation of 7.

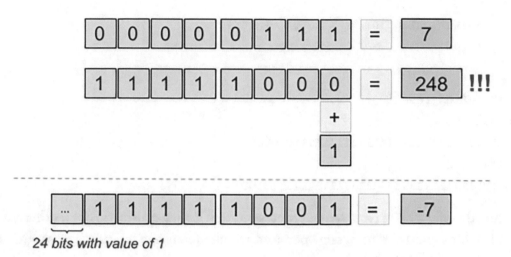

Figure 6-8. *Representing negative numbers internally in 2's complement*

The -7 value in 2's complement representation is out of the byte range, so internally negative numbers are represented as integers. This means that the print8Bits(..) method needs to be replaced with a version that prints all 32 bits of an int value. Listing 6-38 shows the >> unsigned shift right operator applied to a negative number.

Listing 6-38. Testing the >> Operator with Negative Numbers

```java
package com.apress.bgn.six;

public class ShiftDemo {
    public static void main(String... args) {
        System.out.println( " -- " );
        int i1 = -96;
        print32Bits(i1);
        int i2 =  i1 >> 3;
        print32Bits(i2);
    }

    public static void print32Bits(int arg) {
      System.out.println("decimal:" + arg);
      String str = arg > 0 ?
       String.format("%32s", Integer.toBinaryString(arg)).replace(' ', '0'):
       String.format("%32s", Integer.toBinaryString(arg)).replace(' ', '1');
```

```
        System.out.println("binary:" + str);
    }
}
```

```
// execution result
decimal:-96
binary:11111111111111111111111110100000
decimal:-12
binary:11111111111111111111111111110100
```

An advantage of 2's complement representation is that arithmetic operations are identical for signed and unsigned operators, which means half the circuitry is required in the cpu's arithmetic logic unit.

⚠ A peculiar thing about 2's complement representation is that `-Integer.MAX_VALUE` and `Integer.MIN_VALUE` are represented in the same way.

The >>> Unsigned Shift Right Operator

The >>> unsigned shift right operator is also called logical shift. Given a number represented in binary, this operator is used to shift bits to the right, and the remaining positions are replaced with 0, regardless of whether the value is positive or negative. This is why the result will always be a positive number.

Listing 6-39 shows the >>> unsigned shift right operator in action on a negative value.

Listing 6-39. Testing the >>> Operator with Negative Values

```
package com.apress.bgn.six;

public class ShiftDemo {
    public static void main(String... args) {
        int i1 = -16;
        print32Bits(i1);
        int i2 = i1 >>> 1;
        print32Bits(i2);
    }
```

```
    // print32Bits method omitted
}
// execution result
decimal:-16
binary:11111111111111111111111111110000
decimal:2147483640
binary:01111111111111111111111111111000
```

The code in Listing 6-39 can be written like as i1 >>>= 1, using the composed operator, without the need to declare another variable. The result is a very big positive number. The bits are shifted as displayed in Figure 6-9.

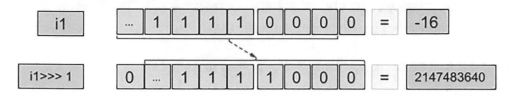

Figure 6-9. *The effect of the `>>>` operator on a negative value*

As with all bitwise operators, shifting operators promote char, byte, or short type variables to int, which is why an explicit conversion is necessary. As you have probably noticed, shifting bits on negative numbers is tricky; it is quite easy for the resulted number to be outside the interval of allowed values for a type, and an explicit conversion can lcad to loss of prccision or even serious anomalies. So why use them? Because they are fast. Just make sure to test intensively when using shifting operators.

The Elvis Operator

The Elvis Operator is the only ternary operator in Java. Its function is equivalent to a Java method that evaluates a condition and depending on the outcome, returns a value. The template of the Elvis operator is depicted here:

```
variable = (condition) ? val1 : val2
```

The method equivalent to this operator is depcited in Listing 6-40.

Listing 6-40. The Elvis Operator Equivalent Method

```
variable = methodName(..);

type methodName(..) {
    if (condition) {
        return val1;
    } else {
        return val2;
    }
}
```

The reason this operator is named the Elvis operator is because the question mark resembles Elvis Presley's hair, and the colon resembles the eyes. The Elvis operator can be easily tested in jshell, as depicted in Listing 6-41.

Listing 6-41. The Elvis Operator Being Tested in jshell

```
jshell> int a = 4
a ==> 4
|  created variable a : int

jshell> int result = a > 4 ? 3 : 1;
result ==> 1
|  created variable result : int

jshell> String a2 = "test"
a2 ==> "test"
|  created variable a2 : String

jshell> var a3 = a2.length() > 3 ? "hello" : "bye-bye"
a3 ==> "hello"
|  created variable a3 : String
```

This operator is quite practical when you have a simple `if` statement that contains only one expression per branch, because using this operator you can compact the whole thing in one expression, one line of code. Just make sure when using it that the readability of the code is improved. From a performance point of view, there is no difference between an `if` statement and the equivalent Elvis operator expression. Another advantage of using the Elvis operator is that the expression can be used to initialize a variable.

Summary

In this chapter we learned that:

- Java has a lot of operators, simple and composed.

- Bitwise operators are fast, but dangerous.

- Negative numbers are represented internally in 2's complement.

- The + operator does different things in different contexts.

- Java has a ternary operator that accepts three operands: a boolean expression and two objects of the same type. The result of the evaluation of the boolean expression decides which operand is the result of the statement.

The purpose of this chapter is just to make you familiar with all the operators that will be used throughout the book, to help you understand the provided solutions and even design and write your own.

CHAPTER 7

Controlling the Flow

The previous chapters have covered ways to create statements, and what operators to use depending on the operand types. Sometimes in the previous chapters elements of logic were added to make the code runnable for you, and this chapter is dedicated to explaining in detail how you can manipulate the execution of your code using fundamental programming conditional and repetitive statements. A solution, an algorithm can be represented using flow charts.

Most of the programming we did up to this chapter contains declaration and printing statements, simple one-step statements. Take a look at the piece of code in Listing 7-1.

Listing 7-1. Java Code Made of a Few Statements

```
package com.apress.bgn.seven;

public class Main {
    public static void main(String... args) {
        String text = "sample";
        System.out.println(text);
    }
}
```

If we were to design a flowchart for it, the schema would be simple and linear, no decision, and no repetition, as depicted in Figure 7-1.

© Iuliana Cosmina 2022
I. Cosmina, *Java 17 for Absolute Beginners*, https://doi.org/10.1007/978-1-4842-7080-6_7

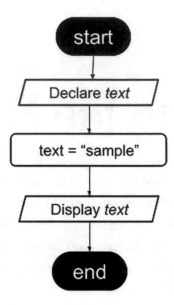

Figure 7-1. *Simple flowchart sample*

Resolving real-world problems often requires a more complicated logic than that, so more complicated statements are necessary. Before getting into that, let's describe the components of a flow chart, because we will make use of that a lot during this chapter. In Table 7-1 all flowchart elements are listed and their purpose is explained.

Table 7-1. *Flowchart Elements*

Shape	Name	Scope
▬	Terminal	Indicates beginning or end of a program, and contains a text relevant to its scope.
→	Flowline	Indicates the flow of the program and the order of operations.
▱	Input/Output	Indicates declaration of variables and outputting values.
▭	Process	Simple process statement: assignment, change of values, and so on.
◇/◁	Decision	Shows a conditional operation that will decide a certain path of execution.

(continued)

Table 7-1. (*continued*)

Shape	Name	Scope
⬜⋯⬜	Predefined Process	This element indicates a process defined elsewhere.
◯	On-page Connector	This element is usually labeled and indicates the continuation of the flow on the same page.
⬠	Off-page Connector	This element is usually labeled and indicates the continuation of the flow on a different page.
⬜	Comment (Or annotation)	When a flow or an element requires extra explanation, it is introduced using this type of element.

The flowchart elements presented in the previous table are pretty standard; you will probably find very similar elements used in any programming course or tutorial. After this consistent introduction, it is only fit to get into it.

`if-else` Statement

The most simple decisional flow statement in Java is the `if-else` statement (probably in other languages as well). You've probably seen the `if-else` statement being used in code samples for the previous chapters; there was no way to avoid it, because providing runnable code that encourages you to write your own is important. In this section the focus will be strictly on this type of statement.

Let's imagine this scenario: we run a Java program with a numeric argument provided by the user. If the number is even we print EVEN in the console; otherwise, we print ODD. The flowchart matching this scenario is depicted in Figure 7-2.

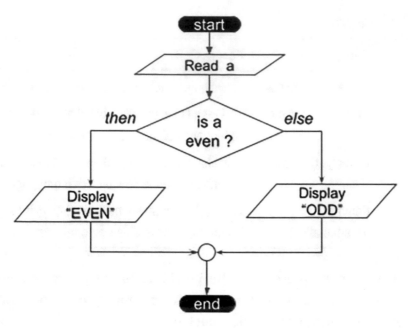

Figure 7-2. *if-else flowchart sample*

The condition is evaluated to a boolean value: if the result is true the statement corresponding to the if branch is executed, and if the result is false, the statement corresponding to the else branch is executed.

The Java code that implements the process described by this flowchart is depicted in Listing 7-2.

Listing 7-2. Java Code with if-else Statement

```java
package com.apress.bgn.seven;

public class IfFlowDemo {
    public static void main(String... args) {
        int a = Integer.parseInt(args[0]);

        if (a % 2 == 0) { // is even
            //Display EVEN
            System.out.println("EVEN");
        } else {
```

```
        //Display ODD
        System.out.println("ODD");
      }
    }
}
```

To run this class with different arguments you have to create an IntelliJ launcher and add your argument into the Program arguments text field, like explained at the beginning of this book. Each Java statement in the previous code snippet was paired with a comment matching the flowchart element, to make the implementation obvious. The fun thing is that not both branches of an if statement are mandatory, the else branch is not always necessary.

Sometimes you just want to print something if a value just matches a condition, and you are not interested in what happens otherwise. For example, given a user provided argument, we just want to print a message if the number is negative, but we are not interested to printing or doing anything else if the number is positive. The flowchart for that is depicted in Figure 7-3.

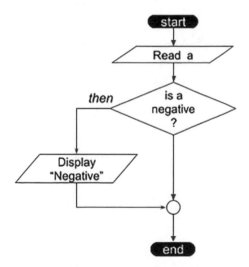

Figure 7-3. *if flowchart sample, missing the else branch*

And the Java code is depicted in Listing 7-3.

Listing 7-3. Java Code with `if` Statements

```java
package com.apress.bgn.seven;

public class IfFlowDemo {
    public static void main(String... args) {
        int a = Integer.parseInt(args[0]);

        if (a < 0) {
            System.out.println("Negative");
        }
    }
}
```

In the same way as the statement can be made simple, in the same way, if we need it, we can link more `if-else` statements together. Let's consider the following example: the user inserts a number from 1 to 12, and we have to print the season the month with that number corresponds to. How would the flowchart look like? Do you think Figure 7-4 fits the scenario?

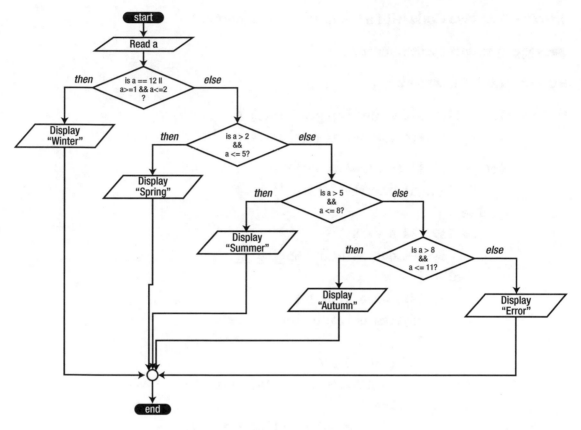

Figure 7-4. *Complex* `if-else` *flowchart sample*

---

❶   Also, when the code blocks for `if` or `else` contain is a single statement, the curly brackets are not mandatory, but most developers keep them for code clarity and to help IDEs indent the code properly.

Looks complicated, right? Wait until you see the code, which is depicted in Listing 7-4.

Listing 7-4. Java Code with a Lot of `if-else` Statements

```java
package com.apress.bgn.seven;

public class SeasonDemo {

    public static void main(String... args) {
        int a = Integer.parseInt(args[0]);

        if(a == 12 || (a>=1 && a<= 2)) {
            System.out.println("Winter");
        } else {
            if (a>2 && a <= 5 ) {
                System.out.println("Spring");
            } else {
                if (a>5 && a <= 8 ) {
                    System.out.println("Summer");
                } else {
                    if (a>8 && a <= 11 ) {
                        System.out.println("Autumn");
                    } else {
                        System.out.println("Error");
                    }
                }
            }
        }
    }
}
```

It looks ugly, right? Fortunately, Java provides a way to simplify it, especially because it really makes no sense having so many `else` blocks that only contain another `if` statement. The simplified code connects the `else` statements with the contained `if(s)` statements. The code ends up looking like Listing 7-5.

Listing 7-5. Java Code with Compacted `if-else` Statements

```java
package com.apress.bgn.seven;

public class CompactedSeasonDemo {
    public static void main(String... args) {
        int a = Integer.parseInt(args[0]);

        if (a == 12 || (a >= 1 && a <= 2)) {
            System.out.println("Winter");
        } else if (a > 2 && a <= 5) {
            System.out.println("Spring");
        } else if (a > 5 && a <= 8) {
            System.out.println("Summer");
        } else if (a > 8 && a <= 11) {
            System.out.println("Autumn");
        } else {
            System.out.println("Error");
        }
    }
}
```

Any argument provided by the user that is not the [1,12] that will cause the program to print Error. You can test it for yourself by modifying your IntelliJ Idea launcher. The elements to focus on are underlined in Figure 7-5.

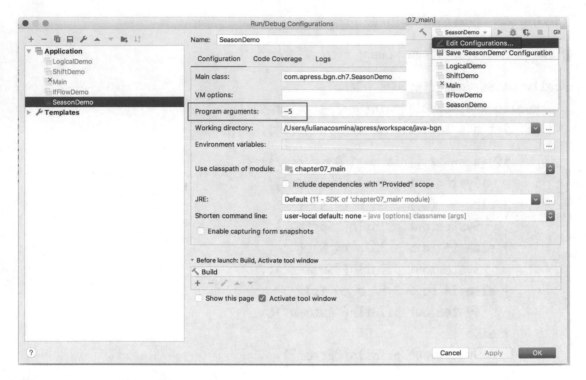

Figure 7-5. *IntelliJ IDEA launcher and parameters*

`switch` Statement

When a value requires different actions for a fixed set of values, the `if` might get more complex, and the more the set of values increases. In this case the more suitable statement is the `switch` statement. Let's look at the code in Listing 7-6 first, and then check what more can be improved.

Listing 7-6. Java Code with Detailed `switch` Statement

```
package com.apress.bgn.seven.switchst;

public class SeasonSwitchDemo {
    public static void main(String... args) {
        int a = Integer.parseInt(args[0]);

        var season = "";
        switch (a) {
```

```
case 1:
    season = "Winter";
    break;
case 2:
    season = "Winter";
    break;
case 3:
    season = "Spring";
    break;
case 4:
    season = "Spring";
    break;
case 5:
    season = "Spring";
    break;
case 6:
    season = "Summer";
    break;
case 7:
    season = "Summer";
    break;
case 8:
    season = "Summer";
    break;
case 9:
    season = "Autumn";
    break;
case 10:
    season = "Autumn";
    break;
case 11:
    season = "Autumn";
    break;
```

```
    case 12:
        season = "winter";
        break;
    default:
        System.out.println("Error");
    }
    System.out.println(season);
  }
}
```

That does not look very practical, at least not for this scenario. Before showing how the switch statement can be written differently, let's explain the structure and logic of it first. The general template of the switch statement is depicted in Listing 7-7:

Listing 7-7. General Template of the switch Statement

```
switch ([onvar]) {
    case [option]:
        [statement;]
        break;
    ...
    default:
        [statement;]
}
```

The terms in square brackets are detailed in the list here:

- [onvar] is the variable that is tested against the case statements to select a statement. It can be of any primitive type, enumerations, and starting with Java 7, String. Clearly the switch statement is not limited by conditions evaluated to boolean results, which allows for a lot of flexibility.

- case [option] is a value the variable mentioned previously is matched upon to make a decision regarding the statement to execute. A case, as the keyword states.

- [statement] is a statement or a group of statements to execute when [onvar] == [option]. Considering that there is no else branch, we have to make sure that only the statement(s) corresponding to the first match is executed, which is where the break; statement comes in. The break statement stops the current execution path and moves the execution point to the next statement outside the statement that contains it. Without break; statements the behavior switches to fall through and this means every case statement after the match is executed until a break; is found. We'll cover it more later in the chapter. Without it, after the first match, all subsequent cases are traversed and statements corresponding to them will be executed.

  If we execute the preceding program and we provide number 7 as an argument, the text *Summer* will be printed. But if the break statements for case 7 and 8 are commented, the output changes to *Autumn*.

- default [statement;] is a statement that is executed when no match on a case has been found; the default case does not need a break statement. If the previous program is run with any number outside the [1-12] interval, *Error* will be printed, because the default statement will be executed.

Now that you understand how switch works, let's see how we can reduce the previous statement. The months example is suitable here, because it can further be modified to show how the switch statement can be simplified, when a single statement should be executed for multiple cases. In our code, writing each assignment statement three times is a little redundant. There are also a lot of break; statements. There are two ways in which the previous switch statement be improved.

The first way of simplifying the switch statement in Listing 7-6 is by grouping together the cases that return the same value, as shown in Listing 7-8.

Listing 7-8. Simplified switch Statement

```java
package com.apress.bgn.seven.switchst;

public class SimplifiedSwitchDemo {
    public static void main(String... args) {
        int a = Integer.parseInt(args[0]);

        var season = "";
        switch (a) {
            case 1:
            case 2:
            case 12:
                season = "winter";
                break;
            case 3:
            case 4:
            case 5:
                season = "Spring";
                break;
            case 6:
            case 7:
            case 8:
                season = "Summer";
                break;
            case 9:
            case 10:
            case 11:
                season = "Autumn";
                break;
            default:
                System.out.println("Error");
        }
        System.out.println(season);
    }
}
```

The grouping in this case represents the alignment of the cases that require the same statement to be executed. This still looks a little weird, but it reduces the statement repetition a little. The behavior in the previous case is possible because each `case` without a `break` statement is followed by the next `case` statement.

The second way is to use a `switch` expression introduced in Java 12. The `switch` returns the season directly instead of storing it into a variable, and this allows for a simpler syntax, as depicted in Listing 7-9.

Listing 7-9. switch Expression Example

```
package com.apress.bgn.seven.switchst;

public class ExpessionSwitchDemo {
    public static void main(String... args) {
        int a = Integer.parseInt(args[0]);

        String season = switch (a) {
            case 1 -> "Winter";
            case 2 -> "Winter";
            case 3 -> "Spring";
            case 4 -> "Spring";
            case 5 -> "Spring";
            case 6 -> "Summer";
            case 7 -> "Summer";
            case 8 -> "Summer";
            case 9 -> "Autumn";
            case 10 -> "Autumn";
            case 11 -> "Autumn";
            case 12 -> "winter";
            default -> "Error";
        };
        System.out.println(season);
    }
}
```

The switch expression was introduced as a way to treat a switch statement as an expression, evaluate it to a single value, and thus use it in statements. The switch expression does not require break; statements to prevent fall through. When blocks of code are executed following a match with a case value, the value is returned using the yield statement, introduced in Java 13.

The code in Listing 7-10 shows a different version of the previous switch expression, where case values that require the same result are grouped and extra System.out.println(..) is added to show the yield usage. The returned value is printed directly by the System.out.println(..) that encloses the switch expression.

Listing 7-10. switch Expression Example Using yield Statements

```
package com.apress.bgn.seven.switchst;

public class AnotherSwitchExpressionDemo {
    public static void main(String... args) {
        int a = Integer.parseInt(args[0]);

        System.out.println( switch (a) {
            case 1, 2, 12 -> {
                System.out.println("One of 1,2,12 is tested.");
                yield "Winter";
            }
            case 3,4,5 -> {
                System.out.println("One of 3,4,5 is tested.");
                yield "Spring";
            }
            case 6,7,8 -> {
                System.out.println("One of 6,7,8 is tested.");
                yield "Summer";
            }
            case 9,10,11 -> {
                System.out.println("One of 9,10,11 is tested.");
                yield "Autumn";
            }
```

```
            default ->
                throw new IllegalStateException("Unexpected value");
        });
    }
}
```

In Java 7, the switch statement started supporting String values. The main problem with switch supporting String values is that there is always a possibility of unexpected behavior, because the equals(..) method is used to find a match and obviously, the method is case-sensitive. The previous example is modified to ask the user for a text representing the month. The switch statement is used to decide the season to print and unless the text in case options matches the text introduced by the user exactly, the text printed is *Error*. Also, since the switch expression was mentioned, the code changes to the one in Listing 7-11.

Listing 7-11. switch Statement Using String Values

```
package com.apress.bgn.seven.switchst;

public class StringSwitchSeasonDemo {
    public static void main(String... args) {
        //Read a
        String a = args[0];
        var season = "";
        switch (a) {
            case "january", "february", "december" -> season = "winter";
            case "march", "april", "may" -> season = "Spring";
            case "june", "july", "august" -> season = "Summer";
            case "september", "october", "november" -> season = "Autumn";
            default -> System.out.println("Error");
        }
        System.out.println(season);
    }
}
```

If we run the previous program with argument *january*, winter will be printed in the console. If we run it with *January* or null, *Error* will be printed in the console.

Before support for `String` value, `switch` statements supported enum values as well. This is practical when the values are grouped into a fixed set, such as the names of the months in a year. By using enums, support for `String` values can be achieved. The user introduces the month as a text value. This value is converted to upper case and used to extract the corresponding enum value. This allows for support of `String` values that are not case sensitive in a `switch` statement. The code in Listing 7-12 shows such an implementation.

Listing 7-12. switch Statement Using Enums Values

```
package com.apress.bgn.seven.switchst;

public class EnumSwitchDemo {

    enum Month {
        JANUARY, FEBRUARY, MARCH, APRIL, MAY, JUNE, JULY, AUGUST,
        SEPTEMBER, OCTOBER, NOVEMBER, DECEMBER
    }

    public static void main(String... args) {
        //Read a
        String a = args[0];
        try {
            Month month = Month.valueOf(a.toUpperCase());
            var season = "";
            switch (month) {
                case JANUARY:
                case FEBRUARY:
                case DECEMBER:
                    season = "Winter";
                    break;
                case MARCH:
                case APRIL:
                case MAY:
                    season = "Spring";
                    break;
                case JUNE:
                case JULY:
```

```
            case AUGUST:
                season = "Summer";
                break;
            case SEPTEMBER:
            case OCTOBER:
            case NOVEMBER:
                season = "Autumn";
                break;
        }
        System.out.println(season);
    } catch(IllegalArgumentException iae) {
        System.out.println("Unrecognized enum value: " + a);
    }
  }
}
```

Notice how using enums, the same season is returned for *january*, *January*, *JANuary*, and so on. Also, no `default` option is needed, because an exception is thrown if an enum value cannot be found matching the user provided data.

This is all that can be said about the switch statement. In practice, depending on the solution you are trying to develop, you might decide to use a combination of `if` and `switch` statements. Unfortunately, because of its peculiar logic and its flexible number of options, it is difficult to draw a flowchart for the `switch` statement, but nevertheless I've tried, and it's depicted in Figure 7-6.

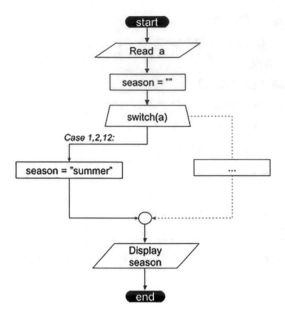

Figure 7-6. *The* switch *statement flowchart*

Looping Statements

Sometimes in programming, we need repetitive steps that involve the same variables. To write the same statement over and over again to get the job done would be ridiculous. Let's take the example of sorting an array of integer values. The most known algorithm to do this, and the one that is taught first in programming courses because it is simple, is called *Bubble Sort*. The algorithm compares the elements of an array two by two, and if they are not in the correct order, it swaps them. It goes over the array again and again until no more swaps are needed. The effects of the algorithm are depicted in Figure 7-7.

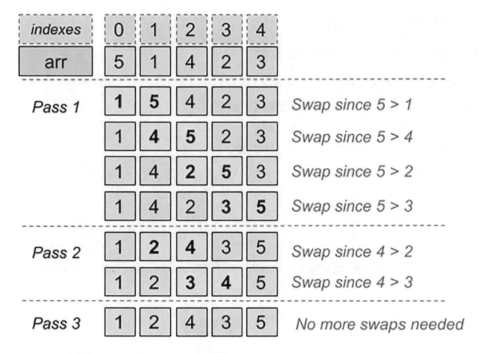

Figure 7-7. *Bubble sort phases and effect*

This algorithm performs two types of loops: one iterates each element of the array using indexes. This traversal is repeated until no swaps are necessary. In Java this algorithm can be written in more than one way using different looping statements. But we'll get there; let's take it slow.

There are three types of looping statements in Java:

- `for` statement
- `while` statement
- `do-while` statement

The `for` looping statement is the most used, but `while` and `do-while` have their uses as well.

for Statement

For is recommended for iterating on objects like array and collections that can be counted. For example, traversing an array and printing each one of its values is as simple as depicted in Listing 7-13.

Listing 7-13. Simple for Loop

```java
package com.apress.bgn.seven.forloop;

public class ForLoopDemo {
    public static void main(String... args) {
        int arr[] = {5, 1, 4, 2, 3};
        for (int i = 0; i < arr.length; ++i) {
            System.out.println("arr[" + i + "] = " + arr[i]);
        }
    }
}
```

Based on the previous example, a flowchart for the for statement can be drawn, depicted as in Figure 7-8.

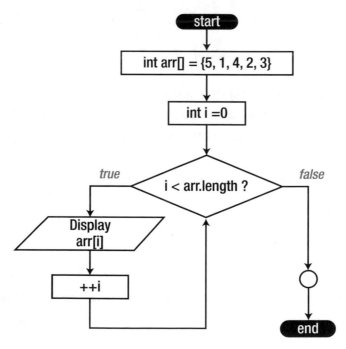

Figure 7-8. *The for statement flowchart*

The code snippet in Listing 7-14 depicts the for loop template:

Listing 7-14. The for Loop Template

```
for ([int_expr]; [condition];[step]){
    [code_block]
}
```

Each of the terms between square brackets have a specific purpose that is explained in the following list:

- [init_expr] is the initialization expression that is used to set the initial value of the counter used by this loop. It ends with ; and is not mandatory, as the declaration initialization can be done outside the statement, especially if we are interested in using the counter variable later in the code and outside the statement. The preceding code can be very well written as in Listing 7-15:

Listing 7-15. The for Loop with Termination Condition and Counter Modification Expression

```
package com.apress.bgn.seven.forloop;

public class AnotherForLoopDemo {
    public static void main(String... args) {
        int arr[] = {5, 1, 4, 2, 3};
        int i = 0;
        for (; i < arr.length; ++i) {
            System.out.println("arr[" + i + "] = " + arr[i]);
        }
        System.out.println("Loop exited with index: " + i);
    }
}
```

- [condition] is the termination condition of the loop; as long as this condition is evaluated to true, the loop will continue executing. The condition ends with ; and funny enough it is not mandatory either, as the termination condition can be placed inside the code to be executed repeatedly by the loop. So the preceding code can be modified further and be written as in Listing 7-16:

Listing 7-16. The for Loop with Only Counter Modification Statement

```
package com.apress.bgn.seven.forloop;

public class AndAnotherForLoopDemo {
    public static void main(String... args) {
        int arr[] = {5, 1, 4, 2, 3};
        int i = 0;
        for (; ; ++i) {
            if (i >= arr.length) {
                break;
            }
            System.out.println("arr[" + i + "] = " + arr[i]);
        }
        System.out.println("Loop exited with index: " + i);
    }
}
```

- [step] is the step expression or increment, this is the expression that increases the counter on every step of the loop. Being the last term, it does not end in ;. As you probably already expected, it is not mandatory either, as nothing stops the developer from manipulating the counter inside the code block. So the preceding code can also be written as in Listing 7-17:

Listing 7-17. The for Loop with No Initialization, Condition, or Counter Modification Expression

```
package com.apress.bgn.seven.forloop;

public class YeyAnotherForLoopDemo {
    public static void main(String... args) {
        int arr[] = {5, 1, 4, 2, 3};
        int i = 0;
        for (; ;) {
            if (i >= arr.length) {
                break;
            }
```

```
            System.out.println("arr[" + i + "] = " + arr[i]);
            ++i;
        }
        System.out.println("Loop exited with index: " + i);
    }
}
```

The modification of the counter does not even have to be done inside the step expression; it can be done in the termination condition. The initialization expression and the termination condition must be modified accordingly to still fit the purpose. The code depicted in Listing 7-18 has the same effect as all samples before it.

Listing 7-18. The `for` Loop with Counter Modification in Termination Condition

```
package com.apress.bgn.seven.forloop;

public class LastForLoopDemo {
    public static void main(String... args) {
        int arr[] = {5, 1, 4, 2, 3};
        int i;
        for (i = -1; i++ < arr.length -1;) {
            System.out.println("arr[" + i + "] = " + arr[i]);
        }
        System.out.println("Loop exited with index: " + i);
    }
}
```

You should also know that the step expression does not really have to be an incrementation. It can be any expression that modifies the value of the counter. Instead of `++i` or `i++`, you can use `i= i+1`, or `i=i+3`, or even decrementation, if the array or collection is traversed starting with a bigger index toward a lower one. Any mathematical operations that keep the counter within the boundaries of the type and within the collection boundaries can be used safely.

- [code_block] is a block of code executed repeatedly in every step of the loop. If there is no exit condition within this code, this block of code will be executed by as many times as the counter passes the termination condition.

> ❶ When the code block contains a single statement the curly brackets are not mandatory, but most developers keep them for code clarity and to help IDEs indent the code properly.
>
> ⚠ Since it was mentioned that the initialization expression, the termination condition, and the iteration expression are optional, this means the following is a valid for statement:
>
> ```
> for ( ; ; ) {
>     \\ statement(s) here
> }
> ```
>
> Just be careful when using the for statement like that. The code block must contain a termination condition to avoid an **infinite loop**.

This is the basic form of the for looping statement, but in Java there are other ways to iterate a group of values. Let's say that instead of an array we have to iterate over a list, as depicted in Listing 7-19.

Listing 7-19. The for Loop Over a List

```java
package com.apress.bgn.seven.forloop;

import java.util.List;

public class ListLoopDemo {
    public static void main(String... args) {
        List<Integer> list = List.of(5, 1, 4, 2, 3);
        for (int j = 0; j < list.size(); ++j) {
            System.out.println("list[" + j + "] = " + list.get(j));
        }
    }
}
```

The code seems somehow impractical, and that is why List<E> instances can be traversed with a different type of for statement that was known as forEach until Java 8. You will see immediately why, but first let's see the forEach in action in Listing 7-20.

Listing 7-20. The forEach Loop Over a List<E>

```java
package com.apress.bgn.seven.forloop;

import java.util.List;

public class ForEachLoopDemo {
    public static void main(String... args) {
        List<Integer> list = List.of(5, 1, 4, 2, 3);
        for (Integer item : list) {
            System.out.println(item);
        }
    }
}
```

This type of for statement is also called as having enhanced syntax and executes the code block for each item in the collection used in its expression. This means that it works on any implementation of Collection<E> interface, and it works on arrays too. So the code given as example until now can also be written as depicted in Listing 7-21.

Listing 7-21. The forEach Loop Over an Array

```java
package com.apress.bgn.seven.forloop;

import java.util.List;

public class ForLoopDemo {
    public static void main(String... args) {
        int arr[] = {5, 1, 4, 2, 3};
        for (int item : arr) {
            System.out.println(item);
        }
    }
}
```

Clearly the best part in this case is that we no longer need a termination condition or counter at all. Starting with Java 8, the name forEach can no longer be used for the for statement with enhanced syntax, because the forEach default method was added to all Collection<E> implementations. Combine that with lambda expressions, and the code to print the elements of a list becomes the one in Listing 7-22.

Listing 7-22. The forEach Method Used to Loop Over a List<E>

```java
package com.apress.bgn.seven.forloop;

import java.util.List;

public class ForLoopDemo {
    public static void main(String... args) {
        List<Integer> list = List.of(5, 1, 4, 2, 3);
        list.forEach(item -> System.out.println(item));
        //or
        list.forEach(System.out::println);
    }
}
```

Pretty neat, right? But wait, there's more: it works on arrays too, but a small conversion to a suitable implementation of java.util.stream.BaseStream is necessary first. This is provided by the Arrays utility class, which was enriched in Java 8 with methods to support lambda expressions. So yes, the code with the arr array written so far can be written starting Java 8 as shown in Listing 7-23.

Listing 7-23. The forEach Method Used to Loop Over an Array

```java
package com.apress.bgn.seven.forloop;

import java.util.List;

public class ForLoopDemo {
    public static void main(String... args) {
        int arr[] = {5, 1, 4, 2, 3};
        Arrays.stream(arr).forEach(System.out::println);
    }
}
```

In Java 17, all the preceding examples will compile and will execute just fine, so use whatever syntax you prefer most when writing your solutions.

while Statement

The while statement is different from the for statement. There is not a fixed number of steps that have to be executed, so a counter is not always needed. The number of repetitions a while statement executes depends only on how many times the continuation condition that controls this number is evaluated to true. The generic template for this statement is depicted in Listing 7-24.

Listing 7-24. The while Statement Template

```
while ([eval(condition)] == true) {
    [code_block]
}
```

A while statement does not really require an initialization statement either, but if needed it can be inside the while code block, or outside it. The while statement can replace the for statement, but the advantage of the for statement is that it encapsulates the initialization, the termination condition, and the modification of the counter in a single block so that it is more concise. The array traversal code sample can be rewritten using the while statement. The code is depicted in Listing 7-25:

Listing 7-25. The while Statement Used to Loop Over an Array

```java
package com.apress.bgn.seven.whileloop;

public class WhileLoopDemo {
    public static void main(String... args) {
        int arr[] = {5, 1, 4, 2, 3};
        int i = 0;
        while(i < arr.length) {
            System.out.println("arr[" + i + "] = " + arr[i]);
            ++i;
        }
    }
}
```

As you can see, the declaration and initialization of the counter variable int i = 0; is done outside the while code block. The incrementation of the counter is done inside the code block to be repeated. At this point, if we design the flowchart for this scenario, it will look the same as the one for the for statement depicted in Figure 7-8. As incredible as it sounds, the [condition] is not mandatory either as it can be replaced directly with true, but in this case you have to make sure there is an exit condition inside the block of code that will definitely be executed, otherwise the execution will most likely end with an error, since the JVM will not allow an infinite loop. This condition must be placed at the beginning of the block of code, to prevent the execution of the useful logic in a situation where it shouldn't be. For our simple example, clearly we do not want to call System.out. println for an element with an index outside the array range, as depicted in Listing 7-26.

Listing 7-26. The while Statement Used to Loop Over an Array, Without a Continuation Expression

```java
package com.apress.bgn.seven.whileloop;

public class AnotherLoopDemo {
    public static void main(String... args) {
        int arr[] = {5, 1, 4, 2, 3};
        int i=0;
        while(true){
            if (i >= arr.length) {
                break;
            }
            System.out.println("arr[" + i + "] = " + arr[i]);
            ++i;
        }
    }
}
```

The while statement is best used when we are working with a resource that is not always online. Let's say we are using a remote database for our application that is in a network that is unstable. Instead of giving up trying to save our data after the first timeout, we could try until we succeed, right? This is being done by using a while statement, which will keep trying to initialize a connection object in its code block. The code looks roughly as depicted in Listing 7-27.

Listing 7-27. The while Statement Used to Repeatedly Try to Obtain a Database Connection

```java
package com.apress.bgn.seven.whileloop;

import java.sql.*;

public class WhileConnectionTester {
    public static void main(String... args) throws Exception {
        Connection con = null;
        while (con == null) {
            try {
                Class.forName("com.mysql.cj.jdbc.Driver");
                con = DriverManager.getConnection(
                        "jdbc:mysql://localhost:3306/mysql",
                        "root", "mypass");
            } catch (Exception e) {
                System.out.println("Connection refused. Retrying in 5
                seconds ...");
                Thread.sleep(5000);
            }
        }
        // con != null, do something
        Statement stmt = con.createStatement();
        ResultSet rs = stmt.executeQuery("select * from user");
        while (rs.next()) {
            System.out.println(rs.getString(1) + " " + rs.getString(2));
        }
        con.close();
    }
}
```

The problem with this code is that will run forever. If we want to give up trying after a certain time, we have to introduce a variable counting the number of tries and exit the loop using a break; statement, as shown in Listing 7-28.

Listing 7-28. The while Statement Used to Repeatedly Try to Obtain a Database Connection Until the Number of Tries Expires

```java
package com.apress.bgn.seven.whileloop;

import java.sql.*;

public class AnotherWhileConnectionTester {
    public static final int MAX_TRIES = 10;

    public static void main(String... args) throws Exception {
        int cntTries = 0;
        Connection con = null;
        while (con == null && cntTries < MAX_TRIES) {
            try {
                Class.forName("com.mysql.cj.jdbc.Driver");
                con = DriverManager.getConnection(
                        "jdbc:mysql://localhost:3306/mysql",
                        "root", "mypass");
            } catch (Exception e) {
                ++cntTries;
                System.out.println("Connection refused. Retrying in 5
                seconds ...");
                Thread.sleep(5000);
            }
        }
        if (con != null) {
            // con != null, do something
            Statement stmt = con.createStatement();
            ResultSet rs = stmt.executeQuery("select * from user");
            while (rs.next()) {
                System.out.println(rs.getString(1) + " " +
                rs.getString(2));
            }
            con.close();
```

```
        } else {
            System.out.println("Could not connect!");
        }
    }
}
```

---

❶ As a rule of thumb, always make sure there is an exit condition when using looping statements.

Since we've now covered all the statements needed to implement the Bubble sort algorithm depicted in Figure 7-7, let's see what the code looks like. Be aware that this algorithm can be written in many ways, but the following code best matches the explanation provided earlier. So while there are elements in the array that are not in the proper order, the array is traversed again and again and adjacent elements are swapped to fit the desired order—ascending, in this case. The simplest version of the Bubble sort algorithm is depicted in Listing 7-29.

Listing 7-29. The Simplest Version of the Bubble sort Algorithm

```java
package com.apress.bgn.seven;

import java.util.Arrays;

public class BubbleSortDemo {
    public static final int arr[] = {5, 1, 4, 2, 3};

    public static void main(String... args) {
        boolean swapped = true;
        while (swapped) {
            swapped = false;
            for (int i = 0; i < arr.length - 1; ++i) {
                if (arr[i] > arr[i + 1]) {
                    int temp = arr[i];
                    arr[i] = arr[i + 1];
                    arr[i + 1] = temp;
                    swapped = true;
                }
```

```
        }
    }
    Arrays.stream(arr).forEach(System.out::println);
  }
}
```

When run, the previous code swaps elements of the arr array until they are all in ascending order, so the last line in the previous code prints the modified arr:

```
1
2
3
4
5
```

do-while Statement

The do-while statement is similar to the while statement, with one difference: the continuation condition is evaluated after executing the code block. This causes the code block to be executed at least once, which is useful to show a menu, for example, unless there is a condition embedded in it that prevents it. The generic template for this statement is depicted in the Listing 7-30.

Listing 7-30. The do-while Statement Template

```
do {
    [code_block]
} while ([eval(condition)] == true)
```

Most times statements while and do-while can be easily interchanged, and with minimum or no changes of the logic of the code block. For example, traversing an array and printing the values of its elements can be written using do-while as well, without changing the code block at all. In Figure 7-9 you can see the two implementations side by side, the while on the left and do-while on the right.

```
  WhileLoopDemo.java ×                                              DoWhileDemo.java ×
 1   /.../                                               ☒   1   /.../
28   package com.apress.bgn.ch7;                            28   package com.apress.bgn.ch7;
29                                                          29
30   /**                                                    30   /**
31    * @author Iuliana Cosmina                             31    * @author Iuliana Cosmina
32    * since 1.0                                           32    * since 1.0
33    */                                                    33    */
34 ▶ public class WhileLoopDemo {                            34 ▶ public class DoWhileDemo {
35                                                          35
36 ▶     public static void main(String... args) {          36 ▶     public static void main(String... args) {
37          int arr[] = {5, 1, 4, 2, 3};                    37          int arr[] = {5, 1, 4, 2, 3};
38          int  i=0;                                       38          int i = 0;
39                                                          39
40          while(i < arr.length){                          40          do {
41              System.out.println("arr[" + i + "] = " + arr[i]);  41              System.out.println("arr[" + i + "] = " + arr[i]);
42              ++i;                                        42              ++i;
43          }                                               43          } while (i < arr.length);
44      }                                                   44      }
45   }                                                      45   }
46                                                          46
```

Figure 7-9. *while and do-while implementation for printing elements of an array*

The flowchart for these two examples is quite different, however, and reveals the different logic of the two statements. You can compare them by taking a look at Figure 7-10.

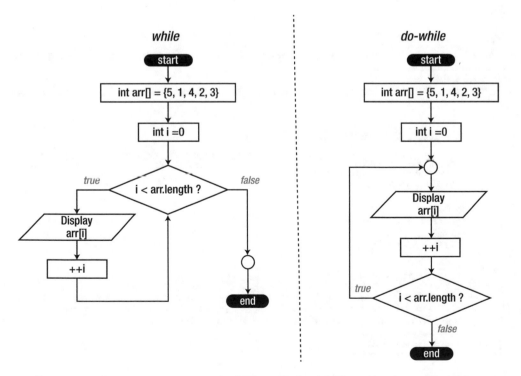

Figure 7-10. *Comparison between while and do-while statements flowcharts*

In the examples in Figure 7-9, if the array is empty, the do-while statement causes an ArrayIndexOutOfBoundsException exception to be thrown, because the contents of the code block are executed even thought they shouldn't be, because the index value is equal to the array length (zero), but there is no element with the index equal to 0, since the array is empty. However, because the condition is evaluated after the code block, there's no way to know that. In Figure 7-11 you can see the previous code samples modified to run with an empty array and the output of each side by side.

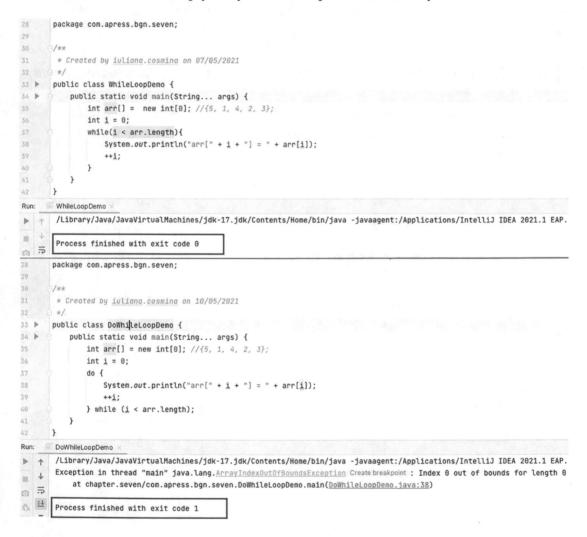

Figure 7-11. *while and do-while implementation for printing elements of an empty array*

To fix the do-while implementation to have the same behavior as the while implementation, the code block execution must be conditioned by the array having at least one element. Listing 7-31 shows one way to do it.

Listing 7-31. do-while Statement Implementation That Works Correctly for an Empty Array Too

```java
package com.apress.bgn.seven.whileloop;

public class DoWhileLoopDemo {
    public static void main(String... args) {
        int arr[] = new int[0];
        int i = 0;
        do {
            if(arr.length >=1) {
                System.out.println("arr[" + i + "] = " + arr[i]);
                ++i;
            }
        } while (i < arr.length);
    }
}
```

> 💡 The do-while statement works best when the code block must be executed at least once, otherwise we evaluate the condition once unnecessarily.

The Bubble Sort algorithm introduced earlier is a good example where while and do-while statements can be used interchangeably with no extra code modifications.

Since it has been mentioned that there is more than one way to write this algorithm, Listing in 7-32 shows an improved version that not only uses do-while, but decreases the size of the array being traversed each time. This is possible because according to Figure 7-7, after each traversal the last index of the array holds the biggest number of the subset being traversed.

Listing 7-32. Optimized Version of the Bubble Sort Algorithm Using do-while
Statement

```java
package com.apress.bgn.seven;

import java.util.Arrays;

public class BubbleSortDemo {
    public static final int arr[] = {5, 1, 4, 2, 3};

    public static void main(String... args) {
        boolean swapped = true;
        do {
            swapped = false;
            for (int i = 0, n = arr.length -1; i < n - 1; ++i, --n) {
                if (arr[i] > arr[i + 1]) {
                    int temp = arr[i];
                    arr[i] = arr[i + 1];
                    arr[i + 1] = temp;
                    swapped = true;
                }
            }
        } while (swapped);
        Arrays.stream(arr).forEach(System.out::println);
    }
}
```

❶   The initialization and the step expressions in the for statement allow for
multiple terms separated by ','. So the following code is valid and works just fine.

```java
for (int j = 0, k =2; j < 10; ++j, ++k) {

    System.out.println("composed indexes:
    [" + j + ", " + k + "]");

}
```

Remember the code sample that was trying to connect to a database that was in an unstable network (Listing 7-27)? When while was used, the execution started by testing to see if the connection was not null, but the connection was not even initialized with a valid value yet. It's illogical to perform that test, right? See the snippet shown in Listing 7-33.

Listing 7-33. while Implementation to Check Connection to a Database

```java
Connection con = null;
while (con == null) {
    try {
        Class.forName("com.mysql.cj.jdbc.Driver");
        con = DriverManager.getConnection(
                "jdbc:mysql://localhost:3306/mysql", "root", "mypass");
    // some code omitted
```

This implementation, although functional, is a bit redundant, and the logic is not really following best programming practices. A do-while implementation is most suitable because it avoids the initial testing if the con instance is null, when there is no way it could be otherwise. One variant of writing the code is depicted in Listing 7-34.

Listing 7-34. do-while Implementation to Check Connection to a Database

```java
package com.apress.bgn.seven.whileloop;

import java.sql.*;

public class DoWhileConnectionTester {
    public static final int MAX_TRIES = 10;

    public static void main(String... args) throws Exception {
        int cntTries = 0;
        Connection con = null;
        do {
            try {
                Class.forName("com.mysql.cj.jdbc.Driver");
                con = DriverManager.getConnection(
                        "jdbc:mysql://localhost:3306/mysql",
                        "root", "mypass");
```

```java
        } catch (Exception e) {
            ++cntTries;
            System.out.println("Connection refused. Retrying in 5
            seconds ...");
            Thread.sleep(5000);
        }
    } while (con == null && cntTries < MAX_TRIES);

    if (con != null) {
        Statement stmt = con.createStatement();
        ResultSet rs = stmt.executeQuery("select * from user");
        while (rs.next()) {
            System.out.println(rs.getString(1) + " " +
            rs.getString(2));
        }
        con.close();
    } else {
        System.out.println("Could not connect!");
    }
  }
}
```

Sure, skipping the evaluation of the condition a single time is not a big optimization, but in a big application, every little optimization counts.

Breaking Loops and Skipping Steps

In the previous examples we have mentioned exiting a loop using the break; statement, and a promise was made to come back and ad more details. There are three ways to manipulate the behavior of a loop:

- **the break statement** exits the loop and if accompanied by a label, will break the loop that is labeled with it; this is useful when we have more nested loops, because we can break from any of the nested loops, not just the one containing the statement.

- **the continue statement** skips the execution of any code after it and continues with the next step.

- **the return statement** is used to exit a method, so if the loop or if or a switch statement is within the body of a method, it can be used to exit the loop as well.

⚠ As for best practices, usage of return statements to exit a method should not be abused, as they might make the execution flow difficult to follow.

---

break Statement

The break statement can only be used within switch, for, while, and do-while statements. You have already seen how it can be used within the switch statement, so let's show you how to use it in all the others. Breaking out of a for, while, or do-while loop can be done using the break statement, but it must be controlled by an exit condition, otherwise no step will be executed. In Listing 7-35 we print only the first three elements in an array, even if the for loop is designed to traverse all of them. If we get the index equal to 3, we exit the loop.

Listing 7-35. Breaking Out of a for Loop

```
package com.apress.bgn.seven.forloop;

public class BreakingForDemo {
    public static final int arr[] = {5, 1, 4, 2, 3};

    public static void main(String... args) {
        for (int i = 0; i < arr.length ; ++i) {
            if (i == 3) {
                System.out.println("Bye bye!");
                break;
            }
            System.out.println("arr[" + i + "] = " + arr[i]);
        }
    }
}
```

If we have a case of nested loops, a label can be used to decide the looping statement to break out of. As an example, in Listing 7-36 we have three nested for loops, and we exit the middle loop when all indexes are equal.

Listing 7-36. Breaking Out of a Nested for Loop

```java
package com.apress.bgn.seven.forloop;

public class BreakingNestedForLoopDemo {
    public static final int arr[] = {5, 1, 4, 2, 3};

    public static void main(String... args) {
        for (int i = 0; i < 2; ++i) {
            HERE: for (int j = 0; j < 2; ++j) {
                for (int k = 0; k < 2; ++k) {
                    if (i == j && j == k) {
                        break HERE;
                    }
                    System.out.println("(i, j, k) = (" + i + "," + j + ","
                    + k + ")");
                }
            }
        }
    }
}
```

The label used in the previous code sample is named HERE and it is declared in front of the for statement that is exited when the condition is fulfilled. The same label follows the break statement. Writing label names with all all-caps letters is considered a best practice in development, as it avoids confusing labels with variables or class names when reading the code.

Breaking loops with labels is actually pretty much frowned upon, since it causes a code jump and makes the execution flow more difficult to follow. So if you must do it, make sure your labels are visible.

To make sure this works, you can take a look in the console. You should see that some combinations of (i, j, k) including the one with i = j = k are missing. The output is listed here.

```
(i, j, k) = (1,0,0)
(i, j, k) = (1,0,1)
(i, j, k) = (1,1,0)
```

continue Statement

The continue statement does not break a loop, but can be used to skip certain steps based on a condition. Essentially the continue statement stops the execution of the current step of the loop and moves to the next one, so you could say that this statement continues the loop. Let's continue experimenting with the array traversal example, and this time, let's skip from printing the elements with odd indexes by using the continue statement. The code is shown in Listing 7-37.

Listing 7-37. Skipping Printing Elements with Odd Indexes Using a for Loop and continue Statement

```java
package com.apress.bgn.seven.forloop;

public class ContinueForDemo {
    public static final int arr[] = {5, 1, 4, 2, 3};

    public static void main(String... args) {
        for (int i = 0; i < arr.length; ++i) {
            if (i % 2 != 0) {
                continue;
            }
            System.out.println("arr[" + i + "] = " + arr[i]);
        }
    }
}
```

Obviously, this statement must be conditioned, otherwise, the loop will just iterate uselessly.

The continue statement can be used with labels too. Let's take a similar example to the three for nested loops used earlier, but this time, when the k index is equal to 1, nothing is printed, and we skip to the next step of the loop enclosing the k loop. The code is shown in Listing 7-38.

Listing 7-38. Continue a Nested for Loop

```java
package com.apress.bgn.seven.forloop;

public class ContinueNestedForLoopDemo {
    public static final int arr[] = {5, 1, 4, 2, 3};

    public static void main(String... args) {
        for (int i = 0; i < 3; ++i) {
        HERE: for (int j = 0; j < 3; ++j) {
                for (int k = 0; k < 3; ++k) {
                    if (k == 1) {
                        continue HERE;
                    }
                    System.out.println("(i, j, k) = (" + i + "," + j + ","
                    + k + ")");
                }
            }
        }
    }
}
```

To make sure this works, you can take a look in the console and see that what combinations are printed, and we clearly notice that no combination with k=1 or k=2 is printed. The output is listed here.

```
(i, j, k) = (0,0,0)
(i, j, k) = (0,1,0)
(i, j, k) = (0,2,0)
(i, j, k) = (1,0,0)
(i, j, k) = (1,1,0)
(i, j, k) = (1,2,0)
```

```
(i, j, k) = (2,0,0)
(i, j, k) = (2,1,0)
(i, j, k) = (2,2,0)
```

---

❶ The usage of labels to break out of loops is frowned upon in the Java community, because jumping to a label resembles the goto statement that can be found in certain old school programming languages. goto is a Java reserved keyword, because this statement used to exist in the first version of the JVM, but it was later removed. Using jumping makes code less readable, less testable, and promotes bad design. That is why goto was removed in later versions, but any need of such operation can be implemented break and continue statements.

---

return Statement

The return statement is an easy one: as already mentioned, it can be used to exit the execution of a method body. If the method returns a value, the return statement is accompanied by the value returned. The return statement can be used to exit any of the statements mentioned in this section. It can represent quite a smart way to shortcut the execution of a method, as the execution of the current method stops, and processing continues from the point in the code that called the method.

Let's look at a few examples. The code in Listing 7-39 shows a method that finds the first even element in an array. If found the method returns its index; otherwise, it returns -1.

Listing 7-39. Finding an Even Number Using the do-while Statement

```java
package com.apress.bgn.seven;

public class ReturnDemo {
    public static final int arr[] = {5, 1, 4, 2, 3};

    public static void main(String... args) {
        int foundIdx = findEvenUsingFor(arr);

        if (foundIdx != -1) {
            System.out.println("First even is at: " + foundIdx);
        }
    }
}
```

```java
    public static int findEvenUsingFor(int ... arr) {
        for (int i = 0; i < arr.length; ++i) {
            if (arr[i] %2 == 0) {
                return i;
            }
        }
        return -1;
    }
}
```

The same method can be written using a while statement, but the purpose of the return statement is the same. The code is shown in Listing 7-40.

Listing 7-40. Finding an Even Number Using the while Statement

```java
// enclosing class omitted
public static int findEvenUsingWhile(int ... arr) {
    int i = 0;
    while (i < arr.length) {
        if (arr[i] % 2 == 0) {
            return i;
        }
        ++i;
    }
    return -1;
}
```

As you can see the return statement can be used in any situation when we want to terminate the execution of a method if a condition is met.

Controlling the Flow Using **try-catch** Constructions

Exceptions and try-catch statements have been mentioned before in this book, but not as tools to control flow execution. Before we skip to explanations and examples, let's first discuss the general template of a try-catch-finally statement. This template is shown in Listing 7-41.

Listing 7-41. `try-catch-finally` Statement Template

```
try {
    [code_block]
} catch ([exception_block]} {
    [handling_code_block]
} finally {
    [cleanup_code_block]
}
```

The components of the template are explained in the following list:

- `[code_block]` is the code block to execute.

- `[exception_block]` is a declaration or more of an exception type that can be thrown by the `[code_block]`.

- `[handling_code_block]` is an exception being thrown that marks an unexpected situation that must be handled; once the exception is being caught, this piece of code is executed to treat it, either by trying to return the system to a normal state or by logging details about the cause of the exception.

- `[clean_up_code]` is used to release resources or set objects to null so that they are eligible for collection. When present, this block of code is executed regardless of whether an exception is thrown or not.

Now that you know how a `try-catch-finally` works, you can probably imagine how to use it to control the execution flow. Within the `[code_block]` you can explicitly throw exceptions and decide how they are treated.

Considering the array that we have been using until now, we'll design our piece of code based on it again. Listing 7-42 shows a piece of code that throws an exception when an even value is found.

Listing 7-42. Controlling Flow Using Exceptions

```java
package com.apress.bgn.seven.ex;

public class ExceptionFlowDemo {
    public static final int arr[] = {5, 1, 4, 2, 3};

    public static void main(String... args) {
        try {
            checkNotEven(arr);
            System.out.println("Not found, all good!");
        } catch (EvenException e) {
            System.out.println(e.getMessage());
        } finally {
            System.out.println("Cleaning up arr");
            for (int i = 0; i < arr.length; ++i) {
                arr[i] = 0;
            }
        }
    }

    public static int checkNotEven(int... arr) throws EvenException {
        for (int i = 0; i < arr.length; ++i) {
            if (arr[i] % 2 == 0) {
                throw new EvenException("Did not expect an even number
                at " + i);
            }
        }
        return -1;
    }
}
```

The EvenException type is a custom exception type written for this specific example, and its implementation is not relevant here. If we execute this piece of code the following will be printed:

```
Did not expect an even number at 2
Cleaning up arr
```

As you can see, by throwing an exception we've directed the execution to the handling code, so "Not found, all good!" is not printed, and because there is a `finally` block, that was executed as well. Yes, you can mix-and-match: use different types of exceptions, and you can have multiple catch blocks whatever you need to solve your problem. At a previous company I worked for we had a piece of code that was validating a document and throwing different types of exceptions depending on the validation check that was not passed, and in the `finally` block we had a code that was converting the error object to PDF. The code looked similar to that in Listing 7-43.

Listing 7-43. Code Sample Showing a `try-multi-catch` Statement

```
ErrorContainter errorContainer = new ErrorContainter();
try {
    validate(report);
} catch (FileNotFoundException | NotParsable e) {
    errorContainer.addBadFileError(e);
} catch (InvestmentMaxException e) {
    errorContainer.addInvestmentError(e);
} catch (CreditIncompatibilityException e) {
    errorContainer.addIncompatibilityError(e);
} finally {
    if (errorContainer.isEmpty()) {
        printValidationPassedDocument();
    } else {
        printValidationFailedDocument(errorContainer);
    }
}
```

The code in the `finally` code block was complex and totally not recommended to be in there. However, sometimes in the real world the solutions do not always respect best practices, or even common-sense practices. When dealing with legacy code, you might find yourself in the position to write crappy but functional code that solves the client's problem—because sure, programming is awesome, but in the eyes of some managers results are more important. If you are lucky enough to get a job at a company that is looking to build on the code in the future or hand it to other team members, you might actually end up with a manager who favors best practices. Just remember to do your best and document everything properly, and you'll be fine.

`try-catch-finally` blocks are quite powerful. They are a useful construction for directing execution flow and printing useful information about the overall status of the application and the source of an eventual problem. When designed properly, exception handling can increase the quality and readability of your code. There are a few rules to follow when designing them:

- Try to avoid multiple catch blocks, unless there are used to treat different types of exceptions differently.

- Group together similar types of exceptions that are treated the same way using the | (`pipe`) symbol. Support for this was added in Java 7.

- Be careful when catching exceptions with related types. The first catch that matches an exception type handles the exception, so superclasses should be lower in the catch list. The compiler will even get really upset if the order is not correct, as shown in Figure 7-12.

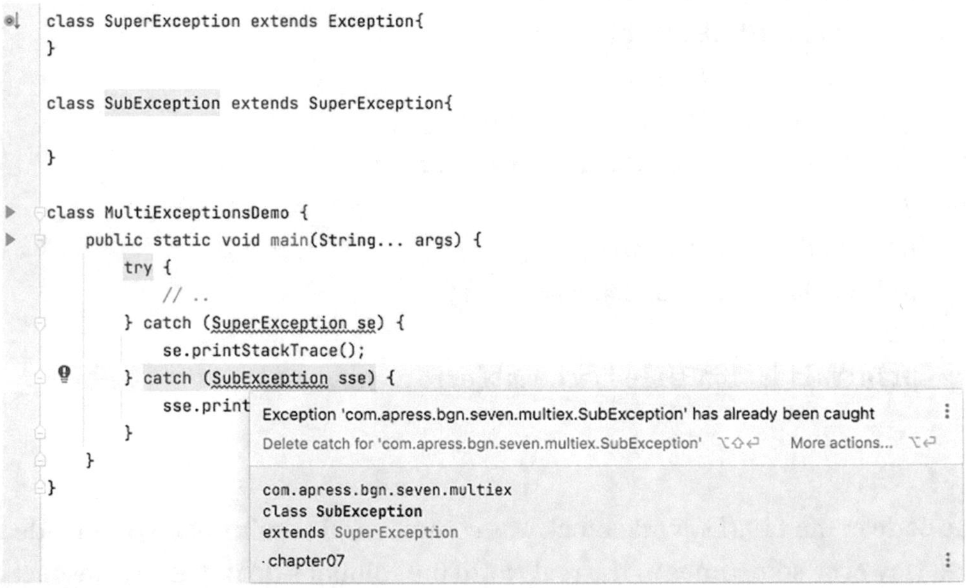

```
class SuperException extends Exception{
}

class SubException extends SuperException{

}

class MultiExceptionsDemo {
    public static void main(String... args) {
        try {
            // ..
        } catch (SuperException se) {
            se.printStackTrace();
        } catch (SubException sse) {
            sse.print
        }
    }
}
```

Exception 'com.apress.bgn.seven.multiex.SubException' has already been caught

Delete catch for 'com.apress.bgn.seven.multiex.SubException'   More actions...

com.apress.bgn.seven.multiex
class SubException
extends SuperException
· chapter07

Figure 7-12.   *IntelliJ IDEA compile error and message showing the wrong order of exception types in a try-catch block*

And of course, you should also respect the basic rules of avoiding exception swallowing and catching `Throwable` that were mentioned earlier in the book.

Summary

This chapter covered one of the most important things in development: how to design your solutions, and the logic of it. You've also been introduced to what flowcharts are and their components as tools for deciding how to write your code and how to control execution paths. And finally, you've learned which statements to use and when, and a few Java best practices have been mentioned, so that you will be able to design the most suitable solutions to your problems. Java provides the following:

- simple and more complex ways to write `if` statements.

- a `switch` statement that works with any primitive type, enumerations, and starting with Java 7, `String` instances.

- a `switch` expression that returns a value and that can be used to write more complex statements.

- a few ways to write `for` statements.

- how to use `forEach` methods and streams to traverse a collection of values.

- `while` statement, used when a step must be repeated until a condition is met.

- `do-while` statement, used when a step must be repeated until a condition is met and the step is repeated at least once, because the continuation condition is evaluated after it.

- how to manipulate loop behavior by using statements such as `break`, `continue`, and `return`.

- how to control the execution flow by using `try-catch-finally` constructions.

CHAPTER 8

The Stream API

The term stream has more than one meaning, as explained on `dictionary.com`:

1. a body of water flowing in a channel or watercourse, as a river, rivulet, or brook

2. a steady current in water, as in a river or the ocean

3. any flow of water or other liquid or fluid

4. a current or flow of air, gas, or the like

5. **a continuous flow or succession of anything**

6. prevailing direction; drift

7. *Digital Technology* **a flow of data**, as an audio broadcast, a movie, or live video, transmitted smoothly and continuously from a source to a computer, mobile device, and so on.

When it comes to programming, the definitions that are closer to what a stream is, are number 5 and a part of number 7 from the previous list. Indeed, a stream is a sequence of objects from a source which supports aggregate operations. In your mind you would be saying right now, so a collection? Well . . . not quite.

Introduction to Streams

Consider a really big collection of songs that we want to analyze and find all songs with duration of at least 300 seconds. For these songs, we want to save the names in a list and sort them in decreasing order of their duration. Assuming we already have the songs in a list, the code looks like Listing 8-1:

© Iuliana Cosmina 2022
I. Cosmina, *Java 17 for Absolute Beginners*, https://doi.org/10.1007/978-1-4842-7080-6_8

Listing 8-1. Java Code Made of a Few Statements

```
// non-relevant code omitted

List<Song> songList = loadSongs();
List<Song> resultedSongs = new ArrayList<>();

//find all songs with duration of at least 300 seconds
for (Song song: songList) {
    if (song.getDuration() >= 300) {
        resultedSongs.add(song);
    }
}

Collections.sort(resultedSongs, new Comparator<Song>(){
    public int compare(Song s1, Song s2){
        return s2.getDuration().compareTo(s1.getDuration());
    }
});

System.out.println(resultedSongs);
List<String> finalList0 = new ArrayList<>();
for (Song song: resultedSongs) {
    finalList0.add(song.getTitle()); // only the song title is required
}
System.out.println("Before Java 8: " + finalList0);
```

One of the problems with this code is that processing large collections is not really efficient. Also, we are traversing lists over and over again and performing checks to get to a final result. Wouldn't it be more efficient if we could execute all those operations on every element one by one, without repeated traversals? It would be, and it is possible to do it so starting with Java 8.

The new **Stream** abstraction introduced in Java 8 represents a sequence of elements that can be processed sequentially or in parallel and supports aggregate operations. Because of the latest evolutions in hardware development, CPUs have become more powerful and more complex, containing multiple cores that can process information in parallel. To make use of these hardware capabilities, in Java, the Fork Join Framework was introduced. And in Java 8, the Stream API was introduced to support parallel data processing, without the boiler-code of defining and synchronizing threads.

The central interface of the *Stream API* is the `java.util.stream.BaseStream`. Any object with stream capabilities is of a type that extends it. A stream does not store elements itself; it is not a data structure, it is just used to compute elements and serve them on-demand to an operation or a set of aggregate operations.

Aggregate operations are special methods in the Stream API with the following characteristics:

- they support behavior as parameters. Most aggregate operations support lambda expressions as parameters.

- they use internal iteration. Internal iteration does not go over the elements sequentially, thus taking advantage of parallel computing. Internal iteration splits a problem into subproblems, solves them simultaneously, then combines the results.

- they process the elements from a stream, not directly from the stream origin.

Serving the elements in a sequence involves an internal automatic iteration. Operations that return a stream can be chained in a pipeline and are called **intermediate operations**. Operations process elements of a stream and return the result as a stream to the next operation in the pipeline. Operations that return a result that is not a stream are called **terminal operations** and are normally present at the end of a pipeline. As a quick example before getting deeper, using streams the code in Listing 8-1 is written as depicted in Listing 8-2.

Listing 8-2. Code in Listing 8-1 Rewritten with Streams

List<String> finalList = songList.stream()

```
    .filter(s -> s.getDuration() >= 300)
    .sorted(Comparator.comparing(Song::getDuration).reversed())
    .map(Song::getTitle)
    .collect(Collectors.toList());
System.out.println(finalList);
```

Yes, programming with streams is awesome. The *Stream API* concept allows developers to transform collections into streams and write code to process the data in parallel and then getting the results into a new collection.

Working with streams is quite a sensitive way of programming, and it is recommended to design the code taking every possibility in mind. `NullPointerException` is one of the most common exceptions to be thrown in Java.

In Java 8, the class `Optional<T>` was introduced to avoid this type of exceptions. `Stream<T>` instances are used to store an infinite instances of type T, while `Optional<T>` is an instance that might or might not contain an instance of type T. Because both of these implementations are basically wrappers for other types, they will be covered together.

---

❶ For practical reasons, `Stream` instances will be referred in this chapter as **streams**, in a similar manner that `List` instances are referred as **lists** and collection instances as **collections**, and many more.

❶ You might notice that the term **function** was introduced and is used to refer to the behavior proved as argument to stream operations. This is because working with streams allows for Java code to be written in *Functional Programming* style. It was mentioned at the beginning of this book that Java is an object-oriented programming language, and the object was its core term. In functional programming the core term is **pure function** and code is written by composing pure functions, which allow to avoid shared state, take advantage of immutable data and thus avoid side-effects of processing contamination.[1]

Pure functions, are software analogues of mathematical functions and have the following properties:

- pure functions return identical values for identical arguments. The implementation does not involve any random value, or nonfinal global variables that might cause a different value to be returned for the same arguments. Pure functions must produce consistent results.

- the return value of the function depends only on the input parameters passed to the function.

---

[1] A very good article about the functional programming paradigm is this one, and I gladly recommend you to read it: see Medium, "Mastering the JavaScript Interview: What Is Functional Programming?," `https://medium.com/javascript-scene/master-the-javascript-interview-what-is-functional-programming-7f218c68b3a0`, accessed October 15, 2021.

- pure functions have no side-effects.(no mutation of local static variables, nonlocal variables, mutable reference arguments, or input/output streams).

The combination of streams, pure functions, and lambda expressions facilitates writing Java **declarative code**. In this chapter we leave behind the typical object-oriented **imperative coding style**, where each step of the algorithm is declared one after the other, and the flow controlled by boolean conditions. Unstead we start designing the chain of pure functions applied to elements of streams.

Creating Streams

Before having fun and optimizing our code using streams, let's see how we can create them. To create a stream we obviously need a source. That source can be anything: a collection (list, set, or map), an array, or I/O resources used as input (such as files, databases, or anything that can be transformed into a sequence of instances).

A stream does not modify its source, so multiple stream instances can be created from the same source and used for different operations.

The biggest difference between collections and streams is that the elements emitted by the stream are consumed by the operations and thus the stream cannot be used more than once. The code here is accepted by the Java compiler.

```
int[] arr = { 50, 10, 250, 100};
IntStream intStream = Arrays.stream(arr);

intStream.forEach(System.out::println);
intStream.forEach(System.out::println);
```

However, an `IllegalStateException` is thrown at runtime when we try traversing the stream a second time.

```
Exception in thread "main" java.lang.IllegalStateException: stream has already
been operated upon or closed at java.base/java.util.stream.AbstractPipeline.
sourceStageSpliterator(AbstractPipeline.java:279) at java.base/java.util.
stream.IntPipeline$Head.forEach(IntPipeline.java:617) at chapter.eigth/com.
apress.bgn.eight.StreamRecyclingDemo.main(StreamRecyclingDemo.java:44)
```

If you need to process the elements of a stream twice, you have to recreate it from the source again.

Creating Streams from Collections

In the introduction of this chapter, the code snippet in Listing 8-2 depicted one method of creating a stream from a list. Starting with Java 8, all collection interfaces and classes were enriched with default methods that return streams. In Listing 8-3, we take a list of integers and transforming it into a stream by calling the stream() method. After having a stream, we traverse it using the forEach(..) method to print the values in the stream, and the name of the execution thread this code is executed on. Why the thread name, you ask? You will see shortly.

Listing 8-3. Creating a Stream of Integer Values from a List of Integers

```java
package com.apress.bgn.eigth;

import java.util.List;

public class IntegerStreamDemo {

    public static void main(String... args) {
        List<Integer> bigList = List.of(50, 10, 250, 100 /*, ... */);

        bigList.stream()
            .forEach(i ->
                    System.out.println(Thread.currentThread().getName() +
                    ": " + i)
        );
    }
}
```

The preceding code creates a stream of integer elements. The Stream<T> interface exposes a set of methods that each Stream<T> implementation provides a concrete implementation for. The most used is the forEach(..) method that iterates over the elements in the stream. The forEach(..) method requires a parameter of type java.util.function.Consumer<T>.

❶ A **consumer** is what we call in this book an inline implementation of the
`java.util.function.Consumer<T>` functional interface. This interface
declares an abstract method that a class implementing it has to provide a concrete
implementation for. This interface is annotated with `@FunctionalInterface` for
this same reason. The method is named `accept(T t)`, and is referred to as a
functional method. It takes an element of type T as argument, processes it, and
returns nothing. For this reason, consumer functions are suitable for the end of a
functional pipeline.

This consumer method is called for each element in the stream. The implementing
class is basically declared inline, by only mentioning the body of the method. The JVM
does the rest, because of the magic of lambda expressions. Without them, you would
have to write code like the one in Listing 8-4.

Listing 8-4. Expanded Declaration of a Consumer

```
package com.apress.bgn.eigth;

import java.util.List;
import java.util.function.Consumer;

public class IntegerStreamDemo {

    public static void main(String... args) {
        List<Integer> bigList = List.of(50, 10, 250, 100 /*, ... */);

        bigList.stream().forEach(
            new Consumer<Integer>() {
                @Override
                public void accept(Integer i) {
                    System.out.println(Thread.currentThread().getName() +
                    ": " + i);
                }
            });
    }
}
```

This was the way you would write code before lambda expressions were introduced in Java 8. When classes implement interfaces this way, inline, using a syntax that looks a lot like a constructor call using the interface type; they are called **anonymous classes**, because they don't have a name, and they are used exactly where declared. Lambda expressions simplified this process a lot, but only for interfaces that define one single method, the interfaces named **functional interfaces**. These interfaces were annotated with @FunctionalInterface annotation starting with Java 8. In the previous example the code prints the thread name and the value of the element. The result is of running that code is depicted here:

```
main: 50
main: 10
main: 250
main: 100
...
```

The fact that each number is prefixed with main means that all integers in the stream are processed sequentially by the same thread, the main thread of the application.

💡 For practical reasons, for collections there is no need to call stream() when a sequential stream is needed only for traversal, because the forEach(..) method defined for them does the job just well. So the preceding code can be reduced to:

```
bigList.forEach(i ->
    System.out.println(Thread.currentThread().getName() +
    ": " + i)
);
```

The name of the thread was printed because there is another way to create a stream: by calling the parallelStream() method. The only difference is that the returned stream is a parallel stream. What this means is that each element of the stream is processed on a different thread. This means the implementation of the Consumer<T> must be thread-safe and not contain code that involves instances that are not meant to be shared amongst threads. The code to print the value of a stream element does not affect the value of the element returned by the stream, nor other external object, so it is safe to parallelize.

Listing 8-5 depicts the use of `parallelStream()` instead of `stream()` to create a stream and print the elements of the stream using the same `Consumer` <T> implementation. The output is depicted at the bottom of the snippet.

Listing 8-5. Creating a Parallel Stream of Integer Values from a List of Integers

```
package com.apress.bgn.eigth;

import java.util.List;
import java.util.function.Consumer;

public class IntegerStreamDemo {

    public static void main(String... args) {
        List<Integer> bigList = List.of(50, 10, 250, 100 /*, ... */);

        bigList.parallelStream()
            .forEach(i ->
                System.out.println(Thread.currentThread().getName() +
                ": " + i)
        );
    }
}
// output
main: 83
ForkJoinPool.commonPool-worker-1: 23
main: 33
ForkJoinPool.commonPool-worker-1: 45
ForkJoinPool.commonPool-worker-2: 50
main: 67
...
```

The first thing you will notice is the thread name: we no longer have one, but a lot of them all named **ForkJoinPool.commonPool-worker-****. The main thread still prints some values, but the other threads do some the work too, and the order—or more like the disorder—of the printed values makes it clear that the threads run in parallel. The threads have similar names that makes it obvious that they are all part of the same **thread pool**. A thread pool is created by the JVM in this case to contain a few thread instances used to process all elements in the stream in parallel. The advantage of using a thread pool is that the threads can be reused, so no new thread instances need to be created and this optimizes the execution time a little.

🔥 Performance improvements when using `parallelStream()` become obvious for more complex solutions. For this simple example, creating a thread pool and managing the threads is actually a waste of CPU and memory. So unless the operation performed for each element in the stream is complex enough for parallel execution to improve performance, avoid using `parallelStream()`.

If you look at the number associated to each thread, the number at the end of the thread name, you can see that the numbers sometimes repeat. This basically means the same thread is reused to process another stream element.

Creating Streams from Arrays

For the previous code samples, the source for our streams is represented by a List<T> instance. The same syntax is used with Set<T> instances as well.

But streams can be created from arrays as well. Just look at Listing 8-6:

Listing 8-6. Creating a Stream of Integer Values from an Array of Integers

```
package com.apress.bgn.eigth;

import java.util.Arrays;

public class ArrayStreamDemo {
    public static void main(String... args) {
        int[] arr = { 50, 10, 250, 100 /* ... */};

        Arrays.stream(arr).forEach(
                i -> System.out.println(Thread.currentThread().getName() +
                ": " + i)
        );
    }
}
```

The static method stream(int[] array) was added to the java.util.Arrays utility class in Java 1.8 and is used in the previous code listing to create a stream of primitives.

For arrays that contain objects, the method called is stream(T[] array), where T is a generic type, that replaces any reference type (also added in Java 1.8). Streams generated from arrays can be parallelized, by calling the same parallel() method.

The novelty with arrays is that a stream can be created from a part of the array by specifying the start and the end indexes for the array chunk. The code in Listing 8-7 shows the creation of a stream from a part of the array and the output of printing the elements of the resulting stream using a simple consumer.

Listing 8-7. Creating a Stream of Integer Values from an Array of Integers

```
package com.apress.bgn.eigth;

import java.util.Arrays;

public class ArrayStreamDemo {
    public static void main(String... args) {
        int[] arr = { 50, 10, 250, 100, 23, 45, 33, 55 /* ... */};

        Arrays.stream(arr, 3,6).forEach(
                i -> System.out.println(Thread.currentThread().getName() +
                ": " + i)
        );
    }
}
// output
main: 100
main: 23
main: 45
```

Creating Empty Streams

When writing Java code, a good practice is to write methods that return objects and avoiding returning null. This to reduces the possibility of NullPointerExceptions being thrown. When methods return streams, the preferred way is to return an empty stream. This can be done by calling the static Stream.empty() method provided by the Stream<T> interface.

The code snippet in Listing 8-8 depicts a method that takes a list of Song instances argument and returns a stream using it as a source. If the list is null or empty, an empty stream is returned. The resulted stream is traversed in the main(..) method, without additional verification. If the stream is empty, nothing will be printed.

Listing 8-8. Creating a Stream of Integer Values from an Array of Integers

```java
package com.apress.bgn.eigth;

import com.apress.bgn.eigth.util.*;

import java.util.List;
import java.util.stream.Stream;

public class SongStreamDemo {
    public static void main(String... args) {
        System.out.println(" -- Testing 'getAsStream(..)' method with
        null -- ");
        getAsStream(null).forEach(System.out::println);

        System.out.println(" -- Testing 'getAsStream(..)' method with empty
        list --");
        getAsStream(List.of()).forEach(System.out::println);

        System.out.println(" -- Testing 'getAsStream(..)' method with a
        list -- ");
        getAsStream(StreamMediaLoader.loadSongsAsList()).forEach(System.
        out::println);
    }

    public static Stream<Song> getAsStream(List<Song> songList) {
        if(songList == null || songList.isEmpty()) {
            return Stream.empty();
        } else {
            return songList.stream();
        }
    }
}
```

```
// output
 -- Testing 'getAsStream(..)' method with null --
 -- Testing 'getAsStream(..)' method with empty list --
 -- Testing 'getAsStream(..)' method with a list --
Song{id=1, singer='John Mayer', title='New Light', duration=206,
audioType=FLAC}
Song{id=2, singer='John Mayer', title='My Stupid Mouth', duration=225,
audioType=M4A}
...
```

Running the previous code results in the first two messages being printed one after the other with nothing in between, since the stream returned by the method is empty.

Creating Finite Streams

Aside from creating streams from actual sources, streams can be created on the spot by calling stream utility methods like `Stream.generate(..)` or `Stream.builder()`. The `builder()` method should be used when building a limited stream with a fixed sets of known values. This method returns an instance of `java.util.stream.Stream.Builder<T>`, an internal interface that declares a default method named `add(T t)` that needs to be called to add the elements of the stream. To create the `Stream <T>` instance, its `build()` method must be finally called. The `add(T t)` method returns a reference to the `Builder<T>` instance, so it can be chained with any other methods of this interface. The code in Listing 8-9 is a sample of how the `builder()` method can be used to create a finite stream of various values.

Listing 8-9. Creating Streams from Finite Sets of Values

```
package com.apress.bgn.eigth;

import com.apress.bgn.eigth.util.AudioType;
import com.apress.bgn.eigth.util.Song;

import java.util.stream.Stream;
```

```java
public class FiniteStreamsDemo {
    public static void main(String... args) {
        Stream<Integer> built = Stream.<Integer>builder()
                .add(50).add(10).add(250)
                .build();

        Stream<String> lyrics = Stream.<String>builder()
                .add("In a world where people never meet,")
                .add("They fall in love looking at some screen")
                .add("And love can only be one-sided")
                .add("Bitter, burning unrequited.")
                .build();

        Stream<Song> songs = Stream.<Song>builder()
                .add (new Song("John Mayer", "New Light", 206,
                AudioType.FLAC))
                .add (new Song("Ben Barnes", "You find me", 420,
                AudioType.FLAC))
                .build();

        Stream data = Stream.builder() // compiler warns about raw use of
parameterized class 'Stream'
                .add("Vultures")
                .add(3)
                .add(List.of("aa"))
                .build();

    }
}
```

As the Builder<T> interface is a generic one, it is mandatory to specify a type
argument, as the type of the elements in the stream. Also, the builder() method is
generic and requires the type to be provided as a parameter in front of it, right before
being called. If no type is specified the default Object is used, and instances of any type
can be added to the stream (as shown in the fourth stream declaration). However, the
compiler warns about *raw use of parameterized class 'Stream'*.

To create a stream, there is another method named generate(..). This method
requires an argument of type java.util.function.Supplier<T>.

❶ A **supplier** is what we call in this book an inline implementation of the java.util.function.Supplier<T> functional interface. This interface requires a concrete implementation to be provided for its single method named get(). This method should return the element to be added to the stream.

So if we want to generate a stream of integers, a proper implementation for get() should return a random integer. The expanded code is depicted in Listing 8-10. Lambda expressions are not used to make it clear that the generate(..) method receives as a parameter a Supplier<Integer> instance created on the spot.

Listing 8-10. Creating Stream Using a Supplier

```
package com.apress.bgn.eigth;

import java.util.stream.Stream;

public class FiniteStreamsDemo {
    public static void main(String... args) {
        Stream<Integer> generated = Stream.generate(
        new Supplier<Integer>() {
            @Override
            public Integer get() {
                Random rand = new Random();
                return rand.nextInt(300) + 1;
            }
        }).limit(15);
    }
}
```

The limit(15) method limits the number of elements generated by the supplier to 15, otherwise the generated stream will be infinite. The code in Listing 8-10 can be simplified by using lambda expressions as depicted in Listing 8-11.

Listing 8-11. Creating Stream Using a Supplier and Lambda Expressions

```java
package com.apress.bgn.eigth;

import java.util.stream.Stream;

public class FiniteStreamsDemo {
    public static void main(String... args) {
        Stream<Integer> generated = Stream.generate(
        () -> {
            Random rand = new Random();
            return rand.nextInt(300) + 1;
        }).limit(15);
    }
}
```

If Supplier<Integer>.get() always returns the same number, no matter how useless such a stream might be, the previous declaration becomes:

```java
Stream<Integer> generated = Stream.generate( () -> 5).limit(15);
```

If more control is needed over the elements emitted by a Stream<T> instance, the iterate(..) method can be used. There are two versions of this method, one added in Java 8 and one in Java 9. Using any of these methods is like having a for statement generate the entries for the stream.

The Java 8 version is used to generate an infinite stream. This version of the method receives as arguments an initial value called a seed and an iteration step.

The Java 9 version is used to generate an finite stream. This version of the method receives as arguments an initial value called a seed, a predicate that determines when the iteration should stop, and an iteration step.

> ❶ A **predicate** is an inline implementation of the functional interface `java.util.function.Predicate<T>`, which declares a single method named `test(T t)` that returns a boolean value. The implementation of this method should test its single argument of type T against a condition and returns `true` if the condition is fulfilled and `false` if not.
>
> ❶ The iteration step is an inline implementation of the functional interface `java.util.function.UnaryOperator<T>` used to represent an operation on a single operand that produces a result of the same type as its operand.

In the following example, stream elements are generated starting from 0, using a step of 5, and they are generated as long as the values are lesser than 50, as defined by the predicate.

```
Stream<Integer> iterated = Stream.iterate(0, i -> i < 50 , i -> i + 5);
```

Just as with the `for` statement, the termination condition is not mandatory, and without it you would be calling the version of this method introduced in Java 8, but in this case the `limit(..)` method must be used to make sure the stream is finite.

```
Stream<Integer> iterated = Stream.iterate(0, i -> i + 5).limit(15);
```

In Java 9 beside the `limit(..)` method there is another way to control the numbers of values in a stream: the `takeWhile(..)` method. This method takes the longest set of elements from the original stream that match the predicate received as argument, starting with the first element. This works fine for ordered streams, but if the stream is unordered the result is any set of elements that matches the predicate, including an empty one. To explain the different streams resilted by calling `takeWhile(..)`, the concept of order for streams has to be discussed first.

The expression **encounter order** represents the order in which a `Stream<T>` encounters data. The encounter order of a stream is defined by the source and intermediate operations. For example: if an array is used as a source the encounter order of the stream is defined by the ordering in the array. If a list is used as a source, the encounter order is the list's iteration order. If a set is used as a source, then there is no encounter order, because a set is inherently unordered.

Each intermediate operation in a stream pipeline acts on the encounter order adn the effects are as follows:

- an encounter order could be imposed on the output. For example the sorted() operation imposes an encounter order on an unordered stream.

- the encounter order is preserved. Some operations like filter(..) might drop a few elements, but the original order is unaffected.

- the encounter order is destroyed. For example the sorted() operation imposes an encounter order on an ordered stream, replacing the existing one.

Collector operations preserve encounter order if accumulating elements into a container with an encounter order. Sequential and parallel streams have the same properties with respect to ordering.

Listing 8-12 shows two usages of the takeWhile(Predicate<? super T> predicate) method.

Listing 8-12. Creating Stream Using a Supplier and the takeWhile(..) Method

```
package com.apress.bgn.eight;

import java.util.stream.Stream;

public class FiniteStreamsDemo {
    public static void main(String... args) {
        // (1)
        Stream<Integer> orderedStream = List.of( 3, 6, 9, 11, 12, 13, 15).
        stream();
        Stream<Integer> result = orderedStream.takeWhile(s -> s % 3 == 0);
        result.forEach(s -> System.out.print(s + " "));
        // output: 3 6 9

        // (2)
        Stream<Integer> unorderedStream = Set.of(3, 6, 9, 2, 4, 8, 12, 36,
        18, 42, 11, 13).stream();
        result = unorderedStream
.parallel()    // this does not affect results
```

```
.takeWhile(s -> s % 3 == 0);
        result.forEach(s -> System.out.print(s + " "));
        // output (maybe): 3 12 36
    }
}
```

The first code chunk uses takeWhile(..) on an ordered stream of integers and returns a stream with elements that divide by 3. The resulted stream contains the elements *3 6 9* because this is the first set of elements that match the given predicate.

If takeWhile(..), is called on an unordered stream (parallel or not) as depicted in the second code chunk, the result will be unpredictable. The result might be 3 12 36 or 12 36 18 42, as the result is a subset of any elements matching the predicate. Also, since the order is not fixed, the code chunk might end up printing 6 3 9, or 18 42, and so on. So the result of takeWhile(..) on an unordered stream is **nondeterministic**.

The takeWhile(..) operation is the "sister" of the dropWhile(..), also introduced in Java 9. As its name says this does exactly the reverse of what takeWhile(..) does: it returns, for an ordered stream, a new stream consisting elements after dropping the longest set of elements that matches the predicate. For an unordered stream, there is only chaos, any subset of elements matching the predicate can be dropped including the empty stream. Listing 8-13 shows two usages of the dropWhile(..) method.

Listing 8-13. Creating Stream Using a Supplier and the dropWhile(..) Method

```
package com.apress.bgn.eigth;

import java.util.stream.Stream;

public class FiniteStreamsDemo {
    public static void main(String... args) {
        Stream.of( 3, 6, 9, 11, 12, 13, 15)
            .dropWhile(s -> s % 3 == 0 )
            .forEach(s -> System.out.print(s + " "));
        // output: 11 12 13 15

        Stream.of(3, 6, 9, 2, 4, 8, 12, 36, 18, 42, 11, 13)
            .dropWhile(s -> s % 3 == 0 )
        .parallel() // this does not affect results
            .forEach(s -> System.out.print(s + " "));
```

```
        // output (maybe): 11 9 8 6 4 2 42 13 36
    }
}
```

If these two operations are applied to parallel streams, the only thing that changes is the order in which the elements are printed, but the result sets will contain the same elements.

Streams of Primitives and Streams of Strings

When we first created a stream of primitives we used an int[] array as a source. However, streams of primitives can be created in many ways, because the Stream API contains more interfaces with default methods to make programming with streams practical. In Figure 8-1 you can see the stream interfaces hierarchy.

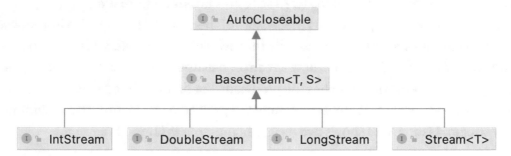

Figure 8-1. *Stream API interfaces*

As you probably imagine after looking at the previous image, the IntStream interface can be used to create primitive streams of integers. This interface exposes many methods to do so, some of them inherited from BaseStream<T,S>. An IntStream instance can be created from a few values specified on the spot, either by using the builder(), generate(..), or iterate(..) method or by using the of range*(..) methods, as depicted in Listing 8-14.

Listing 8-14. Creating IntStream Instances Using Various Methods

```
package com.apress.bgn.eigth;

import java.util.Random;
import java.util.stream.IntStream;

public class NumericStreamsDemo {
```

```java
public static void main(String... args) {
    IntStream intStream0 = IntStream.builder().add(0).add(1).add(2).
    add(5).build();
    IntStream intStream1 = IntStream.of(0,1,2,3,4,5);

    IntStream intStream2 = IntStream.range(0, 10);
    IntStream intStream3 = IntStream.rangeClosed(0, 10);

    Random random = new Random();
    IntStream intStream4 = random.ints(5);
}
}
```

An IntStream instance can be created by giving the start and end of an interval as
arguments to the range(..) and rangeClosed(..) methods. Both of them generate
elements for the stream, with a step of 1, only the last one includes the upper range of the
interval as a value.

Also, in Java 1.8 the java.util.Random class was enriched with a method named
ints(..) that generates a stream of random integers. It declares a single argument that
represents the number of elements to be generated and put in the stream, but there is a
form of this method without the argument that generates an infinite stream.

All the methods mentioned for IntStream can be used to generate LongStream
instances, as equivalent methods are defined in this interface as well.

For DoubleStream there are no range methods, but there is the of(..) method,
builder(), generate(..), and so on. Also, the java.util.Random class was enriched in
Java 1.8 with the doubles(..) method that generates a stream of random double values.
It declares a single argument that represents the number of elements to be generated
and put in the stream, but there is a form of this method without the argument that
generates an infinite stream. In Listing 8-15, a few ways of creating streams of doubles
are depicted.

Listing 8-15. Creating Numeric Stream Instances Using Various Methods

```java
package com.apress.bgn.eigth;

import java.util.Random;
import java.util.stream.DoubleStream;

public class NumericStreamsDemo {
```

```
public static void main(String... args) {
    DoubleStream doubleStream0 = DoubleStream.of(1, 2, 2.3, 3.4,
    4.5, 6);

    Random random = new Random();
    DoubleStream doubleStream1 = random.doubles(3);

    DoubleStream doubleStream2 = DoubleStream.iterate(2.5, d -> d = d +
    0.2).limit(10);
}
}
```

For streams of char values there is no special interface, but IntStream can be used just fine.

```
IntStream intStream = IntStream.of('a','b','c','d');
intStream.forEach(c -> System.out.println((char) c));
```

Another way to create a stream of char values is to use a String instance as a stream source.

```
IntStream charStream = "sample".chars();
charStream.forEach(c -> System.out.println((char) c));
```

In Java 8, the java.util.regex.Pattern was enriched with stream specific methods too; as a class used to process String instances, it is the proper place to add these methods after all. A Pattern instance is useful for splitting an existing String instance and return the pieces as a stream using the splitAsStream(..) method.

```
Stream<String> stringStream = Pattern.compile(" ")
    .splitAsStream("live your life");
```

The contents of a file can also be returned as a stream of strings using the Files. lines(..) utility method.

```
String inputPath = "chapter08/src/main/resources/songs.csv";
Stream<String> stringStream = Files.lines(Path.of(inputPath));
```

The sections so far have shown how to create all types of streams, the next sections will show you how to use them to process data.

❶ If you feel the need to associate stream instances with real objects to make sense of them, I recommend the following: imagine a finite stream (like one created from a collection) as the water dripping from a mug when inclined. The water in the mug will end eventually, but while the water drips, it forms a stream. An infinite stream is like a river that has fountain head, it flows continuously *(unless a serious drought dries the river, of course).*

Short Introduction to `Optional<T>`

The `java.util.Optional<T>` instances are the Schrödinger[2] boxes of the Java Language. They are very useful because they can be used as a return type for methods to avoid returning a `null` value, and cause either a possible `NullPointerException` to be thrown, or the developer using the method to write extra code to treat the possibility of an exception being thrown. `Optional<T>` instances can be created in similar way to streams.

There is an `empty()` method for creating an optional value of any type that does not contain anything.

```
Optional<Song> empty = Optional.empty();
```

There is an `of()` method used to wrap an existing object into an `Optional<T>`.

```
Optional<Long> value = Optional.of(5L);
```

Considering that these type of instances are designed not to allow `null` values, the way the `Optional<T>` instance was created previously, stops us from writing something like this:

```
Song song = null;
Optional<Song> nonNullable = Optional.of(song);
```

The compiler doesn't mind, but at runtime when the code is executed, a `NullPointerException` will be thrown. Still, if we really need an `Optional<T>` instance to

---

[2] Read more about Schrödinger at Wikipedia, "Schrödinger's Cat," `https://en.wikipedia.org/wiki/Schr%C3%B6dinger%27s_cat`, accessed October 15, 2021.

permit null values, it is possible; there's a utility method named ofNullable(T t) that was introduced in Java 9 just for that purpose:

```
Song song = null;
Optional<Song> nullable = Optional.ofNullable(song);
```

Now that we have Optional<T> instances, what can we do with them? We use them. Look at the code in Listing 8-16.

Listing 8-16. Code Showing the Necessity of Optional<T>

```
package com.apress.bgn.eigth;

import com.apress.bgn.eigth.util.MediaLoader;
import com.apress.bgn.eigth.util.Song;

import java.util.List;

public class NonOptionalDemo {
    public static void main(String... args) {
        List<Song> songs = MediaLoader.loadSongs();
        Song song = findFirst(songs, "B.B. King");
        if(song != null && song.getSinger().equals("The Thrill Is Gone")) {
            System.out.println("Good stuff!");
        } else {
            System.out.println("not found!");
        }
    }

    public static Song findFirst(List<Song> songs, String singer) {
        for (Song song: songs) {
            if (singer.equals(song.getSinger())) {
                return song;
            }
        }
        return null;
    }
}
```

The findFirst(..) method looks for the first song in the list that has the singer equal to "B.B. King", returns it and prints a message if found, and another if not. Notice the nullability test and iteration of the list in the previous code listing. In Java 8, both of them are no longer necessary. Listing 8-17 depicts the code in Listing 8-16 redesigned to use Optional<T>.

Listing 8-17. Code Showing Usage of Optional.ifPresent(..)

```java
package com.apress.bgn.eigth;

import com.apress.bgn.eigth.util.MediaLoader;
import com.apress.bgn.eigth.util.Song;

import java.util.List;
import java.util.Optional;

public class OptionalDemo {
    public static void main(String... args) {
        List<Song> songs = MediaLoader.loadSongs();
        Optional<Song> opt = songs.stream()
                .filter(s -> "B.B. King".equals(s.getSinger()))
                .findFirst();
        opt.ifPresent(r -> System.out.println(r.getTitle()));
    }
}
```

If the Optional<T> instance is not empty, the song title will be printed; otherwise, nothing will be printed and the code will continue from that point on without an exception being thrown. But what if we want to print something when the Optional<T> instance is empty? In Java 11 we can do something about that, because a method named isEmpty() was introduced to test the Optional<T> instance contents (Listing 8-18).

Listing 8-18. Code Showing Usage of Optional.isEmpty()

```java
package com.apress.bgn.eigth;

import com.apress.bgn.eigth.util.MediaLoader;
import com.apress.bgn.eigth.util.Song;

import java.util.List;
```

```java
import java.util.Optional;

public class OptionalDemo {
    public static void main(String... args) {
        List<Song> songs = MediaLoader.loadSongs();
        Optional<Song> opt1 = songs.stream()
                .filter(s -> "B.B. King".equals(s.getSinger()))
                .findFirst();
        if(opt1.isEmpty()) {
            System.out.println("Not found!");
        }
    }
}
```

But wait, this is a little bit . . . not right. Can't we just have a method to call on an Optional<T> to get the exact behavior as an if-else statement? Well, that is possible starting with Java 9; the ifPresentOrElse(..) method that takes as arguments a Consumer<T> to process the contents of the Optional<T> instance when is not empty and a Runnable instance to execute when Optional<T> instance when is empty (Listing 8-19).

Listing 8-19. Code Showing Usage of Optional.ifPresentOrElse(..)

```java
package com.apress.bgn.eigth;

import com.apress.bgn.eigth.util.MediaLoader;
import com.apress.bgn.eigth.util.Song;

import java.util.List;
import java.util.Optional;

public class OptionalDemo {
    public static void main(String... args) {
        List<Song> songs = MediaLoader.loadSongs();
        Optional<Song> opt2 = songs.stream()
                .filter(ss -> "B.B. King".equals(ss.getSinger()))
                .findFirst();
        opt2.ifPresentOrElse(
                r -> System.out.println(r.getTitle()),
                () -> System.out.println("Not found!")) ;
```

```
    }
}
```

If the Optional<T> instance is not empty, its contents can be extracted by calling the get() method (Listing 8-20).

Listing 8-20. Code Showing Usage of Optional.get()

```java
package com.apress.bgn.eigth;

import com.apress.bgn.eigth.util.MediaLoader;
import com.apress.bgn.eigth.util.Song;

import java.util.List;
import java.util.Optional;

public class OptionalDemo {
    public static void main(String... args) {
        List<Song> songs = MediaLoader.loadSongs();
        Optional<Song> opt3 = songs.stream()
                .filter(ss -> "Rob Thomas".equals(ss.getSinger()))
                .findFirst();
        System.out.println("Found Song " + opt3.get());
    }
}
```

The previous code does not print anything when the desired object is not found, because the Optional<T> is empty. But if we want to print a default value for example, we can do that as well using a method named orElse(..) (Listing 8-21).

Listing 8-21. Code Showing Usage of Optional.orElse(..)

```java
package com.apress.bgn.eigth;

import com.apress.bgn.eigth.util.MediaLoader;
import com.apress.bgn.eigth.util.Song;

import java.util.List;
import java.util.Optional;

public class OptionalDemo {
```

```java
    public static void main(String... args) {
        List<Song> songs = MediaLoader.loadSongs();
        Optional<Song> opt4 = songs.stream()
                .filter(ss -> "B.B. King".equals(ss.getSinger()))
                .findFirst();
        opt4.ifPresent(r -> System.out.println(r.getTitle()));

        Song defaultSong = new Song();
        defaultSong.setTitle("Untitled");
        Song s = opt4.orElse(defaultSong);
        System.out.println("Found: " + s.getTitle());
    }
}
```

The orElse(T t) method receives as an argument an instance of the type wrapped by Optional<T>. There is another version of it that takes a Supplier<T> that returns an object of the required type. The snippet using that method is shown here:

```java
Song fromSupplier =
    opt4.orElseGet(() -> new Song("None", "Untitled", 0, null));
System.out.println("Found: " + fromSupplier.getTitle());
```

If we were interested to throw a specific exception when the Optional<T> is empty, there is a method for that as well, named orElseThrow(..) (Listing 8-22).

Listing 8-22. Code Showing Usage of Optional.orElseThrow(..)

```java
package com.apress.bgn.eigth;

import com.apress.bgn.eigth.util.MediaLoader;
import com.apress.bgn.eigth.util.Song;

import java.util.List;
import java.util.Optional;

public class OptionalDemo {
    public static void main(String... args) {
        List<Song> songs = MediaLoader.loadSongs();
        Optional<Song> opt5 = songs.stream()
                .filter(st -> "B.B. King".equals(st.getSinger()))
```

```
        .findFirst();
    Song song = opt5.orElseThrow(IllegalArgumentException::new);
  }
}
```

As you probably noticed in the previous code samples, Optional<T> and Stream<T> can be combined to write practical code to solve complex solutions. As there are a lot of methods that can be applied to Optional<T> and Stream<T> instances as well, the next sections will introduce them for streams and randomly make reference to Optional<T> as well.

How to Use Streams Like a Pro

After creating a stream, the next thing is to process the data on the stream. The result of that processing can be another stream that can be further processed as many times as needed. There are quite a few methods to use to process a stream and return the result as another stream. These methods are called **intermediate operations**. The methods that do not return a stream but actual data structures, or nothing, are named **terminal operations**. All these are defined in the Stream<T> interface. The key feature of streams is that the processing of data using streams is only done when the terminal operation is initiated and elements from source consumed only as needed. So you could say that the whole stream process is actually lazy. Lazy loading of source elements and processing them when needed allows significant optimizations.

After the previous affirmations you probably realized that the forEach(..) method that was used a lot previously to print values from the streams is actually a terminal operation. But there are quite a few other terminal operations and a few of them, the ones you'll most likely need for the most commons implementations, will be used in the examples in the rest of the chapter.

This chapter started with an example that was processing a stream of Song instances, but the Song class was not shown. You can see its fields in Listing 8-23.

Listing 8-23. Fields of Class Song

```
package com.apress.bgn.eigth;

public class Song {
    private Long id;
    private String singer;
```

```
    private String title;
    private Integer duration;
    private AudioType audioType;

    //getters and setters
    // toString
}
```

The AudioType is an enum containing the types of audio files and is depicted in Listing 8-24.

Listing 8-24. AudioType Enum

```
package com.apress.bgn.eigth;

public enum AudioType {
    MP3,
    FLAC,
    OGG,
    AAC,
    M4A,
    WMA,
    MP4
}
```

Now that the data type that will be used on the following stream examples, the data should be depicted as well. In the example in the book, the data is contained into a file named songs.csv. The CSV extension denotes a **comma separated file**, and each Song instance matches a line in the file. Each line contains all the property values of each Song instance, separated by columns. The order of the values must match the order of the constructor arguments. Other separators can be used; semicolons are used here for practical reasons (which is the default supported by the library reading the data). The contents of file are depicted in Listing 8-25.

Listing 8-25. Song Entries in the sonds.csv File

```
01;John Mayer;New Light;206;FLAC
02;John Mayer;My Stupid Mouth;225;M4A
03;John Mayer;Vultures;247;FLAC
```

```
04;John Mayer;Edge of Desire;333;MP3
05;John Mayer;In Repair;372;MP3
05;Rob Thomas;Paper Dolls;185;MP3
07;The Script;Mad Love;207;MP3
08;Seth MacFarlane;No One Ever Tells You;244;MP3
09;Nat King Cole;Orange Colored Sky;154;MP3
10;Vertical Horizon;Forever;246;MP3
11;Mario Lanza;Temptation;141;M4A
12;Jack Radics;No Matter;235;MP3
13;George Michael;Fastlove;306;MP3
14;Childish Gambino;Freaks And Geeks;227;M4A
15;Bill Evans;Lover Man;304;MP3
16;Darren Hayes;Like It Or Not;381;MP3
17;Stevie Wonder;Superstition;284;MP3
18;Tony Bennett;It Had To Be You;196;MP3
19;Tarja Turunen;An Empty Dream;322;MP3
20;Lykke Li;Little bit;231;M4A
21;Ben Barnes;You find me;420;FLAC
```

Each line in the file will be transformed into a Song instance by using classes in a library named JSefa.[3] This library is not the topic of this book, but if you are interested, you can use the link in the footnote to get more details from the official site.

Terminal Functions: forEach and forEachOrdered

Now you are ready to start playing with streams. Assuming the songs stream will provide all Song instances declared in the previous listing, let's first print all the elements in the stream. The code in Listing 8-26 prints all Song instances on a Stream<Song> using a simple consumer.

---

[3] JSefa (Java Simple exchange format api) is a simple library for stream-based serialization of Java objects to XML, CSV, and FLR. See more about it at Jsefa, "Java Simple Exchange Format API (Parent)," http://jsefa.sourceforge.net/ accessed October 15, 2021.

Listing 8-26. Using a Stream to Print Song Instances

```
package com.apress.bgn.eigth;

import com.apress.bgn.eigth.util.Song;
import com.apress.bgn.eigth.util.StreamMediaLoader;

import java.util.stream.Stream;

public class MediaStreamTester {
    public static void main(String... args) {
        Stream<Song> songs = StreamMediaLoader.loadSongs();
        songs.forEach(song -> System.out.println(song));
    }
}
```

Method references introduced were introduced in Java 8. Method references are a shortcut for cases when a lambda expression does nothing else than call a method, so the method can be referred by name directly. So this line:

```
songs.forEach(song -> System.out.println(song));
```

Becomes:

```
songs.forEach(System.out::println);
```

The forEach(..) method receives an instance of Consumer<T> as an argument. In the two previous examples the implementation of the accept() method contained only a call to System.out.println(song), and that is why the code is so compact, because method references can be used. But if the implementation of this method needs to contain more statements, then the compact code previously written would not be possible.

Instead of printing the songs directly, let's first uppercase the singer's name, as depicted in Listing 8-27.

Listing 8-27. Using a Consumer Anonymous Class to Print Song Instances

```
package com.apress.bgn.eigth;

import com.apress.bgn.eigth.util.Song;
import com.apress.bgn.eigth.util.StreamMediaLoader;

import java.util.function.Consumer;
import java.util.stream.Stream;
```

```java
public class MediaStreamTester {
    public static void main(String... args) {
        Stream<Song> songs = StreamMediaLoader.loadSongs();
        songs.forEach(new Consumer<Song>() {
            @Override
            public void accept(Song song) {
                song.setSinger(song.getSinger().toUpperCase());
                System.out.println(song);
            }
        });
    }
}
```

It can be simplified using lambda expressions, but since the method body has two lines, it still looks bad. So a different way to do it is to declare a consumer field, and use lambda to call its accept(..) method for every song, as depicted in Listing 8-28.

Listing 8-28. Using a Consumer Field to Print Song Instances

```java
package com.apress.bgn.eigth;

import com.apress.bgn.eigth.util.Song;
import com.apress.bgn.eigth.util.StreamMediaLoader;

import java.util.function.Consumer;
import java.util.stream.Stream;

public class MediaStreamTester {
    public static Consumer<Song> myConsumer = song -> {
        song.setSinger(song.getSinger().toUpperCase());
        System.out.println(song);
    };

    public static void main(String... args) {
        Stream<Song> songs = StreamMediaLoader.loadSongs();

        songs.forEach(song -> myConsumer.accept(song));
    }
}
```

The sister function forEachOrdered(..) does the same thing as forEach(..), with one little difference to ensure that the elements on the stream will be processed in encounter order, if such order is defined for the stream, even if the stream is a parallel one. So basically, the following two lines will print the songs in the same order:

```
songs.forEachOrdered (System.out::println);
songs.parallel().forEachOrdered(System.out::println);
```

Intermediate Operation: filter and Terminal Operation: toArray

In the following example, we will select all MP3 songs and will save them to an array. Selecting all MP3 songs is done using the filter(..) method. This method receives an argument of type Predicate<T>, which is used to define a condition that the elements of the stream must pass to be put into the array that results by calling the terminal method named toArray(..).

The toArray(..) receives an argument of type IntFunction<A[]>. This type of function is also called a *generator* and takes an integer as argument and generates an array of that size. In most cases the most suitable generator is an array constructor reference.

The code to filter the MP3 entries and put them into an array of type Song[] is depicted in Listing 8-29:

Listing 8-29. Using a Generator Function to Collect Stream Elements Into an Array

```
package com.apress.bgn.eigth;

import com.apress.bgn.eigth.util.Song;
import com.apress.bgn.eigth.util.StreamMediaLoader;

import java.util.function.Consumer;
import java.util.stream.Stream;

public class MediaStreamTester {

    public static void main(String... args) {
        Stream<Song> songs = StreamMediaLoader.loadSongs();
```

```
    Song[] sarray = songs.filter(s -> s.getAudioType() == AudioType.
    MP3).toArray(Song[]::new);   // array constructor reference
    Arrays.stream(sarray).forEach(System.out::println);
  }
}
```

Intermediate Operation: map, flatMap and Terminal Operation: collect

In the following example we will process all the songs and calculate the duration in minutes. To do this, we will use the map(..) method to call a pure function for each song instance emitted by the stream that returns the duration in minutes. This will result in a new stream of Integer values.

All its elements will be added to a List<Integer> using the collect(..) method. This method accumulates the elements as they are processed into a Collection<Integer> instance. Listing 8-30 shows these methods being used.

Listing 8-30. Using map(..) and collect(..) Methods

```
package com.apress.bgn.eigth;

import com.apress.bgn.eigth.util.Song;
import com.apress.bgn.eigth.util.StreamMediaLoader;

import java.util.List;
import java.util.stream.Collectors;
import java.util.stream.Stream;

public class SongTransformer {
    public static int processDuration(Song song) {
        int secs = song.getDuration();
        return secs/60;
    }

    public static void main(String... args) {
        Stream<Song> songs = StreamMediaLoader.loadSongs();

        List<Integer> durationAsMinutes = songs
```

411

```
        .map(SongTransformer::processDuration) // method
        reference call
        .collect(Collectors.toList());

    durationAsMinutes.forEach(System.out::println);
    }
}
```

The map(..) method receives an argument of type Function<T,R>(T input type, R result type) which is basically a reference to a function to apply on each element of the stream. The function we applied in the previous example takes a song element from the stream, gets its duration, and transforms it into minutes and returns it. The code in the previous listing can be rewritten as depicted in Listing 8-31 where the method processDuration is declared as a field of type Function<T,R>.

Listing 8-31. Using a Field of Type Function<T,R> to Process Stream Elements

```
package com.apress.bgn.eigth;

import com.apress.bgn.eigth.util.Song;
import com.apress.bgn.eigth.util.StreamMediaLoader;

import java.util.List;
import java.util.function.Function;
import java.util.stream.Collectors;
import java.util.stream.Stream;

public class SongTransformer {

    public static Function<Song, Integer> processDuration = song -> song.
    getDuration()/60;

    public static void main(String... args) {
        Stream<Song> songs = StreamMediaLoader.loadSongs();

        List<Integer> durationAsMinutes = songs
                .map(processDuration)
                .collect(Collectors.toList());

        durationAsMinutes.forEach(System.out::println);
    }
}
```

The first generic type of the Function<T,R> is the type of the processed element, and the second is the type of the result.

A version of the filter(..) method mentioned in the previous section is defined for the Optional<T> type as well and can be used to avoid writing complicated if statements, together with the map(..) method. Let's assume we have a Song instance and we want to check if it is more than three minutes and less than 10 minutes long. Instead of writing an if statement with two conditions connected by an AND operator, we can use an Optional<Song> and those two methods to do the same, as shown in Listing 8-32.

Listing 8-32. Using filter(..) and map(..) to Avoid Writing if Statements

```java
package com.apress.bgn.eigth;

import com.apress.bgn.eigth.util.Song;

public class SongTransformer {

    public static void main(String... args) {
        Song song0 = new Song("Ben Barnes", "You find me", 420,
        AudioType.FLAC);
        if(isMoreThan3MinsAndLessThenTen(song0)) {
            System.out.println("This song is just right!");
        }
    }

    public static boolean isMoreThan3MinsAndLessThenTen(Song song) {
        return Optional.ofNullable(song).map(SongTransformer::proces
        sDuration)
                .filter(d -> d >= 3)
                .filter(d -> d <= 10)
                .isPresent();
    }
}
```

🖌 The previous implementation might not be ideal when it comes to performance, but code like that can be written if you wish. Just make sure to read the documentation properly before abusing stream operations.

So the map(..) is quite powerful, but it has a small flaw. If we take a look at its signature in the Stream.java file this is what we will see:

```
<R> Stream<R> map(Function<? super T, ? extends R> mapper);
```

So if the map(..) function argument applied to each element in the stream returns a stream with the result, which is placed into another stream that contains all results, the collect(...) method is actually called on a Stream<Stream<R>>. The same goes for Optional<T>; the terminal method will be called on a <Optional<Optional<T>>. When the objects are simple, like the Song instances used in these book code samples, the map(..) method works quite well, but if the objects in the original stream are more complex, such as a List<List<T>>, things might get complicated. The easiest way to show the effects of the flatMap(..) is to apply it on a List<List<T>>. Let's take a look at the example in Listing 8-33.

Listing 8-33. Using flatMap(..) to Unwrap Stream Elements

```java
package com.apress.bgn.eigth;

import java.util.Collection;
import java.util.List;
import java.util.stream.Collectors;

public class MoreStreamsDemo {
    public static void main(String... args) {
        List<List<Integer>> testList = List.of (List.of(2,3), List.of(4,5),
        List.of(6,7));
        System.out.println(processList(testList));
    }

    public static List<Integer> processList( List<List<Integer>> list) {
        List<Integer> result = list
                .stream()
                .flatMap(Collection::stream)
```

```
            .collect(Collectors.toList());
        return result;
    }
}
```

The flatMap(..) method receives as argument a reference to a method that takes a collection and transforms it into a stream, the simplest way to create a Stream<Stream<Integer>>. The flatMap(..) does its magic and the result is transformed into Stream<Integer> and the elements are then collected by the collect(..) method into a List<Integer>. The operation of removing the useless stream wrapper is called **flattening**. If it is still not obvious what is happening, Figure 8-2 should make things clearer.

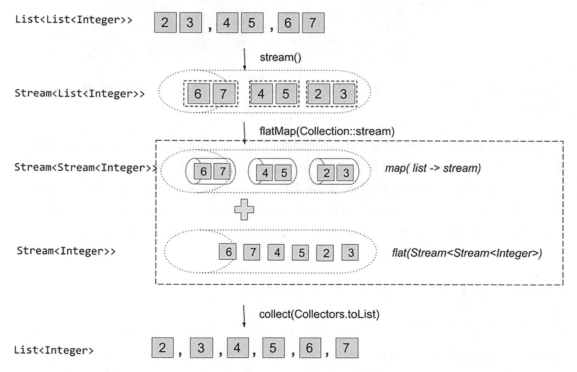

Figure 8-2. *Visual depiction of the effects of flatMap(..)*

In the previous code sample, using the map(..) method doesn't yield the expected result. If the flatMap(..) is replaced with map(..) the final result is not a List<Integer>, but a List<Stream<Integer>>. IntelliJ is smart enough to figure it out, and it provides the appropriate message to help you choose the right method to call, as depicted in Figure 8-3.

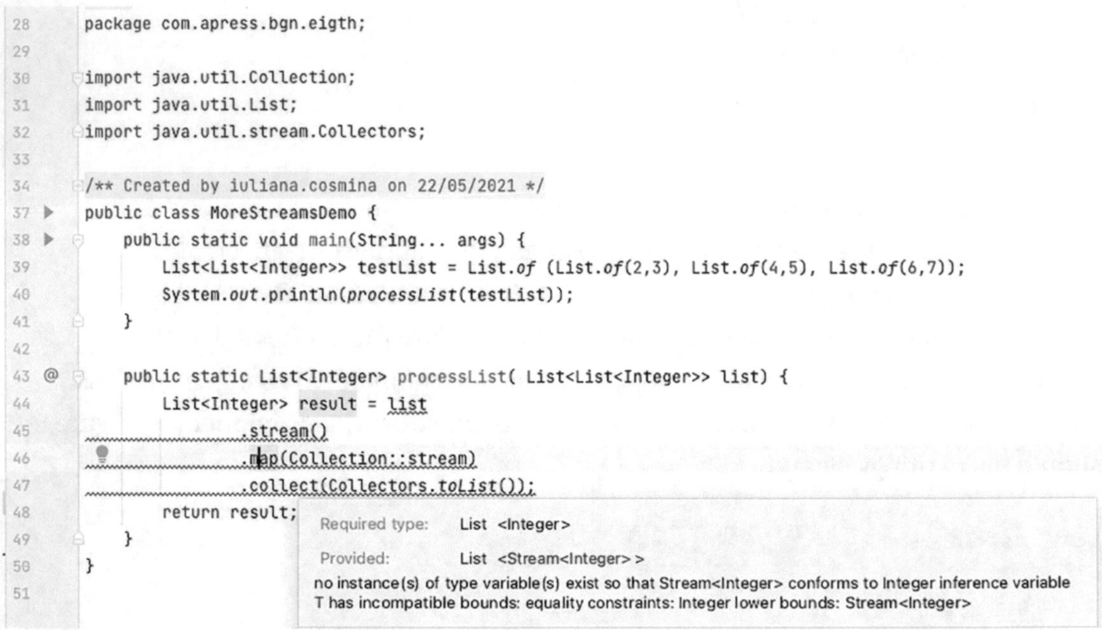

```
28    package com.apress.bgn.eigth;
29
30    import java.util.Collection;
31    import java.util.List;
32    import java.util.stream.Collectors;
33
34    /** Created by iuliana.cosmina on 22/05/2021 */
37    public class MoreStreamsDemo {
38        public static void main(String... args) {
39            List<List<Integer>> testList = List.of (List.of(2,3), List.of(4,5), List.of(6,7));
40            System.out.println(processList(testList));
41        }
42
43    @   public static List<Integer> processList( List<List<Integer>> list) {
44            List<Integer> result = list
45                    .stream()
46                    .map(Collection::stream)
47                    .collect(Collectors.toList());
48            return result;
49        }
50    }
51
```

Required type: List <Integer>

Provided: List <Stream<Integer> >

no instance(s) of type variable(s) exist so that Stream<Integer> conforms to Integer inference variable
T has incompatible bounds: equality constraints: Integer lower bounds: Stream<Integer>

Figure 8-3. *IntelliJ IDEA error message when* map(..) *is used instead of* flatMap(..)

Another way to see the effect of the flatMap(..) method is to write an even more simple example with Optional<T>. Let's say we need a function that transforms a String value into an Integer value. If the String value is not a valid number, we want to avoid returning null. This means that our function must take a String and return Optional<Integer>. The code shown in Listing 8-34 contains an explicit flattening and a flattening done with flatMap(..).

Listing 8-34. Flattening of a Optional<Optional<T>>

```
package com.apress.bgn.eigth;

import java.util.Optional;
import java.util.function.Function;

public class MoreStreamsDemo {

    public static void main(String... args) {
        Optional<String> str = Optional.of("42");
        Optional<Optional<Integer>> resInt = str.map(toIntOpt);
```

```
    // explicit flattening
    Optional<String> str0 = Optional.of("42");
    Optional<Optional<Integer>> resInt0 = str0.map(toIntOpt);
    Optional<Integer> desiredRes0 = resInt0.orElse(Optional.empty());
    System.out.println("finally: " + desiredRes0.get());

    // flatMap(..) flattening
    Optional<String> str1 = Optional.of("42");
    Optional<Integer> desiredRes1 = str1.flatMap(toIntOpt);
    System.out.println("boom: " + desiredRes1.get());
}

// converts a String to int, returns Optional<Integer> with the result,
//Optional.empty if it cannot be converted
public static Function<String, Optional<Integer>> toIntOpt = str -> {
    try {
        return Optional.of(Integer.parseInt(str));
    } catch (NumberFormatException e) {
        return Optional.empty();
    }
};
}
```

So yes, there is a slight difference between map(..) and flatMap(..), and although in most cases you will use the first, it is good to know that the latter exists too.

Intermediate Operation: sorted and Terminal Operation: findFirst

As the name says, the sorted() method has something to do with sorting, element ordering. When called on a stream, it creates another stream with all the elements of the initial stream, but sorted in their natural order. If the type of elements on the stream is not comparable (the type does not implement java.lang.Comparable<T>), a java.lang.ClassCastException is thrown. And since we are going to use this method to get a stream of sorted elements, we will use findFirst() to get the first element in the stream. This method returns an Optional<T>, because the stream might be empty and thus there is no first element. This means to get the value the get() method must be called. For the situation where the stream might be empty, the orElse(..) or the orElseGet(..) method can be used to return a default value in case of the missing first element. Listing 8-35 depicts both situations.

Listing 8-35. Extracting the First Element in an Ordered Stream

```
package com.apress.bgn.eigth;

import java.util.List;

public class MoreStreamsDemo {

    public static void main(String... args) {
        // non empty stream, result 'ever'
        List<String> pieces = List.of("some","of", "us", "we're", "hardly",
        "ever", "here");
        String first0 = pieces.stream().sorted().findFirst().get();
        System.out.println("First from sorted list: " + first0);

        // empty stream, result 'none'
        pieces = List.of();
        String first1 = pieces.stream().sorted().findFirst().
        orElse("none");
        System.out.println("First from sorted list: " + first1);
    }

}
```

Intermediate Operation: `distinct()` and Terminal Operation: `count()`

The distinct() method takes a stream and generates a stream with all the distinct elements of the original stream. And since in the examples in this book we couple intermediary and terminal operations, let's use count(), which counts the elements of the stream. A small example is depicted in Listing 8-36.

Listing 8-36. Counting Elements of a Stream, After Removing Duplicate Elements

```java
package com.apress.bgn.eigth;

public class MoreStreamsDemo {

    public static void main(String... args) {
        List<String> pieces = List.of("as","long", "as", "there", "is",
        "you", "there", "is", "me");
        long count = pieces.stream().distinct().count();
        System.out.println("Elements in the stream: " + count);
    }
}
```

When run, the code prints *Elements in the stream:* 6, because after removing the duplicate terms of *as, there, is* we are left with 6 terms. If the initial stream is empty, the count() method returns 0(zero).

Intermediate Operation: limit(..) and Terminal Operations: min(..), max(..)

The limit(..) method was used in this chapter before to transform an infinite stream into a finite one. As it transforms a stream into another, clearly this is an intermediate function. The terminal methods covered in this section model two mathematical functions:

- to calculate the minimum of the elements in the stream: min(..)

- to calculate the maximum of the elements in the stream: max(..).

The type of elements in the stream must implement java.util.Comparator<T>, otherwise a minimum and maximum value cannot be calculated. Using the limit(..), min(..) and max(..) functions together is depicted in Listing 8-37.

Listing 8-37. Computing the Maximum and Minimum Value in a Stream

```
package com.apress.bgn.eigth;

import java.util.stream.Stream;

public class MoreStreamsDemo {

    public static void main(String... args) {
        Stream<Integer> ints0 = Stream.of(5,2,7,9,8,1,12,7,2);
        ints0.limit(4).min(Integer::compareTo)
                .ifPresent(min -> System.out.println("Min is: " + min));
        // Prints "Min is: 2"

        Stream<Integer> ints1 = Stream.of(5,2,7,9,8,1,12,7,2);
        ints1.limit(4).max(Integer::compareTo)
                .ifPresent(max -> System.out.println("Max is: " + max));
        // Prints "Max is: 9"
    }
}
```

Terminal Operations: sum() and reduce(..)

Let's consider the scenario: we have a finite stream of Song values and we want to calculate the sum of their durations. There are two stream terminator methods that can be used to do this: the sum(..) method and the reduce(..) method. The code to do this is depicted in Listing 8-38.

Listing 8-38. Adding the Elements of a Stream

```
package com.apress.bgn.eigth;

import com.apress.bgn.eigth.util.Song;
import com.apress.bgn.eigth.util.StreamMediaLoader;
import java.util.stream.Stream;
```

```java
public class MediaStreamTester {
    public static void main(String... args) {
        Stream<Song> songs = StreamMediaLoader.loadSongs();
        Integer totalDuration0 = songs
                .mapToInt(Song::getDuration)
                .sum();
        System.out.println("Total duration using sum: " + totalDuration0);

        songs = StreamMediaLoader.loadSongs();
        Integer totalDuration1 = songs
                .mapToInt(Song::getDuration)
                .reduce(0, (a, b) -> a + b);
        System.out.println("Total duration using reduce: " +
        totalDuration1);
    }
}
```

The version of the reduce(..) operation takes two arguments:

- the identity argument represents the initial result of the reduction and the default result if there are no elements in the stream.

- the accumulator function takes two parameters that the operation is applied on to get a partial result (in this case is the addition of those two elements).

The reduce(..) operation accumulator is an instance of java.util.function. BinaryOperator<T> that represents an operation upon two operands of the same type, producing a result of the same type as the operands. On an IntStream, like the one returned by the mapToInt(..) operation, the reduce(..) operation accumulator is an instance of java.util.function.IntBinaryOperator, which is a custom function that takes two int arguments and returns an int result.

Essentially, every time an element of the stream is processed the accumulator returns a new value, which in this case is the result of adding the processed element with the previous partial result. So if the result of the process is a collection, the accumulator's result is a collection, so every time a stream element is processed a new collection is created. This is pretty inefficient, so in scenarios when collections are involved the collect(..) operation is more suitable.

Intermediate Operation: peek(..)

This function is special as it really doesn't affect the stream results in any way. The peek() function returns a stream consisting of the elements of the stream it is called on, while also performing the operation specified by its Consumer<T> argument on each element. This means that this function can be used to debug stream operations using logging statements at that print information at runtime.

Let's take our stream of Song instances, filter them by their duration, select all of them with duration > 300 seconds, and then get their titles and collect them in a list. The code to do this is depicted in Listing 8-39.

Listing 8-39. Calling a Simple map(..) on Stream Elements

```
package com.apress.bgn.eigth;

import com.apress.bgn.eigth.util.Song;
import com.apress.bgn.eigth.util.StreamMediaLoader;
import java.util.stream.Stream;

public class MediaStreamTester {
    public static void main(String... args) {
        Stream<Song> songs = StreamMediaLoader.loadSongs();
        List<String> result = songs.filter(s -> s.getDuration() > 300)
            .map(Song::getTitle)
            .collect(Collectors.toList());
    }
}
```

In the previous code, before the map(..) call, a peek(..) call can be introduced to check if the filtered elements are the ones you expect. Another peek(..) call can be introduced after to inspect the mapped value, as shown in Listing 8-40.

Listing 8-40. Showing What peek(..) Can Do

```
package com.apress.bgn.eigth;

import com.apress.bgn.eigth.util.Song;
import com.apress.bgn.eigth.util.StreamMediaLoader;
import java.util.stream.Stream;
```

```java
public class MediaStreamTester {
    public static void main(String... args) {
        Stream<Song> songs = StreamMediaLoader.loadSongs();
        List<String> result = songs.filter(s -> s.getDuration() > 300)
            .peek(e -> System.out.println("\t Filtered value: " + e))
            .map(Song::getTitle)
            .peek(e -> System.out.println("\t Mapped value: " + e))
            .collect(Collectors.toList());
    }
}
```

Intermediate Operation: skip(..) and Terminal Operations: findAny(), anyMatch(..), allMatch(..) and noneMatch(..)

These are the last operations that will be discussed in this chapter, so they were coupled all together because the skip(..) operation might affect the result of the others when applied together.

The findAny() returns an Optimal<T> instance that contains the some element of the stream or an empty Optimal<T> instance when the stream is empty.

🔥 The behavior of findAny() this operation is explicitly nondeterministic; it is free to select any element in the stream. Its behavior is the same as findFirst() when applied to an unordered stream. So the choice to use one or the other depends on the type of stream is being called on.

Since findAny() is nondeterministic, its result is unpredictable, so applying it to a parallel stream is the same as applying it to a sequential one. The findAny() operation is applied to parallel Song stream, as shown in Listing 8-41.

Listing 8-41. Example Using findAny() on Parallel Stream

```java
package com.apress.bgn.eigth;

import com.apress.bgn.eigth.util.Song;
import com.apress.bgn.eigth.util.StreamMediaLoader;
import java.util.stream.Stream;

public class MediaStreamTester {
    public static void main(String... args) {
        Stream<Song> songs = StreamMediaLoader.loadSongs();
        Optional<Song> optSong = songs.parallel().findAny();
        optSong.ifPresent(System.out::println);
    }
}
```

The anyMatch(..) method receives an argument of type Predicate<T> and returns a boolean true value if there are any elements in the stream that match the predicate, and false otherwise. It works on parallel streams as well. The code in Listing 8-42 returns true if any of the songs in our stream has a title containing the word Paper.

Listing 8-42. Example Using anyMatch(..)

```java
package com.apress.bgn.eigth;

import com.apress.bgn.eigth.util.Song;
import com.apress.bgn.eigth.util.StreamMediaLoader;
import java.util.stream.Stream;

public class MediaStreamTester {
    public static void main(String... args) {
        Stream<Song> songs = StreamMediaLoader.loadSongs();
        boolean bO = songs.anyMatch(s -> s.getTitle().contains("Paper"));
        System.out.println("Are there songs with title containing 'Paper'?
        " + bO);
    }
}
```

The previous code will print true as there is a song in that stream named Paper Dolls. But if we want to change that result, all we have to do is skip the first 6 elements from processing in the original stream by calling skip(6) as depicted in Listing 8-43. This method works on parallel streams as well.

Listing 8-43. Example Using skip(..) and anyMatch(..)

```
package com.apress.bgn.eigth;

import com.apress.bgn.eigth.util.Song;
import com.apress.bgn.eigth.util.StreamMediaLoader;
import java.util.stream.Stream;

public class MediaStreamTester {
    public static void main(String... args) {
        Stream<Song> songs = StreamMediaLoader.loadSongs();
        boolean b1 = songs.parallel()
            .skip(6)
            .anyMatch(s -> s.getTitle().contains("Paper"));
        System.out.println("Are there songs with title containing `Paper`?
        " + b1);
    }
}
```

If the first six elements in the original stream are not processed, the previous code returns false. There is another function that analyzes all elements of a stream checking if they all match a single predicate, and that method is named allMatch(..). In Listing 8-44 we check to see if all Song instances have duration bigger than 300. The function returns a boolean value, and the value is true if all Song instances match the predicate and false otherwise. For the dataset used in the examples for this chapter the expected result is a false value, because not all our Song instances have the duration field value bigger than 300.

Listing 8-44. Showing What allMatch(..) Can Do

```
package com.apress.bgn.eigth;

import com.apress.bgn.eigth.util.Song;
import com.apress.bgn.eigth.util.StreamMediaLoader;
import java.util.stream.Stream;
```

```java
public class MediaStreamTester {
    public static void main(String... args) {
        Stream<Song> songs = StreamMediaLoader.loadSongs();
        boolean b2 = songs.allMatch(s -> s.getDuration() > 300);
        System.out.println("Are all songs longer than 5 minutes? " + b2);
    }
}
```

The *sister* of this function is a function named noneMatch(..) that does exactly the opposite thing: takes a predicate as an argument and returns a boolean value as well, but the value is true if none of the stream elements match the predicate provided as argument, and false otherwise. In Listing 8-45 we check using the noneMatch(..) if there is no Song instance with duration > 300 and we expect the result to be false as well.

Listing 8-45. Showing What noneMatch(..) Can Do

```java
package com.apress.bgn.eigth;

import com.apress.bgn.eigth.util.Song;
import com.apress.bgn.eigth.util.StreamMediaLoader;
import java.util.stream.Stream;

public class MediaStreamTester {
    public static void main(String... args) {
        Stream<Song> songs = StreamMediaLoader.loadSongs();
        boolean b3 = songs.noneMatch(s -> s.getDuration() > 300);
        System.out.println("Are all songs shorter than 5 minutes? " + b3);
    }
}
```

Debugging Stream Code

As mentioned previously the peek(..) method can be used for a light debugging, more like logging the changes that happen on stream elements between one stream method call and another. Another simple way to debug code written with streams is to implement predicates, consumers, and suppliers and add logging statements in their main methods.

These simple methods are not always enough, especially when that code is part of a big application that a big number of users access simultaneously. They might also be tedious to implement, because logging statements must be added during development and then removed before putting the application in production to avoid polluting the application logs and (maybe) slowing it down.

A more advanced way to debug streams is provided by the IntelliJ IDEA editor; starting with May 11, 2017 this editor includes a specialized plug-in for stream debugging named Java Stream Debugger.[4]

💡 If you are reading this book and are not using IntelliJ IDEA as an editor to test the code, you can skip this section and research a Steam debugger plug-in for the editor of your choice. This book is focused of the Java language mostly, and this section is just added here for convenience.

To use the Java Stream Debugger, you must place a breakpoint on the line where a stream processing chain is defined. In Figure 8-4 you can see a piece of code representing the processing of a stream of Song instances being executed in debug and a breakpoint paused the execution in line 44. When the execution is paused, the Stream debugger view can be opened, by clicking on the button that is surrounded in the red rectangle.

---

[4] The official plug-in page from JetBrains, the company that created and maintains IntelliJ IDEA, can be found at JetBrains, "Java Stream Debugger," https://plugins.jetbrains.com/plugin/9696-java-stream-debugger?platform=hootsuite, accessed October 15, 2021.

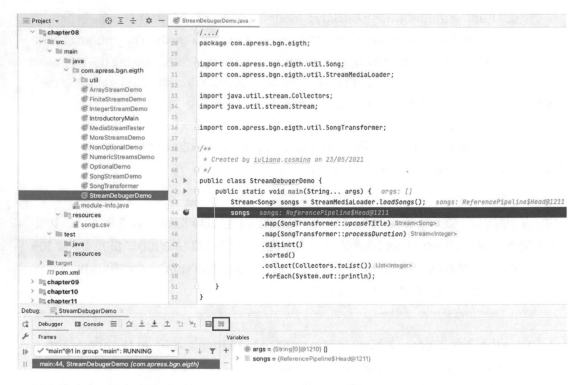

Figure 8-4. *Button to start the Java stream debugger*

If you click the debugger button in the previous image a popup window will appear that will have a tab for each operation of the stream processing. In Figure 8-5 you can see the tabs and their methods underlined and linked to each other.

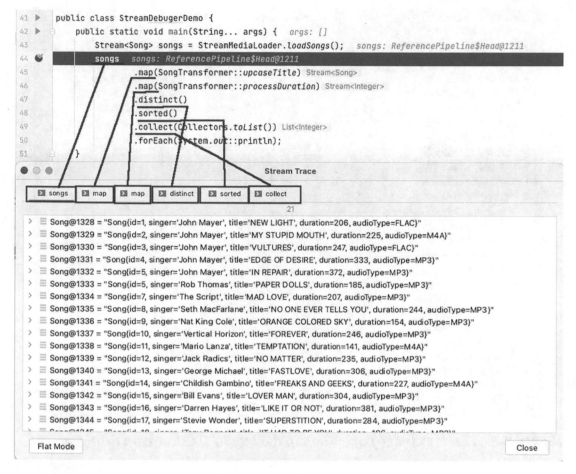

Figure 8-5. *The Java stream debugger window*

In the operation tabs, the text box on the left contains the elements on the original stream. The text box on the right contains the resulting stream with its elements. The following images in the chapter show tabs for various operations. For operations that reduce the number of elements or change their order there are lines from one set of elements to the other. The first map(..) method transforms the song titles to their uppercase version. The second map(..) method transforms the duration of the songs in minutes and returns a stream of integers.

The distinct(..) method produces a new stream that contains only the distinct elements in the previous one, and this operation's effect is depicted quite nice in the debugger and in Figure 8-6.

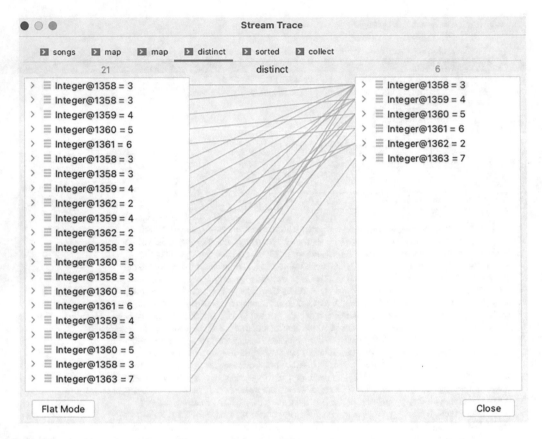

Figure 8-6. *The* `distinct()` *operation in the IntelliJ IDEA stream debugger*

The next operation is `sorted()`, which will sort the entries on the stream returned by the `distinct()` operation. The reordering of the elements and adding them to a new stream is depicted in the debugger also and in Figure 8-7.

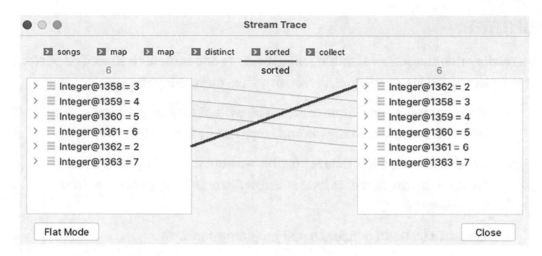

Figure 8-7. *The* sorted() *operation in the IntelliJ IDEA stream debugger*

After inspecting the results in the debugger, even if you want to continue the execution, this won't be possible because all elements in the original stream and the resulting ones were actually consumed by the debugger, so the following exception will be printed in the console:

```
OpenJDK 64-Bit Server VM warning: Sharing is only supported for boot loader
classes because bootstrap classpath has been appended
Exception in thread "main" java.lang.IllegalStateException: stream has
already been operated upon or closed
    at java.base/java.util.stream.AbstractPipeline.<init>(AbstractPipeline.
    java:203)
    at java.base/java.util.stream.ReferencePipeline.<init>
    (ReferencePipeline.java:96)
    at java.base/java.util.stream.ReferencePipeline$StatelessOp.<init>
    (ReferencePipeline.java:800)
    at java.base/java.util.stream.ReferencePipeline$3.<init>
    (ReferencePipeline.java:191)
    at java.base/java.util.stream.ReferencePipeline.map
    (ReferencePipeline.java:190)
    at chapter.eigth/com.apress.bgn.eigth.StreamDebugerDemo.
    main(StreamDebugerDemo.java:45)
```

Summary

After reading this chapter and running the provided code samples it should be obvious why the Stream API is so awesome. Personally, I like three things best:

- more compact and simple code can be written to solve problems without losing readability (ifs and loops can be avoided)

- parallel processing of data is possible without the boilerplate code required before Java 8, as long as the performance angle is taken into consideration

- code can be written in functional programming style

Also, the Stream API is more a declarative way of programming, as most stream methods take arguments of type `Consumer<T>`, `Predicate<T>`, `Supplier<T>`, `Function<T>`, and so on that declare what should be done for each stream element, but the methods are not explicitly called unless there are elements on the stream.

💡 Writing code using the Java Stream API is like designing a Rube Goldberg machine. Nothing happens until an event starts the whole contraption. A Rube Goldberg machine is intentionally designed to perform a simple task in an indirect and overly complicated way. Depending on the problem you are trying to solve, code written using streams can get quote complex too. In the end it is your decision as a developer how much you need to rely on streams.

This chapter also covered how to use `Optional<T>` instances to avoid `NullPointerExceptions` and writing `if` statements.

After you have finished reading this chapter you should have a pretty good idea about the following:

- how to create sequential and parallel streams from collections

- what empty streams are useful for

- terms to remember about streams:

  - sequence of elements

  - predicate

  - consumer

  - supplier

  - method reference

  - source

  - aggregate operations

  - intermediate operation

  - terminal operation

  - pipelining

  - internal automatic iterations

- how to create and use `Optional<T>` instances

CHAPTER 9

Debugging, Testing, and Documenting

Development work does not only require you to design the solution for a problem and write the code for it. To make sure your solution solves the problem, you have to test it. **Testing** involves making sure every component making up your solution behaves as expected in expected and unexpected situations.

The most practical way to test code is to inspect values of intermediary variables by **logging** them and printing them in the console in specific situations.

When a solution is complex, **debugging** provides the opportunity to pause the execution and inspect the state of the variables. Debugging sometimes involves **break points** and requires an IDE. Break points, as the name says, are points where the application pauses its execution and inspection of variables is performed.

After making sure your solution fits the requirements, you have to document it, especially if the problem that is being solved is one that requires complex code to solve it. Or if your solution might be a prerequisite for other applications, it is your responsibility to explain other developers how to use it.

This chapter will cover a few ways to do all these, because these are key talents for a developer.

Debugging

Debugging is a process of finding and resolving defects or problems within a computer program. There are more debugging tactics, and depending on the complexity of an application, one or more can be used. A list of those techniques is noted here:

- logging intermediary states of objects involved in the process and analyzing log files

435

© Iuliana Cosmina 2022
I. Cosmina, *Java 17 for Absolute Beginners*, https://doi.org/10.1007/978-1-4842-7080-6_9

- interactive debugging using breakpoints to pause the execution of the program and inspect intermediary states of objects involved in the process

- testing

- monitoring at the application or system level

- analysis of memory dumps item profiling, a form of dynamic program analysis that measures the memory occupied by a program, or CPU used, duration of method calls, and so on.

Let's start with the simplest way of debugging: **logging**.

Logging

In the real-world logging is a destructive process, is the cutting and processing of trees to produce timber. In software programming **logging** means writing log files that can be later used to identify problems in code. The simplest way to log information is to use the System.out.print*(..) method family, as depicted in Figure 9-1.

```
System.out.
    m print(int i)                                            void
    m print(char c)                                           void
    m print(long l)                                           void
    m print(float f)                                          void
    m print(char[] s)                                         void
    m print(double d)                                         void
    m print(String s)                                         void
    m print(boolean b)                                        void
    m print(Object obj)                                       void
    m printf(String format, Object... args)          PrintStream
    m printf(Locale l, String format, Object... args)  PrintStream
    m println()                                               void
    m println(int x)                                          void
    m println(char x)                                         void
    m println(long x)                                         void
    m println(float x)                                        void
    m println(char[] x)                                       void
    m println(double x)                                       void
    m println(Object x)                                       void
    m println(String x)                                       void
    m println(boolean x)                                      void
```

Figure 9-1. System.out.print method family

The examples in this chapter use a hierarchy of classes that provide methods to sort integer arrays. The class hierarchy is depicted in Figure 9-2.

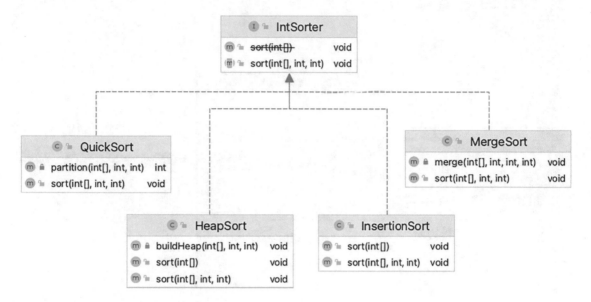

Figure 9-2. *Sorting class hierarchy*

In the next code sample the MergeSort class contents are modified to add System. out.print(..) statements to log the steps of the algorithm.

Merge-Sort is the name of a sorting algorithm with a better performance than Bubble-Sort (introduced in the previous chapter). Merge-Sort describes sorting an array as the following suite of steps:

- The array is split in two halves, each half is split again until the resulting array is one that can be sorted easily, and the sorted arrays are than merged repeatedly, until the result is a single sorted array.

This approach of splitting the array repeatedly until sorting becomes a manageable operation is called **divide et impera,** also known as **divide and conquer**. There are more algorithms that follow the same approach for solving a problem and Merge-Sort is only the first of them that will be covered in this book. In Figure 9-3, you can see what happens in every step of a Merge-Sort algorithm.

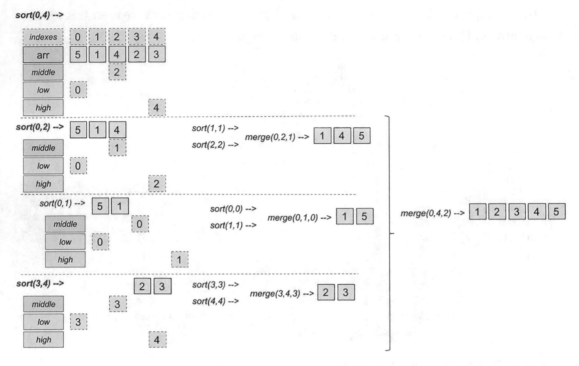

Figure 9-3. *Merge sort algorithm steps*

In each step of the algorithm the middle index of the array is identified. Then the sort(..) method is called for the arrays split in the middle by that index. This continues until there is no middle index, because the array has a single element. That is when the merge(..) method is called; aside from merging pieces of the array, it also sorts them during the merging.

Figure 9-3 depicts the algorithm in a pretty similar way to the output that will be generated by the System.out.print(..) statements. Since it was mentioned that this algorithm is based on the Divide and Conquer method, Figure 9-4 better shows the order of the operations.

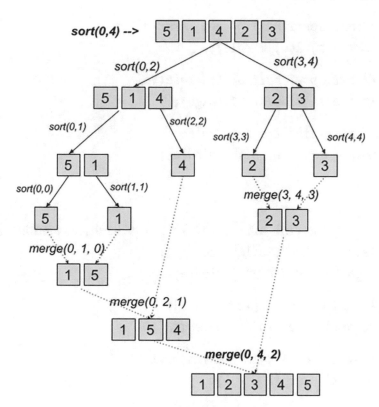

Figure 9-4. *Merge sort algorithm steps shown as a tree*

To write the code that models the Merge-Sort algorithm, we need to write the two methods sort(array, low, high) and merge(array, low, high, middle). The proposed implementation is depicted in Listing 9-1.

Listing 9-1. Merge-Sort Proposed Implementation

```
package com.apress.bgn.nine.algs;

import java.util.logging.Logger;

public class MergeSort implements IntSorter {
    private static final Logger log = Logger.getLogger(MergeSort.class.
    getName());

    public void sort(int[] arr, int low, int high) {
        if (low < high) {

            int middle = (low + high) / 2;
```

```java
        //sort lower half of the interval
        sort(arr, low, middle);

        //sort upper half of the interval
        sort(arr, middle + 1, high);

        // merge the two intervals
        merge(arr, low, high, middle);
    }
}

private void merge(int arr[], int low, int high, int middle) {
    int leftLength = middle - low + 1;
    int rightLength = high - middle;

    int left[] = new int[leftLength];
    int right[] = new int[rightLength];

    for (int i = 0; i < leftLength; ++i) {
        left[i] = arr[low + i];
    }
    for (int i = 0; i < rightLength; ++i) {
        right[i] = arr[middle + 1 + i];
    }

    int i = 0, j = 0;

    int k = low;
    while (i < leftLength && j < rightLength) {
        if (left[i] <= right[j]) {
            arr[k] = left[i];
            i++;
        } else {
            arr[k] = right[j];
            j++;
        }
        k++;
    }
```

```java
    while (i < leftLength) {
        arr[k] = left[i];
        i++;
        k++;
    }

    while (j < rightLength) {
        arr[k] = right[j];
        j++;
        k++;
    }
    }
}
```

Logging with `System.out.print`

The preceding code might look scary, but it does exactly what is depicted in Figure 9-3. A lot of variables are needed though to refer all the indexes used to arrange our elements in the proper order. To make sure our solution is properly implemented, it would be useful to see the values each method is called with and the array pieces that are being handled. We can do this by simply modifying our methods and adding a few `System.out.print` statements, as shown in Listing 9-2.

Listing 9-2. Merge-Sort Proposed Implementation with Logging Using `System.out.print` Statements

```java
package com.apress.bgn.nine.algs;

public class MergeSort implements IntSorter {

    public void sort(int[] arr, int low, int high) {
        System.out.print("Call sort of [low,high]: [" + low + " " + high
        + "] ");
        for (int i = low; i <= high; ++i) {
            System.out.print(arr[i] + " ");
        }
```

```java
        System.out.println();

    if (low < high) {

        int middle = (low + high) / 2;

        //sort lower half of the interval
        sort(arr, low, middle);

        //sort upper half of the interval
        sort(arr, middle + 1, high);

        // merge the two intervals
        merge(arr, low, high, middle);
    }
}

private void merge(int arr[], int low, int high, int middle) {
    int leftLength = middle - low + 1;
    int rightLength = high - middle;

    int left[] = new int[leftLength];
    int right[] = new int[rightLength];

    for (int i = 0; i < leftLength; ++i) {
        left[i] = arr[low + i];
    }
    for (int i = 0; i < rightLength; ++i) {
        right[i] = arr[middle + 1 + i];
    }

    int i = 0, j = 0;

    int k = low;
    while (i < leftLength && j < rightLength) {
        if (left[i] <= right[j]) {
            arr[k] = left[i];
            i++;
        } else {
```

```java
            arr[k] = right[j];
            j++;
        }
        k++;
    }

    while (i < leftLength) {
        arr[k] = left[i];
        i++;
        k++;
    }

    while (j < rightLength) {
        arr[k] = right[j];
        j++;
        k++;
    }
    System.out.print("Called merge of [low, high, middle]: [" + low +
    " " + high + " " + middle + "]) ");
    for (int z = low; z <= high; ++z) {
        System.out.print(arr[z] + " ");
    }
    System.out.println();
    }
}
```

A combination of `System.out.print(..)` and `System.out.println(..)` statements format the output to show the progress of the algorithm. To test the output, we need a class containing a `main(..)` method to execute the algorithm, something similar to the one depicted in Listing 9-3.

Listing 9-3. Main Class to Execute the Merge-Sort Proposed Implementation

```java
package com.apress.bgn.nine;

import com.apress.bgn.nine.algs.IntSorter;
import com.apress.bgn.nine.algs.MergeSort;
import java.util.Arrays;
```

```java
public class SortingDemo {

    public static void main(String... args) {
        int arr[] = {5,1,4,2,3};

        IntSorter mergeSort = new MergeSort();
        mergeSort.sort(arr, 0, arr.length - 1);

        System.out.print("Sorted: ");
        Arrays.stream(arr).forEach(i -> System.out.print(i+ " "));
    }

}
```

If we run the preceding class, the arguments provided to methods sort(..) and merge(..) are printed in the console. So are the values being sorted and array pieces being merged. The output should look like the one depicted in Listing 9-4.

Listing 9-4. Values Being Printed During the Execution of the Merge-Sort Proposed Implementation

```
Call sort of [low,high]: [0 4] 5 1 4 2 3
Call sort of [low,high]: [0 2] 5 1 4
Call sort of [low,high]: [0 1] 5 1
Call sort of [low,high]: [0 0] 5
Call sort of [low,high]: [1 1] 1
Called merge of [low, high, middle]: [0 1 0]) 1 5
Call sort of [low,high]: [2 2] 4
Called merge of [low, high, middle]: [0 2 1]) 1 4 5
Call sort of [low,high]: [3 4] 2 3
Call sort of [low,high]: [3 3] 2
Call sort of [low,high]: [4 4] 3
Called merge of [low, high, middle]: [3 4 3]) 2 3
Called merge of [low, high, middle]: [0 4 2]) 1 2 3 4 5
Sorted: 1 2 3 4 5
```

You can see that the console output matches the algorithm steps depicted in Figure 9-3, so that output is clearly proof that the solution works as expected.

Although all seems well, there is a problem with this code: every time the sort(..) method is called, those printing statements are executed.

🔥 If the sorting is just a step of a more complex solution, the output is not really necessary and can even pollute the output of the bigger solution. Also, if the array is quite big, printing that output could affect the performance of the overall solution.

So a different approach should be considered, one that could be customized and a decision made if the output should be printed or not. This where logging libraries come in.

Logging with JUL

JUL is the name of the logging backend provided by the JDK and is an acronym for java. util.logging. The JDK provides its own logger classes that are grouped under this package. A Logger instance is used to write messages. The Logger instance should be provided a name when is created and log messages are printed by calling specialized methods that print messages at different levels. For the JUL module, the levels and their scope are listed here, but other logging libraries have similar logging levels.

- OFF should be used to turn off all logging

- SEVERE highest level, message indicates a serious failure

- WARNING indicates that this message is being printed because of a potential problem

- INFO indicates that this is an informational message

- CONFIG indicates that this is a message containing configuration information

- FINE indicates that this a message providing tracing information

- FINER indicates that this is a fairly detailed tracing message

- FINEST indicates that this is a very detailed tracing message

- ALL all log messages should be printed

Loggers can be configured using XML or properties files and their output can be directed to external files. For the code sample introduced previously all `System.out.print` statements in the `MergeSort` class are replaced with logger calls. Listing 9-5 depicts the main class to run the algorithm.

Listing 9-5. Main Class to Run the Merge-Sort Proposed Implementation with JUL Logging Statements

```
package com.apress.bgn.nine;

// some imports omitted
import java.util.logging.Level;
import java.util.logging.LogManager;
import java.util.logging.Logger;

public class SortingJulDemo {

    private static final Logger log = Logger.getLogger(SortingJulDemo.
    class.getName());

    static {
        try {
            LogManager logManager = LogManager.getLogManager();
            logManager.readConfiguration(new FileInputStream("./chapter09/
            logging-jul/src/main/resources/logging.properties"));
        } catch (IOException exception) {
            log.log(Level.SEVERE, "Error in loading configuration",
            exception);
        }
    }

    public static void main(String... args) {
        int arr[] = {5,1,4,2,3};

        final StringBuilder sb = new StringBuilder("Sorting  an array with
        merge sort: ");
        Arrays.stream(arr).forEach(i -> sb.append(i).append(" "));
        log.info(sb.toString());
```

```
    IntSorter mergeSort = new MergeSort();
    mergeSort.sort(arr, 0, arr.length - 1);

    final StringBuilder sb2 = new StringBuilder("Sorted: ");
    Arrays.stream(arr).forEach(i -> sb2.append(i).append( " "));
    log.info(sb2.toString());
  }
}
```

There are not many log statements in this class.

The body of the class starts with the declaration and initialization of the Logger instance. The instance is not created by calling the constructor, but obtained by calling the getLogger(..) static method declared in the Logger class. This method looks for a logger instance with the name provided as argument, if found that instance is returned otherwise an instance with that name is created and returned. In this example the name of the logger instance is the fully qualified class name, obtain by calling SortingJulDemo.class.getName().

Right after this statement, there is a static block used to configure the logger from the logging.properties file. The contents of this file are shown in Listing 9-6.

Listing 9-6. Properties Used to Configure the JUL Logger Declared in the logging.properties File

```
handlers=java.util.logging.ConsoleHandler
java.util.logging.ConsoleHandler.level=ALL
java.util.logging.ConsoleHandler.formatter=java.util.logging.
SimpleFormatter
java.util.logging.SimpleFormatter.format=[%1$tF %1$tT] [%4$-4s] %5$s %n
```

This field contains a list of values in the format propertyName=propertyValue that represent the configuration for the JUL logger. Their values specify the following:

- the class used to print the log messages: java.util.logging. ConsoleHandler prints messages in the console.

- the class used to format the log messages: java.util.logging. SimpleFormatter

- a template for printing log messages: [%1$tF %1$tT]
  [%4$-4s] %5$s %n

- the levels of the log messages that are printed, in this case all levels
  log messages because of the the ALL value.

The Logger instance is created by calling the static method Logger.getLogger(..).
The recommended practice is for the logger to be named as the class it is logging
messages for. Without any additional configuration, every message printed with log.
info(..) is printed prefixed with the full system date, full class name, and method name
in front of it. As you can imagine the result is quite verbose, and this is the logging.
properties file comes in handy and the LogManager configured from it. The LogManager
reads the configuration that customizes the Logger instance.

For this section all System.out.print statements are replaced with logger calls in
the MergeSort class. A StringBuilder is introduced to construct longer messages before
writing them with log.info([message]), which is equivalent to calling log.log(Level.
INFO, [message]). The resulting code of the algorithm is shown in Listing 9-7.

Listing 9-7. Merge-Sort Proposed Implementation with Logging Using JUL
Statements

```java
package com.apress.bgn.nine.algs;

import java.util.logging.Logger;

public class MergeSort implements IntSorter {
    private static final Logger log = Logger.getLogger(MergeSort.class.
    getName());

    public void sort(int[] arr, int low, int high) {
        StringBuilder sb = new StringBuilder("Call sort of ")
                .append("[low,high]: [")
                    .append(low).append(" ").append(high)
                .append("] ");
        for (int i = low; i <= high; ++i) {
            sb.append(arr[i]).append(" ");
        }
        log.info(sb.toString());
```

```java
    if (low < high) {

        int middle = (low + high) / 2;

        //sort lower half of the interval
        sort(arr, low, middle);

        //sort upper half of the interval
        sort(arr, middle + 1, high);

        // merge the two intervals
        merge(arr, low, high, middle);
    }
}

private void merge(int arr[], int low, int high, int middle) {
    int leftLength = middle - low + 1;
    int rightLength = high - middle;

    int left[] = new int[leftLength];
    int right[] = new int[rightLength];

    for (int i = 0; i < leftLength; ++i) {
        left[i] = arr[low + i];
    }
    for (int i = 0; i < rightLength; ++i) {
        right[i] = arr[middle + 1 + i];
    }

    int i = 0, j = 0;

    int k = low;
    while (i < leftLength && j < rightLength) {
        if (left[i] <= right[j]) {
            arr[k] = left[i];
            i++;
        } else {
            arr[k] = right[j];
            j++;
        }
    }
```

```java
            k++;
        }

        while (i < leftLength) {
            arr[k] = left[i];
            i++;
            k++;
        }

        while (j < rightLength) {
            arr[k] = right[j];
            j++;
            k++;
        }
        StringBuilder sb = new StringBuilder("Called merge of [low, high,
        middle]: [")
                        .append(low).append(" ").append(high).append("
                        ").append(middle)
                    .append("]) ");
        for (int z = low; z <= high; ++z) {
            sb.append(arr[z]).append(" ");
        }
        log.info(sb.toString());
    }
}
```

Running the `SortingJulDemo` produces the output shown in Listing 9-8.

Listing 9-8. Values Being Printed During the Execution of the Merge-Sort Proposed Implementation When Logging is Done Using JUL with a Custom Configuration

```
[2021-06-06 11:36:06] [INFO] Sorting  an array with merge sort: 5 1 4 2 3
[2021-06-06 11:36:06] [INFO] Call sort of [low,high]: [0 4] 5 1 4 2 3
[2021-06-06 11:36:06] [INFO] Call sort of [low,high]: [0 2] 5 1 4
[2021-06-06 11:36:06] [INFO] Call sort of [low,high]: [0 1] 5 1
[2021-06-06 11:36:06] [INFO] Call sort of [low,high]: [0 0] 5
```

```
[2021-06-06 11:36:06] [INFO] Call sort of [low,high]: [1 1] 1
[2021-06-06 11:36:06] [INFO] Called merge of [low, high, middle]: [0 1 0]) 1 5
[2021-06-06 11:36:06] [INFO] Call sort of [low,high]: [2 2] 4
[2021-06-06 11:36:06] [INFO] Called merge of [low, high, middle]:
[0 2 1]) 1 4 5
[2021-06-06 11:36:06] [INFO] Call sort of [low,high]: [3 4] 2 3
[2021-06-06 11:36:06] [INFO] Call sort of [low,high]: [3 3] 2
[2021-06-06 11:36:06] [INFO] Call sort of [low,high]: [4 4] 3
[2021-06-06 11:36:06] [INFO] Called merge of [low, high, middle]:
[3 4 3]) 2 3
[2021-06-06 11:36:06] [INFO] Called merge of [low, high, middle]: [0 4 2])
1 2 3 4 5
[2021-06-06 11:36:06] [INFO] Sorted: 1 2 3 4 5
```

Without the static initialization block that customizes how log messages are shown, the default class used to specify where the log messages are printed is java.util. logging.ConsoleHandler, and the java.util.logging.SimpleFormatter is configured with a default format that is quite verbose that is declared by the jdk.internal.logger. SimpleConsoleLogger. Formatting.DEFAULT_FORMAT.

The value of this constant is %1$tb %1$td, %1$tY %1$tl:%1$tM:%1$tS %1$Tp %2$s%n%4$s: %5$s%6$s%n, and this makes the logger to prefix the log messages with a line containing the system date and time formatted in a readable manner, the full class name, the method name, and a new line containing the log level. To test this, just comment the static initialization block and run the SortingJulDemo class. The log messages in the console are now printed as depicted in Listing 9-9.

Listing 9-9. Values Being Printed During the Execution of the Merge-Sort Proposed Implementation When Logging is Done Using JUL with the Default Configuration

```
Jun 06, 2021 11:40:46 AM com.apress.bgn.nine.SortingJulDemo main
INFO: Sorting  an array with merge sort: 5 1 4 2 3
Jun 06, 2021 11:40:46 AM com.apress.bgn.nine.algs.MergeSort sort
INFO: Call sort of [low,high]: [0 4] 5 1 4 2 3
Jun 06, 2021 11:40:46 AM com.apress.bgn.nine.algs.MergeSort sort
INFO: Call sort of [low,high]: [0 2] 5 1 4
```

```
Jun 06, 2021 11:40:46 AM com.apress.bgn.nine.algs.MergeSort sort
INFO: Call sort of [low,high]: [0 1] 5 1
Jun 06, 2021 11:40:46 AM com.apress.bgn.nine.algs.MergeSort sort
INFO: Call sort of [low,high]: [0 0] 5
# other log messages omitted
```

Beside thew SimpleFormatter, there is another class that can be used to format log messages named XMLFormatter that formats the messages as XML (Extensible Markup Language). The XML format of writing data is defined by a set of rules for encoding the data that is both human-readable and machine readable. Also, the set of rules makes it easy to validate and find errors.[1] Since for XML it makes no sense for the messages to be written the console, the FileHandler class should be used do direct the log messages to a file. The modifications to be added to the configuration file are depicted in Listing 9-10.

Listing 9-10. Properties Used to Configure the JUL Logger to Write Log Messages as XML to a File

```
handlers=java.util.logging.FileHandler
java.util.logging.FileHandler.pattern=chapter09/out/chapter09-log.xml
.level=ALL
java.util.logging.ConsoleHandler.formatter=java.util.logging.XMLFormatter
```

Using the configuration file with the contents shown in Listing 9-10 when running the SortingJulDemo class, a file named chapter09-log.xml is generated under chapter09/out and contains entries that look like the one depicted in Listing 9-11:

Listing 9-11. Logging Messages as XML

```xml
<?xml version="1.0" encoding="UTF-8" standalone="no"?>
<!DOCTYPE log SYSTEM "logger.dtd">
<log>
    <record>
        <date>2021-06-06T11:03:44.200054Z</date>
        <millis>1622977424200</millis>
        <nanos>54000</nanos>
```

---

[1] You can read more about XML at Wikipedia, "XML," https://en.wikipedia.org/wiki/XML, accessed October 15, 2021.

```xml
        <sequence>0</sequence>
        <logger>com.apress.bgn.nine.SortingJulDemo</logger>
        <level>INFO</level>
        <class>com.apress.bgn.nine.SortingJulDemo</class>
        <method>main</method>
        <thread>1</thread>
        <message>Sorting  an array with merge sort: 5 1 4 2 3 </message>
    </record>
<!-- other log messages omitted-->
</log>
```

The logging output can also be customized by providing a custom class, the only condition is for the class to extend the `java.util.logging.Formatter` class, or any of its JDK subclasses.

In the previous code samples only `log.info(..)` calls were used, because the code is quite basic; there is little room for anything unexpected to happen (there are no external resources involved that might be unavailable).

The code can be modified to allow the user to insert the elements of the array. Code to treat the case when the user does not provide any data and code to treat the case when user inserts bad data should be added to the class. For example, if the user does not provide any data, a `SEVERE` log message should be printed, and the application should terminate. If the user introduces invalid data, the valid data should be used, and warning should be printed for elements that are not integers. This means that the SortingJulDemo class changes as depicted in Listing 9-12.

Listing 9-12. SortingJulDemo Using an Array of Elements Provided as Argument for the `main(..)` Method

```java
package com.apress.bgn.nine;

// imports omitted

public class SortingJulDemo {

    private static final Logger log = Logger.getLogger(SortingJulDemo.
    class.getName());
```

```java
    static {
        try {
            LogManager logManager = LogManager.getLogManager();
            logManager.readConfiguration(new FileInputStream("./chapter09/
            logging-jul/src/main/resources/logging.properties"));
        } catch (IOException exception) {
            log.log(Level.SEVERE, "Error in loading configuration",
            exception);
        }
    }

    public static void main(String... args) {
        if (args.length == 0) {
            log.severe("No data to sort!");
            return;
        }
        int[] arr = getInts(args);

        final StringBuilder sb = new StringBuilder("Sorting  an array with
        merge sort: ");
        Arrays.stream(arr).forEach(i -> sb.append(i).append(" "));
        log.info(sb.toString());

        IntSorter mergeSort = new MergeSort();
        mergeSort.sort(arr, 0, arr.length - 1);

        final StringBuilder sb2 = new StringBuilder("Sorted: ");
        Arrays.stream(arr).forEach(i -> sb2.append(i).append( " "));
        log.info(sb2.toString());
    }

    /**
     * Transforms a String[] to an int[] array
     * @param args
     * @return an array of integers
     */
```

```java
    private static int[] getInts(String[] args) {
        List<Integer> list = new ArrayList<>();
        for (String arg : args) {
            try {
                int toInt = Integer.parseInt(arg);
                list.add(toInt);
            } catch (NumberFormatException nfe) {
                log.warning("Element " + arg + " is not an integer and
                cannot be added to the array!");
            }
        }
        int[] arr = new int[list.size()];
        int j = 0;
        for (Integer elem : list) {
            arr[j++] = elem;
        }
        return arr;
    }
}
```

As you can see the `arr` array is no longer hardcoded in the `main(..)` method, but the values that this method receives as arguments become the array to be sorted and are converted from `String` values to `int` values by the `getInts(..)` method. The person executing this program, can provide the arguments from the command line, but because we are using IntelliJ IDEA, there is an easier way to do that. If you now run the program without providing any arguments, this is what will be printed in the console:

```
[2021-06-06 12:16:14] [SEVERE] No data to sort!
```

The execution stops right there, because there is nothing to sort. Since you've probably run this class a few times, IntelliJ IDEA probably created a launcher configuration for you that you can customize and provide arguments for the execution. Just take a look at Figure 9-5 and try to edit your configuration as it is depicted there, by adding the recommended values as program arguments.

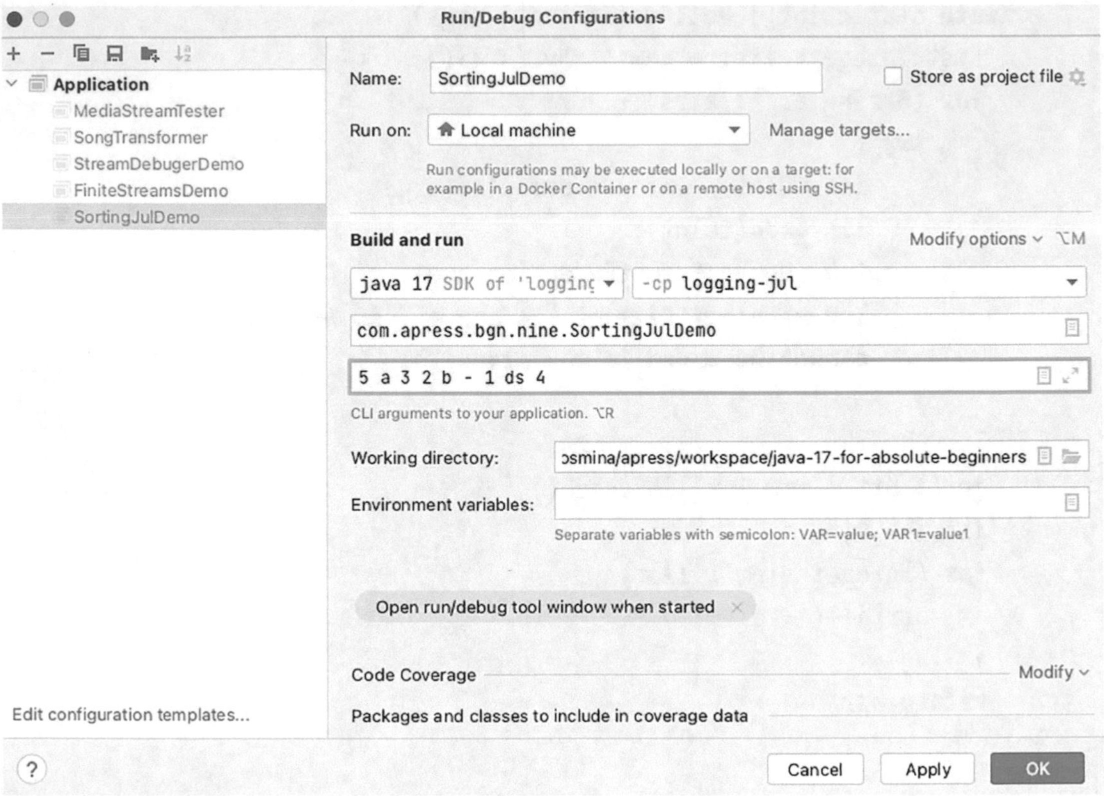

Figure 9-5. *IntelliJ IDEA launcher for the* `SortingJulDemo` *class*

Running this version of the `SortingJulDemo` with the default console logging configured produces a few extra log messages, as depicted in Listing 9-13.

Listing 9-13. Logging Messages of Level WARNING Being Shown During Execution of the New Version of `SortingJulDemo`

[2021-06-06 12:21:35] [WARNING] Element a is not an integer and cannot be added to the array!
[2021-06-06 12:21:35] [WARNING] Element b is not an integer and cannot be added to the array!
[2021-06-06 12:21:35] [WARNING] Element - is not an integer and cannot be added to the array!
[2021-06-06 12:21:35] [WARNING] Element ds is not an integer and cannot be added to the array!

```
[2021-06-06 12:21:35] [INFO] Sorting an array with merge sort: 5 3 2 1 4
[2021-06-06 12:21:35] [INFO] Call sort of [low,high]: [0 4] 5 3 2 1 4
# other log messages omitted
```

We mentioned in the previous section that writing logs can affect performance in some cases. When the application is running in a production system, we might want to refine the logging configuration to filter out less important log messages and keep only those that notify the risk of a problem. In the previous configuration examples, there was a configuration line that enabled all log messages to be printed:

```
java.util.logging.ConsoleHandler.level=ALL
```

Or the more general format that works for any `java.util.logging.Handler` subclass:

```
.level=ALL
```

If the value of this property is changed to `OFF`, nothing will be printed. The log levels have integer values assigned to them, and those values can be used to compare the severity of the messages. As a rule, if you configure a certain level of messages, more severe messages will be printed as well. So if we set that property to `INFO`, `WARNING` messages will be printed as well. The values for the severity levels of messages are defined in the `java.util.logging.Level` class and if you open that class in your editor, you can see the integer values assigned to each of them as depicted in Listing 9-14.

Listing 9-14. The Integer Valued Specific to the Log Levels

```java
package java.util.logging;
// import statements omitted

public class Level implements java.io.Serializable {

    public static final Level OFF = new Level("OFF",Integer.MAX_VALUE,
    defaultBundle);
    public static final Level SEVERE = new Level("SEVERE",1000,
    defaultBundle);
    public static final Level WARNING = new Level("WARNING", 900,
    defaultBundle);
    public static final Level INFO = new Level("INFO", 800, defaultBundle);
    public static final Level CONFIG = new Level("CONFIG", 700,
    defaultBundle);
```

```java
public static final Level FINE = new Level("FINE", 500, defaultBundle);
public static final Level FINER = new Level("FINER", 400, defaultBundle);
public static final Level FINEST = new Level("FINEST", 300,
defaultBundle);
public static final Level ALL = new Level("ALL", Integer.MIN_VALUE,
defaultBundle);
// other comments and code omitted
}
```

In the previous configuration by changing `.level=ALL` to `.level=WARNING`, we would expect to see all log messages of levels WARNING and SEVERE. Running the `SortingJulDemo` class with the previous arguments we should see only the `WARNING` level messages, as depicted in Listing 9-15.

Listing 9-15. Only Logging Messages of Level `WARNING` Being Shown During Execution of the `SortingJulDemo`

```
[2021-06-06 17:12:29] [WARNING] Element a is not an integer and cannot be
added to the array!
[2021-06-06 17:12:29] [WARNING] Element b is not an integer and cannot be
added to the array!
[2021-06-06 17:12:29] [WARNING] Element - is not an integer and cannot be
added to the array!
[2021-06-06 17:12:29] [WARNING] Element ds is not an integer and cannot be
added to the array!
```

To define log messaging formatting there are more ways: system properties can be used or programmatically, a formatter can be instantiated and set on a logger instance. It really depends on the specifics of the application. This won't be covered in the book, however, and if you are interested in reading more about Java logging with JUL I recommend this tutorial: `https://www.vogella.com/tutorials/Logging/article.html`. The reason for this is because JUL is known for its weak performance compared to other logging libraries. Another thing you have to take into account is that if the application you are building is a complex one with a lot of dependencies, these dependencies might use different logging libraries. How do you configure and use them all? This is where a logging facade proves useful. The next section will show you how to use the most renown Java logging facade: SLF4J.

Logging with SLF4J and Logback

The most renown Java logging facade is Simple Logging Facade for Java (SLF4J),[2] which serves as a logging abstraction for various logging frameworks. This means that in your code you will use the SLF4J interfaces and classes, and behind the scenes all the work will be done by a concrete logging implementation found in the classpath. The best part? You can change the logging implementation any time, and your code will still compile and execute correctly and there will be no need to change anything in it.

In the code samples covered until now in this chapter the code is tied to JUL; if we want for some reason to change the logging library, we need to change the existing code as well. The first step is to change our code to use the SLF4J Application Programming Interface (API).[3] Another advantage of using SLF4J is that the configuration is read automatically if the logging configuration file is on the classpath. This means the `LogManager` initialization block that we needed for JUL is not needed for SLF4J, as long as the configuration file is named according to the standard of the concrete logging implementation used. This section starts with the transformation of main `SortingJulDemo` class in Listing 9-5 to the `SortingSlf4jDemo` shown in Listing 9-16, by replacing JUL configuration and log statements with SLF4J specific ones.

Listing 9-16. The `SortingSlf4jDemo` Class

```
package com.apress.bgn.nine;

import org.slf4j.Logger;
import org.slf4j.LoggerFactory;
// other imports omitted

public class SortingSlf4jDemo {

    private static final Logger log = LoggerFactory.
    getLogger(SortingSlf4jDemo.class);
```

---

[2] See the official site at SLF4j, `https://www.slf4j.org`, accessed October 15, 2021.

[3] The API describes the publicly available components of a library: interfaces, classes, methods, and so on.

```java
public static void main(String... args) {
    if (args.length == 0) {
        log.error("No data to sort!");
        return;
    }

    final StringBuilder sb = new StringBuilder ("Sorting an array with
    merge sort: ");
    Arrays.stream(arr).forEach(i -> sb.append(i).append(" "));
    log.debug(sb.toString());

    IntSorter mergeSort = new MergeSort();
    mergeSort.sort(arr, 0, arr.length - 1);

    final StringBuilder sb2 = new StringBuilder("Sorted: ");
    Arrays.stream(arr).forEach(i -> sb2.append(i).append( " "));
    log.info(sb2.toString());
  }
}
```

SLf4J defines an API that maps to the concrete implementation provided by a logging library that hasn't been mentioned yet. The SLf4J log statements look pretty similar, but the log levels are a little different. The following list explains the most common SLf4J log statements:

- `log.error(..)` is used for logging messages at the ERROR level; usually these are messages that are used when there is a critical failure of the application and normal execution cannot continue. There is more than one form for this method, and exceptions and objects can be passed as arguments to it so that the state of the application at the moment of the failure can be assessed.

- `log.warn(..)` is used for logging messages at the WARN level; usually these messages are printed to notify that the application is not functioning normally and there might be reason to worry, in the same way as for the previous method, that there is more than one form of for it and exceptions and objects can be passed as arguments to better assess the current state of the application.

- `log.info(..)` is used for logging messages at the INFO level; this type of messages is informational, to let the user know that everything is okay and working as expected.

- `log.debug(..)` is used for logging messages at the DEBUG level; usually these messages are used to print intermediary states of the application, to check that things are going as expected and eventually in case of a failure you can trace the evolution of the application objects.

- `log.trace(..)` is used for logging messages at the TRACE level; this type of messages is informational of a very low importance.

The logging concrete implementation used for this example is called Logback,[4] and it was chosen for the previous edition of this book because at the time it was the only library that worked with SLF4J after modules were introduced in Java 9.

Logback is viewed as the successor of Log4j,[5] another popular logging implementation.

---

❶ Fun fact   Log4j, SLF4j and Logback were all founded by the same person: Ceki Gülcü. He is currently working in the latter two. As for Log4j, it is currently being replaced by Log4j2, an upgrade that provides significant improvements over its predecessor.

Logback implements SLF4J natively, there is no need to add another bridge library and it is faster as the Logback internals have been rewritten to perform faster on critical execution points. After modifying our classes to use SLF4J all we have to do is to add Logback as a dependency of our application and add a configuration file under the `src/main/resources` directory. The configuration file can be written in XML or Groovy and the standard requires for it to be named `logback.xml`. Listing 9-17 depicts the contents of this file for this sections' example:

---

[4] See the logback official site at Logback, `https://logback.qos.ch`, accessed October 15, 2021.
[5] See the Log4j official site at LOG4J, `https://logging.apache.org/log4j`, accessed October 15, 2021.

Listing 9-17. The Contents of the `logback.xml` Configuration File

```xml
<?xml version="1.0" encoding="UTF-8"?>
<configuration>
    <appender name="console" class="ch.qos.logback.core.ConsoleAppender">
        <encoder>
            <pattern>%d{HH:mm:ss.SSS} %-5level %logger{5} - %msg%n
            </pattern>
        </encoder>
    </appender>
    <logger name="com.apress.bgn.nine" level="debug"/>
    <root level="info">
        <appender-ref ref="console" />
    </root>
</configuration>
```

The `ch.qos.logback.core.ConsoleAppender` class writes log messages in the console and the `<pattern>` element value defines the format of the log messages. Lobgack can format fully qualified class names by shortening up package names to their initials; thus, it allows for a compact logging without losing details. This makes Logback one of the favorite logging implementation of the Java development world at the moment.

The package names, if they are made up of more than one part, are reduced to the first letter of each part. The logging calls in the `MergeSort` class were all replaced with `log.debug(..)` because these messages are intermediary and not really informational, just samples of state of the objects used by the application during the execution of the process. The general logging level of the application can be set using a `<root>` element to the desired level, but different logging levels can be set for classes or packages or subset of packages using `<logger>` elements.

Using the previous configuration, running the `SortingSlf4jDemo` yields the output shown in Listing 9-18.

Listing 9-18. Log Messages Printed by SLF4J + Logback

```
18:59:32.473 WARN  c.a.b.n.SortingSlf4jDemo - Element a is not an integer
and cannot be added to the array!
18:59:32.475 WARN  c.a.b.n.SortingSlf4jDemo - Element b is not an integer
and cannot be added to the array!
18:59:32.475 WARN  c.a.b.n.SortingSlf4jDemo - Element - is not an integer
and cannot be added to the array!
18:59:32.475 WARN  c.a.b.n.SortingSlf4jDemo - Element ds is not an integer
and cannot be added to the array!
18:59:32.477 DEBUG c.a.b.n.SortingSlf4jDemo - Sorting  an array with merge
sort: 5 3 2 1 4
18:59:32.479 DEBUG c.a.b.n.a.MergeSort - Call sort of : [0 4] 5 3 2 1 4
18:59:32.479 DEBUG c.a.b.n.a.MergeSort - Call sort of : [0 2] 5 3 2
18:59:32.479 DEBUG c.a.b.n.a.MergeSort - Call sort of : [0 1] 5 3
18:59:32.480 DEBUG c.a.b.n.a.MergeSort - Call sort of : [0 0] 5
18:59:32.480 DEBUG c.a.b.n.a.MergeSort - Call sort of : [1 1] 3
18:59:32.480 DEBUG c.a.b.n.a.MergeSort - Called merge of: [0 1 0],) 3 5
18:59:32.480 DEBUG c.a.b.n.a.MergeSort - Call sort of : [2 2] 2
18:59:32.480 DEBUG c.a.b.n.a.MergeSort - Called merge of: [0 2 1],) 2 3 5
18:59:32.480 DEBUG c.a.b.n.a.MergeSort - Call sort of : [3 4] 1 4
18:59:32.480 DEBUG c.a.b.n.a.MergeSort - Call sort of : [3 3] 1
18:59:32.480 DEBUG c.a.b.n.a.MergeSort - Call sort of : [4 4] 4
18:59:32.480 DEBUG c.a.b.n.a.MergeSort - Called merge of: [3 4 3],) 1 4
18:59:32.480 DEBUG c.a.b.n.a.MergeSort - Called merge of: [0 4 2],)
1 2 3 4 5
18:59:32.481 INFO  c.a.b.n.SortingSlf4jDemo - Sorted: 1 2 3 4 5
```

As you can see, the fully qualified class name com.apress.bgn.nine.
SortingSlf4jDemo was shortened to c.a.b.n.SortingSlf4jDemo. The configuration
file can be provided to the program as a VM argument, which means logging
format can be configured externally. When launching the class just use -Dlogback.
configurationFile=\temp\ext-logback.xml as a VM argument if you want to provide a
different log file.

Logback can direct output to a file as well, all we have to do is add a configuration using the ch.qos.logback.core.FileAppender class and direct the output to the file by adding an <appender> element in the <root> configuration. A configuration sample is depicted in Listing 9-19.

Listing 9-19. Logback Configuration to Direct Log Messages to a File

```xml
<?xml version="1.0" encoding="UTF-8"?>
<configuration>
    <appender name="file" class="ch.qos.logback.core.FileAppender">
        <file>chapter09/logging-slf4j/out/output.log</file>
        <append>true</append>
        <encoder>
            <pattern>%d{HH:mm:ss.SSS} %-5level %logger{5} - %msg%n
            </pattern>
        </encoder>
    </appender>
    <appender name="console" class="ch.qos.logback.core.ConsoleAppender">
        <encoder>
            <charset>UTF-8</charset>
            <pattern>%d{HH:mm:ss.SSS} %-5level %logger{5} - %msg%n
            </pattern>
        </encoder>
    </appender>
    <logger name="com.apress.bgn.nine" level="debug"/>
    <root level="info">
        <appender-ref ref="file"/>
        <appender-ref ref="console" />
    </root>
</configuration>
```

In the previous example, the original configuration was kept so that log messages are also printed in the console. Thus, proving that log messages can be directed to two destinations at once.

What if the log file becomes too big and cannot be opened? There's an approach for that. A different class named `ch.qos.logback.core.rolling.RollingFileAppender` can be configured to write a file up to a configured limit in size and then start another file. The `RollingFileAppender` and requires two arguments:

- an instance of a type that implements `ch.qos.logback.core.rolling.RollingPolicy` that provides functionality to write a new log file (operation also called roll-over)

- and an instance of a type that implements `ch.qos.logback.core.rolling.TriggeringPolicy<E>` that configures the conditions under which the rollover will happen.

Also, a single instance of a type that implements both of the interfaces can be used to configure the logger. Rolling over a log file means that the log file is renamed according to the configuration, usually—the last date the file was accessed is added to its name, and a new log file is created with the log file named configured (and without a date suffix, to make it clear this is the file logs are currently dumped in). Such a Logback configuration is depicted in Listing 9-20.

Listing 9-20. Logback Configuration to Direct Log Messages to a File of a Reasonable Limit

```xml
<?xml version="1.0" encoding="UTF-8"?>
<configuration scan="true">

    <appender name="r_file" class="ch.qos.logback.core.rolling.
    RollingFileAppender">
        <file>chapter09/logging-slf4j/out/output.log</file>
        <rollingPolicy class="ch.qos.logback.core.rolling.
        TimeBasedRollingPolicy">
            <fileNamePattern>chapter09/logging-slf4j/out/output_%d
            {yyyy-MM-dd}.%i.log</fileNamePattern>

            <timeBasedFileNamingAndTriggeringPolicy class="ch.qos.logback.
            core.rolling.SizeAndTimeBasedFNATP">
                <maxFileSize>10MB</maxFileSize>
            </timeBasedFileNamingAndTriggeringPolicy>
            <maxHistory>30</maxHistory>
        </rollingPolicy>
```

```xml
        <encoder>
            <charset>UTF-8</charset>
            <pattern>%d{HH:mm:ss.SSS} %-5level %logger{5} - %msg%n
            </pattern>
        </encoder>
    </appender>

    <appender name="console" class="ch.qos.logback.core.ConsoleAppender">
        <encoder>
            <pattern>%d{HH:mm:ss.SSS} %-5level %logger{5} - %msg%n
            </pattern>
        </encoder>
    </appender>

    <logger name="com.apress.bgn.nine" level="info"/>

    <root level="info">
        <appender-ref ref="r_file"/>
        <appender-ref ref="console" />
    </root>
</configuration>
```

In the previous configuration the `<file>` element configures the location and the name of the log file.

The `<rollingPolicy>` element configures the name the log file will receive when log messages will no longer be written in it, using the `<fileNamePattern>` element.

In the previous configuration the `output.log` file will be renamed to `output_2020-07-22.log`, for example, and then a new `output.log` file will be created for next day the application is running.

The `<timeBasedFileNamingAndTriggeringPolicy>` element configures when the new log file should be created and how big the `output.log` file should be before a new file is created. The configured size in the previous example is 10MB. If a log file gets bigger that 10MB before the end of the day, the file is renamed to `output_2018-07-22.1.log`. An index is added to the name and a new `output.log` is created.

The `<maxHistory>` element configures the lifespan of a log file, and in this example is 30 days.

Logging is a powerful tool when used properly. When not used properly can easily lead to performance problems. Also, logging everything is not really useful, because looking for a problem in a big logging file is like looking a needle in a haystack.

Another thing worth noticing is that in the previous code, `StringBuilder` instances are used to construct big log messages, that are to be printed at a certain level. What happens if logging for that level is disabled via configuration? If you guessed that time and memory is consumed creating those messages, even if they are not logged, you are right. So what do we do? The creators of SLF4J have thought of this as well, and added methods to test if a certain logging level is enabled and statements creating elaborate log messages can be encapsulated in an `if` statement. This being said, the `SortingSlf4jDemo.main(..)` method can be made more effective by rewriting it as shown in Listing 9-21.

Listing 9-21. Logging Efficiently in Class `SortingSlf4jDemo`

```
package com.apress.bgn.nine;
// import statements omitted

public class SortingSlf4jDemo {

    private static final Logger log = LoggerFactory.
    getLogger(SortingSlf4jDemo.class);

    public static void main(String... args) {
        if (args.length == 0) {
            log.error("No data to sort!");
            return;
        }
        int[] arr = getInts(args);

        if (log.isDebugEnabled()) {
            final StringBuilder sb = new StringBuilder("Sorting  an array
            with merge sort: ");
            Arrays.stream(arr).forEach(i -> sb.append(i).append(" "));
            log.debug(sb.toString());
        }
```

```
        IntSorter mergeSort = new MergeSort();
        mergeSort.sort(arr, 0, arr.length - 1);

        if (log.isInfoEnabled()) {
            final StringBuilder sb2 = new StringBuilder("Sorted: ");
            Arrays.stream(arr).forEach(i -> sb2.append(i).append(" "));
            log.info(sb2.toString());
        }
    }
}
```

In the previous code sample, if the SLF4J configuration for the com.apress.bgn.nine package is set to info, the message starting with *Sorting an array with merge sort: ...* is no longer created nor printed because the log.isDebugEnabled() returns false, so the code enclosed in the if statement is no longer executed. The Logger class contains if..Enabled() methods for any logger level.

This is all that can be said in this section about logging. Just keep in mind that you should use it moderately, pay very close attention when you decide to log messages in loops, and for big application always use a logging façade; in Java, for 99% projects this facade is SLF4J.

Debug Using Assertions

Another way to debug your code is using assertions. If you remember the section about Java keywords, you probably remember the assert keyword. The assert keyword is used to write an assertion statement that is just a test of your assumptions on the program execution. In the previous examples we had the user provide the input for our sorting program, so in order for our program to do the right thing, it is assumed that the user will provide the proper input; this means an array with size bigger than 1, because there is no point to run the algorithm for a single number. So what does this assertion look like in the code? The answer to this question is depicted in Listing 9-22.

Listing 9-22. Asserting the Size of User-Provided Array

```java
package com.apress.bgn.nine;
// other import statements omitted
import static com.apress.bgn.nine.SortingSlf4jDemo.getInts;

public class AssertionDemo {
    public static void main(String... args) {
        int[] arr = getInts(args);

        assert arr.length > 1;

        IntSorter mergeSort = new QuickSort();
        mergeSort.sort(arr, 0, arr.length - 1);

        final StringBuilder sb2 = new StringBuilder("Sorted: ");
        Arrays.stream(arr).forEach(i -> sb2.append(i).append(" "));
        System.out.println(sb2);
    }
}
```

Running the previous code without providing any arguments to the program is possible even if we have an assertion statement in it. As expected, it does nothing, because there is no array to be sorted.

---

❶ The reason for this is that assertions need to be enabled using a VM argument: -ea.

To specify this argument, you add it to the command when executing from the command line, but as we've used the editor until now, you can add it in the VM options text box of the IntelliJ IDEA launcher, as depicted in Figure 9-6.

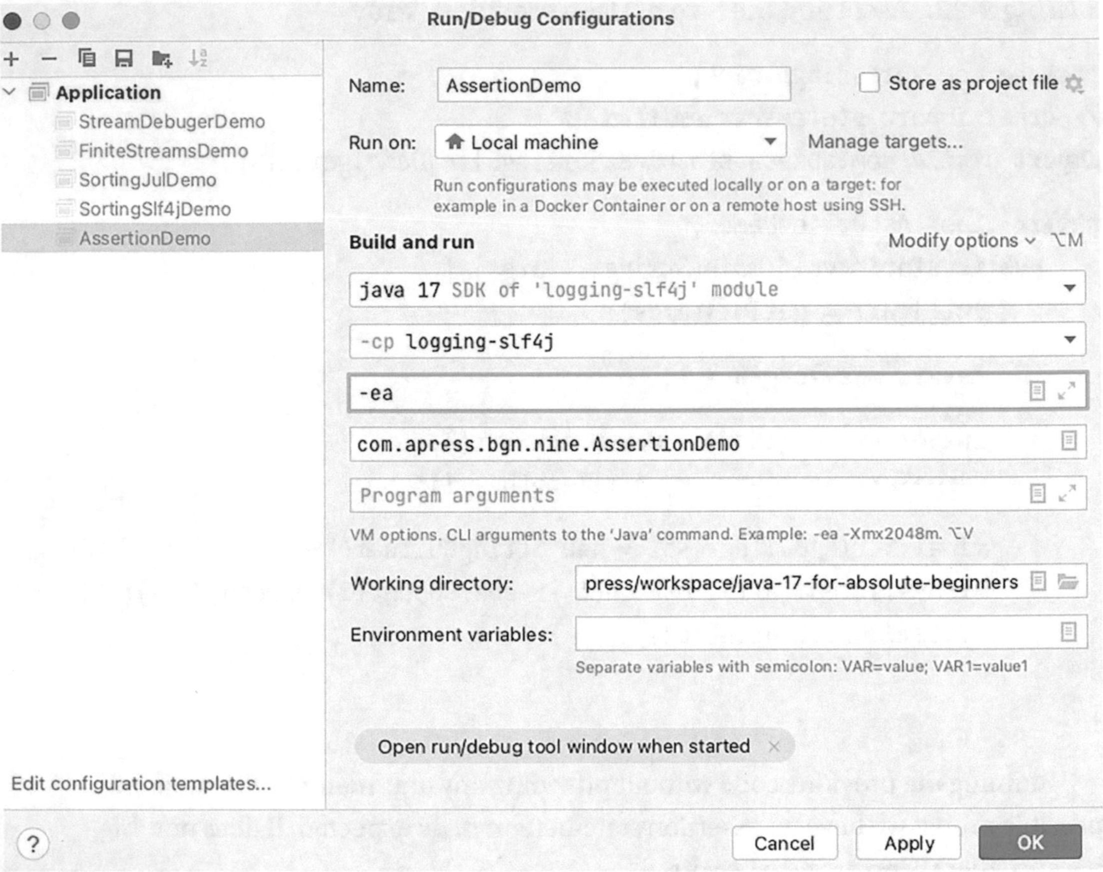

Figure 9-6. *IntelliJ IDEA launcher for the AssertionDemo class with the `-ea` VM argument set*

When assertions are enabled, running the previous code ends with an `java.lang.AssertionError` being thrown, because the expression of the assertions is evaluated to `false`, since obviously the `arr.length` is clearly not bigger than 1 when no argument is provided. Assertions have two forms. There is the simple form, when they have just the expression to evaluate, the assumption to test:

```
assertion [expression];
```

In this case, the `java.lang.AssertionError` being thrown just prints the line where the assumption is asserted for the current run of the program, together with the module and the full classname:

```
Exception in thread "main" java.lang.AssertionError
at chapter.nine.slf4j/com.apress.bgn.ch9.AssertionDemo.main(AssertionDemo.
java:48)
```

The most complex form of an assertion adds in another expression to be evaluated or a value to be used in the stack to tell the user which assumption was wrong.

```
assertion [expression1] : [expression2];
```

So if we replace:

```
assert arr.length > 1;
```

with

```
assert arr.length > 1 : "Not enough data to sort!";
```

When the java.lang.AssertionError is thrown, now it also depicts the *"Not enough data to sort!"* message, which makes it clear why the assertion statement is preventing the rest of the code from being executed.

```
Exception in thread "main" java.lang.AssertionError: Not enough data
to sort!
at chapter.nine.slf4j/com.apress.bgn.nine.AssertionDemo.main(AssertionDemo.
java:47)
```

Or we could just print the size of the array:

```
assert arr.length > 1 : arr.length;
```

Or both:

```
assert arr.length > 1 : "Not enough data to sort! Number of values: " +
arr.length;
```

Assertions can be used before and after the piece of code that needs to be debugged. In the previous case, the assertion was used as a precondition of the execution because the failure of the assertion prevents code from being executed.

Assertions can also be used as postconditions, to test the outcome of executing a piece of code.

In the previous code snippet, the assertion was used to test the correctness of the user provided input. In situations like this the restriction of a valid input should be obeyed, whether assertions are enabled or not. Sure, if our array is empty or contains just a single element, this is not a problem, as the algorithm is not executed and this does not lead to a technical failure. There are a few rules to obey or things to look for when writing code using assertions, and they are listed here:

- **Assertions should not be used to check the correctness of arguments provided to public methods**. Correctness of arguments should be something tested in the code, and a proper RuntimeException should be thrown. Validating public methods arguments should not be avoidable.

🔥 Unfortunately, to keep things simple, the previous code samples showing how assertions work, break this rule. After all, the presence of valid arguments for the main(..) is method is checked using an assertion.

- **Assertions should not be used to do work that is required for your application to run properly**. The main reason for this is obviously that assertions are disabled by default and having them disabled leads to that code not being executed, so the rest of the application will actually not function properly because of the missing code. Assuming no arguments are provided to the main(..) method in the previous example, and assertion could be used to initialize the array being processed with a default value. But that doesn't mean you should! Code like the next line is bad, because disabling assertions, removes the initialization of the array with a default value.

```
assert arr.length > 1 : arr = new int[]{1, 2, 3};
```

- **For performance reasons, do not use expressions that are expensive to evaluate in assertions**. This rule requires no explanation, even if assertions are disabled by default, imagine that somebody enables them by mistake on a production application, that would be quite unfortunate, wouldn't it? The next example shows an assertion expression, that initializes the array with a default value if none is suppiled, but after waiting five minutes. The next assertions breaks all three rules.

```
assert arr.length > 1 : sleepFiveMinsThenInit.apply(5L);
```

```
//the function body
Function<Long, int[]> sleepFiveMinsThenInit =  aLong ->   {
    try {Thread.sleep(Duration.ofMinutes(aLong).toMillis()); }
    catch (InterruptedException e) {}
    return new int[]{1, 2, 3};
};
```

If you are interested in using assertions, just keep in mind those three rules, and you should be fine.

Step-By-Step Debugging

If you do not want to write log messages or use assertions, but you still want to inspect values of variables during the execution of a program, there is a way to do that using an IDE, which was mentioned in previous chapters: pausing the execution using breakpoints and using the IDE to inspect variable contents or execute simple statements to check if your program is performing as expected.

A breakpoint is a mark set on an executable line of code (not a comment line, nor an empty line, and not a declaration). In IntelliJ IDEA, to set a breakpoint you just have to click the gutter area on the line you are interested in, or select the line and from the **Run** menu select **Toggle Line Breakpoint**. When a breakpoint is in place a red bubble appears on the line in the gutter section. In Figure 9-7 you can see a few breakpoints in IntelliJ IDEA.

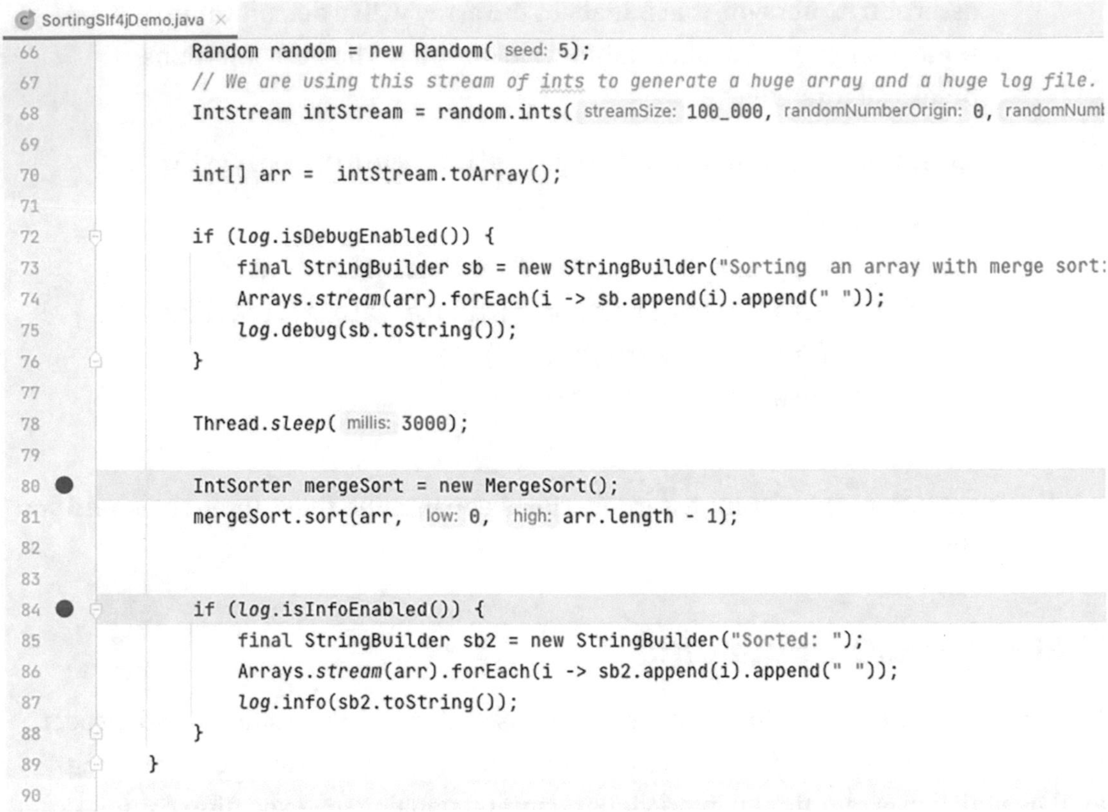

```
  SortingSlf4jDemo.java  ×
66          Random random = new Random( seed: 5);
67          // We are using this stream of ints to generate a huge array and a huge log file.
68          IntStream intStream = random.ints( streamSize: 100_000, randomNumberOrigin: 0, randomNumt
69
70          int[] arr =  intStream.toArray();
71
72          if (log.isDebugEnabled()) {
73              final StringBuilder sb = new StringBuilder("Sorting  an array with merge sort:
74              Arrays.stream(arr).forEach(i -> sb.append(i).append(" "));
75              log.debug(sb.toString());
76          }
77
78          Thread.sleep( millis: 3000);
79
80 ●        IntSorter mergeSort = new MergeSort();
81          mergeSort.sort(arr,  low: 0,  high: arr.length - 1);
82
83
84 ●       if (log.isInfoEnabled()) {
85              final StringBuilder sb2 = new StringBuilder("Sorted: ");
86              Arrays.stream(arr).forEach(i -> sb2.append(i).append(" "));
87              log.info(sb2.toString());
88          }
89     }
90
```

Figure 9-7. *IntelliJ IDEA breakpoints*

Once the breakpoints are in place, when the application runs in debug mode, it will pause on each of the marked lines. During the pause you can continue the execution step by step, inspect values of the variables, and even evaluate expressions in the context of the running application. IntelliJ IDEA is very helpful with this, as it shows you the contents of every variable in each line of the code currently being executed. In Figure 9-8 the SortingSlf4jDemo class is running in debug mode and is paused during execution using breakpoints.

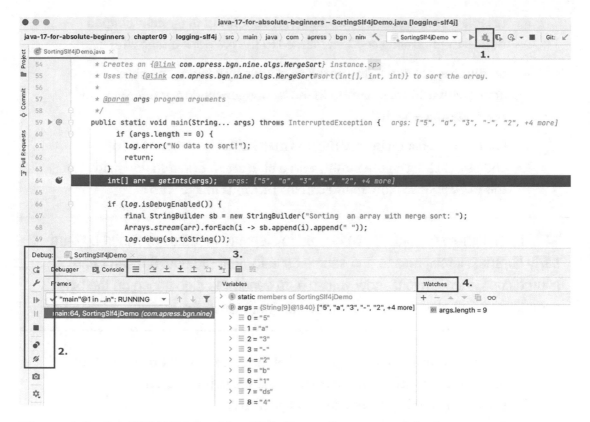

Figure 9-8. *IntelliJ IDEA* `SortingSlf4jDemo` *class paused during execution*

To run an application in debug mode, instead of starting the launcher normally, you can start it by clicking on the green bug-shaped (marked with 1. in the previous image) button that is right next to the green triangle-shaped button that is used to run the application normally.

The application runs and stops at the first line marked with a breakpoint. From that point on the developer can do the following things:

- inspect values of the variables used on the line with the breakpoint, by reading the values depicted by the editor there.

- continue the execution until the next breakpoint by clicking the green triangle in the **Debug** section, marked in the previous image with 2.

- stop the execution by clicking the red square-shaped button in the **Debug** section, marked in the previous image with 2.

- disable all breakpoints by clicking red bubble cut diagonally shaped button in the **Debug** section, marked in the previous image with 2.

- continue execution to the next line of code by clicking the blue arrow with a 90 angle button in the **Debugger** section, marked in the previous image with 3.

- continue execution by entering the method in the current line of code by clicking on the button with a blue arrow oriented down, in the **Debugger** section, marked in the previous image with 3.

ℹ The red arrow oriented down is used to step into methods provided by third-party libraries. Intellij tries to find source code for that method. If it can't find source code, then it might show you an auto generated stub based on the byte code/library. The blue arrow only jumps into methods in the project.

- continue execution by stepping out of the current method by clicking on the button with a blue arrow oriented up, in the **Debugger** section, marked in the previous image with 3.

- or continue the execution to the line pointed at by the cursor, by clicking on the button with a diagonal arrow pointing to a cursor sign in the **Debugger** section, marked in the previous image with 3.

- evaluate your own expressions by adding them to the **Watches** section, marked in the previous image with 4. The only condition is that the expressions only use variables that are accessible in the context of the breakpoint line (e.g., are part of the same method body or class body, and the accessor is not important, private fields can be inspected too).

Another way to evaluate expression in the context of the application currently running is just to click right on the file where your execution is currently paused and from the menu opened select option **Evaluate Expression**. A dialog window is opened where complex expressions can be written and evaluated on the spot, as depicted in Figure 9-9.

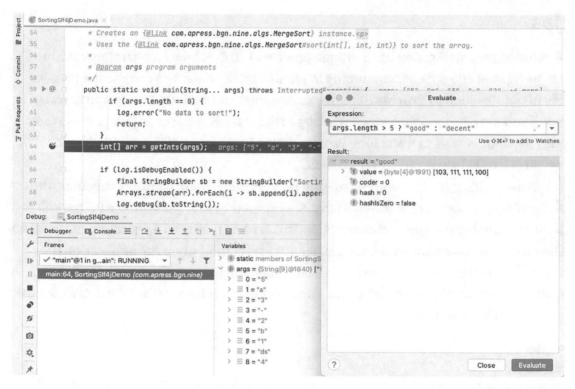

Figure 9-9. *IntelliJ IDEA expression evaluation during debugging session*

Most Java smart editors provide means to run a Java application in debug mode; just make sure to clean up your watches section from time to time. If the expressions added in the watches section expressions are expensive to evaluate, it might affect the performance of the application. Also, be aware of expressions that use streams, since these might make the application fail, as proven in the previous chapter.

Inspecting Running Application Using Java Tools

Aside from the executables to compile Java code and execute or packaging of Java byte code, the JDK provides a set of utility executables that can be used to debug and inspect the state of a running Java application. This section covers the most useful of them. Without further ado, let's do this!

jps

A running Java application has a unique process id. This is how an operating system keeps track of all applications running in parallel at the same. You can see the process ids in utilities such as **Process Explorer** in Windows and **Activity Monitor** in macOs, but if you are comfortable enough working in the console, you might prefer using the **jps** (short for Java Virtual Machine Process Status Tool), executable provided by the JDK because it only focuses on Java processes.

When calling jps from the console, all Java process ids will be listed, together with the main class name or some details that are exposed by the application API that will help you identify the application running. This is useful when an application crashes, but the process remains in a hanging state. This can be painful when the application uses resources such as files or network ports, because it might block them and prevent you from using them. When executing jps on my computer (I have a Mac) these are the Java processes I see running:

```
> jps
41066
51099 Launcher
51100 SortingSlf4jDemo
51101 Jps
```

As you can see from the previous listing, jps includes itself in the output, because it is after all a Java process. The process with id 51100 is the execution of the SortingSlf4jDemo class, obviously. The 51099 process is a launcher application that IntelliJ IDEA uses to start the execution of the SortingSlf4jDemo class. The 41066 process does not have any description, but at this point I can identify the process myself because I know I have IntelliJ IDEA opened, which is itself a Java application. The advantage of being able to know the process ids is that you can kill them when they end up hanging and blocking resources. Let's assume that the process started by the execution of SortingSlf4jDemo ended up hanging. To kill a process all operating systems, provide a version of the kill command. For macOS and Linux you should execute the following:

```
kill -9 [process_id]
```

For this example, if I call `kill -9 51100` and then call jps I can see that `SortingSlf4jDemo` process is no longer listed.

```
> jps
41066
51099 Launcher
51183 Jps
```

I still have the Launcher process, but that is a child process of IntelliJ IDEA so there is no point in killing it because next time I run a main class in the IDE, the process will be started again.

`jps` is quite a simple tool to use for this specific purpose, but sometimes when applications are installed on servers with minimal setup, it might be all you have. So it's good to know it exists.

jcmd

The **jcmd** is another JDK utility that can be useful. It can be used to send diagnostic command requests to the JVM that can help to troubleshoot and diagnose JVM and running Java applications. It must be used on the same machine where the JVM is running, and the result of calling it without any arguments is that it shows all Java processes currently running on the machine, including itself. Beside the process ids, jcmd also displays the command used to start their execution.

```
> jcmd
51205 org.jetbrains.jps.cmdline.Launcher /Applications/IntelliJ IDEA 2021.1
EAP.app/Contents/lib/util.jar:
...
# IntelliJ IDEA command details omitted
51206 chapter.nine.slf4j/com.apress.bgn.nine.SortingSlf4jDemo 5 a 3 - 2
b 1 ds 4
51207 jdk.jcmd/sun.tools.jcmd.JCmd
```

When jcmd is run with a Java process id and the text help as argumens, it displays all additional commands you can use on that process. This will work if the application is currently running and not paused using a breakpoint. The `SortingSlf4jDemo` is currently paused when I am writing this; also, its execution takes too little for the jcmd to be used. Another Java process created for running the `BigSortingSlf4jDemo` class that sorts an array of 100.000.000 randomly generated numbers is used as an example to produce the output depicted in Listing 9-23.

Listing 9-23. The Output of jcmd [pid] help on a Java Process Doing Some Serious Work

```
> jcmd 51301 help
51301:
The following commands are available:
Compiler.CodeHeap_Analytics
Compiler.codecache
Compiler.codelist
Compiler.directives_add
Compiler.directives_clear
Compiler.directives_print
Compiler.directives_remove
Compiler.queue
GC.class_histogram
GC.finalizer_info
GC.heap_dump
GC.heap_info
GC.run
GC.run_finalization
JFR.check
JFR.configure
JFR.dump
JFR.start
JFR.stop
JVMTI.agent_load
JVMTI.data_dump
ManagementAgent.start
ManagementAgent.start_local
ManagementAgent.status
ManagementAgent.stop
Thread.print
VM.class_hierarchy
```

```
VM.classloader_stats
VM.classloaders
VM.command_line
VM.dynlibs
VM.events
VM.flags
VM.info
VM.log
VM.metaspace
VM.native_memory
VM.print_touched_methods
VM.set_flag
VM.stringtable
VM.symboltable
VM.system_properties
VM.systemdictionary
VM.uptime
VM.version
help
```

It is not the objective of this book to cover them all, as these are quite advanced features of Java, but probably you have a basic idea of the scope of each command. As an example, in Listing 9-24 you can see the output of calling jcmd 51301 GC.heap_info:

Listing 9-24. The Output of jcmd [pid] GC.heap_info on a Java Process Doing Some Serious Work

```
> jcmd 51301 GC.heap_info
51301:
 garbage-first heap   total 3923968K, used 2534849K [0x0000000700000000,
 0x0000000800000000)
  region size 2048K, 766 young (1568768K), 1 survivors (2048K)
 Metaspace       used 5386K, committed 5504K, reserved 1056768K
  class space    used 595K, committed 640K, reserved 1048576K
```

If you remember, in **Chapter 5** the different types of memory used by the JVM were discussed, and **heap** was the memory where all the objects used by an application are stored. This command prints the heap details, how much of it is used, reserved, how big is a region, and so on. All these details will be covered more in detail in **Chapter 13**.

jconsole

jconsole is JDK utility that can be used to inspect various JVM statistics. To use it, you just have to start it from the command line and connect it to a Java application that is already running. This application is quite useful, as it can monitor both local and remote JVMs. It can also monitor and manage an application. The application must expose a port for jconsole to connect to.

To start a Java application and expose a port for an external application, you just have to start the application with the following VM parameters:

```
-agentlib:jdwp=transport=dt_socket,server=y,suspend=y,address=1044
```

The `transport=dt_socket` instructs the JVM that the debugger connections will be made through a socket. The `address=1044` parameter informs it that the port number will be 1044. The `port` can be any port bigger than 1024, because those are restricted by the operating system. The `suspend=y` instructs the JVM to suspend execution until a debugger such as jconsole is connected to it. To avoid that, `suspend=n` should be used.

For our simple example and considering we will use jconsole to debug a Java application on the same machine, we do not need all that. We just need to start jconsole from the command line and look in the **Local Processes** section and identify the Java process we are interested in debugging.

In Figure 9-10 you can see the first jconsole dialog window.

Figure 9-10. jconsole *first dialog window*

When the process is running locally it can be easily identified, because it will be named using the module and the fully qualified main class name. For an application as simple as ours we need to make a few tweaks to make sure that we can actually see a few statistics with jconsole during the run of the application. A few Thread.sleep(..) statements were added to pause the execution enough for jconsole to connect. Also, we'll use quite a big array of data to make sure the statistics are relevant. The BigSortingSlf4jDemo class is depicted in Listing 9-25.

Listing 9-25. The Contents of the BigSortingSlf4jDemo Class

```
package com.apress.bgn.nine;

// import statements omitted

public class BigSortingSlf4jDemo {

    private static final Logger log = LoggerFactory.
    getLogger(BigSortingSlf4jDemo.class);
```

```java
public static void main(String... args) throws InterruptedException {
    Thread.sleep(3000);

    Random random = new Random(5);
    IntStream intStream = random.ints(100_000_000,0,350);

    int[] arr =  intStream.toArray();

    if (log.isDebugEnabled()) {
        final StringBuilder sb = new StringBuilder("Sorting  an array
        with merge sort: ");
        Arrays.stream(arr).forEach(i -> sb.append(i).append(" "));
        log.debug(sb.toString());
    }

    Thread.sleep(3000);

    IntSorter mergeSort = new MergeSort();
    mergeSort.sort(arr, 0, arr.length - 1);

    if (log.isInfoEnabled()) {
        final StringBuilder sb2 = new StringBuilder("Sorted: ");
        Arrays.stream(arr).forEach(i -> sb2.append(i).append(" "));
        log.info(sb2.toString());
    }
  }
}
```

With this modification the class can be executed normally and connect jconsole to it. After a successful connection, a window like the one in Figure 9-11 is opened and graphs of the JVM memory consumption, number of threads of classes loaded, and CPU usage are displayed.

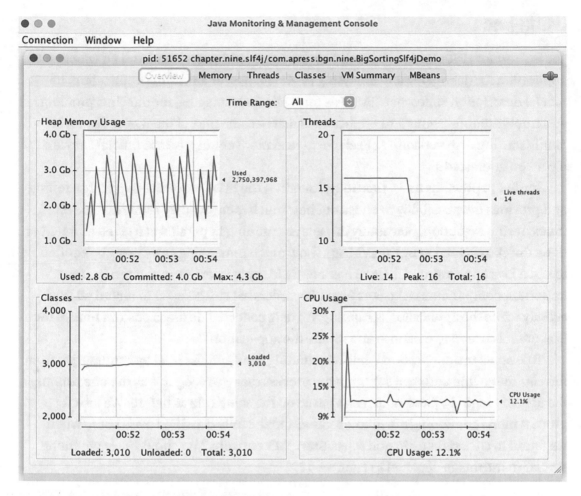

Figure 9-11. *jconsole statistics window*

There is a tab for each of these statistics that provides more information, and in case of a more complex application this information can be used to improve performance, identify potential problems, and even estimate application behavior for desired cases. For our small application the jconsole graphs do not reveal much, but if you really want to see valuable statistics, install an application like mucommander[6] use it for a while without closing it, and then connect jconsole to it and have fun.

---

[6] See the official MuCommander site at MuCommander, http://www.mucommander.com, accessed October 15, 2021.

Using jmc

jmc is short for JDK Mission Control. The jmc command starts an advanced Oracle application for debugging and analysing JVM statistics for a running application. Its official description states that "JMC is a tool suite for managing, monitoring, profiling, and troubleshooting your Java applications that became part of the JDK utility tools family starting with version 7." (Feel free to read more about it on the official Oracle site, if you are interested.)

Similar to previous tools, this utility identifies the JAVA processes currently running and provides the possibility to check out how much memory they require at specific times during execution, how many threads are running in parallel at a given moment in time, the classes loaded by the JVM, and how much processing cpu power is required to run a Java application. The JMC has a more friendly interface and one of its most important components is the Java Flight Recorder that can be used to record all JVM activity while the application is running. All data collected during a custom time of the execution is useful to diagnose and profile the application.

To inspect the application while it is running, we open the JMC by running jmc from the command line and then selecting the process that we recognize as the one running the BigSortingSlf4jDemo main class based on the same rule as before. We look for a process name containing the module name and the fully classified class name when we found it, click right on it, and select **Start JMX console**. You should see something similar to the image depicted in Figure 9-12.

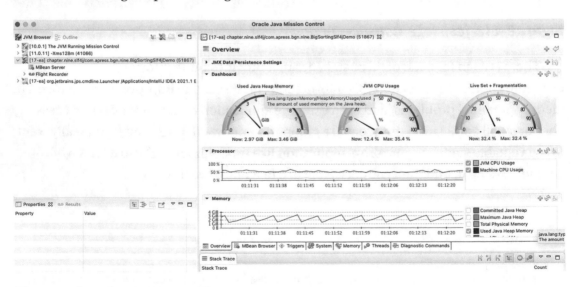

Figure 9-12. jmc JMX console

As you probably noticed, the interface is definitely more friendly, and the provided statistics are definitely more detailed. Using JMC, everything that happens with the application and JVM during a run can be recorded and analyzed later, even if the application has stopped running since. The **Memory** tab at the bottom of the figure provides a lot of information regarding the memory used by the application, including what types of objects are occupying it. Recording detailed information about a Java process requires it to be started with

```
-XX:+UnlockCommercialFeatures -XX:+FlightRecorder.
```

OpenJDK and early access JDKs do not have commercial features or Flight Recorder. These are part of the Oracle JDK designed to be used only commercially, and requires a paid subscription.

The JMC subject is too advanced and wide for this section; probably an entire book could be written about its usage and how to interpret the statistics, so we'll stop here.[7]

Accessing the Java Process API

Java 9 came with a lot of other improvements beside the Jigsaw modules, one of them being a new and improved Process API. The Java Process API allows you to start, retrieve information, and manage native operating system processes. The ability to manipulate processes was there in previous versions of Java, but it was quite rudimentary. Listing 9-26 shows how a process was created before Java 5:

Listing 9-26. Creating a Process Using Pre-Java 5 API

```
package com.apress.bgn.nine;
// import section omitted

public class ProcessCreationDemo {

    private static final Logger log =
            LoggerFactory.getLogger(ProcessCreationDemo.class);
```

---

[7] If you have an Oracle JDK subscription and want to learn more about using JMC, Oracle provides very good resources for that at Oracle, "JDK Mission Control," `https://www.oracle.com/java/technologies/jdk-mission-control.html`, accessed October 15, 2021.

```java
public static void main(String... args) {
    try {
        Process exec = Runtime.getRuntime()
                .exec(new String[] { "/bin/sh", "-c", "echo Java home:
                $JAVA_HOME" });
        exec.waitFor();
        InputStream is = exec.getInputStream();
        StringBuilder textBuilder = new StringBuilder();
        Reader reader = new BufferedReader(new InputStreamReader
                (is, Charset.forName(StandardCharsets.UTF_8.name())));
        try {
            int c = 0;
            while ((c = reader.read()) != -1) {
                textBuilder.append((char) c);
            }
        } finally {
            reader.close();
        }
        log.info("Process output -> {}", textBuilder.toString());
        log.info("process result: {}", exec.exitValue());
    } catch (Exception e) {
        e.printStackTrace();
    }
}
}
```

Intercepting output of the started process is a pain, and you can also see that we need to wrap a BufferedReader instance around the InputStream instance connected to the normal output of the process.

The process API made things a little more practical. It has at its core a few classes and interfaces, all having names that start with the Process term. What we've done so far with Java executables can be directly done by writing Java code. The interface that provides an API to access native processes is named ProcessHandle, and is part of the core Java java.lang package. Similar to the Thread class, there is a static method named current to call on this interface to retrieve the ProcessHandle instance of the current running process. Once we have this, we can use its methods to access more process details.

The ProcessHandle provides several static utility methods to access native processes. Java code can be written to list all processes running on a computer, and they can be sorted based on various criteria. The piece of code in Listing 2-27 lists all processes that were created by running the java command.

Listing 9-27. Listing All java Processes Using Java 9 Process API

```
package com.apress.bgn.nine;
// import section omitted

public class ProcessListingDemo {

    private static final Logger log = LoggerFactory.
    getLogger(ProcessListingDemo.class);

    public static void main(String... args) {
        Optional<String> currUser = ProcessHandle.current().info().user();

        ProcessHandle.allProcesses().filter(ph -> ph.info().user().
        equals(currUser) && ph.info().commandLine().isPresent())
                .filter(ph -> ph.info().commandLine().get().
                contains("java"))
                .forEach(p -> {
                    log.info("PID: " + p.pid());
                    p.info().arguments().ifPresent(s -> Arrays.stream(s).
                    forEach(a -> log.info("   {}", a)));
                    p.info().command().ifPresent(c -> log.info("\t Command:
                    {}", c));
                });
    }
}
```

The code listed previously extracts the user from the current running process by obtaining its handle and calling info() to obtain an instance of the ProcessHandle. Info, an interface that declares a set of methods that are implemented by the ProcessHandleImpl.Info class to access snapshot information about the process as the command and arguments that were used to create the process. The output of running the previous code is printed in the console and might look pretty similar to the output listed in Listing 9-28. *Except, you know, different user, different processes. ;)*

Listing 9-28. Output Produced By Running the Code in Listing 9-27

```
INFO  c.a.b.n.ProcessListingDemo - PID: 58820
INFO  c.a.b.n.ProcessListingDemo -     -javaagent:/Applications/IntelliJ
IDEA.app/Contents/lib/idea_rt.jar=55299:/Applications/IntelliJ IDEA.app/
Contents/bin
INFO  c.a.b.n.ProcessListingDemo -     -Dfile.encoding=UTF-8
INFO  c.a.b.n.ProcessListingDemo -     -p
INFO  c.a.b.n.ProcessListingDemo -     /workspace/java-17-for-absolute-
beginners/chapter09/processapi/target/classes...*.jar
INFO  c.a.b.n.ProcessListingDemo -     -m
INFO  c.a.b.n.ProcessListingDemo -     chapter.nine.processapi/com.apress.
bgn.nine.ProcessListingDemo
INFO  c.a.b.n.ProcessListingDemo -   Command: /Library/Java/
JavaVirtualMachines/jdk-17.jdk/Contents/Home/bin/java
INFO  c.a.b.n.ProcessListingDemo - PID: 58819
INFO  c.a.b.n.ProcessListingDemo -     -Xmx700m
INFO  c.a.b.n.ProcessListingDemo -     -Djava.awt.headless=true
// some output omitted
INFO  c.a.b.n.ProcessListingDemo -     -classpath
INFO  c.a.b.n.ProcessListingDemo -     /Applications/IntelliJ IDEA.app/
Contents/plugins/java/lib/jps-launcher.jar
INFO  c.a.b.n.ProcessListingDemo -     org.jetbrains.jps.cmdline.Launcher
INFO  c.a.b.n.ProcessListingDemo -     /Applications/IntelliJ IDEA.app/
Contents/lib/netty-common-4.1.52.Final...*.jar
INFO  c.a.b.n.ProcessListingDemo -     org.jetbrains.jps.cmdline.BuildMain
INFO  c.a.b.n.ProcessListingDemo -     127.0.0.1
INFO  c.a.b.n.ProcessListingDemo -     52130
INFO  c.a.b.n.ProcessListingDemo -     de98ca31-a7d8-4fe3-b268-44545198d08b
INFO  c.a.b.n.ProcessListingDemo -     /Users/iulianacosmina/Library/Caches/
JetBrains/IntelliJIdea2020.3/compile-server
INFO  c.a.b.n.ProcessListingDemo -   Command: /Library/Java/
JavaVirtualMachines/jdk-17.jdk/Contents/Home/bin/java
```

In the previous log only the IntelliJ IDEA Launcher used to run the ProcessListingDemo class and the process spawned to run it were depicted, but the output could be much bigger. Some arguments were skipped all together, as it is quite useless to waste pages of the book with logs that you can produce yourself. Nevertheless, some depiction of the log format was necessary if you will never run the code yourself.

The previous code sample showed you roughly how to access native processes and print information about them. Using the improved Java process API, new processes can be created, and commands of the underlying operation system can be started. For example, we can create a process that prints the value of the JAVA_HOME environment variable and capture the output to display it in the IntelliJ console, as depicted in Listing 9-29. (This code works on macOS and Linux, for Windows the equivalent PowerShell command should be used.)

Listing 9-29. Java Sample Code to Create a Process

```java
package com.apress.bgn.nine;

// other import statements omitted
import java.util.concurrent.CompletableFuture;
import java.util.concurrent.ExecutionException;

public class NewApiProcessCreationDemo {
    private static final Logger log = LoggerFactory.getLogger(NewApiProcess
    CreationDemo.class);

    public static void main(String... args) throws IOException,
    InterruptedException, ExecutionException {
        ProcessBuilder processBuilder = new ProcessBuilder();
        processBuilder.command("/bin/sh", "-c", "echo Java home:
        $JAVA_HOME");
        processBuilder.inheritIO();

        Process process = processBuilder.start();
        CompletableFuture<Process> future = process.onExit();
        int result = future.get().exitValue();
        log.info("Process result: " + result);

        CompletableFuture<ProcessHandle> futureHandle = process.toHandle().
        onExit();
```

```
    ProcessHandle processHandle = futureHandle.get();
    log.info("Process ID: {}", processHandle.pid());
    ProcessHandle.Info info = processHandle.info();
    info.arguments().ifPresent(s -> Arrays.stream(s).forEach(a -> log.
    info("    {}", a)));
    info.command().ifPresent(c -> log.info("\t Command: {}", c));
  }
}
```

New processes can be created by using instances of `ProcessBuilder` that receive as arguments a list of commands and arguments for them. The class has many constructors and methods with different signatures that can be used to create and start processes easily. The `inheritIO()` method is used to set the source and destination for the subprocess standard I/O to be the same as the current process. This means the process output is printed directly in the console, without the need of reading it using an `InputStream`. The `onExit()` method in the `Process` class returns a `CompletableFuture<Process>` that can be used to access the process at the end of its execution to retrieve the exit value of the process. For a process terminating normally the value should be 0(zero). The `onExit()` method in the `ProcessHandle` class returns a `CompletableFuture<ProcessHandle>` that can be used to access the process can be used to wait for process termination, and possibly trigger dependent actions.

When a Java program creates a process, that process becomes a child of the process that created it. To be able to list all children processes we need to make sure they last a while, because once terminated they obviously no longer exist. The code sample in Listing 9-30 creates three identical processes, each of them executing three linux shell commands:

- `echo "start"` to notify that the process has started execution

- `sleep 3` that pauses the process for 3 seconds

- `echo "done."` is executed right before the parent process finishes its execution.

Once a process is started it can no longer be controlled, so to make sure the child processes actually finish their execution, we'll ask the user to press a key to decide when the current process finishes by adding a `System.in.read();` statement.

Listing 9-30. Java Sample Code to Create Three Processes

```java
package com.apress.bgn.nine;

// import statements omitted

public class ThreeProcessesDemo {
    private static final Logger log =
            LoggerFactory.getLogger(ThreeProcessesDemo.class);

    public static void main(String... args) {
        try {
        List<ProcessBuilder> builders = List.of(
                new ProcessBuilder("/bin/sh", "-c",
                        "echo \"start...\" ; sleep 3; echo \"done.\"").
                        inheritIO(),
                new ProcessBuilder("/bin/sh", "-c",
                        "echo \"start...\" ; sleep 3; echo \"done.\"").
                        inheritIO(),
                new ProcessBuilder("/bin/sh", "-c",
                        "echo \"start...\" ; sleep 3; echo \"done.\"").
                        inheritIO()
        );
        builders.parallelStream().forEach(pbs -> {
            try {
                pbs.start();
            } catch (Exception e) {
                log.error("Oops, could not start process!", e);
            }
        });
        ProcessHandle ph = ProcessHandle.current();
        ph.children().forEach(pc -> {
            log.info("Child PID: {}", pc.pid());
            pc.parent().ifPresent(parent ->
                    log.info(" Parent PID: {}", parent.pid()));
        });
```

```
                System.out.println("Press any key to exit!");
                System.in.read();
            } catch (Exception e) {
                e.printStackTrace();
            }
        }
    }
}
```

As you can see, we have grouped the ProcessBuilders in a list and processed the instances using a parallel stream to make sure that all processes were started almost at the same time. We printed the results of each of them after termination, to make sure all were executed correctly. The children() method returns a stream containing ProcessHandle instances corresponding to the processes started by the current Java process.

The parent() method was called for each child ProcessHandle instance to obtain the ProcessHandle corresponding to the process that created it, if there is one. When running the previous code in the console, you should see an output similar to what is depicted in the Listing 9-31. (If you run it on a Mac or Linux, that is. Windows will probably have no idea what is being asked to do.)

Listing 9-31. Output of a Java Application That Creates Three Processes

```
start...
start...
start...
INFO  c.a.b.n.ThreeProcessesDemo - Child PID: 59368
INFO  c.a.b.n.ThreeProcessesDemo -  Parent PID: 59365
INFO  c.a.b.n.ThreeProcessesDemo - Child PID: 59366
INFO  c.a.b.n.ThreeProcessesDemo -  Parent PID: 59365
INFO  c.a.b.n.ThreeProcessesDemo - Child PID: 59367
INFO  c.a.b.n.ThreeProcessesDemo -  Parent PID: 59365
Press any key to exit!
done.
done.
done.
```

In the past, developers who needed to work with processes on a more advanced level needed to resort to native code. The improved Java Process API provides a lot more control over running and spawned processes, so if you ever need it, now you know it exists. A full list of the Java process API improvements added in Java 9 can be found here: `https://docs.oracle.com/javase/9/core/process-api1.htm`.

Testing

Debugging is a part of a software process named **testing** and involves identifying and correcting code errors. But just avoiding technical errors is not enough, testing an application means much more than that. There is even an organization providing very good materials for training and certifications for software testers. The **International Software Testing Qualifications Board** is a software testing qualification certification organization that operates internationally. It established a syllabus and a hierarchy of qualifications and guidelines for software testing.[8] If you think you are more interested in software testing, then you should look into getting an ISTQB certification.

The ISTQB definition of testing is "the process consisting of all lifecycle activities, both static and dynamic, concerned with planning, preparation and evaluation of software and related work products to determine that they satisfy specified requirements to demonstrate that they are fit for purpose and to detect defects."

The previous is a technical, academic definition. The definition I propose is "the process of verifying that an implementation does what it is supposed to, in the amount of time it is expected to, with an acceptable resources consumption."

---

❶   Testing is an essential part of the development process and should start as early as possible, because the effort of fixing a defect grows exponentially with the time it takes to be discovered.[9]

---

[8] The ISTQB certification path can be found at ISTQB, "Why ISTQB Certification?," `https://www.istqb.org/certification-path-root/why-istqb-certification.html`, accessed October 15, 2021.

[9] See Robert Martin's book *Clean Code* (City: Publisher, year), **Chapter 9**.

During the development phase, aside from writing the actual solution, you can also write code to test your solution. Those tests can be either run manually or by a build tool when you build your project. When writing your code, aside from thinking how you can write it so that the solution solves the problem, you should be thinking also about how to test the solution. This approach is named **TDD** (**Test Driven Development**), a programming paradigm that states that you should think about how to test your solution before implementing it, because if it is difficult to test, it will probably be difficult to implement, maintain in the long run, and extend to solve related problems.

The simplest tests you can write are called **unit tests,** and they are very simple methods that tests small units of functionality. If unit tests cannot be written easily, your design might be rotten. Unit tests are the first line of defence against failures. If unit tests fail, the foundation of your solution is bad.

The tests that span across multiple components, testing the communication between units of functionality and the results of their interactions against an expected results, are called **integration tests**.

The last type of tests a developer should write are **regression tests**, which are tests that are run periodically to make sure that code that was previously tested still performs correctly after it was changed. This type of tests is crucial for big projects where code is written by a considerable number of developers, because sometimes dependencies among components are not obvious and code a developer wrote might break somebody else's code.

This section will only show you how to write unit tests using a Java framework named JUnit and describe a few typical testing components a developer can build to set up a context for the unit tests. Thus, as my Scottish colleagues say: *Let's get cracking!*

Testing Code Location

As you probably remember, in **Chapter 3** the java-bgn project structure was explained. The discussion about tests must start with the structure of the lowest level modules of the project, the ones that contain the source code and tests. In Figure 9-13 you can see the structure of the module containing the sources and test code for the module used in this section.

Figure 9-13. *The Maven (Gradle too) module structure*

The structure depicted in the previous example can be explained as follows:

- the src directory contains all code and resources of the project. The contents are split into two directories main and test.

  - the main directory contains the source code and the application configuration files, split into two directories. The java directory contains the Java source code and the resources directory contains configuration files, nonexecutable text files (that can be written according to various formats: XML, SQL, CSV, etc), media files, PDFs, and so on. When the application is built and packed into a jar (or war, or ear) only the files in the Java directory are taken onto account; the *.class files together with the configuration files are packed.

  - the test directory contains code used to test the source code in the src directory. The Java files are kept under the java directory and in the resources directory contains configuration files needed to build a test context. The classes in the test directory are part of the project and have access to the classes declared in the main directory as described by accessors in **Chapter 3**. However, the contents of the test directory are not part of the project that will be delivered to a client. They exist just to help test the application during development. The files in the test/resources directory usually override configuration files in the main/resources to provide an isolated, smaller execution context for the test classes.

Building an Application to Test

For the examples in this section, we will build a simple application that uses an embedded Derby[10] database to store data. This will be the production database. For the test environment the database will be replaced with various pseudo-constructions that will mimic the database behavior.

The application is quite rudimentary. An AccountService implementation takes data from the input and uses it to manage Account instances. The Account class is a very abstract an unrealistic implementation of a banking account. It has a holder field which is the account owner, an accountNumber field, and an amount field. The AccountService implementation uses a AccountRepo implementation to perform all related database operations with Account instances using an implementation of DBConnection. The classes and interfaces that are making up this simple application and relationships between them are depicted in Figure 9-14.

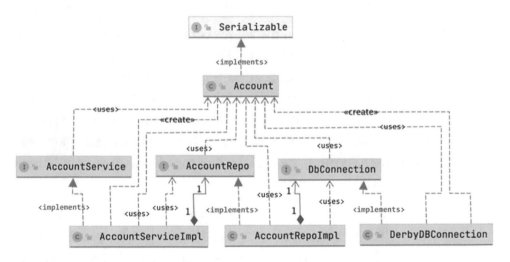

Figure 9-14. *Simple account management application components (as shown by IntelliJ IDEA)*

The implementation of these classes is not relevant for this section, but if you are curious you can find the full code on the official repository of this book. So let's start testing. The easiest way would be to write a main class and perform some account operations. However, it is useless to do that once the application is in production,

---

[10] If you are interested in finding out more about the Derby database, see Apache Derby, https://db.apache.org/derby, accessed October 15, 2021.

since testing new features on it comes with risks of data corruption. Also, production databases are usually hosted on costly products, such as Oracle RDBMS (Oracle Relational Database Management System) or Microsoft SQL Server. They are not really appropriate for development or testing. The intention is to run tests automatically during an automated build, so in-memory or implementations that can be instantiated are more suitable. So let's start by testing the `AccountRepoImpl`.

Introducing JUnit

JUnit is undoubtedly the most-used testing framework in the Java development world. At the end of 2017, JUnit 5[11] was released, which is the next generation of this framework. It comes with a new engine, is compatible with Java 9+, and comes with a lot of lambda-based functionalities. JUnit provides annotations to mark test methods for automated execution, annotations for initialization and destruction of a test context, and utility methods to practically implement test methods. There are multiple JUnit annotations that you can use, but five of them and a utility class represent the core of the JUnit framework and this is the best place to start to learn testing. The following list covers each of them with a short description, to build a general picture of how JUnit can be used to test your application:

- `@BeforeAll` from package `org.junit.jupiter.api` is used on a nonprivate static method that returns void used to initialize objects and variables to be used by all test methods in the current class. This method will be called only once, before all test methods in the class, so test methods should not modify these objects, because their state is shared, and it might affect the test results. Eventually, the static fields to be initialized by the annotated method can be declared final, so once initialized they can no longer be changed. More than one method annotated with `@BeforeAll` can be declared in a test class, but what would be the point?

- `@AfterAll` from package `org.junit.jupiter.api` is the counterpart of `@BeforeAll`. It is also used to annotate nonprivate static methods that return `void`, and their purpose is to destroy the context the test methods were run in and perform cleanup actions.

---

[11] See the official JUnit 5 site at `https://junit.org/junit5`, accessed October 15, 2021.

- @BeforeEach from package org.junit.jupiter.api is used on nonprivate, nonstatic methods that return void, and methods annotated with it are executed before every method annotated with @Test. These methods can be used to further customize the test context to populate objects with values that will be used to test assertions in the test methods.

- @AfterEach from package org.junit.jupiter.api is used on nonprivate, nonstatic methods that return void, and methods annotated with it are executed after every method annotated with @Test.

- @Test from package org.junit.jupiter.api is used on nonprivate, nonstatic methods that return void, and the method annotated with it is a test method. A test class can have one or more, depending on the class that is being tested.

- Utility class org.junit.jupiter.api.Assertions that provides a set of methods that support asserting condition in tests.

Another annotation that you might be interested to know it exists is @DisplayName. It is declared in the same package as all the others and receives a text argument that will represent the test display name, which will be displayed by the IDE and in the resulting reports created by the build tool. Listing 9-32 shows a pseudo test class, so you can get an idea of how test classes look.

Listing 9-32. Pseudo Test Class Using JUnit Annotations

```
package com.apress.bgn.nine.pseudo;

import org.junit.jupiter.api.*;
import org.slf4j.Logger;
import org.slf4j.LoggerFactory;

import static org.junit.jupiter.api.Assertions.assertFalse;
import static org.junit.jupiter.api.Assertions.assertTrue;
```

```java
public class PseudoTest {

    private static final Logger log = LoggerFactory.
    getLogger(PseudoTest.class);

    @BeforeAll
    static void loadCtx() {
        log.info("Loading general test context.");
    }

    @BeforeEach
    void setUp(){
        log.info("Prepare  single test context.");
    }

    @Test
    @DisplayName("test one")
    void testOne() {
        log.info("Executing test one.");
        assertTrue(true);
    }

    @Test
    @DisplayName("test two")
    void testTwo() {
        log.info("Executing test two.");
        assertFalse(false);
    }

    @AfterEach
    void tearDown(){
        log.info("Destroy  single test context.");
    }

    @AfterAll
    static void unloadCtx(){
        log.info("UnLoading general test context.");
    }
}
```

Keeping in mind the information that you now have about these annotations, when running this class we expect the log messages that each method prints to be in the exact order that we have defined, because the methods have been strategically placed in the previous code so the JUnit order of execution is respected. The only thing that cannot be guaranteed is the order the tests are executed in. Also parallel execution of tests is possible by adding a file named junit-platform.properties under test\resources that contains the following properties:

```
junit.jupiter.execution.parallel.enabled = true
junit.jupiter.execution.parallel.mode.default = concurrent
junit.jupiter.execution.parallel.mode.classes.default = same_thread
```

The previous set of properties represents the configuration parameters to execute top-level classes sequentially, but their methods in parallel. More configuration examples are provided in the official JUnit documentation.

Most Java smart editors like IntelliJ IDEA provide you with an option to do so when you click right on the class. In Figure 9-15 you can see the menu option to execute a test class in IntelliJ IDEA.

Figure 9-15. *Menu option to execute a test class in IntelliJ IDEA*

After right-clicking on the class, from the menu that appears select **Run PseudoTest** and the test class is executed. A launcher is created so you can launch it from the typical launch menu as well. Test classes can be executed in debug and break points used too. When executing the previous class, even if the test methods are run in parallel the output is consistent with the order of the methods matching the annotation specifications mentioned previously. To make sure that test methods are executed in parallel, the logger was configured to print the thread id as well. A sample output is depicted in Listing 9-33.

Listing 9-33. Output of the Execution of `PseudoTest`

```
[1-worker-1] INFO  c.a.b.n.p.PseudoTest - Loading general test context.
Jun 12, 2021 1:44:13 PM org.junit.jupiter.engine.config.
EnumConfigurationParameterConverter get
INFO: Using parallel execution mode 'CONCURRENT' set via the 'junit.
jupiter.execution.parallel.mode.default' configuration parameter.
[1-worker-1] INFO  c.a.b.n.p.PseudoTest - Prepare  single test context.
[1-worker-2] INFO  c.a.b.n.p.PseudoTest - Prepare  single test context.
[1-worker-1] INFO  c.a.b.n.p.PseudoTest - Executing test two.
[1-worker-2] INFO  c.a.b.n.p.PseudoTest - Executing test one.
[1-worker-2] INFO  c.a.b.n.p.PseudoTest - Destroy  single test context.
[1-worker-1] INFO  c.a.b.n.p.PseudoTest - Destroy  single test context.
[1-worker-1] INFO  c.a.b.n.p.PseudoTest - UnLoading general test context.
```

Notice how there is a log message about parallel execution of tests method being configured. The `testOne()` method contains this statement: `assertTrue(true);` which is put there to show you how assertion methods look like. The true value is replaced with a condition in a real test. The same goes for the `assertFalse(false);` assertion in method `textTwo()`. That's about all the space we can dedicate to JUnit in this book. My recommendation is to look more into it, because a developer can write code, but a good developer knows how to make sure it works as well.

Using Fakes

A **Fake** object is an object that has working implementations, but not the same as the production object. The code written to implement such an object has simplified functionality of the one deployed in production.

To test the AccountRepoImpl class, we have to replace the DerbyDBConnection with a FakeDBConnection that is not backed up by a database but by something more simple, more accessible like a Map<?,?>. The DerbyDBConnection uses a java.sql.Connection and other classes in that package to perform data operations on the Derby database.

The FakeDBConnection will implement the DBConnection interface so that it can be passed to a AccountRepoImpl and all its methods will be called on it.

The rule of thumb when writing tests and test supporting classes is to put them in the same packages with the objects tested or replaced, but in the test/java directory. This is because test classes must access the classes being tested, without extra configurations needed in the module-info.java. Supporting classes to test the application classes using fakes are declared in the com.apress.bgn.nine.fake package.

Another rule of thumb when writing tests is to write a method to test the correct outcome of the method being tested, and one to test the incorrect behavior. In unexpected cases with unexpected data your application will behave in unexpected ways, so although this seems paradoxical, you have to expect the unexpected and write tests for it.

The AccountRepoImpl class implements the basic methods to persist or delete an Account instance to/from the database. The implementation is depicted in Listing 9-34.

Listing 9-34. The AccountRepoImpl Implementation

```java
package com.apress.bgn.nine.repo;

import com.apress.bgn.nine.Account;
import com.apress.bgn.nine.db.DbConnection;

import java.util.List;
import java.util.Optional;

public class AccountRepoImpl implements AccountRepo {

    private DbConnection conn;

    public AccountRepoImpl(DbConnection conn) {
        this.conn = conn;
    }
```

```java
@Override
public Account save(Account account) {
    Account dbAcc = conn.findByHolder(account.getHolder());
    if(dbAcc == null) {
        return conn.insert(account);
    }
    return conn.update(account);
}

@Override
public Optional<Account> findOne(String holder) {
    Account acc = conn.findByHolder(holder);
    if(acc != null) {
        return Optional.of(acc);
    }
    return Optional.empty();
}

@Override
public List<Account> findAll() {
    return conn.findAll();
}

@Override
public int deleteByHolder(String holder) {
    Account acc = conn.findByHolder(holder);
    conn.delete(holder);
    if(acc != null) {
        return 0;
    }
    return 1;
}
}
```

The deleteByHolder(..) method in the AccountRepoImpl is used to delete an account. If the entry is present, it deletes it and returns 0, otherwise it returns 1. The deleteByHolder(..) method is depicted in the next code snippet.

To test this class, we need to provide a DbConnection implementation that simulates a connection to a database. This is where the previously mentioned FakeDBConnection comes in. The code is shown in Listing 9-35.

Listing 9-35. The FakeDBConnection Implementation

```java
package com.apress.bgn.nine.fake.db;

import com.apress.bgn.nine.Account;
import com.apress.bgn.nine.db.DBException;
import com.apress.bgn.nine.db.DbConnection;

import java.util.*;

public class FakeDBConnection implements DbConnection {
    // pseudo-database {@code Map<holder, Account>}
    Map<String, Account> database = new HashMap<>();

    @Override
    public void connect() {
        // no implementation needed
    }

    @Override
    public Account insert(Account account) {
        if (database.containsKey(account.getHolder())) {
            throw new DBException("Could not insert " + account);
        }
        database.put(account.getHolder(), account);
        return account;
    }

    @Override
    public Account findByHolder(String holder) {
        return database.get(holder);
    }
```

```java
@Override
public List<Account> findAll() {
    List<Account> result = new ArrayList<>();
    result.addAll(database.values());
    return result;
}

@Override
public Account update(Account account) {
    if (!database.containsKey(account.getHolder())) {
        throw new DBException("Could not find account for " + account.
        getHolder());
    }
    database.put(account.getHolder(), account);
    return account;
}

@Override
public void delete(String holder) {
    database.remove(holder);
}

@Override
public void disconnect() {
    // no implementation needed
}
}
```

The FakeDBConnection behaves exactly like a connection object that can be used to save entries to a database, search for them, or delete them, only instead of a database it is backed up by a Map<String, Account>. The map key will be the holder's name, because in our database the holder name is used and an unique identifier for an Account entry in the table. Now that we have the fake object, we can test that our AccountRepoImpl behaves as expected. Because of practical reasons only one method will be tested in this section, but the full code is available on the official GitHub repo for the book.

Listing 9-36 shows a test class that test methods that verify the behavior of the findOne(..) method. It contains a positive test method when there is an entry matching the criteria and a negative test method when there isn't.

Listing 9-36. The FakeAccountRepoTest Test Class

```java
package com.apress.bgn.nine;

// other import statements omitted

import static org.junit.jupiter.api.Assertions.*;

public class FakeAccountRepoTest {
    private static final Logger log = LoggerFactory.
    getLogger(FakeAccountRepoTest.class);
    private static DbConnection conn;

    private AccountRepo repo;

    @BeforeAll
    static void prepare() {
        conn = new FakeDBConnection();
    }

    @BeforeEach
    public void setUp(){
        repo = new AccountRepoImpl(conn);

        // inserting an entry so we can test update/findOne
        repo.save(new Account("Pedala", 200, "2345"));
    }

    @Test
    public void testFindOneExisting() {
        Optional<Account> expected = repo.findOne("Pedala");
        assertTrue(expected.isPresent());
    }
```

```
@Test
public void testFindOneNonExisting() {
    Optional<Account> expected = repo.findOne("Dorel");
    assertFalse(expected.isPresent());
}

    @AfterEach
void tearDown(){
    // delete the entry
    repo.deleteByHolder("Pedala");
}

@AfterAll
public static void cleanUp(){
    conn = null;
    log.info("All done!");
}

}
```

Notice how we are creating exactly one entry that is added to our fake database.

Now that we are sure the repository class does its job properly, the next one to test is the AccountServiceImpl. To test this class, we will look into a different approach. Fakes are useful, but writing one for a class with complex functionality can be quite cost-inefficient in regards to development time. So what are the alternatives? There are a few. In the next section, we'll look at stubs.

Using Stubs

A **Stub** is an object that holds predefined data and uses it to answer test calls. An instance of AccountServiceImpl uses an instance of AccountRepo to retrieve data from the database or save data to a database. When writing unit tests for this class, each test method must cover the functionality from a method in service class so that we can write a stub class to simulate the behavior of AccountRepo. For the AccountServiceImpl instance to be able to use it, the stub must implement AccountRepo. In this section the tests will cover the method createAccount(..), because this method can fail in many ways. Thus, more than one test method can be written for it. Listing 9-37 shows the createAccount(..) method.

Listing 9-37. The AccountServiceImpl#createAccount(..) Method

```java
package com.apress.bgn.nine.service;
// import section omitted

public class AccountServiceImpl implements AccountService {

    AccountRepo repo;

    public AccountServiceImpl(AccountRepo repo) {
        this.repo = repo;
    }

    @Override
    public Account createAccount(String holder, String accountNumber,
    String amount) {
        int intAmount;
        try {
            intAmount = Integer.parseInt(amount);
        } catch (NumberFormatException nfe) {
            throw new InvalidDataException("Could not create account with
            invalid amount!");
        }

        if (accountNumber == null || accountNumber.isEmpty() ||
        accountNumber.length() < 5 || intAmount < 0) {
            throw new InvalidDataException("Could not create account with
            invalid account number or invalid amount!");
        }

        Optional<Account> existing = repo.findOne(holder);
        if (existing.isPresent()) {
            throw new AccountCreationException("Account already exists for
            holder " + holder);
        }
        Account acc = new Account(holder, intAmount, accountNumber);
        return repo.save(acc);
    }
    // other code omitted
}
```

The `createAccount(..)` method takes as parameters the holder name, the number of the account to be created, and the initial amount. All of them are provided as `String` instances intentionally, so that the method body contains a little bit of logic that would require serious testing. Let's analyze the behavior of the previous method and make a list with all possible returned values and returned exceptions:

- if the `amount` is not a number, an `InvalidDataException` is thrown. (The `InvalidDataException` is a custom type of exception created soecifically for this project, which is not relevant at the moment.)

- if the `accountNumber` argument is empty, an `InvalidDataException` is thrown.

- if the `accountNumber` argument is null, an `InvalidDataException` is thrown.

- if the `accountNumber` argument has less than 5 characters, an `InvalidDataException` is thrown.

- if the `amount` argument converted to a number is negative, an `InvalidDataException` is thrown.

- if the `account` for the `holder` argument already exists, an `AccountCreationException` is thrown.

- if all the inputs are valid and there is no account for the holder argument, an `Account` instance is created, saved to the database and the result is returned.

If we were to be really obsessive about testing, we would have to write a test scenario for all those cases. In the software world there is something called **test coverage,** which is a process that determines whether test cases cover application code and how much of it. The result is a percentage value, and companies usually define a test coverage percentage[12] that represents a warranty of quality for the application. Before showing the test methods for the `createAccount(..)` method, take a look at Listing 9-38 that shows the repo stub code.

---

[12] A good read about the subject by Martin Fowler, one of the most renown Java gurus of this generation, can be found at his website, "Test Coverage," `https://martinfowler.com/bliki/TestCoverage.html`, accessed October 15, 2021.

Listing 9-38. The AccountRepoStub Class

```java
package com.apress.bgn.nine.service.stub;
// other import statements omitted
import com.apress.bgn.nine.repo.AccountRepo;

public class AccountRepoStub implements AccountRepo {

    private Integer option = 0;

    public synchronized void set(int val) {
        option = val;
    }

    @Override
    public Account save(Account account) {
        return account;
    }

    @Override
    public Optional<Account> findOne(String holder) {
        if (option == 0) {
            return Optional.of(new Account(holder, 100, "22446677"));
        }
        return Optional.empty();
    }

    @Override
    public List<Account> findAll() {
        return List.of(new Account("sample", 100, "22446677"));
    }

    @Override
    public int deleteByHolder(String holder) {
        return option;
    }
}
```

The option field can be used to change behavior of the stub, to cover more test cases. As we have one stub repository, this means tests might fail when run in parallel, but for this example with this simple stub, it works.

There are two ways to write test using JUnit, depending on the assert*(..) statements used. Listing 9-39 shows two negative test methods that validate the behavior when an invalid amount is provided as argument.

Listing 9-39. The AccountServiceTest Unit Test Class Using a Stub Repo

```java
package com.apress.bgn.nine.service;

import com.apress.bgn.nine.Account;
import com.apress.bgn.nine.service.stub.AccountRepoStub;
import org.junit.jupiter.api.*;

import static org.junit.jupiter.api.Assertions.*;

public class AccountServiceTest {

    private static AccountRepoStub repo;
    private AccountService service;

    @BeforeAll
    static void prepare() {
        repo = new AccountRepoStub();
    }

    @BeforeEach
    void setUp() {
        service = new AccountServiceImpl(repo);
    }

    @Test
    void testNonNumericAmountVersionOne() {
        assertThrows(InvalidDataException.class,
                () -> {
                    service.createAccount("Gigi", "223311", "2I00");
                });
    }
}
```

```java
@Test
void testNonNumericAmountVersionTwo() {
    InvalidDataException expected = assertThrows(
            InvalidDataException.class, () -> {
                service.createAccount("Gigi", "223311", "2I00");
            }
    );
    assertEquals("Could not create account with invalid amount!",
    expected.getMessage());
}

@AfterEach
void tearDown() {
    repo.set(0);
}

@AfterAll
static void destroy() {
    repo = null;
}
}
```

The testNonNumericAmountVersionOne() method makes use of assertThrows(..) that receives two parameters: the type of exception expected to be thrown when the second parameter of type Executable is executed. Executable is functional interface defined in the org.junit.jupiter.api.function, which can be used in a lambda expression to get the compact test that you see in Listing 9-39.

The testNonNumericAmountVersionTwo() method saves the result of the assertThrows(..) call, which allows for the message of the exception to be tested as well, to make sure that the execution flow worked exactly as expected.

Similar methods can be written to test all other service methods. The AccountServiceTest class hosted on the repository for this book depicts a few other testing methods. Feel free to add your own to cover situations that were missed.

The last test technique covered in this chapter: writing tests using mocks.

Using Mocks

Mocks are objects that register calls they receive. During execution of a test, using assert utility methods, the assumption that all expected actions were performed on mocks are tested. Thankfully, code for mocks does not have to be written by the developer, there are three well known libraries that provide the type of classes needed to test using mocks: Mockito, JMock, and EasyMock.[13] Also, if you are ever in need to mock static methods—the most common reason being bad design—there is PowerMock.[14]

Using mocks, you can jump directly to writing the tests. Listing 9-40 shows two tests for the `createAccount(..)` method that focus on the repository class actually calling its methods, because the repository class is the one being replaced with a mock.

Listing 9-40. The `AccountServiceTest` Unit Test Class Using a Mock Repo

```
package com.apress.bgn.nine.mock;
// other import statements omitted
import org.junit.jupiter.api.extension.ExtendWith;
import org.mockito.Mock;
import org.mockito.junit.jupiter.MockitoExtension;

import static org.junit.jupiter.api.Assertions.*;
import static org.mockito.ArgumentMatchers.any;
import static org.mockito.Mockito.when;

@ExtendWith(MockitoExtension.class)
public class AccountServiceTest {

    private AccountService service;

    @Mock
    private AccountRepo mockRepo;
```

---

[13] See the official sites for these libraries at Mockito, `https://site.mockito.org/`; JMock, `https://jmock.org/`; and EasyMock, `https://easymock.org/`, all accessed October 15, 2021.

[14] See the official site for PowerMock at `https://powermock.github.io/`, accessed October 15, 2021.

```java
    @BeforeEach
    public void checkMocks() {
        assertNotNull(mockRepo);
  service = new AccountServiceImpl(mockRepo);
    }

    @Test
    public void testCreateAccount() {
        Account expected = new Account("Gigi", 2100, "223311");
        when(mockRepo.findOne("Gigi")).thenReturn(Optional.empty());
        when(mockRepo.save(any(Account.class))).thenReturn(expected);

        Account result = service.createAccount("Gigi", "223311", "2100");
        assertEquals(expected, result);
    }

    @Test
    public void testCreateAccountAlreadyExists() {
        Account expected = new Account("Gigi", 2100, "223311");
        when(mockRepo.findOne("Gigi")).thenReturn(Optional.of(expected));

        assertThrows(AccountCreationException.class,
                () -> service.createAccount("Gigi", "223311", "2100"));
    }
}
```

The tests are quite self-explanatory, and the Mockito utility methods names make it easy to understand what is actually happening during a test execution. Wait, you might ask, how are the mocks created and injected? Who does that? The @ExtendWith(MockitoExtension. class) is necessary for JUnit 5 tests to support Mockito annotations. Without it, annotations like @Mock have no effect on the code. The @Mock annotation is to be used on references to mocks created by Mockito. The preferred way to work with mocks is to specify a reference of an interface type that is implemented by the real object type and the mock that will be created for the test scenario. But @Mock can be placed on a concrete type reference as well, and the created mock will be a subclass of that class. The @InjectMocks annotation is used on the object to be tested, so that Mockito knows to create this object and inject mocks instead of the dependencies. This is all you need to know to start using Mockito mocks in your test. Declaring the objects to be replaced with mocks and the object to be injected in is the only setup a class containing unit tests using mocks needs.

The body of test methods using mocks have a typical structure as well. The first lines must declare objects and variables passed as arguments to the method called on the object being tested or passed as arguments to Mockito utility methods that declare what mocks take as arguments and what they return. The next lines establish the behavior of the mock when its methods are called by the object to be tested.

The following two lines depict this for the findOne(..) method. The first line creates an account object. The second line defines the behavior of the mock. When mockRepo.findOne("Gigi") will be called, then the previously created account instance will be returned wrapped in an Optional<T> instance.

```
Account expected = new Account("Gigi", 2100, "223311");
when(mockRepo.findOne("Gigi")).thenReturn(Optional.of(expected));
```

There are many other libraries to make writing tests as effortlessly as possible for developers, and big frameworks like Spring provide their own testing library to help developers write test for application using this framework. Build tools like Ant, Maven, and Gradle can be used to automatically run the tests when the project is built and generate useful reports related to the failures.

Using Maven, the project can be build by calling mvn clean install in the console. All test classes declared in the test module, are picked up automatically if they are named *Test.java. When writing tests and not changing application code, you can just run the tests only by calling mvn test. This is a configuration that can be changed by configuring the Maven Surefire Testing Plug-in configured in the pom.xml file.

In a Maven project tests are run by the maven-surefire-plugin. The Maven test results are saved in txt and XML format, and the files are located under target/surefire-reports directory. The test results can be grouped into an HTML report by adding the maven-surefire-report-plugin to the project configuration and configuring it to run during the test phase. This is practical, since it causes the report to be generated by running mvn clean install or mvn test. The generated report is readable, but without being part of the site generated for the project there is no css styling. The report is represented by a file named surefire-report.html located under target/site directory.

For the following example, a test failure was introduced intentionally, and the build was modified to record the failure without failing the full build. Otherwise, the report is not generated. This is all done via Maven configurations that you can take a peek at in the code for this book. You can see the generated report in Figure 9-16.

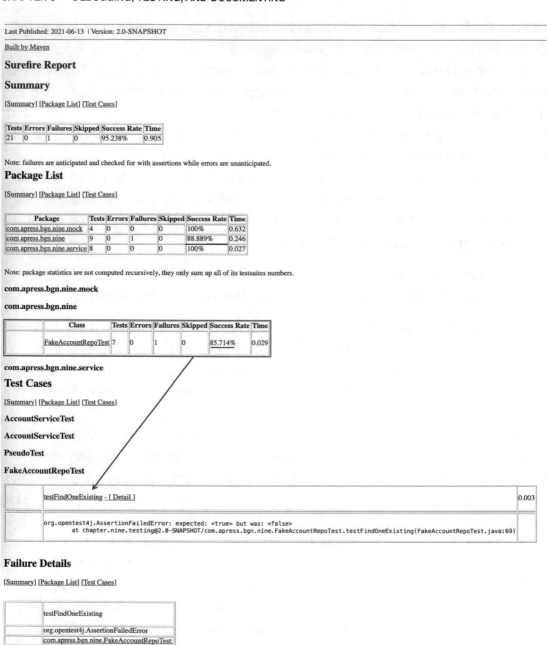

Figure 9-16. *The Maven test report with a test failure and no styling*

It doesn't look pretty, but it is readable. Upon fixing the test the report becomes simpler, and the last two sections are not generated. When included into the site generated for this project using the `maven-site-plugin` (used in the next section of this chapter) the generated report looks a lot better, as depicted in Figure 9-17.

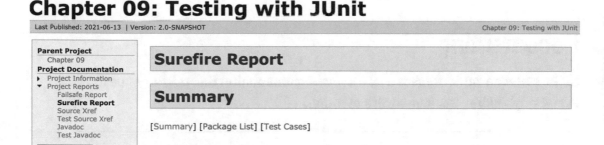

Chapter 09: Testing with JUnit

Last Published: 2021-06-13 | Version: 2.0-SNAPSHOT   Chapter 09: Testing with JUnit

Parent Project
  Chapter 09
Project Documentation
▶ Project Information
▼ Project Reports
    Failsafe Report
    Surefire Report
    Source Xref
    Test Source Xref
    Javadoc
    Test Javadoc

Built by:
maven

Surefire Report

Summary

[Summary] [Package List] [Test Cases]

Tests	Errors	Failures	Skipped	Success Rate	Time
21	0	0	0	100%	1.259

Note: failures are anticipated and checked for with assertions while errors are unanticipated.

Package List

[Summary] [Package List] [Test Cases]

Package	Tests	Errors	Failures	Skipped	Success Rate	Time
com.apress.bgn.nine.mock	4	0	0	0	100%	0.842
com.apress.bgn.nine	9	0	0	0	100%	0.393
com.apress.bgn.nine.service	8	0	0	0	100%	0.024

Note: package statistics are not computed recursively, they only sum up all of its testsuites numbers.

Figure 9-17. *The Maven test report with no test failures and typical Maven generated site styling*

ℹ   The previous edition of this book used Gradle to build this project. Because of various incompatibilities with newer versions of Java and the difficulty of configuration, it was dropped in favor of Maven, which is widely used and pretty stable. Unfortunately, generating test reports requires multiple Maven plug-ins and the reports are not as pretty.

As a conclusion of this section remember this: no matter how good a development team is, without a great testing team, the resulting application might actually be far away from an acceptable quality standard. So if you ever come across companies that do not have a dedicated testing team, or a company culture that compromises in techniques such as code review and writing tests, think twice before accepting that job.

Documenting

In the software world there is a joke about documentation that might not be to everybody's liking, but it is worth a mention.

🔥 Documentation is like sex. When it's good, is really, really good. And when it's bad, it's still better than nothing.

A common-sense rule and best practice of programming is to write code that is self-explanatory, to avoid writing documentation. Basically, if you need to write too much documentation, you're doing it wrong. There are a lot of things you can do to avoid writing documentation, such as using meaningful names for classes and variables, respecting the language code conventions, and many others. However, when you are building a set of classes that will be used by other developers, you need to provide a little documentation for the main APIs. If your solution requires a very complicated algorithm to be written you might want to add comments about it here and there, although in this case, proper technical documentation with schemas and diagrams should be written too.

In **Chapter 3** the different types of comments were mentioned, and a promise was made to come back with more detail regarding Javadoc comments. The Javadoc block comments, also named the **Documentation comments**, can be found associated with a public class, interface, method body, public field, and sometimes even protected or private, if really necessary. The Javadoc comments contain special tags that link documented elements together or mark the different type of information. The Javadoc comments and their associated code can be processed by Javadoc tools, extracted, and wrapped together into a HTML site, which is called the Javadoc API of the project. The Maven configuration of this project declares a few reporting plug-ins and the previously mentioned `maven-site-plugin` that is configured to wrap together all reports into a static site for the project that can be found under `target/site`.

❶ The project site is generated by executing `mvn site`.

🔥 As expected, it is difficult for teams developing and maintaining Maven plug-ins to keep up with the Oracle JDK release schedule. While setting up the configuration for this module several bugs were noticed.[15] It did not seem to affect the success of the build, or its result too much. Hopefully, but the time this book is release there will be no warning and errors messages when running this build.

Smart editors can download and access documentation of a project and display it when the developer tries to write code using the documented components, so good code documentation considerably increases the speed of the development process. Let's start with a few examples of Javadoc comments, to explain the most important tags used.

Whenever we create a class or interface, we should add Javadoc comments to explain their purpose, to add the version of the application when they were added, and eventually link some existing resources. At the beginning of this chapter we mentioned the IntSorter hierarchy, a hierarchy of classes implementing the IntSorter interface that provide implementations of different sorting algorithms. When these classes are used by other developers, one of them might want to add a customised algorithm to our hierarchy. A little information about the IntSorter interface would help them a lot in designing a proper solution. List 9-41 shows a Javadoc comment added to the IntSorter interface.

Listing 9-41. The Documentation Comment on the IntSorter Interface

```
/**
 * Interface {@code IntSorter} is an interface that needs to be implemented
 * by classes that provide a method to sort an array of {@code int}
   values. <p>
 *
 * {@code int[]} was chosen as a type because this type
 * of values are always sortable. ({@link Comparable})
 *
```

---

[15] For example, you might see the message mentioned at Apache, "JDK 16+: Error Fetching Link," `https://issues.apache.org/jira/browse/MJAVADOC-680`, accessed October 15, 2021.

```
 * @author Iuliana Cosmina
 * @since 1.0
 */
public interface IntSorter {
    // interface body omitted
}
```

In the Javadoc comments, HTML tags can be used to format information. In the previous code a <p> element was used to make sure the comment will be made of multiple paragraphs. The @author tag was introduced in JDK 1.0 and it is useful when the development team is quite big, because if you end up working with somebody else's code, you know who to look for if issues appear. The @since tag is used to provide the version of the application when this interface was added. For an application that has had a long development and release cycle, this tag can be used to mark elements (methods, classes, fields, etc.) of a specific version so that a developer using the codebase of your application knows when elements were added, and in case of a rollback to a previous version will know where in his application compile-time errors will appear.

The best example here is the Java official Javadoc; let's take the String class. It was introduced in Java version 1.0, but more constructors and methods were added to it with every Java version being released. Each of them is marked with the specific versions. Listing 9-42 depicts code snippets and documentation comments that prove the previous affirmation.

Listing 9-42. The Documentation Comments in the String Class

```
package java.lang;
// import section omitted

/**
 * ...
 * @since 1.0
 */
public final class String
    implements java.io.Serializable, Comparable<String>, CharSequence,
                Constable, ConstantDesc {
```

```java
// some code omitted

/**
 * ...
 * @since  1.1
 */
public String(byte[] bytes, int offset, int length, String
charsetName) {
    // method body omitted
}

/**
 * ...
 * @since  1.4
 */
public boolean contentEquals(StringBuffer sb) {
    // method body omitted
}

/**
 * ...
 * @since  1.5
 */
public String(int[] codePoints, int offset, int count) {
    // method body omitted
}

/**
 * ...
 * @since  1.6
 */
public String(byte[] bytes, int offset, int length, Charset charset) {
    // method body omitted
}
```

```java
/**
 * ...
 * @since 1.8
 */
public static String join(CharSequence delimiter, CharSequence...
elements) {
    // method body omitted
}

 /**
 * ...
 * @since 9
 */
@Override
public IntStream codePoints() {
    // method body omitted
}

/**
 * ...
 * @since 11
 */
public String strip() {
    // method body omitted
}

/**
 * ...
 * @since 12
 */
public String indent(int n) {
    // method body omitted
}

/**
 * ...
 * @since 15
 */
```

```java
    public String stripIndent() {
        // method body omitted
    }
}
```

In the IntSorter example you might have noticed the @code tag. This tag was introduced in Java 1.5 version and is used to display text in code form, using a special font and escaping symbols that might break the HTML syntax.(ex: < or >).

The @link tag was added in Java 1.2 and is used to insert a navigable link to relevant documentation.

Listing 9-43 shows an even better documented version of the IntSorter interface, which contains documentation comments for the methods so that developers implementing it know how its methods should be used.

Listing 9-43. The Documentation Comments for Method in the IntSorter Interface

```java
/**
 * Interface {@code IntSorter} is an interface that needs to be implemented
 * by classes that provide a method to sort an array of {@code int}
   values. <p>
 *
 * {@code int[]} was chosen as a type because this type
 * of values are always sortable. ({@link Comparable})
 *
 * @author Iuliana Cosmina
 * @since 1.0
 */
public interface IntSorter {

    /**
     * Sorts {@code arr}
     *
     * @param arr int array to be sorted
     * @param low lower limit of the interval to be sorted
     * @param high higher limit of the interval to be sorted
     */
```

```
    void sort(int[] arr, int low, int high);

    /**
     * Implement this method to provide a sorting solution that does not
       require pivots.
     * @deprecated As of version 0.1, because the
     *               {@link #sort(int[], int, int) ()} should be used
                     instead.<p>
     * To be removed in version 3.0.
     * @param arr int array to be sorted
     */
    @Deprecated (since= "0.1", forRemoval = true)
    default void sort(int[] arr) {
        System.out.println("Do not use this! This is deprecated!!");
    }
}
```

The IntelliJ IDEA editor (and other smart editors) can generate small pieces of Javadoc for you. Once you have declared a class or method body that you want to document, type /** and press <Enter>. The generated block of comment contains entries for everything that can be inferred from the component's declaration. The following list describes the most common:

- one or more @param tags together with the parameter names. All is left for the developer to do is to add extra documentation to explain their purpose.

- if the method returns a value of a type different than void a @return tag is generated. Documentation must be provided by the developer to explain what the result represents and if there are special cases when a certain value is returned.

- if the methods declare an exception to be thrown, a @throws tag is generated together with the exception type, and the developer's job is to explain when and why is that type of exception thrown.

Listing 9-44 depicts a snippet from the Optional<T> class containing the filter(..) method and its documentation comment.

Listing 9-44. The Documentation Comments for
Optional<T>#filter(..) Method

```
/**
 * ...
 * @param predicate the predicate to apply to a value, if present
 * @return an {@code Optional} describing the value of this
 *         {@code Optional}, if a value is present and the value
           matches the
 *         given predicate, otherwise an empty {@code Optional}
 * @throws NullPointerException if the predicate is {@code null}
 */
public Optional<T> filter(Predicate<? super T> predicate) {
    Objects.requireNonNull(predicate);
    if (!isPresent()) {
        return this;
    } else {
        return predicate.test(value) ? this : empty();
    }
}
```

The @link to can be used to create a documentation link to a class, or a method in that class or interface, a method documentation section, a field, or even an external web page. Listing 9-45 depicts a class implementing IntSorter. Its documentation comment contains a link to the abstract method in the IntSorter interface.

Listing 9-45. The Documentation Comments for the InsertionSort Class

```
package com.apress.bgn.nine.algs;

/**
 * The {@code InsertionSort} class contains a single method that is a
   concrete implementation of {@link IntSorter#sort(int[])}.<p>
 * Instances of this class can be used to sort an {@code int[] } array
   using the insertion-sort algorithm.
 *
```

```
 * @author Iuliana Cosmina
 * since 1.0
 * @see IntSorter
 */
public class InsertionSort implements IntSorter {
    // class body omitted
}
```

The @see tag is a simple alternative to @link that is supposed to direct developer's attention to documentation specific to the element this tag references. The @deprecated tag is used to add a text explaining the reasons of deprecation, version when the component is meant to be removed, and what to use instead. Javadoc generation tools will take the text for this tag, use italic font for its display, and add it to the main description of the component (class, field, method, etc). Beside this tag, the @Deprecated annotation was introduced in Java 1.5. Annotating a component with it should discourage developers from using it. The advantage of this annotaton is that compilers pick it up and issues warnings when a deprecated component is used or overridden in nondeprecated code. This annotation can be used on any Java language component, including modules.

Smart Java IDEs, like IntelliJ IDEA, are aware of the @deprecated tag and the @Deprecated annotation and show deprecated components in strikethrough format to warn the developer not to use them. The Maven maven-compiler-plugin responsible with compiling Java source code provides a configuration option to show or hide deprecation warnings. All these are depicted in Figure 9-18.

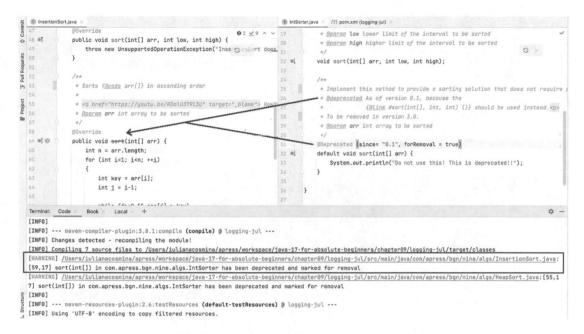

Figure 9-18. *IntelliJ IDEA recognizes the @deprecated tag. Maven build is configured to show deprecation warnings*

With this, we have covered the most-used tags when writing Javadoc comments. If you want to check out the complete list you can find it here: https://www.oracle. com/java/technologies/javase/javadoc-tool.html#javadocdocuments. Javadoc documentation is also a wide subject that could provide material for an entire book. We are just scratching the surface in this section and covering the basics so that you have a good understanding of it.

> ❶ The Maven plug-in configuration for generating the site for a project is an advanced subject, not suitable for this book. However, Maven plug-ins have been mentioned by name, and some comments have been added in the pom.xml files to explaining their purpose and their configuration, if you are curious about these details.

To generate the HTML site for the logging-jul module, open the Maven project view and navigate to **Chapter 09: Logging with SLF4J ➤ Lifecycle** node and under it, we will find the site phase, as depicted in Figure 9-19.

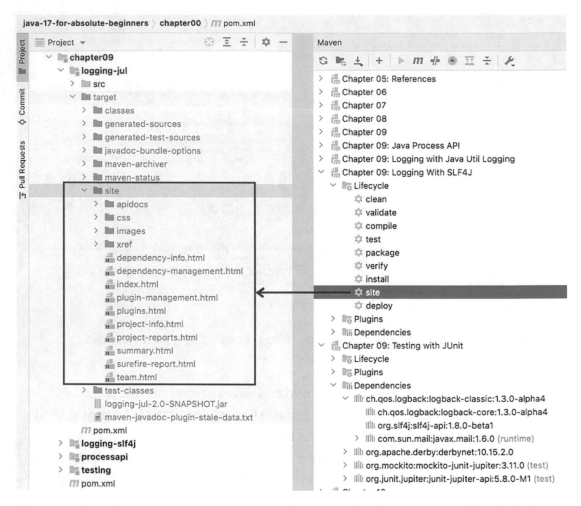

Figure 9-19. *The Maven site phase and the result for the* `logging-jul` *module*

Double-clicking this in the IDE is the same as executing `mvn site` in the console. It triggers the execution of the Maven site generation phase and all the phases it depends on, and the result of the build is a directory named `site`, located under the `target` directory. It contains a static site and its starting page is named `index.html`. The site is quite simple, since a default configuration was used.

Right-click on that file and from the context sensitive menu that appears select **Open in Browser** and select your preferred browser.

The main page of the project depicts information from the `pom.xml` such as project name, description, and so on. On the left side of the page there is a menu that contains a few entries one of them named `Project Reports`. Expand this menu item and a list of items is shown one of them named `Javadoc`. Click on that directs you to the project

Javadoc page. If you think the page resembles the JDK official Javadoc page, you are not imagining it; the same Doclet API was used to generate that official one as well. The project menu and the Javadoc main page are depicted in Figure 9-20.

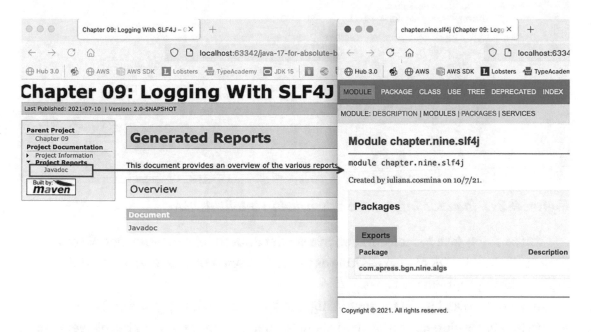

Figure 9-20. *The Maven project site and the main Javadoc site for the* `logging-slf4j` *module*

The documentation is not particularly rich, but it is usable.

It was previously mentioned that Javadoc documentation, when present, is picked up by IntelliJ IDEA and other smart editors and depicted on the spot, while the developer uses the documented components in the code. Smarter editors, when selecting a class, method name, interface method, and so on, provide some kind of combination of keys that include F1 that the developer must press so that the documentation is depicted in a pop-up window. In IntelliJ IDEA, just click an element and press F1 and the Javadoc documentation is shown in a pop-up window, formatted quite nicely, as depicted in Figure 9-21.

```
33    /**
34     * Created by iuliana.cosmina on 14/06/2021
35     */
36    public class DocDemo {
37
38        public static void main(String... args) {
39            IntSorter sorter = new QuickSort();
40
41            sorter.s|
42        }           sort(int[] arr, int low, int high)        void      com.apress.bgn.nine.algs.IntSorter
43    }               sort(int[] arr)                           void      void sort(int[] arr,
44                    souf                  System.out.printf("", expr)             int low,
                      serr                  System.err.println(expr)               int high)
                      sout                  System.out.println(expr)    Sorts arr
                      toString()                         String
                      equals(Object obj)                boolean         Params: arr – int array to be sorted
                      hashCode()                            int                 low – lower limit of the interval to be
                      getClass()         Class<? extends IntSorter>               sorted
                      soutv                 System.out.println(expr)              high – higher limit of the interval to
                      synchronized          synchronized (expr)                   be sorted
            Press ^. to choose the selected (or first) suggestion and insert a dot afterwards  Next Tip    · logging-jul
```

Figure 9-21. *Javadoc information depicted in IntelliJ IDEA*

You can view Javadoc information in a smart editor for any dependency of your project (including JDK classes) as long as the code is open source, and the module exports the appropriate packages.

In Java 9 the Doclet API for generating Javadoc received an upgrade and a facelift. Before Java 9, developers complained about the performance issues of the old version, the cryptic API, the lack of support, and the shallowness of it overall. In Java 9 most of the problems were tackled down and resolved. The detailed description and list of improvements can be found here: http://openjdk.java.net/jeps/221.

Documentation is really valuable, and can make development practical and pleasant when it is really good. So when writing code, document it as you would expect the dependencies of your project to be. You might probably have heard of the expression **RTFM**, which is an abbreviation for **Read The F*ing Manual!** This expression is used quite a lot in software by experienced developers when working with newbie developers. Problem is, what should you do when there is no manual? Most companies on a deadline might have the tendency to allocate little or no time to documenting a project, so this section was added to this book to emphasize the importance of good documentation in software development, and to teach you how to write your documentation while you write your code, because you might not have time to do it afterward.

Summary

This chapter has covered important development tools and techniques, the classes in JDK that provide support for them, and important Java libraries and frameworks that you will most likely end up working with that could make your development job practical and pleasant. A complete list of topics is in the following list, and hopefully after reading this chapter you have a good point to start in using any of them.

- How to configure and use logging in a Java application.

- How to log messages in the console.

- How to log messages to a file.

- How to use Java Logging.

- What a logging facade is and why it is recommended to be used.

- Configure and use SLF4J with Logback.

- How to program using assertions.

- How to debug step by step using IntelliJ IDEA.

- How to monitor and inspect JVM statistics while an application is running using various JDK tools like: `jps`, `jcmd`, `jconsole` and `jmc`.

- How to use the Process API to monitor and create processes.

- How to test an application using JUnit.

- How to write tests using fakes.

- How to write tests using stubs.

- How to write tests using mocks.

- How to document a Java application and generate documentation in HTML format using Maven.

## CHAPTER 10

Making Your Application Interactive

So far in the book, input for our Java programs data was provided via arrays or variables that were initialized inside the code or via program arguments. In real life, however, most applications require interaction with the user. The user can be provided access by entering a username and a password, and the user is sometimes required to type in details to confirm his/her identity or to instruct the application what to do. Java supports multiple methods for user input to be read. In this chapter we will be covering a few ways to build interactive Java applications. Interactive Java application takes their input either from the console, from Java-built interfaces, and from either desktop or web.

JShell is a command line interface where a developer can enter variable declarations and one-line statements that are executed when <Enter> is pressed. Command line interface shells like bash and terminals like Command Prompt from Windows can be used to issue commands to programs in the form of successive lines of text. JShell was covered at the beginning of the book for the simple reason that it was a Java 9 novelty. The following sections will cover how to read user-provided data and instructions using the command-line interface. The sections after that will focus on building Java applications with a desktop/web interface.

Reading Data from the Command Line

This section is dedicated to reading user input from the command line, whether it is the IntelliJ IDEA console or whether the program is run from an executable jar from any terminal specific to an operating system. In the JDK there are two classes that can be used to read user data from the command line: java.util.Scanner and java.io.Console, and this section will cover them both in detail. Without further ado, let's get into it.

© Iuliana Cosmina 2022
I. Cosmina, *Java 17 for Absolute Beginners*, https://doi.org/10.1007/978-1-4842-7080-6_10

Reading User Data Using `System.in`

Before introducing logging in **Chapter 9** to print data in the console methods under `System.out`, they were used often in the code samples for this book. There is also a counterpart utility object named `System.in` used to read data from the console: data that a user of the program introduces to control the application flow. You might have noticed that until now all Java programs when executed would be started, would process the data, would execute the declared statements, and then they would terminate, exit gracefully, or with an exception when something went wrong. The most simple and common way to pass decision of termination to the user is to end the main method with a call to `System.in.read()`. This method reads the next byte of data from the input stream and the program is paused until the user introduces a value; as the value is returned, we can even save it and print it. Listing 10-1 shows the code to read user input using `System.in.read`.

Listing 10-1. Reading a Value Provided By the User in the Console

```java
package com.apress.bgn.ten;

import java.io.IOException;

public class ReadingFormStdinDemo {

    public static void main(String... args) throws IOException {
        System.out.print("Press any key to terminate:");
        byte[] b = new byte[3];
        int read = System.in.read(b);
        for (int i = 0; i < b.length; ++i) {
            System.out.println(b[i]);
        }
        System.out.println("Key pressed: " + read);
    }
}
```

The user input is saved in the byte[] b array; its size is arbitrary. You can type anything you want. Only the first three bytes will be kept in the array. However, this way of reading information is not really useful, is it? I mean, look at the following snippet, which depicts the previous code being executed and a random text being inserted.

```
Press any key to terminate: ini mini miny moo.  # inserted text
32
105
110
Key pressed: 3
```

Let's see how we can read full text from the user: enter class java.util.Scanner.

Using java.util.Scanner

The System.in variable is of type java.io.InputStream, which is a JDK special type extended by all classes representing an input stream of bytes. You will learn more about the class InputStream in **Chapter 11**. This means that System.in can be wrapped in any java.io.Reader extension (read **Chapter 11** for more information), so bytes can be read as readable data. The one that is really important is a class named Scanner from package java.util. An instance of this type can be created by calling its constructor and providing System.in as an argument. The Scanner class provides a lot of next*() methods that can be used to read almost any type from the console. In Figure 10-1 you can see the next*() methods list.

⋆ ⓜ next ()	String
ⓜ next (String pattern)	String
ⓜ next (Pattern pattern)	String
ⓜ nextLine ()	String
ⓜ nextBoolean ()	boolean
ⓜ nextBigDecimal ()	BigDecimal
ⓜ nextBigInteger ()	BigInteger
ⓜ nextBigInteger (int radix)	BigInteger
ⓜ nextByte ()	byte
ⓜ nextByte (int radix)	byte
ⓜ nextDouble ()	double
ⓜ nextFloat ()	float
ⓜ nextInt ()	int
ⓜ nextInt (int radix)	int
ⓜ nextLong ()	long
ⓜ nextLong (int radix)	long
ⓜ nextShort ()	short
ⓜ nextShort (int radix)	short
ⓜ hasNext ()	boolean
ⓜ hasNext (String pattern)	boolean
ⓜ hasNext (Pattern pattern)	boolean
ⓜ hasNextBigDecimal ()	boolean
ⓜ hasNextBigInteger ()	boolean
ⓜ hasNextBigInteger (int radix)	boolean
ⓜ hasNextBoolean ()	boolean
ⓜ hasNextByte ()	boolean
ⓜ hasNextByte (int radix)	boolean
ⓜ hasNextDouble ()	boolean
ⓜ hasNextFloat ()	boolean
ⓜ hasNextInt ()	boolean

Figure 10-1. *Scanner methods for reading various types of data*

The advantage of using Scanner to read data from the console is that the values read are automatically converted to the proper types when possible; when it is not, a java.util.InputMismatchException is thrown.

The following piece of code was designed so you can select the type of value you want to read by inserting a text and then the value. In Listing 10-2 the appropriate method of the Scanner instance is called to read the value.

Listing 10-2. Reading a Value Provided By the User in the Console Using
`java.util.Scanner`

```java
package com.apress.bgn.ten;

import java.math.BigInteger;
import java.util.ArrayList;
import java.util.List;
import java.util.Scanner;

public class ReadingFromStdinUsingScannerDemo {
    public static final String EXIT = "exit";
    public static final String HELP = "help";
    public static final String BYTE = "byte";
    public static final String SHORT = "short";
    public static final String INT = "int";
    public static final String BOOLEAN = "bool";
    public static final String DOUBLE = "double";
    public static final String LINE = "line";
    public static final String BIGINT = "bigint";
    public static final String TEXT = "text";
    public static final String LONGS = "longs";

    public static void main(String... args) {
        Scanner sc = new Scanner(System.in);
        String help = getHelpString();
        System.out.println(help);

        String input;
        do {
            System.out.print("Enter option: ");
            input = sc.nextLine();

            switch (input) {
                case HELP:
                    System.out.println(help);
                    break;
```

```java
        case EXIT:
            System.out.println("Hope you had fun. Buh-bye!");
            break;
        case BYTE:
            byte b = sc.nextByte();
            System.out.println("Nice byte there: " + b);
            sc.nextLine();
            break;
        case SHORT:
            short s = sc.nextShort();
            System.out.println("Nice short there: " + s);
            sc.nextLine();
            break;
        case INT:
            int i = sc.nextInt();
            System.out.println("Nice int there: " + i);
            sc.nextLine();
            break;
        case BOOLEAN:
            boolean bool = sc.nextBoolean();
            System.out.println("Nice boolean there: " + bool);
            sc.nextLine();
            break;
        case DOUBLE:
            double d = sc.nextDouble();
            System.out.println("Nice double there: " + d);
            sc.nextLine();
            break;
        case LINE:
            String line = sc.nextLine();
            System.out.println("Nice line of text there: " + line);
            break;
```

```java
            case BIGINT:
                BigInteger bi = sc.nextBigInteger();
                System.out.println("Nice big integer there: " + bi);
                sc.nextLine();
                break;
            case TEXT:
                String text = sc.next();
                System.out.println("Nice text there: " + text);
                sc.nextLine();
                break;
            default:
                System.out.println("No idea what you want bruh!");
        }

    } while (!input.equalsIgnoreCase(EXIT));
}

private static String getHelpString() {
    return new StringBuilder("This application helps you test various
    usage of Scanner. Enter type to be read next:")
            .append("\n\t help >  displays this help")
            .append("\n\t exit >  leave the application")
            .append("\n\t byte > read a byte")
            .append("\n\t short > read a short")
            .append("\n\t int > read an int")
            .append("\n\t bool > read a boolean")
            .append("\n\t double > read a double")
            .append("\n\t line > read a line of text")
            .append("\n\t bigint > read a BigInteger")
            .append("\n\t text > read a text value").toString();
    }
}
```

As you probably noticed, in the previous code sample most scanner methods are called together with a nextLine(). This is because every input you provide is made of the actual token and a new line character (the <Enter> pressed to end your input), and before you can enter your next value, you need to take that character from the stream as well.

Listing 10-3 depicts the code in Listing 10-2 being used to read a few user values.

Listing 10-3. Running the ReadingFromStdinUsingScannerDemo Class

```
This application helps you test various usage of Scanner. Enter type to be
read next:
     help >  displays this help
     exit >  leave the application
     byte > read a byte
     short > read a short
     int > read an int
     bool > read a boolean
     double > read a double
     line > read a line of text
     bigint > read a BigInteger
     text > read a text value
Enter option: byte
12
Nice byte there: 12
Enter option: bool
true
Nice boolean there: true
Enter option: line
some of us are hardly ever here
Nice line of text there: some of us are hardly ever here
Enter option: text
john
Nice text there: john
Enter option: text
the rest of us are made to disappear...
Nice text there: the
Enter option: double
4.2
Nice double there: 4.2
Enter option: int
AAAA
```

```
Exception in thread "main" java.util.InputMismatchException
    at java.base/java.util.Scanner.throwFor(Scanner.java:939)
    at java.base/java.util.Scanner.next(Scanner.java:1594)
    at java.base/java.util.Scanner.nextInt(Scanner.java:2258)
    at java.base/java.util.Scanner.nextInt(Scanner.java:2212)
    at chapter.ten.scanner/com.apress.bgn.ten.
ReadingFromStdinUsingScannerDemo.main(ReadingFromStdinUsingScannerDemo.
java:80)
```

The output that is highlighted in the previous listing represents the test case for
the next() method. This method should be used to read a single String token. The
next token gets converted to a String instance, and obviously the token ends when
a whitespace is encountered. That is why in the previous example the only read text
ends up being *the*. In the last case the expected option is an integer value, but *AAAA* is
entered, and that is why the exception is thrown.

When you need to repeatedly read the same type of values from the console you
can peek at the value you want to read and check it before reading it to avoid the
InputMismatchException being thrown. For this particular scenario, each of the next*()
methods has a pair method named hasNext*(). To show an example how these methods
can be used, let's add an option to the previous code to be able to read a list of long
values, as depicted in Listing 10-4.

Listing 10-4. Using java.util.Scanner to Read a List of Long Values

```
...
public static final String LONGS = "longs";
...
    String input;
    do {
        System.out.print("Enter option: ");
        input = sc.nextLine();
        switch (input) {
            case LONGS:
                List<Long> longList = new ArrayList<>();
                while (sc.hasNextLong()) {
                    longList.add(sc.nextLong());
                }
```

```
                System.out.println("Nice long list there: " + longList);
                // else all done
                sc.nextLine();
                sc.nextLine();
                break;
            default:
                System.out.println("No idea what you want bruh!");
        }
    } while (!input.equalsIgnoreCase(EXIT));
...
```

Although it seems weird, we need to call the nextLine() method twice: once for the character that cannot be converted to long, so the while loop ends, and once for the end of the line character, so the next read is the type of the following read value.

There are a few other methods in the Scanner class that can be used to filter the input and read only desired tokens, but the methods listed in this section are the ones you will use the most.

Using java.io.Console

The java.io.Console class was introduced in Java version 1.6, one version later than Scanner, and provides methods to access the character-based console device, if any, associated with the current Java virtual machine.

The methods of class java.io.Console can thus be also used to write to the console, not only read user input. If the JVM is started from a background process or a Java editor the console will not be available, as the editor redirects the standard input and output streams to its own window. That is why if we were to write code using Console we can only test it by running the class or jar from a terminal, by calling java ReadingUsingConsoleDemo.class or java -jar using-console-1.0-SNAPSHOT.jar The console of a JVM, if available, is represented in the code by a single instance of class Console that can be obtained by calling System.console().

In Figure 10-2 you can see the methods that can be called on the console instance.

```
37 ▶    public class ReadingUsingConsoleDemo {
38
39 ▶  ⊖    public static void main(String... args) {
40            Console console = System.console();
41  ⊖        if (console == null) {
42              console.|
43            Syste  ⓜ flush()                                        void
44            retur  ⓜ format(String fmt, Object... args)          Console
45        } else {  ⓜ readLine()                                    String
46            cons   ⓜ printf(String format, Object... args)       Console
47            cons   ⓜ readLine(String fmt, Object... args)         String
48            Strir  ⓜ reader()                                      Reader
49            cons   ⓜ readPassword()                                char[]
50                   ⓜ readPassword(String fmt, Object... args)     char[]
                     ⓜ writer()                                 PrintWriter
```

Figure 10-2. *Scanner methods for reading various types of data*

Obviously, the read*(..) methods are for reading user input from the console and printf(..) and format(..) are for printing text in the console. The special case here are the two readPassword(..) methods that allow for a text to be read from the console, but not depicted while is being written. This means that a Java application supporting authentication can be written without any actual user interface. Listing 10-5 depicts a sample code to see all that in action.

Listing 10-5. Using java.io.Console to Read and Write Values

```java
package com.apress.bgn.ten;

import java.io.Console;
import java.util.Calendar;
import java.util.GregorianCalendar;

public class ReadingUsingConsoleDemo {

    public static void main(String... args) {
        Console console = System.console();
        if (console == null) {
            System.err.println("No console found.");
            return;
        } else {
            console.writer().print("Hello there! (reply to salute)\n");
            console.flush();
```

```
String hello = console.readLine();
console.printf("You replied with: '" + hello + "'\n");

Calendar calendar = new GregorianCalendar();
console.format("Today is : %1$tm %1$te,%1$tY\n", calendar);
char[] passwordChar = console.readPassword("Please provide
password: ");
String password =  new String(passwordChar);
console.printf("Your password starts with '" + password.
charAt(0) + "' and ends with '" + password.charAt(password.
length()-1) + "'\n");
        }
    }
}
```

In the previous code sample, various methods to read and write data using the console were used intentionally to show you how they should be used.

The console.writer() returns an instance of java.io.PrintWriter that can be used to print messages to the console. The catch is that the messages are not printed until console.flush() is called. This means that more messages can be queued up by the java.io.PrintWriter instance and printed only when flush() is called or when its internal buffer is full. The console.format(..) is called to print a formatted message, in this case a Calendar instance is used to extract the current date and print it according to the following template: dd mm,yyyy defined by this argument %1$tm %1$te,%1$tY. Templates accepted by the Console methods that use formatters are defined in class java.util.Formatter.

The complicated part: running this code in IntelliJ is not possible, so we have to either execute the class or the jar.

---

❶ To avoid creating new OS console windows when running code most IDEs, like IntelliJ IDEA, are using window-less Java. Since there is no window, there is no console for the user to access and insert data. So applications using must java.io.Console be executed in the command line.

The easiest way is to configure the Maven `maven-jar-plugin` to create an executable jar with the main class to be executed being `ReadingUsingConsoleDemo`. The jar produced by Maven can be found here: `/chapter10/using-console/target/using-console-2.0-SNAPSHOT.jar`. Just open a terminal in IntelliJ IDEA if you want to, by clicking the Terminal button, and go to the `target` directory. Once there, execute `java -jar using-console-2.0-SNAPSHOT.jar` and have fun. In Listing 10-6 you can see the entries I used to test the program.

Listing 10-6. Running the Class `ReadingUsingConsoleDemo`

```
> cd chapter10/using-console/target
> java -jar using-console-2.0-SNAPSHOT.jar
Hello there! (reply to salute)
Salut!
You replied with: 'Salut!'
Today is: 06 21,2021
Please provide password:
Your password starts with 'g' and ends with 'a'
```

This is all that is worth covering about using the console, since once working on a real production-ready project you might never need it.

Build Applications Using Swing

Swing is a GUI widget toolkit for Java. It is part of the JDK starting with version 1.2 and was developed to provide more pleasant looking and practical components for building user applications with complex interfaces with all types of buttons, progress bars, selectable lists, and so on. Swing is based on an early version of something called AWT (short for **Abstract Window Toolkit)**, which is the original Java user-interface widget toolkit. AWT is pretty basic and had a set of graphical interface components that were available on any platform, which means AWT is portable, but this did not imply that AWT code written on one platform would actually work on another, because of the platform specific limitations. AWT components depend on the native equivalent components, which is why they were named heavyweight components. In Figure 10-3 you can see a simple Java AWT application.

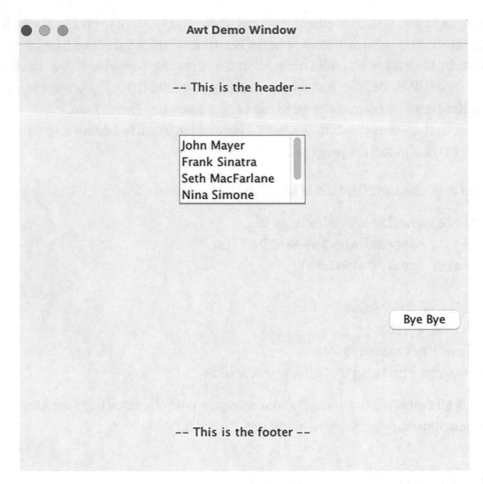

Figure 10-3. *Simple Java AWT application*

It's a simple window that contains a list, a text area, and a button. The theme, also called look-and-feel of the application, is the same one as the operating system it was built on—macOS in the examples in this chapter. It cannot be changed because of the reason mentioned earlier: AWT taps into the OS native Graphical interface. If you run the same code on a Windows machine the window will look different, because it will use the Windows theme.

Swing components are built in Java and follow the AWT model, but provide a pluggable look-and-feel. Swing is implemented entirely in Java and includes all features of AWT, but they are no longer depending on the native GUI; this is why they are called *light-weight* components. Swing provides everything AWT does and also extends the set of components with higher-level ones such as tree-view, list box, and tabbed panes.

Also, the look and feel and the theme is pluggable and can be easily changed. This obviously implies a much better portability than AWT applications: a possibility to write more complex application design with components that are not platform-specific, and because Swing is an alternative to AWT, there was a lot more development done on it.

When web applications took flight, their UI was pretty basic because browsers had quite limited capabilities. AWT was introduced to build Java web applications called applets. Java applets were small applications that were launched from the browser and then executed within the JVM installed on the users operating system in a process separate from the browser itself. That is why an applet can be run in a frame of the web page, a new application window, or standalone tools designed for testing applets. Java applets were using the GUI from the operating system, which made them prettier than the bulky initial look of HTML at the time. They are now deprecated and were scheduled to be removed in Java 11.

As for Java desktop applications written in Swing or AWT, they are rarely used anymore and you might learn to build one during school, but are otherwise quite antique. Nevertheless, there are legacy applications used by certain institutions and companies that have had a long run in their business that are built with Swing. I've seen Swing applications used by restaurants to manage tables and orders, and I think most supermarkets use Swing applications to manage shopping items as well. This is why this section exists in this book, because you might end up working on maintaining such application and it is good to know the basics, because Swing is still a part of the JDK. All Swing components (AWT too) are part of the `java.desktop` module. So if you want to use Swing components, you have to declare a dependence on this module. In Listing 10-7 a configuration snippet is shown. You can see that the module of our project that uses Swing declares its dependency on the `java.desktop` module, by using the `requires` directive in its module-info.java.

Listing 10-7. Module Configuration for the `using-swing` Project

```
module chapter.ten.swing {
    requires java.desktop;
}
```

The application depicted in Figure 10-3 was build using AWT. This section will cover building something similar in Swing and even adding more components to it. The main class of any Swing application is named `JFrame`, and instances of this type are used to create windows with border and title. The code in Listing 10-8 does just that.

Listing 10-8. Swing Application with a Simple Title

```
package com.apress.bgn.ten;

import javax.swing.*;
import java.awt.*;

public class BasicSwingDemo extends JFrame {
    public static void main(String... args) {
        BasicSwingDemo swingDemo = new BasicSwingDemo();
        swingDemo.setTitle("Swing Demo Window");
        swingDemo.setSize(new Dimension(500,500));

        swingDemo.setVisible(true);
    }
}
```

In the previous code an instance of `javax.swing.JFrame` is created, a title is set for it, and we also set a size so when the window is created we can actually see something. To actually display the window the `setVisible(true)` must be called on the JFrame instance. When running the previous code, a window the one in Figure 10-4 is displayed.

Figure 10-4. *Simple Java Swing application*

By default, the window is positioned in the upper left corner of your main monitor, but that can be changed by using some Swing components to compute a position relative to the screen size. Determining size and position of a Swing window relative to screen size is only limited by the amount of math you are willing to get into.

At this moment, if we close the displayed window, the application keeps running. By default, closing the window just makes it invisible by calling `setVisible(false)`. If we want to change the default behavior to exiting the application, we have to change the default operation done when closing. This can be easily done by adding the following line of code after creating the JFrame instance.

```
swingDemo.setDefaultCloseOperation(JFrame.EXIT_ON_CLOSE);
```

The `JFrame.EXIT_ON_CLOSE` constant is part of a set of constants that define application behavior when the window is closed. This one is used to declare that application should exit when the window is closed. The other related options are:

- `DO_NOTHING_ON_CLOSE` does nothing, including closing the window.

- `HIDE_ON_CLOSE` is the default option that causes `setVisible(false)` to be called.

- `DISPOSE_ON_CLOSE` is used when an application has more than one window; this option is used to exit the application when the last displayable window was closed.

Most Swing applications are written by extending the `JFrame` class to gain more control over its components, so the preceding code can also be written as depicted in Listing 10-9:

Listing 10-9. Swing Application That Exits When Closed

```
package com.apress.bgn.ten;

import javax.swing.*;
import java.awt.*;

public class ExitingSwingDemo extends JFrame {

    public static void main(String... args) {
        ExitingSwingDemo swingDemo = new ExitingSwingDemo();
        swingDemo.setDefaultCloseOperation(JFrame.EXIT_ON_CLOSE);
```

```
        swingDemo.setTitle("Swing Demo Window");
        swingDemo.setSize(new Dimension(500,500));

        swingDemo.setVisible(true);
    }
}
```

Now that we have a window, let's start adding components, because changing the look-and-feel is pointless if we do not have more components so that we can notice the change. Each Swing application has at least one `JFrame` that is the root, the parent of all other windows, because windows can be created by using the `JDialog` class as well. The `JDialog` is the main class for creating a dialog window, a special type of window that contains mostly a message and buttons to select options. Developers can use this class to create custom dialog windows or use `JOptionPane` class methods to create a variety of dialog windows.

Back to adding components to a `JFrame` instance: components are added to a `JFrame` by adding them to its container. A reference to the `JFrame` container can be retrieved by calling `getContentPane()`. The default content pane is a simple intermediate container that inherits from JComponent, which extends `java.awt.Container` (Swing being an extension of AWT, most of its components are AWT extensions). For `JFrame` the default content pane is actually an instance of JPanel. This class has a field of type `java.awt.LayoutManager` that defines how other components are arranged in a `JPanel`. The default content pane of a `JFrame` instance uses a `java.awt.BorderLayout` as its layout manager that splits a pane in five regions: EAST, WEST, NORTH, SOUTH, and CENTER. Each of the zones can be referred by a constant with a matching name defined in the `BorderLayout`, so if we would like to add an exit button to our application, we could add it to the south region by writing the code like the one depicted in Listing 10-10.

Listing 10-10. Swing Application using `BorderLayout` to Arrange Components

```
package com.apress.bgn.ten;

import javax.swing.*;
import java.awt.*;
import java.awt.event.ActionEvent;
import java.awt.event.ActionListener;
```

```java
public class LayeredSwingDemo extends JFrame {
    private JPanel mainPanel;
    private JButton exitButton;

    public LayeredSwingDemo(String title) {
        super(title);
        mainPanel = (JPanel) this.getContentPane();
        exitButton = new JButton("Bye Bye!");
        exitButton.addActionListener(new ActionListener() {
            @Override
            public void actionPerformed(ActionEvent e) {
                System.exit(0);
            }
        });
        mainPanel.add(exitButton, BorderLayout.SOUTH);
    }

    public static void main(String... args) {
        LayeredSwingDemo swingDemo = new LayeredSwingDemo("Swing Demo
        Window");
        swingDemo.setDefaultCloseOperation(JFrame.DO_NOTHING_ON_CLOSE);
        swingDemo.setSize(new Dimension(500, 500));
        swingDemo.setVisible(true);
    }
}
```

In Figure 10-5 you can see the modified application. We've added an exit button in the SOUTH area of the content pane and underlined the overall region arrangement of the BorderLayout.

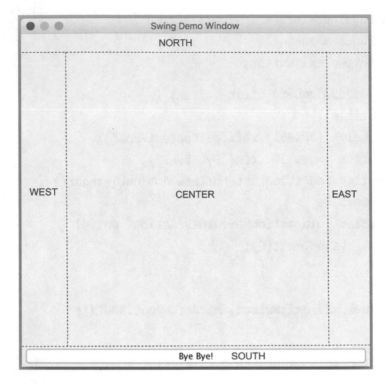

Figure 10-5. *Border layout zones*

Also, because the new button has to be the only way to exit our application, the

setDefaultCloseOperation(JFrame.EXIT_ON_CLOSE);

was replaced with

setDefaultCloseOperation(JFrame.DO_NOTHING_ON_CLOSE);

and an java.awt.event.ActionListener instance was attached to the button so that it could record the event of the button being clicked and react accordingly, in this case exiting the application. Most Swing components support listeners that can be defined to capture events performed on the object by the user and react in a certain way. As we can see the button expands and fills the entire space of the region, because it inherits the dimension of the region. To avoid that, the button should be put in another container and that container should use a different layout: the FlowLayout. As the name implies, this layout allows for Swing components to be added in a directional flow, as in a paragraph. Adjustments can be made similar to a text formatting in text document and constants are defined for components being aligned: in the center (CENTER), left-justified (LEFT), and so on. In the previous example, we will wrap the exitButton in another JPanel that will make use of the FlowLayout. Listing 10-11 shows how FlowLayout can be used to place a button in the right corner of the JFrame instance.

Listing 10-11. Swing Application Using BorderLayout and FlowLayout to Arrange Components

```
...
public LayeredSwingDemo(String title) {
        super(title);
        mainPanel = (JPanel) this.getContentPane();
        exitButton = new JButton("Bye Bye!");
        exitButton.addActionListener(e -> System.exit(0));
        JPanel exitPanel = new JPanel();
        FlowLayout flowLayout = new FlowLayout();
        flowLayout.setAlignment(FlowLayout.RIGHT);
        exitPanel.setLayout(flowLayout);
        exitPanel.setComponentOrientation(ComponentOrientation.RIGHT_
        TO_LEFT);
        exitPanel.add(exitButton);
        mainPanel.add(exitPanel, BorderLayout.SOUTH);
    }
...
```

There are more layouts that can be used, but let's complete the application by adding a list with a number of entries and add a listener to it so when you click an element is added to a text area added to the center of the frame. A swing list can be created by instantiating the JList<T> class. This will create an object that displays a list of objects and allows the user to select one or more items. The swing JList<T> class contains a field of type ListModel<T> that manages the data contents displayed by the list. When created and elements were added, each object is associated with an index, and when the user selects an object, the index can be used for processing as well. In the next snippet the JList object is declared, initialized, a ListSelectionListener is associated with it, to define the action to perform when an element from the list is selected. In our case the element value must be added to a JTextArea. This object is depicted in Listing 10-12.

Listing 10-12. Swing Application Using Layouts and JTextArea to Arrange Components

```
private static String[] data = {"John Mayer", "Frank Sinatra",
    "Seth MacFarlane", "Nina Simone", "BB King", "Peggy Lee"};
private JList<String> list;
private JTextArea textArea;
...
    textArea = new JTextArea(50, 10);
    //NORTH
    list = new JList<>(data);
    list.addListSelectionListener(new ListSelectionListener() {
        @Override
        public void valueChanged(ListSelectionEvent e) {
            if (!e.getValueIsAdjusting()) {
                textArea.append(list.getSelectedValue() + "\n");
            }
        }
    });
    mainPanel.add(list, BorderLayout.NORTH);
    //CENTER
    JScrollPane txtPanel = new JScrollPane(textArea);
    textArea.setBackground(Color.LIGHT_GRAY);
    mainPanel.add(txtPanel, BorderLayout.CENTER);
...
```

When clicking on a list element two things happen: the previous element is deselected and one that was clicked the most recently is selected, so the selected element changes. The getValueIsAdjusting() method returns whether or not this is one in a series of multiple events (selection events, click events, whatever is supported), where changes are still being made, and we test if this method returns false to check that the selection has been already made, so we can get the value of the current selected element and add it to the text area.

Regarding the JTextArea instance, this one is added to a JScrollPane instance that allows for the textArea contents to still be visible as it fills with text by providing a scrollbar or two, depending on the configuration. The JScrollPane can also be wrapped around a list with too many items as well, to make sure all of them are accessible. Also, as we are not interested in user-provided input via the text area, the `setEditable(false);` method is called.

Now that we have a more complex application, it is time to play with the look-and-feel of the application. Until now we've used the default one provided by the underlying Operating System. Using Swing, the look-and-feel can be configured as one of the defaults supported by the JDK or extra custom ones can be used, that are provided as dependencies in the project class path, or developers can create their own. To specify a look-and-feel explicitly, the following line of code must be added in the main method, before any swing component is created:

`UIManager.setLookAndFeel(..).`

This method receives as parameter a `String` value representing the fully qualified name of the appropriate subclass of look-and-feel. This class must extend the abstract `javax.Swing.LookAndFeel`. Although not necessary, you could specify explicitly that you want to use the native GUI by calling:

`UIManager.setLookAndFeel(UIManager.getCrossPlatformLookAndFeelClassName());`

Knowing this, let's do something interesting. The `UIManager` class contains utility methods and nested classes used to manage look-and-feel for swing applications. One of these methods is `getInstalledLookAndFeels()`, which extracts the list of supported look-and-feels and returns them as an `LookAndFeelInfo[]`. Knowing this, let's do the following: list all the supported look-and-feels, add them to our list, and when the user selects one of them, let's apply them. Unfortunately, as swing is rarely used these days, there are not that many custom look-and-feels that we could use in our application, so the only thing to do is to work with what JDK has. The code in Listing 10-13 initializes the data array with the look and feel fully qualified class names.

Listing 10-13. Code Sample to Initialize the List of Supported Look-and-Feels

```
private static String[] data;
...
    public static void main(String... args) throws Exception {
        UIManager.setLookAndFeel(UIManager.
getCrossPlatformLookAndFeelClassName());
```

```
        UIManager.LookAndFeelInfo[] looks = UIManager.
        getInstalledLookAndFeels();
        data = new String[looks.length];
        int i =0;
        for (UIManager.LookAndFeelInfo look : looks) {
            data[i++] = look.getClassName();
        }
        SwingDemo swingDemo = new SwingDemo("Swing Demo Window");
        swingDemo.setDefaultCloseOperation(JFrame.DO_NOTHING_ON_CLOSE);
        swingDemo.setSize(new Dimension(500, 500));
        swingDemo.setVisible(true);
    }
...
```

Now the ListSelectionListener implementation becomes a little complicated, because after selecting a new look and feel class, we have to call repaint() on the JFrame instance to apply the new look and feel, so we'll take the declaration out into its own class and provide the SwingDemo object as argument so that repaint() can be called on it, inside the valueChanged(..) method. The code snippet is depicted in Listing 10-14.

Listing 10-14. Code Sample Showing repaint() Being Called

```
private class LFListener implements ListSelectionListener {
    private JFrame parent;
    public LFListener(JFrame swingDemo) {
        parent = swingDemo;
    }
    @Override
    public void valueChanged(ListSelectionEvent e) {
        if (!e.getValueIsAdjusting()) {
            textArea.append(list.getSelectedValue() + "\n");
            try {
                UIManager.setLookAndFeel(list.getSelectedValue());
                Thread.sleep(1000);
                parent.repaint();
```

```
        } catch (Exception ee) {
            System.err.println(" Could not set look and feel! ");
        }
    }
  }
}
```

If we run the modified program and select each item in the list one by one, we should see the window look change a little bit. In Figure 10-6 you can see all windows side by side; the differences are barely noticeable, but they are there.

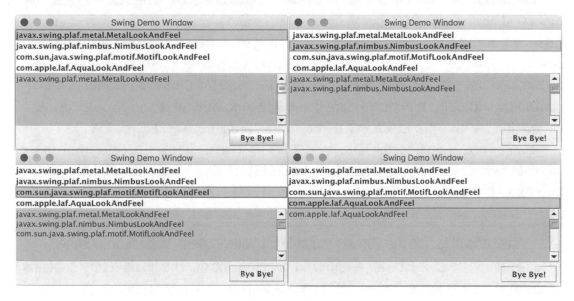

Figure 10-6. *Different look-and-feel provided by JDK*

This is what you can do with Swing components with a few lines of code. There are a lot more components in the Swing library, but Swing is not used that much anymore. As the focus nowadays is on mobile and web applications, this section will have to end here. If you ever need to create or maintain a Swing application, Oracle provides quite an extensive tutorial with a lot of examples that you can directly copy-paste and adapt to your necessities.[1]

---

[1] The Oracle extensive Swing tutorial is available at Oracle, "The Java Tutorials," https://docs.oracle.com/javase/tutorial/uiswing/examples/layout/index.html, accessed October 15, 2021.

Introducing JavaFX

JavaFX Script was a scripting language designed by Sun Microsystems forming part of the JavaFX family of technologies on the Java Platform. It was released shortly after JDK 6 in December 2008 and for a while developers expected it would be dropped because it really did not catch on that much, being a totally different language. After acquiring Sun Microsystems, Oracle decided to keep it and they transformed into the JavaFX library, which is a set of graphics and media packages that can be used by developers to design, create, test, debug, and deploy rich client applications that operate consistently across diverse platforms, including mobile ones. Java FX was intended to replace Swing as the main GUI library of the JDK, but so far both Swing and JavaFX have been part of all JDK versions until 10. This changed in JDK 11. Starting with JDK 11, JavaFX is available as a separate module, decoupled from the JDK. JavaFX is still not used as much as Oracle hoped, and separating it from the JDK might encourage the OpenJFX community to contribute with some innovative ideas that might transform this library into an actual competitor for the other existing GUI toolkits on the market (e.g., Eclipse SWT).[2]

After its exclusion from the JDK, Java FX has evolved on its own, keeping itself in sync with the Java versions being released. At the time this chapter was written, there was a Java FX 17 EAP version available for download at `https://openjfx.io`.

🖋 After downloading the version suitable for your system, unpack the archive. There should be at least a legal and a lib directory inside. The lib directory contains the JavaFX binaries packed as JAR files. Depending on the operating system, the lib might contain other library files. For the examples in this chapter you have to copy the following three files: javafx.base.jar, javafx.controls.jar, and javafx. graphics.jar in the chapter10/using-javafx/libs.

---

[2] SWT is an open-source widget toolkit for Java designed to provide efficient, portable access to the user-interface facilities of the operating systems on which it is implemented. You can learn more about it on the official site at Eclipse, "SWT: The Standard Widget Toolkit," `https://www.eclipse.org/swt`, accessed October 15, 2021.

🔥 On some computers, like new macOS laptops, the examples might not run because some library files must be copied in a specific location. To find out the location where to copy them, run the main JavaFxDemo class with the -Dprism. verbose=true VM argument. This will cause the error log to be more verbose amd tell you where the library files must be copied.

For example, for macOS the directory is /Users/[user]/Library/Java/ Extensions and the files to be copied there are all the files with the dylib extension from the javafx-sdk-17/lib directory.

Java FX used to be part of the JDK, so it has classes and other components. Java FX code is currently normal Java code, so no more scripting. Java FX components are defined under a list of java.fx modules. In the following configuration snippet you can see that the module of our project that uses Java FX declares its dependency on a few java.fx modules, by using the requires directive in its module-info.java as depicted in Listing 10-15.

Listing 10-15. Configuration Sample for a Project Using java.fx Modules

```
module chapter.ten.javafx {
    requires javafx.base;
    requires javafx.graphics;
    requires javafx.controls;
    opens com.apress.bgn.ten to javafx.graphics;
}
```

Java FX Application launcher uses reflection to launch an application, so we need to open the com.apress.bgn.ten package to allow reflection using the opens directive. Without that directive a java.lang.IllegalAccessException is thrown and the application does not start.

The easiest start is a simple window that has just a closing option and explain. The code to display a plain square window is depicted in Listing 10-16.

Listing 10-16. Simple JavaFx Application

```java
package com.apress.bgn.ten;

import javafx.application.Application;
import javafx.scene.Scene;
import javafx.scene.layout.StackPane;
import javafx.stage.Stage;

public class JavaFxDemo extends Application {
    public static void main(String... args) {
        launch(args);
    }

    @Override
    public void start(Stage primaryStage) {
        primaryStage.setTitle("Java FX Demo Window!");
        StackPane root = new StackPane();
        primaryStage.setScene(new Scene(root, 500, 500));
        primaryStage.show();
    }
}
```

The first thing you need to know is that the main class of the application must extend the javafx.application.Application class, because this is the entry point for a Java FX application. This is required because JAVA FX applications are run by a new performance graphics engine named **Prism** that sits on top of the JVM. Aside from Prism, the graphic engine, Java FX comes with its own windowing system named **Glass**, a media engine and a web engine. They are not exposed publicly; the only thing available to developers is the Java FX API that provides access to any components you might need to build application with fancy interfaces. All these engines are tied together by the **Quantum** toolkit that is the interface between these engines and the layer above in the stack. The Quantum toolkit is the one that manages execution threads and rendering.

The launch(..) method is a static method in the Application class that is used to launch a standalone application. It is usually called from the main method and can only be called once, otherwise a java.lang.IllegalStateException will be thrown. The launch method does not return until the application is exited, by closing all windows or calling Platform.exit(). The launch method creates an JavaFxDemo instance, calls the init() method on it and then calls start(..). The start(..) method is declared abstract in the Application class, so the developer is forced to provide a concrete implementation.

A Java FX application is build using components defined under the javafx.scene and has a hierarchical organization. The core class of the javafx.scene package is the javafx.scene.Node that is the root of the Scene hierarchy. Classes in this hierarchy provide implementations for all the visual elements of the application's user interface. Because all of them have Node as a root class, visual elements are called nodes which makes an application a scene graph of nodes and the initial node of this graph is called a root. Each node has a unique identifier, a style class, and a bounding volume, and with the exception of the root note, each node in the graph has a single parent and zero or more children. Beside that, a node has the following properties:

- effects, such as blurs and shadow, are useful when you hover with your mouse over the interface to make sure you click the right component.

- opacity.

- transformations for changing visual state or position.

- event handlers similar to listeners in Swing, used to define reaction on mouse, key, and input method.

- application specific state.

The scene graph simplifies building rich interfaces a lot, and because it also includes primitive graphics such as rectangles, text, images, and media, and animating various graphics can be accomplished by the animation APIs for package javax.animation. If you are interested in finding out more about what's under the hood of Java FX, here is a detailed article about it: https://docs.oracle.com/javafx/2/architecture/jfxpub-architecture.htm. The focus of this book is more on how to do things and not now they work, so reading that article might help with the design of your future solutions.

We've started again with a simple window. The first step is to add a button that will quit the application. As rendering a Java FX application involves a rendering engine, this means it has to shutdown gracefully, so calling System.exit(0) is not a preferred option. The contents of the start(..) method must call a special JavaFX method to close the application gracefully. The code is shown in Listing 10-17.

Listing 10-17. Simple JavaFx Application with a Button

```java
package com.apress.bgn.ten;

import javafx.application.Application;
import javafx.application.Platform;
import javafx.event.ActionEvent;
import javafx.event.EventHandler;
import javafx.scene.*;
import javafx.stage.*;

public class SimpleJavaFxDemo extends Application {
    public static void main(String... args) {
        launch(args);
    }

    @Override
    public void start(Stage primaryStage) {
        primaryStage.setTitle("Java FX Demo Window!");

        Button btn = new Button();
        btn.setText("Bye bye! ");
        btn.setOnAction(new EventHandler<ActionEvent>() {
            @Override
            public void handle(ActionEvent event) {
                Platform.exit();
            }
        });

        StackPane root = new StackPane();
        root.getChildren().add(btn);
        primaryStage.setScene(new Scene(root, 300, 300));
        primaryStage.show();
    }
}
```

Running the SimpleJavaFxDemo class causes the window depicted in Figure 10-7 to pop up on your screen, and if you click the Bye, bye! button the application will be gracefully closed because of the Platform.exit() call.

Figure 10-7. JavaFX window demo

The button was just thrown in there, inside the window and put by default in the center, because no code was written to position it. Java FX supports arranging nodes[3] in a window in a manner similar to Swing, but Java FX provides layout panes that support several different styles of layouts. The equivalent of a JPanel with BorderLayout manager in JavaFX is a built-in layout name named BorderPane. The BorderPane provides five regions where to place your nodes, with distribution similar to BorderLayout, but different names. Listing 10-18 shows the code to place our button in the bottom region in the right corner and then discuss more about it.

Listing 10-18. Simple JavaFx Application with a Properly Positioned Button

```
package com.apress.bgn.ten;

import javafx.application.*;
import javafx.geometry.Insets;
import javafx.geometry.Pos;
import javafx.scene.*;
import javafx.stage.*;
```

---

[3] It was mentioned that the root class for all Java FX components is named Node, so instead of components, Java FX components will be referred as nodes in this section.

```java
public class PannedJavaFxDemo extends Application {
    public static void main(String... args) {
        launch(args);
    }

    @Override
    public void start(Stage primaryStage) {
        primaryStage.setTitle("Java FX Demo Window!");

        Button exitButton = new Button();
        exitButton.setText("Bye bye! ");
        exitButton.setOnAction(event -> Platform.exit());

        BorderPane borderPane = new BorderPane();
        HBox box = new HBox();
        box.setPadding(new Insets(10, 12, 10, 12));
        box.setSpacing(10);
        box.setAlignment(Pos.BASELINE_RIGHT);
        box.setStyle("-fx-background-color: #85929e;");
        box.getChildren().add(exitButton);
        borderPane.setBottom(box);

        StackPane root = new StackPane();
        root.getChildren().add(borderPane);
        primaryStage.setScene(new Scene(root, 500, 500));
        primaryStage.show();
    }
}
```

Running the PannedJavaFxDemo class causes the window depicted in Figure 10-8 to pop up on your screen, and the figure has been modified to show the regions of a BorderPane.

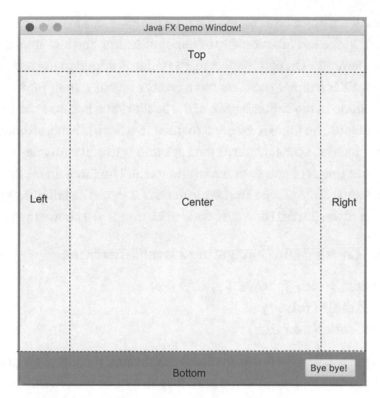

Figure 10-8. *JavaFX Window with* BorderPane *demo*

As you can see, the approach to decide where our button should be located is similar to Swing, with a few differences. The BorderPane has five regions named: Top, Bottom, Center, Left, and Right. To place a node in each of those regions a set*(..) method for each of them has been defined: setTop(..), setBottom(..), setCenter(..), setLeft(..), and setRight(..). To further customise the position of the node it should be placed in a HBox node, another JavaFX element that can be customized quite extensively. As you can see from the code, we are setting the background using CSS style elements. We customize the space between nodes in it and borders of the containing node by using an instance of class Insets and we customize the alignment of the contained nodes by calling box. setAlignment(Pos.BASELINE_RIGHT). There are many more things that HBox supports, so what you can do with a box is limited (mostly) only by your imagination.

So beside all making pretty code in the preceding code sample, the following was done: the root node became parent to a BorderPane node, in the bottom region of the BorderPane a HBox was added, and this HBox instance became parent for a Button. As you can see, this organization is hierarchic, with the button being the last node in the hierarchy.

We also avoided using a layer pane by styling the HBox node properly.

It is time to add the last functionality to our application, the text area, and the list with selectable elements. On being selected, the value is added to the text area. To create a text area in JavaFX is simple. The class has a pretty obvious name: TextArea. We can directly add the node in the center region of the BorderPane because the JavaFX text area is scrollable by default. So there is no need to put it in a ScrollPane, although the class does exist in the javafx.scene.control package and is useful to display nodes inside it that make a form that is bigger than the window size. The three lines of code in Listing 10-19 create a node of type TextArea, declare it to not be editable, and add it to the center region of the BorderPane. The code in Listing 10-19 shows the code to do this.

Listing 10-19. Creating and Configuring a JavaFX TextArea

```
TextArea textArea = new TextArea();
textArea.setEditable(false);
borderPane.setCenter(textArea);
```

Next one is the list. The list is a little more complicated but also a lot more fun to work with, because by using JavaFX there is a lot you can do with a list. The class that needs to be instantiated to create a list object is named ComboBox<T>. This class is just one of a bigger family of classes used to create lists, the root class being the abstract class ComboBoxBase<T>. Depending on the desired behavior of the list, if we want support for single or multiple selection and if we want the list to be editable or not, the proper implementation should be chosen. In our case, the ComboBox<T> class matches the following requirements: we need a noneditable list that supports single element section. A ComboBox<T> has a valueProperty() method that returns the current user input. The user input can be based on a selection from a drop-down list or the input manually provided by the user when the list is editable. Listing 10-20 shows how to add a list to the top section of the BorderPane and add a listener to record the selected value and save it the TextArea that we previously declared.

Listing 10-20. Creating and Configuring a JavaFX ComboBox<T>

```
import javafx.scene.control.ComboBox;
...
private static String data = {"John Mayer", "Frank Sinatra",
    "Seth MacFarlane", "Nina Simone", "BB King", "Peggy Lee"};
...
```

```
ComboBox<String> comboBox = new ComboBox<>();
comboBox.getItems().addAll(data);
borderPane.setTop(comboBox);

comboBox.valueProperty().addListener(
    new ChangeListener<String>() {
        @Override
        public void changed(ObservableValue<? extends String> observable,
        String oldValue, String newValue) {
            textArea.appendText(newValue + "\n");
        }
});
```

The ComboBox<T> value field is an ObservableValue<T> instance. The listener is
added to this instance, and it is notified anytime its value changes and its changed(..)
method is called. As you can see, the changed(..) method receives as argument
the previous list selected value as well, because maybe we have some logic that
requires both.

In AWT and Swing there was not much that you could do with a list visually. You
had that look and feel, and that was that. JavaFX supports more visual customization
for nodes as it even supports CSS. That is why in the next section we'll make our
ComboBox<T> list interesting. In Java FX each entry in a list is a cell that can be drawn
differently. To do that, we have to add a CellFactory<T> to this class that will create for
each item in a list an instance of ListCell<T>.

If a CellFactory<T> is not specified the cells will be created with the default style.
Listing 10-21 shows the code to customize a ComboBox<T>.

Listing 10-21. Creating and Customizing Colors of Cells of a JavaFX ComboBox<T>

```
comboBox.setCellFactory(
    new Callback<>() {
        @Override
        public ListCell<String> call(ListView<String> param) {
            return new ListCell<>() {
            {
                super.setPrefWidth(200);
            }
```

```
            @Override
            public void updateItem(String item, boolean empty) {
                super.updateItem(item, empty);
                if (item != null) {
                    setText(item);
                    if (item.contains("John") || item.contains("BB")) {
                        setTextFill(Color.RED);
                    } else if (item.contains("Frank") || item.
                    contains("Peggy")) {
                        setTextFill(Color.GREEN);
                    } else if (item.contains("Seth")) {
                        setTextFill(Color.BLUE);
                    } else {
                        setTextFill(Color.BLACK);
                    }
                } else {
                    setText(null);
                }
            }
        };
    }
});
```

The javafx.util.Callback interface is a practical utility interface that can be used every time after a certain action, a callback is needed. In this case, after a String value is added to the ListView of the ComboBox<T> node (ListView as the name says is the visual, the interface type of a ComboBox<T> that displays a horizontal or vertical list of items), a cell is being created and some piece of logic was inserted there to decide the color of the text depicted in the cell based on its value.

Inside the ListCell<T> declaration there is a block of code that seems out of place.

```
{
    super.setPrefWidth(200);
}
```

The previous block is an interesting way to call a method from the parent class inside the declaration of an anonymous class. The setPrefWidth(200) is called here to make sure all the ListCell<T> instances will have the same size. The logic in the updateItem(..) is quite obvious, and thus it does not need any extended explanation. The result of adding the cell factory can be viewed in Figure 10-9.

Figure 10-9. *JavaFX colored ComboBox demo*

Internationalization

Interactive applications are usually created to be deployed on more than one server and available 24/7 and in multiple locations. As not all of us speak the same language, the key to convince people to become your clients and use your application is to build it in multiple languages. The process of designing an application so that it meets user needs in multiple countries and easily adapts to satisfy those needs is called **internationalization**. For example, take the initial Google page. Depending on the location where it is accessed, it changes language according to that area. When you create an account, you can select the language you prefer. This does not mean that the Google has built a web application for each region; it's a single web application that displays text in different languages depending on the location of the user. Internationalization should always be taken into consideration in the design phase of an application, because adding it later is quite difficult. We do not have a web application, but we will internationalize the Java FX application built so far in this chapter.

When you start reading about internationalization you might notice that files or directories containing the internationalization property files are named *i18n*, which is because there are 18 letters between *i* and *n* in the English alphabet.

Internationalization is based on locale. **Locale** is the term given to a combination of language and region. The application locale is the one that decides which internationalization file will be used to customize the application. The locale concept is implemented in Java by the `java.util.Locale` class, and a `Locale` instance represents a geographical, political, or cultural region. When an application depends on the locale we say that it is locale-sensitive, as most applications are nowadays. Selecting a locale can be something a user has to do as well. Each `Locale` can be used to select the corresponding *locale resources*, which are files containing locale specific configurations. These files are grouped per locale and can usually be found under the `resources` directory. These resources are used to configure an instance of `java.util.ResourceBundle` that can be used to manage locale-specific resources.

To build a proper use case for localization, the previous JavaFX application will be modified; instead of singer names, the list will contain a list of animal names with labels that can be translated in various languages. A list with the available languages will be added as well, and when a language will be selected from this list a `Locale` static variable will be set with the corresponding locale and the window will be reinitialized so that all labels can be translated to the new language. Let's start by creating the resource files.

Resource files are files with `properties` extensions that contain, as the name says, a list of properties and values. Each line respects the following pattern: `property_name=property_value`, and if it doesn't it is considered an internationalization resource file. Each property name must be unique in the file; if there is a duplicate it will be ignored and IntelliJ IDEA will complain by underlining the property with red. For every language that needs to be supported we need to create one property file that contains the same property names, but different values, as the values will represent the transaction of that value in each language. All files must have names that contain a common suffix and end with the language name and the country, separated by underscores, because these are the two elements needed to create a Locale instance. For our JavaFX application we have three files, depicted in Figure 10-10.

Figure 10-10. *Resource bundle with three resource files*

The suffix is global, and this will be our resource bundle name as well. This is made quite obvious by IntelliJ IDEA, which figures out what our files are used for and depicts them in a most obvious way. The contents of the files are depicted in Table 10-1.

Table 10-1. *Contents of Resource Files*

Property Name	Property value in global_en_GB	Property value in global_fr_FR	Property value in global_it_IT
English	English	Anglais	Inglese
French	French	Français	Francese
Italian	Italian	Italien	Italiano
Cat	Cat	Chat	Gatto
Dog	Dog	Chien	Cane
Parrot	Parrot	Chien	Pappagallo
Mouse	Mouse	Souris	Topo
Cow	Cow	Perroquet	Mucca
Pig	Pig	Porc	Maiale
WindowTitle	Java FX Demo Window!	Java FX Démo Fenêtre!	Java FX Dimostratione Finestra!
Byebye	Bye bye!	Bye bye!	Ciao!
ChoosePet	Choose Pet:	Choisir un animal de compagnie:	Scegli un animale domestico:
ChooseLanguage	Choose Language:	Choisissez la langue:	Scegli la lingua:

IntelliJ IDEA can help you to edit resource bundle files easily and make sure you are not missing any keys from any of them by providing a special view for them. When you open a resource file, in the bottom left corner you should see two tabs: one is named Text and when clicked it allows you to edit a properties file as a normal text file, and one is named Resource Bundle and when clicked it opens a special view that has on the left all the property names in the resource files and on the right views from all resource files containing values for property names selected. In Figure 10-11 you can see this view and the values for property ChooseLanguage.

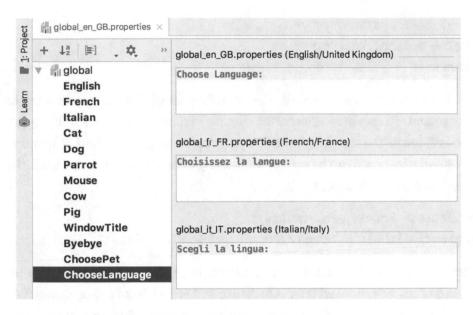

Figure 10-11. *Resource bundle IntelliJ IDEA editor*

The property names can contain special characters as underscore and dots to separate parts of them. In this book example the property names are simple, because we have so few of them. In bigger applications property names usually contain a prefix that is relevant to their purpose; for example, if the property value is a title the name will be prefixed with `title`. The property names in our files could be changed to the one listed in Listing 10-22.

Listing 10-22. Recommended Internationalization Property Names

```
English --> label.lang.english
French --> label.lang.french
Italian --> label.lang.italian
Cat --> label.pet.cat
Dog --> label.pet.dog
Parrot --> label.pet.parrot
Mouse --> label.pet.mouse
Cow --> label.pet.cow
Pig --> label.pet.pig
WindowTitle --> title.window
```

```
Byebye --> label.button.byebye
ChoosePet --> label.choose.pet
ChooseLanguage --> label.choose.language
```

Now that we have covered how the resource files should be written, let's see how they can be used. To create a ResourceBundle, we first need a locale. Applications have a default locale that can be obtained by calling Locale.getDefault(), and a ResourceBundle instance can be obtained by using a bundle name and a locale instance, as depicted in the code snippet here:

```
Locale locale = Locale.getDefault();
ResourceBundle labels = ResourceBundle.getBundle("global", locale);
```

When there is a valid ResourceBundle is obtained, it can be used to replace all hardcoded String instances with calls to return text values from the resource file matching the selected locale. So every time we need to set a label for a node, instead of using the actual text, we use a call to: resourceBundle.getString("[property_name]") to get the localized text.

When a JavaFX window is reloaded, all its nodes are recreated. To be able to influence how, we need to add a couple of static properties to keep the selected locale set. For the application that we've build so far, after internationalizing it, the code looks like the one in Listing 10-23.

Listing 10-23. JavaFX Internationalized Application

```
package com.apress.bgn.ten;

import javafx.application.*;
import javafx.geometry.*;
import javafx.scene.*;
import javafx.stage.*;

import java.io.File;
import java.net.URL;
import java.net.URLClassLoader;
import java.util.Locale;
import java.util.ResourceBundle;
```

```java
public class JavaFxDemo extends Application {

    private static final String BUNDLE_LOCATION = "chapter10/using-javafx/
    src/main/resources";

    private static ResourceBundle resourceBundle = null;
    private static Locale locale = new Locale("en", "GB");
    private static int selectedLang = 0;

    public static void main(String... args) {
        Application.launch(args);
    }

    @Override
    public void start(Stage primaryStage) throws Exception {
        loadLocale(locale);
        primaryStage.setTitle(resourceBundle.getString("WindowTitle"));

        String[] data = {resourceBundle.getString("Cat"),
                resourceBundle.getString("Dog"),
                resourceBundle.getString("Parrot"),
                resourceBundle.getString("Mouse"),
                resourceBundle.getString("Cow"),
                resourceBundle.getString("Pig")};

        BorderPane borderPane = new BorderPane();

        //Top
        final ComboBox<String> comboBox = new ComboBox<>();
        comboBox.getItems().addAll(data);

        final ComboBox<String> langList = new ComboBox<>();
        String[] languages = {
                resourceBundle.getString("English"),
                resourceBundle.getString("French"),
                resourceBundle.getString("Italian")};

        langList.getItems().addAll(languages);
        langList.getSelectionModel().select(selectedLang);
```

```
GridPane gridPane = new GridPane();
gridPane.setHgap(10);
gridPane.setVgap(10);

Label labelLang = new Label(resourceBundle.
getString("ChooseLanguage"));
gridPane.add(labelLang, 0, 0);
gridPane.add(langList, 1, 0);

Label labelPet = new Label(resourceBundle.getString("ChoosePet"));
gridPane.add(labelPet, 0, 1);
gridPane.add(comboBox, 1, 1);

borderPane.setTop(gridPane);

//Center
final TextArea textArea = new TextArea();
textArea.setEditable(false);
borderPane.setCenter(textArea);

comboBox.valueProperty().addListener((observable, oldValue,
newValue)
        -> textArea.appendText(newValue + "\n"));

langList.valueProperty().addListener((observable, oldValue,
newValue)
        -> {
    int idx = langList.getSelectionModel().getSelectedIndex();
    selectedLang = idx;
    if (idx == 0) {
        //locale = Locale.getDefault();
        new Locale("en", "GB");
    } else if (idx == 1) {
        locale = new Locale("fr", "FR");
    } else {
        locale = new Locale("it", "IT");
    }
```

```java
        primaryStage.close();
        Platform.runLater(() -> {
            try {
                new JavaFxDemo().start(new Stage());
            } catch (Exception e) {
                System.err.println("Could not reload application!");
            }
        });
    });

    HBox box = new HBox();
    box.setPadding(new Insets(10, 12, 10, 12));
    box.setSpacing(10);
    box.setAlignment(Pos.BASELINE_RIGHT);
    box.setStyle("-fx-background-color: #85929e;");
    Button exitButton = new Button();
    exitButton.setText(resourceBundle.getString("Byebye"));
    exitButton.setOnAction(event -> Platform.exit());
    box.getChildren().add(exitButton);
    borderPane.setBottom(box);

    //Bottom
    StackPane root = new StackPane();
    root.getChildren().add(borderPane);
    primaryStage.setScene(new Scene(root, 500, 500));
    primaryStage.show();
}

private void loadLocale(Locale locale) throws Exception {

    File file = new File(BUNDLE_LOCATION);
    URL[] url = {file.toURI().toURL()};
    ClassLoader loader = new URLClassLoader(url);

    resourceBundle = ResourceBundle.getBundle("global", locale, loader);
}
}
```

You might be wondering why we used another way of loading the resource bundle and why the full relative path to the bundle location was used. If we want the application to be runnable from the IntelliJ Interface, we have to provide a path relative to the execution context of the application. When the application is built and packed up in a runnable Java archive, the resource files are part of it and in the classpath. When running the application by executing the `main()` method in an Java IDE, the classpath is relative to the actual location of the project.

The code snippet in Listing 10-24 restarts the scene by closing the `Stage`, then instantiates a JavaFxDemo object and calling `start(..)`. This means the whole hierarchical node structure is recreated and the only state that is kept is the one that was defined in static objects. This is needed for the locale setting, because the `start(..)` method execution now starts with a call to `loadLocale(locale)`, which selects the locale of the application and loads the `ResourceBundle` so that all nodes can be labeled with texts returned by it.

Listing 10-24. JavaFX Code Snippet to Restart the Scene

```
primaryStage.close();
Platform.runLater(() -> {
    try {
        new JavaFxDemo().start(new Stage());
    } catch (Exception e) {
        System.err.println("Could not reload application!");
    }
});
```

The application we have built until now and played with is quite a simple one. If you will ever need to build interfaces that will be more complex and internationalization will be needed, this will mean more than translations are configured. You might need to have files with different number and date formats, or multiple resource bundles. Internationalization is quite a big topic and a quite important one, as an application is rarely built nowadays to be used in a single region. For a Java beginner, just knowing what the supporting classes are and how they can be used is a very good starting point.

Building a Web Application

Here we are, building a web application. A web application is an application that runs on a server and can be accessed using a browser. Until recently most Java applications needed Web servers like Apache Tomcat or Glassfish or Enterprise Servers like JBoss (currently known as WildFly) or TomEE to be hosted on so that they could be accessed. You would write the web application with the classes and HTML or JSP files, pack it in a WAR (Web ARchive) or a EAR (Enterprise ARchive), deploy it to a server, and start the server. The server would provide the context of the application and map requests to classes that would provide the answer to be served as response. Assuming the application would be deployed on a Tomcat server, in Figure 10-12 you can see an abstract schema of the deployed application functionality.

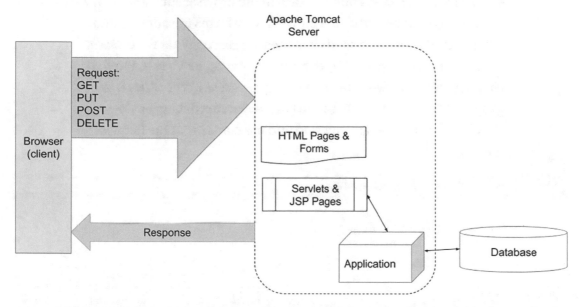

Figure 10-12. *Web application deployed on a Apache Tomcat server*

Requests to a web application can come from other clients than browsers (e.g., mobile applications), but because this section covers web applications, we'll assume all requests to our application come from a browser.

Let's explain the Internet a little first. The Internet is an information system made up of a lot of computers linked together. Some computers host application servers that provide access to applications, some computers access these applications, and some do both. The communication between these computers is done over a network through a list of protocols: HTTP, FTP, SMTP, POP, and so on. The most popular protocol is HTTP which stands for Hypertext Transfer Protocol, and it is an asymmetric request-response client-server protocol, which means that the client makes a request to the server and then the server sends a response. Subsequent requests have no knowledge of one another, and they do not share any state, thus they are stateless. HTTP requests can be of different types, being categorized by the action they require the application on server to perform, but there are four types that are more commonly used by developers (the one listed in Figure 10.12 in the request arrow). We won't go into details regarding request components as this is not really related to Java, but we'll just cover enough details to understand how a web application works. The four request types and the types of responses the server sends back for each of them are in the following list.

- **GET**: whenever a user enters an URL in the browser such as `http://my-site.com/index.html` the browser transforms the address into a Request message and sends it to the web server. What the browser does can be easily viewed by opening the debugger view in **Firefox**, clicking on the **Network** tab and trying to access `https://www.google.com/`. In Figure 10-13 you can see Firefox debugger view showing the URL being requested and the contents of the Request message.

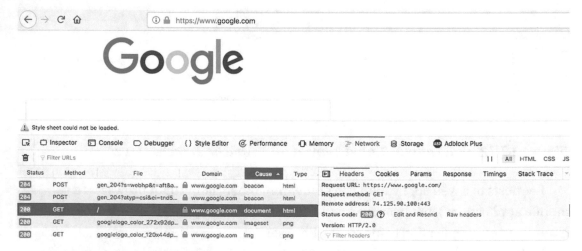

Figure 10-13. *Network debugger view in Firefox*

In the right part of the image, you can see the URL being Requested, the type of request (which is also named a **Request Method** which is GET in this case), and the **Remote address** of the server where the request was sent to. There is also a button named **Raw headers** that will open a view depicting the contents of the the request and response as text. GET requests are used to retrieve something from the server, in this example, a web page. If the web page can be found, the response is sent with the page to be displayed by the browser and other attributes such a status code to communicate that all went fine. There is a list of HTTP status codes and the most important one is the 200 code, which means all went okay. In the previous image you can see that to display the page a lot of additional requests are done, after the initial request is replied, and all subsequent requests are successful, because the status returned by the server is put in the first column in the table and it's always 200.

- **PUT**: this type of request is used when data is sent to the server to be used to updated existing data. In enterprise applications, a PUT requests is interpreted as a request to update an existing object. The request contains the updated version of the object and means to identify it. A successful PUT request generates a response with a status code of 204.

- **POST**: this type of request is used when the server needs to be instructed to save data for storage as well. The difference from PUT request is that this data does not exist on the server yet. In enterprise applications a POST request is either used to send credentials so the user can be authenticated or to send data that will be used to create a new object. When a POST request is used to send credentials the response status code is 200 when the user is authenticated and 401(Unauthorized) when the user credentials are not good, when a POST request is used to send data to be save, the 201-status code is returned if the object was created.

- **DELETE**: this type of request is used when the server is asked to delete data. The response code is 200 when all went okay, and if it did not, any other error code related to the cause.

There are a few other HTTP methods that are used in more complex applications. If you are more curious about Request methods, status codes, and HTTP basics overall, I confidently recommend you look at this tutorial: `http://www.steves-internet-guide.com/http-basics`.

Now let's get back to Writing Java Web applications.

We've mentioned that until a while ago, we needed a server to host a web application. This is no longer the case as of a few years ago. As databases were replaced for testing purposes and applications with minimum functionality with embedded databases, the same happened to web servers as well. If you want to quickly write a simple web application, you have now the option of using an embedded server like Jetty or Tomcat Embedded. Supporting complex pages with an embedded server is pretty difficult, but embedded servers are usually used for microservices which only need simple REST APIs.

Java Web Application with an Embedded Server

For this section of the chapter an embedded Tomcat server is used to display a few simple web pages, using Java servlets *(Patience young padawan, they will be explained shortly)*. Tomcat 10.0.7 version is used, which means Java modules are supported. The advantage of using an embedded Apache Tomcat server is that you can run a web application by executing a main method.

The code is depicted in the Listing 10-25 and it declares a single, very simple servlet that serves as the main page of the application.

Listing 10-25. Simple Java Application with an Embedded Server

```
package com.apress.bgn.ten;

import jakarta.servlet.http.HttpServlet;
import jakarta.servlet.http.HttpServletRequest;
import jakarta.servlet.http.HttpServletResponse;
import org.apache.catalina.Context;
import org.apache.catalina.LifecycleException;
import org.apache.catalina.startup.Tomcat;
// other import statements omitted
```

```java
public class WebDemo {

    private static final Logger LOGGER = Logger.getLogger(Main.class.
    getName());

    public static final Integer PORT = Optional.ofNullable(System.
    getenv("PORT")).map(Integer::parseInt).orElse(8080);
    public static final String TMP_DIR = Optional.ofNullable(System.
    getenv("TMP_DIR")).orElse("/tmp/tomcat-tmp");
    public static final String STATIC_DIR = Optional.ofNullable(System.
    getenv("STATIC_DIR")).orElse("/tmp/tomcat-static");

    public static void main(String... args) throws IOException,
    LifecycleException {
        Tomcat tomcat = new Tomcat();
        tomcat.setBaseDir(TMP_DIR);
        tomcat.setPort(PORT);
        tomcat.getConnector();

        tomcat.setAddDefaultWebXmlToWebapp(false);

        String contextPath = ""; // root context
        boolean createDirs =  new File(STATIC_DIR).mkdirs();
        if(createDirs) {
            LOGGER.info("Tomcat static directory created successfully.");
        } else {
            LOGGER.severe("Tomcat static directory could not be created.");
        }
        String docBase = new File(STATIC_DIR).getCanonicalPath();
        Context context = tomcat.addWebapp(contextPath, docBase);

        addIndexServlet(tomcat, contextPath, context); // omitted

        Runtime.getRuntime().addShutdownHook(new Thread(() -> {
            try {
                tomcat.getServer().stop();
            } catch (LifecycleException e) {
                e.printStackTrace();
            }
        }));
```

```
        tomcat.start();
        tomcat.getServer().await();
    }
}
```

Writing an application with an embedded Tomcat server is quite easy when you don't complex web pages making use of templating libraries for HTML generation like JSP, for example. The code snippet in Listing 10-24 only requires the `tomcat-embed-core` library as dependency, and the steps to create the server are pretty simple and explained here:

- Create a `org.apache.catalina.startup.Tomcat` instance and select the port to expose it. In this case it is 8080, the default value of the `PORT` variable, unless declared using a system environment variable with the same name.

- Set a base directory for the `Tomcat` instance, where the running server will save its various generated files such as logs. In this case, the directory is configured to be `/tmp/tomcat-tmp` unless declared using a system environment variable with the `TMP_DIR` name is declared. The user running the application should have writing rights over that location.

- Set a directory where static files for `Tomcat` are located. In this case, the directory is configured to be `/tmp/tomcat-static` unless declared using a system environment variable with the `STATIC_DIR` name is declared. The user running the application should have writing rights over that location.

- Disable default configurations for a `Tomcat` by calling `tomcat.setAddDefaultWebXmlToWebapp(false)`. In this case this prevents the `org.apache.jasper.servlet.JspServlet` from being registered. This servlet enables using JSP files in the webapp, but when configured automatically takes over and assumes any request must resolve to a JSP page, so the Java Servlets are ignored. Since we want to keep the application simple and use Java servlets, we disable it.

- Make sure the server shuts down gracefully when the application is closed, by adding shutdown hook.

- Write a simple servlet to display the main page of the application to test that the server was started correctly and works as intended. This is done by the addIndexServlet(..) method that was omitted from the previous listing to make sure the focus would be on the Tomcat instance. The method is shown in Listing 10-26.

Listing 10-26. A Simple Method That Creates a Very Simple Servlet and Registers It with a Tomcat Instance

```java
private static void addIndexServlet(Tomcat tomcat, String contextPath,
Context context) {
    HttpServlet indexServlet = new HttpServlet() {
        @Override
        protected void doGet(HttpServletRequest req,
        HttpServletResponse resp)
                throws IOException {
            PrintWriter writer = resp.getWriter();
            writer.println("<html><title>Welcome</title><body
            style=\"background-color:black\">");
            writer.println("<h1 style=\"color:#ffd200\"> Embedded
            Tomcat 10.0.7 says hi!</h1>");
            writer.println("</body></html>");
        }
    };
    String servletName = "IndexServlet";
    String urlPattern = "/";
    tomcat.addServlet(contextPath, servletName, indexServlet);
    context.addServletMappingDecoded(urlPattern, servletName);
}
```

The servlet instance must be associated with a name and a URL pattern, and when the user tries to open the serverURL/contextPath/urlPattern page, the doGet(..) method is called that returns the response constructed in its body.

A Java web application deployed on a server (even an embedded one) needs a context path. The context path value is a part of the URL to access the application. An URL is made up of four parts:

- `protocol`: the application-level protocol used by client and server to communicate, such as `http`, `https`, `ftp`, and so on.

- `hostname`: the DNS domain name (e.g., `www.google.com`) or ip-address (e.g., 192.168.0.255) or any alias recognized in a network. For example, when an application is accessed from the same computer the server is installed on either `127.0.0.1`, localhost, or `0.0.0.0` can be used.

- `path` and `filename`: the name and location of the resource, under the server document base directory. Users usually request to view specific pages hosted on servers, which is why URLs look like this: `https://docs.oracle.com/index.html`. A very used practice is to hide the paths and filenames by using internal mappings (called URL redirection) because of security reasons.

So where does the `contextPath` mentioned previously value come in? When we have an embedded server declared as in the previous code sample, any files that are hosted by it can be accessed by using the `http://localhost:8080/`. But on a dedicated server, more than one application can be running at the same time, and there must be a way to separate them, right? This is where the `contextPath` value comes in handy. By setting the context path to `/demo` instead of the empty string, the `WebDemo` application and the resources it provides to the users can be accessed at `http://localhost:8080/demo/`.

Anyway, back to Java web applications. Java Web Applications are dynamic; the pages are generated from Java code using `Servlets` and `JSP(Java Server Pages)` pages. Because of that, Java Web applications are not running on a server but inside a web container on the server. (This is why Tomcat or Jetty are sometimes called Servlet Containers.) The web container provides a Java runtime environment for Java Web applications. Apache Tomcat is such a container running in the JVM, which supports execution of servlets and JSP pages. A **servlet** is a Java class that is a subclass of `jakarta.servlet.http.HttpServlet`. Instances of this type answer HTTP Requests within a web container.

🔥   Apache Tomcat 10.x is an open-source software implementation of a subset of the Jakarta EE (formally Java EE) technologies. Tomcat is based on Servlet 5.0, JSP 3.0, EL 4.0, WS 2.0, and JASIC 2.0. Up to Tomcat 9.x a servlet is a Java class that is a subclass of `javax.servlet.http.HttpServlet`. The migration from `javax.` packages to `jakarta.</emphasis>` was needed in Tomcat 10.x to separate Oracle official Java products from the open-source ones, built using Eclipse build servers.[4]

A **JSP page** is a file with .jsp extension that contains HTML and Java Code. A JSP page gets compiled into a servlet by the web container the first time the page is accessed. In essence, the servlet is the core element of a Java Web application. The server must also know that the servlet exists and how to identify it, which where the call `tomcat.addServlet(contextPath, servletName, servlet)` comes in. It basically says to add the servlet with name `servletName` to the application context with the `contextPath` value context path, and then associate an URL pattern to the servlet, the `context.addServletMapping(urlPattern, servletName)` is called.

When a Java Web Application is running all its servlets and JSP are running into its context, but they have to be added into the context in the code and mapped to an URL pattern. The requests URL which matches that URL pattern will access that servlet. In Listing 10-26 the servlet was created on the spot by instantiating the `HttpServlet` abstract class and resulting in an anonymous servlet instance. Listing Listing 10-27 depicts a concrete class named `SampleServlet` that extends the `HttpServlet` class. The advantage of doing this is that the URL pattern and the servlet name can become properties of this class simplifying the syntax of adding them to the application context.

Listing 10-27. The `SampleServlet` Class

```
package com.apress.bgn.ten;

import jakarta.servlet.http.HttpServlet;
import jakarta.servlet.http.HttpServletRequest;
import jakarta.servlet.http.HttpServletResponse;
```

---

[4] This blog entry explains the whole thing: see Java Magazine, "Transition from Java EE to Jakarta EE," `https://blogs.oracle.com/javamagazine/transition-from-java-ee-to-jakarta-ee`, accessed October 15, 2021.

```java
import java.io.IOException;
import java.io.PrintWriter;
import java.util.logging.Logger;

public class SampleServlet extends HttpServlet {
    private static final Logger LOGGER = Logger.getLogger(SampleServlet.
    class.getName());

    private final String servletName = "sampleServlet";
    private final String urlPattern = "/sample";

    @Override
    protected void doGet(HttpServletRequest req, HttpServletResponse resp)
            throws IOException {
        PrintWriter writer = resp.getWriter();
        try {
            writer.println(WebResourceUtils.readResource("index.html"));
        } catch (Exception e) {
            LOGGER.warning("Could not read static file : " + e.getMessage());
        }
    }

    @Override
    public String getServletName() {
        return servletName;
    }

    public String getUrlPattern() {
        return urlPattern;
    }
}
```

The urlPattern property was added to this class for practical reasons, to keep everything related to this servlet in one place. The same goes for servletName. If the intention were to instantiate this class multiple times to create multiple servlets, these two properties should be declared as configurable. Adding this servlet to the application is pretty easy. An object of this type needs to be created and then the tomcat. addServlet(..) and context.addServletMappingDecoded(..) must be called, as depicted in Listing 10-28.

Listing 10-28. Adding the SampleServlet Class to the Web Application

```
SampleServlet sampleServlet = new SampleServlet();
tomcat.addServlet(contextPath, sampleServlet.getServletName(),
sampleServlet);
context.addServletMappingDecoded(sampleServlet.getUrlPattern(),
sampleServlet.getServletName());
```

Inside the doGet(..) method the contents of the index.html file are read (using WebResourceUtils that is part of the project for this chapter, but not relevant to this chapter) and are written in the response object using the response PrintWriter.

As you can see, the doGet(..) method receives as arguments two objects: the HttpServletRequest instance is read and all contents of the request sent from the client can be accessed using appropriate methods and the HttpServletResponse instance, which is used to add information to the response. In the previous code sample, we are just writing HTML code read from another file. Extra methods that can be called is the response.setStatus(HttpServletResponse.SC_OK) that sets the response status.

Aside from the doGet(..) method, there are do*(..) methods matching each HTTP method that declare the same type of parameters.

Starting with Servlet 3.0, servlets can be written using the @WebServlet annotation, which removes the necessity to be explicitly added to the web application and mapped in the context as shown in Listing 10-28, because they are picked automatically when Tomcat starts. Also, there is no need to instantiate the servlet class either.

The SampleServlet class after Servlet 3.0 is shown in Listing 10-29.

Listing 10-29. Adding the SampleServlet Class to the Web Application

```
package com.apress.bgn.ten;

import jakarta.servlet.annotation.WebServlet;
import jakarta.servlet.http.*;
// other import statements omitted

@WebServlet(
        name = "sampleServlet",
        urlPatterns = {"/sample"}
)
```

```java
public class SampleServlet extends HttpServlet {
    private static final Logger LOGGER = Logger.getLogger(SampleServlet.
    class.getName());

    @Override
    protected void doGet(HttpServletRequest req, HttpServletResponse resp)
            throws IOException {
        PrintWriter writer = resp.getWriter();
        try {
            writer.println(WebResourceUtils.readResource("index.html"));
        } catch (Exception e) {
            LOGGER.warning("Could not read static file : " + e.getMessage());
        }
    }
}
```

So this is how we handle servlets, but how do we handle JSP pages using an embedded server? It's not impossible, but it is not easy either. That is why, for this task, usually people reply on smarter frameworks such as Spring Boot.[5]

To avoid going through a lot of setup code and details, JSP syntax will be explained on a WEB application that has to be deployed on a standalone instance of a Tomcat Server.

Java Web Application on a Standalone Server

Java Applications that are designed to be deployed on an application server are either packaged as a Web Archive (war) or Enterprise Application Archive (ear). These are special type of Java Archives (jar) that are used to group together other Jars, JSPs (Java Server Pages), Java classes, static pages, and other resources that are part of a web application. There is a maven plug-in named maven-war-plugin that packs an artifact as a war. The EAR is a file format used by Jakarta EE to package one or more modules into a single deployment onto an application server; it basically links a group of jars and wars together into a single application.

---

[5] See the official project page at Spring, https://spring.io/projects/spring-boot, accessed October 15, 2021.

In this chapter a very simple web application, packaged as a war, containing Java Server Pages is built and deployed to a standalone instance of an Apache Tomcat server.

To install Apache Tomcat server locally, go to the official site at `https://tomcat.apache.org/download-10.cgi` and download Apache Tomcat version 10.0.7 and follow the instructions for your operating system. Since Apache Tomcat is provided as an archive, the installation process should be as simple as unpacking it somewhere on your computer. In this chapter and IntelliJ IDEA Tomcat launcher is used to run the web application, so the interaction with the server will be minimal.

A Java web application has a different structure than a typical Java application. It contains the typical `main` and `test` directories, but it also contains a `webapp` directory that contains the web resources. The project structure is depicted in Figure 10-14.

Figure 10-14. *Web application structure change*

Notice the `web.xml` file located under the `WEB-INF` directory. This file defines the structure of the web application. Before Servlet 3.0 this file was the only way to map servlets onto **urlPatterns** and configure them to be part of the application. After Servlet 3.0 and the introduction of annotations, this file is mostly empty.

When the web application is built the bytecode of the application is saved under `WEB-INF/classes`. If the application uses 3rd party libraries, they are all saved into `WEB-INF/lib`.

Now, back to Java Server Pages.

There are two ways of writing JSP pages. The simplest one, which is rarely used these days because it couples HTML code with Java code, is to use **JSP scriptlets.** JSP scriptlets are pieces of Java code embedded in HTML code using directive tags. There are three type of directive tags:

- <%@ page ... %> declarative directive used to provide instructions to the container. Instructions declared using this directive belong to the current page and can be used anywhere in the page. Such a directive can be used to import Java Types or define page properties. Example:

```
<%@ page import="java.util.Date" %>
<%@ page language="java" contentType="text/html; charset=US-ASCII"
pageEncoding="US-ASCII" %>
```

- <%@ include ... %> declarative is used to include a file during translation phase. Thus, the current JSP file, where this directive is used, is a composition of its content and the content of the file that is declared using this directive.

- <%@ include file = "footer.jsp" >

- <%@ taglib ... %> declarative is used to declare a tag library with elements that will be used in the JSP page. This declarative is important because it is used to import a library with custom tags and element that will be used to write the JSP page. These tags provide dynamic functionality without the need for scriptlets.

The index.jsp ahown in Figure 10-14 is quite simple and its content is depicted in Listing 10-30:

Listing 10-30. The Very Simple index.jsp Page Contents

```
<%@ page import="java.util.Date" %>
<%@ page language="java" contentType="text/html; charset=US-ASCII"
pageEncoding="US-ASCII" %>
<!DOCTYPE html PUBLIC "-//W3C//DTD HTML 4.01 Transitional//EN" "http://www.
w3.org/TR/html4/loose.dtd">
```

```
<html>
    <head><title>Web Application Demo JSP Page</title></head>
    <body style="background-color:black">
            <h1 style="color:#ffd200"> Today is <%= new Date() %></h1>
    </body>
</html>
```

It does nothing else but print today's date, and it does so by calling new Date(). As you can see, we are using Java code in what it looks like an HTML page. Because those directives are in there and the extension is .jsp, the container knows this file must be compiled into a servlet. The default page a web application opens with when its root domain is accessed, if nothing was mapped to the default url pattern "/" is a file named index.html or index.htm or index.jsp in this case. Beside from adding the file named index.jsp in the WEB-INF directory and thus making sure the container can find it, all that is left to do is to configure an Apache Tomcat Launcher in IntelliJ IDEA and configure it to deploy the war that results when this application is built before starting Tomcat.

To configure an Apache Tomcat launcher, IntelliJ IDEA needs to have the Tomcat and TomEE plug-in enabled. If you install IntelliJ IDEA without customizing it, this plug-in is installed by default. If you managed somehow to uninstall it, just open the IntelliJ IDE **Preferences** window, select **Plug-ins**, and look for it in the **Marketplace** and tick its box, as depicted in Figure 10-15.

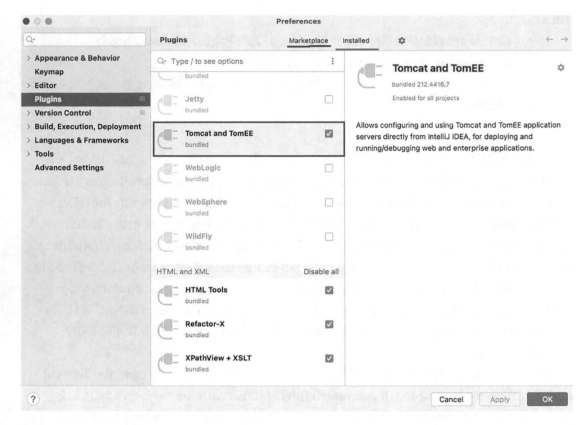

Figure 10-15. *Enabling Tomcat and TomEE plug-in in IntelliJ IDEA*

Once the plug-in is installed, click on the Launch section and select **Edit Configurations…**, and from the list on the left select **Tomcat Server ➤ Local**, as depicted in Figure 10-16.

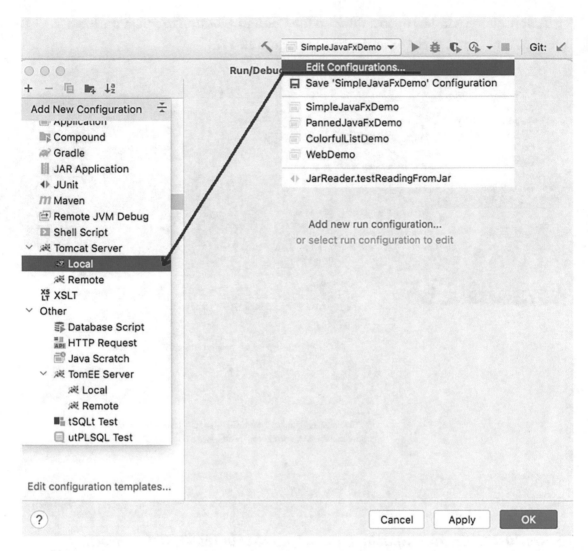

Figure 10-16. *Creating Apache Tomcat launcher in IntelliJ IDEA*

A new dialog window opens. Click on the **Configure** button to select the local Apache Tomcat and click **Ok**, as depicted in Figure 10-17.

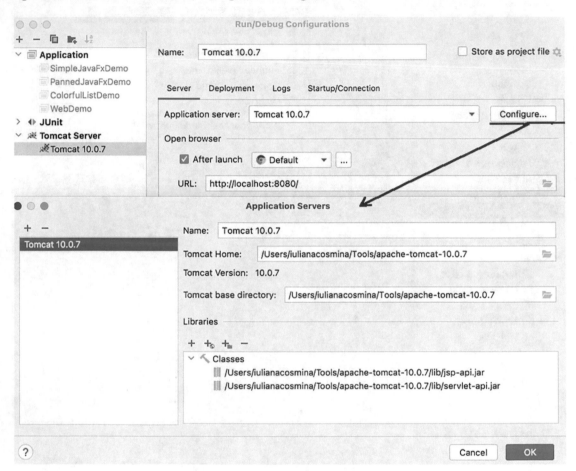

Figure 10-17. *Creating Apache Tomcat Launcher in IntelliJ IDEA: selecting Tomcat Server*

After selecting the server, click on the **Fix** button or on the **Deployment** tab and click the + sign to select an artifact. IntelliJ IDEA will identify all web applications in the project and provide a list to choose from. Select simple-webapp, as depicted in Figure 10-18.

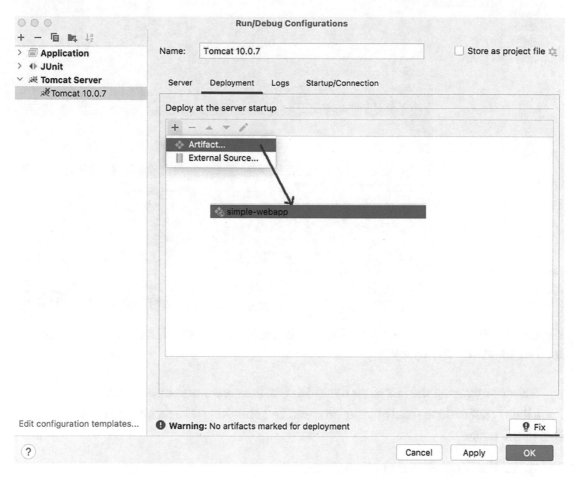

Figure 10-18. *Creating Apache Tomcat launcher in IntelliJ IDEA: selecting the web application to deploy*

Feel free to edit the name of the launcher and the context path, as shown in Figure 10-19.

Figure 10-19. *Creating Apache Tomcat launcher in IntelliJ IDEA: selecting the web application to deploy*

After configuring the launcher like this, start the server and open the `http://localhost:8080/demo` page in your browser. You should just see a simple message like this in the page:

```
Today is Mon Aug 20 01:41:29 BST 2018
```

The depicted date will be the one on your system when you run the application yourself.

Since **taglibs** have been mentioned, let's talk a little about them as well. The most basic tag library is named **JSTL** and stands for **JSP Standard Tag Library**. Other more evolved tag libraries are provided by JSF (Java Server Faces), Thymeleaf, or Spring. Tags defined in this library can be used to write JSP pages that change behavior depending on request attributes, which can be used to iterate, test values, internationalization and formatting. Based on the JSTL functions provided, the tags are grouped into five categories, and they can be used in a JSP page only after specifying the appropriate directive. Following are the five directives listed together with the overall topic the tags are covering:

- `<%@ taglib uri="http://java.sun.com/jsp/jstl/core" prefix="c" %>` JSTL core tags provide support for displaying values, iteration, conditional logic, catch exception, url, forward, or redirect response.

- `<%@ taglib uri="http://java.sun.com/jsp/jstl/fmt" prefix="fmt" %>` JSTL formatting tags are provided for formatting of numbers, dates, and i18n support through locales and resource bundles.

- `<%@ taglib uri="http://java.sun.com/jsp/jstl/sql" prefix="sql" %>` JSTL SQL tags provide support for interaction with relational databases, but never use SQL in a web page because it is very easily hackable (just look up the term SQL Injection on Google).

- `<%@ taglib uri="http://java.sun.com/jsp/jstl/xml" prefix="x" %>` JSTL XML tags provide support for handling XML documents, parsing, transformations, and XPath expressions evaluation.

- `<%@ taglib uri="http://java.sun.com/jsp/jstl/functions" prefix="fn" %>` JSTL function tags provide a number of functions that can be used to perform common operations such as text manipulations.

Now that we know the basic tag categories, which ones do you think we will need to use to redesign our `index.jsp` page? If you thought about **FMT** and **Core,** you are right. Also, JSP pages that use taglibs are most always backed up by a servlet that sets the proper attributes on the request that will be used within the JSP page. So let's modify the `index.jsp` page, as depicted in Listing 10-31.

Listing 10-31. Using FMT adn Core Taglibs to Rewrite `index.jsp`

```
<%@ page language="java" contentType="text/html;charset=US-ASCII"
pageEncoding="US-ASCII"%>
<%@ taglib uri="http://java.sun.com/jsp/jstl/fmt" prefix="fmt" %>
<%@ taglib uri="http://java.sun.com/jsp/jstl/core" prefix="c" %>
```

```
<!DOCTYPE html PUBLIC "-//W3C//DTD HTML 4.01 Transitional//EN" "http://www.
w3.org/TR/html4/loose.dtd">
<html>
    <head>
        <title>Web Application Demo JSP Page</title>
    </head>
    <body style="background-color:black">
        <fmt:formatDate value="${requestScope.today}" pattern="dd/MM/yyyy"
        var="todayFormatted"/>
        <p style="color:#ffd200"> Today is <c:out
        value="${todayFormatted}" /> </p>
    </body>
</html>
```

And while we are at it, let's rename it to make it obvious what it is used for: to
date.jsp and write a servlet class named DateServlet to add to the request the today
attribute, which will be formatted by the <fmt:formatDate> tag and the result saved into
the todayFormatted variable and later printed out by the <c:out> tag. The DateServlet
is depicted in Listing 10-32.

Listing 10-32. DateServlet Class That Provides the today Attribute for the
date.jsp Page

```
package com.apress.bgn.ten;

import jakarta.servlet.RequestDispatcher;
import jakarta.servlet.ServletException;
import jakarta.servlet.annotation.WebServlet;
import jakarta.servlet.http.HttpServlet;
import jakarta.servlet.http.HttpServletRequest;
import jakarta.servlet.http.HttpServletResponse;

import java.io.IOException;
import java.util.Date;
```

```java
@WebServlet(
        name = "dateServlet",
        urlPatterns = {"/date"}
)
public class DateServlet extends HttpServlet {

    @Override
    protected void doGet(HttpServletRequest request, HttpServletResponse
    response)
            throws IOException, ServletException {
        System.out.println(" ->>> Getting date ");
        request.setAttribute("today", new Date());
        RequestDispatcher rd = getServletContext().getRequestDispatcher
        ("/date.jsp");
        rd.forward(request, response);
    }
}
```

Now we just restart the application, and the first page will now display Today is 06/07/2021, and you will see the date on your system when the code is run.

If you think writing Java web applications is cumbersome, you are quite right. Pure Java is quite tedious for such a task. Professional Java web applications are usually written by using frameworks that make the job of creating pages and linking them to the backend easily. Even more, nowadays the tendency is to create interfaces in JavaScript using powerful JavaScript frameworks like Angular and React; using advanced CSS4, many UI Designs can now also be done 100% in CSS3 or CSS4 and communicate to a Java backend application hosted on an enterprise server using Web Service calls, usually REST. Anyway, look it up if you are curious; the subject is vast, but frameworks such as Spring make it quite easy to set your environment up and start developing. Just don't fall into the trap of using a framework without understanding its fundamentals.

Summary

This chapter has covered important development tools and techniques, the classes in JDK that provide support for them, and important Java libraries that you will must likely end up working with that could make your development job practical and pleasant. The JDK has never shined when it comes to GUI support, but JavaFX is quite an evolution from AWT and Swing and just might have a future. A complete list of topics from this chapter is here:

- how to write an interactive console application

- how to write an interactive application with a Swing interface

- the basics of JavaFX architecture

- how to write an interactive application with a JavaFX interface

- how to internationalize your application

- how to write a web application using an embedded server

- what a servlet is

- what a JSP Scriptlet is

- how to use taglibs to write JSP pages

- how to deploy a Java web application to Apache Tomcat

Working With Files

One of the most important functions in software is information organizing and storage, with the goal of using it and sharing it. Information is written on paper and stored in organized cabinets in real life where it can be retrieved from. Software applications do something similar. Information is written in files, files are organized in directories, and eventually when in even more complex structures, named databases. Java provides classes to read information from files and databases and classes to write files and write information to databases. In previous chapters databases have been mentioned, and in **Chapter 9** a simple example using a Derby in-memory database was introduced to show you how heavy dependencies like databases can be mocked, to allow unit testing. This chapter is not about using databases, because writing Java applications to use databases would require extra software to be installed. Instead, the chapter focuses on reading and writing files, and in how many ways this can be done.

Java IO and NIO APIs

Before starting to show you how to read or write files we need to show you how access them from the code, how to check if they exist, check for their size and list their properties, and so on. The core packages for file handling in Java are named `java.io` and `java.nio`.[1] The package names give a pretty good hint about the components they contain. `java.io` is pretty much an acronym for Java Input/Output and groups together component designed to facilitate input and output operations for accessing the file system through data streams and serialization. `java.nio` is an acronym for Java Nonblocking Input/Output. This package was introduced in version 1.4 and

---

[1] See the official java.io package Javadoc page at Oracle, `https://docs.oracle.com/en/java/javase/17/docs/api/java.base/java/io/package-summary.html`; see the official java.nio package Javadoc page at Oracle, `https://docs.oracle.com/en/java/javase/17/docs/api/java.base/java/nio/package-summary.html`, both accessed October 15, 2021.

© Iuliana Cosmina 2022
I. Cosmina, *Java 17 for Absolute Beginners*, https://doi.org/10.1007/978-1-4842-7080-6_11

is a collection of Java programming language APIs that offer features for intensive I/O operations. A package named `java.nio.file` was added in JDK 1.7 containing a collection of utility classes providing comprehensive support for file I/O and for accessing the file system.

The main big difference between Java NIO and IO is that IO is stream oriented, where NIO is buffer oriented. What this means is with the old Java IO API, files are read one or more bytes at the time from a stream. Bytes are not cached anywhere and stream traversal is unidirectional. So once the stream is exhausted, there is no way to traverse it again. If you need to walk the stream in both directions, data must be stored in a buffer first.

With the Java NIO, the data is read directly into a buffer, which means bytes are cached in a web browser and the browser supports bidirectional operations. This gives more flexibility during processing, but extra checks are required to make sure the buffer contains all the data needed for processing.

The second main difference is that Java IO operations are blocking. Once a method to read or write a file was called, the thread is blocked until there is no more data to read or the data was fully written.

Java NIO operations are nonblocking. A thread can request data from a resource (e.g., a file) via an open channel and only get what is currently available, or nothing at all, if no data is currently available. Rather than waiting until some data is there, the thread can go ahead and do something else, and later check to see if the data buffer was populated.

The third difference is not so much a difference but something that Java NIO has extra: **selectors**. These components allow a thread to monitor multiple input channels, and select for processing only the ones that have available data. By comparison, you cannot have that with the classic Java IO, because a thread blocks until a file operation is done.

Depending on the problem you are trying to solve, you can use one or the other, but it all starts with a **file handler**.

File Handlers

The most important class when working with files in Java is the `java.io.File class`. This class is an abstract representation of a file and directory pathname. Instances of this class are named **file handlers** because they allow developers to handle files and directories in the Java code using references of this type, instead of complete path names. A File instance can be created by using different arguments.

The most simple way is to use the constructor that receives as an argument a String value containing the absolute file pathname. In the code sample in Listing 11-1, the printFileStats(..) method is used to print file details.

Listing 11-1. Printing File Details

```java
package com.apress.bgn.eleven.io;

import org.slf4j.Logger;
import org.slf4j.LoggerFactory;

import java.io.File;

public class Main {
    private static final Logger log = LoggerFactory.getLogger(Main.class);

    public static void main(String... args) {
        // replace [workspace] with your workspace path
        var file = new File("[workspace]/java-17-for-absolute-beginners/
        README.adoc");
        printFileStats(file);
    }

    private static void printFilcStats(File f) {
        if (f.exists()) {
            log.info("File Details:");
            log.info("Type : {}", f.isFile() ? "file" : "directory or
            symlink");
            log.info("Location :{}", f.getAbsolutePath());
            log.info("Parent :{}", f.getParent());
            log.info("Name : {}", f.getName());

            double kilobytes = f.length() / (double)1024;
            log.info("Size : {} ", kilobytes);
```

```
            log.info("Is Hidden : {}", f.isHidden());
            log.info("Is Readable? : {}", f.canRead());
            log.info("Is Writable? : {}", f.canWrite());
        }
    }
}
```

In the previous example the file handler instance is created by providing the absolute file pathname on my computer. If you want to run the previous code on your computer, you must provide a pathname to a file on your computer. If you are using Windows, keep in mind that the pathname will contain the "\" character that is a special character in Java and must be escaped by doubling it.

The `printFileStats(..)` method makes use of a lot of methods that can be called on a file handler. The full list of methods that you can call is bigger and you can see them all in the official API documentation here: `https://docs.oracle.com/en/java/javase/17/docs/api/java.base/java/io/File.html`. The methods are explained in the following list:

- `isFile()` returns `true` if the pathname points to a file and `false` if the pathname points to a directory or a symlink (a special type of file that exists with the only purpose to link to another file and can be quite useful when you want to shorten the pathname to a file and incredibly useful on Windows where the pathname length limit is of 256 characters). In the previous code sample the method returns true, and the log prints:

  ```
  INFO  c.a.b.e.Main - Type : file
  ```

  If we want to see if the method works for a directory, just delete the file name from the pathname.

  `File file = new File("/[workspace]/java-17-for-absolute-beginners /");` And the log prints

  ```
  INFO  c.a.b.e.Main - Type : directory or symlink
  ```

- `getAbsolutePath()` returns the absolute pathname to a file or a directory. When creating a file handler, the absolute pathname is not always needed, but if you need to use it later in the code or make sure the relative path was resolved correctly, this method is just what you need. The following piece of code creates a file handler to a file in the resources directory by using the path relative to the root project directory (in our case the java-17-for-absolute-beginners directory).

```
File d = new File("chapter11/read-write-file/src/main/resources/input/");
```

The getAbsolutePath() method returns the full pathname, which is printed by the log statement as:

```
INFO  c.a.b.e.Main - Location :/[workspace]/java-17-for-absolute-beginners/
chapter11/read-write-file/src/main/resources/input
```

The Java File class is quite powerful; it can be used to point to a shared file on another computer. There is a special constructor for that which receives an argument of type java.net.URI, where **URI** stands for **Uniform Resource Identifier**. To test this constructor, just select a file on your computer and open it in a web browser, so you can get its URI from the browser address bar. The code in Listing 11-2 depicts the File class being instantiates using a local URI.

Listing 11-2. Printing File Details for a File Instance Create Using an URI

```
package com.apress.bgn.eleven.io;

import java.net.URI;
import java.net.URISyntaxException;
// other imports omitted

public class Main {
    public static void main(String... args) {
        try{
            // replace [workspace] with your workspace path
            var localUri = new URI("file:///[workspace]/java-17-for-
            absolute-beginners/README.adoc");
            var localFile =  new File (localUri);
            printFileStats(localFile);
```

```
        } catch (URISyntaxException use) {
            log.error("Malformed URI, no file there", use);
        }
    }
}
```

Because the URI might have an incorrect prefix or not exactly point to a file, the URI constructor is declared to throw a `java.net.URISyntaxException`, so in the code you have to handle this as well. In the case of a URI being used to create a file handler, the `getAbsolutePath()` method returns the absolute pathname of the file, on the computer and drive where the file is.

- `getParent()` returns the absolute path to the directory containing the file, because hierarchically, a file cannot have another file as a parent.

- `getName()` returns the file name. The file name contains the extension as the suffix after "`.`" is called, which is used to indicate they type of file and what is intended to be used for.

- `length()` returns the length of the file in bytes. This method does not work for directories, as directories can contain files restricted to the user executing the program and exceptions might be thrown. So if you ever need the size of a directory, you have to write the code yourself.

- `isHidden()` returns `true` is the file is not visible to the current user, returns `false` otherwise. On a macOs/ Linux system, files with names starting with "`.`" are hidden, so if we want to see that method returning `true` we have to create a handler to one of the system configuration files, such as `.gitconfig`. So calling the `printFileStats(..)` on a file handler created using a pathname to a hidden file results in an output similar to the one in Listing 11-3:

Listing 11-3. Printing File Details for a Hidden File

```
INFO  c.a.b.e.Main - File Details:
INFO  c.a.b.e.Main - Type : file
INFO  c.a.b.e.Main - Location :/Users/[userDir]/.gitconfig
INFO  c.a.b.e.Main - Parent :/Users/[userDir]
```

```
INFO  c.a.b.e.Main - Name : .gitconfig
INFO  c.a.b.e.Main - Size : 3.865234375
INFO  c.a.b.e.Main - Is Hidden : true
INFO  c.a.b.e.Main - Is Readable? : true
INFO  c.a.b.e.Main - Is Writable? : true
```

- canRead() and canWrite() are obvious, as files can be secured
  from normal users. Both methods return true when the user has the
  specific right on the file and false otherwise.

File handlers can be created for pathnames pointing to directories, which means there there are available methods to call that are specific only to directories. The most common thing to do with a directory is to list its contents. The list() method returns a String array, containing the names of the files (and directories) under this directory. Lambda expressions makes printing the items in a directory pretty practical.

```
var d = new File("/[workspace]/java-17-for-absolute-beginners");
Arrays.stream(Objects.requireNonNull(d.list())).forEach(ff -> log.info("\t
File Name : {}", ff));
```

Files names are not really useful in most cases; having a File array with file handlers to each of them would be better. That is why listFiles() method was added in version 1.2.

```
Arrays.stream(Objects.requireNonNull(d.listFiles())).forEach(ff → log.
info("\t File : {}", ff.getAbsolutePath()));
```

This method has more than one form, because it can be used to filter the files and return file handlers only for files or directories matching a certain requirement, when called with an instance of FileFilter. The code sample in Listing 11-4 filters the entries under the directories and keeps only the directories with names that start with 'chapter'.

Listing 11-4. Filtering Content of a Directory Using a FileFilter Instance

```
package com.apress.bgn.eleven.io;

import java.io.File;
import java.io.FileFilter;
// other imports omitted
```

```java
public class Main {
    public static void main(String... args) {
        // replace [workspace] with your workspace path
        var d = new File("/[workspace]/java-17-for-absolute-beginners");
        Arrays.stream(d.listFiles(new FileFilter() {
            @Override
            public boolean accept(File childFile) {
                return childFile.isDirectory() && childFile.getName().
                startsWith("chapter");
            }
        })).forEach(ff -> log.info("Chapter Source : {}", ff.getName()));
    }
}
```

The previous code sample is written in expanded form to make it obvious that you should provide a concrete implementation for the accept(..) method. Using lambda expressions, the previous code can be simplified and even made less prone to exceptions being thrown.

```java
Arrays.stream(
    Objects.requireNonNull(d.listFiles(
        childFile -> childFile.isDirectory() && childFile.getName().
        startsWith("chapter")))
    ).forEach(ff -> log.info("Chapter Source : {}", ff.getName())
);
```

In the previous example we implemented the accept(..) to filter by file type and name, but the filter can involve anything. When the filter you need strictly involves the file name, you can reduce use the other version of the method, which receives a FilenameFilter instance as argument.

```java
Arrays.stream(Objects.requireNonNull(d.listFiles(new FilenameFilter() {
        @Override
        public boolean accept(File dir, String name) {
            return dir.getName().startsWith("chapter");
        }
}))).forEach(ff -> log.info("\t File : {}", ff.getAbsolutePath()));
```

Aside from listing properties of file, a file handler can also be used to create a file. To create a file the `createNewFile()` method must be called after creating a file handler with a specific pathname, as shown in Listing 11-5.

Listing 11-5. Creating a File

```
package com.apress.bgn.eleven.io;

import java.io.IOException;
// other imports omitted

public class Main {
    public static void main(String... args) {
        var created = new File(
                "chapter11/read-write-file/src/main/resources/output/
                created.txt");
        if (!created.exists()) {
            try {
                created.createNewFile();
            } catch (IOException e) {
                log.error("Could not create file.", e);
            }
        }
    }
}
```

The `exists()` method returns `true` when the file hander is associated with a concrete file or directory, and `false` otherwise. It can be used to test if the file we are trying to create is already there. If the file exists, the method has no effect. If the user does not have proper rights to create the file at the specified pathname, a `SecurityException` will be thrown. In certain cases we might need to create a file that needs only to be used during the execution if the program. This means we either have to create the file and delete it explicitly, or we can create a temporary file. Temporary files are created by calling `createTempFile(prefix, suffix)` and they are created in the temporary directory defined for the operating system. The prefix argument is of type String and the created file will have the name starting with its value. The suffix argument is of type String as well and it can be used to specify an extension for the file. The rest of the file name is generated by the operating system. The code to create a temporary file is depicted in Listing 11-6.

Listing 11-6. Creating a Temporary File

```
package com.apress.bgn.eleven.io;

import java.io.IOException;
// other imports omitted

public class Main {
    public static void main(String... args) {
        try {
            File temp = File.createTempFile("java_bgn_", ".tmp");
            log.info("File created.txt at: {}", temp.getAbsolutePath());
            temp.deleteOnExit();
        } catch (IOException e) {
            log.error("Could not create temporary file.", e);
        }
    }
}
```

Files in the temporary directory of an operating system are periodically deleted by the operating system, but if you want to make sure it will be deleted, you can explicitly call deleteOnExit() on the file handler for the temporary file. In the previous code sample the absolute path to the file is printed to show the exact location where the temporary file was created and on a macOS system the full pathname looks very similar to this:

```
/var/folders/gg/nm_cb2lx72q1lz7xwwdh7tnc0000gn/T/java_
bgn_14652264510049064218.tmp
```

A file can also be renamed using a Java file handler, there is a method for that called rename(f) that is called with a file handler argument, pointing to the location and desired name that the file should have. The method returns true if the renaming succeeded and false otherwise. The code for doing this is depicted in Listing 11-7.

Listing 11-7. Renaming a File

```java
package com.apress.bgn.eleven.io;

import java.io.IOException;
// other imports omitted

public class Main {
    public static void main(String... args) {
        var file = new File(
                "chapter11/read-write-file/src/main/resources/output/
                created.txt");
        var renamed = new File(
                "chapter11/read-write-file/src/main/resources/output/
                renamed.txt");
        boolean result = file.renameTo(renamed);
        log.info("Renaming succeeded? : {} ", result);
    }
}
```

Most methods in the class File throw IOException, because manipulating a file can fail because of a hardware problem, or because of an operating system problem. This type of exception is a checked exceptions and developers using file handlers are forced to catch and treat this type of exceptions.

Methods that require special rights for accessing a file throw SecurityException. This type extends RuntimeException so exceptions are not checked. They become obvious when the application is running.

Now that all the basis of working with file handlers have been covered, it is time for the next section.

Path Handlers

The java.nio.file.Path interface was introduced in Java 1.7 together with utility classes java.nio.file.Files and java.nio.file.Paths to provide new and more practical ways to work with files. A Path instance may be used to locate a file in a file system, and thus represents a system dependent file path. Path instances are more practical than File as they can provide methods to access components of a path, to combine paths, and compare paths. Path instances cannot be directly created, because an interface cannot be instantiated, but the interface provides static utility methods to create them, and so does the class Paths. Use whichever you want depending on your situation.

The simplest way to create a Path instance is to start with a file handler and call Paths.get(fileURI), as shown in Listing 11-8.

Listing 11-8. Creating a Path Instance

```java
package com.apress.bgn.eleven.io;

// other imports omitted
import java.io.File;
import java.nio.file.Path;
import java.nio.file.Paths;

public class PathDemo {
    private static final Logger log = LoggerFactory.
    getLogger(PathDemo.class);

    public static void main(String... args) {
        // replace [workspace] with your workspace path
        File file = new File(
                "/[workspace]/java-17-for-absolute-beginners/README.adoc");
        Path path = Paths.get(file.toURI());
        log.info(path.toString());
    }
}
```

Starting with Java 11, Paths.get(file.toURI()) can be replaced with Path. of(file.toURI()). The other way to create a Path instance is to use the other form of the Paths.get(..), which receives as arguments, multiple pieces of the path.

```java
Path composedPath = Paths.get("/[workspace]",
    "java-17-for-absolute-beginners",
    "README.adoc");
log.info(composedPath.toString());
```

Both paths created previously point to the same location, thus if compared with each other using the compareTo(..) method (because Path extends interface Comparable<Path>, the result returned will be 0(zero) which means the paths are equal.

```
log.info("Is the same path? : {} ", path.compareTo(composedPath) ==0 ?
"yes" : "no");
// prints : INFO com.apress.bgn.eleven.PathDemo - Is the same path? : yes
```

In the next code sample, a few Path methods are called on the path instance. The code is depicted in Listing 11-9.

Listing 11-9. Inspecting Path Details

```java
package com.apress.bgn.eleven.io;
// import section omitted

public class PathDemo {
    private static final Logger log = LoggerFactory.
getLogger(PathDemo.class);

    public static void main(String... args) {
        var path = Paths.get("/[workspace]",
                "java-17-for-absolute-beginners",
                "README.adoc");
        printPathDetails(path);
    }

    private static void printPathDetails(Path path) {
        log.info("Location :{}", path.toAbsolutePath());
        log.info("Is Absolute? : {}", path.isAbsolute());
        log.info("Parent :{}", path.getParent());
        log.info("Root :{}", path.getRoot());
        log.info("FileName : {}", path.getFileName());
        log.info("FileSystem : {}", path.getFileSystem());
        log.info("IsFileReadOnly : {}", path.getFileSystem().isReadOnly());
    }
}
```

617

The following list explains each method and its outcome:

- `toAbsolutePath()` returns a Path instance representing the absolute path of this path. When called on the path instance created previously, as it is already absolute, the method will just return the path object the method is called on. Also, calling `path.isAbsolute()` will return `true`.

- `getParent()` returns the parent Path instance. Calling this method on the path instance will print:

- `INFO com.apress.bgn.eleven.PathDemo - Parent :/[workspace]/ java-17-for-absolute-beginners`

- `getRoot()` returns the root component of this path as a `Path` instance. On a Linux or macOS system prints "/", on Windows something like "C:\".

- `getFileName()` returns the name of the file or directory denoted by this path as a `Path` instance; basically, the path is split by the system path separator, and the most far away from the root element is returned.

- `getFileSystem()` returns the file system that created this object, for macOS it is an instance of type `sun.nio.fs.MacOSXFileSystem`.

Another useful `Path` method is `resolve(..)`. This method takes a `String` instance that is a representation of a path and resolves it against the Path instance it is called on. This means that path separators are added to combine the two paths according to the operating system the program runs on and a `Path` instance will be returned. This is depicted in Listing 11-10.

Listing 11-10. Resolving a Path Instance

```
package com.apress.bgn.eleven.io;
// import section omitted

public class PathDemo {
    private static final Logger log = LoggerFactory.
    getLogger(PathDemo.class);
```

```java
    public static void main(String... args) {
        // replace [workspace] with your workspace path
        var chapterPath = Paths.get("/[workspace]",
                "java-17-for-absolute-beginners/chapter11");
        Path filePath = chapterPath.resolve(
                "read-write-file/src/main/resources/input/data.txt");
        log.info("Resolved Path :{}", filePath.toAbsolutePath());
    }
}
```

The preceding sample code will print the following:

```
INFO c.a.b.e.PathDemo - Resolved Path :/[workspace]/java-17-for-absolute-
beginners/chapter11/read-write-file/src/main/resources/input/data.txt
```

Using Path instances, writing code that manages files or retrieves their properties becomes easier to write in combination with Files utility methods. The code sample in Listing 11-11 makes use of a few of these methods to print properties of a file, in the same way we did previously using a File handler.

Listing 11-11. Printing a Path Details

```java
package com.apress.bgn.eleven.io;
// import section omitted

public class PathDemo {
    private static final Logger log = LoggerFactory.
    getLogger(PathDemo.class);

    public static void main(String... args) {
        try {
            var outputPath = FileSystems.getDefault()
                .getPath("/[workspace]" +
                        "java-17-for-absolute-beginners/chapter11/read-
                        write-file/src/main/resources/output/sample");
            Path dirPath = Files.createDirectory(outputPath);
            printPathStats(dirPath);
        } catch (FileAlreadyExistsException faee) {
            log.error("Directory already exists.", faee);
```

```
        } catch (IOException e) {
            log.error("Could not create directory.", e);
        }
    }

    private static void printPathStats(Path path) {
        if (Files.exists(path)) {
            log.info("Path Details:");
            log.info("Type: {}", Files.isDirectory(path) ? "yes" : "no");
            log.info("Type: {}", Files.isRegularFile(path) ? "yes" : "no");
            log.info("Type: {}", Files.isSymbolicLink(path) ? "yes" : "no");
            log.info("Location :{}", path.toAbsolutePath());
            log.info("Parent :{}", path.getParent());
            log.info("Name : {}", path.getFileName());

            try {
                double kilobytes = Files.size(path) / (double)1024;
                log.info("Size : {} ", kilobytes);
                log.info("Is Hidden: {}", Files.isHidden(path) ? "yes"
                    : "no");
            } catch (IOException e) {
                log.error("Could not access file.", e);
            }
            log.info("Is Readable: {}", Files.isReadable(path) ? "yes"
                : "no");
            log.info("Is Writable: {}", Files.isWritable(path) ? "yes"
                : "no");
        }
    }
}
```

As you can see, the Files class provides the same functionality as the File class. This class consists exclusively of static methods that operate on files, directories, or other types of files. It was introduced in Java 1.7 and its advantage is the clearer syntax. The power and practicality of using java.nio classes is more obvious when managing files, creating them, renaming them, and deleting them and when reading and writing them.

The code sample in Listing 11-12 shows a file being created, renamed, and deleted using NIO classes.

Listing 11-12. Managing Files Using NIO Classes

```
package com.apress.bgn.eleven.io;
// import section omitted
import java.nio.FileAlreadyExistsException;

public class PathDemo {
    private static final Logger log = LoggerFactory.
getLogger(PathDemo.class);

    public static void main(String... args) {
        Path filePath = chapterPath.resolve(
                "read-write-file/src/main/resources/input/data.txt");
        Path copyFilePath = Paths.get(outputPath.toAbsolutePath().
        toString(), "data.adoc");
        try {
            Files.copy(filePath, copyFilePath);
            log.info("Exists? : {}", Files.exists(copyFilePath)?
            "yes": "no");
            log.info("File copied to: {}", copyFilePath.toAbsolutePath());
        } catch (FileAlreadyExistsException faee) {
            log.error("File already exists.", faee);
        } catch (IOException e) {
            log.error("Could not copy file.", e);
        }
        Path movedFilePath = Paths.get(outputPath.toAbsolutePath().
        toString(), "copy-data.adoc");
        try {
            Files.move(copyFilePath, movedFilePath);
            log.info("File moved to: {}", movedFilePath.toAbsolutePath());
            Files.deleteIfExists(copyFilePath);
        } catch (FileAlreadyExistsException faee) {
            log.error("File already exists.", faee);
```

```
      } catch (IOException e) {
         log.error("Could not move file.", e);
      }
   }
}
```

Notice the `FileAlreadyExistsException`, an exception type added in Java 1.7 that extends `IOException` (indirectly through the `FileSystemException`) and is used to provide more data about the situation that determined the failure if a file operation. It is thown by methods `createDirectory(..)`, `createFile(..)`, and `move(..)`.

The `delete(..)` method that is not used in the previous code sample throws a `java.nio.file.NoSuchFileException` if the file to be deleted does not exist. To avoid an exception being thrown, in the previous code sample `deleteIfExists(..)` is used.

The list of methods is even bigger, but since the size of this chapter is limited, you can go ahead and check it out yourself in the official Javadoc API.

Reading Files

Files are a succession of bits on a hard drive. A `File` handler does not provide methods to read the content of a file, but a group of other classes can be used to do so, but all of them are created using a file handler instance. Depending on what is actually needed to be done with the contents of a file, there is more than one way to read file contents in Java. There are a lot of ways and this section will cover the most common.

Using Scanner to Read Files

The `Scanner` class was used previously to read input from the command line. `System.in` can be replaced with a `File` and `Scanner` methods can be used to read file contents, as depicted in Listing 11-13.

Listing 11-13. Using Scanner to Read a File

```
package com.apress.bgn.eleven.io;

import org.slf4j.Logger;
import org.slf4j.LoggerFactory;
```

```java
import java.io.File;
import java.io.IOException;
import java.nio.charset.StandardCharsets;
import java.nio.file.Paths;
import java.util.Scanner;

public class ScannerDemo {
    private static final Logger log = LoggerFactory.
    getLogger(ScannerDemo.class);

    public static void main(String... args) {
        try {
            var scanner = new Scanner(new File("chapter11/read-write-file/
            src/main/resources/input/data.txt"));
            var content = "";
            while (scanner.hasNextLine()) {
                content += scanner.nextLine() + "\n";
            }
            scanner.close();
            log.info("Read with Scanner --> {}", content);
        } catch (IOException e) {
            log.error("Something went wrong! ", e);
        }
    }
}
```

Instead of a file, a `java.nio.file.Path` instance can be used as well:

```java
scanner = new Scanner(Paths.get(new File("chapter11/read-write-file/src/
main/resources/input/data.txt").toURI()), StandardCharsets.UTF_8.name());
```

Files can be written using different sets of characters, referred to in Java by `java.nio.charset.Charset` instances. To ensure they are read correctly, it is a good practice to read them using the same charset. There is a Scanner constructor, which receives a charset name as an argument. The `StandardCharsets.UTF_8.name()` method is called to extract the name of the UTF-8 charset.

Using `Files` Utility Methods to Read Files

The first code sample in Listing 11-14 shows the simplest way to read a file.

Listing 11-14. The Simplest Way to Read a File

```
package com.apress.bgn.eleven.io;
// import section omitted

public class FilesReadDemo {
    private static final Logger log = LoggerFactory.
    getLogger(FilesReadDemo.class);

    public static void main(String... args) {
        try {
            var file= new File("chapter11/read-write-file/src/main/
            resources/input/data.txt");
            var content = new String(Files.readAllBytes(Paths.get(file.
            toURI()))));
            log.info("Read with Files.readAllBytes --> {}", content);
        } catch (IOException e) {
            log.info("Something went wrong! ", e);
        }
    }
}
```

This approach works well when the file size can be approximated (the file size can be estimated and is relatively small) and it would not be a problem storing it into a `String` object.

The advantage of using `Files.readAllBytes(..)` is that no loop is needed and we do not have to construct the `String` value line by line, because this method just reads all the bytes in the files that can be given as an argument to the `String` constructor. The disadvantage is that no `Charset` is used, so the text value might not be the one we expect. There is a way to overcome this, by calling `Files.readAllLines(..)` that returns the file content as a list of `String` values, and has two forms one of them declaring a `Charset` as a parameter. This version of reading a file is depicted in Listing 11-15.

Listing 11-15. A Simple Way to Read a File Specifying a Charset

```java
package com.apress.bgn.eleven.io;
// import section omitted

public class FilesReadDemo {
    private static final Logger log = LoggerFactory.
    getLogger(FilesReadDemo.class);

    public static void main(String... args) {
        try {
            var file= new File("chapter11/read-write-file/src/main/
            resources/input/data.txt");
            List<String> lyricList = Files.readAllLines(Paths.get(file.
            toURI()), StandardCharsets.UTF_8);
            lyricList.forEach(System.out::println);
        } catch (IOException e) {
            log.info("Something went wrong! ", e);
        }
    }
}
```

But what if we do not need a List<String>, but the one String instance? In Java 11 a method was introduced for that and is called readString(..). The code sample using it is shown in Listing 11-16.

Listing 11-16. The Simplest Way to Read a File Specifying a Charset

```java
package com.apress.bgn.eleven.io;
// import section omitted

public class FilesReadDemo {
    private static final Logger log = LoggerFactory.
    getLogger(FilesReadDemo.class);
```

```
public static void main(String... args) {
    try {
        var content = Files.readString(Paths.get(file.toURI()),
        StandardCharsets.UTF_8);
        log.info("Read with Files.readString --> {}", content);
    } catch (IOException e) {
        log.info("Something went wrong! ", e);
    }
}
}
```

Using Readers to Read Files

Before the Files class and its fancy methods were introduced, there were other ways to read filesThe fancy methods are also not designed for reading big files, or for reading only parts of a file. Let's take a trip to the past and slowly analyze how things have evolved.

Before Java 1.6 to read a file line by line, you would have to write a contraption such as the one in Listing 11-17.

Listing 11-17. Reading a File Line By Line, Before Java 1.6

```
package com.apress.bgn.eleven.io;

import java.io.BufferedReader;
import java.io.FileReader;
// other imports omitted

public class ReadersDemo {
    private static final Logger log = LoggerFactory.
    getLogger(ReadersDemo.class);

    public static void main(String... args) {
        BufferedReader reader = null;
        try {
            reader = new BufferedReader(new FileReader(new File("chapter11/
            read-write-file/src/main/resources/input/data.txt")));
            StringBuilder sb = new StringBuilder();
```

```java
        String line;
        while ((line = reader.readLine()) != null) {
            sb.append(line).append("\n");
        }
        log.info("Read with BufferedReader --> {}", sb.toString());
    } catch (Exception e) {
        log.error("File could not be read! ", e);
    } finally {
        if (reader != null) {
            try {
                reader.close();
            } catch (IOException ioe) {
                log.error("Something went wrong! ", ioe);
            }
        }
    }
}
}
```

Whoa, what is that, right? After Java 1.6 the syntax was simplified a little, but the biggest changes came in 1.7. Before Java 1.7 if you wanted to read a file line by line, this is pretty much the code you had to write:

- You had to create a File handler.

- Then you needed to wrap the file handler into a FileReader. This type of instance could do the job of reading, but only in chunks of char[], which is not very useful when you need the actual text.

- The FileReader instance needs to be wrapped into an instance of BufferedReader that provides this functionality by reading the characters in an internal buffer. The way it works is that reader. readLine() is called until there is nothing more to read because the end of the file was reached, when this method returns null.

- At the end of the reading reader.close() needed to be called explictly otherwise a lock might be kept on the file and it might become unreadable until a restart.

In Java 1.7 a lot of changes were introduced to reduce the boilerplate needed to work with files. One of those things was that all classes used to access file contents and that could keep a lock on the file were enriched by being declared to implement the `java.io.Closeable` interface, which marks resources of these types as **closable** and a `close()` method is invoked to release resources transparently by the JVM before execution ends. Also, in Java 7, the `try-with-resources` statement was introduced. Making use of all these features, the previous code can be written as depicted in Listing 11-18.

Listing 11-18. Reading a File Line By Line, Starting with Java 1.7

```java
package com.apress.bgn.eleven.io;
// other imports omitted

public class ReadersDemo {
    private static final Logger log = LoggerFactory.
    getLogger(ReadersDemo.class);

    public static void main(String... args) {
            try (var br = new BufferedReader(new FileReader(new
            File("chapter11/read-write-file/src/main/resources/input/data.
            txt")))){
             StringBuilder sb = new StringBuilder();
             String line;
             while ((line = br.readLine()) != null) {
                 sb.append(line).append("\n");
             }
             log.info("Read with BufferedReader --> {}", sb.toString() );
        } catch (Exception e) {
            log.info("Something went wrong! ", e);
        }
    }
}
```

The code can be further simplified as the `FileReader` can take the absolute path to a file as `String` as a parameter. But the code can not be made to take encoding into consideration. This became possible in Java 1.8, when a constructor was introduced for the `FileReader` class that accepts a `Charset` argument. Still, we have nested constructor calls in the previous example, and it is quite ugly. Here is where Java 8 comes to the rescue, by introducing the `Files.newBufferedReader(Path)` and the `Files.newBufferedReader(Path, Charset)` method.

So the preceding code can be written as shown in Listing 11-19.

Listing 11-19. Reading a File Line By Line, Taking Encoding Into Consideration Starting with Java 1.8

```java
package com.apress.bgn.eleven.io;
// other imports omitted

public class ReadersDemo {
    private static final Logger log = LoggerFactory.
    getLogger(ReadersDemo.class);

    public static void main(String... args) {
      File file = new File("chapter11/read-write-file/src/main/resources/
    input/data.txt");
      try (var br = Files.newBufferedReader(file.toPath(),
      StandardCharsets.UTF_8)){
            StringBuilder sb = new StringBuilder();
            String line;
            while ((line = br.readLine()) != null) {
                sb.append(line).append("\n");
            }
            log.info("Read with BufferedReader --> {}", sb.toString() );
        } catch (Exception e) {
            log.info("Something went wrong! ", e);
        }
    }
}
```

If it is known that the size of the file is manageable, and we are interested no in just logging the contents, but saving the individual lines for futher processing, the easiest way to do this is by using `Files.readAllLines(..)` method combined with lambda expressions. Streams can be added in the mix, so the lines can be filtered or processed on the spot as shown here:

```
List<String> dataList = Files.readAllLines(Paths.get(file.toURI()),
StandardCharsets.UTF_8)
    .stream()
    .filter(line -> line!= null && !line.isBlank())
    .map(line -> line.toUpperCase())
    .collect(Collectors.toList());
```

Or we can write it another way, using the `Files.lines(..)` method, also introduced in Java 1.8, and get all contents as a stream directly:

```
List<String> dataList = Files.lines(Paths.get(file.toURI()),
StandardCharsets.UTF_8)
    .filter(line -> line!= null && !line.isBlank() )
    .map(line -> line.toUpperCase())
    .collect(Collectors.toList());
```

Anyway, back to file readers. The `BufferedReader` class if a member of a class group that extend the `Reader` class. The `Reader` class is an abstract class used for reading characters streams and is part of the `java.io` package. A simplified hierarchy showing the most commonly used implementations is depicted in Figure 11-1.

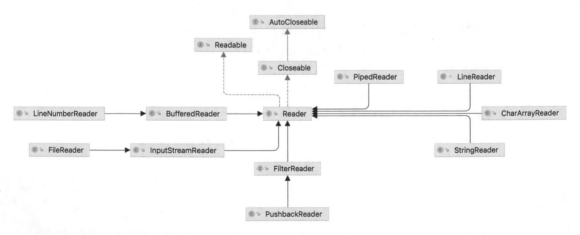

Figure 11-1. *Reader class hierarchy (as shown in IntelliJ IDEA)*

Character streams can have different sources, files being the most common. They provide sequential access to data stored in the file. The `BufferedReader` does not provide support for character encoding, but a `BufferedReader` is based on another `Reader` instance. And as you have noticed in the previous examples, a `FileReader` instance was used as argument when instantiating a BufferedReader, and FileReader was modified in Java 1.8 to support character encoding. Before Java 1.8, to read from a file and taking character encoding into consideration, an InputStreamReader instance was used as depicted in Listing 11-20.

Listing 11-20. Reading a File Line By Line, Taking Encoding Into Consideration Before Java 1.8

```java
package com.apress.bgn.eleven.io;

import java.io.FileInputStream;
import java.io.InputStreamReader;
// other imports omitted

public class ReadersDemo {
    private static final Logger log = LoggerFactory.
getLogger(ReadersDemo.class);

    public static void main(String... args) {
        File file = new File("chapter11/read-write-file/src/main/resources/
        input/data.txt");
        try (var br = new BufferedReader(new InputStreamReader(new
        FileInputStream(file), StandardCharsets.UTF_8))){
            StringBuilder sb = new StringBuilder();
            String line;
            while ((line = br.readLine()) != null) {
                    sb.append(line).append("\n");
            }
            log.info("Read with BufferedReader(InputStreamReader(FileInputS
            tream(..))) --> {}", sb.toString() );
        } catch (Exception e) {
            log.info("Something went wrong! ", e);
        }
    }
}
```

In Java 11, the Reader class was enriched with the nullReader() method, which returns a Reader instance that does nothing. This was requested by developers for testing purposes and is nothing else but a pseudo-Reader implementation.

Using InputStream to Read Files

Classes in the Reader family are advanced classes for reading data as text, but technically speaking files are just a sequence of bytes, so these classes are themselves wrappers around classes in a family of classes used for reading byte streams. This becomes quite obvious when trying to use the proper character encoding, and when reading text (as shown at the end of the previous section) using the BufferedReader, as the InputStreamReader instance given as argument is based on a java.io.FileInputStream instance, a type that is a subclass of java.io.InputStream.

The root class of this hierarchy is java.io.InputStream. A simplified hierarchy showing the most commonly used implementations is depicted in Figure 11-2.

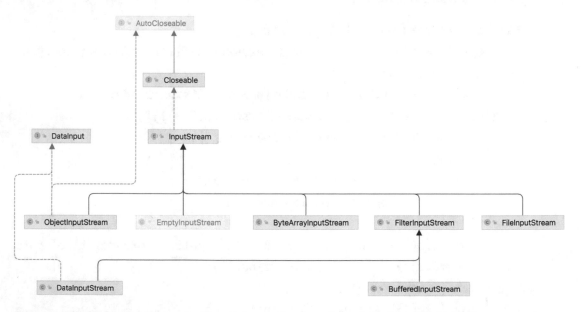

Figure 11-2. *InputStream class hierarchy (as shown in IntelliJ IDEA)*

The class BufferedInputStream is the equivalent of BufferedReader for reading streams of bytes. The System.in that we previously used to read user data from the console is of this type, and the Scanner instance converts the bytes from its buffer into user understandable data. When the data we are interested in is not text that was stored using Unicode conventions, but raw numeric data (binary files such as images, media files, PDFs, etc.) classes for using streams of bytes are more suitable. Just for the purpose of showing you how it's done, we'll read the contents of the data.txt file using FileInputStream. The code is depicted in Listing 11-21.

Listing 11-21. Reading a File Using FileInputStream

```java
package com.apress.bgn.eleven.io;

import java.io.FileInputStream;
// other imports omitted

public class FileInputStreamReadingDemo {
    private static final Logger log = LoggerFactory.getLogger(FileInputStre
    amReadingDemo.class);

    public static void main(String... args) {
        File file = new File("chapter11/read-write-file/src/main/resources/
        input/data.txt");

        try {
            FileInputStream fis = new FileInputStream(file);
            byte[] buffer = new byte[1024];
            StringBuilder sb = new StringBuilder();
            while (fis.read(buffer) != -1) {
                sb.append(new String(buffer));
                buffer = new byte[1024];
            }
            fis.close();

            log.info("Read with FileInputStream --> {}", sb.toString() );
        } catch (IOException e) {
            log.error("Something went wrong! ", e);
        }
    }
}
```

If you run the previous code you will notice that in the console the expected output will be printed, but you might notice something strange: after the text is printed, a set of strange characters are printed too. On a macOS system they look as depicted in Figure 11-3.

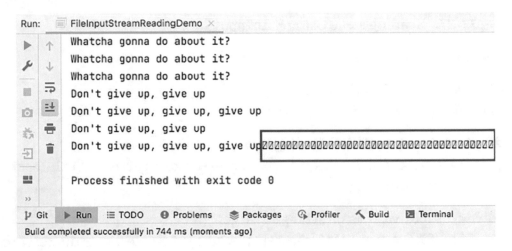

Figure 11-3. *Text read with* `FileInputStream`

Do you have any idea what those characters might be?

It's okay if you have no idea; I did not either the first time I had to use `FileInputStream` to read a file. Those characters appear there because the file size is not a multiple of 1024, so the `FileInputReader` ends up filling the rest of the last buffer with zeroes. A fix for this involves computing the size of the file in bytes and making sure we adapt the `byte[]` buffer size accordingly. You can try doing that as an exercise if you are in the mood for some coding. And now that we've shown you how to read file in a lot of ways, we can continue by showing you how to write files, since you already know how to create them.

In Java 11, the `InputStream` was also enriched with a method that returns an `InputStream` that does nothing. It is named `nullInputStream()` method and is designed for testing purposes and is nothing else but a pseudo-`InputStream` implementation.

All classes presented so far are the ones you will encounter most while working with files in Java. If you need more specialized readers feel free to read te official documentation or use custom implementation provided by third party libraries such as Apache Commons IO.[2]

---

[2] See the official page at Apache Commons, "Apache Commons IO," `https://commons.apache.org/proper/commons-io`, accessed October 15, 2021.

Writing Files

Writing files in Java is quite similar to reading them, only different classes have to be used, because streams are unidirectional. A stream that is used for reading data cannot be used for writing data as well. Almost for any class or method of reading files there is one for writing files. Without further ado, let's start.

Writing Files Using Files Utility Methods

Smaller files can be easily written starting with Java 1.7, using the `Files.write(Path, byte[], OpenOption... options)` method. It takes two arguments: a `Path` representing the location of a file and an array of bytes representing the data to be written. This method is a practical one-liner when the data required to be written is small enough. The last argument is actually a **Varargs** that was introduced in **Chapter 4** and represents none, one, or more operations the file is opened for. The method can be used without specifying any argument of that type as shown in Listing 11-22.

Listing 11-22. Writing a `String` to a File Starting with Java 1.7

```java
package com.apress.bgn.eleven.io;
// other import statements omitted
import java.io.File;
import java.io.IOException;
import java.nio.file.Files;
import java.nio.file.Path;

public class FilesWritingDemo {
    private static final Logger log = LoggerFactory.
    getLogger(FilesWritingDemo.class);

    public static void main(String... args) {
        var file = new File("chapter11/read-write-file/src/main/resources/
        output/data.txt");

        byte[] data = "Some of us, we're hardly ever here".getBytes();
        try {
            Path dataPath = Files.write(file.toPath(), data);
            log.info("String written to {}", dataPath.toAbsolutePath());
```

```
        } catch (IOException e) {
            e.printStackTrace();
        }
    }
}
```

If the file already exists, the contents will be simply overwritten. This means that since no argument was specified to configure what we want to do with the file, the default beavior was to open the file for writing and truncate its size to zero and start writing from there, thus overwriting it. The list of available options is modelled by the values in the `java.nio.file.StandardOpenOption` enum. The value corresponding to the default behavior is `TRUNCATE_EXISTING`. So this line in the previous example:

```
Path dataPath = Files.write(file.toPath(), data);
```

is equivalent to

```
import java.nio.file.StandardOpenOption
...
Path dataPath = Files.write(file.toPath(), data, StandardOpenOption.
TRUNCATE_EXISTING);
```

If the desired behavior is to modify a file if it exists and append the new data at its end, the option to use as argument for the `Files.write(..)` method is `APPEND`. `Path dataPath = Files.write(file.toPath(), data, StandardOpenOption.APPEND);`

Also, notice how the string needs to be converted to an array of bytes before being written. In Java 11 this is no longer necessary, because finally some JDK developer thought that most people would probably write a simple `String` to a file and forcing them to explicitly call `getBytes()` is pretty silly. As a result the `Files.writeString(..)` methods were introduced, and one of them also supports specifying an encoding. An example of this method being used to write a string into a file can be seen in Listing 11-23.

Listing 11-23. Writing a String to a File Starting with Java 11

```java
package com.apress.bgn.eleven.io;
// import statements omitted

public class FilesWritingDemo {
    private static final Logger log = LoggerFactory.
    getLogger(FilesWritingDemo.class);

    public static void main(String... args) {
        var file = new File("chapter11/read-write-file/src/main/resources/
        output/data.txt");
         try {
            Path dataPath = Files.writeString(file.toPath(),
                    "\nThe rest of us, we're born to disappear",
                    StandardCharsets.UTF_8,
                    APPEND);
            log.info("String written to {}", dataPath.toAbsolutePath());
        } catch (IOException e) {
            e.printStackTrace();
        }
    }
}
```

Another version of the Files.write(..) takes an argument of type Iterable<?
extends CharSequence> which means that a list of String valued can be written using it,
as shown in Listing 11-24.

Listing 11-24. Writing a List<String> to a File Using Files.write(..)

```java
package com.apress.bgn.eleven.io;
// import statements omitted

public class FilesWritingDemo {
    private static final Logger log = LoggerFactory.
    getLogger(FilesWritingDemo.class);
```

```java
    public static void main(String... args) {
        var file = new File("chapter11/read-write-file/src/main/resources/
        output/data.txt");

         List<String> dataList = List.of(
                "How do I stop myself from",
                "Being just a number?");
        try {
            Path dataPath = Files.write(file.toPath(), dataList,
                    StandardCharsets.UTF_8,
                    APPEND);
            log.info("String written to {}", dataPath.toAbsolutePath());
        } catch (IOException e) {
            e.printStackTrace();
        }
    }
}
```

Next we are going to look into writing files using classes in the Writer hierarchy.

Using Writer to Write Files

Similar to the Reader hierarchy for reading files, there is an abstract class named Writer, but before we get to that let's introduce the BufferedWriter, the correspondent of BufferedReader for writing file, because this is one of the most used in practice. This class too has an internal buffer, and when write methods are called the arguments are stored into the buffer, and when the buffer is full, its contents are written to the file. The buffer can be emptied earlier by calling the flush() method. It is definitely recommended to call this method explicitly before calling close() to make sure all output was written to the file. The code snippet in Listing 11-25 depicts how a list of String instances is written to a file.

Listing 11-25. Writing a List<String> to a File \Using BufferedWriter

```java
package com.apress.bgn.eleven.io;
// other import statements omitted
import java.io.BufferedWriter;
import java.io.FileWriter;
```

```java
public class FilesWritingDemo {
    private static final Logger log = LoggerFactory.
getLogger(FilesWritingDemo.class);

    public static void main(String... args) {
        var file = new File("chapter11/read-write-file/src/main/resources/
        output/data.txt");

        var dataList = List.of ("How will I hold my head" ,
                "To keep from going under");
        BufferedWriter writer = null;
        try {
            writer = new BufferedWriter(new FileWriter(file));
            for (String entry : dataList) {
                writer.write(entry);
                writer.newLine();
            }
        } catch (IOException e) {
            log.info("Something went wrong! ", e);
        } finally {
            if(writer!= null) {
                try {
                    writer.flush();
                    writer.close();
                } catch (IOException e) {
                    log.info("Something went wrong! ", e);
                }
            }
        }
    }
}
```

Yet another code contraption is needed, because writing files is a sensitive operation that can fail for many reasons. The code in the previous listing is what you had to write before Java 1.7, when try-with-resources reduced the boilerplate and allowed for the previous code to be reduced as shown in Listing 11-26.

Listing 11-26. Writing a List<String> to a File Using BufferedWriter

```
package com.apress.bgn.eleven.io;
// other import statements omitted
import java.io.BufferedWriter;
import java.io.FileWriter;

public class FilesWritingDemo {
    private static final Logger log = LoggerFactory.
getLogger(FilesWritingDemo.class);

    public static void main(String... args) {
        var file = new File("chapter11/read-write-file/src/main/resources/
        output/data.txt");

        var dataList = List.of ("How will I hold my head" ,
                "To keep from going under");
        try (final BufferedWriter wr = new BufferedWriter(new
        FileWriter(file))){
            dataList.forEach(entry -> {
                try {
                    wr.write(entry);
                    wr.newLine();
                } catch (IOException e) {
                    log.info("Something went wrong! ", e);
                }
            });
            wr.flush();
        } catch (IOException e) {
            log.info("Something went wrong! ", e);
        }
    }
}
```

Notice how there is no need to call wr.close(), because in Java 1.7 the java.io.Closeable interface was modified to extend java.lang.AutoCloseable, which declares a version of the close() method that is called automatically when exiting a try-with-resources block. Still, the code looks pretty stuffy, right? Especially since a

BufferedWriter needs to be declared and needs to be wrapped around a FileWriter instance. This was simplified in Java 1.8 with the addition of the Files utility class, which contains a method named newBufferedWriter(Path path) that returns a BufferedWriter instance so that the developer no longer has to write that code explicitly. So the initialization expression in the try-with-resources in Listing 11-26 can be replaced with:

```
final BufferedWriter wr = Files.newBufferedWriter(file.toPath())
```

Also, there is a version of this method taking a charset argument:

```
final BufferedWriter wr = Files.newBufferedWriter(file.
toPath(),StandardCharsets.UTF_8)
```

Before this method was introduced, writing text to a file with a specified charset required a java.io.OutputStreamWriter instance.

```
final OutputStreamWriter wr = new OutputStreamWriter(new
FileOutputStream(file), StandardCharsets.UTF_8)
```

There is also a version of this method taking an argument of type OpenOption that allows you to specify how the file should be opened.

```
final BufferedWriter wr = Files.newBufferedWriter(file.
toPath(),StandardCharsets.UTF_8, StandardOpenOption.APPEND)
```

This is very useful, since a BufferedWriter created explicitly (without specifying a file option) overrides an existing file, unless the FileWriter that is wrapped around is configured to append data to an existing file, as depicted here:

```
final BufferedWriter wr = new BufferedWriter(new FileWriter(file, true))
```

The second parameter is a boolean value representing if the file should be opened for appending text (true) or not(false).

Now that the basics of using BufferedWriter have been covered, it's time to meet he most useful members of the Writer family that are depicted in Figure 11-4.

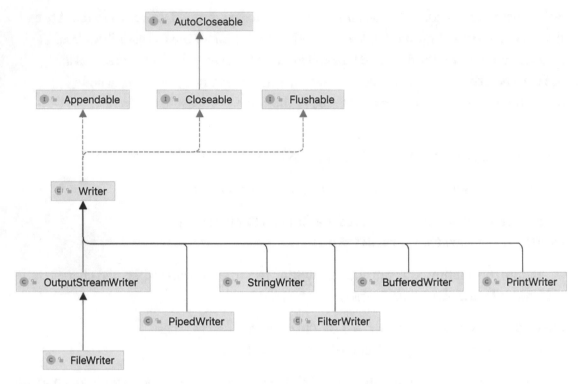

Figure 11-4. *The* Writer *class hierarchy*

The Writer class is abstract, so it cannot be used directly; the appending API comes from the java.io.Appendable interface that Writer implements. The other Writer classes are used for different purposes. As we've already seen, the OutputStreamWriter is used to write text using a special character encoding.

The PrintWriter is used to write formatted representations of objects to a text-output stream (we've already used it to write HTML code, in the previous chapter).

The StringWriter is used to collect output into its internal buffer and write it to a String instance.

In Java 11, the Writer class was enriched with the nullWriter() method, which returns a Writer instance that does nothing. This was requested by developers for testing purposes.

Using OutputStream to Write Files

Classes in the Writer family are advanced classes for writing data as text using character streams, but essentially, before data is written it is turned into bytes. This obviously means that files can be written by using stream of bytes as well. This probably became obvious when trying to use the proper character encoding when writing text using the OutputStreamWriter, as the OutputStreamWriter instance given as argument is based on a FileOutputStream instance, a type that is used to write byte streams to a file.

The root class of this hierarchy is java.io.OutputStream and the most common members of the hierarchy are depicted in Figure 11-5.

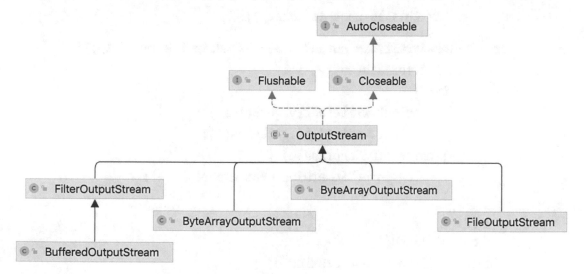

Figure 11-5. *The OutputStream class hierarchy*

Since FileOutputStream has been mentioned, Listing 11-27 shows how to use it to write a list of String entries.

Listing 11-27. Writing a List<String> to a File Using FileOutputStream

```
package com.apress.bgn.eleven.io;
// other import statements omitted
import java.io.FileNotFoundException;
import java.io.FileOutputStream;
```

```java
public class OutputStreamWritingDemo {
    private static final Logger log = LoggerFactory.getLogger(OutputStreamW
    ritingDemo.class);

    public static void main(String... args) {
        var file = new File("chapter11/read-write-file/src/main/resources/
        output/data.txt");

        var dataList = List.of("Down to the wire" ,
                "I wanted water but" ,
                "I'll walk through the fire" ,
                "If this is what it takes");

        try (FileOutputStream output = new FileOutputStream(file)){
            dataList.forEach(entry -> {
                try {
                    output.write(entry.getBytes());
                    output.write("\n".getBytes());
                } catch (IOException e) {
                    log.info("Something went wrong! ", e);
                }
            });
            output.flush();
        } catch (FileNotFoundException e) {
            log.info("Something went wrong! ", e);
        } catch (IOException e) {
            e.printStackTrace();
        }
    }
}
```

The OutputStream family class is used for writing streams of bytes which represent raw data, unreadable by users directly, such as the one contained in binary files like images, media, PDFs, and so on. For example, the code in Listing 11-28 makes a copy of an image using FileInputStream to read it and FileOutputStream to write the copy.

Listing 11-28. Making a Copy of an Image File Using FileOutputStream

```java
package com.apress.bgn.eleven.io;
// other import statements missing
import java.io.*;

public class DuplicateImageDemo {
    private static final Logger log = LoggerFactory.
    getLogger(DuplicateImageDemo.class);

    public static void main(String... args) {
        File src = new File(
                "chapter11/read-write-file/src/main/resources/input/the-
                beach.jpg");
        File dest = new File(
                "chapter11/read-write-file/src/main/resources/output/copy-
                the-beach.jpg");
        try(FileInputStream fis = new FileInputStream(src);
            FileOutputStream fos = new FileOutputStream(dest)) {
            int content;
            while ((content = fis.read()) != -1) {
                fos.write(content);
            }
        } catch (FileNotFoundException e) {
            log.error("Something bad happened.", e);
        } catch (IOException e) {
            log.error("Something bad happened.", e);
        }
    }
}
```

However, writing code like this is no longer necessary, thanks to the introduction of the Files.copy(src.toPath(), dest.toPath()) method in Java 1.7.

In Java 11, the OutputStream was enriched with the nullOutputStream() method that returns a OutputStream instance that does nothing. This was requested by developers for testing purposes and is designed for testing purposes and is nothing else but a pseudo-OutputStream implementation.

Using NIO to Manage Files

The java.nio package was introduced at the beginning of the chapter in comparison with the java.io package. Most classes and methods used up to this section of this book were part of the java.io package and blocked the main thread while the data was read/written. The utility classes java.nio.file.Paths and java.nio.file.Files introduced in previous section contain methods that make use of classes in the java.nio package as well as in the java.io package. It is time to show you how to manipulate files using java.nio classes as well.

Manipulating a file using java.nio requires an instance of java.nio.channels.FileChannel. This a special abstract class that describes a channel for reading, writing, mapping, and manipulating a file. A FileChannel instance is connected to a file and holds a position within a file that can be queried and modified.

To read data from a file using a FileChannel instance the following are needed:

- A file handler instance

- A FileInputStream instance the channel is based on

- A FileChannel instance

- A java.nio.Buffer instance

Being nonblocking, a thread can ask a channel to read data from a buffer and then do other things, until the data is available. Java NIO's buffers allow moving back and forth in the buffer as needed. The data is read into a buffer and cached there until is processed. There are buffer implementations for all primitive types in the java.nio package and depending on the purpose of the data you can use any of them. Listing 11-29 shows how to read data from a file into a ByteBuffer. Since the ByteBuffer can be instantiated with an initial size, by configuring the ByteBuffer catacity in bytes to be the same as the file size, the file can be read in one go.

Listing 11-29. Reading a file Using FileChannel Using a ByteBuffer

```
package com.apress.bgn.eleven.nio;
// other import statements omitted
import java.nio.ByteBuffer;
import java.nio.channels.FileChannel;
```

```java
public class ChannelDemo {
    private static final Logger log = LoggerFactory.
    getLogger(ChannelDemo.class);

    public static void main(String... args) {
        var sb = new StringBuilder();
        try (FileInputStream is = new FileInputStream("chapter11/read-
        write-file/src/main/resources/input/data.txt");
            FileChannel inChannel = is.getChannel()) {
            long fileSize = inChannel.size();
            ByteBuffer buffer = ByteBuffer.allocate((int)fileSize);
            inChannel.read(buffer);
            buffer.flip();
            while(buffer.hasRemaining()){
                sb.append((char) buffer.get());
            }
        } catch (IOException e) {
            log.error("File could not be read! ", e);
        }
        log.info("Read with FileChannel --> {}", sb.toString());
    }
}
```

The method getChannel() returns the unique FileChannel object associated with this file input stream. The most important statement in the previous code sample is the buffer.flip() call. Calling this method *flips the buffer*, meaning that a buffer is switched from writing mode to reading mode. This means initially the channel is the able to write data in the buffer because it is in writing mode, but after the buffer is full the buffer is switched to reading mode, so the main thread can read its contents.

After reading the contents of a buffer, if there is need to do it again, the buffer. rewind() method sets the position to zero.

If the file is big the ByteBuffer can be reinitialized multiple times, but in this case the buffer must be cleared before new data is written by the channel, and this can be done by calling buffer.close(). Also, using a FileInputStream to obtain a channel is not the correct way to do it, since it limits it to reading from the file. But a channel can both read and write from a file, so the recommended way is to use a java.io.RandomAccessFile instance as a file handler, as depicted in Listing 11-30.

Listing 11-30. Reading a File Using FileChannel Using a Smaller ByteBuffer

```java
package com.apress.bgn.eleven.nio;
// other import statements omitted
import java.io.RandomAccessFile;
import java.nio.ByteBuffer;
import java.nio.channels.FileChannel;

public class ChannelDemo {
    private static final Logger log = LoggerFactory.
    getLogger(ChannelDemo.class);

    public static void main(String... args) {
        var sb = new StringBuilder();
        sb = new StringBuilder();
        try (RandomAccessFile file = new RandomAccessFile("chapter11/read-
        write-file/src/main/resources/input/data.txt", "r");
            FileChannel inChannel = file.getChannel()) {

            ByteBuffer buffer = ByteBuffer.allocate(48);
            while(inChannel.read(buffer) > 0) {
                buffer.flip();
                for (int i = 0; i < buffer.limit(); i++) {
                    sb.append((char) buffer.get());
                }
                buffer.clear();
            }
        } catch (IOException e) {
            log.error("File could not be read! ", e);
        }
        log.info("Read with FileChannel --> {}", sb.toString());
    }
}
```

Making a copy of a file is simple as well; it's just about moving the data from a channel to another using a buffer, as shown in Listing 11-31.

Listing 11-31. Duplicating an Image Using `FileChannel` and a `ByteBuffer`

```java
package com.apress.bgn.eleven.nio;
// other import statements omitted
import java.nio.ByteBuffer;
import java.nio.channels.FileChannel;

public class DuplicateImageDemo {
    private static final Logger log = LoggerFactory.
    getLogger(DuplicateImageDemo.class);

    public static void main(String... args){
        final String inDir = "chapter11/read-write-file/src/main/resources/
        input/";
        final String outDir = "chapter11/read-write-file/src/main/
        resources/output/";
        try(FileChannel source =
                    new RandomAccessFile(inDir + "the-beach.jpg", "r").
                    getChannel();
                FileChannel dest =
                    new RandomAccessFile(outDir + "copy-the-beach.jpg",
                    "rw").getChannel()) {
            ByteBuffer buffer = ByteBuffer.allocateDirect(48);
            while (source.read(buffer) != -1) {
                buffer.flip();
                while (buffer.hasRemaining()) {
                    dest.write(buffer);
                }
                buffer.clear();
            }
        } catch (Exception e) {
            log.error("Image could not be copied! ", e);
        }
    }
}
```

Another way to do it is to use dedicated ReadableByteChannel and WritableByteChannel, as shown in listing 11-32.

Listing 11-32. Duplicating an Image Using ReadableByteChannel and a ByteBuffer

```java
package com.apress.bgn.eleven.nio;
// other import statements omitted
import java.nio.channels.ReadableByteChannel;
import java.nio.channels.WritableByteChannel;

public class DuplicateImageDemo {
    private static final Logger log = LoggerFactory.
getLogger(DuplicateImageDemo.class);

    public static void main(String... args){
        final String inDir = "chapter11/read-write-file/src/main/resources/
        input/";
        final String outDir = "chapter11/read-write-file/src/main/
        resources/output/";
        try(ReadableByteChannel source = new FileInputStream (inDir + "the-
        beach.jpg").getChannel();
            WritableByteChannel dest = new FileOutputStream (outDir + "2nd-
            copy-the-beach.jpg").getChannel()) {
            ByteBuffer buffer = ByteBuffer.allocateDirect(48);
            while (source.read(buffer) != -1) {
                buffer.flip();
                while (buffer.hasRemaining()) {
                    dest.write(buffer);
                }
                buffer.clear();
            }
        } catch (Exception e) {
            log.error("Image could not be copied! ", e);
        }
    }
}
```

Because of their nonblocking nature, Java channels are suitable for applications that handle data provided by multiple sources. Such us applications that manage connections with multiple sources over a network. Figure 11-6 depicts the most important members of the Channel hierarchy.

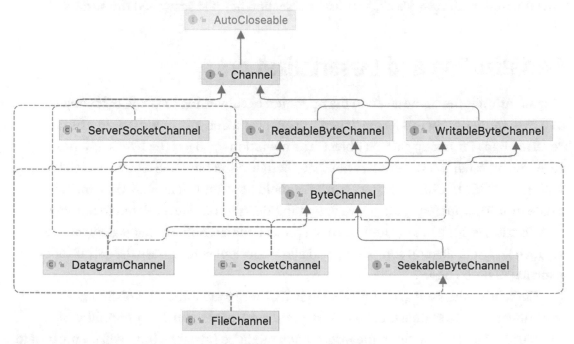

Figure 11-6. *The channel class/interface hierarchy (as shown in IntelliJ IDEA)*

The DatagramChannel can read and write data over the network via UDP. The SocketChannel can read and write data over the network via TCP and the ServerSocketChannel allows you to listen for incoming TCP connections, like a web server does. For each incoming connection a SocketChannel is created.

The NIO components (interfaces and classes) were introduced to complement existing IO functionality. Java IO reads or writes one byte or character at a time. Buffering makes used of Java Heap memeory which can become problematic when files of considerable sizes are used. When NIO was released there was a statement that NI0 was more efficient and had better performance than pure Java I/O, but it all depends on the application you are trying to build. NIO introduces the possibility to handle raw bytes in bulk, the possibility of asynchronous operations, and off-heap buffering. Buffers are created outside the central memory of the JVM, in portions of memory not handled by the garbage collector. This allows for larger buffers to be created, so bigger files can be read without the danger of an OutOfMemoryException being thrown because the JVM is out of memory.

If you ever find yourself needing to handle a lot of data make sure to read the JDK NIO documentation very well, because this section has just scratched the surface.

Serialization and Deserialization

Serialization is the name given to the operation of converting the state of an object to a byte sequence. In this format it can be sent over a network or written to a file and reverted back into a copy of that object. The operation to covert the byte sequence back to an object is named **Deserialization**. Java Serialization has been a controversial topic, with Java Platform Chief Architect Mark Reinhold describing it as a horrible mistake made in 1997. Apparently most Java vulnerabilities are somehow related to the way serialization is done in Java, and there is a project named Amber[3] that is dedicated to remove Java serialization completely and allow developers to choose the serialization in a format of their choice.

Currently things are quite unstable in JAVA; there were quite a lot of changes introduced in a short time that an industry addicted to backward compatibility was unable to adapt to. Sources in the next section might be unstable, but I will do my best to keep them at least compilable by the time the book is published and I will maintain the repository and answer questions as much as possible.

Byte Serialization

The java.io.Serializable interface has no methods or fields and serves only to mark classes as being serializable. When an object is serialized, the information that identifies the object type is serialized as well. Most Java classes are serializable. Any subclass of a serializable class is by default considered serializable. If any fields are nonserializable then an exception of type NotSerializableException will be thrown. Classes written by developers that contain nonserializable fields must implement the

---

[3] See the Project Amber official page at OpenJDK, http://openjdk.java.net/projects/amber, accessed October 15, 2021.

Serializable interface and provide a concrete implementation for the methods shown in Listing 11-33.

Listing 11-33. Methods That Need to Be Emplemented to Make a Custom Class Serializable

```
private void writeObject(java.io.ObjectOutputStream out)
    throws IOException;
private void readObject(java.io.ObjectInputStream in)
    throws IOException, ClassNotFoundException;
private void readObjectNoData()
    throws ObjectStreamException;
```

These are not methods that are part of a specific Java interface, so implementing them in this context just means writing a body for them in the class you want to make serializable. The reason they were grouped in the previous listing, was to depict the signatures of these methods.

The writeObject(..) method is used for writing the state of the object, so that the readObject(..) method can restore it. The readObjectNoData() method is used to initialize the state of the object when the deserialization operation failed for some reason, so this method provides a default state despite the issues (e.g., incomplete stream, client application does not recognize the deserialized class, etc.). This method is not really mandatory, if you are an optimist.

Also, when making a class serializabile, a static field of type long must be added as a unique identifier for the class to make sure both the application that sends the object as a byte stream and the client application receiving it have the same loaded classes. If the application that receives the byte stream has a class with a different identifier, a java.io.InvalidClassException will be thrown. When this happens it means that the application was not updated, or you might even suspect some foul play from a hacker. The field has to be named serialVersionUID, and if the developer does not explicitly add one, the serialization runtime will. The following code snippet in Listing 11-34 depicts a class named Singer that contains serialization and deserialization methods mentioned in the previous code snippet.

Listing 11-34. Serializable Singer Class

```java
package com.apress.bgn.eleven;

import java.io.*;
import java.time.LocalDate;
import java.util.Objects;

public class Singer  implements Serializable {
    private static final long serialVersionUID = 42L;

    private String name;

    private Double rating;

    private LocalDate birthDate;

    public Singer() {
        /* required for deserialization */
    }

    public Singer(String name, Double rating, LocalDate birthDate) {
        this.name = name;
        this.rating = rating;
        this.birthDate = birthDate;
    }

    private void writeObject(ObjectOutputStream out) throws IOException {
        out.defaultWriteObject();
    }

    private void readObject(ObjectInputStream in) throws IOException,
    ClassNotFoundException {
        in.defaultReadObject();
    }

    private void readObjectNoData() throws ObjectStreamException {
        this.name = "undefined";
        this.rating = 0.0;
        this.birthDate = LocalDate.now();
    }
```

```java
    @Override
    public String toString() {
        return "Singer{" +
                "name='" + name + '\'' +
                ", rating=" + rating +
                ", birthDate=" + birthDate +
                '}';
    }

    @Override
    public boolean equals(Object o) {
        if (this == o) return true;
        if (o == null || getClass() != o.getClass()) return false;
        Singer singer = (Singer) o;
        return Objects.equals(name, singer.name) &&
                Objects.equals(rating, singer.rating) &&
                Objects.equals(birthDate, singer.birthDate);
    }

    @Override
    public int hashCode() {
        return Objects.hash(name, rating, birthDate);
    }
}
```

Now that we have the class, let's instantiate it, serialize it, save it to a file, and then deserialize the contents of the file into another object that we will compare with the initial object. All these operations are depicted in Listing 11-35.

Listing 11-35. Serializing and Deserializing a Singer Class

```java
package com.apress.bgn.eleven;

import org.slf4j.Logger;
import org.slf4j.LoggerFactory;

import java.io.*;
import java.time.LocalDate;
import java.time.Month;
```

```
public class SerializationDemo {
    private static final Logger log = LoggerFactory.
    getLogger(SerializationDemo.class);

    public static void main(String... args) throws ClassNotFoundException {
        LocalDate johnBd = LocalDate.of(1977, Month.OCTOBER, 16);
        Singer john = new Singer("John Mayer", 5.0, johnBd);
        File file = new File("chapter11/serialization/src/test/resources/
        output/john.txt");
        try (var out = new ObjectOutputStream(new FileOutputStream(file))){
            out.writeObject(john);
        } catch (IOException e) {
            log.info("Something went wrong! ", e);
        }
        try(var in = new ObjectInputStream(new FileInputStream(file))){
            Singer copyOfJohn = (Singer) in.readObject();
            log.info("Are objects equal? {}", copyOfJohn.equals(john));
            log.info("--> {}", copyOfJohn);
        } catch (IOException e) {
            log.info("Something went wrong! ", e);
        }
    }
}
```

When the previous code is run, everything works as expected, and the
writeObject(..) and the readObject(..) are called by the ObjectOutputStream,
ObjectInputStream respectively. If you want to test that they are actually called you can
add logging, or you can place breakpoints inside them and run the program in debug. If
you open the john.txt you won't be able to understand much. The text written in there
does not make much sense, because it is binary, raw data. If you open the file, you might
see something like what is depicted in Figure 11-7.

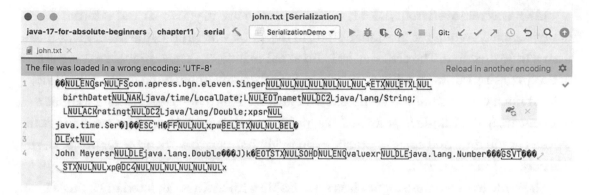

Figure 11-7. *Serialized Singer instance*

XML Serialization

Java serialization does not have to result in cryptic files, however. Objects can be serialized to readable formats. One of the most-used serialization formats is XML, and JDK provides classes to convert objects to XML and from XML back to the initial object. **Java Architecture for XML Binding (JAXB)** used to provide a fast and convenient way to bind XML schemas and Java representations, making it easy for Java developers to incorporate XML data and processing functions in Java applications. The operation to serialize an object to XML is named **marshalling**. The operation to deserialize an object form XML is named **unmarshalling**. For a class to be serializable to XML, it has to be decorated with JAXB specific annotations:

- @XmlRootElement(name = "...") is a top level annotation that is placed at class level to tell JAXB that the class name will become an XML element at serialization time; if a different name is needed for the XML element, it can be specified via the name attribute.

- @XmlElement(name = "..") is a method or field level annotation that is used to tell JAXB that the field or method name will become an XML element at serialization time; if a different name is needed for the XML element, it can be specified via the name attribute.

- @XmlAttribute(name = "..") is a method or field level annotation that is used to tell JAXB that the field or method name will become an XML attribute at serialization time; if a different name is needed for the XML attribute, it can be specified via the name attribute.

JAXB was removed from JDK 11, so if you want to use it, you must add external dependencies.[4] When the previous edition of this book was written, the library was more than a little unstable. The `com.sun.xml.internal.bind.v2.ContextFactory` was part of the `jaxb-impl` library which could not be found on any public repository at the time, at least not a version that was compiled with Java 11. This made configuring modules a pain because of multiple dependencies exporting the same packages. However, the code worked at the time and since in practice you might happen to work on older projects, so it is good to know it exists.

The code to make the `Singer` class serializable with JAXB is depicted in Listing 11-36. Notice how the annotations listed previously are used on the class header and class public getters.

Listing 11-36. A Singer Class with JAXB Annotations

```java
package com.apress.bgn.eleven.xml;

import javax.xml.bind.annotation.XmlAttribute;
import javax.xml.bind.annotation.XmlElement;
import javax.xml.bind.annotation.XmlRootElement;
import java.io.Serializable;
import java.time.LocalDate;
import java.util.Objects;

@XmlRootElement(name = "singer")
public class Singer implements Serializable {
    private static final long serialVersionUID = 42L;

    private String name;

    private Double rating;

    private LocalDate birthDate;

    public Singer() {
        /* required for deserialization */
    }
```

---

[4] Its successor, JAXB2 is now part of JEE; see Java Enterprise Edition, JAXB," https://javaee.github.io/jaxb-v2/, accessed October 15, 2021.

```java
public Singer(String name, Double rating, LocalDate birthDate) {
    this.name = name;
    this.rating = rating;
    this.birthDate = birthDate;
}

@XmlAttribute(name = "name")
public String getName() {
    return name;
}

@XmlAttribute(name = "rating")
public Double getRating() {
    return rating;
}

@XmlElement(name = "birthdate")
public LocalDate getBirthDate() {
    return birthDate;
}
// other code omitted
}
```

Listing 11-37 depicts the code needed to serialize an instance of the Singer class.

Listing 11-37. Marshalling and Unmarshalling a Singer Class with JAXB

```java
package com.apress.bgn.eleven.xml;
// other imports omitted
import javax.xml.bind.JAXBContext;
import javax.xml.bind.JAXBException;
import javax.xml.bind.Marshaller;
import javax.xml.bind.Unmarshaller;

public class JAXBSerializationDemo {

    private static final Logger log = LoggerFactory.
    getLogger(JAXBSerializationDemo.class);
```

```
public static void main(String... args) throws ClassNotFoundException,
JAXBException {
    LocalDate johnBd = LocalDate.of(1977, Month.OCTOBER, 16);
    Singer john = new Singer("John Mayer", 5.0, johnBd);

    File file = new File("chapter11/serialization/src/main/resources/
    output/john.xml");
    JAXBContext jaxbContext = JAXBContext.newInstance(Singer.class);

    try {
        Marshaller marshaller = jaxbContext.createMarshaller();
        marshaller.setProperty(Marshaller.JAXB_FORMATTED_OUTPUT, true);
        marshaller.marshal(john, file);
    } catch (Exception e) {
        log.info("Something went wrong! ", e);
    }

    try {
        Unmarshaller unmarshaller = jaxbContext.createUnmarshaller();
        Singer copyOfJohn = (Singer) unmarshaller.unmarshal(file);
        log.info("Are objects equal? {}", copyOfJohn.equals(john));
        log.info("--> {}", copyOfJohn.toString());
    } catch (Exception e) {
        log.info("Something went wrong! ", e);
    }
}
}
```

Using JAXB with JDK 17 is not an option, because the community library has been unmaintained since 2018. A choice was made to introduce XML serialization in this edition of book using one of the most stable, versatile, and up-to-date libraries: Jackson.[5]

Jackson has been known for quite a wile in the Java ecosystem as the ultimate Java JSON library, but it has modules that support serialization to quite a few formats, among them XML, JSON, CSV, TAML, and YAML. Just check the project page; chances are that

---

[5] See the official page at Github, "FasterXML Jackson," https://github.com/FasterXML/jackson, accessed October 15, 2021.

if there is a new catchy serialization format emerging, there might already be a module for that.

There are a few things to keep in mind when serializing to XML using Jackson.

- there is a different set of annotations to use, the most important are listed here:

  - `@JacksonXmlRootElement(localName = "...")` is a top level annotation that is placed at class level to tell Jackson that the class name will become an XML element at serialization time; if a different name is needed for the XML element, it can be specified via the `localName` attribute.

  - `@JacksonXmlProperty(localName = "...")` is a method or field level annotation that is used to tell Jackson that the field or method name will become an XML element at serialization time; if a different name is needed for the XML element, it can be specified via the `localName` attribute.

  - `@JacksonXmlProperty(localName = "...", isAttribute = true)` with the `isAttribute = true` parameter is used when the property is configured to become an XML attribute.

- to serialize and deserialize with Jackson, an instance of `com.fasterxml.jackson.dataformat.xml.XmlMapper` is used.

- the `XmlMapper` instance has to be configured to support special types such as the new Java 8 Date API types, and this is done by registering and configuring the `com.fasterxml.jackson.datatype.jsr310.JavaTimeModule`.

- when using Java modules you have to make sure they are configured correctly. Exceptions will not always be easy to read and solving them might require a combination of Maven and module configuration to solve.

This being said, let's start with the modules configuration shown in Listing 11-38.

Listing 11-38. Module Configuration for XML Serialization with Jackson

```
module chapter.eleven.serialization {
    requires org.slf4j;
    requires com.fasterxml.jackson.databind;
    requires com.fasterxml.jackson.dataformat.xml;
    requires com.fasterxml.jackson.datatype.jsr310;

    opens com.apress.bgn.eleven.xml to com.fasterxml.jackson.databind;
}
```

The first two requires com.fasterxml.jackson.* directives are needed so that Jackson annotations and XmlMapper can be used. The jsr310 is required for serialization of Java 8 Date API types.

The last statement opens com.apress.bgn.eleven.xml to com.fasterxml.jackson.databind is necessary so that Jackson can access the classes in package com.apress.bgn.eleven.xml, because that is where the version of the Singer class written using the Jackson annotation is located. The class is depicted in Listing 11-39.

Listing 11-39. A Singer Class with Jackson XML Annotations

```
package com.apress.bgn.eleven.xml;
// other imports omitted
import com.fasterxml.jackson.dataformat.xml.annotation.JacksonXmlProperty;
import com.fasterxml.jackson.dataformat.xml.annotation.
JacksonXmlRootElement;

@JacksonXmlRootElement(localName = "singer")
public class Singer implements Serializable {
    private static final long serialVersionUID = 42L;

    private String name;

    private Double rating;

    private LocalDate birthDate;

    public Singer() {
        /* required for deserialization */
    }
```

```java
public Singer(String name, Double rating, LocalDate birthDate) {
    this.name = name;
    this.rating = rating;
    this.birthDate = birthDate;
}

@JacksonXmlProperty(localName = "name", isAttribute = true)
public String getName() {
    return name;
}

@JacksonXmlProperty(localName = "rating", isAttribute = true)
public Double getRating() {
    return rating;
}

@JacksonXmlProperty(localName = "birthdate")
public LocalDate getBirthDate() {
    return birthDate;
}
// other code omitted
}
```

Notice the location where the annotations were placed. Based on the placement of the annotations and their configurations in the previous code when the john object is serialized, the john.xml file is expected to contain the snippet depicted in Listing 11-40.

Listing 11-40. The john Singer Instance in XML Format

```xml
<singer name="John Mayer" rating="5.0">
  <birthdate>1977-10-16</birthdate>
</singer>
```

More readable than the binary version, right? Listing 11-41 depicts the code that saves the Singer instance to the john.xml file, and then it loads it back into a copy and then the two instances are compared.

Listing 11-41. Serializing and Deserializing a Singer Class with Jackson's
`XmlMapper`

```java
package com.apress.bgn.eleven.xml;
// some import statements omitted
import com.fasterxml.jackson.databind.SerializationFeature;
import com.fasterxml.jackson.dataformat.xml.XmlMapper;
import com.fasterxml.jackson.datatype.jsr310.JavaTimeModule;

public class XMLSerializationDemo {

    private static final Logger log = LoggerFactory.
    getLogger(XMLSerializationDemo.class);

    public static void main(String... args) {
        LocalDate johnBd = LocalDate.of(1977, Month.OCTOBER, 16);
        Singer john = new Singer("John Mayer", 5.0, johnBd);

        var xmlMapper = new XmlMapper();
        xmlMapper.registerModule(new JavaTimeModule());
        xmlMapper.configure(SerializationFeature.WRITE_DATES_AS_
        TIMESTAMPS, false);
        xmlMapper.enable(SerializationFeature.INDENT_OUTPUT);

        try {
            String xml = xmlMapper.writeValueAsString(john);
            Files.writeString(Path.of("chapter11/serialization/src/test/
            resources/output/john.xml"), xml,
                    StandardCharsets.UTF_8);
        } catch (Exception e) {
            log.info("Serialization to XML failed! ", e);
        }

        try {
            Singer copyOfJohn = xmlMapper.readValue(Path.of("chapter11/
            serialization/src/test/resources/output/john.xml").toFile(),
            Singer.class);
            log.info("Are objects equal? {}", copyOfJohn.equals(john));
            log.info("--> {}", copyOfJohn);
```

```
        } catch (IOException e) {
            log.info("Deserialization of XML failed! ", e);
        }
    }
}
```

The XmlMapper instance can be used to serialize any class in the project that contains Jackson annotations. In the previous example it is also configured to support default serialization of Java 8 Date API types and keep types readable, by not converting them to numeric time stamps using the following two lines:

```
xmlMapper.registerModule(new JavaTimeModule());
xmlMapper.configure(SerializationFeature.WRITE_DATES_AS_TIMESTAMPS, false);
```

Since the chosen format is XML it would look pretty ugly if all of it was written in a single line, so indented formatting is supported using this statement `xmlMapper.enable(SerializationFeature.INDENT_OUTPUT)`.

XML serialization has been dominating the development field for many years, being used in most web services and remote communication. However, XML files tend to become crowded, redundant, and painful to read as they become bigger, so a new format stole the show: JSON.

JSON Serialization

JSON (JavaScript Object Notation) is a lightweight data-interchange format. It is readable for humans and is easy for machines to parse and generate. JSON is the favorite format for data being used in JavaScript applications, for REST based applications, and the internal format used by quite a few NoSQL databases. Therefore it is only appropriate that we show you how to serialize/deserialize Java objects using this format as well. The advantage of serializing Java objects to JSON is that there is more than one library providing classes to do so, which means at least one of them is stable with Java 9+ versions.

JSON format is in essence a collection of key-pair values. The values can be arrays, or collection of key-pairs themselves. The most preferred library for JSON serialization is the Jackson library as well, because it can convert Java objects to JSON objects and back again without much code being needed to be written. The best part for this chapter is that the same module configuration can be used for JSON too. All we need is to just change the annotations used and change the type of mapper used to do the serialization/deserialization. Jackson supports a multitude of annotation for JSON Serialization, but for the simple example in this book, we don't really need any. A Jackson `com.fasterxml.jackson.databind.json.JsonMapper` instance is smart enough to auto-detect the publicly accessible properties (public fields, or private fields with public getters) of a class and use them when serializing/deserializing instances of this class.

The `@JsonAutoDetect` annotation from the package `com.fasterxml.jackson.annotation` can be used to annotate a class. It can be configured to tell the mapper which class members should be serialized. There are a few options, grouped in the `Visibility` enum declared within the annotation body:

- ANY all kinds of access modifiers (public, protected, private) are auto-detected.

- NON_PRIVATE all modifiers except `private` are auto-detected.

- PROTECTED_AND_PUBLIC, only `protected` and `public` modifiers are auto-detected.

- PUBLIC_ONLY only `public` modifiers are auto-detected.

- NONE disable auto-detection for fields or methods. In this case configuration has to be done explicitly using `@JsonProperty` annotations on fields.

- DEFAULT defult rules apply, depending on the context (sometimes inherited from a parent).

This single annotation placed on the `Singer` class combined with the proper mapper and the `JavaTimeModule` ensures that an instance of `Singer` class can be serialized to JSON correctly; and also deserialized from JSON. Listing 11-42 shows the simple configuration of the `Singer` class (even if redundant).

Listing 11-42. Annotating a `Singer` Class with Jackson `@JsonAutoDetect` Just to Show How It's Done

```
package com.apress.bgn.eleven.json;
// some import statements omitted
import com.fasterxml.jackson.annotation.JsonAutoDetect;
```

```java
@JsonAutoDetect(getterVisibility = JsonAutoDetect.Visibility.PUBLIC_ONLY)
public class Singer  implements Serializable {
    private static final long serialVersionUID = 42L;
    private String name;
    private Double rating;
    private LocalDate birthDate;

    public String getName() { // auto-detected
        return name;
    }

    public Double getRating() { // auto-detected
        return rating;
    }

    public LocalDate getBirthDate() { // auto-detected
        return birthDate;
    }
    // other code omitted
}
```

For serializing a Singer instance, an instance of JsonMapper is needed. This class was introduced in Jackson version 2.10. Up to that version the com.fasterxml.jackson. databind. ObjectMapper was used for the same purpose. ObjectMapper is intended to become the root class for all mappers in future versions. The XmlMapper used in the previous section extends ObjectMapper too. The JsonMapper is a JSON-format specific ObjectMapper implementation and is intended to replace the generic implementation and Listing 11-43 depicts an example how it can be used to serialize/deserialize a Singer instance.

Listing 11-43. Serializing and Deserializing a Singer Class with Jackson's JsonMapper

```java
package com.apress.bgn.eleven.json;
// other import statements omitted
import com.apress.bgn.eleven.xml.Singer;
import com.fasterxml.jackson.databind.SerializationFeature;
import com.fasterxml.jackson.databind.json.JsonMapper;
```

```java
import com.fasterxml.jackson.datatype.jsr310.JavaTimeModule;

public class JSONSerializationDemo {
    private static final Logger log = LoggerFactory.
getLogger(JSONSerializationDemo.class);

    public static void main(String... args) {
        LocalDate johnBd = LocalDate.of(1977, Month.OCTOBER, 16);
        com.apress.bgn.eleven.xml.Singer john = new Singer("John Mayer",
        5.0, johnBd);

        JsonMapper jsonMapper = new JsonMapper();
        jsonMapper.registerModule(new JavaTimeModule());
        jsonMapper.enable(SerializationFeature.INDENT_OUTPUT);
        jsonMapper.configure(SerializationFeature.WRITE_DATES_AS_
        TIMESTAMPS, false);

        try {
            String xml = jsonMapper.writeValueAsString(john);
            Files.writeString(Path.of("chapter11/serialization/src/test/
            resources/output/john.json"), xml,
                    StandardCharsets.UTF_8);
        } catch (Exception e) {
            log.info("Serialization to XML failed! ", e);
        }

        try {
            Singer copyOfJohn = jsonMapper.readValue(Path.of("chapter11/
            serialization/src/test/resources/output/john.json").toFile(),
            Singer.class);
            log.info("Are objects equal? {}", copyOfJohn.equals(john));
            log.info("--> {}", copyOfJohn);
        } catch (IOException e) {
            log.info("Deserialization of XML failed! ", e);
        }
    }
}
```

As you can see, except fir the type of mapper user, not much in this code sample has changed when making the switch from XML. Jackson is pretty great, right?

The field birthDate in clas Singer is of type java.time.LocalDate. Registering the JavaTimeModule allows control over how this type of fields is serialized/deserialized at the mapper level. The other way to do it, is to declare a custom serializer and deserializer class for this type of data and configure them to be used by annotating the birthDate with the @JsonSerialize and @JsonDeserialize annotation. Listing 11-44 shows the custom serializer and deserializer classes configured on the birthdate field.

Listing 11-44. Configuring Custom Serialization and Deserialization for java.time.LocalDate Fields

```
package com.apress.bgn.eleven.json2;
// other import statements omitted
import com.fasterxml.jackson.databind.annotation.JsonDeserialize;
import com.fasterxml.jackson.databind.annotation.JsonSerialize;

@JsonAutoDetect(getterVisibility = JsonAutoDetect.Visibility.PUBLIC_ONLY)
public class Singer  implements Serializable {
    private static final long serialVersionUID = 42L;

    private String name;

    private Double rating;

    @JsonSerialize(converter = LocalDateTimeToStringConverter.class)
    @JsonDeserialize(converter = StringToLocalDatetimeConverter.class)
    private LocalDate birthDate;
    // other code omitted
}
```

Listing 11-45 shows the custom implementation of two serializer and deserializer classes.

Listing 11-45. Custom Serialization and Deserialization Classes

```java
package com.apress.bgn.eleven.json2;

import com.fasterxml.jackson.databind.util.StdConverter;
import java.time.LocalDateTime;
import java.time.format.DateTimeFormatter;
import java.time.format.FormatStyle;

class LocalDateTimeToStringConverter extends StdConverter<LocalDateTime,
String> {
    static final DateTimeFormatter DATE_FORMATTER = DateTimeFormatter.
    ofLocalizedDateTime(FormatStyle.LONG);
    @Override
    public String convert(LocalDateTime value) {
        return value.format(DATE_FORMATTER);
    }
}

class StringToLocalDatetimeConverter extends StdConverter<String,
LocalDateTime> {
    @Override
    public LocalDateTime convert(String value) {
        return LocalDateTime.parse(value, LocalDateTimeToStringConverter.
DATE_FORMATTER);
    }
}
```

This is all that can be said about JSON serialization with Jackson. Feel free to read more yourself if this subject looks appealing to you.

ⓘ There is also a Jackson library for serializing Java instances to YAML, which is *the* new boy in town when it comes to configuration files. The library is named `jackson-dataformat-yaml`.

The Media API

Beside text data, Java can be used to manipulate binary files such as images. The Java Media API contains a set of image encoder/decoder (codec) classes for several popular image storage formats: BMP, GIF (decoder only), FlashPix (decoder only), JPEG, PNG, PNM3, TIFF, and WBMP.

In Java 9, the Java media API was transformed as well and functionality to encapsulate many images with different resolutions into a multiresolution image was added. The core of the Java Media API is the `java.awt.Image` abstract class that is the super class of all classes used to represent graphical images. The most important image representing classes and the relationships between them are depicted in Figure 11-8.

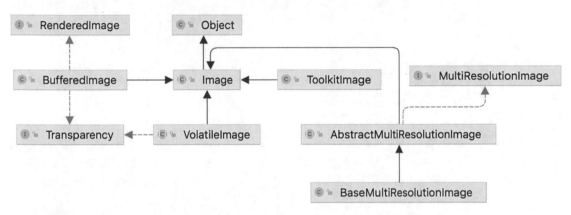

Figure 11-8. *Image classes hierarchy (as shown by IntelliJ IDEA)*

Although the `java.awt.Image` class is the root class in this hierarchy, the most used is `java.awt.BufferedImage`, which is an implementation with an accessible buffer of image data. It provides a lot of methods that can be used to create an image, to set its size and its contents, to extract its contents and analyze them, and so much more. In this section we will make use of this class to read and write images.

An image file is a complex file. Aside from the picture itself it contains a lot of additional information; the most important nowadays is the location where that image was created. If you ever wondered how a social network proposes a check-in location for an image you are posting, this is where the information is found. This might not seem that important, but posting a picture of your cat taken in your house exposes your location to the whole world getting their hands on it. I'm not sure what you think about it, but to me this is terrifying. I used to post pictures of my cat sitting comfortably on the computer where I was writing this book on my personal blog, which meant that I basically exposed my location and that of a quite expensive laptop to the whole world. Sure, most people do not care about my cat, nor the laptop, but somebody who might be looking to make an easy buck might. So after a friendly and knowledgeable reader sent me a private email telling me about something called EXIF data and how he knows where I live because of the last picture I've posted on my blog, I looked into it. A photo's EXIF data contains a ton of information about your camera and where the picture was taken (GPS coordinates). Most smartphones embed EXIF data into pictures taken with their camera.

In Figure 11-9 you can see the EXIF information depicted by the macOS Preview application.

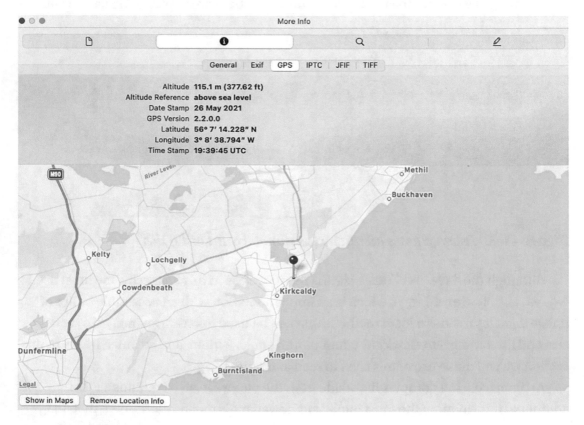

Figure 11-9. *EXIF information on a JPG image*

Notice that the EXIF info contains the exact location, latitude and longitude included, where the picture was taken. EXIF stands for Exchangeable Image File Format and there are utilities to remove it, but when you post a lot of pictures on your blog (like I do), it takes too much time to clean them one by one. This is where Java comes in, and I will share with you a snippet of code I use to clean my pictures of EXIF data (Listing 11-46).

Listing 11-46. Code Snippet to Strip EXIF Data from Images

```java
package com.apress.bgn.eleven;
// some import statement omitted
import javax.imageio.ImageIO;
import java.awt.*;
import java.awt.image.BaseMultiResolutionImage;
import java.awt.image.BufferedImage;
import java.awt.image.MultiResolutionImage;

/**
 * Created by iuliana.cosmina on 23/07/2021
 */
public class MediaDemo {
    private static final Logger log = LoggerFactory.
    getLogger(MediaDemo.class);

    public static void main(String... args) {
        File src = new File("chapter11/media-handling/src/main/resources/
        input/the-beach.jpg");

        try {
            log.info(" --- Removing EXIF info ---");
            File destNoExif = new File("chapter11/media-handling/src/main/
            resources/output/the-beach.jpg");
            removeExifTag(src, destNoExif);
             } catch (Exception e) {
            log.error("Something bad happened.", e);
        }
    }
}
```

```
private static void removeExifTag(final File src, final File dest)
throws Exception {
    BufferedImage originalImage = ImageIO.read(src);
    ImageIO.write(originalImage, "jpg", dest);
}
}
```

Removing EXIF data is pretty easy, since `javax.imageio.ImageIO` does not persist EXIF information or any other information in the image file that is not linked to the actual image.

ℹ   In the previous edition of this book Apache Sanselan was used. This utility library provided classes that do the stripping of the EXIF information with better performance, but unfortunately it is currently unmaintained, and it cannot be used in a modular application.

The `removeExifTag(..)` method is given as an argument the source of the image and a `File` handler managing the location where the new image should be saved. To test that the resulting image has no EXIF data, just open it in an image viewer. Any option that shows EXIF should either be disabled or should display nothing. In the Preview image viewer from macOS the option is greyed out.

Now that we got that out of the way, let's resize the original image. To resize an image we need to create a `BufferedImage` instance from the original image to get the image dimensions. After that, we modify the dimensions and use them as arguments to create a new `BufferedImage` that will be populated with data by a `java.awt.Graphics2D` instance, a special type of class that is used to render 2-D shapes, text, and images. The code is depicted in the Listing 11-47. And the method is called to create an image 25% smaller, an image 50% smaller, and one 75% smaller.

Listing 11-47. Code Snippet to Resize an Image

```
package com.apress.bgn.eleven;

import javax.imageio.ImageIO;
import java.awt.*;
import java.awt.image.BaseMultiResolutionImage;
import java.awt.image.BufferedImage;
```

```java
public class MediaDemo {
    private static final Logger log = LoggerFactory.
getLogger(MediaDemo.class);

    public static void main(String... args) {
        File src = new File("chapter11/media-handling/src/main/resources/
        input/the-beach.jpg");

        try {
            log.info(" --- Creating 25% image ---");
            File dest25 = new File("chapter11/media-handling/src/main/
            resources/output/the-beach_25.jpg");
            resize(dest25, src, 0.25f);

            log.info(" --- Creating 50% image ---");
            File dest50 = new File("chapter11/media-handling/src/main/
            resources/output/the-beach_50.jpg");
            resize(dest50, src, 0.5f);

            log.info(" --- Creating 75% image ---");
            File dest75 = new File("chapter11/media-handling/src/main/
            resources/output/the-beach_75.jpg");
            resize(dest75, src, 0.75f);
        } catch (Exception e) {
            log.error("Something bad happened.", e);
        }
    }

    private static void resize(final File dest, final File src, final float
percent) throws IOException {
        BufferedImage originalImage = ImageIO.read(src);
        int scaledWidth = (int) (originalImage.getWidth() * percent);
        int scaledHeight = (int) (originalImage.getHeight() * percent);

        BufferedImage outputImage = new BufferedImage(scaledWidth,
        scaledHeight, originalImage.getType());

        Graphics2D g2d = outputImage.createGraphics();
```

```
        g2d.drawImage(originalImage, 0, 0, scaledWidth,
        scaledHeight, null);
        g2d.dispose();
        outputImage.flush();

        ImageIO.write(outputImage, "jpg", dest);
    }
}
```

To make things easier, the ImageIO class utility methods come in handy for reading images from files or for writing them to a specific location. If you want to test to see that the resizing works, you can just look in the resources directory. The output files have already been named accordingly, but just to make sure, you can double-check in a file viewer. You should see something similar to what is depicted in Figure 11-10.

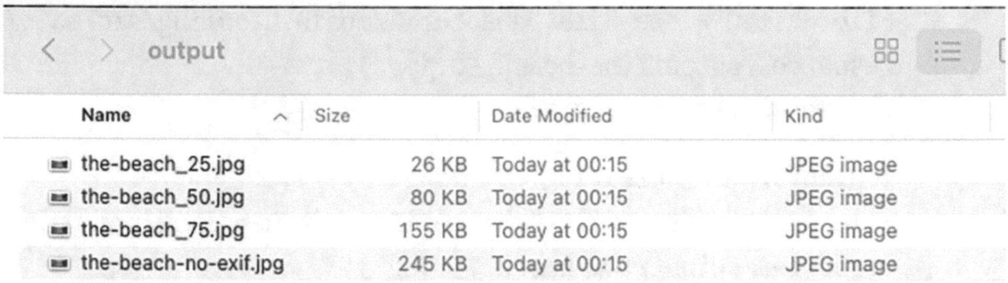

Figure 11-10. *Images resized using Java code*

The resulting images are not so high in quality as the original image, because compressing the pixels does not result in high quality, but they do fit the sizes we intended.

Now that we have all these versions of the same image, we can use them to create a multiresolution image using class BaseMultiResolutionImage introduced in Java 9. An instance of this class is created from a set of images, all copy of a single image, but with different resolutions. This is why earlier we created more than one resized copy of the image. A BaseMultiResolutionImage can be used to retrieve images based on specific screen resolutions and it is suitable for applications designed to be accessed from multiple devices. Let's see the code first and then explain the results (Listing 11-48).

Listing 11-48. Code Snippet to Create a Multiresolution Image

```
package com.apress.bgn.eleven;

import org.slf4j.Logger;
import org.slf4j.LoggerFactory;

import javax.imageio.ImageIO;
import java.awt.*;
import java.awt.image.BaseMultiResolutionImage;
import java.awt.image.BufferedImage;
import java.awt.image.MultiResolutionImage;
import java.io.File;
import java.io.IOException;

public class MediaDemo {
    private static final Logger log = LoggerFactory.
    getLogger(MediaDemo.class);

    public static void main(String... args) {
        File src = new File("chapter11/media-handling/src/main/resources/
        input/the-beach.jpg");

        try {
            // code to create images omitted, check previous Listing
            Image[] imgList = new Image[]{
                    ImageIO.read(dest25), // 500 x 243
                    ImageIO.read(dest50), // 1000 x 486
                    ImageIO.read(dest75), // 1500 x 729
                    ImageIO.read(src) // 2000 x 972
            };

            log.info(" --- Creating multi-resolution image ---");
            File destVariant = new File("chapter11/media-handling/src/main/
            resources/output/the-beach-variant.jpg");
            createMultiResImage(destVariant, imgList);

            BufferedImage variantImg = ImageIO.read(destVariant);
```

```
        log.info("Variant width x height :  {} x {}", variantImg.
        getWidth(), variantImg.getHeight());

        BufferedImage dest25Img = ImageIO.read(dest25);
        log.info("dest25Img width x height :  {} x {}", dest25Img.
        getWidth(), dest25Img.getHeight());
        log.info("Are identical? {}", variantImg.equals(dest25Img));
    } catch (Exception e) {
        log.error("Something bad happened.", e);
    }
}

private static void createMultiResImage(final File dest, final Image[]
imgList) throws IOException {
    MultiResolutionImage mrImage = new
    BaseMultiResolutionImage(0,imgList);
    var variants = mrImage.getResolutionVariants();
    variants.forEach(i -> log.info(i.toString()));

    Image img = mrImage.getResolutionVariant(500, 200);
    log.info("Most fit to the requested size<{},{}>: <{},{}>", 500,
    200, img.getWidth(null), img.getHeight(null));

    if (img instanceof BufferedImage) {
        ImageIO.write((BufferedImage) img, "jpg", dest);
    }
}
}
```

The BaseMultiResolutionImage instance is created from an array of Image instances. This class is an implementation of the MultiResolutionImage interface designed to be an optional additional API supported by some implementations of Image to allow them to provide alternate images for various rendering resolutions.

To be really obvious which image will be selected, the resolution of each image was put in a comment next to it. When getResolutionVariant(..) is called, the arguments are compared to the corresponding image properties and even if both are less than equal to one of the images, that image is returned. In Listing 11-49, the code of the BaseMultiResolutionImage.getResolutionVariant(..) is depicted:

Listing 11-49. Code for Getting an Image Variant Based on Size

```
@Override
public Image getResolutionVariant(double destImageWidth,
                                  double destImageHeight) {

    checkSize(destImageWidth, destImageHeight);

    for (Image rvImage : resolutionVariants) {
        if (destImageWidth <= rvImage.getWidth(null)
                && destImageHeight <= rvImage.getHeight(null)) {
            return rvImage;
        }
    }
    return resolutionVariants[resolutionVariants.length - 1];
}
```

The code looks suited for its purpose. If you call `mrImage.getResolutionVariant(500, 200)` you get the `dest25` image with resolution 500 x 243. If you call `mrImage.getResolutionVariant(500, 300)` you get the `dest50` image with resolution 1000 x 486, because the `destImageHeight` argument is 300, which is bigger than 243, so the next image in the list with width and height bigger than the arguments is returned. But—and this is a big but—this works only if the images in the array are sorted in the order of their sizes. If the `imgList` were to be modified to:

```
Image[] imgList = new Image[]{
                ImageIO.read(src),  // 2000 x 972
                ImageIO.read(dest25), // 500 x 243
                ImageIO.read(dest50), // 1000 x 486
                ImageIO.read(dest75) // 1500 x 729
        };
```

Then both calls return the original image, because that is the first one in the list, and width is bigger then 500 and height is bigger than both 200 and 300.

So if the algorithm is not efficient and it depends on the order of the images in the array used to create the multiresolution image, what can be done? It's simple: we can create our own `MultiResolutionImage` implementation that extends `BaseMultiResolutionImage` and overrides the `getResolutionVariant()` method. Since we know that all images are resized copies of the same image, this means that width and height are proportional. So an algorithm that will always return the variant of the image that is most suitable to the desired resolution can be written that will not really care of the order of the images in the array and that will return the image that fits most. The implementation might look quite similar to the one in Listing 11-50.

Listing 11-50. Better Code for Getting an Image Variant Based on Size

```java
package com.apress.bgn.eleven;
// other import statements omitted
import java.awt.image.BaseMultiResolutionImage;

public class SmartMultiResolutionImage extends BaseMultiResolutionImage {

    public SmartMultiResolutionImage(int baseImageIndex, Image...
resolutionVariants) {
        super(baseImageIndex, resolutionVariants);
    }

    @Override
    public Image getResolutionVariant(double destImageWidth,
                                      double destImageHeight) {

        checkSize(destImageWidth, destImageHeight);
        Map<Double, Image> result = new HashMap<>();

        for (Image rvImage : getResolutionVariants()) {
            double widthDelta = Math.abs(destImageWidth - rvImage.
            getWidth(null));
            double heightDelta = Math.abs(destImageHeight - rvImage.
            getHeight(null));
            double delta = widthDelta + heightDelta;
            result.put(delta, rvImage);
        }
        java.util.List<Double> deltaList = new ArrayList<>(result.keySet());
        deltaList.sort(Double::compare);

        return result.get(deltaList.get(0));
    }
```

```
    private static void checkSize(double width, double height) {
        if (width <= 0 || height <= 0) {
            throw new IllegalArgumentException(String.format(
                    "Width (%s) or height (%s) cannot be <= 0", width,
                    height));
        }

        if (!Double.isFinite(width) || !Double.isFinite(height)) {
            throw new IllegalArgumentException(String.format(
                    "Width (%s) or height (%s) is not finite", width,
                    height));
        }
    }
}
```

The checkSize(..) method must be duplicated, as it is private and used inside getResolutionVariant(..), so it cannot be called inside a superclass, but that is a minor inconvenience to having an implementation that has a proper behavior. With the previous implementation, we no longer need a sorted array, thus calls to getResolutionVariant(500, 200), getResolutionVariant(500, 300), getResolutionVariant(400, 300), and getResolutionVariant(600, 300) all return image dest25.

To use the new class, in Listing 11-48 this line:

```
MultiResolutionImage mrImage = new BaseMultiResolutionImage(0,imgList);
```

must be replaced with

```
MultiResolutionImage mrImage = new SmartMultiResolutionImage(0, imgList);
```

You can reposition the images in the imgList array too, if you want to test it properly. Then running the MediaDemo class produces the output depicted in Listing 11-51.

Listing 11-51. Output Produced By Running the MediaDemo

```
[main] INFO MediaDemo -  --- Creating multi-resolution image ---
[main] INFO MediaDemo - BufferedImage@47c62251: type = 5 ColorModel:
#pixelBits = 24 numComponents = 3 color space = java.awt.color.ICC_
ColorSpace@e25b2fe transparency = 1 has alpha = false isAlphaPre = false
```

```
ByteInterleavedRaster: width = 2000 height = 972 #numDataElements 3
dataOff[0] = 2
[main] INFO MediaDemo - BufferedImage@3c0ecd4b: type = 5 ColorModel:
#pixelBits = 24 numComponents = 3 color space = java.awt.color.ICC_
ColorSpace@e25b2fe transparency = 1 has alpha = false isAlphaPre = false
ByteInterleavedRaster: width = 500 height = 243 #numDataElements 3
dataOff[0] = 2
[main] INFO MediaDemo - BufferedImage@14bf9759: type = 5 ColorModel:
#pixelBits = 24 numComponents = 3 color space = java.awt.color.ICC_
ColorSpace@e25b2fe transparency = 1 has alpha = false isAlphaPre = false
ByteInterleavedRaster: width = 1000 height = 486 #numDataElements 3
dataOff[0] = 2
[main] INFO MediaDemo - BufferedImage@5f341870: type = 5 ColorModel:
#pixelBits = 24 numComponents = 3 color space = java.awt.color.ICC_
ColorSpace@e25b2fe transparency = 1 has alpha = false isAlphaPre = false
ByteInterleavedRaster: width = 1500 height = 729 #numDataElements 3
dataOff[0] = 2
[main] INFO MediaDemo - Most fit to the requested size<500,200>: <500,243>
[main] INFO MediaDemo - Are identical? false
```

Wait, what? Why are the images not identical? They do have the same resolution, but as objects they are not identical because drawing pixels is not really that precise. But if you really want to make sure, you could print the width and height of the two images and open them with an image viewer, and with the naked eye you would see they look identical, using code like this:

```
log.info("variant width x height : {} x {}", variantImg.getWidth(),
    variantImg.getHeight());
log.info("dest25Img width x height : {} x {}", dest25Img.getWidth(),
    dest25Img.getHeight());
```

The previous code prints the width and height of the two images, making it obvious that the two images have the same dimensions, just as expected.

```
[main] INFO MediaDemo - variant width x height :  500 x 243
[main] INFO MediaDemo - dest25Img width x height :  500 x 243
```

Anyway, as you've noticed most of the images classes are part of the old `java.awt`, which is rarely used nowadays and is known to be quite slow. So if you want to build an application and image processing is required, you might want to look for alternatives. One of such alternatives is using JavaFx, presented in the following section.

Using JavaFX Image Classes

Beside the Java Media API that is centered on components of the `java.awt` package, another way to display and edit images is provided by JavaFX. The core class for the `javafx.scene.image` package is named Image and can be used to handle images in a few common formats: PNG, JPEG, BMP, GIF, and others. JavaFX applications display images using an instance of `javafx.scene.image.ImageView` and the part that I like most about this class is that the images can be also displayed scaled, without the original image being modified.

To create a `javafx.scene.image.Image` instance all we need is either a `FileInputStream` instance to read the image from the user-provided location, or a URL location given as `String`. The code snippet in Listing 11-52 creates a JavaFX application that displays an image with its original width and height, which can be accessed using methods in class `javafx.scene.image.Image`.

Listing 11-52. Using JavaFX to Display Images

```java
package com.apress.bgn.eleven;

import javafx.application.Application;
import javafx.geometry.Rectangle2D;
import javafx.scene.Scene;
import javafx.scene.image.Image;
import javafx.scene.image.ImageView;
import javafx.scene.layout.StackPane;
import javafx.stage.Stage;

import java.io.File;
import java.io.FileInputStream;
```

```java
public class JavaFxMediaDemo extends Application {

    public static void main(String... args) {
        Application.launch(args);
    }

    @Override
    public void start(Stage primaryStage) throws Exception {
        primaryStage.setTitle("JavaFX Image Demo");
        File src = new File("chapter11/media-handling/src/main/resources/
        cover.png");
        Image image = new Image(new FileInputStream(src));
        ImageView imageView = new ImageView(image);
        imageView.setFitHeight(image.getHeight());
        imageView.setFitWidth(image.getWidth());
        imageView.setPreserveRatio(true);
        //Creating a Group object
        StackPane root = new StackPane();
        root.getChildren().add(imageView);
        primaryStage.setScene(new Scene(root,
        image.getWidth()+10,
        image.getHeight()+10));
        primaryStage.show();
    }
}
```

The Image instance cannot be added to the Scene of the JavaFX instance directly, as it does not extend the Node abstract class that is required to be implemented by all JavaFX elements that make a JavaFxApplication. That is why this instance must be wrapped in a javafx.scene.image.ImageView instance that is a class extending Node, and it is a specialized class for rendering images loaded with Image class.

This class resizes the displayed image, with or without preserving the original aspect ratio, by calling the setPreserveRatio(..) method with the appropriate argument, true to keep the original aspect ratio, false otherwise.

🔥 Check out **Chapter 10** to learn how to install the JavaFX for your system, so the examples in this chapter can be run correctly.

As you can see, in the previous code we use the values retuned by `image.getWidth()` and `image.getHeight()` to set the size of the `ImageView` object and the size of the `Scene` instance. But let's get creative and display the scaled image, still preserving the aspect ratio and also using a better-quality filtering algorithm when scaling the image by using the `smooth(..)` method, as shown here.

```
...
ImageView imageView = new ImageView(image);
imageView.setFitWidth(100);
imageView.setPreserveRatio(true);
imageView.setSmooth(true);
...
```

Another thing that the `ImageView` class can do is to support a `Rectangle2D` view port that can be used to rotate the image.

```
...
ImageView imageView = new ImageView(image);
Rectangle2D viewportRect = new Rectangle2D(2, 2, 600, 600);
imageView.setViewport(viewportRect);
imageView.setRotate(90);
...
```

Being an implementation of node `ImageView` supports clicking events, and it is quite easy to write some code to resize an image on click. Just take a look at code in Listing 11-53.

Listing 11-53. Using JavaFX to Resize Images on Click Events

```
...
    ImageView imageView = new ImageView(image);
    imageView.setFitHeight(image.getHeight());
    imageView.setFitWidth(image.getWidth());
    imageView.setPreserveRatio(true);
```

```
    root.getChildren().add(imageView);
    imageView.setPickOnBounds(true);
    imageView.setOnMouseClicked(mouseEvent -> {
        if(imageView.getFitWidth() > 100) {
            imageView.setFitWidth(100);
            imageView.setPreserveRatio(true);
            imageView.setSmooth(true);
        } else {
            imageView.setFitHeight(image.getHeight());
            imageView.setFitWidth(image.getWidth());
            imageView.setPreserveRatio(true);
        }
    });
...
```

In the previous code snippet by calling the setOnMouseClicked(..) we attached an EventHandler<? super MouseEvent> instance to the mouse clicking event on the imageView. The EventHandler<T extends MouseEvent> is a functional interface containing a single method named handle, and its concrete implementation is the body of the lambda expression in the previous code listing.

As JavaFX was taken out of JDK 11, there is no real value into going over more image processing classes in this section. But if you are interested in learning more about this subject, this tutorial from Oracle should do the job: https://docs.oracle.com/javafx/2/image_ops/jfxpub-image_ops.htm. Also, as practice, you can try writing your own code based on the code in the book to add a mouse event that rotates the image. This is all the space we can dedicate for playing with images in the Java. I hope you found this section useful and that you might get the chance to test your Java Media API skills in the future—if not for anything else, at least for cleaning EXIF data from your images.

Summary

This chapter has covered most of the details you need to know to be able to work with various types of files, how to serialize Java objects and save them to a file, and then recover them through deserialization. When writing Java applications you will most likely need to save data to files or read data from files, and this chapter provided quite a wide list of components to do so. This is a short summary of this chapter:

- how to use File and Path instances

- how to use utility methods in Files and Paths

- how to serialize/deserialize Java objects to/from binary, XML, and JSON

- how to resize and modify images using the Java Media API

- how to use images in JavaFX applications

CHAPTER 12

The Publish-Subscribe Framework

All the programming concepts explained so far in the book involved data that needed to be processed. Regardless of the form in which data is provided, the Java programs we've written so far took that data, modified it, and printed out the results, whether to console, files, or another software component. You could say that all these components were communicating with each other and passing processed data from one to another. For example, take Figure 12-1, which abstractly describes the interaction between Java components in a program.

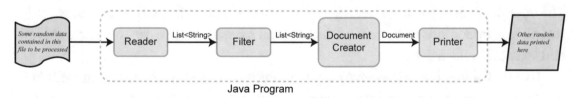

Figure 12-1. *Interactions between Java components within a program*

On each of the arrows is marked with the type of information being passed from one to another. In this image you can identify a starting point where information enters the program, by being read by the Reader and an end point where the information is printed to some output component by the Printer. You could say that the Reader provides the data, the Filter and the DocumentCreator are some internal processors, and processing the data and the Printer is the consumer of the data.

What was described so far is something resembling a **point-to-point (p2p) messaging model**, which describes a concept of one message being send to one consumer. The p2p model is specific to a Java API named Java Message Service (JMS) that supports the formal communication known as messaging between computers

© Iuliana Cosmina 2022

I. Cosmina, *Java 17 for Absolute Beginners*, https://doi.org/10.1007/978-1-4842-7080-6_12

in a network. In the example that begins this chapter, an analogy was made to show that communication between components of a Java Program works in a similar manner. The design of a solution to implement a process as described by the previous figure could be created by considering all components linked into a messaging style communication model.

There is more than one communication model: producer/consumer, publish/subscribe, and sender/receiver, each with its own specifics,[1] but the one this chapter is focused on is the **publish/subscribe,** because this is the model the reactive programming is based on.

Reactive Programming and the Reactive Manifesto

Reactive programming is a declarative programming style that involves using data streams and propagation of change. Reactive programming is programming with asynchronous data streams. Reactive streams is an initiative to provide a standard for asynchronous stream processing with nonblocking back-pressure. They are extremely useful for solving problems that require complex coordination across thread boundaries. The operators allow you to gather your data on to the desired threads and ensures thread-safe operations without requiring, in most cases, excessive uses of synchronized and volatile constructs.

Java took a step toward reactive programming after introducing the Streams API in version 8, but reactive streams were not available until version 9. We've already learned how to use streams a few chapters ago **(Chapter 8)**, so we're one step closer. Now all we must do is understand how to use reactive streams do to some reactive programming.

Using reactive streams is not a new idea. The Reactive Manifesto was first made public in 2014,[2] and it made a request for software to be developed in such a way that **systems are Responsive, Resilient, Elastic and Message Driven**—in short, they should be **Reactive**.

---

[1] If you are interested more in communication models, you can search the web for Enterprise Integration Patterns.

[2] Read it at Reactive Man, "The Reactive Manifesto," https://www.reactivemanifesto.org, accessed October 15, 2021.

Each of the four terms is shortly explained here:

- **Responsive**: should provide fast and consistent response times.

- **Resilient**: should remain responsive in case of failure and be able to recover.

- **Elastic**: should remain responsive and be able to handle various workloads.

- **Message Driven**: should communicate using asynchronous messages, avoid blocking, and applying backpressure when necessary.

Systems designed this way are supposed to be more flexible, loosely coupled, and scalable, but at the same time they should be easier to develop, amendable to change, and more tolerant of failure. To be able to accomplish all that, the systems need a common API for communication. Reactive streams is an initiative to provide such a standard API for asynchronous, nonblocking stream processing that also supports back-pressure. We'll explain what **back-pressure** means in a moment. Let's start with the basics of reactive stream processing.

Any type of stream processing involves a producer of data, a consumer of data, and components in the middle between them that process the data. Obviously, the direction of the data flow is from the producer to the consumer. The abstract schema of a system that was described so far is depicted in Figure 12-2.

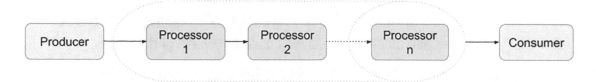

Figure 12-2. *Producer/consumer system*

The system might end up in a pickle when the producer is faster than the consumer, so the extra data that cannot be processed must be dealt with. There is more than one way of doing that:

- the extra data is discarded (this is done in network hardware).

- the producer is blocked so the consumer has time to catch up.

- the data is buffered, but buffers are limited and if we have a fast producer and a slow consumer there is a danger of the buffer overflowing.

- applying **back-pressure**, which involves giving the consumer the power to regulate the producer and control how much data is produced. Back-pressure can be viewed as a message being sent from the consumer to the producer to let it know it has to slow its data production rate. With this in mind, we can complete the design in the previous image, which will result in Figure 12-3.

Figure 12-3. *Reactive producer/consumer system*

If producer, processors, and consumer are not synchronized, solving the problem of too much data by blocking until each one is ready to process it is not an option, as it would transform the system into a synchronous one. Discarding it is not an option either, and buffering is unpredictable, so all we're left with for a reactive system is applying **nonblocking back-pressure**.

💡 If the software example is too puzzling for you, imagine the following scenario.

You have a friend named Jim. You also have a bucket of differently colored balls. Jim tells you to give him all the red balls. You have two ways of doing this:

1. You pick all the red balls, put them in another bucket, and hand the bucket to Jim. This is the typical request—complete response model. It is an asynchronous model, and if selecting the red balls takes too long, Jim just goes and does other things while you do the sorting and when you are done, you just notify him his bucket of red balls is ready. It is asynchronous because Jim is not blocked by you sorting the balls but goes and does other things and gets them when they are ready.

2. You just get the red balls one by one from your bucket and throw them at Jim. This is your data flow, or a ball flow, in this case. If you are faster at finding them and throwing them than Jim is at catching them, you have a blockage. So Jim tells you to slow down. This is him regulating the flow of balls, which is the real-world equivalent of back-pressure.

Writing applications that can be aggregated in reactive systems was not possible in Java before version 9, so developers had to make do with external libraries. A reactive application must be designed according to principle of reactive programming and use reactive streams for handling the data. The standard API for reactive programming was first described by the **reactive-streams** library that could be used with Java 8 as well. In Java 9, the standard API was added to the JDK and the next version of the **reactive-streams** included a set of classes declared nested into the org.reactivestreams. FlowAdapters class that represent bridges between the analogous components in the two APIs (the Reactive Streams API and the Reactive Streams Flow API).

In Figure 12-4 you can see the interfaces that are meant to be implemented by components with the roles defined previously.

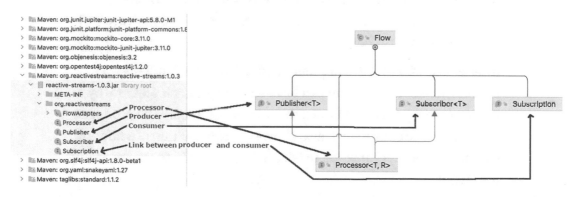

Figure 12-4. *Reactive streams interfaces (as shown in IntelliJ IDEA)*

The reactive streams API is made of four very simple interfaces:

- interface Publisher<T> exposes one method named void subscribe(Subscriber<? super T>), which is called to add a Subscriber<T> instance and produces elements of type T that will be consumed by the Subscriber<T>. The purpose of a Publisher<T> implementation is to publish values according to the demand received from its subscribers.

- interface Subscriber<T>, consumes elements from the Publisher<T> and exposes four methods that must be implemented to define concrete behavior of the instance depending on the event type received by the Publisher<T> instance.

  - void onSubscribe(Subscription) is the first method called on a subscriber and this is the methods that links the Publisher<T> to the Subscriber<T> instance using the Subscription argument; if this method throws an exception the following behavior is not guaranteed.

  - void onNext(T) is the method invoked with a Subscription's next item to receive the data; if it throws an exception, the Subscription might be cancelled.

  - void onError(Throwable) is the method invoked upon an unrecoverable error encountered by a Publisher<T> or Subscription<T>.

  - void onComplete() is the method called when there is no more data to consume, thus no additional Subscriber<T> method invocations will occur.

- interface Processor<T,R> extends both Publisher<T> and Subscriber<R>, because it needs to consume data and produce it to send it further upstream.

- interface Subscription's implementation links the Publisher<T> and the Subscriber<T> and can be used to apply back-pressure by calling the request(long) to set the number of items to be produced and sent to the consumer. It also allows the cancellation of a flow, by calling the cancel() method to tell a Subscriber<T> to stop receiving messages.

In the JDK all the previously listed interfaces are defined within the java.util. concurrent.Flow class. The name of this class is obvious in nature, as the previous interfaces are used to create flow-controlled components that can be linked together to create a reactive application. Aside from these four interfaces there is a single JDK implementation: the java.util.concurrent.SubmissionPublisher<T> class implementing Publisher<T>, which is a convenient base for subclasses that generate items and use the methods in this class to publish them.

The `Flow` interfaces are quite basic and can be used when writing reactive applications, but this requires a lot of work. Currently there are multiple implementations, by various teams, that provide a more practical way to develop reactive applications. Using implementation of these interfaces, you can write reactive applications without needing to write the logic for synchronization of threads processing the data.

The following list contains the most well-known reactive streams API implementations (and there are more, because in a big-data world reactive processing is no longer a luxury but a necessity):

- Project Reactor (`https://projectreactor.io`) embraced by Spring for its Web Reactive Framework

- Akka Streams (`https://doc.akka.io/docs/akka/current/stream/stream-flows-and-basics.html`)

- MongoDB Reactive Streams Java Driver (`http://mongodb.github.io/mongo-java-driver-reactivestreams`)

- Ratpack (`https://ratpack.io`)

- RxJava (`http://reactivex.io`)

Using the JDK Reactive Streams API

As the JDK provided interfaces for reactive programming are quite basic, implementation is quite cumbersome, but nevertheless in this section an attempt is being made. In this section we will be trying to build an application that generates an infinite number of integer values. Filter these values and select the ones that are smaller than 127. For the ones that are even and between 98 and 122, subtract 32 (basically converting small letters to upper case). Then convert them to a character and print them. The most basic solution, without reactive streams is depicted in Listing 12-1.

Listing 12-1. Generating an Infinite Number of Integers <127

```
package com.apress.bgn.twelve.dummy;

// some input statements omitted
import java.security.SecureRandom;

public class BasicIntTransformer {
    private static final Logger log = LoggerFactory.
getLogger(BasicIntTransformer.class);
    private static final SecureRandom random = new SecureRandom();

    public static void main(String... args) {

        while (true){
            int rndNo = random.nextInt(130);
            if (rndNo < 127) {
                log.info("Initial value: {} ", rndNo);
                if(rndNo % 2 == 0 && rndNo >=98 && rndNo <=122) {
                    rndNo -=32;
                }
                char res = (char) rndNo;
                log.info("Result: {}", res);
            } else {
                log.debug("Number {} discarded.", rndNo);
            }
        }
    }
}
```

Each line of code in the previous code listing has a purpose, a desired outcome. This approach is called imperative programming, because it sequentially executes a series of statements to produce a desired output.

However, this is not what we are aiming for. In this section we will implement a reactive solution using implementations of the JDK reactive interfaces, so we'll need the following:

- A publisher component that makes use of an infinite stream to generate random integer values. The class should implement the `Flow.Publisher<Integer>` interface.

- A processor that selects only integer values that can be converted to visible characters, let's say all characters with codes between [0,127). The class should implement the `Flow.Processor<Integer, Integer>`.

- A processor that modified elements received and that are even, and between 98 and 122, by subtracting 32. This class should also implement the `Flow.Processor<Integer, Integer>`.

- A processor that will transform integer elements into the equivalent characters. This is a special type or processor that maps one value to another of another type, and should implement `Flow.Processor<Integer, Character>`.

- A subscriber that will print the received elements from the last processor in the chain. This class will implement the `Flow.Subscriber<Character>` interface.

Let's start by declaring the `Publisher<T>` that will wrap around an infinite stream to produce values to be consumed. We will implement the `Flow.Publisher<Integer>` interface by providing a full concrete implementation to submit the elements asynchronously. To buffer them in case of need a lot of code would need to be added. Fortunately the class `SubmissionPublisher<T>` does that already, so internally, in our class we'll make use of a `SubmissionPublisher<Integer>` object. The code for the publisher is depicted in Listing 12-2.

Listing 12-2. Publisher Generating an Infinite Number of Integers

```
package com.apress.bgn.twelve.jdkstreams;

import java.util.Random;
import java.util.concurrent.Flow;
import java.util.concurrent.SubmissionPublisher;
import java.util.stream.IntStream;
```

```java
public class IntPublisher implements Flow.Publisher<Integer> {
    private static final Random random = new Random();
    protected final IntStream intStream;

    public IntPublisher(int limit) {
        intStream = limit == 0 ? IntStream.generate(() -> random.
        nextInt(150)) :
                IntStream.generate(() -> random.nextInt(150)).limit(30);
    }

    private final SubmissionPublisher<Integer> submissionPublisher = new
    SubmissionPublisher<>();

    @Override
    public void subscribe(Flow.Subscriber<? super Integer> subscriber) {
        submissionPublisher.subscribe(subscriber);
    }

    public void start() {
        intStream.forEach(element -> {
            submissionPublisher.submit(element);
            sleep();
        });
    }

    private void sleep() {
        try {
            Thread.sleep(1000);
        } catch (InterruptedException e) {
            throw new RuntimeException("could not sleep!");
        }
    }
}
```

💡 Notice how the constructor of the `IntPublisher` class takes a single argument. If the value provided as argument at instantiation time is 0(ZERO), an infinite stream is created. If the argument value is different than 0, a finite stream is created. This is useful if you want to run the example and not forcefully stop the execution.

As expected, we've provided an implementation for the `subscribe()` method and in this case what we have to do is just to forward the `subscriber` to the internal `submissionPublisher`. Since we've created our publisher by wrapping it around `submissionPublisher` this is necessary, otherwise our flow won't work as expected. Also, we've added a `start()` method that takes elements from the infinite `IntStream` and submits them using the internal `submissionPublisher`.

The `IntStream` makes use of a `Random` instance to generate integer values in the [0,150] interval. This interval is chosen so that we can see how values bigger than 127 are discarded by the first `Flow.Processor<T,R>` instance connected to the publisher. To be able to slow down the elements submission we added a call to `Thread.sleep(1000)` that basically guarantees one element per second will be forwarded up the chain.

The name of the first processor will be `FilterCharProcessor` and will make use of an internal `SubmissionPublisher<Integer>` instance to send the elements it processes onward to the next processor.

Exceptions thrown will be also forwarded using the `SubmissionPublisher<Integer>`. The processor acts as a publisher but as a subscriber as well, so the implementation on the `onNext(..)` method will have to include a call to `subscription.request(..)` to apply back pressure. From the figures presented earlier in the chapter you could see that the processor is basically a component that allows data flow in both directions, and it does that by implementing both `Publisher<T>` and `Subscriber<T>`.

The processor must subscribe to the publisher and when the publisher `subscribe(..)` method is called, will cause the `onSubscribe(Flow.Subscription subscription)` method to be invoked. The subscription must be stored locally, so that it can be used to apply back pressure. But when accepting a subscription we must make sure that the field was not already initialized, because according to reactive streams specification there can only be one subscriber for a publisher, otherwise the results are unpredictable. If and when a new subscription arrives it must be cancelled, and this is done by calling `cancel()`. The full code for the processor is depicted in Listing 12-3.

Listing 12-3. Flow.Processor<T,R> Implementation FilterCharProcessor<Integ er,Integer> That Filters Integers > 127

```java
package com.apress.bgn.twelve.jdkstreams;

import java.util.concurrent.Flow;
import java.util.concurrent.SubmissionPublisher;
// some input statements omitted

public class FilterCharProcessor implements Flow.Processor<Integer,
Integer> {
    private static final Logger log = LoggerFactory.
getLogger(FilterCharProcessor.class);

    private final SubmissionPublisher<Integer> submissionPublisher = new
SubmissionPublisher<>();
    private Flow.Subscription subscription;
    @Override
    public void subscribe(Flow.Subscriber<? super Integer> subscriber) {
        submissionPublisher.subscribe(subscriber);
    }
    @Override
    public void onSubscribe(Flow.Subscription subscription) {
        if (this.subscription == null) {
            this.subscription = subscription;
            // apply back pressure - request one element
            this.subscription.request(1);
        } else {
            subscription.cancel();
        }
    }
    @Override
    public void onNext(Integer element) {
        if (element >=0 && element < 127){
            submit(element);
        } else {
            log.debug("Element {} discarded.", element);
        }
```

```
        subscription.request(1);
    }
    @Override
    public void onError(Throwable throwable) {
        submissionPublisher.closeExceptionally(throwable);
    }

    @Override
    public void onComplete() {
        submissionPublisher.close();
    }
    protected void submit(Integer element){
        submissionPublisher.submit(element);
    }
}
```

This processor is very specific, and a processing flow usually requires more than one. In this scenario we need a few, and since beside the onNext(..) method the rest of the implementation is mostly boilerplate code that allows for processors to be linked together in the flow we are designing, it would be more practical to wrap up this code in an AbstractProcessor that all processors needed for this solution can extend.

As the last processor in the flow needs to convert the received Integer value to a Character, the returned type of this implementation is to be kept generic. The code is depicted in Listing 12-4.

Listing 12-4. AbstractProcessor<Integer,T> Implementation

```
package com.apress.bgn.twelve.jdkstreams;

import java.util.concurrent.Flow;
import java.util.concurrent.SubmissionPublisher;

public abstract class AbstractProcessor<T> implements Flow.
Processor<Integer, T> {
    protected final SubmissionPublisher<T> submissionPublisher = new
    SubmissionPublisher<>();
    protected Flow.Subscription subscription;
```

```java
    @Override
    public void subscribe(Flow.Subscriber<? super T> subscriber) {
        submissionPublisher.subscribe(subscriber);
    }

    @Override
    public void onSubscribe(Flow.Subscription subscription) {
        if (this.subscription == null) {
            this.subscription = subscription;
            // apply back pressure - ask one or more than one
            this.subscription.request(1);
        } else {
            // avoid more than one Publisher sending elements to this
            Subscriber
            // do not accept other subscriptions
            subscription.cancel();
        }
    }

    @Override
    public void onError(Throwable throwable) {
        submissionPublisher.closeExceptionally(throwable);
    }

    @Override
    public void onComplete() {
        submissionPublisher.close();
    }

    protected void submit(T element) {
        submissionPublisher.submit(element);
    }
}
```

This simplifies the implementation of the FilterCharProcessor<Integer, Integer> and the other processors as well. The FilterCharProcessor<Integer, Integer> simplified implementation is depicted in Listing 12-5.

Listing 12-5. `FilterCharProcessor` Extending `AbstractProcessor<Integer>`

```java
package com.apress.bgn.twelve.jdkstreams;

import org.slf4j.Logger;
import org.slf4j.LoggerFactory;

public class FilterCharProcessor extends AbstractProcessor<Integer> {
    private static final Logger log = LoggerFactory.
    getLogger(FilterCharProcessor.class);

    @Override
    public void onNext(Integer element) {
        if (element >= 0 && element < 127) {
            submit(element);
        } else {
            log.debug("Element {} discarded.", element);
        }
        subscription.request(1);
    }
}
```

We have a publisher and a processor, so now what? We connect them, of course. The dots (..) in Listing 12-6 replace all the processors and the subscribers being connected to each other that are yet to be built in this section.

Listing 12-6. Executing a Reactive Flow

```java
package com.apress.bgn.twelve.jdkstreams;

public class ReactiveDemo {
    public static void main(String... args) {
        IntPublisher publisher = new IntPublisher(0);
        FilterCharProcessor filterCharProcessor = new FilterCharProcessor();

        publisher.subscribe(filterCharProcessor);
        // ..
        publisher.start();
    }
}
```

The next processor implementation is the one that transforms smaller letters in big letters by subtracting 32. It can be easily implemented by extending AbstractProcessor<Integer, T> as well, and the implementation is depicted in Listing 12-7.

Listing 12-7. The TransformerProcessor Implementation

```
package com.apress.bgn.twelve.jdkstreams;

public class TransformerProcessor extends AbstractProcessor<Integer>{
    @Override
    public void onNext(Integer element) {
        if(element % 2 == 0 && element >=98 && element <=122) {
            element -=32;
        }
        submit(element);
        subscription.request(1);
    }
}
```

To plug in this processor in the flow, we just need instantiate it and call the filterCharProcessor.subscribe(..) and provide this instance as an argument. Listing 12-8 shows the next step in creating our reactive flow.

Listing 12-8. A TransformerProcessor Instance Being Added to a Reactive Flow

```
package com.apress.bgn.twelve.jdkstreams;

public class ReactiveDemo {
    public static void main(String... args) {
        IntPublisher publisher = new IntPublisher(0);
        FilterCharProcessor filterCharProcessor = new
        FilterCharProcessor();
        TransformerProcessor transformerProcessor = new
        TransformerProcessor();

        publisher.subscribe(filterCharProcessor);
        filterCharProcessor.subscribe(transformerProcessor);
```

```
        // ..
        publisher.start();
    }
}
```

The next one to implement is the final processor that we need for this solution and is the one that converts an `Integer` value to a `String` value. To keep the implementation as declarative as possible, the processor will be provided the mapping function as an argument. The code is shown in Listing 12-9.

Listing 12-9. The `MappingProcessor` Implementation

```java
package com.apress.bgn.twelve.jdkstreams;

import java.util.function.Function;

public class MappingProcessor extends AbstractProcessor<Character> {
    private final Function<Integer, Character> function;

    public MappingProcessor(Function<Integer, Character> function) {
        this.function = function;
    }
    @Override
    public void onNext(Integer element) {
        submit(function.apply(element));
        subscription.request(1);
    }
}
```

In Listing 12-10, you can see a `MappingProcessor` instance being added to the reactive flow.

Listing 12-10. A `MappingProcessor` Instance Being Added to a Reactive Flow

```java
package com.apress.bgn.twelve.jdkstreams;

public class ReactiveDemo {
    public static void main(String... args) {
        IntPublisher publisher = new IntPublisher();
        FilterCharProcessor filterCharProcessor = new FilterCharProcessor();
```

```
        TransformerProcessor transformerProcessor = new
        TransformerProcessor();
        MappingProcessor mappingProcessor =
                        new MappingProcessor(element -> (char) element.
                        intValue());
        publisher.subscribe(filterCharProcessor);
        filterCharProcessor.subscribe(transformerProcessor);
        transformerProcessor.subscribe(mappingProcessor);
        //...
        publisher.start();
    }
}
```

The last component of this flow is the subscriber. The subscriber is the most important component in a flow; until a subscriber is added to it and a Subscription instance is created, nothing actually happens. Our subscriber implements the Flow. Subscriber<Character>, and most of it is identical to the code we've isolated in the AbstractProcessor<T>, which might look a little bit redundant, but makes things very easy as well. Listing 12-11 depicts the Subscriber implementation.

Listing 12-11. Subscriber<Character> Implementation

```
package com.apress.bgn.twelve.jdkstreams;
// some import statements omitted
import java.util.concurrent.Flow;

public class CharPrinter implements Flow.Subscriber<Character> {
    private static final Logger log = LoggerFactory.
getLogger(CharPrinter.class);
    private Flow.Subscription subscription;

    @Override
    public void onSubscribe(Flow.Subscription subscription) {
        if (this.subscription == null) {
            this.subscription = subscription;
            this.subscription.request(1);
```

```java
        } else {
            subscription.cancel();
        }
    }

    @Override
    public void onNext(Character element) {
        log.info("Result: {}", element);

        subscription.request(1);
    }

    @Override
    public void onError(Throwable throwable) {
        log.error("Something went wrong.", throwable);
    }

    @Override
    public void onComplete() {
        log.info("Printing complete.");
    }
}
```

Using this subscriber class, the flow can now be completed as shown in Listing 12-12.

Listing 12-12. Reactive Pipeline Complete Implementation

```java
package com.apress.bgn.twelve.jdkstreams;

public class ReactiveDemo {
    public static void main(String... args) {
        IntPublisher publisher = new IntPublisher(0);
        FilterCharProcessor filterCharProcessor = new
        FilterCharProcessor();
        TransformerProcessor transformerProcessor = new
        TransformerProcessor();
        MappingProcessor mappingProcessor = new MappingProcessor(element ->
        (char) element.intValue());
        CharPrinter charPrinter = new CharPrinter();
```

```
        publisher.subscribe(filterCharProcessor);
        filterCharProcessor.subscribe(transformerProcessor);
        transformerProcessor.subscribe(mappingProcessor);
        mappingProcessor.subscribe(charPrinter);
        publisher.start();
    }
}
```

It would be nice if the subscribe(..) method would return the caller instance so that we could chain the subscribe(..) calls, but we work with what is provided for us. When the previous code is run, a log similar to the one depicted in Listing 12-13 is printed in the console:

Listing 12-13. Console Output of a Reactive Flow Being Executed

```
...
INFO  c.a.b.t.j.CharPrinter - Result: .
INFO  c.a.b.t.j.CharPrinter - Result: ,
INFO  c.a.b.t.j.CharPrinter - Result: A
DEBUG c.a.b.t.j.FilterCharProcessor - Element 147 discarded.
DEBUG c.a.b.t.j.FilterCharProcessor - Element 127 discarded.
INFO  c.a.b.t.j.CharPrinter - Result: E
INFO  c.a.b.t.j.CharPrinter - Result: Z
...
```

The previous example uses an infinite IntStream to generate elements to be published, processed, and consumed. This leads to the execution program running forever, so you will have to stop it manually. Another consequence of this is that the onComplete() methods will never be called. If we want to use it we must make sure the number of items being published is a finite one, but initializing the IntPublisher with a value different than 0(ZERO).

Another thing to mention is that back-pressure handling is done more in a conceptual way. The Flow API doesn't provide any mechanism to signal about back-pressure or to deal with it. So the subscription.request(1) just makes sure that when onNext(..) is called, the element producing rate is reduced to one. Various strategies can be devised to deal with back-pressure based on the fine-tuning of the subscriber, but it is difficult to show something like this in a very simple example that does not involve two microservices reactively interacting with each other.

Support for reactive streams is quite thin in the JDK, even in version 17, released on September 14, 2021. It was expected that more useful classes will be added in future versions, but apparently Oracle is focused on other aspects, such as reorganizing the module structure and deciding how to better monetize usage of the JDK. That is why the last section of this chapter covers a short example of reactive programming done with the Project Reactor library.

Reactive Streams Technology Compatibility Kit

When building applications that use reactive streams, a lot of things can go wrong. To make sure things go as expected, the **Reactive Streams Technology Compatibility Kit** project, also known as **TCK**,[3] is a very useful library to write tests. This library contains classes that can be used to test reactive implementations against the reactive streams specifications. TCK is intended to verify the interfaces contained in the JDK `java.util.concurrent.Flow` class and for some reason the team that created the library decide to use TestNG as a testing library.

🔥 In version 1.0.3 TCK was modified to verify the interfaces contained in the Reactive Streams API.

Wait, what? You might exclaim.

Then how can it be used verify the interfaces contained in the JDK java.util. concurrent.Flow class?

Patience young padawan, all will be explained at the right time.

TCK contains four classes that have to be implemented to provide their `Flow.Publisher<T>`, `Flow.Subscriber<T>`, and `Flow.Processor<T,R>` implementations for the test harness to validate. The four classes are:

- `org.reactivestreams.tck.PublisherVerification<T>` used to test `Publisher<T>` implementations

---

[3] See the official GitHub Repo at Github, "Reactive-Streams," https://github.com/reactive-streams/reactive-streams-jvm/tree/master/tck, accessed October 15, 2021.

- `org.reactivestreams.tck.SubscriberWhiteboxVerification<T>` used for whitebox testing `Subscriber<T>` implementations and `Subscription` instances

- `org.reactivestreams.tck.SubscriberBlackboxVerification<T>` used for blackbox testing `Subscriber<T>` implementations and `Subscription` instances

- `org.reactivestreams.tck.IdentityProcessorVerification<T>` used to test `Processor<T,R>` implementations

To make the purpose of each test obvious, the library test methods names follow this pattern: TYPE_spec#_DESC where TYPE is one of `required, optional, stochastic,` or `untested,` which refers to the importance of the rule being tested. The hash signs in `spec</emphasis></emphasis>#` represent the rule number with the first one being 1 for `Publisher<T>` instances and 2 for `Subscriber<T>` instances. The `DESC` is a short explanation of the test purpose.

Let's see how we could test the `IntPublisher` that we defined previously. The `PublisherVerification<T>` class requires implementation of two test methods: one to test a working `Publisher<T>` (the `createPublisher(..)` method) instance that emits a number of elements, and one to test a "failed" `Publisher<T>` (the `createFailedPublisher(..)`)instance, which was unable to initialize a connection it needs to emit elements.

The instance tested by the `createPublisher(..)` is created by passing an argument with a value different from 0(ZERO), so the `IntPublisher` instance emits a limits set of elements, and the test execution is finite as well.

The `PublisherVerification<Integer>` implementation is depicted in Listing 12-14.

Listing 12-14. TestNG Test Class for Testing a `IntPublisher` Instance

```
package com.apress.bgn.twelve.jdkstreams;

import org.reactivestreams.FlowAdapters;
import org.reactivestreams.Publisher;
import org.reactivestreams.tck.PublisherVerification;
import org.reactivestreams.tck.TestEnvironment;
import java.util.concurrent.Flow;
// other import statements omitted
```

```java
public class IntPublisherTest extends PublisherVerification<Integer> {
    private static final Logger log = LoggerFactory.
    getLogger(IntPublisherTest.class);

    public IntPublisherTest() {
        super(new TestEnvironment(300));
    }

    @Override
    public Publisher<Integer> createPublisher(final long elements) {
        return FlowAdapters.toPublisher(new IntPublisher(30) {
            @Override
            public void subscribe(Flow.Subscriber<? super Integer>
            subscriber) {
                intStream.forEach(subscriber::onNext);
                subscriber.onComplete();
            }
        });
    }

    @Override
    public Publisher<Integer> createFailedPublisher() {
        return FlowAdapters.toPublisher(new IntPublisher(0) {
            @Override
            public void subscribe(Flow.Subscriber<? super Integer>
            subscriber) {
                subscriber.onError(new RuntimeException("There be dragons!
                (this is a failed publisher)"));
            }
        });
    }
}
```

Another thing that that should be mentioned about the previous test class is that since the implementation is designed to work with the Reactive Streams API, it cannot be used to test the JDK based IntPublisher. However, it was mentioned previously that in version 1.0.3 the Reactive Stream API was enriched with a set of classes used as bridges between the Reactive Stream and the JDK Reactive Stream API. Thus, IntPublisher must be provided as an argument to the FlowAdapters.toPublisher(..) method that converts it to an equivalent org.reactivestreams.Publisher that the IntPublisherTest can test.

A Publisher<T> implementation might not pass all the tests, because of design decisions that are specific to the application you are building. In our case the IntPublisher implementation is quite simplistic and when running the createPublisher(..) method, of all the executed tests, not many of them pass and most are ignored, as depicted in Figure 12-5.

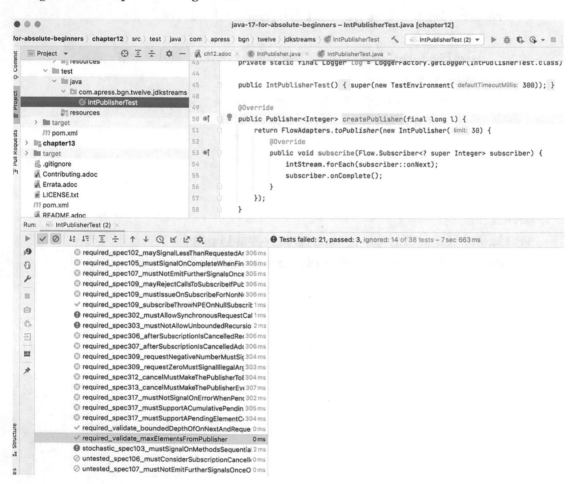

Figure 12-5. *TestNG reactive publisher*

The reason tests do not pass or are ignored is that our implementation does not implement behaviors targeted by those specific tests (e.g., `maySupportMultiSubscribe`, `maySignalLessThanRequestedAndTerminateSubscription`, `mustSignalOnMethodsSequentially`).

We can test the processor and subscriber we defined in the previous section by extending the previously mentioned testing classes as well, but we'll leave that as an exercise to you, because there is one more interesting thing we would like to cover in this chapter.

Using Project Reactor

As mentioned previously, the JDK support for reactive programming is quite scarce. Publishers, processors, and subscribers should function asynchronously, and all that behavior must be implemented by the developer which can be a bit of a pain. The only thing that the JDK is suitable for at the moment is providing a common interface between all the other already existing implementations. There are a lot of them, providing many more useful classes for more specialized reactive components and utility methods to create and connect them easier. The one I personally fancy the most as a Spring aficionado is **Project Reactor**, the same one favored by the Spring development team.

Project Reactor is one of the first libraries for reactive programming and its classes provide a nonblocking stable foundation with efficient demand management for building reactive applications. It works with Java 8 but does provide adapter classes for JDK9+ reactive streams classes.

Project reactor is suitable for microservices applications and provides a lot more classes designed to make programming reactive application practical than the JDK does. Project reactor provides two main publisher implementations: `reactor.core.publisher.Mono<T>`, which is a reactive stream publisher limited to publishing zero or one element, and `reactor.core.publisher.Flux<T>`, which is a reactive stream publisher with basic flow operators.

The advantage of using Project React is that we have a lot more classes and methods to work with, there are static factories that can be used to create publishers, and operations can be chained way more easily.

The Project Reactor team did not like the name `Processor,` though, so the intermediary components are named **operators**.

If you look in the official documentation you will most likely encounter the schema in Figure 12-6.[4]

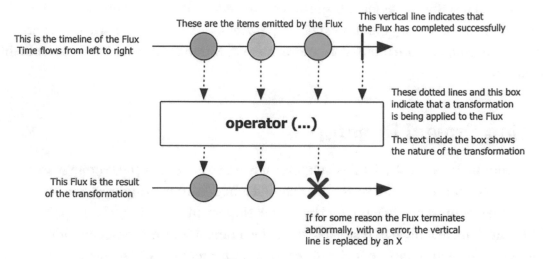

Figure 12-6. *Project Reactor Flux Publisher implementation*

This is an abstract schema of how the `Flux<T>` publisher works. The `Flux<T>` emits elements, can throw exceptions, and completed when there are no more elements to publish, the same behavior it was explained previously, the Project Reactor team just found a prettier way to draw it.

The drawing for the `Mono` implementation is quite similar (see `http://projectreactor.io/docs/core/release/api/reactor/core/publisher/Mono.html`).

But let's put that aside and look at a few code samples. Creating `Flux<T>` instances is very easy using the multiple utility methods in this class. Before starting to publish elements, let's design a general subscriber that does nothing else than print values, because we will need it to make sure our `Flux<T>` publishers work.

To write a subscriber using Project Reactor API, you have multiple options. You can implement the `org.reactivestreams.Subscriber<T>` directly, as shown in Listing 12-15.

---

[4] Image source: Project Reactor, "Public API JavaDoc," `http://projectreactor.io/docs/core/release/api/reactor/core/publisher/Flux.html`, accessed October 15, 2021.

Listing 12-15. `org.reactivestreams.Subscriber<T>` Implementation

```
package com.apress.bgn.twelve.reactor;

import org.reactivestreams.Subscriber;
import org.reactivestreams.Subscription;
// other import statements omitted

public class GenericSubscriber<T> implements Subscriber<T> {
    private static final Logger log = LoggerFactory.
getLogger(GenericSubscriber.class);
    private Subscription subscription;
    @Override
    public void onSubscribe(Subscription subscription) {
        if (this.subscription == null) {
            this.subscription = subscription;
            this.subscription.request(1);
        } else {
            subscription.cancel();
        }
    }
    @Override
    public void onNext(T element) {
        log.info("consumed {} ", element);
        subscription.request(1);
    }
    @Override
    public void onError(Throwable t) {
        log.error("Unexpected issue!", t);
    }
    @Override
    public void onComplete() {
        log.info("All done!");
    }
}
```

To avoid implementing that many methods with boilerplate code, there is also the option of implementing `reactor.core.CoreSubscriber<T>`, the reactor base interface for subscribers, or even better, by extending `reactor.core.publisher.BaseSubscriber<T>` class, which provides basic subscriber functionality. The behavior of subscriber typical methods can be modified by overriding methods with then same name but prefixed with hook. In Listing 12-16, you can see how easy it is to write a subscriber using project reactor.

Listing 12-16. `reactor.core.publisher.BaseSubscriber<T>` Extension

```java
package com.apress.bgn.twelve.reactor;

import reactor.core.publisher.BaseSubscriber;
// other import statements omitted

public class GenericSubscriber<T> extends BaseSubscriber<T> {
    private static final Logger log = LoggerFactory.
getLogger(GenericSubscriber.class);

    @Override
    protected void hookOnNext(T value) {
        log.info("consumed {} ", value);
        super.hookOnNext(value);
    }

    @Override
    protected void hookOnComplete() {
        log.info("call done.");
        super.hookOnComplete();
    }
}
```

Ta da! Now we have a subscriber class, so let's create a reactive publisher that serves integers from an infinite integer stream, to use an instance of this class. The implementation is shown in Listing 12-17.

Listing 12-17. Creating a Reactive Publisher Using Project Reactor's Flux<T>

```
package com.apress.bgn.twelve.reactor;

import reactor.core.publisher.Flux;
import java.util.Random;
import java.util.stream.Stream;

public class ReactorDemo {

    private static final Random random = new Random();

    public static void main(String... args) {
        Flux<Integer> intFlux = Flux.fromStream(
                Stream.generate(() -> random.nextInt(150))
        );
        intFlux.subscribe(new GenericSubscriber<>());
    }
}
```

If you run the preceding code, you will see that all the generated integer values are printed by the subscriber. A Flux<T> can be created from a multitude of sources, including arrays and other publishers. For special situations, to avoid returning a null value, an empty Flux<T> can be created by calling the empty() method.

```
String[] names = {"Joy", "John", "Anemona", "Takeshi"};
Flux.fromArray(names).subscribe(new GenericSubscriber<>());

Flux<Integer> intFlux = Flux.empty();
intFlux.subscribe(new GenericSubscriber<>());
```

The most awesome method in my opinion is named just(..), and it is provided for both Flux and Mono. It takes one or more values and returns a publisher, a Flux<T> or a Mono<T>, depending on the type being called on.

```
Flux<String> dummyStr = Flux.just("one", "two", "three");
Flux<Integer> dummyInt = Flux.just(1,2,3);

Mono<Integer> one = Mono.just(1);
Mono<String> empty = Mono.empty();
```

Another method that you might find useful is concat(..), which allows you to concatenate two Flux<T> instances.

```
String[] names = {"Joy", "John", "Anemona", "Takeshi"};
Flux<String> namesFlux = Flux.fromArray(names);

String[] names2 = {"Hanna", "Eugen", "Anthony", "David"};
Flux<String> names2Flux = Flux.fromArray(names2);
Flux<String> combined = Flux.concat(namesFlux, names2Flux);
combined.subscribe(new GenericSubscriber<>());
```

Another thing that you might like: remember how the IntPublisher class had to be slowed down using a Thread.sleep(1000) call? With Flux<T> you do not need to do that, because there are two utility methods that combined lead to the same behavior.

```
Flux<Integer> infiniteFlux = Flux.fromStream(
        Stream.generate(() -> random.nextInt(150))
    );

Flux<Long> delay = Flux.interval(Duration.ofSeconds(1));
Flux<Integer> delayedInfiniteFlux = infiniteFlux.zipWith(delay,
(s,l) -> s);
delayedInfiniteFlux.subscribe(new GenericSubscriber<>());
```

The interval(..) method creates a publisher that emits long values starting with 0 and incrementing at specified time intervals on the global timer; it receives as an argument of type Duration, in the previous example seconds were used. The zipWith(..) method zips the Flux<T> instance received as a parameter. The zip operation is a specific stream operation that translates as both publishers emitting one element and combining these elements using a java.util.function. BiFunction<T, U, R>. In our case the function just discards the second element and returns the elements of the calling stream slowed down by the generated seconds of the second stream.

The good part about the components provided by project reactor is that they return mostly the same type of objects they are being called on, and this means they can be easily chained.

A reactive piece of code equivalent to the previously implemented JDK based implementation can be written with reactor API, as shown in Listing 12-18.

Listing 12-18. Writing a Reactive Pipeline Using Project Reactor

```
Flux<Integer> infiniteFlux = Flux.fromStream(
        Stream.generate(() -> random.nextInt(150))
    );

Flux<Long> delay = Flux.interval(Duration.ofSeconds(1));
Flux<Integer> delayedInfiniteFlux = infiniteFlux.zipWith(delay, (s, l) -> s);

delayedInfiniteFlux
    .filter(element -> (element >= 0 && element < 127))
    .map(item -> {
        if (item % 2 == 0 && item >= 98 && item <= 122) {
            item -= 32;
        }
        return item;
    })
.map(element -> (char) element.intValue())
.subscribe(new GenericSubscriber<>());
```

Most functions that you remember from the Stream API have been implemented for a reactive usage in project Reactor, so if the previous code seems familiar, this is the reason why.

Regarding Project Reactor API, if you are ever in need of a reactive library, you could consider this one first. You can find the official documentation at `http://projectreactor.io/docs/core/milestone/reference/`, and it is quite good and full of examples. If Oracle ever decides to provide their own rich API for programming reactive applications using reactive streams, they will probably be a little bit too late to the table anyway.

Summary

Reactive programming is not an easy topic, but it does seem to be the future of programming. This book would need to get into really advanced topics to show the true power of a reactive solution. Being a book for absolute beginners in Java, this is not a suitable subject for it. However, after reading this book, if you are interested in learning more about building reactive applications, the *Pro Spring MVC with WebFlux*[5] book, published by Apress in January 2021, has a few great chapters about building reactive applications with Spring and Project Reactor.

What you must keep in mind is that reactive implementations are quite useless with implementations that are not reactive. There is no use in designing and using reactive components with nonreactive components, because you might actually introduce failure points and slow things down. For example, if you are using an Oracle database, there is no point in defining a repository class that returns elements using reactive streams, because an Oracle database does not support reactive access. You would just be adding a reactive layer that adds extra implementation, because there are no real benefits in this case. But if your database of choice is MongoDB, you can use reactive programming confidently, because MongoDB databases support reactive access. Also, if you are building a web application with a ReactJS or angular interface, you can design your controller classes to provide data reactively to be displayed by the interface.

The contents of this chapter can be summarized as follows:

- reactive programming was explained

- the behavior of reactive streams was explained

- the JDK reactive streams support was covered

- how to use the Reactive Streams Technology Compatibility Kit to test your reactive solution was addressed

- a small introduction to Project Reactor components for building reactive applications was provided

---

[5] Marten Deinum and Iuliana Cosmina, *Pro Spring MVC with WebFlux* (New York: Apress, 2021), https://www.apress.com/us/book/9781484256657, accessed October 15, 2021.

CHAPTER 13

Garbage Collection

When executing Java code, objects are created, used, and discarded repeatedly from memory. The process through which unused Java objects are discarded is called **memory management**, but is most commonly known as **garbage collection (GC)**. Garbage collection was mentioned in **Chapter 5,** as it was needed for explaining the difference between primitive and reference types, but in this chapter we will go deep under the hood of the JVM to resolve yet another mystery of a running Java application.

When the Java garbage collector does its job properly, the memory is cleaned up before new objects are created and it does not fill up, so you could say that the memory allocated to a program is *recycled*. Programs of low complexity, like the ones we've been writing so far, do not require that much memory to function, but depending on their design (remember recursivity?) they could end up using more memory than available. In Java, the garbage collector runs automatically. In more low-level languages like C/C++ there is no automatic memory management and the developer is responsible for writing the code to allocate memory as needed, and deallocate it when it is no longer needed. Although it seems practical to have automatic memory management, the garbage collector can be a problem if managed incorrectly. This chapter provides enough information about the garbage collector to ensure that it is used wisely and that when problems arise, at least you will have a good place to start fixing them.

Although some ways to tune the garbage collector will be introduced, just keep in mind that garbage collection tuning should not be necessary; a program should be written in such a way that it creates only the objects needed to perform its function, references are managed correctly, estimations of memory capacity for the server to run the application should be done before the application is put into production, and the maximum amount of memory needed by it should be known and configured before that. If the memory allocated to a Java program is not enough, there is usually something rotten in the implementation.

© Iuliana Cosmina 2022
I. Cosmina, *Java 17 for Absolute Beginners*, https://doi.org/10.1007/978-1-4842-7080-6_13

Garbage Collection Basics

The Java automatic garbage collection is one of the major features of the of the Java Programming language. The JVM is a virtual machine used to execute Java programs, as mentioned at the beginning of this book. A Java program uses resources of the system the JVM is running on top of, so it must have a way to release those resources safely. This job is done by the garbage collector.

To understand what the place of the garbage collector is we must take a look at the JVM architecture.

Oracle Hotspot JVM Architecture

Over the years some big companies have produced their own variations of the JVM (e.g., IBM) and now that Java is moving into the module age and the rapid delivery style, more and more companies will appear that maintain a specific version of the JDK/JVM (e.g., Azul, Amazon Coretto, GraalVM) because migration to 9+ is difficult for big applications with legacy dependencies.

Another important economic factor here is that Java Support is paid as of January 2019, for all LTS versions after the two years grace period, so companies will eventually have to pay for the JDK running their Java based software. The official Oracle JDK can be used on personal computers by developers learning to code, or building small projects, but running their software on a server, accessing enterprise features such as full-fledged JMC, and turning that software profitable requires a paid subscription.

Currently, the Oracle's HotSpot is still the most common JVM being used by many applications. When it comes to garbage collection, this JVM provides a mature set of garbage collection options. An abstract representation of its architecture is depicted in Figure 13-1.

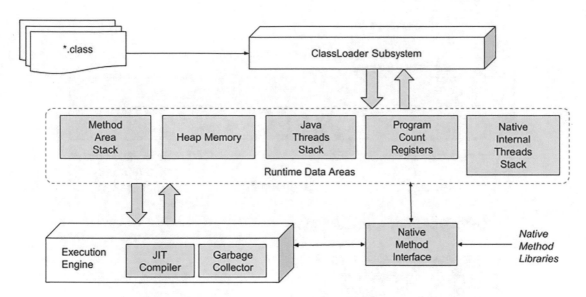

Figure 13-1. *Oracle HotSpot JVM architecture (abstract representation)*

The **heap** memory area is managed by the garbage collector and is split into multiple zones. Objects are moved between these zones until being discarded. The zones depicted in Figure 13-2 are for old-styles garbage collectors, and the new style of garbage collector, which will probably follow the model of the current default garbage collector used by the JDK, the G1GC, that was introduced in JDK 8.

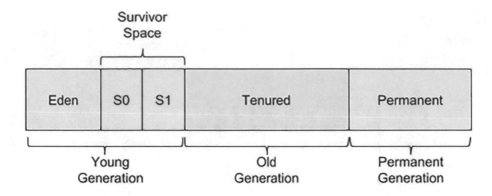

Older GCs: serial, parallel, CMS

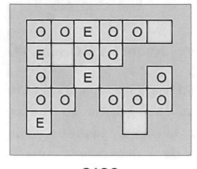

G1GC

Figure 13-2. *The heap structure*

The G1GC is a next-generation garbage collector designed for machines with a lot of resources, which is why its approach to the partitioning of the heap is different. Its heap is partitioned into a set of equal-sized heap regions, each a contiguous range of virtual memory. Certain region sets are assigned the same roles (eden, survivor, old) as in the older collectors, but there is not a fixed size for them. This provides greater flexibility in memory usage. You can read more about the different types of garbage collectors in the next section, for now the focus will remain on the heap memory and its zones that are named **generations**.

When an application is running, objects created by it are stored in the **young generation area**. When an object is created it starts its life in a subdivision of this generation named the **eden space**. When the eden space is filled, this triggers a **minor garbage collection (minor GC run)** that cleans up this area of unreferenced objects, and moves referenced objects to the **first survivor space (S0)**. The next time the eden space is filled another minor GC run is triggered, which again deletes unreferenced objects, and referenced objects are moved to the **next survivor space (S1)**.

The objects in S0 have been there for a minor GC run, so their age is incremented. They are moved to S1 as well, so S0 and the eden can be cleaned up.

At the next minor GC run, the operation is performed again, but this time referenced objects are saved into the empty S0. The older objects from S1 have their age incremented and moved to S0 as well, so the S1 and eden can be cleaned up.

After the objects in survivor space reach a certain age (value specific to each type garbage collector), they are moved to **the old generation space** during minor GC runs.

The previously described steps are depicted in image 13-3, and the objects o1 and o2 are aged until they are moved to the old generation area.

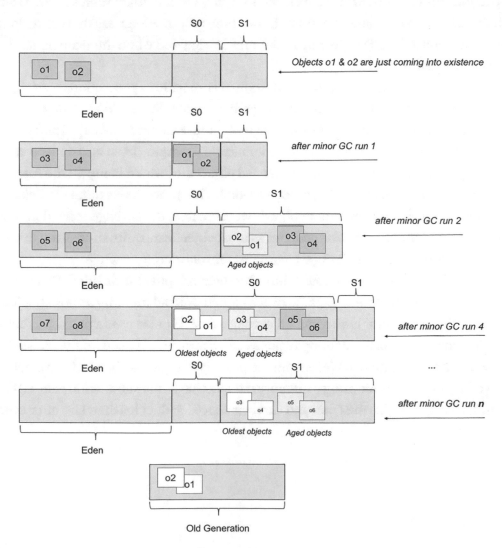

Figure 13-3. *Minor GC runs on the young generation space*

Minor GC collections will happen until the old generation space is filled. That is when a **major garbage collection (major GC run)** is triggered, which will delete unreferenced objects and will compact the memory, moving objects around, so that the empty memory left is one big compact space.

The minor garbage collection event is a stop-the-world event. This process basically takes over the run of the application and pauses its execution, so it can free the memory. As the young generation space is quite small in size (as you will see this in the next section), the application pause is usually negligible. If no memory can be reclaimed from the young generation area after a minor GC run takes place, a major GC run is triggered.

The **permanent generation** area is reserved for JVM metadata such as classes and methods. This area is cleaned too from time to time to remove classes that are no longer used in the application. The cleanup of this area is triggered when there are no more objects in the heap.

The garbage collection process just described is specific to generational garbage collectors, such as the G1GC. Before JDK 8, garbage collection was done using an older garbage collector that uses an algorithm called **Concurrent Mark Sweep**. This type of garbage collector runs in parallel with the application marking used and unused zones of memory. Then it would delete unreferenced object and would compact the memory into a contiguous zone, by moving objects around. This process was quite inefficient and time-consuming. As more and more objects were created, the garbage collection took more and more time to be performed, but as most objects are quite short-lived this was not really a problem. So the CMS garbage collector was okay for a while.

The G1GC has a similar approach, but after the mark phase is finished, G1 focuses on regions that are mostly empty to recover as much unused memory as possible. That is why this garbage collector is also named **garbage-first**. G1 also uses a pause prediction model to decide how many memory regions can be processed based on the pause time set for the application. Objects from the processed region are copied to a single region of the heap, thus realizing a memory compaction at the same time. Also, G1GC does not have a fixed size the eden and survivor spaces, it decides their size after every minor GC run.

How Many Garbage Collectors Are There?

The garbage collectors the Oracle HotSpot JVM provides the following types of garbage collectors:

- **the serial collector**: all garbage collection events are conducted serially in one thread. Memory compaction happens after each garbage collection.

- **the parallel collector**: multiple threads are used for minor garbage collection. A single thread is used for a major garbage collection and Old Generation compaction.

- **CMS (Concurrent Mark Sweep)**: multiple threads are used for minor garbage collection using the same algorithm as the parallel GC. Major garbage collection is multithreaded as well, but CMS runs concurrently alongside application processes to minimize stop the world events. No memory compaction is done. This type of garbage collector is suitable for or applications requiring shorter garbage collection pauses and that can afford to share processor resources with the garbage collector while the application is running. This was the default garbage collector until Java 8, when G1 was introduced as default.

- **G1 (Garbage First)**: introduced in Oracle JDK 7, update 4 was designed to permanently replace the CMS GC and is suitable for applications that can operate concurrently with CMS collector, that need memory compaction, that need more predictable GC pause durations and do not require a much larger heap. The Garbage-First (G1) collector is a server-style garbage collector, targeted for multiprocessor machines with large memories, but considering that most laptops now have at least 8 cores and 16GB RAM it is quite suitable for them as well. G1 has both concurrent (runs along with application threads, e.g., refinement, marking, cleanup) and parallel (multithreaded, e.g., stop-the-world) phases. Full garbage collections are still single threaded, but if tuned properly your applications should avoid full garbage collections.

- **Z Garbage Collector**: the Z Garbage Collector (ZGC) is a scalable low latency garbage collector introduced in Java 11. ZGC performs all expensive work concurrently, without stopping the execution of application threads for more than 10ms, which makes is suitable for applications which require low latency and/or use a very large heap (multiterabytes)

- **Shenandoah Garbage Collector**: Shenandoah is the low pause time garbage collector, introduced in Java 12, that reduces GC pause times by performing more garbage collection work concurrently with the running Java program. Shenandoah does the bulk of GC work concurrently, including the concurrent compaction, which means its pause times are no longer directly proportional to the size of the heap.

- **Epsilon no-op collector**: introduced in Java 11, this type of collector is actually a dummy GC, that does not recycle or clean up the memory. When the heap is full, the JVM just shuts down. This type of collector can be used for performance tests, for memory allocation analysis, VM interface testing, and extremely short-lived jobs and applications that are super-limited when it comes to memory usage and developers must estimate the application memory footprint as exactly as possible.

⚠ The Concurrent Mark Sweep Garbage Collector has been removed from the JDK, and the `-XX:+UseConcMarkSweepGC` VM option is no longer recognized.

We've listed the garbage collector types, but how do we know which is the one used by our local JVM? There is more than one way. The most simple way is to add the `-verbose:gc` as a VM option when running a simple class with a `main(..)` method.

Using Java 17 JDK without any other configuration, the following output is shown:

```
[0.011s][info][gc] Using G1
```

It becomes clear that by default, the G1 garbage collector is used. To show even more details of this garbage collector the -Xlog:gc*[1] can be added to the VM arguments when running a Java class. For the simple class com.apress.bgn.thirteen.ShowGCDemo that contains only a System.out.println statement, the output shown in Listing 13-1 is printed in the console when the class is executed with the two VM options mentioned previously.

Listing 13-1. Showing G1GC details Using -verbose:gc -Xlog:gc* as VM Arguments When Running ShowGCDemo

```
[0.010s][info][gc] Using G1
[0.012s][info][gc,init] Version: 17+35-2724 (release)
[0.012s][info][gc,init] CPUs: 8 total, 8 available
[0.012s][info][gc,init] Memory: 16384M
[0.012s][info][gc,init] Large Page Support: Disabled
[0.012s][info][gc,init] NUMA Support: Disabled
[0.012s][info][gc,init] Compressed Oops: Enabled (Zero based)
[0.012s][info][gc,init] Heap Region Size: 2M
[0.012s][info][gc,init] Heap Min Capacity: 8M
[0.012s][info][gc,init] Heap Initial Capacity: 256M
[0.012s][info][gc,init] Heap Max Capacity: 4G
[0.012s][info][gc,init] Pre-touch: Disabled
[0.012s][info][gc,init] Parallel Workers: 8
[0.012s][info][gc,init] Concurrent Workers: 2
[0.012s][info][gc,init] Concurrent Refinement Workers: 8
[0.012s][info][gc,init] Periodic GC: Disabled
[0.012s][info][gc,metaspace] CDS archive(s) mapped at: [0x0000000800000000-
0x0000000800bd0000-0x0000000800bd0000), size 12386304, SharedBaseAddress:
0x0000000800000000, ArchiveRelocationMode: 0.
[0.012s][info][gc,metaspace] Compressed class space mapped at: 0x0000000800
c00000-0x0000000840c00000, reserved size: 1073741824
[0.012s][info][gc,metaspace] Narrow klass base: 0x0000000800000000, Narrow
klass shift: 0, Narrow klass range: 0x100000000
Hey ma' look the GC!
```

---

[1] This VM option replaced the deprecated -XX:+PrintGCDetails.

```
[0.123s][info][gc,heap,exit] Heap
[0.123s][info][gc,heap,exit] garbage-first heap   total 266240K, used
6098K [0x0000000700000000, 0x0000000800000000)
[0.123s][info][gc,heap,exit]   region size 2048K, 3 young (6144K), 0
survivors (OK)
[0.123s][info][gc,heap,exit]  Metaspace       used 397K, committed 576K,
reserved 1056768K
[0.123s][info][gc,heap,exit]   class space      used 20K, committed 128K,
reserved 1048576K
```

We can see the heap maximum size (4G), the memory region size (2M), and size and occupation for each generation.

In **Chapter 5**, the java -XX:+PrintFlagsFinal -version command was introduced to show all JVM flags. Filtering the results returned by the "GC" and "NewSize" shows all the GC specific flags and their values. There are quite a few of them, and they are shown in Listing 13-2.

Listing 13-2. Showing G1GC Flags Using java -XX:+PrintFlagsFinal
-version | grep 'GC\|NewSize'

```
$ java -XX:+PrintFlagsFinal -version | grep 'GC\|NewSize'
    uintx AdaptiveSizeMajorGCDecayTimeScale   = 10           {product} {default}
     uint ConcGCThreads                        = 2            {product}
                                                              {ergonomic}
     bool DisableExplicitGC                    = false        {product} {default}
     bool ExplicitGCInvokesConcurrent          = false        {product} {default}
    uintx G1MixedGCCountTarget                 = 8            {product} {default}
    uintx G1PeriodicGCInterval                 = 0            {manageable}
                                                              {default}
     bool G1PeriodicGCInvokesConcurrent        = true         {product} {default}
   double G1PeriodicGCSystemLoadThreshold      = 0.000000     {manageable}
                                                              {default}
    uintx GCDrainStackTargetSize               = 64           {product}
                                                              {ergonomic}
    uintx GCHeapFreeLimit                      = 2            {product} {default}
    uintx GCLockerEdenExpansionPercent         = 5            {product} {default}
    uintx GCPauseIntervalMillis                = 201          {product} {default}
```

uintx GCTimeLimit	= 98	{product} {default}	
uintx GCTimeRatio	= 12	{product} {default}	
bool HeapDumpAfterFullGC	= false	{manageable} {default}	
bool HeapDumpBeforeFullGC	= false	{manageable} {default}	
size_t HeapSizePerGCThread	= 43620760	{product} {default}	
uintx MaxGCMinorPauseMillis	= 18446744..	{product} {default}	
uintx MaxGCPauseMillis	= 200	{product} {default}	
size_t MaxNewSize	= 2575302656	{product} {ergonomic}	
size_t NewSize	**= 1363144**	**{product} {default}**	
size_t NewSizeThreadIncrease	= 5320	{pd product} {default}	
int ParGCArrayScanChunk	= 50	{product} {default}	
uintx ParallelGCBufferWastePct	= 10	{product} {default}	
uint ParallelGCThreads	= 8	{product} {default}	
bool PrintGC	= false	{product} {default}	
bool PrintGCDetails	= false	{product} {default}	
bool ScavengeBeforeFullGC	= false	{product} {default}	
bool UseAdaptiveSizeDecayMajorGCCost	= true	{product} {default}	
bool UseAdaptiveSizePolicyWithSystemGC	= false	{product} {default}	
bool UseDynamicNumberOfGCThreads	= true	{product} {default}	
bool UseG1GC	**= true**	**{product} {ergonomic}**	
bool UseGCOverheadLimit	= true	{product} {default}	
bool UseMaximumCompactionOnSystemGC	= true	{product} {default}	
bool UseParallelGC	= false	{product} {default}	
bool UseSerialGC	= false	{product} {default}	
bool UseShenandoahGC	= false	{product} {default}	
bool UseZGC	= false	{product} {default}	

The UseG1GC is set to true by default, which means when the JVM is used to execute a Java application, the G1 garbage collector is used. The NewSize filter picks up flags with values relevant for the Young Generation size. All these flags can be used as VM options preceedded by -XX:+ when running an application to customize the GC behavior or show extra details in the logs. For example, we can instruct the JVM to use any of the garbage collectors listed previously by using their specific VM options:

- -XX:+UseSerialGC to use the serial GC, in this case adding -verbose: gc -Xlog:gc* as VM option as well produces the output in Listing 13-3 (notice the lack of parallel, concurrent workers and the different heap structure).

Listing 13-3. Showing Serial GC Details

```
[0.013s][info][gc] Using Serial
[0.013s][info][gc,init] Version: 17+35-2724 (release)
[0.013s][info][gc,init] CPUs: 8 total, 8 available
[0.013s][info][gc,init] Memory: 16384M
[0.013s][info][gc,init] Large Page Support: Disabled
[0.013s][info][gc,init] NUMA Support: Disabled
[0.013s][info][gc,init] Compressed Oops: Enabled (Zero based)
[0.013s][info][gc,init] Heap Min Capacity: 8M
[0.013s][info][gc,init] Heap Initial Capacity: 256M
[0.013s][info][gc,init] Heap Max Capacity: 4G
[0.013s][info][gc,init] Pre-touch: Disabled
[0.014s][info][gc,metaspace] CDS archive(s) mapped at: [0x0000000800000000-
0x0000000800bd0000-0x0000000800bd0000), size 12386304, SharedBaseAddress:
0x0000000800000000, ArchiveRelocationMode: 0.
[0.014s][info][gc,metaspace] Compressed class space mapped at: 0x0000000800
c00000-0x0000000840c00000, reserved size: 1073741824
[0.014s][info][gc,metaspace] Narrow klass base: 0x0000000800000000, Narrow
klass shift: 0, Narrow klass range: 0x100000000
Hey ma' look the GC!
[0.180s][info][gc,heap,exit] Heap
[0.180s][info][gc,heap,exit] def new generation   total 78656K, used 9946K
[0x0000000700000000, 0x0000000705550000, 0x0000000755550000)
[0.180s][info][gc,heap,exit]   eden space 69952K,   14% used
[0x0000000700000000, 0x00000007009b6a70, 0x0000000704450000)
[0.180s][info][gc,heap,exit]   from space 8704K,    0% used
[0x0000000704450000, 0x0000000704450000, 0x0000000704cd0000)
```

```
[0.180s][info][gc,heap,exit]    to    space 8704K,    0% used
[0x0000000704cd0000, 0x0000000704cd0000, 0x0000000705550000)
[0.180s][info][gc,heap,exit]  tenured generation   total 174784K, used 0K
[0x0000000755550000, 0x0000000760000000, 0x0000000800000000)
[0.180s][info][gc,heap,exit]    the space 174784K,   0% used
[0x0000000755550000, 0x0000000755550000, 0x0000000755550200,
0x0000000760000000)
[0.180s][info][gc,heap,exit]  Metaspace       used 774K, committed 960K,
reserved 1056768K
[0.180s][info][gc,heap,exit]    class space    used 67K, committed 192K,
reserved 1048576K
```

- -XX:+UseParallelGC to use the parallel GC, in this case
  adding -verbose:gc -Xlog:gc* as VM option as well produces the
  output in Listing 13-4 (notice the parallel workers and the different
  heap structure).

Listing 13-4. Showing Parallel GC Details

[0.016s][info][gc] Using Parallel
```
[0.018s][info][gc,init] Version: 17+35-2724 (release)
[0.018s][info][gc,init] CPUs: 8 total, 8 available
[0.018s][info][gc,init] Memory: 16384M
[0.018s][info][gc,init] Large Page Support: Disabled
[0.018s][info][gc,init] NUMA Support: Disabled
[0.018s][info][gc,init] Compressed Oops: Enabled (Zero based)
[0.018s][info][gc,init] Alignments: Space 512K, Generation 512K, Heap 2M
[0.018s][info][gc,init] Heap Min Capacity: 8M
[0.018s][info][gc,init] Heap Initial Capacity: 256M
[0.018s][info][gc,init] Heap Max Capacity: 4G
[0.018s][info][gc,init] Pre-touch: Disabled
```
[0.018s][info][gc,init] Parallel Workers: 8
```
[0.018s][info][gc,metaspace] CDS archive(s) mapped at: [0x0000000800000000-
0x0000000800bd0000-0x0000000800bd0000), size 12386304, SharedBaseAddress:
0x0000000800000000, ArchiveRelocationMode: 0.
[0.018s][info][gc,metaspace] Compressed class space mapped at: 0x0000000800
c00000-0x0000000840c00000, reserved size: 1073741824
```

```
[0.018s][info][gc,metaspace] Narrow klass base: 0x0000000800000000, Narrow
klass shift: 0, Narrow klass range: 0x100000000
Hey ma' look the GC!
[0.187s][info][gc,heap,exit] Heap
[0.187s][info][gc,heap,exit]  PSYoungGen       total 76288K, used 9337K
[0x00000007aab00000, 0x00000007b0000000, 0x0000000800000000)
[0.187s][info][gc,heap,exit]   eden space 65536K, 14% used [0x00000007aab
00000,0x00000007ab41e680,0x00000007aeb00000)
[0.187s][info][gc,heap,exit]   from space 10752K, 0% used [0x00000007af
580000,0x00000007af580000,0x00000007b0000000)
[0.187s][info][gc,heap,exit]   to   space 10752K, 0% used [0x00000007aeb
00000,0x00000007aeb00000,0x00000007af580000)
[0.187s][info][gc,heap,exit]  ParOldGen        total 175104K, used 0K
[0x0000000700000000, 0x000000070ab00000, 0x00000007aab00000)
[0.187s][info][gc,heap,exit]   object space 175104K, 0% used
[0x0000000700000000,0x0000000700000000,0x000000070ab00000)
[0.187s][info][gc,heap,exit]  Metaspace       used 746K, committed 896K,
reserved 1056768K
[0.187s][info][gc,heap,exit]   class space     used 65K, committed 128K,
reserved 1048576K
```

- -XX:+UseG1GC, the default garbage collector, already covered this one.

- -XX:+UseShenandoahGC to use the Shenandoah GC. Although the flag exists, Oracle has chosen not to build Shenandoah, it is however available in various OpenJDK builds listed on the Shenandoah official documentation: https://wiki.openjdk.java.net/display/shenandoah/Main#Main-JDKSupport.

- -XX:+UseZGC to use the ZGC, in this case adding -verbose:gc -Xlog:gc* as VM option as well produces the output in Listing 13-5 (notice the GC and Runtime workers and the different heap structure).

Listing 13-5. Showing ZGC Details

[0.031s][info][gc,init] Initializing The Z Garbage Collector

[0.031s][info][gc,init] Version: 17+35-2724 (release)

[0.031s][info][gc,init] NUMA Support: Disabled

[0.031s][info][gc,init] CPUs: 8 total, 8 available

[0.031s][info][gc,init] Memory: 16384M

[0.031s][info][gc,init] Large Page Support: Disabled

[0.031s][info][gc,init] GC Workers: 2 (dynamic)

[0.031s][info][gc,init] Address Space Type: Contiguous/Unrestricted/
Complete

[0.031s][info][gc,init] Address Space Size: 65536M x 3 = 196608M

[0.032s][info][gc,init] Min Capacity: 8M

[0.032s][info][gc,init] Initial Capacity: 256M

[0.032s][info][gc,init] Max Capacity: 4096M

[0.032s][info][gc,init] Medium Page Size: 32M

[0.032s][info][gc,init] Pre-touch: Disabled

[0.032s][info][gc,init] Uncommit: Enabled

[0.032s][info][gc,init] Uncommit Delay: 300s

[0.032s][info][gc,init] Runtime Workers: 5

[0.032s][info][gc   ] Using The Z Garbage Collector

[0.033s][info][gc,metaspace] CDS archive(s) mapped at: [0x0000000800000000-
0x0000000800ba4000-0x0000000800ba4000), size 12206080, SharedBaseAddress:
0x0000000800000000, ArchiveRelocationMode: 0.

[0.033s][info][gc,metaspace] Compressed class space mapped at: 0x0000000800
c00000-0x0000000840c00000, reserved size: 1073741824

[0.033s][info][gc,metaspace] Narrow klass base: 0x0000000800000000, Narrow
klass shift: 0, Narrow klass range: 0x100000000

Hey ma' look the GC!

[0.283s][info][gc,heap,exit] Heap

[0.283s][info][gc,heap,exit] **ZHeap**   used 10M, capacity 256M, max
capacity 4096M

[0.283s][info][gc,heap,exit] Metaspace   used 754K, committed 896K,
reserved 1056768K

[0.283s][info][gc,heap,exit] class space   used 66K, committed 128K,
reserved 1048576K

- -XX:+UseEpsilonGC, the no-op garbage collector. If in the console
  you will see a message asking you to also add the -XX:+UnlockExpe
  rimentalVMOptions before the option to enable the Epsilon garbage
  collector do so. This VM option is needed to unlock experimental
  features and at the time this book was written this garbage collector
  is an experimental feature. Adding -verbose:gc -Xlog:gc* as VM
  option as well produces the output in Listing 13-6 (notice the lack of
  any workers and the TLAB options).

Listing 13-6. Showing Epsilon GC Details

[0.012s][info][gc] Using Epsilon
[0.012s][info][gc,init] Version: 17+35-2724 (release)
[0.012s][info][gc,init] CPUs: 8 total, 8 available
[0.012s][info][gc,init] Memory: 16384M
[0.012s][info][gc,init] Large Page Support: Disabled
[0.012s][info][gc,init] NUMA Support: Disabled
[0.012s][info][gc,init] Compressed Oops: Enabled (Zero based)
[0.012s][info][gc,init] Heap Min Capacity: 6656K
[0.012s][info][gc,init] Heap Initial Capacity: 256M
[0.012s][info][gc,init] Heap Max Capacity: 4G
[0.012s][info][gc,init] Pre-touch: Disabled
[0.012s][warning][gc,init] Consider setting -Xms equal to -Xmx to avoid
resizing hiccups
[0.012s][warning][gc,init] Consider enabling -XX:+AlwaysPreTouch to avoid
memory commit hiccups
[0.012s][info   ][gc,init] TLAB Size Max: 4M
[0.012s][info   ][gc,init] TLAB Size Elasticity: 1.10x
[0.012s][info   ][gc,init] TLAB Size Decay Time: 1000ms
[0.013s][info   ][gc,metaspace] CDS archive(s) mapped at:
[0x0000000800000000-0x0000000800bd0000-0x0000000800bd0000), size 12386304,
SharedBaseAddress: 0x0000000800000000, ArchiveRelocationMode: 0.
[0.013s][info   ][gc,metaspace] Compressed class space mapped at:
0x0000000800c00000-0x0000000840c00000, reserved size: 1073741824
[0.013s][info   ][gc,metaspace] Narrow klass base: 0x0000000800000000,
Narrow klass shift: 0, Narrow klass range: 0x100000000

```
Hey ma' look the GC!
[0.179s][info    ][gc,heap,exit] Heap
[0.179s][info    ][gc,heap,exit] Epsilon Heap
[0.179s][info    ][gc,heap,exit] Allocation space:
[0.179s][info    ][gc,heap,exit]  space 262144K,   1% used
[0x0000000700000000, 0x00000007003364a0, 0x0000000710000000)
[0.180s][info    ][gc,heap,exit]  Metaspace       used 751K, committed 896K,
reserved 1056768K
[0.180s][info    ][gc,heap,exit]   class space    used 65K, committed 128K,
reserved 1048576K
[0.180s][info    ][gc           ] Heap: 4096M reserved, 256M (6.25%)
committed, 3289K (0.08%) used
[0.180s][info    ][gc,metaspace] Metaspace: 1032M reserved, 896K (0.08%)
committed, 752K (0.07%) used
```

As you can see, the data printed for these garbage collectors has common elements, such as the size of heap, which will always be 256M at the start of the application and has a maximum size of 4GB on my system. The eden and the young generation differs between them as well, the G1 using just 4096K for the young generation, when the CMS requires 78656K. (a lot more)

The most interesting here is the Epislon garbage collector, because as expected it does not have a heap split into generation areas, as this type of garbage collector does not perform garbage collection at all. The **TLAB** is an acronym for **Thread Local Allocation Buffer**, which is a memory area where objects are stored. Only bigger objects are stored outside of TLABs. The TLABs are dynamically resized during the execution for each thread individually. So if a thread allocates very much, the new TLABs that it gets from the heap will increase in size. The minimum size of a TLAB can be controlled using the VM -XX:MinTLABSize option.

For the small empty class that we ran with the previous VM options this output is not really relevant, but you can play with these options when running the code from the next sections, because that is when the statistics printed here have some relevance.

Also, there is a VM option named -XX:+PrintCommandLineFlags that can be used when a class is run to depict configurations of the garbage collector, as the number of threads it makes use of, heap size, and so on. These options are shown in Listing 13-7.

Listing 13-7. G1GC VM Options

```
-XX:ConcGCThreads=2
-XX:G1ConcRefinementThreads=8
-XX:GCDrainStackTargetSize=64
-XX:InitialHeapSize=268435456
-XX:MarkStackSize=4194304
-XX:MaxHeapSize=4294967296
-XX:MinHeapSize=6815736
-XX:+PrintCommandLineFlags
-XX:ReservedCodeCacheSize=251658240
-XX:+SegmentedCodeCache
-XX:+UseCompressedClassPointers
-XX:+UseCompressedOops
-XX:+UseG1GC
```

Most of these VM options have obvious names that allow a developer to infer himself or herself what they are used for; for those that do not, there is such a thing as the official documentation from Oracle. If you ever need to dissect the Oracle memory management, this article is very good for this: `https://www.oracle.com/java/technologies/javase/javase-core-technologies-apis.html`.

Working with GC from the Code

For most applications garbage collection is not something a developer must really consider. The JVM starts a GC thread from time to time, which does its job usually without hindering the execution of the application. For developers who want to have more than Java basic skills, understanding how the Java garbage collection works and how can it be tuned is a must. The first thing a developer must accept about Java garbage collection is that it cannot be controlled at runtime. As you will see in the next section there is a way to suggest the JVM that some memory cleaning is necessary, but there is no guarantee that a memory cleaning will actually be performed. The only thing that can be done from the code specifying some code to be run when an object is discarded.

Using the `finalize()` Method

At the beginning of this book it was mentioned that every Java class is automatically a subclass of the JDK `java.lang.Object` class. This class is at the root of the JDK hierarchy and is the root of all classes in an application. It provides quite a few useful methods that can be extended or overwritten to implement behavior specific to the subclass. The `equals()`, `hashcode()` and `toString()` have already been mentioned. The `finalize()` method was deprecated in Java 9, but it was not yet removed from the JDK in the interest of backward compatibility. The finalization mechanism is somewhat problematic. Finalization can lead to performance issues, deadlocks, and hangs. Errors in finalizers can lead to resource leaks, also there is no way to cancel finalization if it is no longer necessary.

Since some developers might end up working with Java projects using earlier versions of the JDK, it is good to know that this method exists in case you might ever need it, or just to know where to look for weird bugs.

This method is called by the garbage collector when there are no longer any references to that object in the code. Before we move forward, take a look at the code in Listing 13-8.

Listing 13-8. Class Generating an Infinite Number of `Singer` Instances

```
package com.apress.bgn.thirteen;

import com.apress.bgn.thirteen.util.NameGenerator;
import org.slf4j.Logger;
import org.slf4j.LoggerFactory;

import java.time.LocalDate;
import java.util.Random;

public class InfiniteSingerGenerator {
    private static final Logger log = LoggerFactory.getLogger(InfiniteSinge
rGenerator.class);
    private static NameGenerator nameGenerator = new NameGenerator();
    private static final Random random = new Random();
```

```java
public static void main(String... args) {
    while (true) {
        genSinger();
    }
}

private static void genSinger() {
    Singer s = new Singer(nameGenerator.genName(), random.nextDouble(),
    LocalDate.now());
    log.info("JVM created: {}", s.getName());
}
}
```

The action performed by the previous code should be obvious even without knowing how the NameGenerator or the Singer class look like. The main method calls the genSinger() method in an infinite loop. This means that an infinite Singer instances are created. So what happens? Will the code run? For how long? If you were able to reply to these questions in your mind, my work here is complete; you can stop reading the book now. ☺

In **Chapter 5** there were some figures representing the memory contents for a small program. Figure 13-4 represents how the Java heap and stack memory might look during the execution of the previous program.

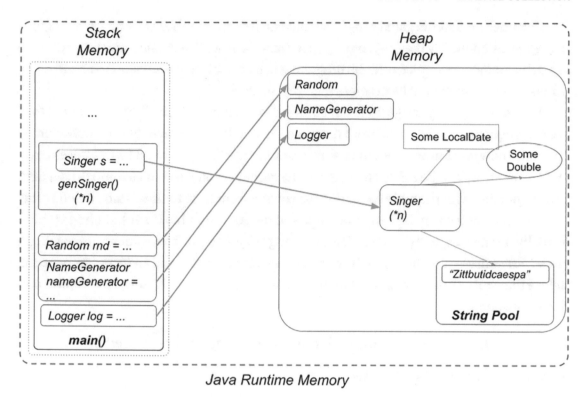

Figure 13-4. Java stack and heap memory during execution of the InfiniteSingerGenerator class

Only one genSinger() call was represented and only one Singer instance, for obvious reasons. As you can see, when the main(..) method is called, references to the static instances are created, that will be relevant to the program until the end of its execution. Then, genSinger() methods are called. Each of these methods has its own stack where it saves references to the objects created within the context of that method, in this case the Singer instance. This reference is used just to print the name of the Singer instance that was created in the body of this method. Then the method exists, without returning the reference. This means that the instance that was created, is no longer necessary, as it was created to be used only in the context of this method. When the execution of thegenSinger() method ends, the reference to the Singer is discarded from the stack. The Singer instance still exists in the heap memory, but can no longer be accessed from the program, thus it is no longer necessary to it. It now just keeps a memory block occupied with its own contents and its references to other instances, in this case, a String, a Double and a LocalDate.

Considering that the genString() is called an infinite number of times (in the figure we represented this by the (*n), more Singer instances will be created and they will keep the memory occupied and the program will be unable at some point to create others, because there will be no more memory available.

This is where the garbage collector comes into the picture. The Singer instances that are no longer being referenced from the program, and thus unreachable, are considered garbage, (now you know where the name is coming from): they are no longer necessary, and the memory can be safely cleaned up. The garbage collector is a cleanup thread that runs in parallel with the main execution thread and from time to time, starts deleting the unreferenced objects in the heap memory. And because the finalize() method is still available for use, we will overwrite it for the Singer type to print a log message, so we can see in our console directly when the garbage collector is destroying an instance, because before that will call the finalize() method. The code snippet in Listing 13-9 depicts our Singer instance.

Listing 13-9. The Singer Class with the Overriden finalize() Method

```
package com.apress.bgn.thirteen;

import org.slf4j.Logger;
import org.slf4j.LoggerFactory;

import java.time.LocalDate;
import java.util.Objects;

public class Singer {
    private static final Logger log = LoggerFactory.
    getLogger(Singer.class);
    private static final long serialVersionUID = 42L;
    private final long birthtime;

    private String name;

    private Double rating;

    private LocalDate birthDate;

    public Singer(String name, Double rating, LocalDate birthDate) {
        this.name = name;
        this.rating = rating;
```

```
        this.birthDate = birthDate;
        this.birthtime = System.nanoTime();
    }

    // some code omittted

    @Override
    protected void finalize() throws Throwable {
        try {
            long deathtime = System.nanoTime();
            long lifespan = (deathtime - birthtime) / 1_000_000_000;
            log.info("GC Destroyed: {} after {} seconds", name, lifespan);

        } finally {
            super.finalize();
        }
    }
}
```

The field birthtime was added just to be able to calculate the time that passes between when the constructor for an instance is called and the time the garbage collector calls the finalize() method. As the time is counted in nanoseconds, we are dividing the difference by 10^9 to get the time in seconds.

The code sample used in this section gives the garbage collector a lot of work to do, as every Singer instance being created is being used very little before being discarded. If you run the code you will see a lot of log messages in the console: first a lot of messages about objects being created, and if you wait a little, messages about objects being discarded will appear as well. All output is directed to a file, because the IntelliJ IDEA console is based on a buffer that resets from time to time to prevent the editor from crashing. You will have to stop the program manually, because the while(true) never ends, because its condition will never evaluate to false. After you stopped the program you will notice a log file at the following location: /chapter13/out/gc.log. If you don't, modify the IntelliJ IDEA launcher for this class and add the following VM option:

-Dlogback.configurationFile=chapter13/src/main/resources/logback.xml and run it again.

The gc.log contents should look a lot like the snippet depicted in Listing 13-10:

Listing 13-10. The `gc.log` File Showing the `finalize()` Method in Class Singer Being Called

```
INFO  c.a.b.t.InfiniteSingerGenerator - JVM created: Acnefqlspvwekzq
INFO  c.a.b.t.InfiniteSingerGenerator - JVM created: izyfkluhimlpkt
INFO  c.a.b.t.InfiniteSingerGenerator - JVM created: Tcyrpvgyfbpobym
INFO  c.a.b.t.InfiniteSingerGenerator - JVM created: Akmvyeazowdavpy
INFO  c.a.b.t.Singer - GC Destroyed: Kjidllzezjjdjge after 1 seconds
INFO  c.a.b.t.InfiniteSingerGenerator - JVM created: Llsghambpgetl c
INFO  c.a.b.t.Singer - GC Destroyed: Bffmcezvrzflhlh after 1 seconds
INFO  c.a.b.t.InfiniteSingerGenerator - JVM created: Pg vjmfwzhujzv
INFO  c.a.b.t.Singer - GC Destroyed: wrlaqutybuzvsj after 1 seconds
INFO  c.a.b.t.InfiniteSingerGenerator - JVM created: Kdzlsyiteskleka
INFO  c.a.b.t.Singer - GC Destroyed: Lqzdgeqqguitbgg after 1 seconds
INFO  c.a.b.t.Singer - GC Destroyed: Ddpzqlbiryelzvr after 1 seconds
INFO  c.a.b.t.Singer - GC Destroyed: Ozkzfubi  vpmj  after 1 seconds
INFO  c.a.b.t.InfiniteSingerGenerator - JVM created: Uegz isigjcrlfj
...
```

When you have the file you can open it and start analyzing its contents, but because IntelliJ might not open such a big file, try to open it with a specialized text editor like Notepad++ or Sublime. Or, if you use a Unix/Linux operating system, just open your console and use the grep command like this:

```
grep -a 'seconds' gc.log
```

This will display all log entries printed when the `finalize()` method is called. Then you can select the name of an instance and do something like this:

```
$ grep -a 'Lybhpococssuoz' gc.log
INFO c.a.b.c.Main - JVM created: Lybhpococssuoz
INFO c.a.b.c.Singer - GC Destroyed: Lybhpococssuoz after 7 seconds
```

As you can see, the time it takes for a `Singer` instance to be deleted from the heap varies, and this is because the GC is called randomly; the developer has no control over it. There is a way to explicitly request garbage collection to be done— well, two ways. You can call: `System.gc()` or

`Runtime.getRuntime().gc().`

`System.gc()` calls `Runtime.getRuntime().gc()` anyway.

This doesn't mean that the GC will immediately start cleaning up the memory, though; it is more like a suggestion to the JVM that it should make an effort to recycle unused objects and reclaim unused memory, because it is being needed.

Now, back to the `finalize()` method. It was mentioned that it was marked as deprecated in Java 9. This method is meant to be overridden by classes that handle resources that are stored outside of the heap. The obvious example here are the I/O handling classes, used to read resources as files or URLs and databases. The `finalize()` would be called by the JVM when an object can no longer be accessed by any alive thread of the running application, to make sure that those resources were released and available for other external and unrelated programs to use.

ℹ   In older versions of Apache Tomcat (a Java based web server) on Windows there was a bug related to release of resources. When the server would crash or would be stopped forcefully, it couldn't be started again because some of its log files handlers were not released properly, and the new server instance could not get access to them to start writing the new log entries. (This is an observation from my personal experience when working with Apache Tomcat on Windows from a long, long time ago.)

With the introduction of the `java.lang.AutoCloseable` interface in JDK 1.7, the `finalize()` method became less and less used. A few problems with this method have been mentioned previously, but the following list gives more context:

- The JVM cannot guarantee which thread will call this method for any given object, so any thread that has access to it can call it, and we might end up with resources being released while the object is still needed. The method is public, and thus it can be called explicitly in the code even if it is supposed to be called only by the GC thread.

- What happens if the custom implementation is not correct, throws exceptions, or does not release resources properly?

- The `finalize()` method should be called only once by the JVM, but this cannot be guaranteed.

- Another downside is that `finalize()` calls are not automatically chained, so a custom implementation of a `finalize()` method must always explicitly call the `finalize()` method of the superclass.

- Another problem that was previously mentioned: once a `finalize()` was called, there is no way to stop the method from executing or undo its effect, so you are basically left with a reference to an object that no longer exists.

As you have probably figured out by now, there is a lot of freedom given to the developer when it comes to implementing this method, and this means there is a lot of room for errors to happen.

This is why the finalization mechanism in Java is flawed and was deprecated in JDK 9 to discourage its use. Improper `finalize()` implementations could lead to:

- memory leaks (memory contents are not discarded)

- deadlocks (resource is blocked by two processes)

- hangs (process is in a waiting state it cannot go out of)

In order to help with memory management, the `java.lang.ref.Cleaner` class was introduced in Java 9. Before getting into that, I must show you how to check out that status of your memory programatically.

Heap Memory Statistics

The `Runtime` class is quite useful when trying to interact with the internals of the JVM while a program is running. As previously mentioned in this chapter, its `gc()` method can be called to suggest to the JVM that the memory should be cleaned, and a few chapters ago we used methods in this class to start processes from the Java code. There are three methods in this class are useful to see the status of the memory assigned to a Java program:

- `runtime.maxMemory()` returns the maximum amount of memory the JVM will attempt to use for its heap, in case of need. The value returned by this method varies from machine to machine and is being set implicitly to a quarter of the total existing RAM memory on the machine, unless is set it is set explicitly by using the following JVM option -Xmx followed by the amount of memory (e.g., -Xmx8G will allow the JVM to use a maximum of 8 GB of memory).

- `runtime.totalMemory()` returns the total amount of memory of the JVM. The value returned by this method varies from machine to machine too and is implementation-dependent, unless explicitly set by using the following JVM option -Xms followed by the amount of memory (e.g., -Xms1G will tell the JVM that is the initial size of its heap memory should be 1 GB of memory).

- `runtime.freeMemory()` returns an approximation of the amount of free memory for the Java Virtual Machine. Using the `runtime.totalMemory()` and the `runtime.freeMemory()` methods we can write some code to check how much of our memory is occupied at various times during the execution of the program. For this a class named `MemAudit` is created that will use the current logger to print memory values. The implementation of this class is shown in Listing 13-11.

Listing 13-11. The `MemAudit` Class Shown Memory Statistics During the Execution of a Java Application

```
package com.apress.bgn.thirteen.util;

import org.slf4j.Logger;

public class MemAudit {
    private static final long MEGABYTE = 1024L * 1024L;
    private static final Runtime runtime = Runtime.getRuntime();

    public static void printBusyMemory(Logger log) {
```

```
        long memory = runtime.totalMemory() - runtime.freeMemory();
        log.info("Occupied memory: {} MB", (memory / MEGABYTE));
    }
    public static void printTotalMemory(Logger log) {
        log.info("Total Program memory: {} MB", (runtime.
        totalMemory()/MEGABYTE));
        log.info("Max Program memory: {} MB", (runtime.maxMemory()/MEGABYTE));
    }
}
```

The methods of this class will be called during the execution of our program, as shown in Listing 13-12.

Listing 13-12. The MemAuditDemo Class Using the Class in Listing 13-11 to Print Memory Statistics in the Console

package *com.*apress.bgn.thirteen;

```
// some imports omitted
import static com.apress.bgn.thirteen.MemAudit.*;

public class MemAuditDemo {
    private static final Logger log = LoggerFactory.
    getLogger(MemAuditDemo.class);
    private static NameGenerator nameGenerator = new NameGenerator();
    private static final Random random = new Random();

    public static void main(String... args) {
        printTotalMemory(log);
        int count =0;
        while (true) {
            genSinger();
            count++;
            if (count % 1000 == 0) {
                printBusyMemory(log);
            }
        }
    }
```

```
    private static void genSinger() {
        Singer s = new Singer(nameGenerator.genName(), random.nextDouble(),
        LocalDate.now());
        log.info("JVM created: {}", s.getName());
    }
}
```

After we delete the old log file we should run this class, and leave it running for a while. Since it will be impossible again to see the output, this command

```
grep -a 'memory' gc.log
```

is useful to extract all lines containing the 'memory' word, and the result should look quite similar to one in Listing 13-13.

Listing 13-13. Memory Statistics Printed By Methods in the MemAudit Class During Java Application Execution

```
$ grep -a 'memory' gc.log
INFO  c.a.b.t.MemAuditDemo - Total Program memory: 260 MB
INFO  c.a.b.t.MemAuditDemo - Max Program memory: 4096 MB
INFO  c.a.b.t.MemAuditDemo - Occupied memory: 21 MB
INFO  c.a.b.t.MemAuditDemo - Occupied memory: 7 MB
INFO  c.a.b.t.MemAuditDemo - Occupied memory: 12 MB
...
INFO  c.a.b.t.MemAuditDemo - Occupied memory: 98 MB
INFO  c.a.b.t.MemAuditDemo - Occupied memory: 104 MB
...
```

The max memory is 4096MB, which means my machine has a total of 16 GB of RAM and the occupied memory is very little, not even close to the initial 260MB the JVM is given to use. If we want to see real memory being occupied we can modify the genSinger() method to return the created references and add them to a list. Since the Singer instances are referenced in the main class, the memory is no longer emptied. The modifications mentioned previously are shown in Listing 13-14.

Listing 13-14. Saving the Singer Instances to a List to Avoid Them Being Collected by the GC and the Memory Cleared

```java
import com.apress.bgn.thirteen.util.NameGenerator;
// some import statements omitted
import java.util.ArrayList;
import java.util.List;
import static com.apress.bgn.thirteen.util.MemAudit.*;

public class MemoryConsumptionDemo {
    private static final Logger log = LoggerFactory.
getLogger(MemoryConsumptionDemo.class);
    private static NameGenerator nameGenerator = new NameGenerator();
    private static final Random random = new Random();

    public static void main(String... args) {
        printTotalMemory(log);
        List<Singer> singers = new ArrayList<>();
        for (int i = 0; i < 1_000_000; ++i) {
            singers.add(genSinger());
            if (i % 1000 == 0) {
                printBusyMemory(log);
            }
        }
    }
    private static Singer genSinger() {
        Singer s = new Singer(nameGenerator.genName(), random.nextDouble(),
        LocalDate.now());
        log.info("JVM created: {}", s.getName());
        return s;
    }
}
```

After running the previous program, we can actually see the memory being used gradually increasing. A look in the log filtered magically by grep will show us that the program keeps the memory occupied until its end, since the references now are saved into the List<Singer> instance, as shown in Listing 13-15.

Listing 13-15. Memory Statistics Printed By Methods in the MemAudit Class During a Java Application Execution Where Instances Are Saved to a List<Singer>

```
$ grep -a 'memory' gc.log
INFO  c.a.b.t.MemoryConsumptionDemo - Total Program memory: 260 MB
INFO  c.a.b.t.MemoryConsumptionDemo - Max Program memory: 4096 MB
INFO  c.a.b.t.MemoryConsumptionDemo - Occupied memory: 14 MB
INFO  c.a.b.t.MemoryConsumptionDemo - Occupied memory: 17 MB
INFO  c.a.b.t.MemoryConsumptionDemo - Occupied memory: 19 MB
INFO  c.a.b.t.MemoryConsumptionDemo - Occupied memory: 22 MB
...
INFO  c.a.b.t.MemoryConsumptionDemo - Occupied memory: 99 MB
INFO  c.a.b.t.MemoryConsumptionDemo - Occupied memory: 101 MB
INFO  c.a.b.t.MemoryConsumptionDemo - Occupied memory: 104 MB
...
INFO  c.a.b.t.MemoryConsumptionDemo - Occupied memory: 474 MB
INFO  c.a.b.t.MemoryConsumptionDemo - Occupied memory: 477 MB
```

And as we print the occupied memory every 1,000 steps, we can draw the conclusion that 1,000 Singer instances occupy approximatively 2 MB. The preceding code no longer uses an infinite loop to generate instances; if it did, at some point the program would abruptly crash, throwing the following exception:

```
Exception in thread "main" java.lang.OutOfMemoryError: Java heap space
    at chapter.thirteen/com.apress.bgn.thirteen.MemoryConsumptionDemo
        .genSinger(MemoryConsumptionDemo.java:64)
    at chapter.thirteen/com.apress.bgn.thirteen.MemoryConsumptionDemo
        .main(MemoryConsumptionDemo.java:55)
```

Remember the value returned by the runtime.maxMemory()? On my machine, it was 4096MB. If I look in the console, right before the exception just depicted, here is what I see:

```
INFO c.a.b.c.MemoryConsumptionDemo - Occupied memory: 4094 MB
INFO c.a.b.c.MemoryConsumptionDemo - Occupied memory: 4094 MB
INFO c.a.b.c.MemoryConsumptionDemo - Occupied memory: 4095 MB
INFO c.a.b.c.MemoryConsumptionDemo - Occupied memory: 4095 MB
INFO c.a.b.c.MemoryConsumptionDemo - Occupied memory: 4095 MB
```

So the JVM was struggling to create another Singer instance, but there was no more memory left. The last value printed before the exception was 4095MB, which is 1 MB less than 4096MB the maximum amount of memory that the JVM was allowed to use. So the poor JVM crashed because there was no more heap memory available. If a program ever ends like that, the problem is always in the design of the solution. The values for total and maximum memory for the JVM can also influence the behavior of the GC as well. The -Xms and -Xmx introduced previously are quite important, as they decide the initial and the maximum size of the heap memory. Configured properly they can increase performance, but when unsuitable values they have the adverse effect. For example, never set an initial size for the heap too small, because if there is not enough space to fit all objects created by the application the JVM has to allocate more memory, basically rebuilding the heap repeatedly during the execution of the program. So if this happens a few times during the application run, the overall time consumption will be affected. The maximum size for the heap is very important: allocate too little the application will crash, allocating too much might hinder other programming from running. Deciding these values is usually done through repeated experiments and starting with JDK 11, the new Epsilon garbage collector comes quite in handy for this purpose.

If you want to learn more about GC tunning, usually the best documentation is the official one (https://docs.oracle.com/en/java/javase/17/gctuning).

Now that you know what to expect from the GC, let's see other methods of customizing its behavior so problems are avoided.

Using Cleaner

Because of the necessity to ensure backward compatibility, it is not clear when the finalize() method is to be taken out of the JDK. If needed, classes can be developed to implement java.lang.AutoCloseable and provide an implementation for the close() method and make sure you use your objects in a try-with-resources statement. If you want to avoid implementing the interface there is another way: use a java.lang.ref. Cleaner object. This class can be instantiated, and objects can be registered to it together with an action to perform when the object is being discarded by the garbage collector. Using a Cleaner instance, the previous code can be written as depicted in Listing 13-16:

Listing 13-16. Using a Cleaner Instance

```
package com.apress.bgn.thirteen.cleaner;
// some import statements omitted
import java.lang.ref.Cleaner;

public class CleanerDemo {
    private static final Logger log = LoggerFactory.
getLogger(CleanerDemo.class);
    public static final Cleaner cleaner = Cleaner.create();
    private static NameGenerator nameGenerator = new NameGenerator();

    public static void main(String... args) {
        printTotalMemory(log);
        int count = 0;
        for (int i = 0; i < 100_000; ++i) {
            genActor();
            count++;
            if (count % 1000 == 0) {
                printBusyMemory(log);
                System.gc();
            }
        }

        //filling memory with arrays of String to force GC to clean up
        Actor objects
        for (int i = 1; i <= 10_000; i++) {
            String[] s = new String[10_000];
            try {
                Thread.sleep(1);
            } catch (InterruptedException e) {
            }
        }

    }
```

```java
private static Cleaner.Cleanable genActor() {
    Actor a = new Actor(nameGenerator.genName(), LocalDate.now());
    log.info("JVM created: {}", a.getName());
    Cleaner.Cleanable handle = cleaner.register(a, new ActorRunnable(a.
    getName(), log));
    return handle;
}

static class ActorRunnable implements Runnable {
    private final String actorName;
    private final Logger log;

    public ActorRunnable(String actorName, Logger log) {
        this.actorName = actorName;
        this.log = log;
    }

    @Override
    public void run() {
        log.info("GC Destroyed: {} ", actorName);
    }
}
}
```

Because we wanted to make it easier for you to browse the code, as all these sources are part of the same project, we are using here a class modelling an Actor instead of a Singer— but no worries, the implementation is quite similar. The Cleaner instance has a method named register(..) that is called to register the action to be performed when the object is cleaned. The action to be performed is specified as a Runnable instance, and the decision to create a class by implementing it, ActorRunnable in this example, was taken so that we could save the name of the object to be destroyed into a field without actually keeping a reference to the object to be destroyed, otherwise the Cleaner. Cleanable handle would not be used by the GC during the execution of the program, as the object would appear as if it still had references to it. The cleaner.register(..)

method returns an instance of type `Cleaner.Cleanable` that can be used to explicitly perform the action, by calling the `clean()` method. This is the method called by the JVM when the object is deleted from memory, when no longer used. If you run the preceding code, the printed log would look pretty similar to the one in Listing 13-17.

Listing 13-17. Log Printed By an Execution Using a `Cleaner` Instance to Free Up Memory

```
INFO  c.a.b.t.c.CleanerDemo - Total Program memory: 260 MB
INFO  c.a.b.t.c.CleanerDemo - Max Program memory: 4096 MB
INFO  c.a.b.t.c.CleanerDemo - JVM created: Nuyktryvtkewiwd
INFO  c.a.b.t.c.CleanerDemo - JVM created: Brqivlsbvmteihz
INFO  c.a.b.t.c.CleanerDemo - JVM created: Qzvopg ophjcyho
...
INFO  c.a.b.t.c.CleanerDemo - Occupied memory: 17 MB
INFO  c.a.b.t.c.CleanerDemo - JVM created: Jrliwbjadztvwdm
INFO  c.a.b.t.c.CleanerDemo - JVM created: Evdteelpzinfcfh
INFO  c.a.b.t.c.CleanerDemo - JVM created: Hozfatszogfvzfz
...
INFO  c.a.b.t.c.CleanerDemo - GC Destroyed: Giqojswtuqzs s
INFO  c.a.b.t.c.CleanerDemo - GC Destroyed: Lzdjorokvyzwdu
INFO  c.a.b.t.c.CleanerDemo - JVM created: Igmzjiypo ttkzw
INFO  c.a.b.t.c.CleanerDemo - JVM created: Ljmksqzhzzhuzwl
INFO  c.a.b.t.c.CleanerDemo - GC Destroyed: Fny tnsffvyuisp
INFO  c.a.b.t.c.CleanerDemo - GC Destroyed: Qzillviekynpkec
...
```

So the same result as using `finalize()` was obtained, but without implementing a deprecated method.

💡 As a good practice to take from here, if you are writing your application using Java 9+, avoid using `finalize()`, because this method is clearly on the path toward being removed. Use `Cleaner` and you might have less of a hassle when upgrading the Java version your application is using.

Preventing GC from Deleting an Object

In the two previous sections we focused on objects that were eligible for garbage collection. In an application there are objects that should not be discarded while the program runs, because they are needed. The most obvious references in our classes that were discarded only at the end of the execution were the static fields, and they are final, so they cannot be reinitialized.

```
private static final Logger log = LoggerFactory.
getLogger(CleanerDemo.class);
public static final Cleaner cleaner = Cleaner.create();
private static NameGenerator nameGenerator = new NameGenerator();
private static final Random random = new Random();
```

The problem with these static values, however, is that they occupy the memory. What if your application uses a big Map<K,V> that contains a dictionary that is not even needed right when the application starts? To solve this, enter the Singleton design pattern. The Singleton pattern is a specific design of a class that ensures the class will only be instantiated **once** during the execution of the program. This is done by hiding the constructor (declare it private), and declaring a static reference of the class type and a static method to return it. There is more than one way to write a class according to the Singleton pattern, but the most common way is depicted in Listing 13-18.

Listing 13-18. SingletonDictionary Class

```
package com.apress.bgn.thirteen;
// some import statements omitted
import java.util.HashMap;
import java.util.Map;

public final class SingletonDictionary {
    private static final Logger log = LoggerFactory.
getLogger(SingletonDictionary.class);
    private Map<String, String> dictionary = new HashMap<>();

    private static final SingletonDictionary instance = new
    SingletonDictionary();

    private SingletonDictionary() {
```

```
    // init dictionary
    log.info("Starting to create dictionary: {}", System.
    currentTimeMillis());
    final NameGenerator keyGen = new NameGenerator(20);
    final NameGenerator valGen = new NameGenerator(200);
    for (int i = 0; i < 100_000; ++i) {
        dictionary.put(keyGen.genName(), valGen.genName());
    }
    log.info("Done creating dictionary: {}", System.
    currentTimeMillis());
  }

  public synchronized static SingletonDictionary getInstance(){
    return instance;
  }
}
```

In the previous code we simulated a dictionary with 100,000 entries, all generated by a modified version of the NameGenerator class. Log messages were printed in its constructor to be really obvious when the instance is created. There are four things you have to remember about the Singleton pattern:

- the constructor must be private, as it should not be called outside the class

- the class must contain a static reference to an object of its type that can be initialized in place by calling the private constructor

- a method to retrieve this instance must be defined, so it has to be static

- the method to retrieve the static instance also has to be synchronized so no two threads can call it at the same and gain access to the instance, because the core idea of the Singleton pattern is to allow the class to be instantiated only once during the duration of the execution of the program and ensure that no concurrent access is allowed, as it might lead to unexpected behavior. There are multiple ways to initialize and work with a Singleton, feel free to do your own research.

In a singleton class a static reference to an instance is created, and this static reference prevents the garbage collector from cleaning up this instance during the execution of the program. This is because a static reference is a class variable, and classes are the last to be deleted by the GC, toward the end of the program execution. To test this, we'll write a main class that declares a `Cleaner` instance and register a `Cleanable` for the `SingletonDictionary` instance. The main method will create a lot of `String` array to fill up the memory to try to convince the GC to delete the `SingletonDictionary` instance, and we'll even set its own reference to it to `null`, as depicted in Listing 13-19.

Listing 13-19. `SingletonDictionaryDemo` Class

```java
package com.apress.bgn.thirteen;
// import statements omitted

public class SingletonDictionaryDemo {
    public static final Cleaner cleaner = Cleaner.create();
    private static final Logger log = LoggerFactory.getLogger(Singleton
    DictionaryDemo.class);

    public static void main(String... args) {
        log.info("Testing SingletonDictionary...");
        //filling memory with arrays of String to force GC
        for (int i = 1; i <= 10_000; i++) {
            String[] s = new String[10_000];
            try {
                Thread.sleep(1);
            } catch (InterruptedException e) {
            }
        }
        SingletonDictionary singletonDictionary = SingletonDictionary.
        getInstance();

        cleaner.register(singletonDictionary, ()-> {
            log.info("Cleaned up the dictionary!");
        });
        // we delete the reference
        singletonDictionary = null;
```

```
    //filling memory with arrays of String to force GC
    for (int i = 1; i <= 10_000; i++) {
        String[] s = new String[10_000];
        try {
            Thread.sleep(1);
        } catch (InterruptedException e) {
        }
    }
    log.info("DONE.");
  }
}
```

If we run the previous code and expect to see the "Cleaned up the dictionary!" message in the console, we're expecting in vain. That static reference in the SingletonDictionary will not allow GC to touch that object until the program ends. The static reference that we have in class SingletonDictionary is also called a strong reference, because it prevents the object from being discarded from memory.

Using Weak References

Obviously, if there are strong references, we should be able to use weak references as well, for objects that we actually want cleaned, right? Right.

In Java there are three classes can be used to hold a reference to an object that will not protect that object from garbage collection. This is useful for objects that are too big, and it makes it inefficient to keep them in memory. With this kind of object it is worth the cost of time consumed to be reinitialized, because keeping them in memory would slow done the overall performance of the application.

The three classes are:

- java.lang.ref.SoftReference<T>: objects referred by this type of references are cleared at the discretion of the garbage collector in response to memory demand. Soft references are most often used to implement memory-sensitive caches.

- `java.lang.ref.WeakReference<T>`: objects referred by this type of references do not prevent their referents from being made finalizable, finalized, and then reclaimed. Weak references are most often used to implement canonicalizing mappings. Canonicalizing mapping refers to containers where weak references can be kept in and can be accessed by other objects, but their link to the container, does not prevent them from being collected.

- `java.lang.ref.PhantomReference<T>`: objects referred by these type of references are enqueued after the collector determines that their referents may otherwise be reclaimed. Phantom references are most often used to schedule postmortem cleanup actions.

Our `SingletonDictionary` contains a `Map<K,V>` that is actually the big object stored in memory. This map can be wrapped in a `WeakReference`, since weak references are most often used to implement canonicalizing mappings. We can write some logic, that when the dictionary instance is accessed, if it is not there, it should be reinitialized. Because we need to access the map, the implementation will change a little, aside from wrapping the `Map<K,V>` into a `WeakReference`. The new class, named `WeakDictionary`, is depicted in Listing 13-20.

Listing 13-20. WeakDictionary Class

```
package com.apress.bgn.thirteen.util;
// other import statements omitted
import java.lang.ref.WeakReference;

public class WeakDictionary {
    private static final Logger log = LoggerFactory.
getLogger(WeakDictionary.class);
    private static WeakDictionary instance = new WeakDictionary();
    private static Cleaner cleaner;
    private WeakReference<Map<Integer, String>> dictionary;

    private WeakDictionary() {
        cleaner = Cleaner.create();
        dictionary = new WeakReference<>(initDictionary());
    }
```

```
public synchronized String getExplanationFor(Integer key) {
    Map<Integer, String> dict = dictionary.get();
    if (dict == null) {
        dict = initDictionary();
        dictionary = new WeakReference<>(dict);
        return dict.get(key);
    } else {
        return dict.get(key);
    }
}

public WeakReference<Map<Integer, String>> getDictionary() {
    return dictionary;
}

public synchronized static WeakDictionary getInstance() {
    return instance;
}

private Map<Integer, String> initDictionary() {
    final Map<Integer, String> dict = new HashMap<>();
    log.info("Starting to create dictionary: {}", System.
    currentTimeMillis());
    final NameGenerator valGen = new NameGenerator(200);
    for (int i = 0; i < 100_000; ++i) {
        dict.put(i, valGen.genName());
    }
    log.info("Done creating dictionary: {}", System.
    currentTimeMillis());
    cleaner.register(dict, ()-> log.info("Cleaned up the
    dictionary!"));
    return dict;
}
}
```

The getExplanationFor(..) is used to access the map and get the value corresponding a key. Before doing that, however, we have to check if the Map<K,V> is still there. This is done by calling the get() method on the dictionary reference which is of type WeakReference<Map<Integer, String>>. If the map was not collected by the GC, the key is extracted and returned; otherwise, the Map<K,V> is reinitialized and the weak reference is recreated. The Cleaner instance is used here as well, and registered a Cleanable for the Map<K,V>, so we can see the map being collected. So how do we test this? In a similar way that we tested SingletonDictionary. The WeakDictionaryDemo class is not that different. The code is depicted in Listing 13-21.

Listing 13-21. WeakDictionaryDemo Class

```java
package com.apress.bgn.thirteen;

import com.apress.bgn.thirteen.util.WeakDictionary;
import org.slf4j.Logger;
import org.slf4j.LoggerFactory;

public class WeakDictionaryDemo {
    private static final Logger log = LoggerFactory.
getLogger(WeakDictionaryDemo.class);

    public static void main(String... args) {
        log.info("Testing WeakDictionaryDemo...");
        //filling memory with arrays of String to force GC
        for (int i = 1; i <= 10_000; i++) {
            String[] s = new String[10_000];
            try {
                Thread.sleep(1);
            } catch (InterruptedException e) {
            }
        }
        WeakDictionary weakDictionary = WeakDictionary.getInstance();

        //filling memory with arrays of String to force GC
        for (int i = 1; i <= 10_000; i++) {
            String[] s = new String[10_000];
            try {
```

```
        Thread.sleep(1);
      } catch (InterruptedException e) {
      }
    }
    log.info("Getting val for 3 =  {}", weakDictionary.
    getExplanationFor(3));
    log.info("DONE.");
  }
}
```

After retrieving the WeakDictionary reference, a lot of String arrays are created to force GC to delete the map from memory. After that, we try to access the problematic map. Will it work?

Listing 13-22. WeakDictionaryDemo Log

```
INFO  c.a.b.t.WeakDictionaryDemo - Testing WeakDictionaryDemo...
INFO  c.a.b.t.u.WeakDictionary - Starting to create dictionary:
1629635325234
INFO  c.a.b.t.u.WeakDictionary - Done creating dictionary: 1629635325485
INFO  c.a.b.t.u.WeakDictionary - Cleaned up the dictionary!
INFO  c.a.b.t.u.WeakDictionary - Starting to create dictionary:
1629635337852
INFO  c.a.b.t.u.WeakDictionary - Done creating dictionary: 1629635338093
INFO  c.a.b.t.WeakDictionaryDemo - Getting val for 3
=  Lqcnaowqotkzlhckqepogpjdlgkjzenyzzoaunebjsc z nervebnbc
yjjlmuqkjaemmbtjbqzstjsssrwubwvfeoqfynyisba zclhf   lep fdbsnm
cagubzodfpkepblslpypjwsybmwgptyznuymzgcdhkfydtibkjwgojjalctkrloat
luakwwzppledhzdi
INFO  c.a.b.t.WeakDictionaryDemo - DONE.
```

The previous log proves this works, and not only that, we can see the map being discarded by GC and then reinitialized when needed. This is that power of soft references.

The garbage collection process is un-deterministic, because it cannot be controlled much from the code. A Java program cannot tell it to start, pause, or stop, but by using the appropriate VM options we can control the resources it has.

Using the proper implementation, from the code we can tell it what to collect or not, and most times this is enough.[2]

Garbage Collections Exceptions and Causes

It was mentioned before that if objects cannot be discarded from the memory, an exception of type OutOfMemoryError will be thrown. I'm not sure if you noticed, but OutOfMemoryError does not actually extend java.lang.Exception, so calling it an exception is wrong. The exception class hierarchy was mentioned in **Chapter 5**. In that hierarchy there was a class named java.lang.Error that implements java.lang.Throwable, and it was mentioned that when these types of objects where thrown by a program when there was a critical issue that the program cannot recover from. The full hierarchy of the java.lang.OutOfMemoryError is depicted here.

```
java.lang.Object
    java.lang.Throwable
        java.lang.Error
            java.lang.VirtualMachineError
                java.lang.OutOfMemoryError
```

OutOfMemoryError is actually one of those ugly things you do not want thrown when your program is running, because this means your program is actually no longer running. The reason why it is not running is because it has no memory left to store new objects being created.

This error is being thrown by the JVM when anything goes wrong when doing memory management. Although the most common cause is that the heap memory is depleted, there are other causes. When heap memory allocated to the JVM is depleted, the error has the following message:

```
Exception in thread "main" java.lang.OutOfMemoryError: Java heap space
```
But there is another message that you might see:

```
Exception in thread "main" java.lang.OutOfMemoryError: GC Overhead Limit
Exceeded
```

---

[2] If you want more details about GC, see Oracle, "Getting Started with the G1 Garbage Collector," https://www.oracle.com/technetwork/tutorials/tutorials-1876574.html, accessed October 15, 2021.

This message is still related to the heap size. The error is thrown with this message when the data for the program barely fits the size of the heap, so the heap is almost full, which allows the GC to run, but because it cannot redeem any memory, the GC keeps running and it is actually hindering the normal execution of the application. This message is added to the error when the GC spends 98% of execution time and the application spends the other 2%.

These two are the most common error messages you will see when GC cannot do its job properly for whatever reason. A complete list can be found at https://docs.oracle.com/javase/8/docs/technotes/guides/troubleshoot/memleaks002.html, but since most GC issues relate to the heap size, G1GC mostly throws errors with the Java heap space messages.

Summary

This section ends this book. When it comes to the Java ecosystem, there are a lot of book and tutorials on the Internet. This book only scratched the surface to give you a good starting point as a Java developer, and the whole team that worked on it hopes it satisfied your needs and raised your curiosity to fund out more. Just keep in mind that there is no panacea solution to make sure the memory is always managed right, regardless of the application scope. If you get into trouble, experimentation is always a step of determining the right collector for your JVM.

This chapter has covered the following topics:

- what garbage collection is and the steps involved

- how the heap memory is structured

- how many types of garbage collectors there are in the Oracle HotSpot JVM and how can we switch between them

- how to list all GC flags and use them as VM options

- how to view a garbage collector configurations and statistics using VM options

- how to view the garbage collection in action using finalize and Cleaner

- how to stop the garbage collector from collecting important objects

- how to create objects that are easily collected using soft references

APPENDICES

Appendix A

JDK 11 was released on September 25, 2018. Aside from all the novelties already covered in this book, there was also the news that developers had been suspecting since the introduction of modules. Java is still free, but the Oracle JDK isn't. Developers can use the Oracle JDK to learn, but applications that are deployed in production require a license.

The work-around is to use an OpenJDK build (`https://adoptopenjdk.net`), but this does not come with Oracle support. JDK 17 is a major release that will benefit from long-term support and if you are curious about the Oracle terms of use, you can read them at `https://www.oracle.com/technetwork/java/javase/terms/license/javase-license.html`.

The Java world has changed, and Oracle restrictions causes the market to provide more options. Companies like Zulu and IBM developed their own JDKs, Amazon has its own already,[1] and all provide support for JDKs that Oracle doesn't. Probably more companies will emerge to provide cheaper support and open-source JDKs. Now that access to an important resource has been restricted, humanity will do what it does best—become creative to get access to it or develop similar resources. Either way, diversity will be blooming in the following years for the Java open-source community, and I can barely wait to see what is coming.

The purpose of this appendix is to gracefully end the book and to cover more advanced details regarding Java modules that might not be suitable for a Java beginner developer right at the start of the book. It contains an extended version of the modules section in **Chapter 3**, covering configuration of Java modules in a complex project, good, bad, and recommended practices working with modules. The code snippets mentioned in this appendix are already part of the project associated with the book. Enjoy!

---

[1] Amazon Corretto is a no-cost, multiplatform, production-ready distribution of the Open Java Development Kit (OpenJDK).

© Iuliana Cosmina 2022
I. Cosmina, *Java 17 for Absolute Beginners*, https://doi.org/10.1007/978-1-4842-7080-6

Modules

Starting with Java 9 a new concept was introduced: `modules`.[2] Java modules represent a more powerful mechanism to organize and aggregate packages. The implementation of this new concept took more than 10 years. The discussion about modules started in 2005, and the hope was for them to be implemented for Java 7. Under the name **Project Jigsaw** an exploratory phase eventually started in 2008. Java developers hoped a modular JDK will be available with Java 8, but that did not happen.

Modules finally arrived in Java 9 after three years of work (and almost seven of analysis). Supporting them delayed the official release date of Java 9 to September 2017.[3]

A Java module is a way to group packages and configure more granulated access to package contents. A Java module is a uniquely named, reusable group of packages and resources (e.g., XML files and other types of non-Java files) described by a file named `module-info.java`, located at the root of the source directory. This file contains the following information:

- the module's name
- the module's dependencies (that is, other modules this module depends on)
- the packages it explicitly makes available to other modules (all other packages in the module are implicitly unavailable to other modules)
- the services it offers
- the services it consumes
- to what other modules it allows reflection
- native code
- resources
- configuration data

---

[2] Build tools such as Maven or Gradle refer to subprojects as `modules` as well, but their purpose is different from the one of the Java modules.

[3] The full history of the Jigsaw project can be found at OpenJDK, "Project Jigsaw," `http://openjdk.java.net/projects/jigsaw`, accessed October 15, 2021.

In theory, module naming resembles package naming and follows the reversed-domain-name convention. In practice, just make sure the module name does not contain any numbers and that it reveals clearly what its purpose is. The module-info. java file is compiled into a module descriptor, which is a file named module-info. class that is packed together with classes into a plain old JAR file. The file is locatedd at the root of the Java source directory, outside of any package. For the chapter03 project, introduced earlier, the module-info.java file is located in the src/main/java directory, at the same level with the com directory; the root of the com.apress.bgn.three package Figure A-1.

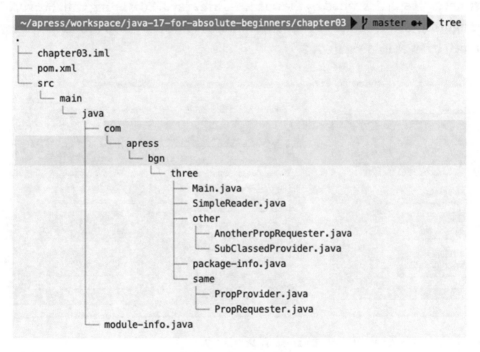

Figure A-1. *Location of the module-info.java file*

As any file with *.java extension, the module-info.java is compiled into a *.class file. As the module declaration is not a part of Java type declaration, module is not a Java keyword, so it can still be used when writing code for Java types; as a variable name, for example. For package the situation is different, as every Java type declaration must start with a package declaration. Just take a look at the SimpleReader class declared in Listing A-1.

Listing A-1. SimpleReader Class

```
package com.apress.bgn.three;

public class SimpleReader {
    private String source;

    // code omitted
}
```

You can see the package declaration, but where is the module? Well, the module is an abstract concept, described by the module-info.java. So starting with Java 9, if you are configuring Java modules in your application, Figure 3-4 (from the short version of **Chapter 3**) evolves into Figure A-2.

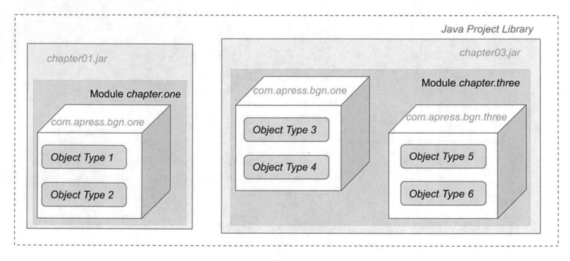

Figure A-2. *Java modules represented visually*

A Java module is a way to logically group Java packages that belong together.

The introduction of modules allows for the JDK to be divided into modules too. The java --list-modules command lists all modules in your local JDK installation. Listing A-2 depicts the output of this command executed on my personal computer where currently JDK 17-ea is installed.

Listing A-2. JDK 17-ea Modules

```
$ java --list-modules
java.base@17-ea
java.compiler@17-ea
java.datatransfer@17-ea
java.desktop@17-ea

# output omitted
```

Each module name is followed by a version string @17-ea in the previous listing, which means that the module belongs to Java version 17-ea.

So if a Java application does not require all modules, a runtime can be created only with the modules that it needs, which reduces the runtime's size. The tool to build a smaller runtime customized to an application needs is called jlink and is part of the JDK executables. This allows for bigger levels of scalability and increased performance. How to use jlink[4] is not an object of this book. The focus of the book is learning the Java programming language; thus the technical details of the Java platform will be kept to a minimum, just enough to start writing and executing code confidently.

There are multiple benefits of introducing modules that more experienced developers have been waiting for years to take advantage of. But configuring modules for bigger and more complex projects is no walk in the park, and most software companies they either preffer to stick to JDK or to avoid configuring modules altogether.

The contents of the module-info.java can be as simple as the name of the module and two brackets containing the body, as shown in Listing A-3.

Listing A-3. A Simple module-info.java Configuration

```
module chapter.three {}
```

---

[4] More information is available at Oracle, "Tools Reference," https://docs.oracle.com/en/java/javase/11/tools/jlink.html, accessed October 15, 2021.

Advanced Module Configurations

A Java module declaration body contains one or more `directives` that are constructed using the keywords in Table A-1. These directives represent access configurations and dependency requirements for the packages and classes contained in the modules.

Table A-1. *Java Module Directives*

Directive	Purpose
`requires`	Specifies that the module depends on another module.
`exports`	One of the module's packages whose `public` types (and their `nested public` and `protected` types) should be accessible to code in all other modules.
`exports ... to`	This is the qualified version of the `exports` directive. It enables specifying in a comma-separated list precisely which modules or module code can access the exported package.
`open`	Used at module level declaration (`open module mm {}`) and allows reflective access to all module packages. Java Reflection is the process of analyzing and modifying all the capabilities of a class at runtime and works on private types and members too. So before Java 9, nothing was really encapsulated.
`opens`	Is used inside the body of a module's declaration to selectively configure access through reflection only to certain packages.
`opens ... to`	This is the qualified version of the `opens` directive. It enables specifying in a comma-separated list precisely which modules or module code can access its packages reflectively.
`uses`	Specifies a service used by this module—making the module a **service consumer**. A service in this case represents the full name of a interface/ abstract class that another module provides an implementation for.
`provides ... with`	Specifies that a module provides a service with a specific implementation— making the module a **service provider**.
`transitive`	Used together with `requires` to specify a dependency on another module and to ensure that other modules reading your module also read that dependency— known as *implied readability*.

Modules can depend on one another. The project for this book is made of 13 modules, and most on them depend on module `chapter.zero`. This module contains the basic components used to build more complex components in the other modules. For example, classes inside module `chapter.three` need access to packages and classes in module `chapter.zero`. Declaring a module dependency is done by using the `requires` directive, as depicted in Listing A-4.

Listing A-4. A Simple `module-info.java` Configuration

```
module chapter.three {
    requires chapter.zero;
}
```

The preceding dependency is an **explicit** one. But there are also **implicit** dependencies. For example, any module declared by a developer implicitly requires the JDK `java.base` module. This module contains the foundational APIs of the Java SE Platform, and no Java application could be written without it. This implicit directive ensures access to a minimal set of Java types, so basic Java code can be written. Listing A-4 is equivalent to Listing A-5.

Listing A-5. A Simple `module-info.java` Configuration with an Explicit Directive of `requires java.base`

```
module chapter.three {
    requires java.base;

    requires chapter.zero;
}
```

---

❶ Declaring a module as required means that that module is required when the code is compiled—frequently referred to as *compile time* and when the code is executed—frequently referred to as *runtime*. If a module is required only at runtime, the **requires static** keywords are used to declare the dependency. Just keep that in mind for now, it will make sense when we talk about web applications.

Now chapter.three depends on module chapter.zero. But does this mean chapter.three can access all public types (and their nested public and protected types) in the all the packages in module chapter.zero? If you are thinking that this is not enough, you are right. Just because a module depends on another, it does not mean it has access to the packages and classes it actually needs to. The required module must be configured to expose its *insides*. How can this be done? In our case, we need to make sure module chapter.zero gives access to the required packages. This is done by customizing the module-info.java for this module by adding the exports directive, followed by the necessary package names. Listing A-6 depicts the module-info.java file for the chapter.zero module that exposes its single package.

Listing A-6. The module-info.java Configuration File for the chapter. zero Module

```
module chapter.zero {
    exports com.apress.bgn.zero;
}
```

💡 Think about it like this: you are in your room cutting out Christmas decorations, and you need a template for your decorations. Your roommate has all the templates. But just because you need it doesn't mean it will magically appear. You need to go and talk to your roommate. Needing your roommate's assistance can be viewed as the *requires room-mate* directive. After talking to your roommate, he will probably say: *Sure, come in, they are on the desk! Take as many as you need.* This can be considered the *exports all-templates-on-desk* directive. The desk is probably a good analogy for a package.

Using the configuration in listing A-6 we have just given access to the com.apress. bgn.zero package, to any module configured with a requires module.zero; directive. What if we do not want that? (Considering the previous tip, your roommate just left the door to his room open, so anybody can enter and get those templates!)

What if we want to limit the access to module contents only to the chapter.three module? (So your roommate has to give his templates only to you.) This can be done by adding the "to" keyword followed by the module name to clarify, that only this module is allowed to access the components. This is the qualified version of the `exports` directive mentioned in Table A-1.

⚠ If you were curious and read the recommended **Jar Hell**[5] article, you noticed that one of the concerns of working with Java sources packed in Jars was security. This is because even without access to Java sources, by adding a Jar as a dependency to an application, objects can be inspected, extended, and instantiated. So aside from providing a reliable configuration, better scaling, integrity for the platform, and improved performance, the goal for introduction of modules was in fact **better security**.

Listing A-7 depicts the `module-info.java` file for the `chapter.zero` module that exposes its single package only to the `chapter.three` module.

Listing A-7. Advanced `module-info.java` Configuration File for the `chapter.zero` Module

```
module chapter.zero {
    exports com.apress.bgn.zero to chapter.three;
}
```

More than one module can be specified to have access, by listing the desired modules separated by commas, as depicted in Listing A-8.

Listing A-8. Advanced `module-info.java` Configuration File for the `chapter.zero` Module with Multiple Modules

```
module chapter.zero {
    exports com.apress.bgn.zero to chapter.two, chapter.three;
}
```

---

[5] A great article about the Jar Hell is available at Tech Read, "What Is Jar Hell?," https://tech-read.com/2009/01/13/what-is-jar-hell, accessed October 15, 2021 (but you might want to read it later, after you have written a little code of your own).

The order of the modules in an `exports` directive is not important. The order of packages being exported by `exports` directives is not important either, and if there are a lot of them you can place them on multiple lines. Just make sure to end the declaration with a ; (semicolon).

🔥 Multiple packages cannot be exported using a single `exports` directive because this would lead to conflicts in the different packages exported from different modules, which defies the purpose of modularizing the code. So a construction like the following, using a wildcard to export multiple packages is not supported.

```
module chapter.zero {
exports com.apress.bgn.* to chapter.two, chapter.three;
}
```

This is all good and well, and we can go even one step further. What if module `chapter.three` requires access to a class defined in a module that is a dependency of `chapter.zero`? In technical language this is called a **transitive** dependency because it is obviously more practical to use a dependency that is already there, instead of declaring it again. Modules support this as well and the keyword to declare such a dependency is (as you probably suspected): `transitive`.

For this scenario, we'll make our module `chapter.zero` depend on external module of the LOG4J (Apache Log4j 2) that is a simple library for logging of application behavior,[6] but we also want any module depending on `chapter.zero` to be able to use classes in the `org.apache.logging.log4j` module. In this case, the contents of the `module-info.java` for module `chapter.zero` become the ones shown in Listing A-9.

---

[6] More details about it can be found at Apache, "Apache Log4j 2," `https://logging.apache.org/log4j/2.x`, accessed October 15, 2021.

Listing A-9. `module-info.java` Configuration File for the `chapter.zero` Requiring a Dependency Being Shared with Its Dependents

```
module chapter.zero {
    requires transitive org.apache.logging.log4j;

    exports com.apress.bgn.zero to chapter.three;
}
```

By using `requires transitive` we have given read access to module `org.apache.logging.log4j` to our `chapter.three`. This means that types in `chapter.three` can be declared by making use of types defined in packages exported by module `org.apache.logging.log4j`. To test this, class `com.apress.bgn.three.transitive.LoggingSample` has been introduced in project chapter03. This class uses a Log4j 2 logger to print a simple log message.

And this is where simple, basic things end. There are a few more module directives to cover, and it makes sense to do so in this appendix, since they use notions spread all throughout this book. So here it goes.

In Java there is a feature named **reflection**. Reflection can be used to inspect a package and access information of all its contents including private members. You can imagine that maybe this is not such a good thing, especially in a productive application that requires higher levels of security. Plus, such a feature makes it useless to have so many types of accessors, right? Up to Java 9 this is how things were, and using reflection leads to problems included in the **Jar Hell** category. By introducing modules, reflection can be restricted as well. As in, reflection is no longer possible unless the module is configured to allow it. There are three forms of the same directive that can be used to configure access using reflection:

- open is used at module declaration level and allows reflective access to all packages in the module. A configuration to allow reflective access to all packages in module `chapter.zero` is depicted in Listing A-10.

Listing A-10. `module-info.java` Configuration File for the `chapter.zero` Allowing Reflective to All Its Packages

```
open module chapter.zero {
    requires transitive org.apache.logging.log4j;
    exports com.apress.bgn.ch0 to chapter.three;
}
```

- opens is used inside the module declaration to selectively configure access through reflection only to certain packages. A configuration to allow reflective access only to package `com.apress.bgn.three.helloworld` is depicted in Listing A-11.

Listing A-11. `module-info.java` Configuration File for the `chapter.three` Allowing Reflective Access Only to Package `com.apress.bgn.three.helloworld`

```
module chapter.three {
    requires chapter.zero;
    opens com.apress.bgn.three.helloworld;
}
```

- opens ... to is used inside the module declaration to selectively configure access through reflection only to certain packages and to a specific module. It's a little difficult to give an example here, but let's imagine this project uses Spring Boot.[7] Spring Boot uses reflection to instantiate objects of types defined in our `chapter.three` module. A configuration to allow reflective access only to package `com.apress.bgn.three.helloworld` only to a specific Spring module named `spring.core` is depicted in Listing A-12.

---

[7] A very popular framework written in Java is Spring; Spring Boot is used to build production-ready Spring applications. Read more about it at Spring, "Spring Boot," `https://spring.io/projects/spring-boot`, accessed October 15, 2021.

Listing A-12. `module-info.java` Configuration File for the `chapter.three`
Allowing Reflective Access Only to Package `com.apress.bgn.three.helloworld`
to a Module Named `spring.core`

```
module chapter.three {
    requires chapter.zero;
    requires spring.boot;
    requires spring.web;
    requires spring.context;
    requires spring.boot.autoconfigure;
    opens com.apress.bgn.three.helloworld to spring.core;
}
```

Beside opening a package or a module for reflection, the preceding directives also
provide access to the package's (respectively all packages in the module) public types
(and their nested public and protected types) at runtime only.

If you are curious about how reflection is used, take a look at class `com.apress.bgn.`
`three.ReflectionDemo` from project `chapter03`. This class inspects the structure of the
Base class and uses this knowledge to try to modify the value of a private field of a Base
instance. The code is depicted in Listing A-13.

Listing A-13. the `ReflectionDemo` Class

```
package com.apress.bgn.three;

import com.apress.bgn.zero.Base;
import org.apache.logging.log4j.Logger;
import org.apache.logging.log4j.LogManager;

import java.lang.reflect.Field;

public class ReflectionDemo {

    private static final Logger LOGGER = LogManager.getLogger();

    public static void main(String... args) {
        //testing access to Base class from module chapter.zero
        Base base = new Base();
        LOGGER.info("Base object was created? >  {} ", (base != null));
```

```
    //testing reflection
    try {
        Field field = base.getClass().getDeclaredField("secret");
        field.setAccessible(true); // make the private field accessible
        field.set(base, 1); // set the value of the private field
        base.printSecret(); // call public method to display value of
        private field
    } catch (NoSuchFieldException nsf) {
        LOGGER.error("Field 'secret' cannot be accessed!" );
    } catch (IllegalAccessException e) {
        LOGGER.error("Field 'secret' cannot be set!" );
    }
  }
}
```

Initially the attempt fails, and this exception is shown in the console:

```
Exception in thread "main" java.lang.reflect.InaccessibleObjectException:
Unable to make field private int com.apress.bgn.zero.Base.secret
accessible: module chapter.zero does not "opens com.apress.bgn.zero" to
module chapter.three
    at java.base/java.lang.reflect.AccessibleObject.checkCanSetAccessible(A
    ccessibleObject.java:354)
    at java.base/java.lang.reflect.AccessibleObject.checkCanSetAccessible(A
    ccessibleObject.java:297)
    at java.base/java.lang.reflect.Field.checkCanSetAccessible(Field.
    java:178)
    at java.base/java.lang.reflect.Field.setAccessible(Field.java:172)
    at chapter.three/com.apress.bgn.three.ReflectionDemo.
    main(ReflectionDemo.java:52)
```

Edit the module-info.java in project chapter00 and remove the comment from line 9 (same line from Listing A-11):

```
opens com.apress.bgn.zero to chapter.three;
```

This enables reflection access to package com.apress.bgn.zero where the Base class is located. If you run the ReflectionDemo class again, the exception is gone and instead, the value is set correctly as shown by the execution of the base.printSecret() method. Expect to see the following message in the console:

```
[main] INFO  com.apress.bgn.three.ReflectionDemo - Base object was
created? >  true
```

There are two directives left to cover that were too difficult to explain in **Chapter 3**, since they make more sense after you understand Java a little more: uses and provides. Module declarations that contain directives provides or provides... with are named service providers because these modules provide a service implementation.

Java has a class named java.util.ServiceLoader that can be used to modularize an application and load implementations of a service. What is a service in this case? It is a Java type that defines only a contract, and that service providers need to provide a concrete implementation for.

💡 Essentially a service is modelled using an interface, and a service implementation is modelled by a class implementing the interface. An interface can be compared with the earliest specification version for a car before being built; it covers what it should do, but not how. When the car is actually being built that is the implementation part, when *the how* is decided. And cars do the same things, but in different ways depending on their type of engine, for example. An electric car will have a different implementation (under the hood) for the braking function (during braking electric cars also recharge their battery) than a diesel based car. More about interfaces can be read in **Chapter 4**.

Assuming the service needed to be implemented is named NakedService, a module that contains a class that provides an implementation for it is declared, as shown in Listing A-14.

Listing A-14. Module Providing an Implementation for the NakedService

```
// yes, import statements are supported in module configuration file
import com.apress.bgn.one.service.Provider;
import com.apress.bgn.zero.service.NakedService;
```

```
module chapter.one {
    requires chapter.zero;

    // needed for Appendix A.
    exports com.apress.bgn.one.service;
    provides NakedService with Provider;
}
```

By using the `provides` declarative like that, this module just became a **service provider**.

The module retrieves the service using the `java.util.ServiceLoader<S>` class and uses it; it is called a **service consumer**. The `ServiceLoader` class is generic, and the S type provided as parameter is the type of service(the interface type) the `ServiceLoader` tries to find and load from the project classpath.

To declare the fact that a service consumer uses an implementation of that service, its `module-info.java` must contain the directive configuration shown in Listing A-15.

Listing A-15. Module Using an Implementation of the `NakedService`

```
import com.apress.bgn.zero.service.NakedService;

module chapter.three {
    requires chapter.zero;
    uses NakedService;
}
```

You might ask now, but what is the difference from normally accessing module contents? If you noticed, there is no `requires chapter.one` directive in the module configuration file depicted previously. Why? Because when using services, it is only needed to have the module that provides the service type as a dependency **in the classpath, at runtime** (this is done in this project by using Maven configurations in the `pom.xml` file). This way module `chapter.three` does not really care who provides the implementation. As long as it is there, it is retrieved by the `java.util.ServiceLoader`. Why is this important? Because it decouples an application and removes explicit dependencies on concrete implementation (the `module-info.java` for module `chapter.three` does not need to explicitly declare a dependency on module `chapter.one`).

This is the Java simple way to support **Inversion of Control**.

❶ It was mentioned in the initial chapter that this book will introduce you into the core components of programming, which are data structures, algorithms, design patterns, and most-used coding principles. They will be explained as they come up in the book, so there is no predefined order or sequence that you should expect.

To explain **Inversion of Control**, the **Dependency Injection** must be explained. The action performed by any program (not only Java) is the result of interaction between its interdependent components, usually named objects.

Dependency injection is a concept that describes how dependent objects are connected at runtime by an external party. Look at Figure A-3. It describes two types of relationships between objects, and how those objects "meet" each other.

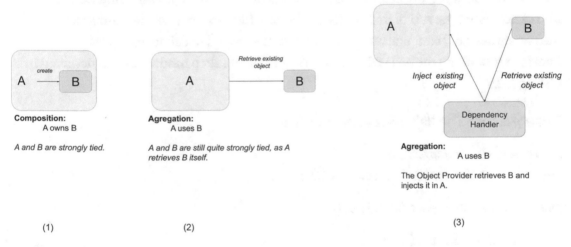

Figure A-3. *Object relationships and how they "meet"*

Because object A that needs an object of type B to perform its functions, *A depends on B*.

Object A can directly create the object B - case (1): composition, or retrieves a reference to an existing object itself - case (2):aggregation, but this ties them up together.

Dependency injection allows severing that tie by using an external party to provide an object of type B to the object of type A - case (3), which is still aggregation, but with no direct ties and a twist.

Inversion of Control is a design principle in which generic reusable components are used to control the execution of problem-specific code, as in retrieving dependencies. Thus, you can say that the `java.util.ServiceLoader` is a **dependency handler** used to perform dependency injection, and it was designed following the inversion of control principle.[8]

This is where the *under the hood* section ends. I hope it has given you enough understanding of Java organization of code and the reasons behind it that you will enjoy reading this book and experimenting with code confidently.

Before I digressed into explaining inversion of control and dependency injection, we had our service provider—module `chapter.one` and our service consumer—module `chapter.three` configurations. Looking at Listings A-14 and A-15, you might have noticed that both require `chapter.zero`. This is because both provider and consumer must know what the API of the service is; the provider, so it can implement it; and the consumer, so it can "consume" it, which in this case is to call its methods. The interface modelling the API is declared in the `chapter.zero` module and is depicted in Listing A-16.

Listing A-16. The `NakedService` Interface

```
// in module 'chapter.zero'
package com.apress.bgn.zero.service;

public interface NakedService {

    String theSecret();
}
```

The service implementation provided by the `Provider` class in `chapter.one` module is depicted in Listing A-17.

---

[8] Also known as the Hollywood Principle, or "Don't call us, we'll call you."

Listing A-17. The NakedService Implementation

```java
// in module 'chapter.one'
package com.apress.bgn.one.service;

import com.apress.bgn.zero.service.NakedService;

public class Provider implements NakedService {
    @Override
    public String theSecret() {
        return "I am the implementation of NakedService provided by module
        'chapter.one'.";
    }
}
```

The ServiceConsumerDemo class using the service in the chapter.three module is depicted in Listing A-18.

Listing A-18. The NakedService Implementation

```java
// in module 'chapter.three'
package com.apress.bgn.three;

import com.apress.bgn.zero.service.NakedService;
import org.apache.logging.log4j.LogManager;
import org.apache.logging.log4j.Logger;

import java.util.ServiceLoader;

public class ServiceConsumerDemo {
    private static final Logger LOGGER = LogManager.getLogger();

    public static void main(String... args) {
        ServiceLoader<NakedService> loader = ServiceLoader.
        load(NakedService.class);
        loader.findFirst().ifPresent( service -> LOGGER.info("Service
        found: {}, with secret '{}'",service.getClass(), service.
        theSecret()));
    }
}
```

When the module configuration is correct, running the class in the previous listing, the following message is printed in the console:

```
[main] INFO com.apress.bgn.three.ServiceConsumerDemo - Service found: class
com.apress.bgn.one.service.Provider, with secret 'I am the implementation
of NakedService provided by module 'chapter.one'.'
```

Figure A-4 shows all the modules configuration files side by side, together with the Maven configuration for the service consumer module (chapter.three):

Figure A-4. *Service api, producer, and consumer module configurations*

This concludes the advanced module configurations section. I hope you enjoyed it and will get to use this knowledge soon.

Appendix B

If you've inspected the structure of the `java-17-for-absolute-beginners` project in IntelliJ IDEA you might have noticed a `Modules` tab. If not, feel free to do it so from the menu: **File ➤ Project Structure…**, as shown in Figure A-5.

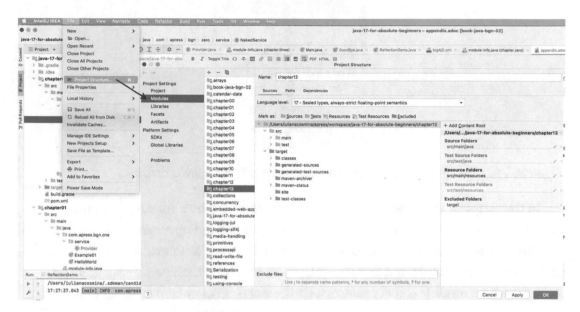

Figure A-5. *IntelliJ IDEA modules tab*

You might think that the `Modules` tab is related to the Java modules, but that is not the case. This section explains the existence of this tab.

Let's consider a banking web application. It probably is quite complex, right? A lot of code must be written to handle user requests, process banking transactions, and saving and retrieving data. Can you imagine how this code is organized?

Most applications have three basic layers: presentation, services, and data access. Figure A-6 depicts this common structure:

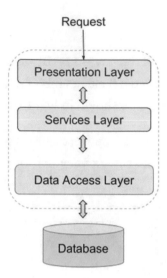

Figure A-6. *The three most common layers of a Java application*

In the simplest applications, each layer is represented by a subproject or module that contains all the code used to perform a group of related operations. For example: all code in the presentation layer implements functionalities for interaction with the user, processing user requests and transforming them into calls for layers under it. Before there were Java modules, Java projects were themselves organized as multimodule projects. That is why in IntelliJ IDEA there is a tab called **Modules**. If the project is configured using a build tool such as Maven of Gradle, the modules in the IntelliJ IDEA Modules tab are the project modules configured by the build tool.

As you've probably noticed in Figure A-5, the java-17-for-absolute-beginners project is multimodular as well. The module names shown in the IntelliJ IDEA Modules tab are not the Java module names configured in the module-info.java files, but the names of the Maven modules configured in pom.xml files.

Index

A

Abstract classes, 156
Abstraction, 141–145
Abstract method, 142
Abstract Window Toolkit (AWT), 10, 547
accept() method, 408, 612
Access modifiers
    AnotherPropRequester, 75
    HiddenBase, 69
    Java class, 70
    member-level, 70
    PropProvider, 71, 74
    top-level, 67
AccountRepoImpl implementation, 504
AccountRepoStub class, 512
AccountServiceImpl#createAccount(..)
    method, 510
AccountServiceTest unit test class,
    513, 515
Actor class, 140
Actor interface, 153
Advanced module configurations,
    772–786
allMatch(..), 425
AND operator, 306, 307
Annotations, 14, 152, 172, 173
Anonymous classes, 384
AnotherPropRequester, 75
anyMatch(..) method, 424
Apache Maven, 101
Apache Tomcat server, 593

Application classpath, 66
Application programming
    interface (API), 459
ArrayDemo class, 228
ArrayIndexOutOfBoundsException,
    107, 360
Arrays, 226–236
Arrays.sort(array), 235
Arrays.stream(array), 235
Arrays.toString(array), 235
Artist interface, 155, 158–160
assert keyword, 468
Assertions, debug, 468–473
Assignment operator, 280–283
Autoboxing/unboxing, 14, 253
Automatic memory management, 8

B

Back-pressure, 691, 692, 708
badList variable, 123
Bad recursive method, 176, 177
Base class, 68
BaseMultiResolutionImage, 676, 678
base.printSecret() method, 781
BasicHumanDemo Class, 133
BigSortingSlf4jDemo Class, 483
Binary numeric representation, 215
Binary operators
    /(divide), 295, 296
    -(minus), 293
    %(modulus), 296–299

789

M

N

Printed in the United States
by Baker & Taylor Publisher Services